Legal Issues of Services of General Interest

Series Editors
Johan Willem van de Gronden
Markus Krajewski
Ulla Neergaard
Erika Szyszczak

For further volumes:
http://www.springer.com/series/8900

Johan Willem van de Gronden · Erika Szyszczak
Ulla Neergaard · Markus Krajewski
Editors

Health Care and EU Law

T·M·C·ASSER PRESS

Springer

Editors
Johan Willem van de Gronden
Faculty of Law
Radboud University
Comeniuslaan 4
6525 HP Nijmegen
The Netherlands
e-mail: J.vandeGronden@jur.ru.nl

Ulla Neergaard
Faculty of Law
University of Copenhagen
Studiestræde 6
1455 Copenhagen K
Denmark
e-mail: ulla.neergaard@jur.ku.dk

Erika Szyszczak
School of Law
University of Leicester
University Road, Leicester
LE1 7RH
UK
e-mail: ems11@leicester.ac.uk

Markus Krajewski
Fachbereich Rechtswissenschaft
Universität Erlangen-Nürnberg
Schillerstraße 1
91054 Erlangen
Germany
e-mail: markus.krajewski@jura.uni-erlangen.de

ISBN 978-90-6704-832-3
ISBN 978-90-6704-728-9 (eBook)

DOI 10.1007/978-90-6704-728-9

Softcover reprint of the hardcover 1st edition 2011

Published by T.M.C. ASSER PRESS, The Hague, The Netherlands, www.asserpress.nl

Produced and distributed for T.M.C. ASSER PRESS by Springer-Verlag, Berlin Heidelberg

Cover design: eStudio Calamar, Berlin/Figueres

Printed on acid-free paper

Springer is part of Springer Science+Business Media (www.springer.com)

Series Information

The aim of the series *Legal Issues of Services of General Interest* is to sketch the framework for services of general interest in the EU and to explore the issues raised by developments related to these services. The Series encompasses, inter alia, analyses of EU internal market, competition law, legislation (such as the Services Directive), international economic law and national (economic) law from a comparative perspective. Sector-specific approaches will also be covered (health, social services). In essence, the present Series addresses the emergence of a European Social Model and will therefore raise issues of fundamental and theoretical interest in Europe and the global economy.

Series Editors

Johan Willem van de Gronden
Faculty of Law
Radboud University
Comeniuslaan 4
6525 HP Nijmegen
The Netherlands
e-mail: J.vandeGronden@jur.ru.nl

Markus Krajewski
Fachbereich Rechtswissenschaft
Universität Erlangen-Nürnberg
Schillerstraße 1
91054 Erlangen
Germany
e-mail: markus.krajewski@jura.uni-erlangen.de

Ulla Neergaard
Faculty of Law
University of Copenhagen
Studiestræde 6
1455 Copenhagen K
Denmark
e-mail: ulla.neergaard@jur.ku.dk

Erika Szyszczak
School of Law
University of Leicester
University Road, Leicester
LE1 7RH
UK
e-mail: ems11@leicester.ac.uk

Preface and Acknowledgments

Over the last 20 years, it has become clear that EU law has had a considerable impact on health care, despite the limited EU competence to legislate in this field. A very important development is the Commission's proposal for a Directive on Patients' Rights in Cross-border Health Care. In response to these controversial developments in October 2009, a conference on Health Care and EU law was held at the Radboud University, Nijmegen, The Netherlands. This book contains the proceedings of this vibrant conference and, in addition, other contributions that were commissioned by the editors to address a wide variety of significant themes related to health care and EU law. Given that the ECJ's case law on the free movement of patients was an important starting point, the present volume places the emphasis on internal market and competition issues.

This book is the second volume of the Series *Legal Issues of Services of General Interest*. The aim of this series is to explore legal developments regarding Services of General Economic Interest from a national, EU, WTO and comparative perspective. In 2009, the first volume, *The Changing Legal Framework for Services of General Interest in Europe. Between Competition and Solidarity* was published stemming from an international conference organised in Potsdam, Germany.

We would like to thank all authors for their interesting and stimulating papers. Their studies greatly contribute to a better understanding of the growing importance of EU Law for health care. Furthermore, we are very grateful for the generous financial support that we received from the Board of the Law Faculty of the Radboud University Nijmegen to organise the conference on health care and EU Law. We are very aware that this conference would not have seen the light of day without the organisational and administrative support of the Centre for Postacademic Legal Education of the Nijmegen Law Faculty. Members of the staff of this centre, especially Wieneke Paulssen, were of great help.

The book was edited in the course of 2010 in close co-operation between the four editors. Additional thanks are owed to Nina Harteveld, student-assistant at the Department of International and European law of the Nijmegen Law Faculty, for her work on the indexes.

Moreover, we are also very grateful for the help and support given by the team of *T.M.C. Asser Press*. Especially, the efforts of Philip van Tongeren and Marjolein Bastiaans, which have led to a timely publication of the present volume, are greatly appreciated.

Nijmegen, Leicester,
Copenhagen and Bremen, Autumn 2010

Johan Willem van de Gronden
Erika Szyszczak
Ulla Neergaard
Markus Krajewski

Post Script

In January 2011 the European Parliament adopted a revised text of the Directive on patient's rights to second reading.

At the moment of the publishing of the present volume, a meeting of the Council was scheduled with regard to this directive in March 2011. These developments are not addressed in this volume.

Contents

List of Contributors

Rita Baeten, holds a master of social sciences and is senior policy analyst at the OSE, European Social Observatory. Her research activities focus on the impact of European integration on national healthcare systems and on their social character. She advises the Belgian federal authorities on EU level developments with a potential impact on healthcare.

Senior Policy Analyst, OSE, European Social Observatory, Paul Emile Janson straat 13, 1050 Brussels. e-mail: baeten@ose.be

Hilde Cadenau, currently works as a lawyer in the section European and Competition Law at Pels Rijcken Droogleever Fortuijn N.V., located in The Hague. She advises and litigates on subjects of European law, including agricultural law, institutional law and state aid. She has a special interest in European and national equal treatment law, and has published on the subject on various occasions.

Lecturer & Coordinator European Law Line, International Bachelor of Law Program, The IIague University, Johanna Wcsterdijkplcin 75, 2521 EN, Thc Haguc

Nathan Cortez, is an Assistant Professor of Law at Southern Methodist University, teaches and writes in the areas of health law, food and drug law, administrative law and the legislative process. His research focuses on regulation of emerging international markets in health care and biotechnology, including cross-border health care. He has published in a number of law reviews and peer-reviewed journals, and is frequently quoted by the media, including the Associated Press, CNN and National Public Radio. Professor Cortez received his B.A. from the University of Pennsylvania and his J.D. from Stanford. Before joining academia, Professor Cortez practiced law in Washington D.C. with the law firm Arnold & Porter.

Assistant Professor, Dedman School of Law, Southern Methodist University, 3315 Daniel Avenue, Dallas, TX 75205, e-mail: ncortez@smu.edu

Julio Baquero Cruz, is a member of the Legal Service of the European Commission and visiting professor at Sciences Po (Paris) and at Universidad San Pablo CEU/Fundación Ortega y Gasset (Madrid). He has been Research Fellow at the Centro de Estudios Políticos y Constitucionales and Associate Professor at Universidad Carlos III of Madrid (2007–2009), and Marie Curie Fellow at the Robert Schuman Centre (2005–2006). He holds a Ph.D. from the EUI and a LL.M. from the College of Europe. From 2000 to 2004, he was a référendaire at the European Court of Justice. He has lectured and published extensively on EU law.

Member of the Legal Service, European Commission, BERL 2/398, B-1049, Brussels, e-mail: Julio.BAQUERO-CRUZ@ec.europa.eu, Tel.: +32-2-2995436, Fax: +32-2-2961846

Gareth Davies, is a Professor of EU law at the VU University Amsterdam. He was previously a lecturer in EU law at the University of Groningen and a barrister. In 2006, he was an Emile Noel scholar at New York University. His research interests are in European economic law, particularly the interaction of economic and non-economic interests, and in EU constitutional law.

Faculty of Law, Department of Transnational Legal Studies, VU University Amsterdam, De Boelelaan 1105, 1081HV Amsterdam, e-mail: g.t.davies@vu.nl

Berend-Jan Drijber, currently works as a lawyer (partner) in the section European and Competition Law at Pels Rijcken Droogleever Fortuijn N.V., located in The Hague. Previously, Berend-Jan was a staff member of the Legal Services of the European Commission and subsequently legal adviser at the Permanent Representation of the Netherlands. He now advises and litigates on a broad range of subjects relating to European law, amongst others institutional issues, the four freedoms and state aid. General and sector-specific competition law is an important part of his practice, and health care is an upcoming subject. Besides his work as a lawyer, he publishes on a regular basis, and has a long list of publications to his name.

Pels Rijcken & Drooglever Fortuijn (state advocate), P.O. Box 11756, 2502 AT, The Hague, The Netherlands, e-mail: bj.drijber@pelsrijcken.nl

Johan W. van de Gronden, is a Professor of European law at the Law Faculty of the Radboud University Nijmegen (The Netherlands). He received his Ph.D. in 1998. His research interest concerns European internal market law, competition law, Services of General (Economic) Interest and the impact of EU law on health care. From 1998 until September 2007, he worked at the Europa Institute of the University Utrecht (the last years as a senior lecturer). On 1 September 2007, he was appointed as a Professor of European law in Nijmegen. Since 2003, he is also a deputy judge at the District Court Rotterdam, where he mainly handles competition law cases. He is also a member of the Committee of Consumer Affairs and of the Committee of International Social and Economic Affairs of the Social and Economic Council.

Professor of European law, P.O. Box 9049, 6500 KK, Nijmegen, The Netherlands, e-mail: j.vandegronden@jur.ru.nl

Jean McHale, is a Professor of Health Care Law and Director of the Institute of Medical Law at the University of Birmingham. She previously held a chair at the University of Leicester and also held posts at the Universities of Manchester, Nottingham and East Anglia. She is a member of the editorial board of Health Economics Policy and the Law, the Medical Law Review and Nursing Ethics.

Professor of Health Care Law and Director of the Institute of Medical Law, Birmingham Law School, University of Birmingham, Edgbaston, Birmingham, B15 2TT, UK

Vassilis Hatzopoulos, is an Associate Professor at the Democritus University of Thrace (Greece), a visiting Professor at the College of Europe, Bruges (Belgium) and a Special (Honorary) Lecturer at the University of Nottingham (UK). He practices as a lawyer at the Athens Bar since 1995 in the fields of Internal Market (emphasis on services and free movement), network industries and public procurement. He has published a couple of books, as well as over one hundred articles and case notes, in English, French and Greek, on various topics of EU law.

Associate Professor, Department of Social Administration, Democritus University of Thrace (Greece), Lycavittou 39-41, 10672 Athens, e-mail: vasshatz@socadm.duth.gr, Visiting Professor at the Legal Department, College of Europe, Bruges, Belgium

Tamara Hervey, is Jean Monnet Professor of European Union Law at the School of Law, University of Sheffield. Her main research interests are in the field of EU social and constitutional law, in particular its application in health fields, and she has written widely on the EU's involvement in health. She is interested in the phenomenon of 'new governance' in the EU, in particular as an alternative or supplement to 'command and control' means of regulation in social fields. She is also interested in socio-legal theory and method, in particular, as applied to the law of the EU.

Jean Monnet Professor of European Union Law, School of Law, University of Sheffield, Bartolomé House, Winter Street, Sheffield, S3 7ND, e-mail: t.hervey@sheffield.ac.uk

Markus Krajewski, is a Professor of International Public Law, Faculty of Law, University of Erlangen-Nuremberg, Germany. His research interests include constitutional and institutional issues of WTO law, trade in services, and the treatment of public services under European and international law.

Professor of Public and International Law, Fachbereich Rechtswissenschaft, Universität Erlangen-Nürnberg, Schillerstraße 1, 91054 Erlangen, Germany, e-mail: Markus.Krajewski@jura.uni-erlangen.de

Ulla Neergaard, holds a Ph.D. degree from the European University Institute, Florence, Italy. Since 1998, Neergaard has been an academic at the Law Department at the Copenhagen Business School, Denmark, most recently as professor of competition law. Since 2009, Neergaard has been Professor of EU market law at the Law Faculty at the University of Copenhagen, however, from the summer of 2010 moving over to a professorship of EU law. Since 1999, Neergaard has been an expert member of the Danish Council of Competition and, since 2005, also of the Danish Energy Regulatory Authority. She has published widely in EU competition law and the more fundamental EU law.

Professor of EU law, Faculty of law, University of Copenhagen, Studiestræde 6, 1455 Copenhagen, e-mail: ulla.neergaard@jur.ku.dk, Tel.: 35323313

Christopher Newdick, is a Professor of Health Law at the University of Reading. He has served on the UK Department of Health's Medicines Commission and the British Medical Association's Working Party on NHS Rationing. He is an Honorary Consultant to health authorities in England and a member of the South Central Priorities Committee which assists the process of health care resource allocation in the NHS.

Professor of Health Law, University of Reading, Foxhill House, Whiteknights Road, Reading RG6 7BA, UK, e-mail: c.newdick@reading.ac.uk

Willy Palm, is the Dissemination development Officer of the European Observatory on Health Systems and Policies. He is responsible for organising and leading policy dialogues with policy-makers in European countries on various health systems-related issues. As a lawyer specialized in European social security law, Willy has been working mainly in the field of statutory health insurance and has been more specifically looking at the impact of EU integration on health systems. Before joining the Observatory in April 2006, Willy was the Managing Director of the International Association of Mutual benefit societies (AIM).

Dissemination Development Officer, European Observatory on Health Systems and Policies, Zelfbestuursstraat 4, 1070 Brussels, e-mail: wpa@obs.euro.who.int

Frans Pennings, is a Professor of labour Law and Social Security Law at Utrecht University and Professor of International Social Security Law at Tilburg University, the Netherlands. He published several books and articles on (European) social law, including the European Coordination Security Regulation. In addition, he is a judge at the Central Appeals Court in Utrecht (The Netherlands).

Professor of Labour Law and Social Security Law, Utrecht University, Achter St Pieter 200, 3512 HT, Utrecht, The Netherlandse-mail: f.pennings@uu.nl

Wolf Sauter, is currently a competition expert at the Dutch Healthcare Authority (NZa) and a Professor of healthcare at the University of Tilburg. He obtained his Ph.D. from the European University Institute in Florence and has previously held academic appointments in Bremen and Groningen. Wolf has also worked in private practice in Brussels as well as with the Dutch ministry of finance, the Dutch telecommunications regulator, and with DG Competition of the European Commission.

Professor of Healthcare Regulation and competition expert at the Dutch Healthcare authority, Nederlandse Zorgauthoriteit, Postbus 3017, 3502 GA, Utrecht, The Netherlands, e-mail: WSauter@nza.nl

Hélène Stergiou, is a Ph.D. fellow and lecturer of European Law at the Department of International and European Law of the Radboud University Nijmegen. As an attorney at law, she practiced European Law at AKD Prinsen Van Wijmen (Brussels) and Pels Rijcken & Droogleever Fortuijn in The Hague. Her research focus lies with EU Public Procurement Law. Hélène holds a law degree from the University of Utrecht and the College of Europe.

Ph.D. Fellow, P.O. Box 9049, 6500 KK, Nijmegen, The Netherlands, e-mail: H.Stergiou@jur.ru.nl

Erika Szyszczak, is a Jean Monnet Professor of European Law ad personam and a Professor of European Competition and Labour Law at the University of Leicester. She is a practising barrister at Littleton Chambers, Temple, London, and an ADR-accredited mediator.

Professor of European law, School of Law, University of Leicester, LE1 7RH, UK, e-mail: ems11@leicester.ac.uk

Sybe A. de Vries, has been an Associate Professor of European law at the Europa Institute of Utrecht University since 2007. Prior to his current position, he has been a research assistant and lecturer in European Law at the Universities of Nijmegen and Utrecht. In 2006, he obtained his Ph.D. at Utrecht University for his dissertation 'Tensions within the Internal Market—The Functioning of the Internal Market and the Development of Horizontal and Flanking Policies'. From 2001 until 2004, he was a legal secretary of the Advisory Appeal Committee of the Netherlands Competition Authority. He has authored and co-authored a number of articles in law journals and books. His research interests are European law and public economic law in general.

Associate Professor in European Law, Europa Institute, Utrecht University, Achter Sint Pieter 200, 3512 HT, Utrecht, e-mail: S.A.deVries@uu.nl, Tel.: +31-30-2537271

Felix Welti, was an academic assistant at the faculty Law II of the University of Hamburg from 1994 until 1997. In 1997, he received his Ph.D. at the University of Hamburg. From 1999 until 2005, he was an academic assistant at the Institute for Social law and Social policy in Europe of the Christian-Albrechts University of Kiel. From 2007 to 2010, he was a Professor of Social and Administrative law at the University of Applied Sciences Neubrandenburg (Department of health, nursing and management). Since 2008, he is an honorary member of the Constitutional Court of Schleswig-Holstein, and since 2010, he is an honorary member of the Federal Social Court. Since 2010 he is a Professor of Social Law at the University of Kassel, Department of Humanities.

Professor of Social law, Universität Kassel, Room 3109, Arnold-Bode-straße 10, 34109, Kassel, Germany, e-mail: mail@felix-welti.de

Abbreviations

BVerfG	Bundesverfassungsgericht (Fed. Rep. of Germany)
CDHP	Consumer-driven health plans
CFI	Court of First Instance (now General Court)
CFREU	Charter of Fundamental Rights of the EU
CNMSS	Caisse nationale militaire de sécurité sociale
CO-OP	Consumer-Oriented and Operated Plan
CPV	Common Public Procurement Vocabulary
DCC	Dublin City Council
DOH	UK Department of Health
DTC	Diagnosis and Treatment Combinations
EC	European Community
ECHR	European Convention on Human Rights
ECJ	European Court of Justice
EEA	European Economic Area
EEC	European Economic Community
ENVI	Committee on Environment, Public Health and Food Safety
EP	European Parliament
EPSCO	Council for Employment, Social Policy, Health and Consumer Affairs
ESC	European Economic and Social Committee
EU	European Union
EUnetHTA	European Union network of Health Technology Agencies
EWCA	England and Wales Court of Appeal
EWHC	England and Wales High Court
FDC	German Federal Court
GATS	General Agreement on Trade in Services
GATT	General Agreement on Tariffs and Trade
GC	General Court
GDP	Gross domestic product
GKV-WSG	Act to Strengthen Competition in the Statutory Health Insurance System

HIA	Health Insurance Authority
HMO	Health Maintenance Organization
ICCPR	International Covenant on Civil and Political Right
ILO	International Labour Organisation
IMF	International Monetary Fund
LOCI	Logit Competition Index
LTHC	Long-term Health Care
LTC	Long-term care
MEP	Member of the European Parliament
MP	Member of Parliament
MISSOC	Mutual Information System on Social Protection
NESGIs	Non-economic services of General Interest
NGO	Non-governmental Organization
NHS	National Health Service
NICE	National Institute for Health and Clinical Excellence
NMa	Nederlandse Mededingingsautoriteit (Dutch Competition Authority)
n.y.r.	not yet reported
NZa	Nederlandse Zorgautoriteit (Dutch Healthcare Authority)
OECD	Organisation for economic co-operation and development
OLG	Öberlandesgericht
OMC	Open method of coordination
PCT	Primary Care Trust
PMI	Private Medical Insurance
PPO	Personal Protection order
QALY	Quality-adjusted life year
RES	Risk Equalisation Scheme
SGEI	Services of General Economic Interest
SGI	Services of General Interest
SHA	Strategic Health Authority
SSGIs	Social Services of General Interest
SMP	Significant Market Power
TEU	Treaty on European Union
TFEU	Treaty on the Functioning of the European Union
WHO	World Health Organisation
WTO	World Trade Organisation

Journals

All ER	All England Reports
BJPIR	British Journal of Politics and International Relations
BMJ	British Medical Journal
BMLR	British Medical Law Reports
CMLRev	Common Market Law Review
Comp. L. Rev	Competition Law Review

CUP	Cambridge University Press
ECLR	European Competition Law Review
ECR	European Court Reports
EIOP	European Integration Online Papers
EJIL	European Journal of International Law
ELJ	European Law Journal
ELRev	European Law Review
Harv LR	Harvard Law Review
Harvard UP	Harvard University Press
JCMS	Journal of Common Market Studies
LIEI	Legal Issues of Economic Integration
Med LR	Medical Law Review
MLR	Modern Law Review
NTER	Nederlands Tijdschrift voor Europees Recht
OJ	Official Journal
OUP	Oxford University Press
P.P.L.R.	Public Procurement Law Review
QJ Med	Quarterly Journal of Medicine
SEW	Sociaal-economische wetgeving (Dutch Journal for European and Economic law)
WLR	Weekly Law Reports

Chapter 1
Introduction

Johan van de Gronden, Erika Szyszczak, Ulla Neergaard and Markus Krajewski

Contents

1.1 Introduction

In 1998 the European Court of Justice of the EU/EC (ECJ) delivered its famous judgments using the free movement provisions in the cases

J. van de Gronden (✉)
The Law Faculty of the Radbouw University Nijmegen, Nijmegen, The Netherlands
e-mail: j.vandegronden@jur.ru.nl

E. Szyszczak
The University of Leicester, Leicester, UK
e-mail: ems11@leicester.ac.uk

U. Neergaard
The Law Faculty of the University of Copenhagen, Copenhagen, Denmark
e-mail: ulla.neergaard@jur.ku.dk

M. Krajewski
Faculty of Law, University of Erlangen-Nuremberg, Erlangen, Germany
e-mail: Markus.Krajewski@jura.uni-erlangen.de

J. W. van de Gronden et al. (eds.), *Health Care and EU Law*,
Legal Issues of Services of General Interest, DOI: 10.1007/978-90-6704-728-9_1,

Kohll[1] and *Decker*.[2] By doing so it signalled that national health care and especially the Member States organisation of health care (such as planning) are not immune from EU law. *Kohll* and *Decker*, and subsequent case law, have attracted attention both in practice and in legal doctrine. Health care issues have not escaped the attention of the competition rules of the EU as Member States increasingly experiment with new forms of funding and delivery of health care and social welfare services. It is timely to consider the future role of EU economic and social law in a field where the EU has limited legislative competence. In September 2006 the Commission started a consultation procedure[3] to clarify and codify in a legislative proposal the conditions for patient mobility in the EU. Attempts to include health care in the Services Directive revealed that this was too audacious a move for the EU and in July 2008 the Commission tried for a second time to legislate in the area of patient mobility and the coordination of health care issues with the adoption of a draft Directive.[4] The differences between the Member States on whether, and how, health care should be regulated at the EU level has left this proposal unadopted at the time of writing of this Introduction (July 2010).

It is clear from the outset that issues of health care and EU law are very topical nowadays. Therefore, in October 2009 a conference dedicated to these issues was held in Nijmegen, The Netherlands. The present volume contains, *inter alia*, the proceedings of this conference. It should be noted that this volume is closely related to the book *The Changing Legal Framework for Services of General Interest in Europe. Between Competition and Solidarity,*[5] published by TMC Asser Press in 2009. This book was the outcome of a conference organised in Potsdam in 2008 with the aim of sketching the contours of the current framework for Services of General Interest in the EU, exploring the issues that have been high on the political agenda in Europe as a result of the liberalisation processes which were speeded up after the completion of the internal market programme in 1992. Of crucial concern are questions of the role of essential services accepted under traditional welfare state models in Europe and still seen as essential in modern society: Services of General Interest. Perhaps not unexpectedly this project unearthed a wide range of issues on the provision and delivery of Services of General Interest which have been transformed into a new series of texts: *Legal Issues of General Interest*. We already have a wide-ranging agenda of books to be published in this series, addressing Services of General Interest both from the perspective of EU law and from other perspectives, for example a comparative approach, WTO law, the role of Social Services of General Interest. It was

[1] Case C-158/96 *Kohll* [1998] *ECR* I-1931.

[2] Case C-120/95 *Decker* [1998] *ECR* I-1831.

[3] Communication from the Commission of 26 September 2006—Consultation regarding Community action on health services, SEC (2006) 1195/4.

[4] Draft Directive on the Application of Patients' Rights in Cross-Border Health Care, COM(2008) 414 final.

[5] This volume was edited by Markus Krajewski, Ulla Neergaard and Johan van de Gronden.

apparent from the first volume of the series that health care raises complicated, significant, interesting and even dazzling issues that deserved further research. The second volume in the series explores how EU law influences the way health care is organised and delivered at the national level.

1.1.1 Aims and Structure of the Book

Not withstanding the difficulties the EU legislature encounters in the adoption process of the Directive on patients' rights, it is clear from the outset that the 'EU market rules' (the free movement rules, competition law and other EU law areas of an economic nature) are capable of interfering with the national organisation of health care, producing disruptive effects and challenging the national solidarity on which health services are based. The focus of the present volume is on the impact of EU internal market and competition law on the organisation of the national health care systems of the Member States. Pursuant to Article 168(7) of the Treaty on the Functioning of the European Union (TFEU) (former Article 152(5) EC) this area rightly belongs to the competences of the Member States. However, the case law of the ECJ shows that the Treaty provisions on free movement and competition have had a great impact on national health care competences. Given this significant impact of EU internal market and competition law on national health care, other branches of EU law that may be of importance for health care issue are not included in this book or not discussed in great detail.[6]

The aim of this volume is to explore the consequences of the impact of the EU rules for the internal market (including the proposed Directive on patients' rights) and competition on national health care systems. It will also address how related areas, such as EU public procurement law and WTO law, influence national health care organisation and Member State autonomy.

The book consists of five parts. Part I is entitled 'Foundations' and the chapters discuss a fundamental issue of health care: what is its place in the European integration process? Part II addresses patient mobility. How did the ECJ foster patient mobility in applying the Treaty provisions on free movement? What is the added value of the proposed Directive on patients' rights? In this Part not only general issues but also the specific consequences of EU internal market law for one particular Member State (UK) will be discussed. In Part III attention is paid to competition issues. This Part of the book explores the consequences of the Treaty provisions on competition and state aid for national health care. To complement the second part the affect of EU competition law is explored in two Member States (Germany and The Netherlands). Competition is at the heart of the US health care system and important enough to devote at least one chapter to the role competition

[6] On, for example, the EU Directives on professional qualifications, which are of great relevance for medical profession, see Barnard (2006), p. 235 et seq. Furthermore, a wide variety of issues are discussed and explored in Hervey and McHale (2004).

plays in a 'foreign' developed economy, to discover whether new lessons could be learnt. Part IV addresses further issues of raised by the application of economic rules to the health care sector. This Part of the book explores how the ECJ is increasingly applying the Treaty provisions beyond the scope of patient mobility and discusses the way EU public procurement law deals with health care cases. Increasingly health care shows that it no longer respects national borders designed to promote solidarity amongst citizens. As health care costs rise, and national provision of expensive or unusual health treatments is rationed patients may seek treatment in low-cost countries in, for example, Central and South America or Asia. It seems appropriate to include a chapter on how WTO law may affect patient mobility. Part V contains a synthesis of the chapters, drawing conclusions and pointing to how future application of economic law may affect the direction of health care provision in the EU.

1.1.2 Foundations of EU Law and Health Care

Neergaard analyses EU health care law in a more constitutional light, limited to the following five issues: distribution of competences and the Treaty, distribution of competences and free movement of services, distribution of competences and services of general economic interest in light of *BUPA*,[7] notions of solidarity, and Social Europe. Her overall research aim is to achieve an understanding of which direction Europe is taking with regard to health care on the basis of the five examined perspectives. She argues that health care constitutes an essential element in a typical European welfare state, and that a welfare state in Europe is originally a nation-state, where contributions to a national health care system normally are provided through taxation or by payments of premiums into an insurance scheme. Also, she explains that although differing in many ways, all health care systems in the Member States of the EU provide near universal coverage based on solidarity.[8] However, in her opinion there is an increasingly blurred line between such states and EU law as part of a more comprehensive multi-level legal system, where EU law and the law of its Member States are mutually embedded, this also includes health care.[9] Neergaard argues that health care law used to be a nation-state matter, but, *inter alia*, the EU has altered this point of departure amongst others through an increased amount of competences. By reference to different models of Social Europe, the author points out that in a larger context, EU health care law at the general level develops heavily in these years, by now being an important element of a newer agenda. In the authors view, it is difficult to see how exactly the organisation will be influenced, whether for example, more privatisation will

---

[7] General Court, Case T-289/03 *BUPA* [2008] *ECR* II-81. Also see General Court, Case T-289/03 (Order) BUPA [2008] *ECR* II-741.

[8] See also Mossialos and McKee (2004), p. 21.

[9] See in this regard Neergaard and Nielsen (2010) ssrn: http://ssrn.com/abstract=1618758.

occur, more cross-border health care will arise, loss of well-functioning national solidarity mechanisms will evolve, negative changes as to the financing of health care will happen, etc., although it is certain that further changes are unavoidable. She warns that in this process it is important to take into account that health care is not a normally traded good, but has particular social traits, which need to be taken into consideration when deciding if a more market economically oriented ideology should rule, and in that case to which degree and how.

An important element of a general EU approach towards a model of Social Europe and health care is the principle of non-discrimination. *Drijber* and *Cadenau* explore the role that this principle plays in the ECJs case law on health care. On the basis of the observation that the EU legislator and courts have extended EU influence in all types of public benefits, or are attempting to, Drijber and Cadenau analyse one of the vehicles that makes the greater part of these changes possible, namely the wide concept of 'restriction' to the free movement of patients and health care suppliers. As the four freedoms started as basically a prohibition of discrimination on the ground of nationality, the concept of discrimination constitutes the point of departure in this analysis. Thus, the authors first explore the actual meaning of the concept of discrimination in general. Subsequently they examine the evolution of the principle of non-discrimination in the wider context of the four freedoms. Finally, they focus on the health care sector and they examine to what extent the principle of non-discrimination on the ground of nationality is relevant in the case law concerning medicinal products, patients, health care providers and pensioners. Amongst their findings are that in cases involving health care-related issues the ECJ by and large follows the same 'scheme' as in other cases involving the freedom of establishment or the free provision of services. They observe that the prohibition of discrimination on the ground of nationality, whilst still underlying the application of internal market rules in the area of health care services, has in practice largely been 'overtaken' by the wider concept of 'restriction'. Also, they argue that parallel to the increasing importance of cases on EU citizens moving to other Member States for reasons other than exercising economic activities, an increasing number of cases involve restrictions imposed by the Member State of origin on its own citizens leaving its territory. In addition, amongst their findings are that discriminatory aspects or effects of a national measure are part of the ECJ's reasoning regarding the justification of the restriction it entails, so that the ECJ takes discriminatory aspects into account when assessing the suitability or the proportionality of a restrictive measure.

1.1.3 The (Draft) Patient Directive and Internal Market Issues

The starting point of the influence of EU law on health care was the application of the EU internal market rules to this sector. So, it is of great importance to map the developments that took place with regard to the internal market and health care.

Julio Baquero Cruz focusses on the freedom of individuals to receive health services in Member States other than that in which they are affiliated for health purposes, that is, the issue of the mobility of patients. He approaches this task through an assessment of the leading judgments in the field. Amongst his findings are that health and the liberty of individuals to receive treatment where they prefer are the main concern, and the economic issues seem to be secondary. Also, he argues that the case law is certainly risky. However, its exact consequences are difficult to predict about and he believes that it could lead to three rather different outcomes, namely: 1. the solidarity element of the public health systems of the Member States could be undermined; 2. 'a more efficient use of the EUs health care resources' could be promoted, and a degree of virtuous competition between health systems could become initiated; or 3. only a marginal effect will occur so that there will only be a negligible impact with no transformative potential on the health systems of the Member States. The author points out that the third possibility could be the most likely outcome, implying that the liberalisation has not been 'wild' and that the accusation of a neoliberal bias is not justified in this field. In his opinion, the aim of the ECJ, as with the case law on citizenship, is individual freedom and freedom of choice, not the liberty of economic actors. Therefore, he thinks that the intervention of the ECJ has in principle been neutral with regard to the debate on the socio-economic model of the Union, meaning that the case law then would only be positive for those few individuals that make use of it.

As the EU law was developed in an incremental way by the ECJ on the basis of the EU free movement rules, the Commission decided to step in and to come up with a proposal for Directive on the Application of Patients' Rights in Cross-Border Health Care.[10] The main aim of this action is to codify (and perhaps—to a certain extent—to modify) the ECJ's case law on patient mobility.

Erika Szyszczak analyses the troubled legislative history of this proposed Directive. In particular she focusses upon the sticking points in finding agreement in the council: the legal base of the proposal, the exclusion of long-term health care, which health care providers should be included in the re-imbursement schemes for health care obtained in another Member State and the reasons for requiring prior authorisation to seek hospital care abroad and the reasons for refusing to make reimbursement. Although the proposal was in response to the ECJ case law she charts the significant role played by the Commission in developing new governance processes to the regulation of health care issues at the EU level from the early 1990s. These processes will be institutionalised within the Directive if it is ever adopted. She concludes that whilst the adoption of the proposal will increase patients' rights the non-adoption of the proposal will not diminish the increasing use of new governance processes to regulate cross-border issues of health care in the EU, despite the limited competence of the EU to legislate in the area.

---

[10] See Commission Communication of 2 July 2008, *Proposal for a directive on the application of patients' rights in cross-border health care*, COM(2008) 414 final.

The contribution of *Frans Pennings* looks upon the draft Directive of the European Parliament and of the Council on the application of patients rights in cross-border health care,[11] which is seen as having been launched in response to case law of the ECJ on reimbursement of cross-border health care, which is discussed in Baquero Cruz's contribution. Pennings views the case law as having resulted in a dual system: health care for which authorisation was given according to the rules of the regulation and health care for which no authorisation was given but which had to be reimbursed on the basis of the Treaty. His aim is to examine whether the draft Directive solves the problems arising from this dual system. In his opinion, the draft Directive (the text published by the Commission) followed very closely the case law of the ECJ, which implies it left the dual system and the ensuing problems intact. This is criticised by the author as he believes that the drafters of the Directive in fact had a unique opportunity to rethink the system. Therefore, he finds it unsatisfactory that not more progress has been established, and he points out various weaknesses, but also some of its all positive sides. He ends up concluding that is indeed a very sensitive issue, as Member States are so fearful of the effects of opening the borders that the chance of harmonising the dual system has not been taken and the negotiations of the Council widen the gap created by this system even more. However, he emphasises that given the lack of support for making a more unified system, the adoption of the Directive would be better than nothing, as it requires Member States to adjust their legislation and thus makes access to EU rights more accessible for the citizens.

A theme from Szyszczak's chapter is carried through to the chapter by *Tamara Hervey*. This is the fact that even without a piece of EU hard law the Member States have discussed issues of health care coordination through new governance processes for a number of years, and are likely to continue to do so in the future, with or without the adoption of a Directive. Hervey's premise is that lawyers, trained in the traditional 'Community' method of EU law-making, have underestimated and ignored the important role of new governance processes to tackle the 'wicked problems' which face the EU and the Member States today.

To redress the imbalance of the limited legal attention given to new governance Hervey analyses the provisions in the draft Directive, which addresses the 'Duty of Cooperation' and 'Mutual Assistance and Cooperation'. Despite the history of cooperation stemming from new governances processes developed in the early 1990s some Member States are unwilling to translate this historical cooperation, often taken in the form of soft law processes, into a hard law Directive and have raised questions as to the competence of the union to legislate in this area. However, as Hervey shows, issues relating to the availability of drugs across borders are already the subject of litigation using the free movement of goods provisions as well as services and bring into play EU law. Thus the problems of cross-border health care may be addressed in different ways if the Member States fail to develop cooperation processes.

[11] Brussels, 2 July 2008, COM(2008) 414 final.

Other parts of the proposed Directive create 'European Reference Networks' which again build upon earlier networks which have developed, for example in relation to rare diseases. These are justified in that a *European* reference network can give 'added value' to heath care provision in the individual Member States. However, as Hervey shows the Commissions attempts to create mandatory cooperation between the Member States do not clarify the purpose or objective of the legal measures and this explains the concern of some of the Member States as to the extend of the cooperation: is it to foster *cross-border* health care issues or to enhance quality and safety across the EU independently of any *cross-border* element? If the latter view is taken the concerns of the proposed Directive over-reaching EU legislative competence, outlined in Szyszczak's chapter, are once again raised.

The theme of whether the Member States can ignore the litigation which gives rise to patients' rights and not address the problems, which flow from the exercise of free movement rights is taken on by *Gareth Davies*. In his chapter Davies addresses squarely the major issues arising from the exercise of free movement rights by patients seeking health care abroad: rights of exit, entry, the facilitation of free movement and harmonisation. Echoing themes found in other chapters (most notably Penning's chapter) Davies explores the relationship between the free movement rights and the Social Security Directive. After discussing the concrete issues relating to the proposed Directive Davies then explores a theme also seen in other chapters (most notably the chapters of Szyszczak and Newdick): what is the purpose of legislation in this area? Is it a Directive which merely consolidates the free movement case law embodying the idea of an *economic freedom*? Or does the proposal do more? Is it an idea of European citizenship? Or is the Directive to be understood primarily in institutional and structural terms, as merely an instrumental realisation of individual rights in the process of European integration? As with the conclusions of Szyszczak and Hervey, Davies also realises that patient mobility and cross-border health care issues will not go away and that the Directive is a first step to structuring *how* this will occur in the future. The adoption of the directive would benefit patients and potentially the EU would see a greater integration of health care systems bringing with it greater social and economic integration. This in turn may bring greater benefits to the EU health care industry in global markets.

Davies also sees the proposed Directive as strengthening the quality of 'citizenship' as an EU concept, by delivering rights to good quality health care and widening the potential for access to faster and different forms of medical treatment in an EU-wide market.

In contrast, *Chris Newdick* challenges the ECJ case law on the free movement of patients' and the propose Directive, seeing the dominance of individual rights over community welfare rights as a disruptive effect. Newdick sees the free movement rights as individualist in nature which may be at odds with long-term planning and strategic decision-making at the national level. Thus he challenges the basic premise of EU market-based rights that health care can be treated like any other traded commodity. For Newdick solidarity and community evolve from cultural, political and economic bonds that have developed over centuries within the nation states. These in turn have developed the evolving notions of citizenship and the rights and obligations which flow from that notion at the national level. In particular, access to health care and difficult choices over the provision of health care are ultimately policy choices made within a particular constitutional setting. In contrast the EU is still under-developed in its notions of an EU 'solidarity' and 'cohesion' and has limited re-distributive effects. Yet the ECJ has been willing to isolate the right to freedom of movement across borders as part of an EU notion of citizenship. For Newdick the result is an enhanced role for the judiciary, both at the national and EU level, which threatens the traditional paradigm of the separation of powers, and with no safety valve of challenging the constitutionality of the acts of the judiciary. Ultimately Newdick argues that there are legal, political and cultural misgivings surrounding the ECJs controversial rulings on cross-border health care, with no constitutional forum to allow dialogues between the EU Institutions as to the proper limits of EU jurisdiction. For him, neither Article 35 of the Charter of Fundamental Rights of the EU nor the proposed Directive remedy this constitutional dilemma but continue with ideas of individualism which, he argues, will continue to divide and disrupt local (State) communities creating an 'impoverished' view of citizenship.

Newdick's contribution touches upon the issue of the impact of EU internal market law on the national health care organisation. This raises the question how national health care authorities respond to this impact. *Jean McHale* explores this question with regard to the UK. She starts with examining how health care issues are being turned into 'rights' through EU case law and developments such as the Charter of Fundamental Rights of the EU and the proposal for a Directive on Patients' Rights discussed by Szyszczak and Hervey. McHale's chapter analyses the effects of the case law of the ECJ (which have been discussed by Baquero Cruz) on the English National Health Service (NHS). The NHS is a distinctive health care scheme in Europe because, by and large, treatment is free at the point of delivery and the English Courts have not recognised a 'right' for patients to demand a particular treatment under the NHS. Initially the free movement case law did not have an impact upon patients seeking treatment abroad but the publicity surrounding the *Watts* case[12] raised awareness of the implications of free movement for patients. As a result the UK government has tried to limit the potential impact of the proposed Patients' Rights Directive and has even attempted to pre-empt the adoption of the Directive with its own guidance for general practitioners set out in the National Health Service (Reimbursement of the Cost of EEA Treatment) Regulations 2010 (and related Directions and Guidance). However, McHale argues that the increased emphasis upon rights in the proposed Directive may lead to a greater litigation culture in the UK as patients seek definition over standards and quality of care. Similarly there are concerns that exchanges of

[12] ECJ, Case C-372/04 R (on the application of *Watts*) v. *Bedford Primary Care Trust, Secretary of State for Health* [2006] *ECR* I-4325.

information, e-health and telemedicine may increase the vulnerability of patients to abuses of information without sufficient legal redress. McHale concludes that whilst the EU encroachment into the area of health care has had an impact upon the UK NHS and the government has developed a policy towards aligning national practices with EU law the impact has not been considerable enough to challenge the basic tenets upon which the NHS is based. In other words, her analysis proves that the assumption made by Baquero Cruz that the effects of the ECJs case law on patient mobility are moderate may turn out to be true.

1.1.4 Competition Issues

The analysis carried out above shows that the ECJs case law has put emphasis on the economic character of health care, which entails that apart from internal market law the EU rules on competition come into play. Unsurprisingly, the ECJ has also handed down cases, in which health care practices are assessed in the light of the Treaty provisions on competition.

Johan van de Gronden analyses the case law on the application of EU competition law to some health care issues. The chapter examines whether health care objectives are accommodated in the application of the Treaty provisions on competition. He argues that in EU law solidarity, universal coverage and high quality are regarded to be important health care objectives. Hence, it may be expected that EU Institutions, when applying the EU competition rules, pay due consideration to these objectives. His contribution analyses various representative judgments on competition law and health care delivered by the European Courts. It appears that at the jurisdictional stage of the competition law assessment (the concept of undertaking), the objectives of solidarity and (to a lesser extent) universal coverage are of importance. If social security schemes are largely based on these objectives, competition law is not applicable to bodies managing these schemes. The issue of high quality does not seem to play a significant role at the jurisdictional stage. When it comes to the application of the competition rules (Articles 101 and 102 TFEU) to practices that do fall within the scope of these rules, the European Courts have failed to develop a clear and coherent approach towards health care. However, it cannot be derived from the case law analysed in this chapter that the extent to which the objectives of solidarity, universal coverage and high quality have an impact on the way the Treaty provisions on competition are applied. van Gronden contends that at the EU level better understanding and guidance could be achieved by a soft law approach, which should address the problems resulting from the lack of clarity on the relationship between health care and competition law. As enhancing efficiency in health care will be one of the challenges to meet in the future in the Western world, it must be clarified how competition law should be applied in this sector. Moreover, in order to ensure access to health care of high quality for all, it must be outlined at EU level how due account may be paid to universal coverage, solidarity and high quality in applying competition law.

Sybe de Vries also focusses on an issue of competition law and health care, as his contribution examines how the Treaty provisions on state aid are applied in health care. His analysis confines itself (mainly) to discussing the *BUPA* case,[13] which concerned the relationship between the EU state aid rules and national measures financing health care. He examines the implications of this case for EU law in general and more specifically for services of general interest (hereafter: SGEI). It appears that the General Court (then the Court of First Instance) has adopted a flexible approach towards national financing mechanisms in health care and by doing so it has shown a great respect for the competences of the Member States in this area. As Neergaard did, De Vries points to the constitutional dimension of the *BUPA* judgment. De Vries even argues that the General Court took an advance on the Treaty of Lisbon 2009: the *BUPA* judgment was handed down in 2008 but anticipated on constitutional issues, such as the reinforced health care competences of the Member States and the increased role of SGEI in the Treaty of Lisbon 2009. However, he advocates that the objective of undistorted competition remains of great interest in the EU. Hence, the Commission has the duty to scrutinise in state aid cases whether the Member States has provided convincing evidence as to whether undertakings are not overcompensated. As a result, Member States are forced to formulate minimum criteria for health care services in their national legislation. It may be expected that this will lead to considerable changes in the health care systems of the Member States, as the competent authorities must offer a more transparent policy on the control and definition of SGEI than they usually do. Conversely, De Vries notes also a drawback to the *BUPA* judgment: it increasingly complicates the application of the concept of SGEI. As a result, at EU level no coherent approach towards this concept is in place and, therefore, the Union legislature should take action.

It is apparent from the analysis carried out by van de Gronden en De Vries that EU competition could have considerable impact on the national health care organisation of the Member States. Therefore, the consequences of this EU law area for two Member States are examined: Germany and The Netherlands.

Exploring the German experience of the impact of EU law on health care reform, *Felix Welti* highlights the interplay between incorporating elements of competition in the domestic organisation of health care and the application of EU law in that sector. In this context three different relationships which may be exposed to competition can be distinguished: competition between public health funds, competition between public and private health insurance and competition between the providers of health care services. This distinction is important because EU competition law may apply in one relationship but not in another as can be seen in the ECJ judgment *AOK Bundesverband*[14] which concerned the introduction of a certain degree of competition in the relationship between public health funds. Due to the fact that there was only a limited amount of competition the ECJ

[13] GC, Case T-289/03, *BUPA* v. *Commission* [2008] *ECR* II-81.

[14] Joined Cases C-264/01, C-306/01, C-453/01 and C-355/01 *AOK* [2004] *ECR* I-2493.

held that the public health funds are not performing economic activities. However, recent changes in the German health system might result in a level of competition which no longer excludes the application of EU competition law to public sickness funds. A related issue concerns the requirement of using procurement law by the health care funds when they conclude contracts with health services suppliers. It should not be surprising that the German special social law courts and social law experts are critical of the applicability of procurement law whilst the commercial courts and civil law experts have supported it. The ECJ sided with the latter in its *Oymanns* judgment.[15] Nevertheless, policy questions on the appropriateness of procurement law in this context remain as discussed in greater detail in the chapter by *Hatzopoulos* and *Stergiou*. Meanwhile the legislator and the German courts have reacted to the growing impact of EU law on German health care system. However, it should also be noted that EU law does not mandate a certain health system. In fact, as Welti rightly concludes the (non-)applicability of EU competition law depends largely on how the state organises its health system. This conclusion is in line with van de Gronden's finding that national health care schemes that are predominantly based on solidarity lack economic nature and do not fall, therefore, within the scope of EU competition law.

Wolf Sauter explains the role competition plays in the Dutch health care system, which is, unlike the German system, market-driven. The general rules of competition, as laid down in the Treaty and in the Dutch Act on Competition, are enforced by the Dutch Competition Authority (NMa), whereas sector specific competition policy is applied by the Dutch Health Care Authority (NZa). He is of the opinion that the arguments in favour of a regulatory framework for sector specific competition rules in health care are strong, due to pervasive market failures. Of importance, moreover, is that the fact that liberalisation of health care markets is taking place gradually, step by step. The Dutch Health Care Authority seems to be more concerned about foreclosure effects on health care markets than about exploitation, as it attributes great importance to market structure (for example, market entry, remaining competition on a given market). As a result, the Dutch Health Care Authority is more sensitive to the effects on market structure caused by merger activity than is the NMa. However, the power to clear mergers in health care rests with the NMa and not with the Dutch Health Care Authority. In any event, Sauter argues that we must wait to see if the existence of two independent bodies enforcing competition rules in health care will turn out to be a success. To date this question remains unanswered because there is no national case law on the competence to review decisions taken by the Dutch Health Care Authority addresses important competition law issues concerning, for example, the definition of 'Significant Market Power'.

Without any doubt, the most significant and striking example of a health care system that is driven by competition could be found in the US. Hence, the US health care system is explored in order to learn lessons as to how a market-driven

---

[15] ECJ, Case C-300/07 *Oymanns* [2009] *ECR* I-0000 (n.y.r.).

system works in practice. *Nathan Cortez* argues that market competition is a persistent but elusive ideal in US health care. However, the ideal of market competition has not delivered what American patients desire. Nonetheless, reforming the US health care system is extremely difficult as the issue of 'market vs. government' is the dividing line in the dominant theme in the health care debate. He notes that the US health care system has embraced several market-based techniques in order to solve problems such as the considerable number of uninsured persons. However, he points out that that the market-oriented measures taken by the government have failed to reduce spending or even to provide health insurance coverage for more persons. Remarkably, the health care reforms proposed by the Obama administration were based on market-driven ideals. Yet, these plans are heavily criticised by market advocates and others, because it is feared that the government's role in health care would irreversibly be amplified. The Health Care Act that was finally adopted by the Congress at the beginning of 2010 amounts more to health *insurance* reform rather than health *system* reform. This Act generally targets access to health care rather than reforming the system of delivery health care. Of interest is that the Act enhances competition on health insurance markets by allowing individuals and small employers to shop around amongst competing health care plans. Consequently, in US health care the point of departure remains private health insurance and competition, although this policy has not and will not produce universal coverage. Conversely, Cortez examines various health care specific market features and concludes, on the basis of the findings of this research, that competition in health care works the best when coupled with strong government regulation.

1.1.5 Further Issues of EU Health Law

EU law has expanded its influence on health care beyond matters of patient mobility and competition. Recent case law of the ECJ on free movement and general issues of capacity planning in health care has drawn much attention lately. Further, EU public procurement law imposes significant obligation on national health care authorities, when contracting out the performance of important public tasks. Therefore, these two topical themes are also explored.

The particularities and requirements of health care capacity planning have played an important role in the ECJs case law on patient mobility. *Rita Baeten* and *Willy Palm* take this as a starting point for their more general enquiry into the compatibility of health care planning and the EU internal market law. They point to the special characteristics of health care planning and the various forms that are being employed in the Member States. Without efficient and rational planning many public health goals such as quality, universal access and affordability are difficult to realise. Health care planning may, however, also be subject to regulatory capture in particular if provider associations are heavily involved in the planning process as it is the case in countries with strong corporatist traditions.

Capacity planning can also become a restriction on free movement because it limits the number of service providers. Nevertheless, the ECJ accepted planning requirements as justifications of the deviation from the market freedoms in a number of health-related cases.[16] In its case law on patient mobility the ECJ has applied a strict delineation between hospital and out-patient treatment only accepting planning with regards to the former as a justification of restrictions on free movement. However, in the recent *Blanco Perez* and *Chao Gomez* case on planning for pharmacies in Spain the ECJ recognised planning restrictions on a more general level. These cases, which are also discussed by Drijber and Cadenau in relation to the principle of non-discrimination, are explored in great detail by Baeten and Palm. It remains to be seen if this new development will influence the case law and/or legislation on patient mobility. In any case, restrictions on free movement due to capacity planning have to be proportionate. The ECJ does not seem to interfere heavily with the substance of the policies pursued by the Member States. Yet, the ECJ requires coherence and consistency of the measure in question.

The impact of public procurement law on health care is the subject of the chapter by *Vassilis Hatzopoulos* and *Hélène Stergiou*. Core health services such as hospital, medical, and dental services are subject to the 'light' procurement regime of Directive 2004/18/EC as they are listed in Annex II B of that Directive. This means that there is no mandatory tendering requirement. However, the general transparency and non-discrimination principles developed by the ECJ for service concessions and procurement not covered by the procurement Directives apply nonetheless. Whilst the exact contents of these principles remain unclear, they may require competitive tendering procedures in certain situations and therefore go beyond the requirements of the Directives. As public procurement law applies only to 'contracting authorities' in the meaning of the procurement Directives, the definition of this term is of crucial importance. According to ECJ case law the specific purpose of a contracting authority must be meeting needs of general interest which do not have an industrial or commercial character. Furthermore, the entity must be financed, supervised or appointed by another contracting authority. So far, the ECJ only handed down one judgment which specifically addressed the question whether a health care entity should be considered a contracting authority. In the *Oymanns* case, discussed from the German perspective in the contribution by Welti, the ECJ held that the German public sickness funds qualified as contracting authorities because they are financed for the most part by compulsory contributions from their members. Other cases have, however, also touched upon this issue. In particular, in a number of cases concerning ambulance services the ECJ has implicitly decided on the character of various public health entities as contracting authorities. However, so far the case law leaves many questions open. The approaches of the Member States also seem to vary considerably. This

[16] On this case law, see also Hancher and Sauter (2010), p. 132 et seq.

is in particular the case if a Member State reformed its health system to include elements of privatisation and liberalisation. The gradual introduction of such elements can lead to hybrid settings which may or may not be considered contracting authorities depending on the facts of the case. Domestic courts faced with adjudicating these issues will often be left with more questions than answers as the example of the Dutch *Amphia* case aptly demonstrates. The case concerned a general hospital which purchased new food distribution trolleys. As the Netherlands considerably reformed their health care system in 2006 the question arose whether such a hospital operating as a privatised entity but still financed through the general health system was a contracting authority. Four Dutch Courts including the Supreme Court addressed this question and reached different results, which indicates the complicated and fact-dependent nature of the issue.

Most debates on the impact of EU law on health policy have focussed on the internal side of EU law, i.e. internal market, competition, state aid and procurement rules. However, the external law of the EU including international trade agreements which are an integral part of the EU legal order may also have an impact on health policies. Furthermore, there has been a debate on the influence of the WTOs General Agreement on Trade in Services (GATS) on public services in general and health care in particular, which remarkably resembles the respective debates about EU law. Hence, it is of great importance that due attention is paid to the WTO dimension of the Europeanisation process of health care. Due to growing importance of this dimension *Markus Krajewski* discusses the application of WTO rules on health care. He takes the WTO debates on public services into account when asking what would have happened if Mrs Watts had gone to the United States, Singapore or Malaysia for her surgery instead of France. In light of the growing numbers of international patients in South-east Asia and elsewhere this is not such a far-fetched scenario. By analysing how Mrs Watts's case would have been solved under GATS law the similarities and differences between EU and WTO law can be compared and analysed on the basis of a concrete example. The GATS clearly applies to health services and it covers four modes of supply which bear striking similarities with the notion of cross-border health care in the original Commissions proposal for the Patients' Rights Directive. However, the actual level of liberalisation of health services achieved through the GATS depends on the scope of commitments of each WTO Member in this sector. If a Member made commitments in medical and hospital services the refusal to reimburse the costs of a medical treatment abroad whilst reimbursing the costs of the treatment at home could violate the principle of national treatment (Article XVII GATS). Such a violation could be justified on the basis of Article XIV(b) GATS if it could be shown that the refusal of reimbursement would be necessary to maintain the financial stability of the respective national health system. If, however, a Member did not undertake specific commitments in health services in the first place or scheduled a special limitation which excluded the reimbursement of costs for treatment abroad the measure would not violate Article XVII GATS. Hence, the scope of the commitments is crucial. However, since the WTO agreements including the GATS do not have direct effect in the EU legal order, an individual could not rely on them in a proceeding before a court.

References

Barnard C (2006) EC Employment Law, Oxford University Press, Oxford

Hancher L, Sauter W (2010) 'One Step Beyond? From Sodemare to Docmorris: The EU's Freedom of Establishment Case Law Concerning Health Care', CML Rev 47

Hervey TK, McHale JV (2004) Health Law and the European Union. Cambridge University Press, Cambridge

Mossialos E, McKee M (2004) EU Law and the Social Character of Health Care. Bruxelles, P.I.E. Lang

Neergaard U, Nielsen R (2010). Blurring Boundaries: From the Danish Welfare State to the European Social Model (ssrn: http://ssrn.com/abstract=1618758)

Part I
Foundations

Chapter 2
EU Health Care Law in a Constitutional Light: Distribution of Competences, Notions of 'Solidarity', and 'Social Europe'

Ulla Neergaard

Contents

2.1 Introduction

On one occasion an expert in the law stood up to test Jesus. "Teacher", he asked, "what must I do to inherit eternal life?"
"What is written in the Law?" he replied. "How do you read it?"
He answered: "'Love the Lord your God with all your heart and with all your soul and with all your strength and with all your mind'; and, 'Love your neighbour as yourself'."
"You have answered correctly", Jesus replied. "Do this and you will live."
But he wanted to justify himself, so he asked Jesus, "And who is my neighbour?"In reply Jesus said: "A man was going down from Jerusalem to Jericho, when he fell into the hands

U. Neergaard (✉)
Law Faculty, University of Copenhagen, Copenhagen, Denmark
e-mail: ulla.neergaard@jur.ku.dk

J. W. van de Gronden et al. (eds.), *Health Care and EU Law*,
Legal Issues of Services of General Interest, DOI: 10.1007/978-90-6704-728-9_2,

> of robbers. They stripped him of his clothes, beat him and went away, leaving him half dead. A priest happened to be going down the same road, and when he saw the man, he passed by on the other side. So too, a Levite, when he came to the place and saw him, passed by on the other side. But a Samaritan, as he travelled, came where the man was; and when he saw him, he took pity on him. He went to him and bandaged his wounds, pouring on oil and wine. Then he put the man on his own donkey, took him to an inn and took care of him. The next day he took out two silver coins and gave them to the innkeeper. 'Look after him', he said, 'and when I return, I will reimburse you for any extra expense you may have'."
> Which of these three do you think was a neighbour to the man who fell into the hands of robbers?
> The expert in the law replied, "The one who had mercy on him."
> Jesus told him, "Go and do likewise."[1]

This parable of the 'Good Samaritan' may be claimed to have worked itself deeply into the European consciousness. It may be taken as one of the explanatory roots for the establishment of the modern sophisticated European public health systems, beginning as these often did back in history through Christian thinking, for example, in the shape of caring tasks in certain periods of time undertaken by monasteries and other organised institutions.[2]

Health care constitutes an essential element in a typical European welfare state. A welfare state in Europe is originally a nation-state, where contributions to a national health care system normally are provided through taxation or by payments of premiums into an insurance scheme. Although differing in many ways, all health care systems in the Member States of the EU provide near universal coverage based on solidarity.[3] However, generally there is an increasingly blurred line between such states and EU law as part of a more comprehensive multi-level legal system, where EU law and the national law of its Member States are mutually embedded.[4] Regarding more specifically healthcare, the same situation seems to have developed. Health care law used to be a nation-state matter, but, inter alia, the EU has altered this point of departure. Also, the market as such is having an increasing influence on the organisation of health care. Thus, there is a wave of liberalisation and privatisation, including the fact that cross-border health care has become a reality, which is changing the traditional way of setting up such systems. Also, certain basic values and principles, for example, non-discrimination, equality, social inclusion, and access to essential services, are becoming increasingly influential. These changes are largely, but not only, due to the influence of the EU.

---

[1] The New Testament of the Christian Bible, Luke 10: 25–37. This quoted English version has been found on the internet. The present chapter constitutes a revised version of a paper presented at the Conference: 'Health Care and EU Law', 1–2 October 2009 (Radboud University Nijmegen). Generally, material which has come to my knowledge after 1 February 2010 has been left out of consideration.

[2] See also, for example, Manow (2004); or Østergaard (2010).

[3] Mossialos and McKee (2004), p. 21.

[4] See in this regard Neergaard et al. (2010).

Against this background, the present chapter has the purpose of analysing the changes of EU health care law in a more constitutional light, but limited to the following five issues: distribution of competences and the Treaty (Sect. 2.2), distribution of competences and free movement of services (Sect. 2.3), distribution of competences and SGEIs[5] in light of *BUPA* (Sect. 2.4),[6] notions of solidarity (Sect. 2.5), and Social Europe (Sect. 2.6).[7] Conclusions are brought forward in the final part (Sect. 2.7). The overall research aim is to achieve an understanding of which direction Europe takes with regard to health care on the basis of the five examined perspectives. The first three perspectives may be viewed as relating to the issue of competence, that is, who has the power (the Member State or the EU?). The last two perspectives may be viewed as relating more directly (compared with the first three perspectives) to which economic model the EU adopts in this area. At the same time, these two latter perspectives do in fact also throw some light on the understanding of distribution of competences. In other words, all five perspectives are inter-related. Taking this road, the changes occurring in this area are placed into a larger context. As a point of departure the approach taken is legal dogmatic, which results in the focus centred on what is valid law.[8]

2.2 Distribution of Competences and the Treaty

The issue of the distribution of competences is a concrete way of examining which direction European health law moves. By including this dimension it is possible to see at which level of governance the legislative competences in the area are placed, and in fact thereby also obtaining an indication of how much economic and/or social integration may be expected. On the one hand, if the legislative competences primarily are vested at the Member State level, they are more likely to be free to go ahead the way they so wish. On the other hand, if competences primarily are vested at the level of the EU, interference in this regard may be expected with an increased economic and social integration as the result.[9] Therefore, in this part, the purpose is to examine the role of health care primarily in the light of the Treaty of Lisbon 2009 with regard to distribution of competences.[10]

The Treaty of Rome, which entered into force in 1958, referred to health in principle only in Articles 36, 48(3), and 56(1) EEC, either as a reference to the

[5] The concept 'SGEIs' refers to 'services of general economic interest'.

[6] General Court, Case T-289/03 *BUPA* [2008] *ECR* II-81. See also General Court, Case T-289/03 (Order) *BUPA* [2008] *ECR* II-741.

[7] In other words, a full account of the subject is not possible here.

[8] See, for example, Hesselink (2009), pp. 20–45.

[9] In this regard, see further Sect. 2.6 *infra*.

[10] The Treaty of Lisbon 2009 entered into force 1 December 2009. Generally about distinction of competences in EU law, see, for example, Bribosia (2007), pp. 389–437; de Búrca and de Witte (2002), pp. 201–222; and Weatherill (2002), pp. 41–73.

'protection of health' or 'public health'.[11] Thus, the context in which health was placed in originally in principle only concerned the expressly stated derogations to the principles of free movement. Therefore, in the absence of harmonisation national measures could take precedence over free movement in the interest of health, of course provided that amongst others the principle of proportionality is fulfilled. As Barnard points out, the Court of Justice[12] has ruled that each Member State had the right to determine the level of health protection desired for its citizens, taking into account various factors such as the climate in the state, the normal diet of the population, and its state of health.[13] The seminal state of law could be seen as a strong indication of the Member States originally being in charge of health matters in a way that most likely not even the otherwise 'strong' free movement principles could disturb.

Today, the situation has changed radically. To date, the Treaty of Lisbon 2009 represents the final step in a rather long process of changes having taken place concerning the area of health in connection with Treaty amendments, but in fact also due to the interpretation of fundamental principles, launched by the progressive Court of Justice.[14] In the Treaty of Lisbon 2009, health issues still constitute an important derogation within the framework of free movement, but regarding legislative competences as such the picture is changed radically

---

[11] Now Articles 36, 45(3), and 52(1) TFEU. In addition to the three provisions mentioned, for the sake of completeness reference could also be made to the original Article 135 EEC.

[12] Pursuant to Article 19 TEU, the terminology regarding the European Courts now is: 'The Court of Justice of the European Union shall include the Court of Justice, the General Court and specialised courts…' This terminology is used throughout the present chapter, also in situations of reference to case law rendered before the entering into force of the Treaty of Lisbon 2009. Therefore, what often has been referred to as the European Court of Justice will here be referred to as the Court of Justice (except for references in footnotes to specific cases, where 'ECJ' is used), and what often has been referred to as the Court of First Instance will here be referred to as the General Court.

[13] Barnard (2007), p. 74. See further Sect. 2.3 *infra*.

[14] The evolution of the changes will not systematically be dealt with here. It is worth emphasising that the Proposal for a Directive of the European Parliament of the Council on the application of patients' rights in cross-border healthcare, COM(2008) 414, Brussels 2 July 2008 (hereinafter referred to as the 'Directive Proposal'), which was launched before the entry into force of the Treaty of Lisbon 2009 would have its legal basis in Article 95 EC (now Article 114 TFEU). It is stated at p. 8 that: 'This proposal respects the fact that health systems are primarily the responsibility of Member States and fully respects the responsibilities of the Member States for the organisation and delivery of health services and medical care in accordance with Article 152 TEC. Article 95(3) of the Treaty further stipulates that the Commission, in its proposals for the establishment and functioning of the internal market concerning health, shall take as a basis high level of protection of health, taking account in particular of any new development based on scientific evidence. In preparation of this proposal, the Commission took fully into account the most recent research results and the current best medical practice. Several expert studies, analyses and research reports were used in the preparatory work. The proposal will thus ensure that the necessary requirements for high-quality, safe and efficient healthcare are also ensured for cross-border healthcare.' Regarding the case law of the Court of Justice, see in particular Sect. 2.5.3 *infra*.

especially when compared with the original stance taken in the Treaty of Rome. Now, it is expressly stated in Article 4(1) and (2) of the TFEU that:

> 1. The Union shall share competence with the Member States where the Treaties confer on it a competence which does not relate to the areas referred to in Articles 3 and 6.
> 2. Shared competence between the Union and the Member States applies in the following principal areas:
>
> (a) internal market;
> (b) social policy, for the aspects defined in this Treaty; ...
> (k) *common safety concerns in public health matters, for the aspects defined in this* Treaty. [emphasis added]

In Article 3 TFEU (to which reference is made in the quoted provision) areas where the Union has exclusive competences are mentioned. Health is not included therein. In Article 6 TFEU (to which reference is also made in the quoted provision) health is mentioned, as it is stated that:

> The Union shall have competence to carry out actions to support, coordinate or supplement the actions of the Member States. The areas of such action shall, at European level, be: (a) *protection and improvement of human health*; ... [emphasis added]

It is thus expressly stated that the Union and the Member States share competences within the area of common safety concerns in public health matters, for the aspects defined in the Treaty. Also, it is expressly stated that the Union shall have competence to carry out actions to support, coordinate or supplement the actions of the Member States regarding the protection and improvement of human health. In other words, the Member States do not in any regard hold an exclusive competence in the area of health. Rather, sharing of competences in different variants is now dominant. It may be, first, added that pursuant to Article 2(1) TFEU, when the Treaties confer on the Union exclusive competence in a specific area, only the Union may legislate and adopt legally binding acts, the Member States being able to do so themselves only if so empowered by the Union or for the implementation of Union acts. Second, it may be added that pursuant to Article 2(2) TFEU when the Treaties confer on the Union a competence shared with the Member States in a specific area, the Union and the Member States may legislate and adopt legally binding acts in that area. Also, in this case, the Member States shall exercise their competence to the extent that the Union has not exercised its competence, and the Member States shall again exercise their competence to the extent that the Union has decided to cease exercising its competence. Third, it may be added that Article 2(5) TFEU provides that in certain areas and under the conditions laid down in the Treaties, the Union shall have competence to carry out actions to support, coordinate or supplement the actions of the Member States, without thereby superseding their competence in these areas. Although there is a distinction between concepts, this latter situation may in certain cases end up being close to the concept of shared competences.

Furthermore, Article 114 TFEU contains the general Internal Market legal base, and it is of some interest that Article 114(3) TFEU requires that harmonisation measures adopted must guarantee a high level of protection of human health[15]:

> The Commission, in its proposals envisaged in paragraph 1 concerning *health*, safety, environmental protection and consumer protection, will take as a base a high level of protection, taking account in particular of any new development based on scientific facts. Within their respective powers, the European Parliament and the Council will also seek to achieve this objective. [emphasis added]

In addition, Title XIV concerns 'public health'. It consists of one provision, namely Article 168 TFEU. In general, this is a provision of importance here, but especially Article 168(7) TFEU should be given particular attention, as it is here stated that:

> Union action shall respect the responsibilities of the Member States for *the definition of their health policy and for the organisation and delivery of health services and medical care*. The responsibilities of the Member States shall *include the management of health services and medical care* and the allocation of the resources assigned to them. The measures referred to in paragraph 4(a) shall not affect national provisions on the donation or medical use of organs and blood.[16] [emphasis added]

The provision (in its earlier formulation) may (according to Hervey and McHale) be viewed as an explicit statement on the application of the principle of subsidiarity in the health field.[17]

In sum, the picture gained from this examination of particularly the Treaty of Lisbon 2009 definitely confirms the above-mentioned impression of a blurred line

---

[15] See the chapter by Szyszczak.

[16] The predecessor in the Treaty of Nice 2000 was Article 152(5) EC where it was stated that: 'Community action in the field of public health shall fully respect the responsibilities of the Member States for the organisation and delivery of health services and medical care. In particular, measures referred to in paragraph 4(a) shall not affect national provisions on the donation or medical use of organs and blood.' Especially, it is of interest that 'fully' has disappeared in the Treaty of Lisbon 2009. It is also of interest that in the Directive Proposal it is stated at p. 9 that: 'According to Article 152(5) of the EC Treaty Community action in the field of public health is to fully respect the responsibilities of the Member States for the organisation and delivery of health services and medical care. As confirmed by the Court, that provision does not, however, exclude the possibility that the Member States may be required under other Treaty provisions, such as Article 49 EC of the EC Treaty, or Community measures adopted on the basis of other Treaty provisions, to make adjustments to their national healthcare and social security systems. As the Court held, this does not mean that this undermines their sovereign powers in the field. In any event, Member States are responsible for the organisation and delivery of health services and medical care. They are in particular responsible for determining which rules will apply to the reimbursement of patients and to the provision of healthcare. This proposal changes nothing in this respect. It is important to underline that this initiative does not alter the Member States' choice of the rules which will be applicable to a specific case.' The provision was first introduced in the Treaty of Maastricht 1992 (as Article 129 EC).

[17] See further Hervey and McHale (2004), Chapter 3.

between Member States and the EU in the area of the regulation of health care.[18] Also, viewed over the time span of the existence of the EEC/EC/EU, health care has increasingly become an area of interest to this level of governance, having the unavoidable consequence of erosion of national competences.[19]

2.3 Distribution of Competences and Free Movement of Services

Within the area of free movement several important cases have been rendered by the Court of Justice. This area is in focus in what follows, at least with regard to the examined issue of distribution of competences, and only including services. As the judgments generally are rather complicated, but also already quite commented upon in legal discourse, the examination will focus on just the main consequences of this case law with regard to the issues at stake, rather than going into very technical details.[20] The most important cases will be analysed chronologically.[21] In general, the cases included in the examination constitute preliminary rulings and they are often decided by either eleven or thirteen judges as an indication in itself of the importance attached to the judgments by the Court of Justice itself.

Compared to the previous section, the level of focus is, in other words, changed here, because that part primarily took its point of departure in the more general understanding of legislative competences to be gained from a reading of the Treaty of Lisbon 2009. Thus, this was largely a matter of when the Institutions are given formal legal power to act. This Part takes its point of departure in the question of *when* Member States can legislate lawfully without contravening the general

[18] For the sake of completeness, it may be added that references to health (besides what has already been indicated) is also made in Articles 9, 114, 153, 169, 191, 202, 207 TFEU as well as Declaration on Article 168(4)(c) of the TFEU. In addition, see especially Article 35 of the Charter of Fundamental Rights of the European Union of 7 December 2000, as adapted at Strasbourg, on 12 December 2007. The Charter shall pursuant to Article 6 of the TEU have the same legal value as the Treaties. Also, besides the many mentioned provisions and the principles of free movement it should for the sake of completeness be emphasised that competition law provisions may be of relevance. Finally, other legal basis provisions and principles may be of relevance. Concerning legal base in the context of the Directive Proposal see the chapter by Szyszczak.

[19] See Hervey and McHale (2004), p. 80.

[20] See for one of the more recent contributions, for example, van de Gronden (2008), pp. 705–760. Also, several other chapters of the present volume deal with this case law in detail; see the chapter of Baquero Cruz.

[21] The analysis is limited to primary law issues, and will not include, for example, social security regulation, which may also be of significance, as a main theme. In this regard, see in particular the chapter of Pennings. Also, as indicated, only primary law concerning free movement of services is included. These delimitations of the analysis may have an impact on the conclusions reached, however, not fundamentally.

principles of free movement of services. The reason why this is of interest is, in somehow simplified terms, that even though a Member State formally has the legislative competence in a given area, most often this is limited as the competence will have to be used in a way not contravening these principles. Thus, a legislative competence in a given area may be thought of as 'vertical' in character, whereas free movement principles may be thought of as 'horizontal' as these principles often will function as cutting across all kinds of areas, and Member States are not protected there from, 'just' because they have a legislative competence in a given area pursuant to the Treaty. This—to some rather surprising—point of departure will be further understood from the following analysis.

Luisi and Carbone in 1984 is the first case to discuss because it paved the road to later case law of more specific importance.[22] In this case, it was established that not only the providers of services, but also the recipients, are included in the scope of protection. Although the case in hindsight is analysed for this new view of the scope of services, it in fact also concerned medical treatment.[23]

Gül decided in 1986 should be the next case to discuss.[24] Here, the importance of the Court of Justice ruling is seen in the statement that:

> … The right to restrict freedom of movement on grounds of public health is intended not to exclude the public health sector, as a sector of economic activity and from the point of view of access to employment, from the application of the principles of freedom of movement but to permit Member States to refuse access to their territory or residence there to persons whose access or residence would in itself constitute a danger for public health.[25]

In its entirety this case represents the somewhat 'older' regime of thinking, which now may be considered as too limited to be representative of today's thinking. The first part of this sentence is of importance, because the Court of Justice in the first case of essential importance, *Kohll*, finds pursuant to *Gül* that, although under Articles 56 and 66 EC (now Articles 52 and 62 TFEU) Member States may limit freedom to provide services on grounds of public health, that does not permit them to exclude the public health sector, as a sector of economic activity and from the point of view of freedom to provide services, from the application of the fundamental principle of freedom of movement.[26]

---

[22] ECJ, Joined Cases 286/82 and 26/83 *Luisi and Carbone* [1984] *ECR 377*. See the chapter by Baquero Cruz.

[23] Para 16 states: 'It follows that the freedom to provide services includes the freedom, for the recipients of services, to go to another member state in order to receive a service there, without being obstructed by restrictions, even in relation to payments and that tourists, persons receiving medical treatment and persons travelling for the purpose of education or business are to be regarded as recipients of services.'

[24] ECJ, Case 131/85 *Gül* [1986] *ECR* 1573.

[25] Ibid., para 17.

[26] ECJ, Case C-158/96 *Kohll* [1998] *ECR* I-1931, paras 45–46. See also the related case, however, concerning free movement of goods, rendered on the same date: ECJ, Case C-120/95 *Decker* [1998] *ECR* I-1831. See for further discussion of this case, Chapter 4.

Kohll is in many respects of great importance regarding free movement of services and health care. On the surface, it has a certain degree of 'innocence' attached to it as it concerns a Luxembourg father stubbornly requesting authorisation for his daughter, who is a minor, to receive treatment from an orthodontist established in Germany. The case arises in proceedings between this father, Mr Kohll, and the Union des Caisses de Maladie, with which he is insured. Inter alia, the Court of Justice states that the fact that the national rules at issue in the main proceedings fall within the sphere of social security cannot exclude the application of Articles 59 and 60 EC (now Articles 56 and 57 TFEU). The Court of Justice holds that whilst the national rules at issue in the main proceedings do not deprive insured persons of the possibility of approaching a provider of services established in another Member State, they nevertheless make reimbursement of the costs incurred in that Member State subject to prior authorisation, and denies such reimbursement to insured persons who have not obtained that authorisation.[27] Also, costs incurred in the State of insurance are not, however, subject to that authorisation.[28] In the ruling of the Court of Justice, the measure is considered as constituting a barrier to freedom to provide services and it is thus examined whether it is objectively justified.[29] Although the Court of Justice in this regard finds that aims of a purely economic nature cannot justify a barrier to the fundamental principle of freedom to provide services it also importantly states that it cannot be excluded that the risk of seriously undermining the financial balance of the social security system may constitute an overriding reason in the general interest capable of justifying a barrier of that kind.[30] However, this is not the situation in the case at hand. In addition, the Court of Justice examines whether the measure in question can be justified on grounds of public health. The conclusion is that it cannot be justified on such grounds. More specifically, the Court of Justice finds in this regard first, that the measure cannot be justified on grounds of public health in order to protect the quality of medical services provided in other Member States.[31] Second, it finds that the objective of maintaining a balanced medical and hospital service open to all, that objective, although intrinsically linked to the method of financing the social security system, may also fall within the derogations on grounds of public health under Article 56 EC (now Article 52 TFEU), in so far as it contributes to the attainment of a high level of health protection.[32] However, the Court of Justice finds that this is not the situation in the measure at hand.

Overall, Articles 59 and 60 EC (now Articles 56 and 57 TFEU) are considered to be infringed, because these provisions preclude national rules under which reimbursement, in accordance with the scale of the State of insurance, of the cost

[27] Ibid., para 34.
[28] Idem.
[29] Ibid., para 35.
[30] Ibid., para 41.
[31] Ibid., para 48.
[32] Ibid., para 50.

of dental treatment provided by an orthodontist established in another Member State is subject to authorisation by the insured person's social security institution. With *Kohll*, it thus becomes clear that the path towards a more general right to have the costs of health treatment incurred in other Member States should in principle be reimbursed is initiated. Thus the case is of considerable significance.

The next case of primary interest, *Smits-Peerbooms*, rendered almost three years later, confirms this new path.[33] This time, the central issue is much more to the point as the case concerns reimbursement of hospital treatment costs. At the overall level, it concerns the issue of whether Articles 59 and 60 EC (now Articles 56 and 57 TFEU) are to be interpreted as precluding legislation of a Member State, which makes the assumption of the costs of care provided in a hospital establishment in another Member State conditional upon prior authorisation by the sickness insurance fund with which an insured person is registered, that authorisation being granted only in so far as two conditions are satisfied.[34] The first condition is that the proposed treatment must be amongst the benefits for which the sickness insurance scheme of the first Member State assumes responsibility, which means that the treatment must be regarded as 'normal in the professional circles concerned'.[35] The second condition is that the treatment abroad must be necessary in terms of the medical condition of the person concerned, which supposes that adequate care cannot be provided without undue delay by a health care provider which has entered into an agreement with a sickness insurance fund in the first Member State.[36]

Regarding the competence of the Member States to arrange their social security systems and the obligation to comply with EU law in exercising that competence, the Court of Justice states that:

> In order to answer the questions as thus reformulated, it should be remembered at the outset that, according to settled case-law, Community law does not detract from the power of the Member States to organise their social security systems... In the absence of harmonisation at Community level, it is therefore for the legislation of each Member State to determine, first, the conditions concerning the right or duty to be insured with a social security scheme... and, second, the conditions for entitlement to benefits... Nevertheless, the Member States must comply with Community law when exercising that power.[37]

In other words, free movement principles may, in a way, be viewed as 'superior' to the competence to organise social security systems, or at least as explained above, as having a 'horizontal' significance.

It is also of relevance to the understanding of distribution of competences in the area of health care that the Court of Justice considers whether the situations at issue in the main proceedings fall within the ambit of the freedom to provide services provided for in Articles 59 and 60 EC (now Articles 56 and 57 TFEU).

---

[33] ECJ, Case C-157/99 *Smits-Peerbooms* [2001] *ECR* I-5473.

[34] Ibid., para 43.

[35] Idem.

[36] Idem.

[37] Ibid., paras 44–46.

More precisely, it is considered whether hospital services can constitute an economic activity within the meaning of Article 60 EC (now Article 57 TFEU), particularly when they are provided in kind and free of charge under the relevant sickness insurance scheme. The Court of Justice responded in the affirmative. Accordingly, medical activities fall within the scope of Article 60 EC (now Article 57 TFEU), there being no need to distinguish in that regard between care provided in a hospital environment and non-hospital care.[38]

The Court of Justice finds that rules such as those at issue in the main proceedings deter, or even prevent, insured persons from applying to providers of medical services established in another Member State and constitute, both for insured persons and service providers, a barrier to freedom to provide services.[39] In this regard, it is emphasised that treatment provided in contracted hospitals situated in the Member State itself, is paid for by the sickness insurance funds without any prior authorisation being required.[40]

Subsequently, the Court of Justice examines whether there are overriding reasons which can be accepted as justifying barriers to freedom to provide medical services supplied in the context of a hospital infrastructure. On the basis of *Kohll*, it acknowledges the following reasons: (1) the possible risk of seriously undermining a social security system's financial balance; (2) maintenance of a balanced medical and hospital service open to all, in so far as it contributes to the attainment of a high level of health protection; and (3) maintenance of treatment capacity or medical competence on national territory being essential for the public health, and even the survival of, the population.[41] Against this background, the Court of Justice concludes that in principle, the measure in question is justified, but under specified conditions.[42] When such conditions are satisfied, Member States are free to legislate.

---

[38] Ibid., para 53.

[39] Ibid., para 69.

[40] Ibid., para 68.

[41] Ibid., paras 72–74.

[42] More specifically, the Court of Justice concludes that: 'Article 59 of the EC Treaty (now, after amendment, Article 49 EC) and Article 60 of the EC Treaty (now Article 50 EC) do not preclude legislation of a Member State, such as that at issue in the main proceedings, which makes the assumption of the costs of treatment provided in a hospital located in another Member State subject to prior authorisation from the insured person's sickness insurance fund and the grant of such authorisation subject to the condition that (i) the treatment must be regarded as 'normal in the professional circles concerned', a criterion also applied in determining whether hospital treatment provided on national territory is covered, and (ii) the insured person's medical treatment must require that treatment. However, that applies only in so far as—the requirement that the treatment must be regarded as 'normal' is construed to the effect that authorisation cannot be refused on that ground where it appears that the treatment concerned is sufficiently tried and tested by international medical science, and—authorisation can be refused on the ground of lack of medical necessity only if the same or equally effective treatment can be obtained without undue delay at an establishment having a contractual arrangement with the insured person's sickness insurance fund.'

Vanbraeckel was rendered on the exact same day as *Smits-Peerbooms*.[43] In principle, it builds on the same understanding as presented above. It is of central interest in the present context that the Court of Justice determines that Article 59 EC (now Article 56 TFEU) is to be interpreted as meaning that, if the reimbursement of costs incurred on hospital services provided in a Member State of stay, calculated under the rules in force in that State, is less than the amount which application of the legislation in force in the Member State of registration would afford to a person receiving hospital treatment in that State, additional reimbursement covering that difference must be granted to the insured person by the competent institution.[44]

In *Müller-Fauré*, decided in 2003, the Court of Justice considered whether Articles 59 and 60 EC (now Articles 56 and 57 TFEU) should be interpreted as precluding legislation of a Member State, which makes assumption of the costs of care provided in another Member State, by a person or an establishment with whom or which the insured person's sickness fund has not concluded an agreement, conditional upon prior authorisation by the fund.[45] This is answered in the negative, in principle.[46] In addition, the Court of Justice examined whether legislation, which has restrictive effects on the freedom to provide services, can be justified by the actual particular features of the national sickness insurance scheme, which provides not for reimbursement of costs incurred but essentially for benefits in kind and is based on a system of agreements intended both to ensure the quality of the care and to control the costs thereof.[47] In connection therewith, it is also examined whether the fact that the treatment at issue is provided in whole or in part in a hospital environment has any effect in that regard.[48] In principle, the

43 ECJ, Case C-368/98 *Vanbraeckel* [2001] *ECR* I-5363.

44 Ibid., para 53.

45 ECJ, Case C-385/99 *Müller-Fauré* [2003] *ECR* I-4509, para 37.

46 More precisely, the Court of Justice concludes that: 'Article 59 of the EC Treaty (now, after amendment, Article 49 EC) [now Article 56 TFEU] and Article 60 of the EC Treaty (now Article 50 EC) [now Article 57 TFEU] must be interpreted as not precluding legislation of a Member State, such as that at issue in the main proceedings, which (i) makes the assumption of the costs of hospital care provided in a Member State other than that in which the insured person's sickness fund is established, by a provider with which that fund has not concluded an agreement, conditional upon prior authorisation by the fund and (ii) makes the grant of that authorisation subject to the condition that such action is necessary for the insured person's health care. However, authorisation may be refused on that ground only if treatment which is the same or equally effective for the patient can be obtained without undue delay in an establishment which has concluded an agreement with the fund…'.

47 Ibid., para 46.

48 Idem.

Court of Justice answers this in the affirmative.[49] With this case, therefore, an important distinction between hospital and non-hospital care is introduced.

Inizan, also decided in 2003, may largely be viewed as a confirmation of its predecessors with regard to the understanding of free movement of health services.[50] More precisely, the Court of Justice holds that Articles 49 and 50 EC (now Articles 56 and 57 TFEU) must be interpreted as not precluding legislation of a Member State, such as that at issue in the main proceedings, which, first, makes reimbursement of the cost of hospital care provided in a Member State other than that in which the insured person's sickness fund is established conditional upon prior authorisation by that fund and, second, makes the grant of that authorisation subject to the condition that it be established that the insured person could not receive within the territory of the Member State where the fund is established the treatment appropriate to his condition.[51] However, the Court of Justice stresses that authorisation may be refused on that ground only if treatment which is the same or equally effective for the patient can be obtained without undue delay in the territory of the Member State in which he resides.[52]

Leichtle, decided in 2004 mainly constitutes a continuation of previously established principles.[53] For instance, it is stated that:

> Moreover, although it is not disputed that Community law does not detract from the power of the Member States to organise their social security systems and that, in the absence of harmonisation at Community level, it is for the legislation of each Member State to determine the conditions on which social security benefits are granted, it is nevertheless the case that, when exercising that power, the Member States must comply with Community law....[54]

It is of some interest that the Court of Justice stated that although travel costs and any visitors' tax are not medical in character, and are not as a rule paid to health care providers, they none the less appear to be inextricably linked to the cure itself, since, as previously stated, the patient is required to travel to and stay at the spa.[55] Therefore, a right to reimbursement of such related costs may also be in existence at times.

---

[49] More precisely, the Court of Justice concludes that: '... Articles 59 and 60 of the Treaty [now Articles 56 and 57 TFEU] do preclude the same legislation in so far as it makes the assumption of the costs of non-hospital care provided in another Member State by a person or establishment with whom or which the insured person's sickness fund has not concluded an agreement conditional upon prior authorisation by the fund, even when the national legislation concerned sets up a system of benefits in kind under which insured persons are entitled not to reimbursement of costs incurred for medical treatment, but to the treatment itself which is provided free of charge.'

[50] ECJ, Case C-56/01 *Inizan* [2003] *ECR* I-12403.

[51] Ibid., para 60.

[52] Idem.

[53] ECJ, Case C-8/02 *Leichtle* [2004] *ECR* I-2641.

[54] Ibid., para 29.

[55] Ibid., para 35.

Watts, decided in 2006 contributes many new interesting aspects to the understanding of the area.[56] It is a rather long and detailed judgment. Inter alia, the Court of Justice was faced with the question of whether, given the particular characteristics of the National Health Service (hereinafter referred to as 'NHS'), a patient resident in the UK is entitled under Article 49 EC (now Article 56 TFEU) to receive hospital treatment in another Member State at the expense of that national service.

It is of significance that the case concerns national health services financed by the State, such as the NHS. In this regard, the Court of Justice states that:

> It must therefore be found that Article 49 EC applies where a patient such as Mrs Watts receives medical services in a hospital environment for consideration in a Member State other than her State of residence, regardless of the way in which the national system with which that person is registered and from which reimbursement of the cost of those services is subsequently sought operates.[57]

Regarding the distribution of competences, the Court of Justice emphasises that:

> Whilst it is not in dispute that Community law does not detract from the power of the Member States to organise their social security systems, and that, in the absence of harmonisation at Community level, it is for the legislation of each Member State to determine the conditions in which social security benefits are granted, when exercising that power Member States must comply with Community law, in particular the provisions on the freedom to provide services... Those provisions prohibit the Member States from introducing or maintaining unjustified restrictions on the exercise of that freedom in the healthcare sector.[58]

The Court of Justice decides that Article 49 EC (now Article 56 TFEU) applies where a person whose state of health necessitates hospital treatment goes to another Member State and receives such treatment for consideration, there being no need to determine whether the provision of hospital treatment within the national health service with which that person is registered is in itself a service within the meaning of the Treaty provisions on the freedom to provide services.[59]

It is of interest that the Court of Justice in connection with the answering of a question as to whether Article 49 EC (now Article 56 TFEU) and Article 22 of Regulation No 1408/71 must be interpreted as imposing an obligation on Member States to fund hospital treatment in other Member States without reference to budgetary constraints and, if so, whether such an obligation is compatible with Article 152(5) EC (now Article 168(7) TFEU), the Court of Justice reasserts its case law that the requirements arising from these provisions are not to be interpreted as imposing on the Member States an obligation to reimburse the cost of hospital treatment in other Member States without reference to any budgetary consideration

---

[56] Case C-372/04 *Watts* [2006] *ECR* I-4325.

[57] Ibid., para 90.

[58] Ibid., para 92. See further the chapter by Baquero Cruz.

[59] Ibid., para 123.

but, on the contrary, are based on the need to balance the objective of the free movement of patients against overriding national objectives relating to management of the available hospital capacity, control of health expenditure and financial balance of social security systems.[60] The Court of Justice also emphasises that:

> Next, it should be noted that, according to Article 152(5) EC [now Article 168(7) TFEU], Community action in the field of public health is to fully respect the responsibilities of the Member States for the organisation and delivery of health services and medical care. That provision does not, however, exclude the possibility that the Member States may be required under other Treaty provisions, such as Article 49 EC [now Article 56 TFEU], or Community measures adopted on the basis of other Treaty provisions, such as Article 22 of Regulation No 1408/71, to make adjustments to their national systems of social security. It does not follow that this undermines their sovereign powers in the field...[61]

The judgment contains certain considerations regarding private hospitals which are of interest. Thus, after having held that the system of prior authorisation in question deters, or even prevents, the patients concerned from applying to providers of hospital services established in another Member State and constitutes, both for those patients and for service providers, an obstacle to the freedom to provide services, the Court of Justice establishes that[62]:

> That conclusion is not undermined by the fact, referred to in Question 1(b), that the NHS is not obliged to authorise and assume the cost of hospital treatment provided to patients in private non-NHS hospitals in England and Wales. In applying the case-law set out in paragraph 94 of the present judgment, the conditions for the NHS's assuming the cost of hospital treatment to be obtained in another Member State should not be compared to the situation in national law of hospital treatment received by patients in private local hospitals. On the contrary, the comparison should be made with the conditions in which the NHS provides such services in its hospitals.[63]

The Court of Justice considers the following three possible justifications: (1) the risk of seriously undermining the financial balance of a social security system; (2) the objective of maintaining a balanced medical and hospital service open to all may also fall within the derogations on grounds of public health under Article 46 EC (now Article 52 TFEU) in so far as it contributes to the attainment of a high level of health protection; and 3) the maintenance of treatment capacity or medical competence on national territory being essential for the public health, and even the survival, of the population.[64] Amongst the results of the examination of the measure in question is that Article 49 EC (now Article 56 TFEU) must be interpreted as meaning that it does not preclude reimbursement of the cost of hospital treatment to be provided in another Member State from being made subject to the grant of prior authorisation by the competent institution and that a refusal to grant

---

[60] Ibid., para 145.

[61] Ibid., paras 146–147.

[62] Ibid., para 98.

[63] Ibid., paras 99–100.

[64] Ibid., paras 103–105.

prior authorisation cannot be based merely on the existence of waiting lists intended to enable the supply of hospital care to be planned and managed on the basis of predetermined general clinical priorities, without carrying out an objective medical assessment of the patient's medical condition, the history and probable course of his illness, the degree of pain he is in and/or the nature of his disability at the time when the request for authorisation was made or renewed.[65] Furthermore, the Court of Justice finds that where the delay arising from such waiting lists appears to exceed an acceptable time having regard to an objective medical assessment of the above-mentioned circumstances, the competent institution may not refuse the authorisation sought on the grounds of the existence of those waiting lists, an alleged distortion of the normal order of priorities linked to the relative urgency of the cases to be treated, the fact that the hospital treatment provided under the national system in question is free of charge, the obligation to make available specific funds to reimburse the cost of treatment to be provided in another Member State and/or a comparison between the cost of that treatment and that of equivalent treatment in the competent Member State.[66]

Finally, it should be mentioned that in *Watts* it is determined that Article 49 EC (now Article 56 TFEU) must be interpreted as meaning that a patient who was authorised to go to another Member State to receive hospital treatment there or who received a refusal to authorise subsequently held to be unfounded is entitled to seek from the competent institution reimbursement of the ancillary costs associated with that cross-border movement for medical purposes provided that the legislation of the competent Member State imposes a corresponding obligation on the national system to reimburse in respect of treatment provided in a local hospital covered by that system.[67]

The last case selected in the present analysis is *Stamatelaki* a judgment rendered in the subsequent year, 2007.[68] The Court of Justice finds that Article 49 EC (now

---

[65] Ibid., para 123.

[66] Idem.

[67] Ibid., para 143.

[68] ECJ, Case C-444/05 *Stamatelaki* [2007] *ECR* I-3185. However, see also ECJ, Case C-212/06 *Gouvernement de la Communauté francaise* [2008] I-1683, where it, amongst others, is held that: 'On a proper construction of Articles 39 EC and 43 EC, legislation of a federated entity of a Member State limiting affiliation to a social security scheme and entitlement to the benefits provided by that scheme only to persons residing in that entity's territory is contrary to those provisions, in so far as such limitation affects nationals of other Member States working in that entity's territory or nationals of the Member State concerned who have made use of their right to freedom of movement within the European Community.' In addition, see also ECJ, Case C-208/07 *von Chamier-Glisczinski*, 16 July 2009, *ECR* I-0000 (n.y.r)., para 76, where it is held, that Article 49 EC (now Article 56 TFEU) is not applicable because the person involved did not move to Member State in question, namely Austria, on a temporary basis, but rather that this person had fixed her residence on a stable basis in that Member State without a foreseeable limit to its duration. This decision contains important guidelines as to Article 18 EC (now Article 21 TFEU) in the context of health care. See in this regard in particular paras 80 et seq. For a discussion of this case, see the chapter by Baquero Cruz.

Article 56 TFEU) precludes legislation of a Member State which excludes all reimbursement by a national social security institution of the costs occasioned by treatment of persons insured with it in private hospitals in another Member State, except those relating to treatment provided to children under 14 years of age.[69] In reaching this conclusion, the Court of Justice puts emphasis on the absolute terms, with the exception of the case of children under 14 years of age, of the prohibition laid down by the scrutinised measure not being appropriate to the objective pursued, since measures which are less restrictive and more in keeping with the freedom to provide services could be adopted, such as a prior authorisation scheme which complies with the requirements imposed by EU law and, if appropriate, the determination of scales for reimbursement of the costs of treatment.[70] Also, it stresses that private hospitals located in other Member States are also subject, in those Member States, to quality controls and that doctors established in those States who operate in those establishments provide professional guarantees equivalent to those of doctors established in Member State involved.[71]

In sum, the principles of free movement of services have become of great importance to the area of health care. In fact, they have become one of the decisive factors as to the changes having taken place by now. From a point of departure where this area was thought of to be under no (or almost no) influence of these principles, today Member States cannot freely define or organise their health systems completely the way they wish. Most importantly and in simplified terms, Member States are supposed to take into account that patients are now in principle free to move to other Member States to obtain health care, and that patients may in many instances be free to bring the financing from the State of affiliation along. Member States may, however, under certain circumstances, demand a prior authorisation. In addition, Member States should take into account that health providers have gained an improved possibility of delivering health services to a wider group of patients than their 'own' nationals.

There may be situations where EU law will not interfere due to reasons such as: (1) the risk of seriously undermining the financial balance of a social security system; (2) the objective of maintaining a balanced medical and hospital service open to all in so far as it contributes to the attainment of a high level of health protection; and (3) the maintenance of treatment capacity or medical competence on national territory being essential for the public health, and even the survival, of the population. In other words, there may exist situations where such reasons may justify legislation which otherwise would be considered a barrier to the free movement of services, this being subject to the principle of proportionality.

[69] Ibid., para 38.

[70] Ibid., para 35.

[71] Ibid., para 36.

Under all circumstances, national health care systems may no longer be viewed as 'closed' systems, which is why a kind of pressure may be perceived to have been placed on these health care schemes.[72] In the short run, this will by many be viewed as a positive development as for instance any seriously ill person will appreciate the possibility of choice, perhaps having the opportunity of finding the best hospital in Europe, perhaps having the possibility of escaping horrible waiting lists, and perhaps even having the possibility of having some, or all, of the costs covered from home. However, in the long run, this will by some be viewed as a negative development, as national health care systems will be challenged, amongst others, on their financing in a not completely predictable manner. However, more positively, they will also be challenged regarding the quality delivered. Altogether, the picture gained from the analysis of this corner of the case law also confirms the above-mentioned impression of a blurred line between Member States and the EU in the area of health care.[73]

2.4 The Distribution of Competences and SGEIs in the Light of *BUPA*

BUPA is one of the more interesting and important judgments which have been rendered in recent times regarding health care, and it will therefore be analysed with regard to the issue of distribution of competences within health care. Compared to Sect. 2.2 the level of focus is of the same reasons as were given above concerning Sect. 2.3 changed here. Section 2.2 primarily took its point of departure in the more general understanding of legislative competences to be gained from a reading of the Treaty of Lisbon 2009. This part rather takes its point of departure in the understanding of the EU concept of SGEIs, which now has an importance as to when Member States can legislate in areas such as competition law, state aid, and perhaps even free movement.[74] In simplified terms, the reason is that if a given health measure is to be considered to concern an SGEI, a possibility of 'immunity' from the requirements of EU law may often exist. This may have an impact on a Member State's rights for example, to grant exclusive or special rights, to establish public undertakings, grant state aid, etc.

Regarding the background and facts of the case as well as the general findings of the General Court, see the chapter by De Vries. I shall provide a more limited

[72] Therefore, it is rather surprising that the Danish Economic Councils in a recent report concerning health expenditure and financing in Denmark did not in any way include the present and future effect of EU law; see De Økonomiske Råd (2009).

[73] See also van de Gronden (2008), p. 759, who finds that the approach of the Court of Justice '... inevitably leads to the harmonization of several aspects of the organization of national health care systems.'

[74] See, however, for example, ECJ, Case C-567/07 *Sint Servatius*, 1 October 2009, *ECR* I-0000 (n.y.r.).

discussion of the concept SGEI and of the placement of the competence to decide what constitutes an SGEI.

2.4.1 The Concept of Services of General Economic Interest

In *BUPA*, the General Court declared that:

> [I]n Community law and for the purposes of applying the EC Treaty competition rules, there is no clear and precise regulatory definition of the concept of an SGEI mission and no established legal concept definitively fixing the conditions that must be satisfied before a Member State can properly invoke the existence and protection of an SGEI mission, either within the meaning of the first *Altmark* condition or within the meaning of Article 86(2) EC.[75]

The definition of SGEIs is as mentioned of concern regarding the distribution of competences between the EU and the Member States. The classification of various services, as for instance either 'market services', SGEIs, 'non-economic services of general interest',[76] or 'exercise of public authority', is of huge importance.[77] The reason is that the legal consequences vary a lot depending on which concept is involved, especially with regard to which degree market economic requirements will rule as well as the degree as to which Member State competence may be claimed. So far, for example, 'exercise of public authority' is largely a matter for the Member States. In contrast, 'market services' are largely completely within the competence of the EU. However, as indicated in the quotation, at present a lack of clarity dominates the definition of SGEI.[78]

BUPA contains certain important interpretational guidelines regarding the understanding of SGEIs. These are given in the context of the first condition of *Altmark,* where strictly speaking the concept 'public service' rather than SGEI is mentioned in the wording, as well as Article 86(2) EC (now Article 106(2) TFEU).[79] In this regard, it was held that the Commission was entitled to consider that the conditions for recognition of PMI services and obligations as relating to an SGEI mission were satisfied and that Ireland had made no manifest error in that regard.[80]

Importantly, pursuant to the General Court the point of departure is the following:

---

[75] *BUPA*, para 165.

[76] Hereinafter referred to as 'NESGIs'.

[77] See for further details regarding these various concepts as well as the concept SGEI itself Neergaard (2009), pp. 30–57, and Neergaard (2009), pp. 191–224.

[78] See in the same direction, for example, Ross (2007), pp. 1057–1059.

[79] See in this context *BUPA*, para 162, where it is stated that: 'It is common ground between the parties that the concept of public service obligation referred to in that judgment corresponds to that of the SGEI as designated by the contested decision and that it does not differ from that referred to in Article 86(2) EC'.

[80] *BUPA*, para 207.

> … even though the Member State has a wide discretion when determining what it regards as an SGEI, that does not mean that it is not required, when it relies on the existence of and the need to protect an SGEI mission, to ensure that that mission satisfies certain minimum criteria common to every SGEI mission within the meaning of the EC Treaty, as explained in the case-law, and to demonstrate that those criteria are indeed satisfied in the particular case.[81]

In the opinion of the General Court, these so-called minimum criteria common to every SGEI mission are:

> … the presence of an act of the public authority entrusting the operators in question with an SGEI mission and the universal and compulsory nature of that mission… Furthermore, it follows from the case-law on Article 86(2) EC that the Member State must indicate the reasons why it considers that the service in question, because of its specific nature, deserves to be characterised as an SGEI and to be distinguished from other economic activities… In the absence of such reasons, even a marginal review by the Community institutions on the basis of both the first *Altmark* condition and Article 86(2) EC with respect to the existence of a manifest error by the Member State in the context of its discretion would not be possible.[82]

The General Court also holds that the provision of the service in question must, by definition, assume a general or public interest, implying that SGEIs are distinguished from services in the private interest, even though that interest may be more or less collective or be recognised by the State as legitimate or beneficial.[83] Furthermore, it is explained that the general or public interest on which the Member State relies must not be reduced to the need to subject the market concerned to certain rules or the commercial activity of the operators concerned to authorisation by the State.[84] In other words, the General Court states that, the mere fact that the national legislature, acting in the general interest in the broad sense, imposes certain rules of authorisation, functioning, or control on all the operators in a particular sector does not in principle mean that there is an SGEI.[85]

Furthermore, it is emphasised that the recognition of an SGEI mission does not necessarily presume that the operator entrusted with that mission will be given an exclusive or special right to carry it out.[86] According to the General Court, this follows from a reading of paragraph 1 together with paragraph 2 of Article 86 EC (now Article 106 TFEU), pursuant to which a distinction must be drawn between a special or exclusive right conferred on an operator and the SGEI mission which, where appropriate, is attached to that right.[87] The General Court views the grant of

---

[81] *BUPA*, para 172.

[82] Idem.

[83] *BUPA*, para 178.

[84] Idem.

[85] Idem.

[86] *BUPA*, para 179.

[87] Idem.

a special or exclusive right to an operator merely as the instrument, possibly justified, which allows that operator to perform an SGEI mission.[88]

In addition, in the General Court's opinion both the first condition laid down by the Court of Justice in *Altmark* and the wording of Article 86(2) EC (now Article 106(2) TFEU), as such, require that the operator in question be entrusted with an SGEI mission by an act of a public authority and that the act clearly defines the SGEI obligations in question.[89]

On this basis, it may be summarised that at least the following descriptors—or in the wording of the General Court the minimum criteria, common to every SGEI mission pursuant to *BUPA* are important:

- the presence of an act of the public authority entrusting the operators in question with an SGEI mission and the universal and compulsory nature of that mission;
- the presence of an indication by the Member State of the reasons why it considers that the service in question, because of its specific nature, deserves to be characterised as an SGEI and to be distinguished from other economic activities; and
- the presence of a general or public interest, implying that the service is distinguished from services in the private interest.

In addition to this, the recognition of an SGEI mission does not necessarily presume that the operator entrusted with that mission will be given an exclusive or special right to carry it out.

2.4.2 Placing the Competence to Decide What Constitutes a Service of General Economic Interest

In the *Olsen* case, it was held that Member States have a wide discretion to define what they regard as SGEIs and that the definition of such services by a Member State can be questioned by the Commission only in the event of a manifest error.[90] This was upheld in *BUPA*.[91] In this regard, it is pointed out that:

> That prerogative of the Member State concerning the definition of SGEIs is confirmed by the absence of any competence specially attributed to the Commission and by the absence of a precise and complete definition of the concept of SGEI in Community law. The determination of the nature and scope of an SGEI mission in specific spheres of action which either do not fall within the powers of the Community, within the meaning of the

88 Idem.

89 *BUPA*, para 181.

90 General Court, Case T-17/02 *Fred Olsen* [2005] *ECR* II-2031, para 216. What exactly could constitute a 'manifest error' is not yet developed.

91 *BUPA*, paras 166–170. In addition, see General Court, Case T-442/03 *SIC* [2008] *ECR* II-1161, para 195. Finally, especially regarding this issue in the context of public broadcasting services, see General Court, Joined Cases T-309/04, T-317/04, T-329/04 and T-336/04 *TV 2/Danmark* [2008] *ECR* II-2935, especially paras 88–124.

> first paragraph of Article 5 EC, or are based on only limited or shared Community competence, within the meaning of the second paragraph of that article, remains, in principle, within the competence of the Member States. As the defendant and Ireland maintain, the health sector falls almost exclusively within the competence of the Member States. In that sector, the Community can engage, under Article 152(1) and (5) EC, only in action which is not legally binding, while fully respecting the responsibilities of the Member States for the organisation and provision of health services and medical care. It follows that the determination of SGEI obligations in this context also falls primarily within the competence of the Member States. That division of powers is also reflected, generally, in Article 16 EC, which provides that, given the place occupied by SGEIs in the shared values of the Union as well as their role in promoting social and territorial cohesion, the Community and the Member States, each within their respective powers and within the scope of application of the Treaty, are to take care that such services operate on the basis of principles and conditions which enable them to fulfil their missions.[92]

A lack of clarity could seem present in respect of the issue of where the competence to decide what constitutes an SGEI is situated.

On the one hand, this concept may be seen as an EU concept in the same way as it is the case with more or less any other Treaty-concept.[93] In fact, it has normally been considered as such,[94] in reality right from the very beginning.[95] One consequence normally following from this is that the definition of the concept in question is then common to all the Member States, independent of various definitions in national legal orders. Another consequence is that the competence to define the content of a given concept then is situated at the EU level rather than at the Member State level. This approach is more or less identical to what Buendia Sierra has designated as the 'Community approach'.[96]

On the other hand, by now it seems that the competence to define the content of the concept is situated at the Member State level. For instance, in the Services Directive, it is, amongst other things, stated in the second sentence of Article 1(3) that it does not affect the freedom of Member States to define what they consider to be SGEIs. This point of view is also expressed in several of the Communications of the

---

[92] *BUPA*, para 167. See also the important para 172.

[93] See amongst others, Due (1997), p. 137. Also compare with ECJ, Case C-242/95 *GT-Link* [1997] *ECR* I-4449, para 50, where the Court of Justice states that: 'Since Article 90(2) [now Article 106 TFEU] is a provision which permits, in certain circumstances, derogation from the rules of the Treaty, there must be a strict definition of those undertakings which can take advantage of it (ECJ, Case 127/73 *BRT* v. *SABAM and NV Fonior* [1974] *ECR* 313, para 19)'. See also ECJ, Case 127/73 *Belgische Radio* [1974] *ECR* 313, para 23; ECJ, Case 41/83 *Italian Republic* v. *Commission* [1985] *ECR* 873, para 30; and ECJ, Case C-179/90 *Merci* [1991] *ECR* I-5889, para 27.

[94] See for instance Page (1982), p. 28.

[95] Papaconstantinou (1988), p. 84.

[96] Buendia Sierra (1999), pp. 280–283.

Commission.[97] This approach is more or less identical to what Buendia Sierra has referred to as the 'national approach'.[98] However, it should be pointed out that in the mentioned provision of the Services Directive, it is stressed that the definition has to be in conformity with EU law. In addition, it is of interest that the Court of Justice recently in *Federutility* has stated that Member States are entitled, whilst complying with the law of the Union, to define the scope and the organisation of their SGEIs, and that they may take account of objectives pertaining to their national policy.[99]

The General Court in *BUPA* focuses on the distribution of competences between the Member States and the EU. It seems to find, of more universal impact, that the absence of any competence specially attributed to the Commission and the absence of a precise and complete definition of the concept in EU law, point in the direction that the definition of SGEIs is the competence of the Member States. In addition, it seems that it is important that the case concerns the health sector, as the General Court points out that this sector falls almost exclusively within the competence of the Member States. This may be understood as indications in the direction, that under all circumstances this field of law will imply 'immunity', at least when viewed on the basis of the standing of the law before the entering into force of the Lisbon Treaty. It is emphasised by the General Court that a discussion of services of general interest is obviously not of relevance when the service in question belongs to a field of law which falls more or less exclusively within the competence of the Member States. Article 16 EC (now Article 14 TFEU) is additionally referred to as further support to the argument.

If assuming that the principle, amongst others stipulated in the Services Directive, that the competence to define what is considered to be SGEIs is vested at the Member State level, is universal in character, one may wonder how this principle may be unified with the characterisation of the concept as an EU concept, as well as with the principle, that the definition created by Member States has to be in accordance with EU law. Thus, it seems that the two principles are in conflict with one another and it may be questioned where the competence to define actually is situated, at the EU level or at the Member State level; or somewhere in between. Also, the exact definition of what constitutes a manifest error is at present completely unsettled.

[97] See amongst others Commission, *Services of general interest in Europe* (96/C281/03), *OJ* C 281/3, Section 26; Commission, *Communication from the Commission. Services of general interest in Europe,* COM(2000) 580 (2001/C17/04), Section 22; Commission, *Green Paper on Services of General Interest,* COM(2003) 270, Sections 30–32; and Commission, *Communication from the Commission to the European Parliament, the Council, the European Economic and Social Committee and the Committee of the Regions. White Paper on services of general interest,* COM(2004) 374, Section 2.

[98] Buendia Sierra (1999), pp. 280–283.

[99] ECJ, Case C-265/08 *Federutility* 20 April 2010, *ECR* I-0000 (n.y.r.), para 29.

2.4.3 Preliminary Considerations

At present, it is not completely settled how health services and related activities shall be categorised in relation to SGEIs and related terms. Most likely, their categorisation will require a concrete evaluation of the exact activities involved, which will imply that the assessment of such activities often has to be carried out on a case-by-case basis.[100] On the basis of the above analysis, there are reasons to estimate that activities within the health sector often will be included within the concept of SGEI, or at times rather the related concepts SSGIs or NESGIs, inter alia, depending on the determination made by the Member States. At the present stage of development a large degree of uncertainty is related to this terminology and its concrete application. This of course is not optimal in relationship to traditional legal standards such as transparency and legal certainty. In the area analysed in the present part an impression of an increasingly blurred line between Member State and EU law may be observed.

2.5 'Solidarity'

This concept has an important role to play in *BUPA*. It is mentioned in paras 199, 200, 204, 292, and 293. The Commission refers to the concept several times in its Decision. In fact, one of the important reasons why the measure is approved of has to do with the fact that it is based on solidarity. For instance, the General Court points out that:

> … In effect, the purpose of community rating, namely that the young, healthy insured persons subsidise the premiums that would normally have to be paid by the elderly and sick insured persons, and, accordingly, *solidarity* between the generations, would be jeopardised if one PMI insurer, in an extreme situation, covered only young persons or

[100] See for example, Recital 34 of the Services Directive. See also Commission, *Commission Staff Working Document. Annexes to the Communication from the Commission on Social services of general interest in the European Union—Socio-economic and legal overview*—COM(2006) 177 final, SEC(2006) 516, Section 1.1.1., where it is stated that: 'It is in this context very important to note that 'social' does not necessarily mean "non-economic". The fact that the functioning is based on solidarity, that certain social objectives are pursued or the non-profit nature of the provider do not rule out that the activity in question is qualified as an *economic* activity. Some operators may agree to take aspects of solidarity into account in the light other benefits they may obtain from intervening in the sector under consideration. Conversely, non-profit-making entities may compete with profit-making undertakings and may, therefore, constitute undertakings within the meaning of Article 87 of the EC Treaty. As a general rule, Community case law classifies as an undertaking any entity engaged in an economic activity, regardless of its legal status in which it is financed [Footnote omitted]. It should also be noted that an entity carrying out primarily non-economic activities might be engaged in secondary activities of an economic nature. In such cases, classification as an undertaking within the meaning of the competition rules will be confined to the economic activities involved.'

> elderly, sick persons.... While such rating appears to be capable of significantly reducing the incentive to employ active risk selection... and, accordingly, of maintaining a certain equilibrium, it does not permit the other objective pursued by the open enrolment and community rating obligations to be achieved, namely *solidarity* between the generations, which ensures easier access to PMI—owing, in particular, to the cross-subsidy of premiums—by the elderly and the sick.[101] [emphasis added]

In Article 5(1) in the Directive Proposal, solidarity is mentioned in the following way:

> The Member States of treatment shall be responsible for the organisation and the delivery of healthcare. In such a context and taking into account principles of universality, access to good quality care, equity and *solidarity*, they shall define clear quality and safety standards for healthcare provided on their territory, and ensure that...[102] [emphasis added]

Solidarity has become one of the more 'fancy' terms in EU law, and it is generally important as to the organisation of healthcare. For instance, Hervey and McHale refer to solidarity as a fundamental value and point out that solidarity may be said to underpin all health regimes within the EU.[103] Mossialos and McKee also agree on this, and point out that the solidarity in the health sector often implies that contributions are made according to the ability to pay and benefits are received according to needs.[104] Thus, in the following part of this chapter some further guidance as to its understanding will be provided. With regard to the issue of distribution of competences, this has an interest because it is central whether certain solidarity mechanisms in Member States may be protected from interference of EU law. For instance, *BUPA* may in generalised terms be viewed as an indication of a certain degree of immunity in these instances to be realistic to obtain. More concretely, in what follows first the background of the concept is briefly stated (Sect. 2.5.1); second, solidarity in the Treaty texts is explained (Sect. 2.5.2); and third, solidarity in the case law of the Court of Justice is examined (Sect. 2.5.3).[105]

---

[101] *BUPA*, paras 292–293.

[102] The concept is also mentioned other places in the Directive Proposal, see pp. 4, 9, and 23 (recital 12).

[103] Hervey and McHale (2004), p. 5. Also, at p. 392, the authors explain that: 'In the context of health law, this could refer to such matters as the cross-subsidisation that takes place within European national health systems (whether through compulsory insurance or taxation) allowing equality of access to health care and treatment, regardless of an individual patient's means; the interference with the normal operation of the market in setting prices for pharmaceuticals and other medical products; and the voluntary and unpaid donation of blood or organs.'

[104] Mossialos and McKee (2004), p. 34.

[105] For a more general account of solidarity in EU law health care law, see for example, Newdick (2006), pp. 1645–1668.

2.5.1 'Solidarity' in the Member States

Although the concept in the context of EU law at present is fairly 'immature', it has for long been a central subject in other disciplines such as for example, philosophy and sociology.[106] Due to the complex and ambiguous nature of the concept, a full account of the content thereof is not possible here. Therefore, the aim here is much more modest: to provide an impression of what it is more or less about.

Many of the welfare services, including health care, in the Member States are organised on the basis of certain solidarity mechanisms, at least with regard to some elements. Through a primarily tax-financed system, citizens may have the right of access to various welfare services, at most times based on certain criteria to be fulfilled.[107] They may be provided at the municipal, regional, or state level. They may largely be said to be based on a premise of the stronger supporting the weaker, but not only, as the system also is constructed as a way of the members of the society getting services which would not be possible for the individual to acquire, had each of us had to do everything ourselves. 'Belongingness' to the society is the main criterion to have the right to access of the services in question. Historically, citizenship has been the dominant determinant of belongingness, but nowadays residence or occupation appears as much more important. At times it may be sufficient just simply physically being there in order to take advantage of a given service. Also, being a member of the society, you will often not be able to escape contributing to it, primarily through tax contributions, but at times also otherwise.[108] Solidarity in national welfare systems are founded on the principle of territoriality.[109] The concept of solidarity may be for the present purposes loosely understood and as amongst others referring to such particular and often complex

---

[106] For an account, see for example, Ottmann (2008), www.icl-journal.com, p. 40.

[107] As explained by Hervey and McHale (2004), p. 125, national public health care systems in the EU may be seen as falling into two main categories: (1) social insurance systems and (2) national health services. About the former category, the authors point out that they are: '... based upon the compulsory insurance of categories of persons (now expanded to include all, or virtually all, the population). Insurance premiums are usually income related, and calculated on the basis of total annual expenditure. Administratively speaking, health care schemes are often integrated into the general social security system. The administration of health insurance may be entrusted to public or semi-public bodies, such as sickness funds. Social insurance schemes may be further subdivided into reimbursement schemes, in which patients have to pay for care, and are reimbursed subsequently by their sickness fund; and benefits-in-kind schemes, in which patients receive care essentially free (to them) from health providers, who are then paid directly by the relevant health insurance institutions.' [all footnotes in the quotation omitted] About the latter category, the authors state that these are: '... funded by public taxation, and operate according to benefits-in-kind system. They may be more or less centralised in terms of their administration.' [all footnotes in the quotation omitted].

[108] See, for example, Mau (2007), pp. 138–139, who points out that: '... the national welfare state represents a system of compulsory solidarity that does not rest on the voluntary contributions of the citizens, but on tax duties or compulsory social contributions...'.

[109] For an account, see, for example, Ottmann (2008), pp. 36–48.

structures in Member States, which are of central importance in holding institutionalised societies together.[110]

Weiler has expressed that:

> Europe prides itself on a tradition of social solidarity which found political and legal expression in the post-war welfare state, which all states of all political colours embraced as an ideal and as a pragmatic commitment for years. Universal health coverage, free education from kindergarten through to university, generous welfare for the less fortunate, notably the unemployed, have been the proud hallmarks of this commitment. This was not just a question of political choice. Like the eventual rejection of the death penalty, this commitment became a source of identity, even pride—especially in comparison with the United States.[111]

In the same direction, Mau points out that:

> Policy makers and social scientists have frequently referred to the nature of European society and the shared traits of the European nation states and people in order to justify the process of supranational community building. In their view, the European Union constitutes more than a random cluster of countries that have opted for a particular form of cooperation; it represents a particular identity and commonness that come together to support the integration process. Indeed, though the European continent has been the locus of the nation state and nationalism, it can also be argued that there is a common ground that unifies the European countries.[112]

Thus, Weiler stresses the importance of solidarity in Europe, and Mau the shared traits of the European nation states and people. But what is this European solidarity all about? One way to approach this question is to understand the results put forward by Karagiannis of her research on the subject.[113] This author provides a useful overview of what the features of European solidarity are characterised by. These are: the issue of inclusion/exclusion; the elusive nature of the centre of 'solidarity'; the issue of inequality; and the simultaneity of commitment and belonging.[114] These features may be further explained.

Regarding the first feature, Karagiannis explains that on the one hand inclusion is an important element in solidarity in the sense that solidarity federates, that is it makes social things come together and then hold together.[115] On the other hand, and perhaps more paradoxical is the widely observed fact that such inclusion entails exclusion.[116]

Regarding the second feature, that is the elusive nature of the centre of solidarity, Karagiannis explains that traditionally, solidarity federated previously

[110] Multiple solidarities may be identified, see, for example, Karagiannis (2007), pp. 1–12.

[111] Weiler (2002), p. 569.

[112] Mau (2007), p. 129.

[113] For further details, see Neergaard (2010), pp. 99–140.

[114] Karagiannis (2007), pp. 4–5.

[115] Ibid., p. 5.

[116] Idem.

separate elements around a specific core of values, ideas or reified categories.[117] For example, western Christian solidarity, federated around entities such as 'God' or 'the Church', and working class solidarity was created around the central category of 'the workers'.[118] In other words, Karagiannis states, a normative commitment to solidarity as a value and a practice is on the one hand upheld, whilst on the other hand there is a recognition that this solidarity no longer has fixed points of reference, such as 'God', or 'the workers'.[119]

Third, the importance of the feature of inequality is explained as equality on the one hand being one of the fundamental traits of the received view of solidarity, together with reasonableness/rationality and abstraction, and on the other hand, solidarity can only exist where there already is inequality.[120] In other words, only if there are for example rich and poor can solidarity be inclusive; or only if there are for instance oppressed and oppressors can there be a dispassionate community; and finally, e.g. only if there are less powerful and more powerful classes can there be class-based solidarity.[121]

Finally, it is central in the understanding of the fourth feature, that is the simultaneity of commitment and belonging, that:

> [T]here is a hiatus between solidarity as a commitment or a value—that is, as something that is pursued—and solidarity as 'belonging', 'belongingness' or 'we-ness', something that is already there... In this sense, we are dealing with a different sense of solidarity when it is attached to particular world views about the good life, to autonomy and to freedom, and when it is viewed as endangered, dissolving or emerging. In the first case, solidarity is seen as the attribute that will keep the good polity together, and thus as an expression of the belief in the future of this polity as polity... In the second case, solidarity is seen as that which, having adequately described a social situation, no longer does so because the situation has become indescribable in social terms... The move from the second to the first case is always necessary before a new sense of 'belonging' can be ascribed to the social.[122]

Admittedly, it is rather difficult to sum up on the roots of solidarity in Europe. In addition to the four features put forward by Karagiannis, certain help from Wilde may be useful here. Thus, it may added that solidarity may largely be understood as the feeling of reciprocal sympathy and responsibility amongst members of a group which promotes mutual support.[123] Also, it is of importance that the difference between moral solidarity and legal solidarity may, with the words of Ottmann, be said to be that in the welfare state, solidarity is no longer seen as a voluntary act of charity, but rather as an obligatory act based on legal rights and duties.[124]

---

[117] Idem.

[118] Idem.

[119] Idem.

[120] Ibid., p. 6.

[121] Idem.

[122] Idem.

[123] Wilde (2007), pp. 171–172.

[124] Ottmann (2008), p. 40.

2.5.2 'Solidarity' in the Treaty Texts

On the basis of the platform established in the previous section, the attention is now turned to the much more concrete level. In what follows, it will be explained what the explicit role of solidarity in primary EU law has been over the years.[125]

In general, a significant increase in the use of the word solidarity over the years can be observed. Also, a change from a more 'external' dimension to an 'internal' dimension has occurred so that a kind of protection or at least acknowledgement of the latter dimension with the Treaty of Lisbon 2009 and the Charter of Fundamental Rights now appears. The concept may thus be understood in light of which of the following words following it, namely either 'between' or 'among' following it. In other words, it is central to understand what relationship it is connected with. Thus, it can be observed that it is no longer only the relationship amongst Member States, amongst the peoples of the EU, and between the Member States and the EU, and between the EU and the wider world which are of interest. Solidarity 'internally' in Member States is becoming of interest in the sense that it is worthwhile protecting. However, it is not clear whether this protection is considered, e.g., only a domestic task or whether it, e.g., also has more European dimensions.

The concept of solidarity is not only to be understood in playing a role regarding these relationships. It also plays an important role in the definition of the European identity. Thus, it appears clear that solidarity is viewed as a special and important virtue of what Europe, including both the EU as such and the individual Member States, is about; something which apparently is viewed as distinguishing it from other continents.

At the same time, it may also be viewed as indicating an ideal, a programmatic commitment, an expression of a value or even an aspect of an ideology, which may be given weight. It seems as if the Treaty texts as a whole may be viewed as moving in the direction of a clearer commitment to the social responsibility of Europe over the years.

In sum, a rather significant re-orientation at the explicit level has taken place seen clearly in the Treaty of Lisbon 2009 and the Charter of Fundamental Rights. However, the exact content of the nature of the concept of solidarity cannot be deduced just on the basis of a reading of the Treaty texts. Therefore, the attention will now be moved to the case law of the Court of Justice.

125 See for further details Neergaard (2010).

2.5.3 'Solidarity' in the Case Law of the Court of Justice

In a search on the EurLex database, the concept solidarity appears 113 times.[126] The first judgment dates back to 1969, some 11 years after the Treaty of Rome entered into force, and the context in which the concept is found in relates to Article 10 EC (previously Article 5 EEC; now repealed but replaced, in substance, by Article 4, paragraph 3 TEU).[127] In fact, in the first many years the references to the concept generally occurred in the context of a more 'external' dimension. This has changed over the years, so that the more 'internal' dimension has become of larger and larger importance. However, references to solidarity in a framework of identity or programmatic commitment, as were identified in the foregoing section, are not truly identifiable.

In general, the referrals to the concept have not surprisingly steadily increased strongly over the years, this also being so already when taking into account the increasing case load of the Court of Justice, which has occurred. It may, however, also be seen as an indication of the concept growing in importance. This may be exemplified in the following manner: from 1958 to 1970 (both years included) 1 reference was made; from 1971 to 1980 (both years included) 6 references were made; from 1981 to 1990 (both years included) 19 references were made; from 1991 to 2000 (both years included) 34 references were made; and from 2001 until 2010 53 references were made.[128]

The important legal areas may on the basis of the results of the query, and when focusing primarily on the 'internal' dimension of solidarity, roughly be limited to competition law,[129] internal market law, and Union Citizenship law as being the areas of possible interest. All of the cases identified have been rendered largely only from the end of the 1980s and onwards.[130]

---

[126] See http://eur-lex.europa.eu (31 August 2009). The search undertaken was 'simple' and limited to judgments from the Court of Justice. The present section 21.5.3 presents only very the very general results of a previous study accomplished; see for further details Neergaard (2010), pp. 99–140.

[127] ECJ, Joined Cases 6 and 11–69, *Commission* v. *French Republic* [1969] *ECR* 523.

[128] 31 August 2009.

[129] For the present purposes here understood as not including state aid law.

[130] It should be stressed that other judgments than those in which the concept explicitly is mentioned may be of importance to national structures involving solidarity. However, these have largely been left out of the analysis, among others due to limitations of space, and that primary interest is taken in the explicit use of the concept rather than subjectively assuming that solidarity implicitly may be of concern. Also, several of the cases in which the term is mentioned, may be not of the least interest. This may for instance be the case, when the term is used in national legislation being reiterated by the Court of Justice or otherwise being an element in the account of the facts of relevance. Also, this may be the case when the more 'external' dimensions of solidarity are involved. In addition, a certain amount of cases concern the ECSC Treaty, which implies that they are also excluded from analysis. Also, cases, in which the reference to solidarity is to a relationship among workers or among trade unions in the context of solidarity actions, are also excluded. This in fact consists of a very large amount of cases.

An analysis of solidarity in its more 'internal' dimension shows that it at present holds a rather complex role and the degree of 'immunity' to be obtained there from is not very clear at present. Generally speaking, it has been observed that it is both used 'negatively' and 'positively'. This terminology has in the context of solidarity been introduced by Barnard whom refers to a 'negative' use of solidarity by the Court of Justice when social welfare policies are defended against erosion from single market principles.[131] Barnard views solidarity to have been used 'positively' when obligations are imposed on Member States.

The 'negative' function clearly dominates in the competition law regime. In the internal market law regime both functions have been seen. Finally, in the union citizenship law regime, the function is largely 'positive'. These findings are of interest to the area of healthcare, as health services in the Member States as mentioned most often are organised within a framework of solidarity mechanisms. The importance of this to those Member States being interested in as little interference of the EU in the organisation of their health services is that the 'negative' function may be viewed as a kind of optimism in that direction, whereas the 'positive' function may be viewed as a threat. Under all circumstances, it should be kept in mind that so far the case law in question is very limited with regard to what kind of solidarity mechanisms which have been under scrutiny by the Court of Justice.

The protection through the principle of solidarity may as mentioned be observed to be stronger in the competition law regime, than what may be observed in the residing regimes.[132] This may to a certain degree be explained by the circumstance that the competition law regime, if coming into force, might be considered to be more dominated by market economics and with fewer possibilities of exemptions. Also, it is an area which is not really constructed to a scrutiny of national legislation, but originally largely was developed with a primary eye on the activities of private undertakings. In addition, the competition law regime works in closer relationship to economic theory than the other regimes which may be a reason to explain the development: the understanding of the issues at stake may simply have been better perceived in this area. In contrast, the internal market and union citizenship law regimes constitute areas in which the individuals and their rights are the driving force. Although possible explanations may be suggested, this is not the same as implying that the difference in treatment between the

---

131 Barnard (2005), p. 159.

132 Pointing in the same direction, it was demonstrated above that the protection of health care in Member States is larger through the concept of SGEI, which is a concept which may be viewed as originating from competition law, than the justifications related to the concept public health and the like, in the area of free movement.

regimes is desirable.[133] The problem by ignoring economic theory in this area in a nuanced manner, and interfering in national systems, is in a nutshell that this sector from an economic point of view largely may be characterised as a public good,[134] which implies that imposing of a market economic ideology may create more problems than necessarily taken into consideration in the above-mentioned case law. In actual fact, it is a sector which is often characterised by market failures.[135] In other words, it is a sector where several factors constitute barriers to competition.[136] Amongst others, the amount of health providers will often be insufficient to ensure competition about demand and thereby prices which will mirror the marginal costs, which is often connected with the fact that health production is characterised with large-scale advantages.[137] In addition, it is seldom the consumers themselves who directly pay for the services, which will often imply an overconsumption of the services in question both by the consumers (often patients) and the producers (often the doctors).[138]

Generally speaking, there is a great deal of truth in the statement by Ross that an analysis of solidarity provides a rather frustratingly mixed picture to the extent that the concept is multifaceted and, as such, likely to send confusing or diluted messages as to its role.[139] In fact, at present transparency and predictability as to its use is not very apparent. Although responsibility for welfare provision based on

---

[133] See, for example, Szyszczak (2009), p. 192, who states: 'Finally the essay concludes with the view that EU law is inconsistent in its treatment of healthcare, finding that under the free movement rules there is a greater ease in accepting the economic nature of healthcare and patient mobility rights thus undermining the principle of solidarity upon which healthcare services were originally built. Whereas under the competition rules the Courts are generous towards national healthcare schemes using ideas of cohesion and solidarity to ring fence healthcare activities, even where such activities are explicitly commercial activities, protecting them from the full force of market principles. It is argued that this is the wrong approach and that the EU could play a role in defining an inner core of healthcare activities which are truly solidaristic in a different, EU-level, spatial setting and that there may be good and defensible reasons for protecting these activities from the full force of competition and market rules.' See also, for example, Hatzopoulos (2009), p. 228, who warns: 'The fully-fledged application of these same rules to public healthcare, a field based on the (non-market) principle of solidarity, could have undesirable—if not unacceptable—effects. Both the provision of health services and national healthcare and social systems themselves could suffer unintended negative consequences.'

[134] Mossialos and McKee (2004), p. 32. See also Chapter 14.

[135] See, for example, De Økonomiske Råd (2009), p. 271 et seq.

[136] Ibid., p. 271.

[137] Ibid., pp. 271–272.

[138] Ibid., p. 272.

[139] Ross (2007), p. 1069.

solidarity mechanisms for long has been considered primarily a domestic responsibility, EU law now has a severe impact thereon.[140]

In Recital 31 of the Directive Proposal it is stated that:

> The evidence available indicates that the application of free movement principles regarding use of healthcare in another Member State within the limits of the cover guaranteed by the statutory sickness insurance scheme of the Member State of affiliation will not undermine the health systems of the Member States or financial sustainability of their social security systems.

In the context of the present discussion of solidarity mechanisms, the prediction in the quotation does not seem completely convincing neither does it seem too correct to speak about 'evidence'. Changes are occurring and will continue to occur—with or without the adoption of the Directive Proposal, and solidarity at a wider scale, eventually at a European scale, will have to be established. As Szyszczak has pointed out the principle of solidarity upon which health care services were originally built on are being undermined.[141] A process towards a not completely known destination has been initiated already with especially the significant case law of the Court of Justice as explained above, this development perhaps to be further supported by such an adoption.

2.6 'Social Europe'

> The allegation made by the complainants re V. that European economic policy is a purely market-oriented policy without a social-policy orientation and that its functional approach restricts the possibilities of the legislature in the Member States to engage in a self-determined social policy is incorrect. Neither is the European Union without any social-policy competences, nor is it inactive in this area. At the same time, the Member States have a sufficient space of competences to take essential social-policy decisions on their own responsibility.[142]

---

[140] This has been expressed by Dougan and Spaventa (2005), p. 181, as: '… the idea that the European Union now constitutes a multi-level welfare system characterized by a complex combination of local, national and Community policies. This is sometimes expressed in the notion that the Member States are now "semi-sovereign welfare states" whose choices about how to provide for the social well-being of their own citizens are increasingly constrained not only by obvious factors such as the demographic pressures posed by an aging population and the need to compete within the globalizing economy but also by the pervasive influence of the Union—which has not, however, evolved into a "newly sovereign welfare state" determining for itself the conditions under which we pay taxes and receive benefits. As a result, the idea of social solidarity can no longer be treated simply as a national or local monopoly. It also has a vital Community component. [footnotes omitted]'.

[141] Szyszczak (2009) at p. 192.

[142] 30 June 2009, para 393. See http://www.bundesverfassungsgericht.de/entscheidungen/es20090630_2bve000208en.html.

This quotation from the judgment of German Constitutional Court on the Treaty of Lisbon 2009 sums up one of the most complicated, controversial and fundamental problems which confronts the EU, namely how to understand and solve the problems of the tensions between economic and social integration. In the specific field of health care, the same characterisation may be given. In what follows, the concept of a European Social Model and the related concept of Social Market Economy will be touched upon and the findings established so far will be related to the scheme of Maduro on models of Social Europe.[143] By doing this, the development of the law on health care is placed into its larger context.

At the level of the EU, it is of significance that provision of welfare was for a long time the concern of, and within the competence of, the Member States. This point of departure has changed to some extent and continues to change further. In that context, it has now become a common theme to talk about a European Social Model as a point of reference. The concept of a European Social Model is several years old; it was applied for the first time by the Commission in 1994.[144] The most important step in this regard may be viewed as having been taken with the formulation of the Lisbon strategy in 2000, which may be interpreted as the result of a compromise between the neo-liberal and the more socially oriented governments of Member States.[145] Some authors have raised doubt as to whether the latter term really can be considered to exist.[146] One author has characterised the term as: '... a rather diffuse amalgam of ideas and principles constructed principally by the Commission to justify social policy interventions on the part of the EU.'[147] Others have characterised it as a concept that has '... an ambiguous and polysemic nature'.[148] Some emphasise the importance of a shared set of values that have given rise to the welfare state in the Member States, which are distinct from those in, for instance, the US.[149] Others again have pointed out that one cannot speak of a single 'European Social Model'. For instance, Kleinman points out that:

> Rather, there is a range of different European social models in existence. As there is no single European model, it logically follows that the idea that European Social Policy is about "defending" a European Social Model against, say, globalization, is logically

[143] Poiares Maduro (2006), pp. 125–141.

[144] Pursuant to Hatzopoulos (2005), p. 1600, whom refers to: Commission, European Social Policy—A Way forward for the Union—A White Paper, COM(94) 333. Here it is stated in the 'Preface': 'The objective in the coming period must be to preserve and develop the European social model as we move towards the 21st century, to give to the people of Europe the unique blend of economic well-being, social cohesiveness and high overall quality of life which was achieved in the post-war period.' See also, for example, Adnett and Hardy (2005).

[145] Hatzopoulos (2005), p. 1634.

[146] Ibid., pp. 1599–1635.

[147] Shaw (2000), p. 3.

[148] Jørgensen and Kongshøj Madsen (2007), p. 25, who point out that already in 1985 Jacques Delors introduced a social dimension of the EU.

[149] Mossialos and McKee (2004), p. 41.

> inconsistent. Rather, what European (supra-national) social policy seeks to do is to *create* a European social model—either by synthesising aspects of all four models or (more realistically) by imposing one model on all. In an analogous way to the national myths that create and sustain both nationalism and nations, the idea of a "European Social Model" should be considered perhaps as a founding myth which helps to create (not defend) the concept and reality of "Europeanisation" and a politically integrated Europe.[150]

Schiek agrees on this point, and states that the European Social Model should be defined as being based on commonalities between the Member States:

> It has been characterised as an "essence of a common political culture (...) which finds it difficult to accept the phenomena of exclusion and excessive inequality, which believes in the legitimacy of state intervention in redressing adverse consequences of the Market Economy in this respect and (...) in (...) a sufficient involvement of social partners", as a combination of "economic efficiency and generous social insurance" and as the "broad acknowledgement of three common features shared by every European state: (...) public commitment to social justice (...) the theoretical approach that social justice is not opposed to economic efficiency (...) and the value of interest representations and negotiations between social actors".[151]

The concept of Social Market Economy is closely related to the concept of European Social Model. In that context, it may be worth pointing out that the Court of Justice has ruled in *Laval* that:

> Since the Community has thus not only an economic but also a social purpose, the rights under the provisions of the EC Treaty on the free movement of goods, persons, services and capital must be balanced against the objectives pursued by social policy, which include, as is clear from the first paragraph of Article 136 EC, inter alia, improved living and working conditions, so as to make possible their harmonisation while improvement is being maintained, proper social protection and dialogue between management and labour.[152]

It is likely that these sentences, as well as for instance the judgment itself in its entirety and other sources of law including soft law, may be understood as an expression of a 'social market economy' as already, that is, before the entry into force of the Treaty of Lisbon 2009, being the actual objective for the EU to strive for.[153] After the Treaty of Lisbon 2009 entered into force, this objective is explicitly introduced, namely in Article 3(3) TEU:

> The Union shall establish an internal market. It shall work for the sustainable development of Europe based on balanced economic growth and price stability, a highly competitive social market economy, aiming at full employment and social progress, and a high level of protection and improvement of the quality of the environment. It shall promote scientific and technological advance. It shall combat social exclusion and discrimination, and shall promote social justice and protection, equality between women and men, solidarity

---

[150] Kleinman (2002), p. 58.

[151] Schiek (2007), p. 26. Footnotes have been omitted from the quotation.

[152] Case C-341/05 *Laval* [2007] *ECR* I-11767, para 105. See also Case C-438/05 *Viking* [2007] *ECR* I-10779, para 79.

[153] See further, for example, Azoulai (2008), pp. 1335–1356; and Jacqueson (2009), no. 5–6.

> between generations and protection of the rights of the child. It shall promote economic, social and territorial cohesion, and solidarity among Member States. It shall respect its rich cultural and linguistic diversity, and shall ensure that Europe's cultural heritage is safeguarded and enhanced.

In other words, it is expressly indicated that the Union should work for 'social market economy'.[154] It is noteworthy that the term 'social market economy' will play an explicit and significant role. Thereby, a culmination of the development away from the original point of departure as a mere economic integrationist Community with a focus on, primarily, a system of undistorted competition, to a rather new situation, has explicitly taken place.[155] However, it may be of some significance and impact that it is a 'highly competitive' social market economy which the development should be based at.

The importance of the European Social Model and the Social Market Economy primarily lies in the function of indicating that Europe is now heading in a different direction. The social dimension of the EU will make the European integration project more acceptable to some than when it was primarily defined as an economic project. However, this change also unavoidably implies a larger impact, and at times limitations, on the national organisation of welfare and of interest here, health services, which will be perceived negatively by others. As it has been put forward by Damjanovic and De Witte, the EU's legitimacy to deal with welfare services is disputed and uneven.[156] The same seems to be the case regarding health care services.

The change may be further explained by reference to the work by Maduro, where he distinguishes between the following three models: (1) The model on economic freedom and social non-discrimination; (2) the model protecting the social model of the Member States; and (3) the social model of Europe.[157] However, first the content of these will be elucidated.

The three models presented by Maduro review the relationship between the constitutionalisation of the project of European integration and social values.[158] It is stressed that the models are heuristic devices rather than 'real-life' representations, and that elements of all are to be found to a greater or lesser extent, in the EU.[159] It is also stressed that they do not simply represent different understandings of the role and place that social values ought to have in the project of European integration, because they embody different processes of decision making

---

[154] It should be noted that the former Article 3(1), litra g) EC, states that the activities of the Community shall include: '... a system ensuring that competition in the internal market is not distorted...' In the Lisbon Treaty this aim could be said to have been 'moved' to Protocol 27. See further, for example, Behrens (2008), p. 193; and Semmelmann (2008), pp. 15–47.

[155] See Joerges (2004), amongst others at pp. 16–17.

[156] Damjanovic and de Witte (2009), p. 55.

[157] Poiares Maduro (2006), pp. 125-141.

[158] Ibid., p. 125.

[159] Idem.

with respect to social values in the EU and these processes provide, in turn, different degrees of participation to different social groups.[160]

The first model more precisely is said to arise from the constitutionalisation of market integration.[161] Accordingly, in this model the focus is on the fact that market integration rules constituted the basis for the initial process of constitutionalisation of the project of European integration, and that they shaped its impact on the European social model.[162] Therefore, in this model both the impact of EU law on national social values and the development of European social values are linked to the logic of market integration and its focus on negative integration.[163]

The second model more precisely is said to have grown out of the policies of social harmonisation.[164] Here, the European social model is viewed as a set of basic social values and rules which are promoted or set by the European Union, but are mainly to be guaranteed and protected by the Member States.[165] Maduro points out that this model either aims at guaranteeing a level playing field in the social sphere so as to prevent social deregulation at the Member State level, or, in certain Member States, attempts to promote further social regulation by shifting the level of decision making of national social policies to what is perceived to be a more social-friendly political sphere.[166]

Finally, the third model assumes that the European social model must entail both a definition of genuinely European social values and mechanisms of distributive justice at the European level[167]:

> The underlying idea is that the European Union needs a political identity and that the latter requires a European definition of a core set of social values (including, in this respect, some core aspects of private law). It can also be argued that the increased redistributive consequences of some EU policies and its increased majoritarian character require a criterion and policies of distributive justice so as to legitimize and compensate for those redistributive consequences and to guarantee the necessary political loyalty of those in the minority. This model would require harmonization policies not as instruments of market integration (to guarantee a level playing field) but as instruments of a set of European social values that the Union ought to pursue. It would also require further instruments of distributive justice at the EU level (including taxation mechanisms).[168]

EU health care law seems to move more in the direction of the second model, but having its roots in the first model, whereas the third model still seems further

---

160 Ibid., p. 127.

161 Ibid., p. 125.

162 Idem, p. 125. Pursuant to Maduro this concept refers in this context both to the social model of the European States and that of the European Union itself.

163 Ibid., p. 125.

164 Idem.

165 Idem.

166 Ibid., pp. 125–126.

167 Ibid., p. 126.

168 Ibid., p. 126.

(perhaps forever) away.[169] In this respect, it is central that within the health care sector a right as such for the EU to legitimately establish and exercise an independent redistributive function is not recognised.

2.7 Conclusions

The ‘Good Samaritan’ has travelled a long way. Thus, the consciousness which may be claimed to have arisen from, amongst others, the parable may be considered to constitute an important element behind EU law, and thus no longer the domain solely of national law. The boundaries between the two levels of governance have become more blurred over the years. By reference to the different models of Social Europe, it seems clear that in a larger context, EU health care law at the general level is evolving and developing rapidly in recent years. It is now an important element of a newer agenda. The implementation of the understanding of the message inherent in, amongst others, the parable for the years to come will probably be less predictable. It is difficult to see how exactly the organisation will be influenced, whether for example, more privatisation will occur, more cross-border health care will arise, loss of well-functioning national solidarity mechanisms will evolve, negative changes as to the financing of health care will happen, and so on. It is certain that further changes are unavoidable. Hopefully, this process will eventually take into account the fact that health care is not a normally traded good, but has particular social traits, which need to be taken into consideration when deciding if a more market economically oriented ideology should rule, and if so, to what degree and how.

References

Adnett N, Hardy S (2005) The European social model. Modernisation or evolution?. Cheltenham, Edward Elgar

Azoulai L (2008) The Court of Justice and the social market economy: the emergence of an ideal and the conditions for its realization. CML Rev 45

[169] See in particular Poiares Maduro, ibid., p. 131: ‘The need to protect the cross-border provision of health services has led the Court to recognize, in several circumstances, the rights of patients to choose the Member State where they wish to be treated. This allows citizens to choose from a broader array of treatments and also to benefit from a faster and better treatment than that which may be available in their country of residence. Some critics have pointed out, however, that this may impose too great a burden on the financial foundations of national health systems. So far, the Court has been careful in this regard but one must recognize that such a system involves a certain degree of cross-subsidization. That such forms of solidarity are inherent in the logic of an internal market which includes a dimension of citizenship appears obvious. The remaining question is how such solidarity should be organized.’

Barnard C (2005) EU citizenship and the principle of solidarity. In: Dougan M et al (eds) Social welfare and EU law. Hart Publishing, Oxford

Barnard C (2007) The substantive law of the EU. The four freedoms, 2nd edn. Oxford University Press, Oxford

Behrens P (2008) Der Wettbewerb im Vertrag von Lissabon [May be translated into: Competition in the Treaty of Lisbon]. Europäische Zeitschrift für Wirtschaftsrecht

Bribosia H (2007) Subsidiarité et repartition des competences entre l'union et ses états membres. In: Amato G, Bribosia H, de Witte B (eds) Genesis and destiny of the European constitution. Bruylant, Brussels

Buendia Sierra JL (1999) Exclusive rights and state monopolies under EC law. Article 86 (formerly Article 90) of the EC Treaty. Oxford University Press, Oxford

Damjanovic D, de Witte B (2009) Welfare integration through EU law: the overall picture in the light of the Lisbon Treaty. In: Neergaard U, Nielsen R, Roseberry L (eds) Integrating welfare functions into EU law—from Rome to Lisbon. DJØF Publishing, Copenhagen

De Búrca G, de Witte B (2002) The delimitation of powers between the EU and its member states. In: Arnull A, Wincott D (eds) Accountability and legitimacy in the European Union. Oxford University Press, Oxford

De Økonomiske Råd (2009) Konjunkturvurdering. Sundhed [May be translated into: Economic survey. Health]. De Økonomiske Råds Sekretariat, Copenhagen

Dougan M, Spaventa E (2005) Wish you weren't here… new models of social solidarity in the European Union. In: Dougan M, Spaventa E (eds) Social welfare and EU law. Hart Publishing, Oxford

Due O (1997) Hvad mener de dog? (Om læsning af EF-domstolens afgørelser). In: Nielsen R, Fejø J, Lynge Andersen L (eds) Festskrift til Ole Lando. GadJura, Copenhagen

Hatzopoulos V (2005) A (more) social Europe: a political crossroad or a legal one-way? Dialogues between Luxembourg and Lisbon. CML Rev 42

Hatzopoulos V (2009) Services of general interest in healthcare: an exercise in deconstruction? In: Neergaard U, Nielsen R, Roseberry L (eds) Integrating welfare functions into EU law—from Rome to Lisbon. DJØF Publishing, Copenhagen

Hervey TK, McHale JV (2004) Health law and the European Union. Cambridge University Press, Cambridge

Hesselink M (2009) A European legal method? On European private law and scientific method. Eur J Law 15

Jacqueson C (2009) Social dumping i EU—på vej mod en social markedsøkonomi? [May be translated into: Social dumping in the EU—on the road to a social market economy?] no. 5–6

Joerges C (2004) What is left of the European economic constitution?. EUI Working Paper LAW No. 2004/13. European University Institute, Florence, among others

Jørgensen H, Kongshøj Madsen P (2007) Flexicurity and beyond. Finding a new agenda for the European social model. DJØF Publishing, Copenhagen

Karagiannis N (ed) (2007) European solidarity. Liverpool University Press, Liverpool

Kleinman M (2002) A European welfare state? European Union social policy in context. Palgrave, Hampshire

Manow P (2004) "The Good, the Bad, and the Ugly"—Esping Andersen's regime typology and the religious roots of the Western Welfare State. MPIfG Working Paper 04/3. Max Planck Institute for the Study of Societies, Cologne

Mau S (2007) Forms and prospects of European solidarity. In: Karagiannis N (ed) European solidarity. Liverpool University Press, Liverpool

Mossialos E, McKee M (2004) EU law and the social character of health care. P.I.E. Lang, Bruxelles

Neergaard U (2009a) Services of general economic interest and related concepts: the nature of the beast. In: Krajewski M, van de Gronden J, Neergaard U (eds) The changing legal framework of services of general interest in Europe—between competition and solidarity. T. M.C. Asser Press, The Hague

Neergaard U (2009b) Services of general (economic) interest: What aims and values count? In: Neergaard U, Nielsen R, Roseberry L (eds) Integrating welfare functions into EU law—from Rome to Lisbon. DJØF Publishing, Copenhagen
Neergaard U (2010) In search of the role of solidarity in primary law and the case law of the European Court of Justice. In: Neergaard U, Nielsen R, Roseberry L (eds) The role of the courts in developing a European social model—theoretical and methodological perspectives. DJØF Publishing, Copenhagen
Neergaard U et al (eds) (2010) Blurring boundaries: from the Danish welfare state to the European social model. Copenhagen Business School Working Paper Series or Social Science Research Network, Copenhagen http://ssrn.com/abstract=1618758
Newdick C (2006) Citizenship, free movement and health care: cementing individual right by corroding social solidarity. CML Rev 43
Østergaard U (2010) Martin Luther og dansk politisk kultur. Nationalkirke, luthersk reformation og dansk nationalisme [May be translated into: Martin Luther and Danish political culture. The national church, reformation and Danish nationalism] Kritik
Ottmann J (2008) The concept of solidarity in national and European Law: the welfare state and the European social model www.icl-journal.com
Page AC (1982) Member states, public undertakings and Article 90'. ELRev 7
Papaconstantinou H (1988) Free trade and competition in the EEC. Law, policy, and practice. Routledge, London
Poiares Maduro M (2006) European constitutionalism and three models of social Europe. In: Hesselink MW (ed) The politics of a European civil code. Kluwer Law International, The Hague
Ross M (2007) Promoting solidarity: from public services to a European model of competition. CML Rev 44
Schiek D (2007) The European social model and the services directive. In: Neergaard U, Nielsen R, Roseberry L (eds) The services directive—consequences for the welfare state and the European social model. DJØF Publishing, Copenhagen
Semmelmann C (2008) The future role of the non-competition goals in their interpretation of Article 81 EC. Global Antitrust Rev 1
Shaw J (2000) Introduction. In: Shaw J (ed) Social law and policy in an evolving European Union. Hart Publishing, Oxford
Szyszczak E (2009) Modernising healthcare: pilgrimage for the Holy Grail? In: Krajewski M, van de Gronden J, Neergaard U (eds) The changing legal framework of services of general interest in Europe—between competition and solidarity. T.M.C. Asser Press, The Hague
Van de Gronden J (2008) Cross-border health care in the EU and the organization of the national health care systems of the member states: the dynamics resulting from the European Court of Justice's Decisions on free movement and competition law. Wisconsin Int Law J 26
Weatherill S (2002) Pre-emption, harmonisation and the distribution of competence to regulate the internal market. In: Barnard C, Scott J (eds) The law of the single European Market. Unpacking the Premises. Hart Publishing, Oxford
Weiler J (2002) A constitution for Europe? Some hard choices. J Common Market Stud 40
Wilde L (2007) The concept of solidarity: emerging from the theoretical shadows? Br J Polit Int Relations 9

Chapter 3
Discrimination and Beyond

Berend Jan Drijber and Hilde Cadenau

Contents

3.1 Introduction

In the previous chapter, written by Neergaard, the relationship between national health policies and EU health issues has been explored. The overall picture is that the sanctity of an exclusively national welfare state is no longer self-evident.

B. J. Drijber (✉) and H. Cadenau
European and Competition Law at Pels Rijcken Droogleever Fortuijn N.V., The Hague, The Netherlands
e-mail: bj.drijber@pelsrijcken.nl

H. Cadenau
e-mail: h.m.cadenau@hhs.nl

J. W. van de Gronden et al. (eds.), *Health Care and EU Law*,
Legal Issues of Services of General Interest, DOI: 10.1007/978-90-6704-728-9_3,

The EU legislator and courts have extended EU influence in all types of public benefits, or are attempting to. The vehicle that makes the greater part of these changes possible has been the wide concept of 'restriction' to the free movement of patients and health care suppliers.

Initially, the four freedoms started as basically a prohibition of discrimination on the ground of nationality. Nationality discrimination is, by its very nature, at odds with the EU and its objectives. The Internal Market could never have come into being and operate effectively, if Member States were free to exclude persons, goods, services and more from their territory.[1]

The backbone of the ban is embodied in Article 18 TFEU (ex Article 12 EC). It is settled case law that the principle of non-discrimination laid down in Article 18 TFEU requires that comparable situations must not be treated differently unless such treatment is objectively justified.[2] Several Treaty provisions are more or less explicitly based on the elimination of discrimination of nationality. Most particularly, the four freedoms and the right to move and reside freely throughout the Union are species of the generic prohibition of discrimination on the ground of nationality. These provisions are the specific expression of this general prohibition and are to be applied as *lex specialis*.[3] They are the main source of liberalisation through market integration, eliminating unjustified barriers to cross-border trade and other activities.

In this contribution, we will first explore the actual meaning of the concept of discrimination in general. Subsequently we will examine the evolution of the principle of non-discrimination in the wider context of the four freedoms. Finally, we will focus on the health care sector. We will examine to what extent the principle of non-discrimination on the ground of nationality is relevant in case law concerning medicinal products, patients, health care providers and pensioners. In many ways, this chapter aims to provide some background and a framework to the more specialist chapters.

3.2 Discrimination: The Concept

3.2.1 Preliminary Observations

At first glance, providing a definition of the concept of discrimination seems simple. A closer look, however, reveals that this is far from the truth. In effect, discrimination and its interpretations come in all forms and shapes. One might

---

1 van der Mei (2004), p. 82.

2 See, for example, ECJ Case C-403/03 *Schempp* [2005] *ECR* I-6421, para 28.

3 See, for example, ECJ, Case C-384/08 *Attanasio* [2010], *ECR* I-0000 (n.y.r.), para 37.

even say that the scope and thus purpose of the concept is in the eye of the beholder.

Equality is the state in which equal situations are treated equally. The difficulty with this definition is that no two situations are ever wholly the same. Absolute equality is impossible. In a legal context, 'equal' means 'equal in all ways that are legally accepted to be legitimately relevant to the decision in question'.[4] Discrimination means that differential treatment has taken place without a legally accepted ground, for example, race or nationality. In order to reach a state of equality in which equal situations are treated equally, the prohibition of discrimination is imperative. Without it, there would be no means to achieve equality. In other words: the one cannot exist without the other.

3.2.2 Discrimination and Nationality

Certain forms of discrimination are widely perceived to be morally and ethically unacceptable, such as discrimination on the ground of race or sex. Others are unacceptable for a combination of reasons, in which practical and political goals play a role. Discrimination on grounds of nationality is an example of the latter. The condemnation of this type of discrimination is by no means as self-evident as other types of discrimination that are clearly morally abject. In a civil society, (direct) discrimination on the highly suspect ground 'race' will not be approved of under any circumstances.[5] Discrimination on nationality, however, has long been a means to form and unite a nation and protect the interests of these sovereign states.[6] Up to this day, it functions as a shield to ensure that civilians of states have privileges in their home state. Part of this system is that enjoyment of these same rights and privileges in host states is absent, or at best limited.

These long established practices can in principle only be abolished by the states themselves through bilateral agreements, conventions and other forms of cooperation. Through the creation of the various EEC/EC/EU Treaties the Member States have accepted the fact that their ability to differentiate between their own subjects, goods and assets is diminished. This sacrifice was (and is) vital to the achievement of an internal market, one of the main goals of the EU. However, the Member States have gradually seen their ability to differentiate, even to regulate in a neutral manner diminish in ways that they themselves could not have foreseen.

---

4 Davies (2003), p. 9.

5 See Schiek et al. (2007), pp. 35–36.

6 Discrimination on grounds of nationality is an accepted standard in important conventions, such as the International Covenant on Civil and Political Rights (ICCPR) and the Convention on the Elimination of Race Discrimination.

3.2.3 Formal and Material Discrimination

A key role in the interpretation of the concept is reserved for the distinction between formal and material discrimination. This distinction might not be the best known, but in fact covers all the more known types of discrimination, such as direct and indirect discrimination. The dichotomy formal-material is pivotal to the extent of the impact any rule will have that attempts to remove unjust differentiation.

The formal approach to discrimination, or formal equality, is the traditional view of the concept of discrimination, and signifies that different rules are applied to comparable situations or similar rules are applied to different situations. Thus, there is no discrimination if comparable situations are treated similarly and dissimilar situations dissimilarly, to the extent of the difference.[7] In other words, the formal conception of equality is a negative concept of discrimination: 'a prohibition of'.[8] Formal discrimination is often put on a par, and overlaps with, direct (overt) discrimination. The term 'distinctly applicable measures', as opposed to 'indistinctly applicable measures', is more or less synonymous. Essential to the concept of direct (or formal) discrimination is that there is a direct link between the differential treatment and the ground of discrimination, here nationality. It means that all provisions and practices that make the enjoyment of a right, benefit or opportunity explicitly conditional upon the nationality of the host state or the receiving state.[9]

The material or substantive approach entails that equal or unequal treatment itself is less important, as an overall assessment is made of the actual effect of a certain rule. The primary task is to create real social, economic and cultural equality and in order for this aim to be achieved, it is necessary to evaluate the results of a certain treatment. The approach means that the principle of equal treatment will lead from a duty to defer from discrimination, which is a rather passive stance, to the active duty to differentiate.[10] One will classify an approach as formal or material depending on the starting position on the scale. If this position is located on the edge of the formal side, anything that is slightly more material will be deemed a material approach and the other way around.[11]

Indirect discrimination can be considered a species of the material approach of equality. Roughly, it can be defined as the situation in which a rule or a practice does not formally discriminate, but has a different effect on different groups. It will not bear a division by nationality on its face, but does have a similar effect: the rule

[7] Burri (2004), p. 39.

[8] Prechal (2004), p. 548.

[9] van der Mei (2004), p. 82.

[10] Burri (2004), p. 40. See also Timmermans (1982), pp. 426–460.

[11] See Prechal (2004), p. 537. In France, which traditionally uses a very formal concept of equality, even the concept of indirect discrimination is considered to be far-reaching material equality.

has a tendency to divide by nationality (statistically) or to affect, in practice, more non-nationals than own nationals.[12] The classic example is a residence requirement.

The most comprehensive (or 'most material') concept of discrimination is the inclusion of rules that are not directly or indirectly discriminatory, but form a burden or obstacle to a national from another state in its own right. The rules are basically completely neutral and are strictly speaking not discriminatory at all. This concept plays a major role in the interpretation an application of the free movement law.

3.2.4 Free Movement Rules: From Discrimination to Market Access and Back Again?

3.2.4.1 From Diskriminierungsverbot to Beschränkungsverbot[13]

In light of the above-discussed different conceptual scopes of discrimination, a further look at the interpretation in the area of free movement is essential. For the purposes of the present contribution, our analysis can only be very succinct.

As we have mentioned before, the principle of non-discrimination is the corner stone of the four freedoms. It requires out-of-state goods, persons, services and capital to enjoy the same treatment as their in-state equivalents.[14] It also presupposes that domestic and imported goods, persons, services and capital are similarly situated and should be treated equally. Direct discrimination is relatively easy to discern. Indirect discrimination presents the courts with more complex matter. Yet, the European Court of Justice will not normally go into any sort of statistical exercise. It will readily assume that a measure will, in practice, predominantly affect non-nationals.[15]

All four freedoms have evolved from a prohibition of discrimination to a prohibition of measures involving a restriction or an obstacle, regardless

---

[12] Davies (2003), at p. 9.

[13] In English: 'From a prohibition on discrimination to a prohibition on obstacles'. Out of the innumerable contributions that have been devoted to the case law on free movement we mention van de Gronden (2004), p. 11.

[14] Barnard (2007), p. 18.

[15] See, for example, ECJ Case C-107/94 *Asscher* [1996] *ECR* I-3089 concerning a Dutch national residing in Belgium who complained about a Dutch tax measure having an adverse affect on persons working inside but living outside the Netherlands. The Court held this to be an indirectly discriminatory measure.

nationality.[16] Rules that make the provisions of services less attractive and, therefore, hinder to any extent the access to the market are caught by the wide notion of 'restriction'. Frequently, measures that are qualified as a restriction could also be seen as measures having *de facto* a discriminatory effect, for example, authorisation schemes that contain requirements that nationals will be able to meet more easily than non-nationals.

The scope of the Treaty prohibitions has, therefore, been considerably widened. At the same time the Court extended the rule of reason exceptions.[17] Indistinctly applicable measures that might give rise to an indirect discrimination may be justified on the basis of a (non-economic) rule of reason exception. An indirect discrimination is no longer treated, for the purposes of the justification, as formally or directly discriminating measures.[18] From an institutional point of view, the shift from discrimination to restriction essentially amounts to reversing the burden of proof in favour of market integration in a larger set of situations. In most free movement cases, the centre of gravity is, therefore, on the justification of the measure, the onus of proof being on the Member State concerned. As a consequence, less measures escape *the control* of the Commission and the Court. That does not necessarily mean, however, that statistically more measures are held to be in breach of the free movement rules, since restrictions may be justified.

With regard to the justification of restrictive measures four well-known criteria must be met: non-discriminatory application, overriding reason in the general interest, appropriateness (or suitability) and proportionality (or necessity).[19] After Gebhard, fulfilment of the first criterion has diminished in importance. In several cases, the Court has shown that it considers the discriminatory nature of a rule more or less 'irrelevant' as it only checks if a rule is an obstacle, regardless of its discriminatory nature.[20] However, as a rule of thumb one might say that measures having a discriminatory effect are less likely to satisfy the proportionality test than measures that are purely neutral in their effects. Such measures may not fulfil either the conditions that they must be applied in a non-discriminatory manner and that they must be suitable for securing the attainment of the objective which they pursue. In other words, restrictive measures having a discriminatory effect may benefit of rule of reason exceptions but they are nonetheless in practice more difficult to justify than strictly neutral measures.

---

[16] See for the free movement of goods: ECJ, Case 8/74 *Dassonville* [1974] *ECR* 837; for the free provision of services: ECJ, Case C-76/90 *Säger* [1991] *ECR* I-4221 and ECJ, Case C-353/89 *Mediawet* [1991] *ECR* I-4069; for the freedom of establishment: ECJ, Case C-55/94 *Gebhard* [1995] *ECR* I-4165; and for the freedom movement of capital: ECJ, Case C-222/97 *Trummer* [1999] *ECR* I-1661.

[17] There is no 'closed' list of rule of reason exceptions, as is shown by the case law on patient mobility. Occasionally the Court 'invents' new ones.

[18] See for an older example, ECJ, Case C-34/95 *De Agostini* [1996] *ECR* I-3843.

[19] Established case law since, notably, ECJ, Case C-55/94 *Gebhard* [1995] *ECR* I-4165, para 37.

[20] An example of such a case is ECJ, Case C-169/07 *Hartlauer* [2009] *ECR* I-1721, a case that we shall discuss in Sect. 3.3.4.

3.2.4.2 The Concept of Mutual Recognition

Ever since *Cassis de Dijon* mutual recognition plays a part in the case law of the Court on the various freedoms. The concept is not always rightly understood. Mutual recognition does not mean that the host state must accept the rules of the state of origin. It means that the host state must *in principle* accept the lawfulness of goods and services that are imported into its territory from another Member State where they are lawful. In all circumstances, the host state may seek to justify measures that limit or hinder such importation. Mutual recognition may be inherent in the Court's case law, *unconditional* mutual recognition is not.

In the absence of any harmonisation of national legislations, there is no place for the principle of mutual recognition.[21] The Union legislator may decide to introduce mutual recognition in combination with the principle of home state control. This is not exactly the same as introducing the country of origin principle. The country of origin rule is essentially a rule of conflict, discarding the applicability of the legislation of other states than the state of origin, save exceptions expressly provided for. The country of origin principle does not flow directly from the Treaty. It may be vested by the Union legislator, but like mutual recognition it will not work without some degree of harmonisation.[22]

3.2.4.3 Discrimination in (Recent) Case Law

One would expect that, with the rise of the 'obstacle theory', the prohibition of discrimination on the basis of nationality (or residence) is no longer a central feature of the Court's case law. That is indeed true to some extent. Discrimination is nonetheless still often at the heart of Court's reasoning. The distinction challenged is not so much that between nationals and non-nationals[23] but rather that between persons moving abroad and persons staying in their home state. For natural persons this follows clearly from the increasing number of cases on citizenship (Article 21 TFEU, ex Article 18 EC).

According to settled case law, the status of Citizen of the European Union is destined to be the fundamental status of nationals of the Member States, enabling those amongst such nationals who find themselves in the same situation to receive the same treatment in law irrespective of their nationality, subject to such exceptions as are expressly provided for in that regard.[24] In addition, when a natural person loses certain rights granted by its state of origin on the sole ground that he or she has moved residence towards another Member State, Article 21

[21] For gambling services, ECJ, Case C-42/07 *Liga Portuguesa de Futebol*, *ECR* I-0000 (n.y.r.). For a critical analysis see, Dawes and Struckmann (2010), p. 236.

[22] In the same sense see the chapter by Davies.

[23] There are still examples though, see ECJ, Case C-164/07 *Wood* [2008] *ECR* I-4143.

[24] See, in particular, ECJ, Case C-224/02 *Pusa* [2004] *ECR* I-5763, para 16; ECJ, Case C-76/05 *Schwarz and Gootjes-Schwarz* [2007] *ECR* I-6849, para 86.

TFEU is likely to be violated.[25] For companies this is not entirely different, as is shown by a series of judgments on direct taxation, the details of which would exceed the scope of this contribution.[26] There will normally be a violation of the freedom of establishment and the free movement of capital when situations which are objectively comparable are not treated equally.[27]

Another area in which the prohibition of indirect discrimination (alongside the principle of equal treatment) has started to play a prominent role is that of the granting of services concessions. For those concessions and other contracts not (fully) covered by the Procurement Directives 2004/17 and 2004/18, primary law imposes on tendering authorities an obligation of transparency. This consistent but still somewhat controversial case law[28] is based on the assumption that a lack of transparency deprives potential bidders of the possibility to show their interest for the contract. A lack of transparency is supposed to amount to indirect discrimination on the ground of nationality,[29] unless it is clear that the contract in question does not present 'a certain cross-border interest' to an undertaking located in another Member State.[30] Recently, this line of case law was in principle extended to administrative authorisations granting an exclusive right to carry out an economic activity.[31]

So far, reverse discrimination has not, as such, been held to violate EU law.[32] In reality, measures hindering a Member State's own nationals to move their domicile or residence to an other Member State, bear features of reverse discrimination. Since such measures will normally be considered to be a 'restriction', there is no need to examine whether they may also give rise to a reserve discrimination. As regards measures equivalent to a quantitative export restriction (Article 35 TFEU, ex Article 29 EC), for a long time the Court has maintained the requirement of discrimination,[33] contrary to its classic case law on measures of equivalent effect to quantitative import restrictions. However, it no longer appears to do so.[34]

---

[25] See for example ECJ, Case C-192/05 *Tas-Hagen and Tas* [2006] *ECR* I-10541 and ECJ, Case C-221/07 *Zablocka-Weyhermüller* [2008] *ECR* I-9029.

[26] For example, ECJ, Case C-446/03 *Marks & Spencer* [2005] *ECR* I-10837. More recently the Court seems to be more receptive for justifications invoked by Member States. See, for example, ECJ, Case C-337/08 *X holding* judgment of 10 February 2010, *ECR* I-0000 (n.y.r.).

[27] See also Banks (2008), p. 482. This author advocates that discrimination be made 'the criterion of the existence of a restriction of a fundamental freedom'.

[28] The first case was ECJ, Case C-324/98 *Telaustria* [2000] *ECR* I-10745, one of the most recent cases is ECJ, Case C-91/08 *Wall AG*, judgment of 13 April 2010, *ECR* I-0000 (n.y.r.).

[29] See the chapter by Hatzopoulos and Stergiou and Drijber and Stergiou (2009), pp. 805–846.

[30] ECJ, Case C-507/03 *Commission/Ireland (An Post)* [2007] *ECR* I-9777 and ECJ, Case C-376/08 *Serrantoni*, judgment of 23 December 2009, *ECR* I-0000 (n.y.r.).

[31] ECJ, Case C-203/08 *Betfair*, judgment of 3 June 2010, *ECR* I-0000 (n.y.r.), paras 46 and 47.

[32] For example, ECJ, Case 86/78 *Peureux* [1979] *ECR* 897.

[33] Ever since ECJ, Case 15/79 *Groenveld* [1979] *ECR* 3409. See, for an analysis, Oliver and Enchelmaier (2007), p. 685.

[34] ECJ, Case C-205/07 *Gysbrechts* [2008] *ECR* I-9947.

In *Keck*, the Court limited the scope of Article 34 TFEU (ex Article 28 EC) to exclude selling arrangements insofar as they have a general application and affect in the same manner, in law and in fact, the marketing of domestic products and those from other Member States.[35] The Court did not reject the applicability of *Keck* to other freedoms as a matter of principle, but denied its application in a number of cases which generally involved problems of market access.[36]

3.3 Discrimination in Health Care: Is It an Issue?

3.3.1 Introduction

In this section we elaborate on what was discussed in the previous sections, thereby specifically focussing on the health care sector. That is clearly not an easy task, not only because there are many interfaces between EU law and the health care sector, but also because many important topics are dealt with separately and more extensively in various other contributions to this book. We will leave aside EU legislation on such matters as the homologation procedures for *medical equipment*[37] or the conditions and the procedures for marketing authorisations in respect of medicinal products.[38] Nor do we deal with EU legislation enacted on the basis of Article 114 TFEU (ex Article 95 EC)[39] or Article 168 TFEU (former Article 152 EC Treaty). Most of these topics have extensively been covered elsewhere.[40] Instead, we will focus on four 'Ps': products, patients, professionals and pensioners.

---

[35] Joined Cases C-267/91 and C-268/*91 Keck and Mithouard* [1993] *ECR* I-6097. As is observed in the chapter by Baquero Cruz, *Keck* was meant to refocus the aim of the freedom of goods towards protectionist measures. *Keck* has always remained rather controversial. See, for example, Wilsher (2008), p. 3.

[36] Sometimes the Court finds another way to get around the problem that the case submitted to it has no real link with cross-border trade, for instance by holding that the effect of the measure on trade is too uncertain or too remote to be qualified as a restriction. See, for example, ECJ, Case C-431/01 *Mertens* [2002] ECR I-7073 and ECJ, Case C-231/03 *Coname* [2005] *ECR* I-7287. This line of case law was applied to the free provision of services in a health care case: ECJ, Case C-211/08, Commission/Spain, judgment of 15 June 2010, ECR I-0000 (n.y.r.) para 72.

[37] Or even more specifically the regime for medical devices; see Frank (2003).

[38] Directive 2001/83 of the European Parliament and of the Council of 6 November 2001 on the Community code relating to medicinal products for human use, *OJ* 2001 L 311/67, and Council Regulation 2309/93 of 22 July 1993 laying down Community procedures for the authorisation and supervision of medicinal products for human and veterinary use and establishing a European Agency for the Evaluation of Medicinal Products, *OJ* 1993 L 214/1.

[39] Such as Directive 2003/33 of the European Parliament and of the Council of 26 May 2003 on the approximation of the laws, regulations and administrative provisions of the Member States relating to the advertising and sponsorship of tobacco products, *OJ* 2003 L 152/16.

[40] See, for an overview, Hervey and Vanhercke (2010), Chap. 2. Chapter 11 of that same volume contains an outstanding contribution by Gekiere et al. (2010).

3.3.2 Products

Under this heading we will refer to an infringement case against Germany on the rules concerning the supply of medicinal products directly to hospitals.[41] German hospitals can procure their medicinal products from an 'internal pharmacy' at their premises or from an 'external pharmacy' located in the proximity. The requirement of proximity was challenged by the Commission. The action by the Commission was based on the free movement of goods only. This is not self-evident: although medicinal products are clearly goods and pharmacists are primarily selling goods rather than providing services, one could argue that the difference of treatment under the German law stemmed from the distinction between the location of the pharmacies and not from the products they sell. This is illustrated by the ground on which the Court rejects the application of *Keck* to the German requirement of geographical proximity:

> 35. It follows that the contested provisions are such as to make the supply of medicinal products to German hospitals more difficult and more costly for pharmacies established in Member States other than the Federal Republic of Germany than for pharmacies established in the latter State. Pharmacies established in other Member States, unless they are in a border region and near to the German hospital concerned, which wish to conclude a supply contract with such a hospital must either transfer their dispensary to the vicinity of the hospital concerned or open another pharmacy near to the hospital.

Essentially this was a discrimination of pharmacists. Somewhat paradoxically, the provision on the free movement of goods, the scope of which goes far beyond encompassing discriminatory measures,[42] is at this instance interpreted as a prohibition of discrimination:

> For a national measure to be characterised as discriminatory or protective within the meaning of the rules on the free movement of goods, it is not necessary for it to have the effect of favouring national products as a whole or of placing only imported products at a disadvantage and not national products.[43]

Be that as it may, the Court found the German measure to be a measure of equivalent effect, which it held to be justified in the protection of public health. The Court emphasised the need to have requirements that are equivalent to those as applicable in the system of internal provision of supplies, thus guaranteeing 'the unity and the balance of that system'. The contested provisions were necessary to

---

[41] ECJ, Case C-141/07 *Commission* v. *Germany* [2008] *ECR* I-6935.

[42] '... all legislation of the Member States that is capable of hindering, directly or indirectly, actually or potentially, intra-Community trade' (ECJ, Case 8/74 *Dassonville* [1974] *ECR* 837, para 5).

[43] At para 39, with reference to ECJ, Joined Cases C-1/90 and C-176/90 *Aragonesa de Publicidad Exterior and Publivía* [1991] *ECR* I-4151, para 24, and Case C-254/98 *TK-Heimdienst* [2000] *ECR* I-151, para 27.

the achievement of the objectives of ensuring a high level of public health protection and clearly do not go beyond what is necessary.[44]

In reply to arguments put forward by the Commission the Court separately examined whether the German requirements also constitute 'the least restrictive measure'. The alternative consisting of hospitals contracting several 'external pharmacies', as the Commission had advocated, would create additional costs for the hospitals. Referring to the two rules of reason exceptions developed in the case law on patient mobility, that is, the maintenance of a balanced medical and hospital service open to all and the planning of the number of hospitals and their facilities, the Court concluded that the German measure was justified.[45]

3.3.3 Patients

The cases *Kohll,*[46] *Smits and Peerbooms,*[47] *Müller-Fauré and van Riet,*[48] *Watts*[49] and *Stamatelaki*[50] have given the Court the opportunity of stating the conditions on which patients may, under Article 56 TFEU (ex Article 49 EC) now receive medical treatment in another Member State and be reimbursed for the costs incurred for that treatment by the national sickness insurance funds of which they are members. This case law is summarised at length elsewhere in this book,[51] as is the proposed Directive on patients' rights.[52] We will, therefore, make just a few observations.

First, these cases involve a state of origin that put limits on the possibility of residents to receive medical services in another Member State. In other words, the restrictions are 'export related'. It was each time the effect of the national rule on the provision of service by a health care provider in the host Member State that triggered the application of the free provision of services. One could possibly argue that those providers were treated differently from health care providers based on the territory where the patient has his insurance. That discussion may, however, be somewhat moot anyhow, since cases of the kind fall to be assessed under the wider concept of 'restriction'.

44 Paras 56 and 57.

45 Paras 60–62.

46 ECJ, C-158/96 *Kohll* [1998] *ECR* I-1931.

47 ECJ, C-157/99 *Smits and Peerbooms* [2001] *ECR* I-5473.

48 ECJ, C-385/99 *Müller-Fauré and van Riet* [2003] *ECR* I-4509.

49 ECJ, C-372/04 *Watts* [2006] *ECR* I-4325.

50 ECJ, C-444/05 *Stamatelaki* [2007] *ECR* I-3185.

51 See the chapter by Baquero Cruz.

52 COM(2008) 414 final. See the chapter by Davies and also Sauter (2009), p. 1.

Secondly, the host state shall grant equal treatment to patients from other Member States.[53] The question may arise how limited medical resources would have to be allocated if, for whatever reason, an influx of patients from other Member States causes delays for 'domestic patients'.

Finally, in private insurance schemes the requirement of prior authorisation may be based on the policy applied by the health care insurer, which is an agreement under private law. If private insurers were bound by the case law on prior authorisation one would construe Article 56 TFEU as having direct horizontal effect.[54]

3.3.4 Professionals

In cases concerning the access to certain health care professions the Court generally follows a rather cautious approach. Two older cases involved national rules reserving the exercise of certain medical activities to physicians.[55] In both cases, the Court considered the restrictions to be justified and necessary to protect public health, showing that the application of the '*Gebhard* scheme' may well result in a favourable outcome for the Member State.

More recently, the Court accepted in *Apothekerkammer des Saarlandes* the German restrictions to reserve the right to operate a pharmacy to pharmacists alone. This restriction of the freedom of establishment was held to be justified in view of the need to the level of reliability and quality in the provision of medicinal products to the public.[56] This was not entirely self-evident, since the actual pharmaceutical activities were not really at stake. These cases could suggest that the review carried out by the Court is considerably less strict than in the cases involving patients.

The *Hartlauer* case on the freedom of establishment shows, however, that the Court may take a critical stand towards a national measure on the establishment of health care providers if such a measure lacks consistency.[57] Hartlauer, a German firm, intended to establish a private health institution in the form of an outpatient dental clinic in Austria. According to Austrian law, authorisation for the establishment of such an institution was mandatory. Authorisation was granted only if

---

[53] Article 5.1.g of the draft Directive on Patients' Rights. See the chapter by Davies.

[54] In Gerechtshof's-Hertogenbosch (Court of Appeal), 3 March 2009, LJN: BJ0679, 08/00334 horizontal effect was accepted.

[55] ECJ, Case C-108/96 *Mac Quen* [2001] *ECR* I-837 and ECJ, Case C-294/00 *Gräbner* [2002] *ECR* I-6515 concerning the prohibition of the exercise of the activity as 'healer' by persons not qualified as medical doctors.

[56] ECJ, Case C-171/07 *Apothekerkammer des Saarlandes*, Judgment of 19 May 2009, *ECR* I-0000 (n.y.r.).

[57] ECJ, Case C-169/07 *Hartlauer* [2009] *ECR* I-1721. This case discussed also in the chapter by Baeten and Palm.

there was a need for such an institution, whilst the presence of such a need is assessed taking into account the already existing care available for patients within a reasonable distance. Such an authorisation was not required for the establishment of a so-called group practice, in which independent professionals (health care professionals outside paid employment) operate in a partnership. In other words, the measure was aimed at controlling and, where necessary, maximising the number of dental professionals in a certain region.

Not surprisingly, the Court starts by saying that any national rule under which the establishment of an undertaking from another Member State is subject to the issue of a prior authorisation constitutes a restriction. In line with the earlier cases in the field of services and establishment, no reference is made to actual discrimination. In fact, the Court emphasises that the presence or absence of discrimination is of no significance:

> Consequently, the legislation constitutes a restriction of freedom of establishment within the meaning of Article 43 EC, notwithstanding the alleged absence of discrimination on grounds of the nationality of the persons concerned.[58]

The Court decides that the rule is not objectively justified. It is in that context that equal treatment reappears in the reasoning of the Court. First, it concludes that the national legislation at issue does not pursue the stated objectives in a consistent and systematic manner, since the two categories of providers of services are in many ways comparable and are likely to have the same potential effect on an increased volume of treatments. Secondly, the Court finds that the national criteria of 'need' is not a non-discriminatory criterion known in advance, in such a way as adequately to circumscribe the exercise of the national authorities' discretion. It must be noted, however, that the comparable situation and the discriminatory criteria referred to do not relate to any discrimination *on the ground of nationality.*

This interesting judgment calls for some comments. On the one hand, the Court has proceeded to an intensive review of the Austrian measure which echoes the approach taken in the patient mobility cases but which is, at the same time, less cautious than the approach recently taken in *Apothekerkammer des Saarlandes* or, previously, in *Sodemare*.[59] The Court is not shying away from giving a full assessment of the Austrian legislator's policy. It gives a clear boost to opening up the market to private clinics, as the authorisation of these more efficient private clinics can improve the market and the allocation of the public funds. The question is whether this approach is desirable. Many States may find that a certain amount of scarcity is acceptable, or even necessary to maintain the health care system at hand. A flux of funds to the private clinics may cause a deterioration of the publicly funded health care system. The Court, as in *Watts*, does not seem very convinced by that argument and will only consider it under strict circumstances.

---

58 See para 39. This may be seen as material equality in *optima forma* (see Sect. 3.2 of this contribution).

59 ECJ, Case C-70/95 *Sodemare* [1997] *ECR* I-3395.

On the other hand, the judgment in *Hartlauer* fits well into case law which concerned the consistency of the national measures under scrutiny as part of the suitability test (the third '*Gebhard* criterion')[60] and the discretion of national authorities when granting or refusing an authorisation as part of the 'proportionality test' (the fourth '*Gebhard* criterion').[61] In that respect, the judgment is also in line with the Services Directive,[62] even if health care services are excluded from the scope of that Directive.[63] Rather than rejecting the public interests advanced by the respondent Member State, the Court strikes down a national measure on its perceived lack of 'internal logic'. In so doing it directly intervenes in the policy choices made by a Member State. In this particular case, one cannot exclude that the whiff of protectionism that arises from the facts of the case may also have influenced the Court to decide the case the way it did.[64]

This line of case law was further pursued in the recent *Asturias* judgment.[65] Pharmacies in Spain are subject to rules on territorial distribution. Under rules of the region of Asturias, in each 'pharmaceutical area' a single pharmacy may be opened, as a general rule, per unit of two 800 inhabitants and there must be a minimum distance of at least 250 metre between two pharmacies. The effect of such rules is to hinder and render less attractive the exercise by pharmacists from other Member States or their activities of Spanish territory through a fixed place of business.

The Court then examines whether this restriction on the freedom establishment, which is applicable without discrimination on grounds of nationality, may be justified. The Court notes that the rules apply without discrimination on grounds of nationality[66] and that they are designed to protect public health. Clearly the most interesting part of the reasoning concerns the third criterion, that is, the suitability of the restriction.

The Court holds that the finding in *Smits–Peerbooms* that public health establishments and infrastructure may be subject to planning is transposable to the provision of public health services in the field of pharmacy.[67] It recognises that a

---

[60] For example, ECJ, Case C-334/04 a.o. *Placanica* [2007] *ECR* I-1891 and ECJ, Case C-500/06 *Corporación Dermoestética* [2008] *ECR* I-5785.

[61] See ECJ, C-483/99 *Commission* v. *France* (golden shares) [2002] *ECR* I-4781; ECJ, C-205/99 *Analir* [2001] *ECR* I-1271, paras. 36 and 38; ECJ, Case C-385/95 *Müller-Fauré en Van Riet,* paras. 84 and 85, and ECJ, C-324/07 *Coditel Brabant* [2008] *ECR* I-8457.

[62] Directive 2006/123 of the European Parliament and of the Council of 12 December 2006 on services in the internal market, *OJ* 2006 L 376/36. See Articles 9, 10 and 14(5) of that Directive.

[63] By virtue of Article 2(2)(f) of that Directive.

[64] See van Harten (2008), p. 222.

[65] ECJ, Joined Cases C-570/07 and C-571/07, *José Manuel Blanco Pérez a.o.* v. *Consejerá de Salud y Servicios Sanitarios and Principado de Asturias*, judgment of 1 June 2010, *ECR* I-0000 (n.y.r.).

[66] At para 62. It has always been somewhat unclear what the test of 'application without discrimination' (the first '*Gebhard* criterion') precisely adds to the finding that a measure is indistinctly applicable (as opposed to discriminatory measures). The Court nonetheless maintains this first condition.

[67] Para 71.

Member State might see a risk that some part of its territory will be left with too few pharmacies and also that the measure at issue may lead to a more even distribution of pharmacies within a given area. Also the 'minimum distance' condition helps to achieve the objective of distributing pharmacies evenly throughout the territory. It furthermore repeats earlier case law that the seriousness of the objectives of the protection of public health may justify restrictions which may have substantial adverse consequences for certain operators.[68]

The Court goes one step further: referring to *Hartlauer* and *Apotheker des Saarlandes* it holds that the national rules must also 'genuinely reflect a concern to attain that objective in a consistent and systematic manner'.[69] The Court then makes an in-depth examination of the consistency of the Spanish rules, including the flexibility needed to ensure that adequate pharmaceutical services are available in more rural areas. It is striking that in a field in which Member States are supposed to enjoy wide discretion, the Court examines the rules at such length and in such an amount of detail. It is also interesting to note that where the Court frequently criticises national authorisation schemes on the ground that national authorities have too wide a discretion, its concern in this case is to make sure that the rules are sufficiently *flexible* to attain in each relevant situation the objectives pursued. Subsequently, in relation to the 'least restrictive measure test' the Court makes again a careful and detailed assessment of the Spanish (and Asturian) rules. It concludes that those rules do not go beyond what is necessary to attain the objective pursued.[70]

The authorisations for opening a pharmacy have an administrative nature. These authorisations are tendered. Two selection criteria were indirectly discriminatory, since they both referred to the applicant having professional experience within the Principality of Asturias. These selection criteria were, therefore, in breach Article 49 TFEU, in conjunction with the directive on the recognition of professional qualifications.[71]

3.3.5 Pensioners

The last category of cases concerns pensioners who receive a pension from one Member State, but reside in another.[72] For this category of persons, Articles 26–34

---

[68] Para 90.

[69] Para 94.

[70] Para 104–112.

[71] See, in particular, Directive 2005/36/EC of the European Parliament and of the Council of 7 September 2005 on the recognition of professional qualifications, *OJ* 2005, L 255, p. 22.

[72] Pensioners with another nationality who still reside in a Member State and receive a pension of that same Member State can simply rely on Article 3 of Regulation 1408/71. They cannot be discriminated against and can claim medical benefits under the same conditions as nationals. See also the chapter by Pennings.

of Regulation 1408/71 are relevant, as well Regulation 574/72.[73] In a nutshell, the complex rules provide that a pensioner is entitled to access the system of health care in the State of migration at the expense of the State or origin, the later being entitled to claim a premium or other form of compensation from the pensioner. At the time, this system was designed to ensure that migrant workers from southern Europe (typically Italy) could, also after their retirement, stay in the Northern state (typically Germany) where they had been working as *Gastarbeiter*.

Today, there is movement from the northern countries towards southern destinations, of more or less well-off persons who stopped working (often long before the age of 65) to settle at a Spanish *costa* or another Mediterranean retreat. The sunny climate, including the tax climate, might get somewhat overshadowed when these *pensionados* become dependent on local public health care services, the quality of which they may perceive as inferior to that of their state of origin. The 'right' granted by the Social Security Regulation may become even more a *cadeau empoisonné* if their home state charges the *pensionados* a substantial amount to compensate for the contribution it has to pay to the authorities of the migrant state under the regulation.

This triangular relationship raises all sort of questions of solidarity but most prominently the question whether a 'Treaty conform' interpretation of a rule of secondary law meant to protect migrant persons[74] implied that the application of such rule may not detract from the subjective rights flowing from, in particular, Article 21 TFEU. This question has now been referred to the Court in a long-standing court battle between Dutch *pensionados* and the Dutch authorities.[75] The case shows that it is now more and more frequently the State of origin which is said to hinder the free movement of persons,[76] and that it is not sufficient to rely on rules of secondary law to know the full range of EU law obligations Member States have to observe.[77] The effects of disparities of legislation are, however, to a large extent unavoidable in a system that 'coordinates' rather than harmonises national legislations.[78] In addition, Article 21 TFEU does not guarantee to an insured person that a move to another Member State will be neutral as regards

[73] Regulation 1408/71 of the Council of 14 June 1971 on the application of social security schemes to employed persons and their families moving within the Community, *OJ* 1971 L 149, p. 2. Regulation 574/72 of the Council of 21 March 1972 fixing the procedure for implementing Regulation 1408/71 on the application of social security schemes to employed persons and their families moving within the Community, OJ 1972 L 74, p. 1.

[74] Articles 28, 28bis and 33 of Regulation 1408/71 and Article 29 of Regulation 574/72.

[75] ECJ, Case C-345/09 *Van Delft a.o.* judgment of 14 October 2010, ECR I-0000 (n.y.r.).

[76] See in that sense also the interesting contribution from the late Advocate General Geelhoed (2006), pp. 31–48.

[77] In that respect there is a parallel with public procurement law, since it is no longer sufficient to know and to apply the Public Procurement Directives.

[78] 'Coordination' has the meaning of 'organising the co-existence of national legislations, *inter alia*, by fixing rules of conflict. 'Coordination' may also mean a form of harmonisation.

social security. This was recently confirmed in *Von Chamier-Glisczinski*, another case on alleged restrictions imposed by the State of origin.[79]

The recent judgment in *Rüffler* concerns a more classic problem of a host state discriminating against a migrant. Polish law excludes tax reduction of compulsory health insurance premiums paid in another Member State where they had not been deducted from income tax. The problem submitted reminds us of the old *Bachmann* case (on the non-deductibility of premiums paid to a life insurance company in another Member State).[80] This time the Court examines the case against the background of Article 21 TFEU. Interestingly, it applies a non-discrimination test:

> 68. With regard to the taxation of their income in Poland, it should be borne in mind that resident taxpayers paying contributions to the Polish health insurance scheme and those falling within a compulsory health insurance scheme of another Member State are not in objectively different situations capable of justifying such a difference in treatment according to the place where the contributions are paid.

This difference in treatment is subsequently linked to the fact that Rüffler had exercised his right of free movement. This difference is not considered to be justified.

3.4 Conclusions

In cases involving health care-related issues the Court by and large follows the same 'scheme' as in other cases involving the freedom of establishment or the free provision of services.

First, the prohibition of discrimination on the ground of nationality, while still underlying the application of Internal Market rules in the area of health care services, has in practice largely been 'overtaken' by the wider concept of 'restriction'. Only in tax-related measures has discrimination remained at the heart of the Court's reasoning.

Secondly, parallel to the increasing importance of cases on EU citizens moving to other Member States for reasons other than exercising economic activities, an increasing number of cases involves restrictions imposed by the Member State of origin on own citizens leaving its territory.

Thirdly, discriminatory aspects or effects of a national measure are part of the Court's reasoning regarding the justification of the restriction it entails. The Court takes discriminatory aspects into account when assessing the suitability or the proportionality of a restrictive measure.

---

[79] ECJ, Case C-208/07, judgment of 16 July 2009, *ECR* I-0000 (n.y.r.). See the contribution by Baquero Cruz.

[80] ECJ, Case C-240/90 *Bachmann* [1992] *ECR* I-249.

Finally, a number of the cases discussed, most prominently the recent *Asturias* case, illustrates that the Court may examine in great detail the consistency and 'internal logic' of a national measure, even in an area as sensitive as health care.

References

Banks K (2008) The application of the fundamental freedoms to member state tax measures: guarding against protectionism or second-guessing national policy choices. ELRev

Barnard C (2007) The substantive law of the EU. The four freedoms. Oxford University Press, Oxford

Burri SD (2004) Gelijke Behandeling m/v. Europees Sociaal Recht (Equal treatment of men and women. European social law). Sdu Uitgevers, Den Haag

Davies G (2003) Nationality discrimination in the European internal market. Kluwer Law International, The Hague

Dawes A, Struckmann K (2010) Rien ne va plus? Mutual recognition and the free movement of services in the gambling sector after the Santa Casa judgment. ELR

Drijber B-J, Stergiou H (2009) Public procurement law and internal market law. CML Rev

Frank S (2003) A new model for European medical devices regulation. Dissertation, University of Leiden. Europa Law Publishing, Groningen

Geelhoed LA (2006) De vrijheid van personenverkeer en de interne situatie: maatschappelijke dynamiek en juridische rafels (The free movement of persons and the internal situation: dynamics in society and legal loose ends). In: Manunza E, Senden L (eds), De EU: de interstatelijkheid voorbij? (The EU: beyond interstate effects?). Wolf Legal Publishers, Nijmegen

Gekiere W et al (2010) Free movement of services in the EU and health care. In: Mossialos E, Permanand G, Baeten R, Hervey T (eds) Health systems governance in Europe: the role of EU law and policy. Cambridge University Press, Cambridge, Chapter 11

Hervey T, Vanhercke B (2010) Health care and the EU: the law and policy patchwork. In: Mossialos E, Permanand G, Baeten R, Hervey T (eds) Health systems governance in Europe: the role of EU law and policy. Cambridge University Press, Cambridge Chapter 2

Oliver P, Enchelmaier S (2007) Free movement of goods: recent developments in the case law. CML Rev

Prechal S (2004) Equality of treatment, non-discrimination and social policy: achievements in three themes. CML Rev 41(2)

Sauter W (2009) Patiëntenrechten bij grensoverschrijdende zorg (Patients' rights in case of cross border care). NTER

Schiek D et al (2007) Cases, materials and text on national, supranational and international non-discrimination law. Hart Publishing, Oxford

Timmermans CWA (1982) Verboden discriminatie of (geboden) differentiatie? (Forbidden discrimination or required differentiation?). SEW (6)

Van de Gronden JW (2004) Zorg tussen lidstaat en interne markt—Zorgverzekeringen, EG-recht en particulier initiatief (Health care from member state to internal market—health insurance, EC law and private initiative). Europese Monografieën 74. Kluwer, The Hague

Van der Mei AP (2004) Free movement of Persons within the European community. Cross border access to public benefits (Non-commercial edition)

Van Harten H (2008) Proportionality in decentralized action: the Dutch court experience in free movement of services and freedom of establishment cases. Legal Issues Econ Integr 35(3)

Wilsher D (2008) Does Keck discrimination make any sense? An assessment of the non-discrimination principle *within* the European single market. ELRev

Part II
The (Draft) Patients' Rights Directive and Internal Market Issues

Chapter 4
The Case Law of the European Court of Justice on the Mobility of Patients: An Assessment

Julio Baquero Cruz

Contents

The opinions expressed in this chapter are purely personal and do not necessarily coincide with those of the Commission or of its Legal Service. Thanks are due to Chiara Cattabriga for comments and suggestions on a first draft. The chapter reflects the law as it stood in January 2010. For more recent case law, see the conclusions to this volume.

J. Baquero Cruz (✉)
Legal Service of the European Commission, Brussels, Europe
e-mail: Julio.BAQUERO-CRUZ@ec.europa.eu

J. W. van de Gronden et al. (eds.), *Health Care and EU Law*,
Legal Issues of Services of General Interest, DOI: 10.1007/978-90-6704-728-9_4,

4.1 Introduction

These pages are devoted to a particular aspect of the relationship between the free movement rules and the provision of health services in the European Union: the freedom of individuals to receive health services in Member States other than that in which they are affiliated for health purposes, that is, the issue of the mobility of patients.

My aim is to offer an overview and an assessment of the leading judgments in the field. More than 10 years have passed since the *Decker* and *Kohll*[1] rulings were rendered and it may be a good moment for this kind of exercise. I shall also reflect on whether the case law is exhausted or still has some space and potential for development. A final aim of this chapter is to assess the line of case law from the point of view of a common critique, according to which these judgments could endanger the solidarity aims of national health systems by putting pressure on their territorial character.[2]

This means that I shall not deal with other interesting issues such as the free movement of health care providers, with the other free movement rules relevant to health policy (for example, the free movement of pharmaceutical products or the freedom of establishment), and with the influence of the competition rules on health care. In all these issues, it seems to me, health is secondary or at most as important as the underlying economic interests. In the cases about the free movement of patients, in contrast, health and the liberty of individuals to receive treatment where they prefer are the main concern and the economic issues seem to be secondary. This is the reason for the specificity of the case law on the mobility of patients, and also what makes it so unusual, problematic and interesting.

In addition, I shall deal only in passing with Regulation 833/2004 on social security,[3] which is often invoked in the cases concerning the mobility of patients alongside the Treaty provision on services. I shall refer only very briefly to the draft Directive on the mobility of patients,[4] a proposal which, in spite of its unlikely future after difficult negotiations, remains very important to assess the future of this line of case law.

---

1 ECJ, Case C-120/95 *Decker* [1998] *ECR* I-1831; Case C-158/96 *Kohll* [1998] *ECR* I-1931.

2 On these issues, see, for example, Scharpf (2002), p. 645, and his more recent views in Scharpf (2009), p. 173; see also my critique in Baquero Cruz (2007), p. 1105.

3 Regulation (EC) No 883/2004 of the European Parliament and of the Council of 29 April 2004 on the coordination of social security systems (*OJ* L 166, of 30 April 2004, p. 1), which replaces Council Regulation (EEC) No 1408/71 of 14 June 1971 on the application of social security schemes to employed persons, to self-employed persons and to members of their families moving within the Community (*OJ* L 149, of 5 July 1971, p. 2). On the Regulation, see the chapter by Pennings.

4 Proposal for a Directive of the European Parliament and of the Council on the application of patients' rights in cross-border healthcare Brussels (2 July 2008, COM(2008) 414 final).

The case law can be read like a chain novel of interconnected episodes, from *Luisi and Carbone*,[5] of 1984, to *von Chamier-Glisczinski*,[6] of July 2009. The leading cases, besides these two, seem to me to be the following: *Kohll*,[7] of 28 April 1998 (rendered the same day as *Decker*,[8] which concerned the free movement of goods), *Vanbraekel* and *Smits-Peerbooms*,[9] of 12 July 2001, *Müller-Fauré and van Riet*,[10] of 13 May 2003, and *Watts*,[11] of 16 May 2006. I shall leave aside other less important cases which more or less repeat the established case law, such as *Inizan*,[12]*Leichtle*[13] or *Stamatelaki*,[14]*Keller*[15] or *Acereda Herrera*.[16]

4.2 An Analysis of the Leading Cases

4.2.1 Luisi and Carbone

Perhaps this whole line of case law would have been impossible without the *Luisi and Carbone* judgment of 1984, in which the Court held, after a complex reasoning and seemingly contrary to the wording of the provision on services, that:

> the freedom to provide services includes the freedom, for the recipients of services, to go to another Member State in order to receive a service there, without being obstructed by restrictions, even in relation to payments and that tourists, persons receiving medical treatment and persons travelling for the purpose of education or business are to be regarded as recipients of services.[17]

This seemingly minor judgment actually changed the whole perspective of the Treaty of Rome on services. After this judgment, it was no longer just the freedom of the *provider* of services which was protected by the provision on services: the freedom of *recipients* was also considered to be protected by means of a judicially enforceable subjective right. This makes sense in economic terms. Indeed, the freedom of service recipients to get those services that they consider better or

---

[5] ECJ, Joined Cases 286/82 and 26/83 *Luisi and Carbone* [1984] *ECR* 377.

[6] ECJ, Case C-208/07, *von Chamier-Glisczinski* [2009] ECR I-6095.

[7] Cited in n. 1 *supra*.

[8] Ibid.

[9] ECJ, Case C-368/98 *Vanbraekel and others* [2001] *ECR* I-5363; ECJ, Case C-157/99 *Smits and Peerbooms* [2001] *ECR* I-5473.

[10] ECJ, Case C-385/99 *Müller-Fauré and van Riet* [2003] *ECR* I-4509.

[11] ECJ, Case C-372/04 *Watts* [2006] *ECR* I-4325.

[12] ECJ, Case C-56/01 *Inizan* [2003] *ECR* I-12403.

[13] ECJ, Case C-8/02 *Leichtle* [2004] *ECR* I-2641.

[14] ECJ, Case C-444/05 *Stamatelaki* [2007] *ECR* I-3185.

[15] ECJ, Case C-145/03 *Keller* [2005] *ECR* I-2529.

[16] ECJ, Case C-466/04 *Acereda Herrera* [2006] *ECR* I-5341.

[17] *Luisi and Carbone*, cited in n. 5 *supra*, para 16.

cheaper in a common market is as conducive to an efficient allocation of resources in service markets as the free movement of providers. Even more so, perhaps, for it may be easier for an individual to move to another Member State in order to receive a service. It was also properly justified in an extensive interpretation by reference to the economic law of the Treaty and to the legislation enacted at the time pursuant to it, even if it seemed to run against the wording of Article 56 TFEU (ex Article 49 EC).

But the judgment has a deeper meaning than its technical legal meaning or its economic meaning. The Court was beginning to change its perspective, moving beyond the purely economic dimension of trade in services, opening a door towards the subjective rights of citizens, as citizens, and not just as economic actors. This intention is clear, in my view, in the fact that the Court expressly mentions education and medical treatment as examples of services that can be received pursuant to the free provision of services.

The judgment paved the way to new developments which may have been quite unthinkable had the Court decided that only providers of services and not their recipients benefited from a subjective right based on the Treaty. But that possibility remained open for many years without anybody using it. Only in 1998, in *Decker* and *Kohll*, did the Court have a chance to move forward.

4.2.2 *Decker and Kohll*

In *Decker* and *Kohll* the Court confirmed that social security as such is not excluded from the purview of the free movement rules, even though the Member States have retained their competences to regulate their social security systems. The Court made it clear that Regulation 1408/71 on social security does not exhaust the field and has to be compatible and interpreted in accordance with the free movement rules. It held that prior authorisation systems are incompatible with the free movement rules insofar as they concern non-hospital treatment, such as orthodontic treatment, or the acquisition of health goods, such as a pair of spectacles with corrective lenses. In such cases, the Member State of affiliation must reimburse the patient on the same terms as if the spectacles had been bought or the treatment had been received within its territory. A prior authorisation condition cannot be justified for reasons related to the quality and guarantee of health services, because the access to the profession has been harmonised at Union level. It cannot be justified either by the need to preserve the financial balance of the medical and hospital system of the Member State. As a matter of fact, since reimbursement is governed by the rules of the Member State of affiliation, the cost remains constant for the national health system concerned regardless of the fact that the spectacles are bought or the treatment is received in another Member State. Finally, as regards the orthodontic treatment, the Court held that the Member State did not prove that prior authorisation was indispensable to maintain a balanced medical and hospital service accessible to all or for the maintenance of an essential treatment facility or medical service on national territory.

Read today, these judgments may appear to be timid exploratory judgments, but in 1998 they were catalytic decisions which, like *Luisi and Carbone*, pointed to new and unforeseen doors that would soon be opened. They introduced the important distinction between hospital and non-hospital treatment. They are also important in what they do not dwell upon the issue of the economic nature of the service provided; it is almost taken for granted. According to *Kohll*, the service of the orthodontist, 'provided for remuneration, must be regarded as a service within the meaning of Article [57 TFEU], which expressly refers to activities of the professions.'[18] No particular importance was attached to the fact that that remuneration was then to be reimbursed by the Caisse de Maladie and thus cancelled out in economic terms, or to the fact that the Caisse de Maladie operated according to principles of solidarity and not along strictly economic interests. The decision to interpret expansively the notion of economic activity and to consider only the part of a complex triangular economic relationship in which there is remuneration will have important consequences for the future development of the case law.

The bottom line of these two judgments was to pierce, for the first time, the territorial veil of national health systems, which until then were only connected through Regulation 1408/71. The free movement rules could thus open up new possible and necessary bridges between those systems. As in *Luisi and Carbone*, the individuals concerned were not seen only, or mainly, as economic actors (in this case, workers affiliated to a system of social security). They were seen as *citizens* who want to move to receive health services in another Member State and who have a right, subject to justified limitations, to receive such services under the same conditions as if they had not moved.

4.2.3 Vanbraekel and Smits–Peerbooms

The next significant step came only 3 years later, in July 2001, when the Court decided the *Vanbraekel* and the *Smits–Peerbooms* cases. Let us first consider the facts. Mrs Vanbraekel wanted an operation to treat bilateral gonarthrosis in France, to avoid the long waiting lists of Belgian hospitals. She sought authorisation from the Belgian Institut national d'assurance maladie-invalidité, but it was refused on the grounds that she had not produced the opinion of a Belgian university professor stating that the operation would be performed in France under better medical conditions than in Belgium. She decided nonetheless to have the operation performed in France and then requested reimbursement of the expenses from the Belgian health insurance organisation. In the course of the national litigation, the necessity of the hospital treatment in France was recognised and also that she had a

[18] *Kohll*, cited in n. 1 *supra*, para 29.

right to be reimbursed. But the Belgian court did not know whether she should be reimbursed within the limits of the scheme of her State of affiliation (Belgium) or according to the French rules, which were less generous than those of Belgium.

Mrs Smits suffered from Parkinson's disease. She underwent treatment in Germany. The reimbursement of the expenses was refused by the health fund to which she was affiliated in the Netherlands, because a similar treatment existed in the Member State of affiliation and there was no additional advantage and no medical necessity in the treatment provided in Germany.

Mr Peerbooms fell into a coma after a road accident. He was transferred to Innsbruck where he was given special intensive therapy using neurostimulation. In the Netherlands such technique was only used experimentally in two clinics and only for persons under the age of 25 years (he was older so he would not have received such a treatment in the Netherlands). The request to pay the cost of his treatment in Austria was rejected by his sickness fund. In the meantime Mr Peerbooms came out of the coma. The refusal was based on similar reasons as in the case of Mrs Smits: adequate treatment existed in the Netherlands, the treatment received was not regarded as 'normal' in the Netherlands, and there was no scientific evidence of its effectiveness.

Part of the *Vanbraekel* case concerned again Article 22 of Regulation 1408/71, on social security, whereas the *Smits–Peerbooms* cases were focused exclusively on the free movement rules. According to the Regulation, Mrs Vanbraekel should have been reimbursed following the French rules, which established a lower scale of reimbursement than the Belgian rules. When confronted with the issue, the Court confirmed the view it held in *Decker* and *Kohll* to the effect that that Regulation was not the end of the matter. One still had to see whether the freedom to receive services granted Mrs Vanbraekel the right to receive the higher reimbursement offered by the French system. The application of primary law, in other words, is not pre-empted by the Regulation, which does not intend to harmonise and exhaust the field, but only aims at coordinating the existing national regimes of social security. At the same time the Court avoided ruling on the compatibility of the Regulation with the Treaty. The two regimes thus appear to be parallel and alternative, and sometimes also complementary.

An important decision taken by the Court in all three cases was, I think, the confirmation of its expansive approach to the notion of economic activity when confronted with health services provided in hospitals. In these cases, the Advocates General strongly argued that no economic activities were involved. In *Vanbraekel*, Advocate General Saggio had considered, following *Humbel*[19] (on public education) and the arguments of a number of intervening Member States, that the fact that these services are provided within the framework of the system of public health, established and organised by the State, and financed with public funds, meant that they were not carrying out economic activities within the purview of the free movement rules. The reasoning, in other words, proposed to

[19] ECJ, Case 263/86 *Humbel* [1988] *ECR* 5365.

extend to the free movement rules the rationale that we find in the context of the competition rules in order to exclude from their scope those entities whose activities are predominantly based on solidarity (the *Poucet and Pistre*[20] line of case law). In his Opinion about *Smits–Peerbooms*, Advocate General Ruiz-Jarabo Colomer defended similar ideas.

The Court disregarded these arguments and in a single paragraph limited itself to affirm that these services constitute an economic activity:

> It is settled case-law that medical activities fall within the scope of Article [57 TFEU], there being no need to distinguish in that regard between care provided in a hospital environment and care provided outside that environment.[21]

As has been argued, this is a mere assertion backed by no reasoning.[22] At no point did the Court consider the possibility that these services may be provided under a system of solidarity and thus be a non-economic activity excluded from the scope of the free movement rules.

After finding that it was in the presence of an economic activity covered by the free movement rules, and with the hole on territoriality opened by *Decker* and *Kohll*, it was not difficult for the Court to go on to decide the cases.

In *Vanbraekel* the Court held that the lower level of reimbursement when a patient moves to France to receive hospital treatment constitutes a potential barrier to free movement, and that no overriding reason could justify it. In particular, the payment of the additional reimbursement due could not possibly affect the maintenance of a balanced medical and hospital service open to all or of a treatment capacity or medical competence on national territory: as such it did not impose any additional financial burden by comparison to the reimbursement due if Mrs Vanbraekel had decided to have the treatment performed in the State of affiliation.

The most important decision taken by the Court in *Smits–Peerbooms* was to consider justified as a matter of principle the requirement of prior authorisation for hospital services to be received in another Member State. This introduced a distinction between intramural services, for which the requirement of prior authorisation may in principle be warranted as long as it satisfies the principle of proportionality, and extramural services, for which such a requirement would be in breach of the Treaty. But the Court was not content to stop there. In order to consider a system of prior authorisation compatible with the principle of proportionality, the Court framed, and interpreted, the conditions imposed by the system of the Netherlands. The standard to determine what is considered to be a normal treatment has to be that of 'international medical science and medical standards generally accepted at international level'.[23] Authorisation

---

[20] ECJ, Joined Cases C-159/91 and C-160/91 *Poucet and Pistre* [1993] *ECR* I-637.

[21] *Vanbraekel* and *Smits–Peerbooms*, cited in n. 9 *supra*, paras 41 and 53.

[22] See Hatzopoulos (2002), p. 683 at p. 693.

[23] *Smits–Peerbooms*, cited in n. 9 *supra*, para 49.

> can be refused on the ground of lack of medical necessity only if the same, or equally effective, treatment can be obtained without undue delay at an establishment having a contractual arrangement with the insured person's sickness insurance fund.[24]

Finally, the Court introduced a number of well-known procedural requirements that are needed for a prior administrative authorisation scheme to be considered proportionate under a fundamental freedom of the Treaty: the system must:

> be based on objective, non-discriminatory criteria which are known in advance, in such a way as to circumscribe the exercise of the national authorities' discretion, so that it is not used arbitrarily.

Such a system must also:

> be based on a procedural system which is easily accessible and capable of ensuring that a request for authorisation will be dealt with objectively and impartially within a reasonable time and refusals to grant authorisation must also be capable of being challenged in judicial or quasi-judicial proceedings.[25]

4.2.4 Müller-Fauré and Van Riet

The next important case was *Müller-Fauré and van Riet,* of May 2003. It concerned the reimbursement of non-hospital medical costs incurred in Belgium and Germany, respectively. Ms Müller-Fauré received dental treatment whilst on holiday in Germany, provided without recourse to any hospital facilities. The reimbursement of the expenses was refused, since no exceptional circumstances justified receiving the treatment in another Member State. Ms Van Riet had an arthroscopy carried out in a Belgian hospital because there it could be performed much sooner than in the Netherlands. Reimbursement was also refused because there was no urgency and she could have waited for the treatment.

The judgment of the Court is a confirmation of the previous case law. Reading it one has the impression that the main principles of the case law were already well established. The issue of the existence of an economic activity is again taken for granted. The judgment develops further the distinction between hospital services and non-hospital services. Even though the Court admits that that distinction 'may sometimes prove difficult to draw',[26] it decided to stick to such a distinction, confirming that it accepts the requirement of prior authorisation with regard to hospital treatment, in view of the need of forward planning. As regards non-hospital services, however, the Court sees no evidence that prior authorisation is really needed to maintain the financial balance of the national social security

---

[24] Ibid., para 108.

[25] Ibid., para 90. These requirements were first mentioned in ECJ, Case C-205/99 *Analir* [2001] *ECR* I-1271, para 38.

[26] *Müller-Fauré and van Riet*, cited in n. 10 *supra*, para 75.

system. As a result, a prior authorisation requirement is deemed to be in breach of the Treaty. Finally, the Court addressed the issue of the essential characteristics of the system of access to health care in the Netherlands (benefits in kind rather than reimbursement), which was presented as a possible justification. Against the position of Advocate General Ruiz-Jarabo Colomer, who thought the system of prior authorisation would be justified even for non-hospital treatment in a system such as that of the Netherlands, where services are provided free of charge, the Court held that the removal of the prior authorisation requirement for non-hospital treatment does not undermine it.

The specific problem in *Müller-Fauré* was that a Member State operating under a system of reimbursement (Belgium) opposed the position of a Member State operating under a system of services in kind (the Netherlands). The former argued that the applicability of the free movement rules should not depend on the specific nature of each system.[27] Thus, what *Muller-Fauré* does is to guarantee a common solution and a level-playing field for both kinds of systems. The same issue was to reappear in *Watts* with regard to a third type of system: a purely national health service. The rationale of the common approach and of the level-playing field was to have the upper hand once again.

4.2.5 Watts

Watts, decided in May 2006, concerned the United Kingdom and its National Health Service (NHS), which, unlike the other systems examined by the Court in previous cases, is a completely public system in its organisation and in the way it is financed. There is no contribution from workers or companies to the system. For obvious reasons, there are no reimbursements in such a system.

Ms Watts had osteoarthritis and needed a hip replacement, but the treatment could only be provided by the NHS within a year. She wanted to have the operation performed sooner abroad but authorisation under the social security Regulation was refused. She had the operation in France anyway instead of waiting and then asked for reimbursement, which was duly refused. She started litigation and a preliminary reference reached the Court.

The first issue to be considered was whether there was an economic activity at all. The Court, following Advocate General Geelhoed, had no doubts that this was the case, because she paid for the treatment received. Indeed, the case was not about a service received within the NHS, which could be excluded in view of the fact that it is financed entirely or mainly by public funds. For the Court, the operation in France was a service received for consideration, 'regardless of the way in which the national system with which that person is registered and from

[27] In this sense, Hervey (2006–2007), p. 261 at p. 268.

which reimbursement of the cost of those services is subsequently sought operates', and 'there being no need [...] to determine whether the provision of hospital treatment in the context of a national health service such as the NHS is in itself a service within the meaning of those provisions.'[28]

Once again, this approach may seem somewhat simplistic: in economic terms the whole transaction is more complex than that. A service is received, paid for, and then reimbursed from a national health system. If you see it as one complex transaction, the fact that part of it, the reimbursement, comes from a non-economic actor in a system characterised by solidarity can really be seen as irrelevant? According to Spaventa, the Court wrongly focused on the economic transaction (between Ms Watts and the French hospital), but this was just an 'hermeneutic trick' to avoid tackling the real issue: 'The relevant relationship to establish entitlement to reimbursement for health services obtained abroad is, in this case, that between patient and health provider/social security fund'; 'there is no economic aspect in the provision of medical services by the NHS, since they are not 'bought' by other providers, and are therefore not part of an economic transaction'. The thrust of her criticism is the following:

> The rulings in *Peerbooms* and *Müller-Fauré* affect the *determination* of the circumstances in which the State *has* to recognize a right to seek health care outside the national health system, rather than just imposing an obligation of non-discrimination between health care providers *once* this right is recognized by national law [this would be the case of *Kohll* and *Decker*].[29]

Oddly enough, the provision on the free movement of services applies because the patient pays first, making it an economic transaction, and then that provision obliges the NHS to reimburse, which means that when Union law is complied with the treatment comes to be financed entirely or mainly by public funds, and thus would normally cease to be an economic transaction. There is something odd in that reasoning.

On other hand, it is true that once one has admitted that the systems of the Belgian and Dutch kind are economic in nature, it would be difficult to say that the treatments received by persons affiliated to a national health system in another Member State are not economic, thus insulating these particular systems from all others because of their specific nature. Once the door of the notion of economic activity has been opened, it is difficult to close it for just one kind of system.

For the rest, *Watts* is a mere repetition of *Smits–Peerbooms* and *Müller-Fauré*. In the application of the principle of proportionality, the system of the United Kingdom is held to be incompatible with the Treaty because the regulations of the NHS 'do not set out the criteria for the grant and refusal of the prior authorisation necessary for reimbursement of the cost of hospital treatment provided in another Member State, and therefore do not circumscribe the exercise of the national competent authorities' discretionary power in that context. The lack of a legal

---

[28] *Watts*, cited in n. 11 *supra*, paras 90 and 91.

[29] Spaventa (2007), pp. 56–58.

framework in that regard also makes it difficult to exercise judicial review of decisions refusing to grant authorisation.'[30] In addition, the refusal cannot be based merely on the existence of waiting lists: an objective individual medical assessment of the medical condition of the patient is needed.[31] And

> where the delay arising from such waiting lists appears to exceed in the individual case concerned an acceptable period having regard to an objective medical assessment of all the circumstances of the situation and the clinical needs of the person concerned, the competent institution may not refuse the authorisation sought on the grounds of the existence of those waiting lists.[32]

4.2.6 Von Chamier-Glisczinski

The most recent judgment in this field is the one rendered in the *von Chamier-Glisczinski* case on 16 July 2009. It is a judgment of a Chamber of the Court and, at this stage, it is not easy to say whether it is a leading case. But whether a case is 'leading' or not can only be known when some years have passed and one can see whether it has been followed consistently by the Court itself and by the other legal and political actors it was intended to lead.

The facts are complex, but we must get acquainted with them in order to understand the underlying issues. Mrs von Chamier-Glisczinski, a German national resident in Munich and reliant on care, received from the Deutsche Angestellten-Krankenkasse, the social security organisation with which she was insured through her husband, combined benefits in kind and in cash as provided for by German law in Austine. When her husband decided to move to Austria in order to look for a job or to start a business there, he put her in a care home in Austria. The Krankenkasse, at that point, continued to give her a cash benefit but no longer gave the full in-patient care which she had been receiving in Germany, since that was a benefit in kind that could not be exported to Austria, for it was not provided for by Austrian law. The Krankenkasse argued that according to the case law of the European Court of Justice only the care allowance, a cash benefit, could be 'exported' to Austria. In the end the couple went back to Germany, but Mrs von Chamier-Glisczinski continued the litigation until reaching the Bayerisches Landessozialgericht, seeking repayment of the costs linked to her stay in the Austrian care home in the amount of the difference between the care allowance granted pursuant to German law and the amount provided for by the German legislation for full in-patient care.

Her argument was that benefits in kind actually correspond to cash benefits, and that nothing could prevent the possibility of 'exporting' them. The refusal to

[30] *Watts*, cited in n. 11 *supra*, para 118.

[31] Ibid., para 119.

[32] Ibid., para 120.

provide benefits in kind in another Member State would be an infringement of Community law. The German court stayed the proceedings and sent a preliminary reference to the Court, asking whether the social security Regulation or the provisions on the free movement of citizens, workers or services were opposed to such a situation.

In his Opinion, Advocate General Mengozzi concluded that the provision on Union citizenship precluded such differential treatment. He argued that Mrs von Chamier-Glisczinski would have been treated better if she had stayed in Germany, that there was no justification for this different treatment, and that the refusal on the part of the Krankenkasse was not based on proper grounds.

The Court did not follow the Advocate General's Opinion as regards the solution. Concerning the Regulation, it simply confirmed what was already clear from *Molenaar*[33]*:* that in-house care is a benefit in kind and the Regulation does not require the State of affiliation to continue serving it. It added, however, that the Regulation does not mean that the competent institution is prevented from granting it,[34] probably meaning, as in *Bosmann*,[35] that the Regulation does neither require nor preclude it.

Concerning the second question, the Court began recalling its case law according to which its:

> interpretation of Regulation No 1408/71 [...] must be understood without prejudice to the solution which flows from the potential applicability of provisions of primary law [...]. The finding that a national measure may be consistent with a provision of a secondary law measure, in this case Regulation No 1408/71, does not necessarily have the effect of removing that measure from the scope of the Treaty's provisions [...]. It follows that the applicability, as the case may be, of Articles 19 or 22 of Regulation No 1408/71 to a situation such as that at issue in the main proceedings does not of itself prevent the person concerned from claiming, pursuant to primary law, the payment of certain costs relating to care received in a care home situated in another Member State, under rules different to those provided for in those articles [...].[36]

This is nothing new: we have known this since *Decker* and *Kohll*.

The Court went on to exclude the applicability of the provisions on the free movement of workers and on services. There was no element, the Court said, proving Mr von Chamier-Glisczsinski's status as a worker. The provision on services was not applicable either, since Mrs von Chamier-Glisczinski moved to Austria on a permanent basis, and that rules out the applicability of the services provision. But there was no doubt, held the Court, that:

> in any event, Mrs von Chamier-Glisczinski, as a German national, enjoyed the status of a citizen of the Union pursuant to Article 17(1) EC [now Article 20(1) of the TFEU].[37]

---

[33] ECJ, Case C-160/96 *Molenaar* [1998] *ECR* I-843.

[34] *Von Chamier-Glisczinski*, cited in n. 6 *supra*, para 55.

[35] ECJ, Case C-352/06 *Bosmann* [2008] *ECR* I-3827.

[36] *Von Chamier-Glisczinski*, cited in n. 6 *supra*, para 66.

[37] Ibid., para 78.

It was just then, when that declaration on citizenship could have created good hopes in the mind of the reader, that the judgment took a surprising turn and the Court departed from the Opinion of Advocate General Mengozzi.

One might have expected the Court to analyse the measure according to the classical technique of barrier, justification and proportionality, as it would have done in the context of Article 56 TFEU, as it did, for example, in all the other cases of this saga, and as it usually does in cases concerning Union citizenship. What the Court did was different: first it admitted that Mrs von Chamier-Glisczinski found herself in a less favourable situation after her move to Austria.[38] 'However', added the Court:

> as Article 42 EC provides for the coordination, not the harmonisation, of the legislation of the Member States, substantive and procedural differences between the social security systems of individual Member States, and hence in the rights of persons who are insured persons there, are unaffected by that provision.[39]

The conclusion:

> In those circumstances, Article 18(1) EC cannot guarantee to an insured person that a move to another Member State will be neutral as regards social security [...]. As the Commission states, in view of the disparities existing between the schemes and legislation of the Member States in this field, such a move may, depending on the case, be more or less advantageous or disadvantageous for the person concerned, according to the combination of national rules applicable pursuant to Regulation No 1408/71.[40]

In other words, it was bad luck that the movement of Mrs von Chamier-Glisczinski and the interaction between the German and the Austrian systems were unfavourable to her. It could have been otherwise.

This could seem to be in contradiction with what the Court itself had held before in paragraph 66 to the effect that the Regulation does not pre-empt the application of primary law. In *Vanbraekel*, a similar case, the disparity of legislation, the negative answer under the Regulation and the fact that Ms Vanbraekel's movement could have been either advantageous or disadvantageous for her did not prevent the Court from entering into the logic of barrier, justification and proportionality. One wonders why the Court accepted that kind of argument now, instead of following the usual path. Why is that final with regard to the free movement of citizens and not final with regard to the free provision of services?

Time will tell us whether this approach will be consolidated as good law.

---

[38] Ibid., para 83.

[39] Ibid., para 84.

[40] Ibid., para 85. A similar approach was followed in ECJ Case C-403/03, Schempp [2005] ECR I-6421, concering EU citizenship, non-discrimination on the basis of nationality and deductions from the revenue tax.

4.3 Some Reflections on the Case Law

After this review of the case law, which has not been exclusively descriptive, I should like to offer a more general reflection structured around various issues: one more technical: on the notion of economic activity; and the others more general: the place of this line of case law in the general case law on free movement; the relationship with Union citizenship and with the fundamental right to health; the room for growth of the case law; its relationship between the draft directive on patients' mobility; and finally the more general theme of the assessment of the case law from the point of view of the socioeconomic model of the European Union.

4.3.1 The Notion of 'Economic Activity'

A striking characteristic of this line of case law is the wide notion of economic activity employed by the Court. This catch-all notion, coupled with the usually wide concept of restriction, means that almost everything will be caught and decided at the stage of justification, normally through the application of the proportionality principle.

On economic activity, the Court could have decided to follow a more cautious approach, as proposed by Advocates General Saggio and Ruiz-Jarabo Colomer. At present that would take a dramatic overruling which is very unlikely, but it may be interesting to take a look at the road not taken. It seems to me that in these judgments the notion of economic activity was crucial, because the Court could have chosen to stop there, and the position of its Advocates General was far from farfetched. Once that threshold was crossed, however, many things were bound to happen, especially in view of the wide notion of restriction. The Member States would be bound to justify themselves, a difficult exercise, for their measures in this field had never or only rarely taken into account the existence of a world beyond their borders and the interests of people not affiliated to their health systems.

A first point to be made on the notion of economic activity is that this line of case law seems to sit rather uncomfortably with two other lines of case law: the *Sodemare* judgment of 1997 and the competition cases on activities based on the solidarity principle, starting with *Poucet and Pistre*.

In *Sodemare*, the Court declared that

> as Community law stands at present, a Member State may, in the exercise of the powers it retains to organize its social security system, consider that a social welfare system of the kind at issue in this case [based on solidarity] necessarily implies, with a view to attaining its objectives, that the admission of private operators to that system as providers of social welfare services is to be made subject to the condition that they are non-profit-making.[41]

---

[41] ECJ, Case C-70/95 *Sodemare* [1997] *ECR* I-3395, para 32. See, in contrast Case C-169/07 *Hartlauer* [2009] *ECR* I-1721. See also the chapter by Baeten and Palm in this volume.

Sodemare was not, however, an application of the *Poucet and Pistre* line of case law to the field of free movement. In *Poucet and Pistre*,[42] the important elements of solidarity of the system in hand meant that the companies involved were not carrying out an economic activity and thus were not undertakings subject to the competition rules of the Treaty (an issue, then, related to the personal and objective scopes of application of the Treaty). In *Sodemare*, in contrast, the Court found that the provisions on establishment were indeed applicable to the State regulation at issue, but the restriction was justified in view of the aims of solidarity of the system. The Court was happy with the fact that the measure applied in a non-discriminatory fashion to both Italian and non-Italian operators. One could argue, therefore, that *Sodemare* remains good law with regard to health operators and professionals, and that that line of case law can be distinguished from that of the free movement of patients, whose rights, connected to issues of citizenship and to the fundamental right to health, deserve stricter protection than the rights of companies looking for economic profit. A difference between services received by patients and the establishment of health companies may be warranted, for the interests at stake and the balance amongst them are clearly different.

In *Poucet and Pistre*, followed by other judgments such as *Albany*,[43] the Court has made clear that a national security system is not an undertaking when it provides services under a system which is predominantly based on solidarity and not on profit. What does this mean for our case law? Is there not a contradiction? Is the solidarity of the health system not relevant for the definition of the scope of the free movement rules?

The Court, as we have seen, has not paid much attention to the issues of solidarity in the context of the patients' mobility cases. In all of them, there was consideration provided against the services received in the cases considered, and that was enough for the activity to be considered economic. In particular, the fact that that consideration would be offset by the reimbursement of the cost of the service in full or in part did not exclude the economic character of the activity. I have already highlighted the somewhat paradoxical character of this argument. By looking just at one segment of a complex transaction, the Court qualifies it as economic and drives it into the scope of application of the free movement rules. This step, in turn, obliges the Member State of affiliation to reimburse, as a result of which the transaction ceases to be strictly economic, for it will then be 'financed entirely or mainly by public funds',[44] according to a system based on solidarity. But without that step, the transaction would not be reimbursed and would remain economic.

Now, the economic or non-economic nature of the transactions depends basically on the point of view and on the aspects one takes into account. In concentrating in just one part of a transaction, the Court is taking the point of view of the

---

42 Cited in n. 20 *supra*.

43 ECJ, Case C-67/96 *Albany* [1999] *ECR* I-5751.

44 See ECJ, Case C-318/05 *Commission* v. *Germany* [2007] *ECR* I-6957, para 68.

person moving abroad to receive a medical treatment, that is, the point of view of the person holding a subjective right of free movement. This choice shows once again that this line of case law is moved by considerations related to the fundamental freedoms of individuals. It has another advantage: it creates a level-playing field and ensures limited openings in all the various systems regardless of the particular technical solutions adopted by each of them. Indeed, a more restrictive notion of economic activity could have meant that some systems would have been insulated against the application of the free movement rules whilst others would have been subject to them.

One may also wonder about whether there is a justification to having a different notion of economic activity under the free movement rules and under the competition rules. Against the common sense intuition that the notion should remain the same throughout the Treaty, the case law now seems to accept that the notion might be different for both sets of rules. The judgment of the Court on appeal in the *Meca-Medina* case makes it clear:

> the Court of First Instance held that the fact that purely sporting rules may have nothing to do with economic activity, with the result that they do not fall within the scope of Articles 39 EC and 49 EC, means, also, that they have nothing to do with the economic relationships of competition, with the result that they also do not fall within the scope of Articles 81 EC and 82 EC.
>
> In holding that rules could thus be excluded straightaway from the scope of those articles solely on the ground that they were regarded as purely sporting with regard to the application of Articles 39 EC and 49 EC, without any need to determine first whether the rules fulfilled the specific requirements of Articles 81 EC and 82 EC [...], the Court of First Instance made an error of law.[45]

Is this approach justified? Can the elements of solidarity of a health system never shield that system from the application of the free movement rules? My impression is that the general notion of economic activity should remain the same for the whole Treaty, but that the different aim and structure of the free movement rules and of the competition rules could entail different consequences of that very same notion.[46] This is compatible with a possible reading of the *Meca-Medina* judgment of the Court of Justice: a distinct analysis is needed for both sets of rules to see whether the activity is to be considered economic. As a result, the same activity or regulation could be economic in its cross-border aspects and remain non-economic in its other aspects.

---

[45] ECJ, Case C-519/04 P *Meca-Medina and Majcen* v. *Commission* [2006] *ECR* I-6991, paras 32 and 33. The same distinction is made in the communication of the Commission on *Services of general interest, including social services of general interest: a new European commitment*, of 20 November 2007, COM(2007) 725 final, p. 5. On these issues, see Odudu (2009), p. 225.

[46] Compare Hatzopoulos (2002), p. 723, for whom the existence of a 'core' solidarity activity will have a different bearing on free movement and on competition. For the competition rules, it would entail their inapplicability. For the free movement rules, the presence of such a conduct would mean that they 'are only infringed by discriminatory measures, not mere hindrances'. The existence of 'core' solidarity activities would thus become 'yet another "overriding reason".'

In sum, what the Court is trying to open up with this wide notion of economic activity is the closed territorial character of national systems. If one remains within the narrow logic of territoriality, then everything can be accepted and natural, even the non-economic nature of the system. But once one starts to look at the issue from a European point of view, where closure is a potential violation of the free movement of individuals, then the economic dimensions come out, as do the restrictive aspects of national regimes based on territoriality, and also the need to justify national policy choices.

A similar thing happens with the notion of restriction. From the national point of view, there is no restriction: the obstacle is just a consequence of the territorial character of social security systems, such consequences do not have any protectionist intent or effect, and they would not be a restriction relevant for the purposes of Article 56 TFEU. If you take the European point of view and that of the individual, however, which are the points of view the European Court of Justice is bound to take, the existence of a restriction goes without saying. The case law is thus aimed at forcing some limited openings into the national health systems, whose closure, beyond the even more limited openings of the social security Regulation, is considered to be problematic from the perspective of the freedom of patients to receive their treatments throughout the Union. The Member States have to justify their choices and no longer think only in national terms when they regulate their health systems.

4.3.2 The Relationship with General Free Movement Law and with Union Citizenship

The case law on the mobility of services was one of the chances the Court had to revitalise its free movement jurisprudence after *Keck*.[47] In a way, it also sits uncomfortably with *Keck*. The latter was meant to restrict the interpretation of the provision on the free movement of goods and to refocus it aim towards protectionist measures. In contrast, the case law on the mobility of patients rests on an expansive interpretation of all the normative elements of the provision on services. The only reason for such disparity is that the line of case law on the mobility of patients, while using an economic freedom, is hybrid, since it also pursues objectives which are not economic. The same happens with the free movement of workers. These non-economic dimensions may justify the more expansive approach the Court followed in these cases. They are related, it seems to me, to the citizenship of the Union and to the fundamental right to health. The same reason can explain other controversial judgments such as *Carpenter*.[48] These are the

[47] ECJ, Joined Cases C-267/91 and C-268/91 *Keck and MithouardECR* [1993] I-6097.

[48] ECJ, Case C-60/00 *Carpenter* [2002] *ECR* I-6279. On this judgment, see Acierno (2003), p. 398.

elements that make a difference with regard to the case law on the free movement of purely economic factors.

In this line of case law, which indeed evolved hand in hand with the case law on citizenship, the deep discourse of the Court is about Union citizenship and about the fundamental right to health, enshrined in Article 35 of the Charter, even if these are never expressly mentioned in the judgments. The paradox is that, as we have just seen, the first time that citizenship could be applied because the economic provisions were not applicable, in *von Chamier-Glisczinski*,[49] the Court did not follow the argument to its natural conclusion: an analysis from the angle of the free movement of citizens according to the scheme of restriction/discrimination, justification and proportionality. This judgment shows that the provisions on citizenship are not a panacea. In addition, in contrast with the case law on the mobility of patients seen from the angle of the reception of services, the case law on citizenship has referred to the citizenship directives as accepting 'a certain degree of financial solidarity between nationals of a host Member State and nationals of other Member States'.[50] This element of solidarity does not seem to exist in the case law on patients' mobility, in view of the system of payments and reimbursements involved, which, if applied correctly, would mean that patients' mobility would have, in the long run, a neutral effect on the health expenditure of national systems.

This difference explains another contrast with the case law on citizenship, in which the grant of a welfare advantage can be made conditional by the host Member State on the existence of a 'genuine link' between the Union citizen and that State. A residence requirement is in principle appropriate in that regard, although the length of residence required must not go beyond of what is necessary in accordance with the proportionality principle.[51] Such a 'genuine link' is not required by the case law on the mobility of patients, which is more flexible: since there is no actual supranational solidarity involved, a 'genuine link' is not needed; the very idea of a reception of a short or limited service is opposed to a requirement of that nature. This is related to some of the problems that the Court may have faced in *von Chamier-Glisczinski*, which concerned long-term care and not a time-limited medical intervention. This is also the reason why the inclusion of long-term care in the draft Directive on the cross-border rights of patients is one of the most disputed issues in the course of the ongoing negotiations. This issue is discussed in the chapter of Szyszczak. Even so, the approach of the Court in the latter case may be problematic, as a degree of coherence must be kept between the interpretation and techniques of adjudication used in the framework of the provisions on Union citizenship and those used with regard to the economic freedoms.

[49] Cited in n. 6 *supra*.

[50] ECJ, Case C-184/99 *Grzelczyk* [2001] *ECR* I-6193, para 44.

[51] ECJ, Case C-138/02 *Collins* [2004] *ECR* I-2703, paras 67–72.

4.3.3 Is There Room for Growth?

It is important to ask whether there is still room for growth in the case law or whether we may see it as established and almost exhausted. I think most of the important issues have already been settled, and it is not likely that the Court will overrule those decisions, although there is always room for a distinguishing in cases and for various nuances. The other points that remain to be decided are minor but not completely negligible. They will, in all probability, be decided by Chambers of the Court, which considers the main principles of its case law in this field to be well established.

One issue that has not been decided yet is what happens when the State of affiliation does not even provide a more expensive or more advanced treatment which is covered in another Member State. *Peerbooms* moves from the assumption that the public health systems of all Member States should take into account the state of 'international medical science' when they decide what treatments to provide, but we now have in the European Union 27 Member States which are very different and have very different degrees of economic development, medical capacities, and even cultural attitudes to medical treatment. So this issue was bound to arise and has arisen. It is at the heart of a pending case, *Elchinov*,[52] a preliminary reference sent by a Bulgarian court, in which the treatment provided in another Member State is not and cannot be provided in Bulgaria. In such a case, is the refusal of reimbursement a breach of the social security Regulation and/or of the freedom to receive health services?

Another unresolved issue is the possibility for the Member State in which the treatment is provided to limit the number of non-nationals that can use its system, since this may have negative effects on the capacity of its facilities to offer treatment to those who are affiliated to it.

Another issue is the contours of the proportionality principle. In the case law, the Court seems to imply that authorisation would always be justified in the case of hospital treatment, but the judgments could also be read to mean that the authorisation requirement has to be analysed case by case, and that in some cases it could well be that proportionality does not justify the requirement of prior authorisation, even for some kinds of hospital treatment. If that were the case (as the initial draft Directive on patients' mobility proposed), with less than 1% of patients receiving cross-border treatment, it would be difficult to justify the requirement of prior authorisation for all kinds of hospital treatment, for the impact of mobility would always be marginal on national health systems and could not possibly affect them. Another issue related to proportionality is the question of whether the neat distinction between hospital and non-hospital treatment introduced by the case law is justified or not. Some may wonder whether it makes sense at all, for the need for

---

[52] ECJ, Case C-173/09. A summary of the reference has been published in the *OJ* C 180, of 1 August 2009, p. 28. The judgment of the Court was delivered on 5 October 2010 (confirming the expansive approach of the Court to the rights of patients).

forward planning applies equally to non-hospital and hospital treatment. Indeed, the need for forward planning has to do with the financial stability of the system, and this is taken care of by controlling in advance all costs, not only those related to hospital services. The distinction between hospital and non-hospital treatment, in which the Court is now stuck, has the advantage of being clear, but its normative basis is fuzzy and its consequences are not necessarily correct in all cases. This is why, no doubt, the draft Directive would supplement it with a number of expensive and complex extramural interventions for which authorisation would be required.

The scope of application of this line of case law is not totally clear either: are long-term and in-house care included or excluded? Are paramedical activities included? *Von Chamier-Glisczinski* does not really settle the issue. The Directive may exclude such activities in the end, but that does not mean that 56 TFEU is not applicable.

And finally, the relationship between the social security Regulation, the new Directive (if finally adopted) and Treaty rules will be important, and the very interpretation of the Directive, which will probably involve new and difficult questions. So there are a number of important issues that will most probably come out. This naturally leads us to a very brief discussion of the draft Directive in its relationship with the case law.

4.3.4 The Draft Directive on Patients' Rights in Cross-Border Health Care

As the Press Release of the Commission recognised, the draft Directive was 'prompted after judgments of the European Court of Justice in a number of cases, concerning the mobility of individual citizens from different Member States'.[53] That already bears witness to the catalytic effect of the case law.

The Directive proposed[54] is basically a codification of the case law. According to its Article 8(4), the 'prior authorisation system shall be limited to what is necessary and proportionate to avoid such impact, and shall not constitute a means of arbitrary discrimination.' If applied strictly, as I have argued, this provision could mean that the States would have to justify case by case their choice for a system of prior authorisation, and could not just decide that all hospital services require prior authorisation. It is just one possible interpretation of the case law of the Court.

The added value of the Directive is clear insofar as it will have to be transposed into national law and will become well known by legal and health actors. Still today, it would seem, some Member States have not changed their legislation or

[53] *Commission adopts proposal for directive on patients' rights in cross-border healthcare*, IP/08/1080, Brussels, 2 July 2008.

[54] Cited in n. 4 *supra*.

their administrative practices to adapt them to the Court's case law, and some have already reached the Court.[55] With the Directive, it will be more difficult for the States to go on ignoring or circumventing the case law.

The added value of the Directive is less clear concerning its substance, for it does not do much to develop what we already find in the case law: it is not really much more precise or detailed than the case law; and as a result it would do little to ensure increased legal certainty, which is, after all, one of the main functions and advantages of legislation when compared with case law. In other words, the draft Directive remains mired in the logic of negative integration, without progressing much in the path of positive integration. Some may consider that legal certainty would have required a more ambitious exercise and not just a pragmatic and timid codification of the case law.

This view comes out with force in the Opinion of the Committee on the internal market and consumer protection of the European Parliament:

> The Commission proposal provides only a very partial answer to this equation, by merely codifying the decisions of the Court of Justice, which are precisely the consequence of an acknowledged legal vacuum.... As regards defining the key concepts... the text is totally insufficient, and increases the legal uncertainty rather than removing it.[56]

These are, in any event, just provisional remarks. The negotiations on the Directive seem to be protracted and difficult, mainly because it is a very sensitive area and also, perhaps, as a result of the general crisis the Union is going through. One cannot take for granted whether the directive will be adopted or not. Its content may also change radically with regard to the initial proposal.[57]

4.4 Conclusion

To conclude this chapter I shall address the more general question of how this line of case law fits with the socioeconomic constitutional model of the European Union. The questions I ask myself here are whether it is guided by neoliberal concerns and whether it is an example of what some have called the social deficit

---

[55] See ECJ, Case C-211/08 *Commission* v. *Spain* (summary publication in *OJ* C 197 of 2 February 2008, p. 12); Case C-512/08 *Commission* v. *France* (*OJ* C 44 of 21 February 2009, p. 29). The cases were respectively decided by judgments of 15 June 2010 and of 5 October 2010. Both were rejected by the Court, perhaps suggesting a shift towards a more restrictive approach in this field (which would however be at odds with the more expansive approach in the Elchinor judgement, mentioned in the previous section), and/or reflecting the increasingly difficult burden of proof that the Commission bears in infringement proceedings pursuant to Article 258 TFEU.

[56] European Parliament, *Report on the proposal for a directive of the European Parliament and of the Council on the application of patients' rights in cross-border healthcare* (*rapporteur*: John Bowis, A6-0233/2009, of 3 April 2009, p. 147).

[57] By the end of January 2011, a political agreement seems to exist on the Directive, but the final text is not known.

of the Union; and whether the limited de-territorialisation of national health systems really endangers those systems.[58]

Whatever we say has, I think, to be based on the practical consequences of the case law rather than on purely theoretical and abstract considerations. The case law is certainly risky, and it could lead to three different outcomes. First, opening up could mean 'pick and choose', undermining the solidarity element of the public health systems of the Member States, penalising the good ones and relieving the bad ones, distorting the priorities established by the managers of national health systems and leading to unequal access to care.[59] But it could well be the other way around. The case law could promote 'a more efficient use of the EU's health care resources' and a degree of virtuous competition between health systems.[60] A third possibility, which few seem to be considering, is that the use of the case law and of the directive, if adopted, will remain so marginal that it will only have a negligible impact with no transformative potential, for good or for bad, on the health systems of the Member States. Only time will tell.

The impact of this line of case law is sometimes exaggerated, in a sensationalistic fashion. Thus, to give only one example amongst many, it has been argued that with this line of case law the Court has 'launched a conceptual transformation in the territorial identity of the national welfare state', and that this may lead to a 'legal de-territorialisation of the welfare state'.[61] Lurking behind is, once again, the fear that this may endanger welfare provision in the Member States. I think that may be an overstatement, for at least two reasons.

The first one is that, with the exception of international agreements, commercial policy measures, tariffs, quantitative restrictions and the like, most of the legislation and policy measures taken by a State are territorial in nature, and necessarily so, for the powers of a State are circumscribed to its own territory. If the territorial character of State legislation and policy measures were a valid justification or excluded the presence of a restriction in the context of the application of the free movement rules, these rules would be emptied of most of their normative content. The fact is that many territorial measures related to many policy fields produce externalities of some sort or another and end up having restrictive and protectionist effects. Such measures are clearly caught by the free movement rules. In those cases the Member States are bound to justify their choices, and that is the correct way to introduce a concern into their policy practice: the concern for the interests of those living in other Member States and the consideration of the possible negative externalities of their policy measures.

The second reason is that the territorial identity of the national welfare states is kept, certainly not intact, but neither radically altered by the Court's case law.

---

58 See the references in n. 2 *supra*.

59 For this view, see Newdick (2006), p. 1645. See also his chapter in this book.

60 For this second view, see Hervey (2006–2007), p. 285; editorial comment, *CML Rev* (2008), p. 1326; and the Report of the European Parliament cited in n. 56 *supra*, p. 77.

61 Dougan (2009), at pp. 121 and 132.

What the Court tries to achieve in the name of the freedom of individuals are limited openings into those systems. To make some openings into previously closed systems cannot be equated with a transformation or a 'de-territorialisation' of the welfare state. What the Court is saying is the following: in the context of the European Union, the welfare states (in our case their health systems) can no longer operate as if they were isolated units. They have to take into account what lies beyond their borders, the other European citizens not affiliated with their systems, and the other systems in the Union. A 'de-territorialisation' of the welfare state would require the creation of an autonomous 'welfare Union', and the blurring of the borders of the Member States. But there is no such thing as a European Union health system or a Union welfare identity. The systems remain national, and the intervention of the Union does not even begin to coordinate the regimes but limits itself to remedy some problems experienced by the few persons that want to move for health care purposes. With these limited openings, the welfare state remains a welfare *state*, and its territorial boundaries remain visible, no longer as absolute borders, but as borders nonetheless.

Realistically, the third possibility mentioned above, that the case law will have little or no impact, for good or for bad, on national health systems, could be the most likely outcome. This means that in any case, whatever the practical effects or lack of effects of the case law, the liberalisation has not been 'wild' and that the accusation of a neoliberal bias is not justified in this field. The aim of the Court, as with the case law on citizenship, is individual freedom and freedom of choice, not the liberty of economic actors. Indeed, the intervention of the Court has in principle been neutral with regard to the debate on the socioeconomic model of the Union. The case law then would only be positive for those few individuals that make use of it. As I have argued, the reduced number of patients, the requirement of prior authorisation for hospital treatment, and the cross-payments involved between national systems (which are based on the rules of the Member State of affiliation) ensure that those systems know in advance the tendencies of cross-border health care and are able to plan accordingly, and also that their priorities and the overall level of expenditure will not be distorted or affected in the medium and long term. Taking that financial neutrality into account, since the perspective of individuals and their rights is that which the Court vindicates and defends, that would already be enough justification for the existence of this line of case law. For the Court is properly engaged in law, rights and justice, not in policy-making, even though its decisions will have a bearing on policy.

It should not overdo it, some may want to add, and there might also be a point in that. For if the Court goes too far we may end up with a situation in which the people that decide to move, those Union citizens who fall under the scope of application of the Treaty, end up having a privileged status. The difficult exercise is to find an interpretation that serves to fight against discrimination and unjustified restrictions of movement without giving a privileged status to those Union citizens that do exercise their rights. In each case, one should ask oneself: is this interpretation leading to the suppression of an unfair or unjustified limit on freedom of movement or are we giving privileged rights to Union citizens just because they happen to move from one Member State to another? That does not give us the answer, but it may be a good starting point.

References

Acierno S (2003) The *Carpenter* judgment: fundamental rights and the limits of the Community legal order. ELRev 28

Baquero Cruz J (2007) The socioeconomic model of the european union: stuck with the status quo? In: Amato G, Bribosia H, de Witte B (eds) Genèse et destinée de la Constitution européenne. Bruylant, Brussels

Dougan M (2009) Expanding the frontiers of union citizenship by dismantling the boundaries of the national welfare states? In: Barnard C, Odudu O (eds) The outer limits of European Union Law. Hart, Oxford

Hatzopoulos V (2002). Killing National Health and Insurance Systems but Healing Patients? The European Market for Health Care Services after the Judgments of the ECJ in Vanbraekel and Peerbooms. CML Rev 3

Hervey TK (2006–2007) The Current Legal Framework on the Right to Seek Healthcare Abroad in the European Union. The Cambridge Yearbook of European Legal Studies, Oxford, Hart

Newdick C (2006) Citizenship, free movement and health care: cementing individual rights by corroding social solidarity. CML Rev 43

Odudu O (2009) Economic activity as a limit to community law. In: Barnard C, Odudu O (eds) The outer limits of European Union Law. Hart, Oxford

Scharpf F (2002) The European social model: coping with the challenges of diversity. J Common Market Stud 40(4)

Scharpf F (2009). Legitimacy in the multilevel European polity. Eur Polit Sci Rev 1(2)

Spaventa E (2007) Free movement of persons in the European Union: barriers to movement in their constitutional context (Alphen aan den Rijn, Kluwer)

Chapter 5
Patients' Rights: A Lost Cause or Missed Opportunity?

Erika Szyszczak

Contents

5.1 Introduction

On 2 July 2008, the Commission put forward a proposal for a Directive of the European Parliament and of the Council on the Application of Patients' Rights in Cross-Border Health Care.[1] The proposal was part of a broader social agenda[2] with

[1] COM (2008) 414 final. Available at: http://ec.europa.eu/health/ph_overview/co_operation/healthcare/docs/COM_en.pdf.

[2] *Commission Communication of 2 July 2008 on the Renewed Social Agenda: Opportunities, Access and Solidarity in 21st Europe*, COM (2008) 412 final.

E. Szyszczak (✉)
School of Law, University of Leicester, University Road, LE1 7RH, Leicester, UK
e-mail: ems11@leicester.ac.uk

J. W. van de Gronden et al. (eds.), *Health Care and EU Law*,
Legal Issues of Services of General Interest, DOI: 10.1007/978-90-6704-728-9_5,

the package of measures on health care explicitly codifying and reinforcing a number of developments in health care coordination in the EU which had taken place in the previous decade.

The purpose of this chapter is three-fold: firstly, to analyse the reasons for a Directive titled 'Patients Rights' against the content of the proposal which, it is argued, goes beyond the issue of patient mobility to colonise a number of issues in health care which are not necessarily inter-state trade (cross-border) issues but invade the autonomy of the Member States' competence in the field of health care and services of general economic interest. Secondly, the chapter charts the troubled legislative background to the proposal, highlighting the sticking points for acceptance—the legal base, the exclusion of long-term care, prior authorisation, the mix of public and private health care providers which may be covered by the Directive and the continued use of soft governance processes [comitology, the open method of coordination (omc) and networks] to promote European integration, through the Europeanisation of health care issues which go beyond the EU's limited competence in the field. Finally, at the time of writing, an amended version of the proposed Directive has been agreed by the Council and has been sent to the European Parliament for a second reading. This raises two questions: Firstly, is the proposal a lost cause, but with the possibility of the EU continuing to coordinate health care with the softer Europeanisation processes of new governance networks and OMC processes? A process of integration through de-legalisation?[3] Secondly, whether the non-adoption of the proposal is a lost opportunity, and if so, for whom?

To analyse these issues, Sect. 5.2 of this chapter examines the political, legal and economic context of the Commission's proposal for a Directive on Patients' Rights. Section 5.3 examines the content of the proposal against the background examined in Sect. 5.2. Section 5.4 traces the historical background, and Sect. 5.5 the troubled legislative history of the proposed Directive. Section 5.6 examines in greater detail points of contention which have emerged as sticking points to achieving and an agreement in the Council: whether the EU has competence to legislate so broadly in the field of health care and what is the correct legal base to use; whether long-term health care (LTHC) should be included in the Directive; in what circumstances can a Member State refuse to give prior authorisation for hospital medical care in another Member State; the range of institutions providing medical care which can be included in the Directive. Section 5.7 discusses the role of accountability and the role of law in the determination of rights which would flow from the adoption of the Directive. It also examines the role of accountability in the use of cooperative networks, which have been deployed for many years in this area but are now explicitly recognised in the draft proposal and will play an important role given the limited EU legislative competence in the field of health care and the need to treat certain emerging issues in a sensitive manner. Section 5.8 examines the different levels of impact the proposed Directive would have if it is ever adopted, and discusses whether the non-adoption of the Directive would be a lost opportunity.

---

[3] Joerges (2008), p. 291.

5.2 The Political, Legal and Economic Context of the Proposal

The legal framework for the regulation of health care issues in the EU is fragmented. The legislative competence of the Community/EU was specifically limited. The original EEC Treaty of 1957 did not contain a specific provision relating to health issues but references to public health issues were found as derogations for the Member States in relation to the free movement principle in the old Article 36 and Article 46 EC. The Treaty of Maastricht 1992 introduced a new Article 129 EC (renumbered Article 152 EC after the Treaty of Amsterdam 1997) setting out the limited competence of the then Community to regulate the area of public health. Essentially, the involvement of the EU is to complement the activities of the Member States, encouraging and promoting the coordination and cooperation between the Member States on issues which may have a cross-border effect. Particularly important was the old Article 152(5) EC stating that any action by the Community in the field of public health shall fully respect the responsibilities of the Member States for the organisation and delivery of health services and medical care.[4] Article 168(7) TFEU now expands the limits of the EU's role in public health. Member States will be responsible for the definition of health policy and the delivery of health services, but the Article now specifically states that the responsibilities of the Member States shall include the management of health services and medical care and the allocation of resources assigned to them:

> *Union* action shall respect the responsibilities of the Member States *for the definition of their health policy* and for the organisation and delivery of health services and medical care. *The responsibilities of the Member States shall include the management of health services and medical care and the allocation of the resources assigned to them.* The measures referred to in paragraph 4(a) shall not affect national provisions on the donation or medical use of organs and blood.[5]

The European Court of Justice (ECJ) of the European Union (EU) has repeated, as a mantra, that the responsibility over the organisation and delivery of health care services is the responsibility of the Member States.[6] Health care is closely linked

---

[4] The Treaty of Amsterdam 1997 raised the profile of public health issues by adding it to the list of activities of the Community in Article 3(1) (p) EC. The new Article 152 EC also mainstreamed a 'high level of human health protection' through Community policies.

[5] Words in italics denote changes made by the Treaty of Lisbon 2009.

[6] Seen in ECJ, Case 238/82 *Duphar* [1984] *ECR* 523 through to the most recent repetitions in ECJ, Case C-208/07 *Petra von Chamier-Glisczinski* [2009] *ECR* I-6095, para 63: 'First of all, it follows, both from the case-law of the Court and from Article 152(5) EC, that Community law does not detract from the power of the Member States to organise their social security systems and to adopt, in particular, provisions intended to govern the organisation and delivery of health services and medical care (Case C-169/07 *Hartlauer* [2009] *ECR* I-0000 (n.y.r.), para 29 and the case-law cited...)' and ECJ, C-211/08 *Commission* v. *Spain,* judgment of 15 June 2010, paras 53 and 75.

to social services and social protection in the EU Member States and viewed as part of the services provided in the [national] general interest.[7] The Protocol [9] on Services of General Interest annexed to the TEU and TFEU by the Treaty of Lisbon 2009 emphasises, in Article 2, that the Treaties do not in any way affect the competence of the Member States to provide, commission and organise non-economic services of general interest.

The acceptance that health care and other social services are services provided in the general interest is matched by a growing recognition at the international and national level that these rights are 'fundamental' rights capable of enforcement at the individual level.[8] A tension has emerged with the conceptual battleground located in an arena where litigation is testing the nature of these modern social, economic rights and fundamental rights. The setting pitches ideas of individual choice against the constraints on public expenditure involving rationing and prioritising social services in the interests of cohesion, solidarity and the general interest. As a result of the Court's case law services provided in the general interest have now assumed a legal identity as individual rights, and citizenship rights, capable of constitutional protection.

As the traditional welfare states of Europe have experimented with reforms in the shape of modernisation, the EU has staked an interest in the use of market-based principles in the provision and delivery of the new social services. This sector saw rapid growth during the 1990s as a result of social and demographic changes in the EU and the corresponding increases of both public and private expenditures in the field. The Commission has assumed a role in the overall management of the different responses from the Member States by using what may generically be called new governance techniques, especially the use of networks and the omc as a process to monitor developments and create a dialogue between the Member States.[9]

A Community interest in the area of social services and protection was found by posing as a negative threat and a positive attribute the transformation the 'old' welfare State in Europe may have for the European integration project. At a negative level, the Commission found a role by linking the fragmentation of social services and social protection as a threat to cohesion and growth within the EU. While public health issues are of cross-border concern to the EU, the legal competence for legislation at the EU level was limited. At a positive level, social

---

[7] See the *Communication from the Commission: Implementing the Community Lisbon programme: Social Services of General Interest in the European Union*, COM (2006) 177, 26 April 2006, where the Commission distinguishes three broad categories of SSGI: (i) health services; (ii) statutory and complementary social security schemes; and (iii) other essential services provided directly to the person. The latter category becomes important in clarifying where health care mobility rights end where such services involve long-term care, see Mossialos and McKee (2002).

[8] In the academic literature, this has been called 'market citizenship', see Everson (1995).

[9] See Szyszczak (2006), p. 486. On health care specifically, see the Special Edition 'Health care and New Governance: The Quest for Effective Regulation', 2.1. *Regulation and Governance* (2008).

services were portrayed as core values of the new Europe and were seen as part of the Lisbon Agenda 2000–2010. Further embedding to the EU was achieved as key aspects of social services were linked to the Lisbon Agenda objectives: a high level of employment, social protection, health protection, equality between men and women, economic, social and territorial cohesion.

The Health Council also agreed that social services, and in particular health services, were part of 'European Values':

> Our health systems are a fundamental part of Europe's social infrastructure. We do not under-estimate the challenges that lie ahead in reconciling individual needs with the available finances, as the population of Europe ages, as expectations rise, and as medicine advances. In discussing future strategies, our shared concern should be to protect values and principles that underpin the health systems of the EU. As Health Ministers in the 25 Member States of the European Union, we invite the European Institutions to ensure that their work will protect these values as work develops to explore the implications of the European Union on health systems as well as the integration of health aspects in all policies.[10]

The moves towards private and hybrid forms of social services' provision increased the risk of the application of the economic rules of EU law and the reconciliation of the application of economic rules to services and goods traditionally still seen as being supplied in the general interest by the Member States. The idea of social services of general interest has now been recognised in Commission soft law as a distinct concept.[11] This is not necessarily the position of the European Courts. Arguably, the issues relating to the application of EU law to social services of general economic interest have been influenced by the limited legal competence of the EU to legislate in the field. The European Courts have reacted in different ways when the competition rules are applied and when the free movement rules have been applied to social services which involve health care issues.

In the more recent application of the free movement provisions to cross-border patient mobility, there has been very little discussion of the economic nature[12] of health care services. The Court has brought health care issues into the remit of EU law emphasising the direct effect and individual nature of the economic right, allowing the justifications and the principle of proportionality to play the mediating role of protecting the general interest missions such service play at the national level.[13] By contrast, the role of exemptions and justifications performs a different role in competition law, where there is a more sensitive approach to including health care matters within the remit of EU law. Article 106(2) TFEU can

---

[10] Statement on Common Values and Principles in EU Health Systems, Health Council 1 June 2006.

[11] *Services of General Interest, including social services of general interest: a new European Commitment* COM (2007) 725. This was part of wider package of proposals to create a Citizens' Agenda, see Szyszczak 2009a, b; Neergaard (2011, forthcoming).

[12] This is in contrast to the earlier case law where public services in education were excluded from the scope of Article 56 TFEU because the essential characteristic of payment for the service was not present: ECJ, Case 263/85 *Belgian State* v. *Humbel* [1988] *ECR* 5365, para 17.

[13] See the chapters by Pennings, Baquero Cruz and Newdick.

be used to protect a service of general economic interest from the full application of free movement and competition rules.[14] In contrast to the free movement principle, competition law has created a protective veil for many issues relating to health care by not ascribing the traditional concepts of 'economic' activity or 'undertaking' to bodies delivering general interest missions.[15] This approach allows significant areas of public and private expenditure to be shielded from the scrutiny of EU law, especially in relation to the proportionality of restrictions to inter-state trade and competition. It may be that this broad approach may be tempered by a more nuanced approach recognising the economic functions of health care providers, but either applying a 'Rule of Reason' to the activity as discussed in van de Gronden's chapter or recognising that Article 101(3) TFEU could be used to justify agreements which are anti-competitive but provide benefits in the general interest.

5.3 The Draft Directive

Against this confused conceptual background, the Commission attempted to deepen the codification of the Court's case law under the free movement provisions which had created an economical free-standing right of patients to travel abroad for medical treatment and recoup some, or all, of the costs of this treatment from their Member State of affiliation. The aim of using a Directive in the area of 'Patients Rights' was, firstly, to establish a general framework for the provision of safe, high quality and efficient cross-border health care. Secondly, to create a framework for re-imbursement by the State of affiliation of health care obtained abroad. Thirdly, to confirm, in a legislative text, that non-hospital care obtained abroad in an EU Member State was not subject to prior authorisation but that prior authorisation may be necessary for hospital care but such authorisation should be limited to what is necessary and proportionate and administratively transparent.[16] Fourthly, the draft

[14] Seen, for example, in ECJ, Case C-475/99 *Firma Ambulanz Glöckner* v. *Landkreis Südwestpfalz* [2001] *ECR* I-8089.

[15] See the chapters by Neergaard, de Vries, van de Gronden and Welti.

[16] In the original draft of the proposal Article 8(1) provided a definition of hospital care, a definition varying between the Member States and a matter neglected by the European Court of Justice. Hospital care would be defined as (a) health care which requires overnight accommodation of the patient for at least one night or (b) health care included in a specific list that does not require overnight accommodation of the patient. The list shall be limited to health care that requires use of highly specialised and cost-intensive medical infrastructure or medical treatment or health care involving treatments presenting a particular risk for the patient or the population. The concept becomes an EU law concept and the Commission would draw up the initial list of treatments covered by the concept of hospital care, updating it regularly. This seems a sensible approach given the experimentation with different kinds of health care delivery in the Member States. The draft also introduced a new concept of 'specialised care' which is not found in the case law. The new draft text does not contain this definition.

Directive creates an EU set of procedural rights and guarantees for patients seeking health care outside of the State of affiliation. Finally, the draft Directive provides a framework for cooperation between the Member States on cross-border health care. Thus, the proposal moves beyond free movement of 'Patients Rights' ideas towards common principles for health care and pan-European cooperation on health care: a process of modernisation and Europeanisation of health care issues which can no longer be accommodated within national boundaries.[17]

The reasons put forward for using a Directive in such a sensitive field of EU competence are ostensibly to bring clarity and legal certainty to an area which has been opened up to cross-border trade as a result of the increased litigation over cross-border rights. The *ad hoc* litigation has been driven by individual litigants using the opportunity of using EU law to liberalise EU health care markets creating new ideas of a consumer-citizenship in health care services. This case law is addressed in detail in other chapters in this book and will not be discussed here. We should note that over the course of the last decade, when the momentum in the litigation took place, only a handful of cases were referred to the Court of Justice of the EU, and official statistics reveal that cross-border patient mobility is limited.

The conceptual legal right at the EU level of an individual to travel between the Member States of the EU to receive medical care has altered over time. It appeared from an employment-based social security route under Regulation 1408/71/EC[18] to a dual system of access to care under Regulation 1408/71 and an individual economic right (or freedom) to receive services in another Member State using Article 56 TFEU.[19] More recently, the right to health care has been found in Article 35 of the Charter of Fundamental Rights of the EU. Article 35 CFREU is found in the Chapter on Solidarity (Title IV) providing a 'right' to preventative health care for everyone. The Article allows the Member States to define other forms of health care. The Charter follows Article 168(1) TFEU by mainstreaming a 'high standard of health protection' as part of the policies and activities of the EU. The Charter also addresses the promotion of the respect for the patient (Article 3), and many Articles address the vulnerable in terms of respecting their dignity, for example, Chapter II of the Charter relating to Equality. Issues relating to data protection are found in Article 8.

The case law applying the free movement (and competition rules) to health care issues received mixed interpretations, from being viewed as creating *positive* ideas

---

[17] See Szyszczak 2009a, b.

[18] See the chapter by Pennings. Social security systems in the EU have been subject to coordination in the EU since 1971 to facilitate the free movement of workers and their families. Under Article 22 of Regulation 1408/71, workers and their families have an immediate right to emergency health care in another Member State and a right to elective health care subject to prior authorisation. See, however, ECJ, Case C-211/08 *Commission* v. *Spain*, judgment of 15 June 2010.

[19] The starting point is ECJ, Joined Cases 286/82 and 26/83 *Graziana Luisi and Giuseppe Carbone* v. *Ministero de Tesoro* [1984] *ECR* 377.

of a European citizenship developed from the free movement principle[20] to a *negative* disruption of national solidarity and a challenge to Member State autonomy and competence in the area of health care.[21] Indeed, looking at some of the headliners to academic writing, a passionate and strong use of language is found in many of the articles: the virus of cross-border patient mobility…' is the opening statement of Kostera[22]; 'Killing National Health and Insurance Systems …' (Hatzopoulos)[23]; '…Corroding Social Solidarity' (Newdick)[24]; 'One Foot in the Grave …' (Hancher and Sauter)[25] are but a few of the titles, implying negative responses to the Court.

As a result of the case law, national solidaristic boundaries have been exposed as porous and aspects of a State's social welfare policy choices can be challenged by individual patient's moving abroad to receive treatment.[26] Elsewhere, I have argued that when intertwined with ideas found in procurement law, state aid and competition law, the free movement rules (and the inherent citizenship rules) have combined to create new public markets and a new public space where providers and recipients of services are liberalised from traditional State constraints in their choice and supply of social and welfare provision.[27] The Court's case law is developed within a negative integration framework, and the search is now on to find ways for the EU to re-regulate this sensitive aspect of free movement.

The proposed Directive is a step to create a broader framework for health care policy despite the fragility of an EU legislative competence to do so. Given the

---

[20] Davies (2007), p. 158. See also Flear, who argues the free movement case law may also foster cross-border solidarity between patients fighting for certain forms of medical treatment as well as improve treatment in the home state by cutting waiting lists for treatment, allowing new forms of medical treatment to be delivered: Flear (2009).

[21] See Newdick (2006), p. 1645 and his chapter in this volume.

[22] Kostera (2007).

[23] Hatzopoulos (2002), p. 883.

[24] Newdick (2006), p. 1645.

[25] Hancher and Sauter (2009). The revised article is published as Hancher and Sauter (2010), p. 117.

[26] The freedom to provide services and establishment under EU law allows foreign health care providers to enter and establish in a Member State but to date there is no European Court of Justice ruling on whether medical treatment provided in a private medical establishment can be reimbursed through a national health care system. At the national level see the claim in: *European Surgeries Ltd* v. *Cambridgeshire Primary Care Trust* [2007] *EWHC* 2758 (Admin).

[27] Szyszczak 2009a, b. The case law on the free movement of patients poses new challenges to legal theories of trans-national integration since the cases are concerned with 'exit' from the State of affiliation where the perceived barrier to free movement occurs. They require a different perspective from traditional views of 'market access' barriers, since in the reported cases the host State has not erected barriers to market entry. It is the State of affiliation which is compelled to open up the choice of traditional social welfare markets and take into account cross-border interests in the planning of its own social welfare provisions. Thus, it is easier for a service provider to enter the State of affiliation's social welfare market through the agent of the patient which is easier and less costly than using the freedom of services and establishment rules of the EU to establish a presence in the State of affiliation. But cf., ECJ, Case C-211/08 *Commission* v. *Spain*, judgment of 15 June 2010.

potential disruptive effects of the individual litigation, which can be idiosyncratically *ad hoc*[28] and difficult to accommodate within existing national systems of health care policy producing disruptive effects, there are efficiency arguments for legislating in the area. Yet, the proposal has met with opposition on many fronts: from the Member States, who view it as over-reaching the limited EU competence to legislate in health care matters, to criticism from public service unions who argue that that it locates health care purely within the economic sphere, addressing the needs of Europeans who are mobile, knowledgeable and can pay in advance for health care in another Member State. Greer[29] has argued that the commoditisation of health care by the EU means that health care now takes its place alongside postal services and telecommunications and that liberalisation is the only available road or direction for health care under EU Regulation. This view is misconceived. It ignores the reasons why the pressures to modernise national health care services are different from other (networked) industries which have been opened up to competition through liberalisation in the EU and the fact that the modernisation of all services of general economic interest are subject to different regulatory approaches in the EU.

Aspects of the proposal are also viewed as discriminatory. The free movement perspective has been driven by patients who are knowledgeable of their EU rights, have the economic means to travel abroad for treatment and stay abroad for fairly short periods to receive treatment, often returning back to the home State system for after care and support. It can be argued that the concept of patient mobility and the proposal for a Directive is biased against chronically ill patients and the long-term sick who need longer and perhaps more complex forms of long-term social and health care and social security support. Thus, the proposal can be seen as discriminatory and out of the social focus of the EU, given that it is part of a package of new EU social values.[30]

The proposal provides for controls over the basket of health care services the home State wishes to provide and also increases the rights of static patients (patients who choose to remain in the State of affiliation) by giving the Member States the ability to protect local needs by not responding to outside demands for treatment, subject to an overriding principle of non-discrimination. Thus, as a counter-argument the proposal can be categorised as part of a new generation of

---

[28] Seen in the different kinds of health care received abroad ranging from complex heart surgery (ECJ, Case C-444/05 *Aikaterini Stamatelaki* v. *NPDD Organismos Asfaliseos Eleftheron Epangelmation* [2007] *ECR* I-3185) to the less complex supply of spa services (ECJ, Case C-8/02 *Ludwig Leichtle* v. *Bundesanstalt für Arbeit* [2004] *ECR* I-2641).

[29] Greer (2006), p. 134; Greer (2009).

[30] On the same day as the original proposal for a Patients' Rights Directive, the Commission also published a proposal to extend the equal treatment principle in the fields of social protection, social advantages, education and goods and services, including housing: European Commission, *Proposal for a Council Directive on Implementing the Principle of Equal Treatment Between Persons Irrespective of Religion or Belief, Disability, Age, Sexual Orientation*, COM (2008) 426. See also the chapter by Davies.

citizenship rights for all citizens who seek medical help within the EU and contribute to the development of EU social values forming an EU social model. However, the thrust of the proposal is to enhance the rights of patients who move to another Member State for treatment. Within the aims of the Commission proposal is the realisation that, by triggering Article 56 TFEU in the context of health care, Europeans have a new relationship with the welfare state: a consumer-citizen who needs ancillary rights to exercise her choice of health care provision. Thus, the proposal is seeking to draw clearer EU rules on the classic triangle of Member State-EU-Citizen relationships.[31] Furthermore, Article 35 Charter of Fundamental Rights of the European Union recognises access to health care as a fundamental right of the EU.[32] If the proposal for a new anti-discrimination Directive is also adopted, then this will enhance the rights to access medical treatment in the Member States and to accommodate diversity in the provision of health care in the home and the host State.[33] This may encompass different forms of treatment as well as the way in which patients are treated. Thus, the content of the new rights agenda moves beyond a purely economic commodification principle to a new status for information on, access to, and treatment within, health care systems as a modern citizenship right in the EU.

5.4 The Historical Background to the Proposed Directive

Most analyses of the draft Directive see the case law of the Court as the main impetus and driver for the Europeanisation of health care issues in the EU. This approach ignores the central role played by the Commission in driving both old governance and new governance processes in the field of health care from the 1990s onwards.[34] The role of the Commission in the modern governance processes tends to be underestimated by academic commentators,[35] citing the diminishing

---

[31] See the most recent Public Consultation on Citizenship which will lead to a Commission Communication on Citizenship in October 2010. The President of the Commission, Barroso had set out political guidelines in September 2009 which included the need to give real effect to citizens' cross-border rights by removing administrative and procedural obstacles. See: http://ec.europa.eu/citizenship/news/news1029_en.htm.

[32] See Hervey (2003). Contrast the criticism of defining health care as a fundamental right in Szyszczak 2009a, b.

[33] Proposal for a Council Directive of 2 July 2008 on implementing the principle of equal treatment between persons irrespective of religion or belief, disability, age or sexual orientation, COM (2008) 426.

[34] This is used here as a broad term embracing organised processes orchestrated in the EU framework as well as the coordination of various interested actors in multi-level networks, alongside communication tools used by the Commission in the publication of a range of official documents, pulling together legal and political documents and suggesting agendas for future evolution and development.

[35] Wincott (2001), p. 897.

central policy-making role for the Commission against the increased legislative role of the European Parliament and the increased use of new governance techniques alongside the 'scandals' which beset, and weakened, the Commission in the late 1990s. In contrast, there are examples, seen in the Services Directive discussed above, and the Patients' Rights proposal, where the Commission is able to seize the opportunity to develop emerging areas of EU governance and position itself as a central agent in developing EU policy.[36]

Despite the existence of a limited legal competence for the EU in areas of health the Commission has coordinated an EU health policy on public health using soft governance techniques.[37] In December 2001, a High Level Committee[38] on health reported to the Commission on the impact of the *Kohll*[39] and *Decker*[40] and *Smits–Peerbooms*[41] cases. This coincided with the launch of the Lisbon Strategy and the use of open method of coordination processes to integrate social policies into the economic strategy of EU rejuvenation.[42] The limited EU competence in this area resulted in a gentle and tentative approach: an 'omc-light'. The findings of the High Level Committee were discussed by the Health Council in February and June 2002 with the Council calling for an ambiguous 'high level process of reflection'. The Commission pulled together government ministers and groups of experts, producing a Report in December 2003 offering 19 recommendations which have been addressed in different ways in the subsequent period.[43] This Report reveals that as far back as 2003, issues of rights and duties of patients, data

---

36 Cram describes the Commission as a 'purposeful opportunist' with the ability 'to respond to opportunities for action as they present themselves and even to facilitate the emergence of these opportunities', Cram (1994), p. 156.

37 The first official documents were issued soon after The Treaty of Amsterdam was signed: *Communication from the Commission on the development of public health policy in the European Community*, COM (1998) final of 15 April 1998. A *Community Action Programme in the field of public health* was adopted in Decision No. 1786/2002/EC *OJ* 2002 L 271/1.

38 This is an informal advisory body composed of 'High Level' officials from the Member States.

39 ECJ, Case C-158/96 *Raymond Kohll* v. *Union des caisses de maladi*e [1998] *ECR* I-1931.

40 ECJ, Case C-120/95 *Nicolas Decker* v. *Caisse de maladie des employés privés* [1998] *ECR* I-1831.

41 ECJ, Case C-157/99 *BSM. Geraets-Smits* v. *Stichting Ziekenfonds VGZ and H.T.M. Peerbooms* v. *Stichting CZ Groep Zorgverzekeringenen* [2001] *ECR* I-5473.

42 See, for example, the linkage between health and economic growth in the Guidance Paper drawn up by DG SANCO, available at: http://ec.europa.eu/health/ph_overview/Documents/byrne_reflection_en.pdf. Entitled 'Enabling Good Health for all: A reflection process for a new EU health Strategy' 15 July 2004. The then Commissioner, David Byrne states: 'Health is closely intertwined with economic growth and sustainable development' (p. 4) and 'Europe needs a paradigm shift from seeing health expenditure as a cost to seeing effective health policies as an investment. Europe should look at what health puts into the economy and what illness takes out.' (p. 6).

43 High Level Reflection Group, High Level Reflection Process on Patient Mobility and Health care Developments in the European Union HLPR/2003/16, 9 December 2003. *Communication from the Commission Follow-up to the high level reflection process on patient mobility and health care developments in the European Union* COM (2004) 301 final.

protection, access, quality and affordability of health care were emerging as an EU agenda for EU health care policy. Around the same time, in 2002, the Active Citizenship Network produced the European Charter of Patients' Rights containing fourteen fundamental rights and values.[44]

The Commission reviewed the impact of the Court's case law in the Member States concluding that the take up of the economic' right to free movement for health care treatment was very sparse. The Report concluded that there were barriers in place which made the right to free movement illusory. For example, Member States continued to require prior authorisation for medical treatment abroad, using the Article 22 of Regulation 1408/71 as the legal justification for demanding prior authorisation before a patient could travel abroad for medical treatment.[45] There was also an assumption that the right to reimbursement for medical care obtained abroad was not available for in-patient hospital treatment[46] or to English NHS-style benefits in kind systems.[47] In May 2010, when the draft Patients' Rights Directive was floundering in the Council that the Commission decided to step up enforcement initiating the infringement proceedings process against three Member States: Spain, Slovakia and Denmark.[48]

The Commission was conscious that the limited EU competence to legislate in health care matters did not cater for, or squeezed out, discussion over cross-border health care issues and patient mobility.[49] A crucial point which is missing in the Commission's analysis, and which is a weakness in viewing health care from an economic perspective, is the failure to appreciate that health care is different from other services, including other welfare or social services which have been found to embrace an economic perspective, for example, social security.

Health care is a complex sensitive personal service requiring dignity and privacy and which relies upon trust and confidence by the patient and a high level of competence, professional and ethical behaviour from the provider of health care services. Patients, and medical practitioners, believe that medical treatment achieves the best results in a local, 'comfort zone' of knowledge. Even in the United Kingdom where, since 2006, patients are given a choice of four to five hospitals to receive care, with a procedure to complain where that choice is not

---

[44] Available at: http://www.activecitizenship.net/content/blogcategory/32/77/.

[45] See the chapter by Pennings.

[46] Although the Court had made the point in ECJ, Case C-368/98 *Vanbraekel* [2001] *ECR* I-5363 and *Kohll* (*supra* n. 39) that in applying Article 56 TFEU there was no need to distinguish between hospital care and care outside of the hospital environment.

[47] An assumption settled by awkward reasoning in ECJ, Case C-372/04 *The Queen ex parte Yvonne Watts* v. *Bedford Primary Care Trust and Secretary of State for Health* [2006] *ECR* I-4325. See the discussion in the chapter by Baquero Cruz.

[48] See Press Release IP/10/505, 'Patient Rights: Commission acts to protect patients' rights in Spain, Slovakia and Denmark' Brussels, 5 May 2010.

[49] A point developed by Robert Madelin, the then Director General of DG Sanco at a *Conference on Patient Mobility Directive: Advance or Threat?* organised by The Madariaga College of Europe Foundation on 29 April 2009. Conference summary available at: http://www.epha.org/a/3490.

given, there is a tendency to rely on the primary care doctor (the GP) to make that choice, with the doctor and patient relying on 'soft' information (local 'word of mouth', reputation of a hospital/clinician, information from friends and family) over hard data (mortality rates, cleanliness) when making the choice.[50] Also, there is often a distrust of medical care provided locally in the home State by unfamiliar medical providers.[51]

From the Commission's consultation on health services, the financial flow of patient mobility was estimated at only 1% of all expenses in health care, which included health care received unexpectedly during holidays abroad. Only in border regions (for example, in the Netherlands where Dutch patients go to Germany) and Luxembourg were the financial flows higher than 1%.[52] Even later, by 2008, in the impact statement of the draft Directive, the Commission quotes Eurobarometer polls revealing that only 4% of respondents had received medical treatment abroad. When asked the hypothetical question of whether they would be willing to travel abroad for treatment, 50% of the respondents were prepared to do so and 70% of respondents thought that they should be reimbursed if they did travel abroad for treatment.[53] The Commission believed that more patients would go abroad for treatment if they received better information and less hindrance from the Member States.

The Report was followed by a Commission Communication in 2004.[54] This Communication effectively created an agenda for future EU action and responses to health care issues in the EU, beyond the remit of the impact of the patient mobility issue. The key elements of the Commission's agenda were to provide better provision of information on patients' rights in cross-border health care matters, establishing an omc process on the reform of health care and an action plan on e-health and the creation of a permanent High Level Group on health care services to coordinate 'Community policy'.

Within the Communication are a variety of responses already activated to achieve an EU colonisation of health care issues, despite the limited EU competence in the field. For example, the use of traditional old governance techniques to

---

50 'Patients Don't Use Quality Measures When Choosing a Hospital', The Kings Fund available at: http://www.kingsfund.org.uk/press/press_releases/patients_dont_use.html; Robertson and Dixon (2010).

51 An example of this is seen in the UK where tabloid newspapers raise concerns over foreign doctors' language ability and qualifications, see for example: Professor Sikora (2010).

52 See also Legido-Quigley et al. (2007), p. 188 and Baeten (2008).

53 A similar disparity is seen between aspiration and practical implementation in the UK where surveys show that respondents consider it important to have choice in hospitals where they may (potentially) be treated but in fact patients continue to use local facilities. See *Choice and Competition in Public Services, Case Studies A Report Prepared for OFT by Frontier Economics*, March 2010, OFT1214case.

54 *Communication from the Commission Follow-up to the high level reflection process on patient mobility and health care developments in the European Union*, COM (2004) 301 final. See Press Release: P/04/508 21 April 2004.

consolidate the developments in case law under the social security Regulation 1408/71/EEC,[55] proposals for a Directive on free movement of services, on the free movement of medical professionals (including mutual recognition aspects)[56] and the use of the Data Protection Directive in health care issues.[57] Another technique using established EU competence was the use of EU funding to collect and disseminate data on health care.[58] Health care issues had also been part of the omc processes addressing the modernisation of social protection within the Lisbon process.[59] These processes create structured and unstructured networks of stakeholders engaged in coordination and cooperation of issues which have a cross-border interest, involving different, and different levels of, public and private actors, engaged in a multi-level dialogue of continuous negotiation.[60]

The then Commissioner for DG SANCO, David Byrne, created an electronic Reflection Process in July 2004. Reading Byrne's Guidance Paper, 'Enabling Good Health for All: a Reflection Process for a New EU Health Strategy'[61] it is clear at this stage that the Commission took an ambitious approach seeking to mainstream health care into all EU policies using multi-level participation.

The Commission included medical services in Article 23 of the draft of the Services Directive of March 2004.[62] In contrast to the later draft of the Patients' Rights Directive, this provision was limited. However, it was a significant, and daring, move for the Commission to include health care services in the de-regulation agenda, viewing them as explicitly economic in character but also starting a process of creating open EU-wide markets for such services.[63]

The Commission's attempt to consolidate the Court's case law into a legislative text and elevate the free movement principle into a citizenship concept underestimated the impact the inclusion of a wide area of social services within the concept of economic services would have. It met with hostile responses at the

---

55 Regulation 883/2004/EC, *OJ* 2004 L 166/1.

56 COM (2002) 119 on mutual recognition of professional qualifications.

57 Directive 95/46/EC on the protection of individuals with regard to the processing of personal data and on the free movement of such data, *OJ* 1995 L. 281/31.

58 The EU was already supporting investments in health using the Structural Funds and the High Level Reflection Report called for EU funds to support health infrastructure and skills development, especially in the new Member States.

59 *Modernising social protection for the development of high-quality, accessible and sustainable health care and long-term care: support for the national strategies using the 'open method of coordination'; Commission Communication The Future of Health care and Care for the Elderly: guaranteeing accessibility, quality, and financial viability* COM (2001) 723 final. The soft law approach to coordination of social protection can be traced back to Council Recommendation 92/442/EEC, *OJ* 1992 L 245/49 on the convergence of social protection objectives and policies.

60 Marks (1993); Kickert (1993); Szyszczak (2006), p. 486.

61 15 July 2004. Available at: http://ec.europa.eu/health/ph_overview/Documents/byrne_reflection_en.pdf.

62 COM (2004) 2 final.

63 See Rowland et al. (2004), p. 1200.

national level. Of significance was the creation of the *collectif ssig-fr* in France, which, with other welfare associations, increased awareness of the impact of the Services Directive on social services and successfully campaigned to keep a range of welfare and social services outside of the scope of the Directive.[64]

The proposed Article 23 was dropped by the Council and the European Parliament, with the latter wanting a wider range of patients' rights, initially discussing the idea of Guidelines rather than binding legislation. The Health Council of June 2006 adopted a statement of Conclusions of Common values and principles in European Union Health Systems[65] and the European Parliament adopted a Resolution on 23 May 2007.[66] Concurrently, the Commission was undertaking a consultation on Community health care especially on how to ensure legal certainty in cross-border health care rights in EU law and to support cooperation between the health systems of the Member with the emerging responses revealing uncertainty over the impact of the Court's case law on national health care services.[67]

5.5 The Legislative History of the Proposal

The fierce resistance to framing health care services within an economic liberalisation agenda did not deter the Commission from proposing a new Directive on patient mobility in 2008. The proposal emphasised 'Patients' Rights' in its title, but went beyond individual rights to the coordination of a range of health care issues.[68] The Commission avoided polarising health care issues by emphasising the role health care systems played in the EU: as a central component of the EU high level of social protection, social cohesion and social justice and sustainable development, as well as part of the framework of services of general interest.[69]

---

[64] Les Services Sociaux et de Santé d'Intérêt Général – Droits fondamentaux versus marché interieur?, Brussels, Editions Bruylant, 2006; Les Services Sociaux et de Santé d'Intérêt Général. Quel cadre communautaire pour les services sociaux d'intérêt général? Une contribution au debat communautaire', Brussels Editions Bruylant 2006; Quatre notes de problematique techniques redigees a l'occasion de la conference 'Droits fondamentaux protection social et integration europeene: Quel cadre communautaire pour les services sociaux d'intérêt general?', Paris, 30 May 2006.

[65] *OJ* 2006 C 146/1.

[66] European Parliament Resolution of 23 May 2007 on the impact and consequences of the exclusion of health services from the Directive on services in the internal market (2006/2275(INI)).

[67] *Communication from the Commission Consultation regarding Community action on health services*, SEC (2006) 1195/4, 26 September 2006.

[68] *Commission Communication of 2 July 2008, Proposal for a Directive of the European Parliament and of the Council on the application of patients' rights in cross-border health care presented by the Commission*, COM (2008) 414 final.

[69] Ibid., at p. 22.

The European Parliament voted in favour of the proposal in April 2009, but made 122 amendments to the text.[70]

A compromise text was discussed in the Council following a Council Presidency Report in public debate in the Council in June 2009.[71] At this meeting, the Commission agreed for a number of concessions, for example, removing LTHC from the scope of the Directive, agreeing to include Article 168 TFEU in the legal base of the proposed Directive. The Czech Presidency drew up a compromise proposal attempting to solve questions by restructuring the text of the Directive, applying consistent definitions but not defining the actual content of many key provisions. The text failed to satisfy the Member States' concerns over the reasons which could be given for refusal to grant prior authorisation for medical care abroad, the reimbursement of prescriptions and the provisions on cooperation over health care.

The Swedish Presidency failed to build upon the progress made by the French and Czech Presidencies of the EU. Committee of permanent representatives of the member states (COREPER) examined the compromise texts on 25 November 2009 but concluded that several issues remained unresolved and invited the Council to consider further deliberation. The discussions in the Council focused upon the re-imbursement of costs where medical treatment had been provided by non-contractual health care providers and the position of pensioners living abroad. The Council reached political agreement on a new text at the Council Meeting in Brussels on 28 May 2010 and the draft Directive was remitted to the European Parliament for a second reading. The indicative date for this second reading is 14 December 2010.

The main areas of difficulty in persuading the Member States to agree to a final text of the Directive are examined in the next section.

5.6 Points of Contention

There are three main points of contention which explain why it has been difficult to find enough consensus within the Council. These are the questions of the legal base for the Directive, whether LTHC should be included within the remit of the

---

[70] Report on the Proposal for a Directive of the European Parliament and of the Council on the application of patients' rights in cross-border health care (COM (2008)0414-C6-0257/2008-2008/0142(COD) A6-0233/2009). The original Rapporteur for the proposal in the EP was John Bovis but, after the June 2009 European Parliament elections, a new Rapporteur from France, Françoise Grossetete, was appointed in September 2009 to steer the proposal through the final legislative processes in the European Parliament. The ESC delivered its Opinion on 2 December 2008 (SOC/322-CESE) and the Committee of the Regions delivered its Opinion on 12 February 2009 (CdR 348/2008 fin –DEVE-IV-032). The European Data Protection Supervisor delivered its Opinion on 2 December 2008 (16855/08).

[71] Public debates can be seen at: http://www.consilium.europa.eu/videostreaming.

Directive and the situations in which the Member States can refuse prior authorisation for hospital treatment sought abroad. Other issues which divide the Member States relate to whether pensioners living abroad should be able to use the Directive and the range of non-affiliated medical care providers who could fall within the Directive.

5.6.1 Legal Base

The initial Proposal for a Directive was based upon the Internal Market legal base of Article 114 TFEU. Article 114(3) TFEU contains a requirement that any harmonisation measures adopted must guarantee a high level of protection of human health, taking into account in particular any new development based upon scientific fact.

The Commission justified the choice of legal base by stating that while the Court had clarified patients' rights to travel abroad for medical treatment, patients were not in a position to exercise the right effectively. This choice of legal base proved to be controversial by its explicit linkage to the free movement right to health care services as an economic right but also by subsuming the progress made through soft law and soft governance processes as part of the functioning of the Internal Market. Interest groups were concerned that the social character of health care and the idea of a service in the general interest[72] would be lost in the context of seeing the proposal only in the context of harmonising measures linked to the exercise of economic rights. The concern was the dominance of economic integration issues over the explicit wording of what is now Article 168(7) TFEU recognising the limited EU competence in the area of health care, invoking concepts of subsidiarity and proportionality.[73] The Commission claimed in its *Explanatory Memorandum* that the objective of the proposal was fully in line with the requirements of both Articles 114 and 168(7) TFEU. The Commission also argued that the proposal met the principles of subsidiarity and proportionality. The European Parliament narrowly rejected proposing a joint legal base of Article 114 TFEU and 168 TFEU by a margin of just four votes.

DG Sanco argued that the Commission was charged with the complex task of finding a legal base for initiatives which was consistent with the political structure

[72] At the time of the original proposal the old Article 16 EC did not provide a legal base for legislation in the area of SGEIs, After the Treaty of Lisbon 2009, Article 14 TFEU allows the European Parliament and the Council to use the ordinary legislative procedure to enact 'regulations'. See Szyszczak 2009a, b for suggestions of how health care as a SGEI could be regulated using this legal base.

[73] The reaction of national responses also ignores the problems faced by devolved and regional governments in the EU. For example, in Scotland, the devolved Scottish Parliament legislated (NHS (Scotland) Reform Act 2004) to abolish the English NHS market-oriented health care system and re-introduced an integrated public health care system for Scotland. This system does not use a system for determining costs of health care in advance and there is opposition to using commercial providers of health care in Scotland.

of the EU and that the legal base used for the proposal allowed the Commission a greater room for manoeuvre to develop a Directive which met the wider needs of cross-border mobility for patients. The Committee of the Regions also supported the use of Article 168 TFEU as the legal base. It is not possible to use Article 168 TFEU as the sole legal base for the proposal since the proposal goes beyond a measure improving public health, preventing human illness and diseases and obviating sources of danger to human health. In fact, many of the objectives of the proposal would seem incompatible with Article 168 TFEU since Article 168(5) is explicit that when incentive measures are adopted the harmonisation of the laws and regulations of the Member States is excluded.

At the June 2009 Council meeting, the legal base issue was linked with the Member States wanting greater certainty over the responsibilities of the Member States to organise their own health care systems especially in relation to the requirement of prior authorisation before medical treatment can take place abroad.

The Commission agreed to add the legal base of Article 168(5) TFEU for Articles 13 and 15 of the proposed Directive.[74] Normally, the Court has expressed a preference for only one legal base to be used for EU legislation, the decisive factor in the choice of legal base being the main object of a proposal.[75] The use of two legal bases for a measure fits uneasily with the Court's acceptance that two legal bases may be used only where a proposed legal instrument has two equal-ranking aims which are indissoluble.[76] Even the combination of Article 114 and Article 168(5) TFEU for a harmonising measure in the field of health care are opposing, rather than indissoluble, aims.

5.6.2 Long-Term Health Care

A second area of difficulty is whether LTHC should be covered by the patient mobility principle. The recognition of a concept of 'long-term care' (LTC) in social services in the EU is part of the process of modernisation: recognising new social risks. The traditional basic text of the ILO categorising social security risks[77] is now outdated by the emergence of new social risks, termed 'dependency' and the need for 'long-term care' and which are the result of demographic changes in the EU stemming from increases in health and life expectancy in Europe. The Commission has used the definition of LTC offered by the Organisation for Economic Co-operation and Development (OECD) as

[74] http://register.consilium.europa.eu/pdf/en/09/st16/st16005.en09.pdf.

[75] ECJ, Case C-377/98 *Netherlands* v. *European Parliament and Council* [2001] *ECR* I-7079, para 27.

[76] ECJ, Case C-165/87 *Commission* v. *Council* [1988] *ECR* 5545, para 11.

[77] ILO Convention C102 Concerning Minimum Standards of Social Security uses the following typology of social risks: medical care, sickness, unemployment, old age, employment injuries, maintenance of children, maternity, invalidity, loss of support as a result of the death of the breadwinner.

> … a cross-cutting policy issue that brings together a range of services for persons who are dependant upon help with basic activities of daily living over an extended period of time.[78]

Thus, the issue with long-term care and LTHC is that the latter is inseparable from other forms of daily care which may need to be provided to the individual 'patient'. It may be difficult to draw the line between *social* care and *health care*. This may be related not only to the nature of the care, and where it takes place, but also in how it is funded, especially where a State uses an individual cash/voucher/social security benefit system to fund the provision of LTHC. This fundamental problem is accentuated by the fact that Member States have changed their policies over time, with the demise of the family as the first point of care to a rise in institutional care for LTC being replaced by experimentation with home care supported by professionals and community care services.[79] The modernisation of LTC has confronted the Member States with new challenges for policy design alongside new structures for the organisation and framework of LTC. As a result, in many Member States, the concept of LTC is fragmentary and the result of piece-meal historical evolution rather than strategic planning. Not all of the Member States have faced the new challenges posed by LTC. In some Member States, there is no definition of LTC,[80] whereas, in other Member States, there is a definition which is detailed and moves beyond the OECD definition[81] In other Member States, the definition is vague.[82] Thus, there are differences between the Member States on how to provide and fund LTC. Should LTC be provided as inpatient or outpatient or ambulatory care? Should it be collective or individual? Should it be a service provided or cash/voucher system to buy an individualised care package? Is it a social security or a health care issue? Should it be provided at a universal level, through State resources or through accredited bodies? What are the benchmarks for quality? The response from the EU has been to monitor the Member States' approaches to LTC largely by collecting information through MISSOC.[83]

The Member States' reluctance to define and include LTHC in the draft Patients' Rights Directive may be misguided as more cases emerge before the Court raising issues of payments under the social security Regulation or where

---

[78] European Commission, Joint Report 2008, p. 81.

[79] European Commission, *Long-term Care in the European Union*, 2008, available at: http://ec.europa.eu/employment_social/spsi/docs/social_protection/ltc_final_2504_en.pdf.

[80] Bulgaria, Greece, Hungary, Malta, Romania, Slovenia, United Kingdom.

[81] For example, in Spain LTC is defined as '… the situation of a person who, on account of age, disease or incapacity, and linked to lack or loss of physical, mental, intellectual or sensorial autonomy, requires assistance from (an)other person(s) or considerable help to carry out essential daily activities or, in the case of persons with a mental disability or illness, other forms of support for their personal autonomy.' European Commission, *supra* n. 79.

[82] For example, LTC is defined in Cyprus as '… need of care due to mental or physical incapacity or social distress.' European Commission, *supra* n. 79, p. 8.

[83] Mutual Information System on Social Protection in the EU Member States, the EEA and Switzerland.

LTC recipients choose to buy LTC in other Member States relying upon the free movement provisions or where foreign LTC providers challenge procurement, state aid and establishment/discrimination rules in the Member States.[84]

At the June 2009 Council meeting, the Commissioner for Health Vassiliou agreed to exclude LTHC from the scope of the proposed Directive. In the version of the proposal discussed by the Permanent Representatives on 25 November 2009, the definition of LTHC excluded from the scope of the Directive is as follows:

> This Directive does not apply to services whose primary purpose is to support people in need of assistance in carrying out routine, everyday tasks. More specifically this refers to those long-term care services deemed necessary to enable the person in need of care to live as full and self-determined life as possible. Thus, this Directive should not apply, for example, to long-term care services provided in residential homes or housing ("nursing homes") by home care services or assisted living facilities.[85]

In the latest draft of the Directive, this definition is reduced to the following:

> Article 2.1 This Directive shall not apply to
> (a) services in the field of long-term care whose purpose is to support people in need of assistance in carrying out routine, everyday tasks.

Notwithstanding the differences in the definition of LTHC amongst the Member States the ECJ may decide upon its own definition as to when different kinds of care fall within the remit of EU law.[86]

5.6.3 Prior Authorisation

A third area of disagreement between the Member States is when the Member State of affiliation may demand that prior authorisation is necessary before a patient can be reimbursed for health care costs incurred abroad. This requirement is seen by the Commission and the Court as a hindrance to free movement. However, prior authorisation from the Member State of affiliation can give greater clarification and certainty of what payments will be made before the patient embarks on the journey abroad for medical treatment.

---

[84] ECJ, Case C-70/95 *Sodemare SA, Anni Azzurri Holding SpA and Anni Azzurri Rezzato Srl* v. *Regione Lombardia* [1997] *ECR* 3395.

[85] Recital 9b COREPER draft of 26 November 2009. Article 2(2)(a) of the revised draft Directive.

[86] Cf., ECJ, Case C-208/07 *Petra von Chamier-Glisczinski* v. *Deutsche Angestellten-Krankenkasse* [2009] *ECR* I-0000 (n.y.r.). The dispute concerned the application of the social security Regulation 1408/71/EC but the claimant brought into play Articles 21, 45 and 56 TFEU. The Court ruled that where a person moves to a Member State on a permanent basis the claim for the provision of services does not fall within Article 56 TFEU since this Treaty measure is designed to cover situations where the provider or recipient of the services is based in another Member State on a temporary basis.

The Court of Justice has held that prior authorisation can be justified in the light of overriding reasons in the general interest, for example, the risk of seriously undermining the financial balance of the social security system, the objective of maintaining on grounds of public health a balanced medical and hospital service open to all or the objective of maintaining treatment capacity or medical competence on national territory, essential for the public health, and even the survival of the population.[87] The Court has also enumerated the reasons which may not be used to justify a restriction on the free movement of patients: prior authorisation may not be based solely on the ground that there are waiting lists for treatment intended to plan and manage predetermined clinical priorities, without making an objective assessment of the patient's medical condition, the history and probable cause of the illness, the degree of pain and/or the nature of the patient's disability at the time the request for authorisation was made (or renewed). The prior authorisation must be necessary and proportionate.

The Member States have argued that, given their competence to create the rules for the organisation and delivery of health care and that planning requirements vary between the Member States, they should have the authority to decide whether there is a need to introduce a system of prior authorisation for medical treatment abroad. They also point out that different criteria may be necessary between, and within, the Member States.[88]

The general rule in the draft of the proposed Directive of June 2010 is that the Member State of affiliation shall ensure re-imbursement of costs incurred by an insured person who has received cross-border health care, if the heath care in question is among the benefits to which the insured person is entitled in the Member State of affiliation.[89] However, there are exceptions. Article 8(1)(1a) states that where a Member State is listed in Annex IV of Regulation No 883/2004 and in compliance with Regulation (EC) No 883/2004 has recognised the rights to sickness benefits for pensioners and members of their families where they are resident in a different Member State it will provide the health care under the Directive at its own expense when they stay on its territory.

A Member State may not make the reimbursement of costs of cross-border health care subject to prior authorisation [Article 8(6)] except in the situations covered by Article 9:

- Where health care is made subject to planning in so far as it involves overnight hospital accommodation for at least one night, or
- Is made subject to planning in so far as it requires highly specialised treatment and cost-intensive medical infrastructure or medical equipment, or
- Involves treatments presenting a particular risk for the patient or population or which could raise serious and concrete concerns related with the quality or

---

87 See the chapter by Baquero Cruz.

88 Recital 31d of COREPER November 2009 draft.

89 Article 8(1). Cf., the ruling pending in ECJ, Case C-173/09 *Elchinov* v. *Natsionalna zdravnoosiguritelna kasa*, Opinion of Advocate General Cruz Villalón of 10 June 2010.

safety of the care (with the exception of Union legislation ensuring a minimum level of safety and quality through out the Union.

Even in these situations, the system of prior authorisation must be limited to what is necessary, proportionate and shall not constitute a means of arbitrary discrimination. Where a patient applies for prior authorisation the Member State of affiliation should check whether the conditions of Regulation (EC) No 883/2004 are met. If this is the situation, then prior authorisation should be granted according to the Regulation.

The draft Directive also sets out the (non-exhaustive) situations where a Member State may refuse prior authorisation in Article 9(4):

(a) the patient is not entitled to the treatment in question (in accordance with Article 8);
(b) if this health care can be provided on its territory within a time-limit which is medically justifiable, taking into account the current state of health and the probable course of the illness of the person concerned;
(c) if the patient according to a clinical evaluation with reasonable certainty will be exposed to a patient safety risk that cannot be considered to be normal, taking into account the potential benefit for the patient of the sought cross-border health care;
(d) if the general public with reasonable certainty will be exposed to a substantial safety hazard as a result of the cross-border health care in question;
(e) if this health care is provided by health care providers that raise serious and concrete concerns related to the respect of standards and guidelines on quality of care and patient safety, including provisions on supervision, whether these standards and guidelines are given by laws and regulations or through accreditation systems established by the Member State of Treatment.

The Member State of affiliation must make publicly available which health care is subject to prior authorisation for the purposes of this Directive as well as all relevant information on the system of prior authorisation.

The use of a Directive to clarify the Court's case law creates new procedural rights for the patient as well as creating the refusal of authorisation to travel for medical care as a justifiable issue capable of review against EU law norms and principles. The Member States should identify the health care requiring prior authorisation, in accordance with the criteria set out in the Directive and the Court's case law. The information concerning prior authorisation should be made publicly available. Where a Member State establishes a system of prior authorisation, the costs of the health care provided in another Member State should be reimbursed up to the same level as the costs which would have been incurred in the treatment had the same taken place in the State of affiliation, without exceeding the costs of the actual health care received. When the conditions set out in Article 22(2) of Regulation 1408/71 or Article 20 of Regulation No 883/2004 are met, the authorisation should be granted and the benefits applied to the patient, unless she or he requests otherwise. Any decisions should be made in an objective, transparent and non-discriminatory and timely manner.

A different solution of amending the provisions of Regulation 1408/71 to extend to patients seeking medical treatment abroad who do not currently fall within the remit of the Regulation was ignored by the Commission but may have been an easier and less confrontational route than the proposals within the draft Directive.[90]

Linked to the question of prior authorisation is the issue of what kind of health care providers will be covered in the draft Directive. Even though the Member States have the competence to organise the internal health care schemes, they are not immune from the free movement rules.[91]

5.7 Accountability in the EU

An aspect of the focus on Patients' Rights in the Directive is the increased accountability the role (and rule) of law can play in the determination of rights and procedures put in place by the Member States. Article 9 of the proposal sets out procedural guarantees distilled from the Court's case law: objective, transparent, non-discriminatory criteria alongside principles of necessity, proportionality and access to judicial review. Courts would become the *fora* for the enforcement of rights. Differences between the various legal systems of the EU in terms of framing social rights, access to the courts and judicial receptiveness to claims can be mediated by the use of the preliminary reference procedures and over-arching principles of EU law such as effectiveness and proportionality resulting in a hierarchical relationship between the national courts and the Court of Justice. More difficult will be the question of whether the judicial arena is the best forum for challenges to the interpretation of concepts found within the proposal on the quality of care.[92] Article 5 of the proposal establishes common principles for

---

90 An idea proposed by Sauter (2008). Also published in Sauter (2009), p. 109.

91 See ECJ, Case C-169/07 *Hartlauer Handelsgesellschaft mbH* v. *Wiener Landesregierung, Oberösterreichische Landesregierung*, judgment of 10 March 2009, discussed in the chapter by Baeten and Palm.

92 'Quality' of health care is a difficult concept to quantify since a patient will be concerned with the quality of the clinical treatment provided and the quality of their experience of the medical system, especially where the treatment involves in-patient care in a hospital (for example, the cleanliness of the hospital, the food, the attitude of the medical staff). The use of performance indicators in the UK NHS has shown that the use of observable indicators may not capture unobservable factors which are important for the patient experience. If certain indicators are given preference over others, then there is an incentive for the institution to concentrate on the quality of only these indicators. By creating performance tables for public services the use of statistical analysis may be have an impact for the institution concerned, such as a hospital, but even small variations in the use of the indicators may also alter the position of an institution in league tables, bringing with it a lack of confidence in the potential consumers of its services. See Jacobs and Goddard (2007), p. 103; Propper (2008), p. 138.

health care. These are based on the Council Conclusions on common values and principles in health care agreed in 2006, the over-arching principles being equity and solidarity.

This raises the question of how far the network governance procedures (discussed in Hervey's chapter in this book) which are in existence[93] and are also envisaged in the proposed Directive[94] can, and should, be brought into the scrutiny of EU and national legal frameworks. If the proposed Directive is delayed, or not adopted, then these networks of new governance will most likely continue to operate without the formal structures and agendas created by the proposal.

The Commission has used such cooperative networks as part of omc processes in the modernisation of social protection.[95] The formal omc relies upon accountability through formal reporting and Commission analysis which may involve highlighting areas of best practice, tacitly condemning bad practice. Under less scrutiny are the wider governance networks which exist in the EU. Such networks are created by, and composed of, a broad range of actors representing many different interests (public, private, commercial, consumer interests, for example). At a formal level, in health care issues the networks create cooperation between public authorities to 'problem-solve' inter-State issues which cannot be resolved at a national level, or which can be resolved better by pooling resources,[96] which in turn may lead to regulation which may sometimes be subject to democratic scrutiny.[97] In the EU, this has been described as a second-best solution when the use of centralised EU processes and EU regulation is not feasible.[98] Picciotto[99] has shown that one of the effects of using networks to create 'networking governance' across inter-State jurisdictions is to create a technocratic approach to issues which may be politically sensitive by depoliticising social issues through the use of technical, scientific and professional standards. This is important in the interpretation of many of the legal issues in the proposed Directive, for example, the commitment to a 'quality' of care which is allegedly an over-arching aim of the proposal, or the level of professional regulation of health care providers. The words 'good quality care' in Article 5 of the Commission's original proposal may have different interpretations and expectations across, and within, the Member States of the EU. Indicators as to quality may be useful as comparison benchmarks but is difficult to transfer indicators across Member States without recognising the

---

93 See Hervey and Vanhercke (2010).

94 In Chapter IV titled 'Cooperation in Healthcare'.

95 For criticisms of the use of these processes see, Scharpf (2002), p. 645; Bernard (2005), p. 261.

96 A good example is the EU programme to coordinate research in rare diseases: Decision No 1295/1999/EC of the European Parliament and the Council of 29 April 1999, adopting a programme of Community action on rare diseases within the framework for action in the field of public health, *OJ* 1999 L 155/1.

97 See Slaughter (2004); Krisch and Kingsbury (2006), p. 1.

98 Thatcher and Coen (2008), p. 56.

99 Piccioto (1996/1997), p. 1014.

culture of health care and its setting. These issues of definition in an EU-context have already appeared as a result of the Court's case law in the interpretation of hospital or long-term care. In the proposed Chapter IV, there the Member States are asked to 'facilitate' cooperation in cross-border health care through information. This is a vague concept. The European Parliament was more clear-sighted in its recognition that what separates health care from other forms of services in the EU is the asymmetry of information and power between a patient and a health care provider/professional. It is a service where a patient may be put in a vulnerable position as a result of this asymmetry. The European Parliament proposed that the co-operation provisions of Chapter IV should be more specific, for example, the Member States should guarantee registers of health professionals which are listed and open to consultation by the relevant authorities in other Member States and Member States should immediately and pro-actively exchange information on disciplinary and criminal investigations against health care professionals where the proceedings impact on the right to provide services. Admittedly there is increased awareness of these networks through self-promotion, publication of documents on the internet as well as academic attention. What is lacking, however, is adherence to the principles of transparency and accountability in the current operation of such networks[100] and ignored in the Commission's proposed Directive.

5.8 Conclusion

The history and the context of the proposed Directive explains why it has been so difficult to find consensus for hard legislation in health care. The stumbling blocks to consensus may result in the Directive becoming a lost cause. For the Member States and for patients, it would be a lost opportunity to rationalise and create an effective framework for cross-border health care issues and an iterative framework for the modernisation of a social service of general interest. This chapter has shown that it is possible to discern different levels of impact the proposed Directive may have on national competence and the formal Europeanisation of health care if it is adopted.[101] The first level impact is that the proposal increases individual rights. It moves beyond patient mobility and (State) financial access to medical treatment to giving patients a deeper set of EU-based rights on access to health care leading towards an overall EU framework involving safeguards of quality, safety, reliability, redress, continuity, information in health care matters. Thus, if it is not adopted, then the individual citizens would be the main losers as they face uncertainty when embarking upon travel abroad. Even for non-mobile (static) patients the proposed Directive brings with it a new raft of substantive and

[100] See for example, Fisher (2004), p. 495.

[101] In this sense, 'Europeanisation' is used to denote the movement away from national competence and processes to EU-level regulation.

procedural rights and accountability in terms of the quality of care that a patient can expect in a Member State of the EU.

The second level impact of the proposal moves the EU from coordinating social security rights to coordinating health systems. These will embrace issues of cross-border activity on e-health and bio-ethical issues which challenge the legal competence of the EU to legislate in an area which impacts on national regulatory autonomy and financial planning. Yet, as we have seen, such coordination processes are a necessary spill-over of increased trade and cooperation in public and commercial markets and operate within networks which are neither fully transparent or accountable. The impact of the proposed Directive would be to further institutionalise existing governance networks and bring them closer to a rule of law framework of good governance practice. A process of Europeanisation of health care issues is already in place in the sense defined and described by Radaelli as a set of processes of construction, diffusion and institutionalisation of formal and informal rules, procedures, policy paradigms, styles, 'ways of doing things' and shared beliefs and norms which are first defined and consolidated in the EU policy process and then incorporated in the logic of domestic (national and sub-national) discourse, political structures and public policies.[102]

The free movement litigation has been complemented by other litigation invoking the EU rules involving procurement, competition and state aid. Economic factors in the shape of rising health care costs and deeper public sector deficits create a greater demand for the liberalisation and privatisation of welfare provision from governments. The liberalisation of health care markets has been facilitated by a new breed of medical tourist facilitators, ranging from the cheap flights offered by 'no frills' airlines, to clinics which can arrange medical package holidays, to insurance companies providing medical tourism insurance schemes. The original EP Rapporteur for the draft Directive, John Bowis, suggested that the rise in medical tourism may lead to a new health care professional emerging: a health broker who can give advice on the best place and form of EU medical treatment.[103]

As the other chapters of this book reveal, the demands of individuals have proved difficult to reconcile with the respect for the solidaristic and the social welfare nature of health care systems in the EU, creating a tension on how to find consistency in promoting new social values of the EU against the current practices and the experimentation of the Member States in modernising not only health care but systems of social security. The right of individuals to travel to another Member State to receive health care is firmly embedded in the free movement principle and viewed as part of the citizenship rights of EU membership. This chapter shows that health care is without firm national frontiers and, for some time, the EU has facilitated aspects of soft and hard governance to coordinate cross-border health care issues. Thus, there is the inevitable varied and fragmented EU involvement in cross-border patient mobility even without the adoption of the proposed Directive.

---

[102] Radaelli (2009).

[103] European Parliament Report A6-0233/2009, p. 76.

The value-added of the proposal is that Member States would be obliged to take positive measures to ensure that the Directive is properly implemented in the Member State to make patient mobility rights accessible and transparent. The Directive's proposals move the issue away from the narrowly formulated issue about 'who pays?' to creating an EU framework on health care on matters relating to quality of medical care, safety issues, liability for botched medical care and redress, alongside issues of maintaining continuity of medical care and information for patients. By doing this, the Directive would make even greater inroads into national regulatory autonomy and move the ownership of health care away from the State and a service of general interest within closed boundaries into the EU regulatory field. In this respect, the Directive begins to over-reach existing EU competence in the health care field by moving away from mere coordination of social security rights to the coordination and the Europeanisation of health care systems. Even if not adopted in its original form, the existence of the proposal and continued litigation in this field have consolidated a Europeanisation of this sector.

The inevitability of cross-border health care issues has led the EU to a response which creates a multi-dimensional dynamic involving different *fora* and different actors responding to the challenges posed by the modernisation of health care. The aim is to enable the EU to respond to new challenges, for example, of e-health and bio-ethical questions, LTHC created by social and demographic changes and the transformation of health care from a national, solidaristic public service to a global cross-border and competitive economic service with distinctively European responses.

Acknowledgments My thanks to comments on a draft of this chapter from the University of Leicester CELI Internal Market research cluster and participants at the conference 'Health Care and EU Law' at Nijmegen University in October 2009.

References

Baeten R (2008) The proposal for a directive on patients' rights in cross-border health care. In: Degryse C (ed) Social developments in the European Union. OSE/ETUC, Brussels

Bernard N (2005) Between a rock and a hard place: internal market v open coordination in EU social welfare law. In: Dougan M, Spaventa E (eds) Social welfare and EU law. Hart, Oxford

Cram L (1994) The European commission as multi-organisation: social policy and IT policy in the EU. J Europ Pub Pol 1

Davies G (2007) The effect of Mrs Watts trip to France on the national health service. Kings Law J 18

Everson M (1995) The legacy of the market citizen. In: Shaw J, More G (eds) New legal dynamics of European Union. OUP, Oxford

Fisher E (2004) The European Union in the age of accountability. Oxf J Leg Stud 24

Flear M (2009) The open method of coordination on health care after the lisbon strategy II: towards a neo-liberal framing? EIOP, Special Issue I, vol 13, available at: http://eiop.or.at/eiop/index.php/eiop/article/view

Greer S (2006) Uninvited Europeanization: neofunctionalism, health services and the EU. J Europ Pub Pol 13

Greer S (2009) The politics of European health policies. Open University Press, Maidenhead
Hancher L, Sauter W (2009) One foot in the grave or one step beyond? From Sodemare to DocMorris: The EU's freedom of establishment case law concerning health care, TILEC discussion paper series, 2009/28, available at: http://dbiref.uvt.nl/iPort?request=full_record&db=wo&language=eng&query=doc_id=3497608
Hancher L, Sauter W (2010) One step beyond? from sodemare to docmorris: the EU's freedom of establishment case law concerning health care. CMLRev 47
Hatzopoulos V (2002) Killing national health and insurance systems but healing patients? the European market for health care services after the judgments of the ECJ in Vanbraekel and Peerbooms. CMLRev 39
Hervey T (2003) The right to health in EU law. In: Hervey T, Kenner J (eds) Economic and social rights under the EU Charter of Fundamental Rights. Hart, Oxford
Hervey T, Vanhercke B (2010) Health care and the EU: the law and policy patchwork. In: Mossialos E, Permanand G, Baeten R, Hervey T (eds) Health systems governance in Europe: the role of European Union law and policy. CUP, Cambridge
Jacobs R, Goddard M (2007) How do performance indicators add up? an examination of composite indicators in public services. PMM 27
Joerges C (2008) Integration through de-legalisation? EL Rev 33(3)
Kickert K (1993) Complexity, governance and dynamics: conceptual explorations of network management. In: Kooiman J (ed) Modern governance: new government-society interactions. Sage, London
Kostera T (2007) Unwelcome Europeanisation—the development of cross-border patient mobility, master of European studies thesis, 2007, College of Europe, Bruges, available at: http://62.102.106.100/Objects/2/Files/Kostera.pdf
Krisch N, Kingsbury B (2006) Introduction: global governance and global administrative law in the international legal order. EJIL 17
Legido-Quigley H et al (2007) Patient mobility in the European Union. BMJ 334
Marks G (1993) Structural policy and multilevel governance in the European community. In: Cafruny A, Rosenthal G (eds) The state of the European community. Lyne Rienner, New York
Mossialos E, McKee M (2002) EU law and the social character of health care. PIE-Peter-Lang, Brussels (Work & Society No. 38)
Newdick C (2006) Citizenship, free movement and health care: cementing individual rights by corroding social solidarity. CML Rev 43
Neergaard U (2011, forthcoming) The Commission's soft law in the area of services of general economic interest. In: Szyszczak E, Davies J, Bekkedal T, Andenas M (eds) Developments in services of general economic interest. TMC Asser Press, The Hague
Piccioto S (1996/1997) Networks in international economic integration: fragmented states and the dilema of neo-liberalism. Northwestern J Internatl Law Bus 17
Propper C (2008) Competition and quality: evidence from the NHS internal markets 1991-9. Th Econ J 118
Radaelli C (2009) Europeanisation: solution or problem? EIoP 8. Available at: http://eiop.or.at/eiop/texte/2004-016.htm
Robertson R, Dixon A (2010) Choice at the point of referral, London, Kings Fund. Available at: http://www.kingsfund.org.uk/publications/choice_at_the_point.html
Rowland D et al (2004) Price and Pollack A, Implications of the draft European Union services directive for health care. Lancet 364
Sauter W (2008) The proposed patient mobility directive and the reform of cross-border health care in the EU, TILEC discussion paper 2008-034, Tilburg University, The Netherlands. Available at: http://papers.ssrn.com/sol3/papers.cfm?abstract_id=1277110
Sauter W (2009) The proposed patient mobility directive and the reform of cross-border health care in the EU Leg Issues Eur Integration 36
Scharpf F (2002) The European social model: coping with the challenges of diversity. JCMS 40

Sikora K (2010) Terrifyingly inept foreign doctors are a symptom of a sickness in the NHS—not the cause, Daily Mail, 18 March 2010. Available at: http://www.dailymail.co.uk/debate/article-1258782/KAROL-SIKORA-Terrifyingly-inept-foreign-doctors-symptom-sickness-NHS-cause.html

Slaughter AM (2004) A new world order. Princeton University Press, Princeton

Szyszczak E (2006) Experimental governance: the open Method of coordination. ELJ 12. Available at: http://papers.ssrn.com/sol3/papers.cfm?abstract_id=913101

Szyszczak E (2009a) Legal tools in the liberalisation of welfare markets. In: Neergaard U, Nielsen R, Roseberry L (eds) Integrating welfare functions into EU law—from Rome to Lisbon. DJØF Publishing, Copenhagen

Szyszczak E (2009b) Modernising health care: pilgrimage for the holy grail? In: Krajewski M, Neergaard U, van de Gronden J (eds) The changing legal framework for services of general interest in Europe between competition and solidarity. TMC Asser Press, The Hague

Thatcher M, Coen D (2008) Network governance and multi-level delegation: European networks of regulatory agencies. J Eur Pub Pol 28

Wincott D (2001) Looking forward or harking back? the Commission and the reform of governance in the European Union. JCMS 39

Chapter 6
The Draft Patient Mobility Directive and the Coordination Regulations of Social Security

Frans Pennings

Contents

F. Pennings (✉)
Labour Law and Social Security Law, Utrecht University, Utrecht, The Netherlands
e-mail: f.pennings@uu.nl

F. Pennings
International Social Security Law, Tilburg University, Tilburg, The Netherlands

J. W. van de Gronden et al. (eds.), *Health Care and EU Law*,
Legal Issues of Services of General Interest, DOI: 10.1007/978-90-6704-728-9_6,

6.1 Introduction

The draft Directive of the European Parliament and of the Council on the application of patients' rights in cross-border health care,[1] hereafter the draft Patient Mobility Directive or simply Directive, was in response to case law of the Court of Justice on reimbursement of cross-border health care. In this case law the authorisation for medical treatment, required under Regulation 1408/71[2] for reimbursement of the expenses of medical care obtained abroad, was overruled by the Treaty provisions on freedom of goods and services (the *Kohll* and *Decker* case law, discussed below in Sect. 6.4.2).[3] As a result a dual system came into existence: health care for which authorisation was given according to the rules of the Regulation and health care for which no authorisation was given but which had to be reimbursed on the basis of the Treaty. In this contribution I will analyse whether the draft Directive solves the problems arising from this dual system.

I will first discuss the system of the coordination regulation in relation to health care, in particular the authorisation requirement system (Sects. 6.2 and 6.3). In Sect. 6.4, I will describe the case law on the basis of Article 49 EC, now Article 56 TFEU, that affected the Regulation. Section 6.5 will deal with the draft Directive's rules on cross-border health care and the discussion on this proposal. In Sect. 6.6 conclusions will be drawn.

6.2 The Coordination Regulation's System to Obtain Medical Care in Another Member State

6.2.1 *The Scope of the Regulation*

On 1 May 2010 Regulation 1408/71 was replaced by Regulation 883/2004.[4] For this reason I will focus on the latter Regulation, but where necessary I will mention Regulation 1408/71; the differences between the Regulations are small in so far as

[1] Brussels, 2 July 2008, COM(2008) 414 final.

[2] Council Regulation (EEC) No 1408/71 of 14 June 1971 on the application of social security schemes to employed persons, to self-employed persons and to members of their families moving within the Community (*OJ* L 149 of 5 July 1971, p. 2).

[3] ECJ, Case C-158/96 *Kohll* [1998] *ECR* I-1931 and Case C-120/95 *Decker* [1998] *ECR* I-1871. Other cases are ECJ, Case C-368/98 *Vanbraekel* [2001] *ECR* I-5363; ECJ, Case C-157/99 *Smits* and *Peerbooms* [2001] *ECR* I-5473; ECJ, Case C-56/01 *Inizan* [2003] *ECR* I-12403; ECJ, Case C-8/02 *Leichtle* [2004] *ECR* I-2641; ECJ, Case C-385/99 *Müller-Fauré* and *Van Riet* [2003] *ECR* I-4503, and ECJ, Case C-372/04 *Watts* [2006] *ECR* I-4325.

[4] Regulation (EC) No 883/2004 of the European Parliament and of the Council of 29 April 2004 on the coordination of social security systems (*OJ* L 166 of 30 April 2004, p. 1).

relevant to the topic of this chapter. It is unnecessary for our purposes to describe the Regulations in great detail; thus I will limit myself to the main aspects.

The personal scope of the Regulation 1408/71 was limited to employed and self-employed persons, terms defined as: persons who are or have been insured on the basis of a social security scheme for employed and self-employed persons, respectively. Regulation 883/2004 has a broader personal scope. It applies to all nationals of a Member State, stateless persons and refugees residing in a Member State who are, or have been, subject to the legislation of one or more Member States, as well as to the members of their families and to their survivors. Both Regulations are limited to persons having the nationality of a Member State. Third country nationals are not completely excluded from the application of the coordination Regulation: in 2003 Regulation 859/2003 was adopted,[5] which extended the provisions of Regulation 1408/71 and Regulation 574/72 to nationals of third countries who are not already covered by those provisions solely on the ground of their nationality, as well as to members of their families and to their survivors provided they are legally resident in the territory of a Member State. An important condition is that they are in a situation which is not confined in all respects within a single Member State. Thus, if a person from Japan moves to Germany, the Regulation is not yet applicable. If the person subsequently accepts a job in Italy the Regulation applies.

The legal basis for this Regulation, Article 69(4) EC allows Denmark, the UK and Ireland to opt in or opt out of instruments made on basis of the latter article. Actually, it was only Denmark that did not opt into Regulation 859/2003. For Regulation 883/2004 a new third country nationals' Regulation needs to be drafted; negotiations on this Regulation are difficult and, if it is adopted, it is uncertain whether more countries will choose not opt in.[6]

The material scope of the Regulation concerns all sickness benefits in kind which are covered by statutory benefit schemes. Thus, benefits provided on the basis of non-statutory schemes, for example, private insurance schemes, are not included in the scope of the Regulation. This is the same for both the old and new Regulation.

6.2.2 The Provisions on Sickness Benefits in Kind

Chapter 1 of Title III of the Regulation provides a set of rules on the coordination of sickness benefits; *inter alia*, these deal with the situation of persons whose residence is outside the competent State (that is, the State where the person is insured); frontier workers and members of their family, and pensioners having a

[5] Council Regulation (EC) No 859/2003 of 14 May 2003 extending the provisions of Regulation (EEC) No 1408/71 and Regulation (EEC) No 574/72 to nationals of third countries who are not already covered by those provisions solely on the ground of their nationality (*OJ L* 124 of 20 May 2003). See the preparatory work for this Regulation in COM 2002, 59.

[6] In 2010 Regulation (EU) No 1231/2010 was adopted as the successor of Regulation 859/2003.

pension from a State other than the State of residence.[7] Although these provisions relate to cross-border health care, these are not the ones which lead to the case law of the Court of Justice on Article 49 EC (now Article 56 TFEU). These provisions concern situations where persons *reside* in a State other than the competent State and are allowed to obtain benefits in kind in the State of residence and/or the State of employment. The proposed Patients' Rights Directive may be beneficial for these persons to the extent that the Directive leads to more cooperation of the authorities and more information on the available services. My chapter is, however, concentrated on persons who obtain medical care in a State where they neither reside nor work. This is the situation in which persons *stay* outside the competent State or State of residence. *Stay* is a situation which is much more temporary than *residence*, and where the centre of interests of the person concerned (his house, family, etc.) is in a State other than the one where s/he stays. The provisions on stay outside the competent State can be found in Article 22 of Regulation 1408/71 and Article 19 of Regulation 883/2004.

6.2.3 Benefits Which Become Necessary

Article 19 of Regulation 883/2004 concerns the situation of a person whose condition requires benefits in kind which become necessary on medical grounds during a stay in the territory of another Member State, taking into account the nature of the benefits and the expected length of the stay. The provision itself is limited to a person who satisfies the conditions of the legislation of the competent State for entitlement to benefits. A person who is not insured under the legislation of that State cannot invoke this condition, apart from members of the family and survivors of this insured person.

If Article 19 of Regulation 883/2004 is applicable, the person concerned is entitled to benefits in kind provided on behalf of the competent State by the institution of the place of stay in accordance with the provisions of the legislation which it administers, as though s/he were insured with it. The length of the period during which benefits are provided is governed by the legislation of the competent State. In this case no authorisation by the competent institution of the State of affiliation is necessary.

For example, if a person breaks his leg during a skiing holiday, and s/he is insured in the home State, s/he receives the medical treatment available under the legislation of the State where s/he is treated, i.e. where s/he stays. The person does not have to pay the bill for the treatment to the health provider; the costs are settled in arrangements between the States involved.

There can, of course, be disputes on when care becomes necessary or whether it was already necessary when crossing the border. If the medical situation of the person concerned was the same as when he entered the State of stay, or when the

[7] For a detailed description, see Pennings (2010).

treatment can be awarded without problems upon return to the State of residence, it is not a matter for Article 19.

However, in order to settle an uncertain situation in which pregnant women close to delivery went to a State with good health care in order to be treated there, the Administrative Commission decided that benefits in kind required in the case of pregnancy and delivery which are provided before the 38th week of pregnancy are considered as immediately required. This was a pragmatic solution in order not to impede the health of pregnant women.

Regulation 883/2004 provides that the Administrative Commission has to establish a list of benefits in kind which, in order to be provided during a stay in another Member State, for practical reasons require a prior agreement between the person concerned and the institution providing the care.[8]

6.3 Going to Another Member State in Order to Receive Planned Care

6.3.1 The Applicable Provisions of the Coordination Regulations

The Articles discussed in this section were the subjects of judgments of the Court of Justice, the *Kohll* and *Decker* case law. Article 22(1)(c) of Regulation 1408/71 provides that an employee or self-employed person, who is authorised by the competent institution to go to the territory of another Member State to receive there the treatment appropriate to his condition, is entitled to benefits in kind provided on behalf of the competent State by the institution of the place of stay in accordance with the provisions of the legislation it administered, as though s/he were insured with it.

Article 22(2), second sentence, provides in relation to the authorisation that it may not be refused when the treatment in question is amongst the benefits provided for by the legislation of the Member State in whose territory the person concerned resided and where he cannot be given such treatment within the time normally necessary for obtaining the treatment in question in the Member State of residence taking account of his current state of health and the probable course of the disease.

Article 20 of Regulation 883/2004 follows the same approach. Paragraph 1 provides that, unless otherwise provided for by this Regulation, an insured person travelling to another Member State with the purpose of receiving benefits in kind during the stay shall seek authorisation from the competent institution. Paragraph 2 provides that an insured person who is authorised by the competent institution to go to another Member State with the purpose of receiving the treatment appropriate to his condition shall receive the benefits in kind provided, on behalf of the competent institution, by the institution of the place of stay, in accordance with the

[8] The decisions are published in *OJ* 2010, C 106.

provisions of the legislation it applies, as though he were insured under the said legislation. The authorisation shall be accorded where the treatment in question is amongst the benefits provided for by the legislation in the Member State where the person concerned resides and where he cannot be given such treatment within a time limit which is medically justifiable, taking into account his current state of health and the probable course of his illness. Paragraph 3 provides that paragraphs 1 and 2 shall apply *mutatis mutandis* to the members of the family of an insured person.

Article 22(1)(b) of Regulation 1408/71 allows an employee or self-employed person, having become entitled to benefits chargeable to the competent institution, to be authorised by that institution to return to the territory of the Member State where he resides, or to transfer his residence to the territory of another Member State. This situation often occurs in the case of migrant workers who fall ill and of whom it is presumed that they will not recover quickly and who want to recover in the State of origin. The Regulation provides that authorisation may be refused only if it is established that movement of the person concerned would be prejudicial to his state of health or the receipt of medical treatment. This provision is not included in Regulation 883/2004, but the situation can be covered by Article 20 of Regulation 883/2004 as well.

6.3.2 The Financial Aspects of the Authorisation

Where a person has received authorisation to go to another Member State to receive treatment which is covered in the competent Member State (hereinafter also referred to as: the State of affiliation), s/he shall be entitled to this treatment in accordance with the legislation of the Member State providing the treatment, as if s/he were insured in that Member State. The cost of that treatment is to be borne by the State of affiliation, which refunds the institution of the Member State of treatment directly, in accordance with Article 36 of the Regulation. Thus, if Article 19 of Regulation 883/2004 is applicable, reimbursement is made in accordance with that Regulation directly to the competent institution of the State of treatment at the rate of reimbursement normally applicable in the Member State of treatment, and not to the patient.

A patient failing to obtain authorisation because the conditions of Article 19 have not been fulfilled is not eligible for reimbursement for treatment received in another Member State. However, if a person has applied for permission to receive medical treatment in another Member State, but that has been wrongfully refused, a different rule applies. The Court found that this person is entitled to be reimbursed directly by the competent institution by an amount equivalent to that which it would ordinarily have borne if authorisation had been granted in the first place. This was decided in the *Vanbraekel* judgment.[9]

---

[9] ECJ, Case C-368/98 *Vanbraekel* [2001] *ECR* I-5363.

6.4 The Regulation Challenged; the Case Law on the Basis of Articles 28 and 49 EC (Now Articles 34 and 56 TFEU)

6.4.1 Introduction

The authorisation system of the coordination Regulation was challenged by patients who sought health treatment in another Member State. Patients do so for various reasons, but Member States are reluctant to give authorisation for this. Reasons for seeking care abroad may be because treatment in another Member State is available sooner than in the Member State of residence; the availability of treatment in another Member State which is not (yet) available in the Member State of residence or which is only available on an experimental basis, or the fact that the patient has more confidence in a medical care provider established in another Member State. Patient mobility is also stimulated through the availability of more information (for example, on the internet) on the possibility of obtaining medical treatment in other countries and through the activities of intermediaries, such as medical care brokers.[10]

Reasons for the reluctance of Member States to give authorisation on the basis of the Regulation include the fear that expenditure for health care will increase since there is now a larger capacity of care providers than on the basis of the national system alone. Foreign care providers may also be more expensive. Finally there is the fear that the quality and safety of treatment is not guaranteed. Under the system of the Regulation, if no authorisation is granted, no reimbursement takes place and the patient has to bear the expenses him/herself.

6.4.2 The Kohll *and* Decker *Case Law*

The authorisation requirement of Article 22(1)(c) of Regulation 1408/71 (the authorisation system) was confronted with the freedom of goods and services guaranteed by Articles 28 and 49 EC (now Articles 38 and 56 TFEU). In the *Kohll* and *Decker* judgments the Court ruled that the condition of authorisation of Article 22 of Regulation 1408/71 was in some cases contrary to the mentioned Articles of the Treaty.[11] Mr. Decker, a Luxembourg national, bought a pair of spectacles from an optician established in Belgium, on a prescription from an ophthalmologist established in Luxembourg. Mr. Kohll required orthodontist treatment in Germany. No authorisation was sought for these treatments and reimbursement was subsequently refused.

The Court argued that Article 22 is not intended to regulate, and hence does not in any way prevent, the reimbursement by Member States, at the tariffs in force in

[10] Advocate General in the *Watts'* case (Opinion delivered on 15 December 2005, Case C-372/04, para 22).

[11] For an analysis of the case law, see Chap. 4 by Baquero Cruz.

the competent State, of costs incurred in connection with treatment provided in another Member State, even without prior authorisation. Subsequently, the Court considered the compatibility of the disputed national rules with the Treaty provisions on freedom to provide services or goods. For this purpose it examined whether the disputed rules constitute a restriction on freedom to provide services or goods and, if so, whether they are objectively justified. It considered that the disputed rules do not deprive persons of the possibility of approaching a provider of services established in another Member State, but the rules deter insured persons from approaching providers of medical services established in another Member State, as the costs incurred in that State are not reimbursed. Therefore, it was relevant whether there was an objective justification. Thereupon the Court considered that the risk of seriously undermining the financial balance of the social security system may constitute an overriding reason in the general interest capable of justifying a barrier of the kind at stake. However, it is clear that reimbursement of the costs of dental treatment provided in other Member States in accordance with the tariff of the State of insurance has no significant effect on the financing of the social security system. Also the fear that the quality of medical care could be in danger was not accepted as an objective justification: the Court referred to several Directives concerning the mutual recognition of diplomas which would guarantee the quality of the health care. In both judgments, the reimbursement had to be given in accordance with the tariffs of the State of insurance. Consequently, the ensuing costs for Luxembourg were not higher than if the glasses and dental treatment were bought in that State.[12]

As a result of this case law the system of reimbursement of the coordination Regulation and Article 49 EC differ: in the first situation reimbursement (to the competent institution) is according to the scales of State of treatment, in the latter situation reimbursement (to the patient) is according to the scales of the State of insurance.[13]

6.4.3 Hospital Care

The *Kohll* and *Decker* judgments led to much discussion in the Member States, as they feared the effects. In order to try to restrict these effects, Member States argued, amongst other things, that the judgments did not apply to hospitals and applied to reimbursement systems only. So if a health insurance does not reimburse the costs of health care but provides care in kind only, the case law would not be applicable. The Court had to deal with these issues.

---

[12] See also van der Mei (2003).

[13] Where the request for authorisation has been refused by the competent institution and it is subsequently established that such refusal was unfounded, and the scales in the host State are lower than in the competent State, reimbursement to the patient is according to the scales of the competent State (*Vanbraekel* judgment, Case 368/98, [2001] *ECR* I-5363). See Jorens (2003), p. 90.

The first question, whether treatment in hospitals was excluded from the *Kohll* and *Decker* approach, was the subject of the *Geraets-Smits* and *Peerbooms* judgment.[14] In this judgment the Court decided that, in so far as medical services provided within a hospital infrastructure are concerned, an authorisation system could be objectively justified.

6.4.3.1 Objective Justifications

The Court mentioned the following arguments for allowing the authorisation system. The first is that the possible risk of seriously undermining a social security system's financial balance may constitute an overriding reason in the general interest capable of justifying a barrier to the principle of freedom to provide services. A second argument is the objective of maintaining a balanced medical and hospital service open to all. Article 46 EC (now Article 52 TFEU) permits Member States to restrict the freedom to provide medical and hospital services in so far as the maintenance of treatment capacity or medical competence on national territory is essential for the public health, and even the survival of the population.

In the judgment the Court accepted that, by comparison with medical services provided by practitioners in their surgeries or at the patient's home, medical services provided in a hospital take place within an infrastructure with, undoubtedly, certain very distinct characteristics. This is because for determining the number of hospitals, their geographical distribution, the mode of their organisation and the equipment with which they are provided, and even the nature of the medical services which they are able to offer, a good planning system is necessary. This has to ensure that there is sufficient and permanent access to a balanced range of high-quality hospital treatment. It also assists in meeting a desire to control costs and to prevent, as far as possible, any wastage of financial, technical and human resources. If insured persons were at liberty to use the services of hospitals with which their sickness insurance fund had no contractual arrangements, all the planning which goes into the contractual system in an effort to guarantee a rationalised, stable, balanced and accessible supply of hospital services would be jeopardised at a stroke.

In the *Müller-Fauré* and *Van Riet* judgment[15] the Court admitted that the distinction between these two forms of care might sometimes prove difficult to draw. In particular, certain services usually provided in a hospital environment but which can also be provided by a practitioner in his surgery or in a health centre could for that reason be placed on the same footing as non-hospital services. Since the national court and the governments did not ask questions on this issue, the Court did not consider it in further detail.[16]

---

[14] ECJ, Case 157/99 [2001] *ECR* I-5473.

[15] ECJ, Case 385/99 [2003] *ECR* I-4503.

[16] See, for the applicability on health spas, ECJ, Case C-8/02 *Leichtle* [2004] *ECR* I-2641.

6.4.3.2 Criteria for the Authorisation Procedure

Subsequently, the Court discussed the criteria for giving authorisation. In exercising the power on deciding on prior authorisation, the Member State must not disregard EU law. A prior administrative authorisation scheme must be based on a procedural system that is easily accessible and capable of ensuring that a request for authorisation will be dealt with objectively and impartially within a reasonable time. Refusals to grant authorisation must also be capable of being challenged in judicial or quasi-judicial proceedings. They must refer to the specific provisions on which they are based. They must be properly reasoned in accordance with them. This was decided in the *Watts* judgment.[17]

Likewise, courts or tribunals hearing actions against such refusals must be able, if they consider it necessary for the purpose of carrying out the review which it is incumbent on them to make, to seek the advice of wholly objective and impartial independent experts.

In relation to the dispute in the *Watts* case itself the Court noted that the regulations on the UK's NHS did not set out the criteria for the grant or refusal of the prior authorisation necessary for reimbursement of the cost of hospital treatment provided in another Member State. Therefore, they do not circumscribe the exercise of the national competent authorities' discretionary power in that context. The lack of a legal framework in that regard also makes it difficult to exercise judicial review of decisions refusing to grant authorisation.

6.4.3.3 Undue Delay

Authorisation may be refused only if the same or equally effective treatment can be obtained without undue delay. In the *Müller-Fauré* and *Van Riet* case, already mentioned above, the Court was asked what this term means. It replied that a refusal to grant prior authorisation which is based not on fear of wastage resulting from hospital overcapacity, but solely on the ground that there are waiting lists, is an unjustified restriction. Instead, it is essential that also account is taken of the specific circumstances attaching to the patient's medical condition. The national authorities are required to have regard to all the circumstances of each specific case. They have to take due account of the patient's medical condition at the time when authorisation is sought. They also have to take account, where appropriate, of the degree of pain or the nature of the patient's disability which might, for example, make it impossible or extremely difficult for him to carry out a professional activity. Finally, they have to take account of his medical history.

The term 'without an undue delay' was also subject of the *Watts* case.[18] The referring court asked whether the criteria for the interpretation of the phrase

---

[17] ECJ, Case 372-04 [2006] *ECR* I-43.

[18] Ibid. See Stergiou (2006), p. 219.

'within the time normally necessary for obtaining the treatment in question' in the second subparagraph of Article 22(2) of Regulation 1408/71 are the same as those used to define the term 'without undue delay' in the context of Article 49 EC. The Court answered that the interpretation is indeed the same; there is no reason which seriously justifies different interpretations. Thus, the second condition of Article 22(2) is not satisfied whenever it is apparent that treatment which is the same or equally effective for the patient can be obtained without undue delay in his Member State of residence.

6.4.3.4 Waiting Lists

The Court continued its reasoning by considering that where the demand for hospital treatment is constantly rising, primarily as a consequence of medical progress and increased life expectancy, and the supply is necessarily limited by budgetary constraints, it cannot be denied that waiting lists may be necessary. However, the competent institution must establish that the waiting time does not exceed the period which is acceptable in the light of an objective medical assessment of the clinical needs of the person concerned in the light of his medical condition and the history and probable course of his illness, the degree of pain he is in and/or the nature of his disability at the time when the authorisation is sought. These were the criteria already mentioned in the *Muller-Fauré* judgment.

A new element in the Court's case law in respect of the waiting lists is that the setting of waiting times should be done flexibly and dynamically, so that the period initially notified to the person concerned may be reconsidered in the light of any deterioration in his state of health occurring after the first request for authorisation. It is for the referring court to determine whether the waiting time invoked by the competent body and based on the planning objectives pursued by the authorities, in order to refuse the initial application for authorisation and the renewed request exceeded a medically acceptable period in the light of the patient's particular condition and clinical needs at those respective times.

6.4.4 The Level of Reimbursement and Travel and Accommodation Costs

Mrs. Watts, in the *Watts* case, asked for reimbursement of the full costs of the treatment, and her travel and accommodation costs. The Court ruled that in the case of Article 49 EC (now Article 56 TFEU), it is for the Member States alone to determine the extent of the sickness cover available to insured persons. If an insured person goes (without prior authorisation) to another Member State for medical treatment, he can claim reimbursement of the cost of the treatment given to him only within the limits of the cover provided by the sickness insurance scheme in the Member State of affiliation. This means that he is only entitled to the amount which would be reimbursed if the treatment had been provided in the competent Member State.

Further, the question arose how the rules should be applied in a situation such as that of the UK's NHS which provides health care free at the point of delivery and does not provide for any system of reimbursement. No rates for reimbursement exist in that system. The Court replied that the absence of a system of rates or tariffs does not as such preclude the application of reimbursement rules. The final point is whether there is a right under Article 49 EC (now 56 TFEU) and Article 22 of Regulation 1408/71 to the reimbursement of travel and accommodation costs related to hospital treatment received in another Member State.

The Court considered that if authorisation is given according to Regulation 1408/71, the patient has the right to receive benefits in kind provided, on behalf of the competent institution, by the institution of the host Member State. The sole purpose of Article 22(1)(c)(i) of the coordination Regulation is to confer to have access to treatment in another Member State on conditions for reimbursement as favourable as those enjoyed by patients covered by the legislation of that other State. The obligation of Articles 22, therefore, relates exclusively to the expenditure connected with the health care received by the patient in the host Member State, namely, in the case of hospital treatment, the cost of medical services strictly defined and the inextricably linked costs relating to the patient's stay in the hospital for the purposes of his treatment. Benefits in kind are designed to cover care received by the person concerned by the direct payment or reimbursement of 'medical expenses' incurred by that patient's state. Since its purpose is thus not to settle the question of ancillary costs, such as the cost of travel and any accommodation other than in the hospital itself, Article 22 of Regulation 1408/71 does not make provision for, but also does not prohibit, the reimbursement of such costs.

Then the Court considered whether an obligation to reimburse such costs might arise under Article 49 EC (now Article 56 TFEU). It adds that the legislation of a Member State cannot, without infringing Article 49 EC, exclude reimbursement of the ancillary costs in another Member State whilst providing for the reimbursement of those costs where the treatment is provided in a hospital covered by the national system in question. By contrast, a Member State is not required to lay down a duty on its competent institutions to reimburse the ancillary costs where there is no such duty in the case of movement within the Member State. It is for the referring court to determine which situation is the case.

6.4.5 Summary

A person authorised by the competent institution to go to the territory of another Member State to receive there the treatment appropriate to his condition is entitled to benefits in kind provided on behalf of the competent State by the institution of the place of stay in accordance with the provisions of the legislation it administered, as though s/he were insured with it. The coordination Regulation provides in relation to the authorisation that it may not be refused when the treatment in question is amongst the benefits provided for by the legislation of the Member State in whose territory the person concerned resided and where s/he cannot be given such treatment within the time normally necessary for obtaining the treatment in question in the Member State of residence taking account of his current state of health and the probable course of the disease. The cost of that treatment is to be borne by the Member State of insurance which refunds the institution of the Member State of treatment directly, in accordance with the regulation.

In the case of non-hospital care, benefits can also be obtained without authorisation on the basis of Article 56 TFEU; in those cases reimbursement is given in accordance with the scale of the State of insurance.

However, if authorisation is refused, and afterwards it appears that it should have been given, the system of the coordination Regulation applies. If this means that costs have to be reimbursed the actual costs of treatment have to be reimbursed to the person concerned.

In the case of hospital care, the possible risk of seriously undermining a social security system's financial balance may constitute an overriding reason in the general interest capable of justifying a barrier to the principle of freedom to provide services. Community law thus does not in principle preclude a system of prior authorisation. In exercising the power to refuse or grant authorisation the Member State must not disregard Community law. A prior administrative authorisation scheme must be based on a procedural system that is easily accessible and capable of ensuring that a request for authorisation will be dealt with objectively and impartially within a reasonable time and refusals to grant authorisation must also be capable of being challenged in judicial or quasi-judicial proceedings.

Refusals to grant authorisation, or the advice on which such refusals may be based, must refer to the specific provisions on which they are based and be properly reasoned in accordance with them. Likewise, courts or tribunals hearing actions against such refusals must be able, if they consider it necessary for the purpose of carrying out the review which it is incumbent on them to make, to seek the advice of wholly objective and impartial independent experts. The lack of a legal framework in that regard also makes it difficult to exercise judicial review of decisions refusing to grant authorisation.

A refusal to grant prior authorisation which is based not on fear of wastage resulting from hospital overcapacity but solely on the ground that there are waiting lists on national territory for the hospital treatment concerned, without account being taken of the specific circumstances attaching to the patient's medical condition, cannot amount to a properly justified restriction on freedom to provide services. Instead, the national authorities are required to have regard to all the circumstances of each specific case and to take due account not only of the patient's medical condition at the time when authorisation is sought and, where appropriate, of the degree of pain or the nature of the patient's disability which might, for example, make it impossible or extremely difficult for him to carry out a professional activity, but also of his or her medical history.

Since there are important differences between the draft Directive and the coordination Regulation it is useful to show the approaches towards planned care and emergency care in a table. The table is derived from the Commission's working Document on the draft Patients' Rights Directive.[19] The coordination Regulation mentioned in the table refers to both Regulation 1408/71 and Regulation 883/2004; there is no difference between these Regulations in so far as the aspects mentioned in the table are concerned.

Overview of the different systems	Emergency care Coordination regulation	Planned care Coordination regulation	Planned care Draft patient directive
Prior authorisation for hospital care	No prior authorisation	Obligatory	May be required by the Member States
Prior authorisation for non-hospital care	No prior authorisation	Obligatory	Not needed
Means of payment	Benefits in kind provided according to the legislation of the Member State of treatment	Benefits in kind provided according to the legislation of the Member State of treatment (i.e. in some countries free of charge, in some countries out-of-pocket payment may be required)	Out-of-pocket payment with subsequent reimbursement from the social security institution of the patient's home Member State
	Settlement of costs between the social security institutions of the two countries concerned	Settlement of costs between the social security institutions of the two countries concerned	
Level of reimbursement	According to the rules of the MS of treatment	According to the rules of the MS of treatment	According to the rules of the patient's home MS
		If this is less than what a patient would receive in his home MS, the additional reimbursement covering that difference must be granted	In any event, only actual costs of the treatment are reimbursed (i.e. a patient cannot make profit)

[19] Commission Staff Working Document, accompanying the proposal for the patient mobility directive, SEC(2008) 2163, p. 27.

6.5 The Draft Patients' Rights Mobility Directive

6.5.1 Objectives of the Directive Relevant to This Chapter

The proposal for the draft Directive on the application of patients' rights in cross-border health care was published in July 2008. A main objective of the draft Directive is to increase legal certainty in the field of cross-border care following the Court of Justice's case law concerning the right of patients to benefit from medical treatment in another Member State. Since the provisions on health care were repealed from the then draft Directive on services in the internal market, a separate instrument was prepared.

Based on the case law discussed in Sect. 6.4, the new instrument aims at ensuring a clear and transparent framework for the provision of cross-border health care within the EU for those occasions where the care patients seek is provided in another Member State than in their home country. The objective is also to avoid unjustified obstacles and to ensure that the care is safe and of good quality. In addition, it wishes to ensure that the procedures for reimbursement of costs are clear and transparent.

After the proposal was published, several meetings of the Council have taken place and amendments have been made to the original text (some proposals for amendments are still pending). On 11 November 2009 a compromise text was published by the Presidency of the Council of the European Union.[20] At the time of completing this chapter, no agreement has been reached on a final version yet. In the meantime the European Parliament has also adopted many amendments to the draft Directive. These have not yet been discussed by the Council. As a result the text of the proposal is still far from final. I will refer to discussions only where relevant to their relation to the coordination Regulation; to the compromise text I will refer to as: Presidency text.

6.5.2 The Relation Between the Directive and the Coordination Regulation

6.5.2.1 The Priority of the Regulation

The system of the coordination Regulation will remain in place next to that of the Directive; if the coordination Regulations have more beneficial rules, these have priority. Thus in the case of medical care which becomes necessary, the Regulation is applied and the competent institutions make arrangements for the settlement of the costs; the patient does not have to pay the costs to the care provider. The

[20] Council of the European Union 15560/09 of 11 November 2009.

Directive does not change anything in this regard; however, it contains requirements on providing information, which may be helpful, as it appears that many care providers do not know these rules and in practice patients often have to pay the costs on the spot.

Secondly, the rules on planned care, which requires authorisation, remain in force, including the provisions which stipulate when authorisation must be given if the appropriate care for the patient's condition cannot be provided in their own country within a time-limit which is medically justifiable, taking into account his current state of health and the probable course of illness. Any additional costs of treatment will be covered by public funds. This follows from the Regulation and is not changed.

This priority of the coordination Regulation is laid down in Article 3(2) of the draft Directive that provides that when the circumstances under which an authorisation to go to another Member State in order to receive appropriate treatment under Article 22 of Regulation 1408/71 must be granted are met, the provisions of that Regulation shall apply and the provisions of Articles 6–9 of this Directive shall not apply. In the Presidency text, Article 3(2) was removed; Article 3(1) still provides that the Directive shall apply without prejudice to the coordination Regulations. Now, in Recital 23, it reads that the patient should not be deprived of the more beneficial rights guaranteed by the Regulations when the conditions are met. Therefore, any patient who requests an authorisation to receive a treatment appropriate to his/her condition in another Member State shall always be granted this authorisation under the conditions provided for in the regulations when the treatment in question cannot be given within the time medically justifiable, taking account of his/her current state of health and the probable course of the disease. However, if a patient instead explicitly requests to seek treatment under the terms of the Directive, the benefits which apply to reimbursement will be limited to those which apply under the Directive.

Thus, the text was amended with the effect that if a patient does not want to, or cannot follow the authorisation procedure, s/he does not have the benefits of the coordination Regulation. In the Presidency text the recital of the draft text was also deleted which read that the patient may choose which mechanism he prefers, but in any case, where the application of Regulation 1408/71 or 883/2004 is more beneficial for the patient, the patient should not be deprived of the rights guaranteed by those Regulations.

We may conclude that Regulation 883/2004 still has priority, but if the patient does not apply for authorisation, it is no longer provided that the more beneficial rules of the Regulation are applied. Thus, if patients are unaware of their rights, or are not willing or do not have the time to wait for the authorisation procedure, they can be worse off under the new text. This seems to constitute a discrepancy with the Court's case law. As we have seen in Sect. 6.3.2, the Court ruled that a person, who, despite the absence of authorisation has gone to another Member State for treatment, is entitled to be reimbursed directly by the competent institution for an amount equivalent to that which it would ordinarily have borne if authorisation had been granted in the first place (*Vanbraekel* judgment).[21] Where the initial text of the draft Directive carefully followed the Court's case law, the Member States in the Council are reluctant to do so. Since the case law of the Court was based on the Regulation itself and the draft Directive does not and cannot change this, the Court will probably stick to the *Vanbraekel* approach. For patients involved, this means lengthy procedures, and it is unfortunate that the Directive does not take such impediments away.

6.5.2.2 Definitions

In Article 4 of both texts of the draft Directive some important terms are defined. In the Presidency text, health care is defined as 'health services provided by health professionals to patients to assess, maintain or restore their state of health, including the prescription, dispensation and provision of medicinal products and medical devices'. This definition is meant to restrict the application of the Directive. Assistance in daily life by a third person, sometimes part of long term care provisions, seems to be excluded by this definition. The exclusion of such care was an important point of discussion in the Council.

Article 4 also defines the insured persons included in the Directive. These are persons, including members of their families and survivors, covered by Article 2 of Regulation 883/2004; also nationals of a third country covered by Regulation 859/2003, or who satisfy the conditions of the legislation of the Member State of affiliation for entitlement to benefits.

The Member State of affiliation is defined in the Presidency text. For persons covered by Regulation 883/2004 it is the Member State that is competent to grant, to the insured person, a prior authorisation to receive appropriate treatment. In the original text it was the State where the patient is an insured person. For third country nationals, the Member State of affiliation is the State which is competent to give authorisation. Thus, the more recent texts focus more on the State which is actually responsible for the payment of benefits, which may be another State than the one where a person is insured. This difference is relevant, in particular, in case a person does not reside in the competent State, and in the case of pensioners.

6.5.2.3 The Systems of Reimbursement

In addition to the system of the Regulation, the draft Directive puts in place an alternative mechanism, based on the Treaty provisions of free movement and the case law of the Court of Justice. This allows patients to seek health care in another Member State if they would have been entitled to this in their State of residence and be reimbursed up to the amount that would have been paid had they obtained

---

[21] ECJ, Case C-368/98 *Vanbraekel* [2001] *ECR* I-5363.

that treatment at home. The patients bear the financial risk of any additional costs arising. For hospital care there is a separate rule in the draft Directive (see, however, also the Presidency text, to be discussed below, which extends this exception).

Consequently, when the costs of health care are reimbursed according to the Directive, the provisions of the Directive apply, unless the patient is granted the authorisation pursuant to the coordination Regulation on the ground that the conditions of its Article 19 of Regulation 883/2004 are met. Member States can, as under the present case law and system, define the benefits they choose to provide. Consequently, if a particular treatment is not included in a national system, for example, forms of plastic surgery and hydro or balno-therapy, or spa cures, patients are not reimbursed if they make use of these in another Member State.

6.5.3 Reimbursement Under the Draft Directive

6.5.3.1 General

Under the judgments on Article 49 EC (now Article 56 TFEU), the patient bears the risk that health care in another Member State costs more than at home—s/he only gets reimbursed up to the amount that would have been paid if s/he had obtained that treatment at home. Under the coordination Regulations, that financial risk is borne by public funds.

The draft Directive closely follows the approach of the Court of Justice to Article 56 TFEU. It thus leaves the different systems of reimbursement intact. The European Commission considered in its memorandum to the draft Directive that patients might prefer health care abroad for two main reasons:

- the health care that they need is just not available in their own system, at least not within a reasonable time; or
- the health care is available at home, but it is more convenient for them to have it abroad because it is closer, quicker, or better.

The Commission argued that these are quite different reasons; one is a matter of need, one is a matter of personal preference. Therefore, the Commission continues, it seems reasonable they should be treated differently. If a patient has to go abroad to get the health care he needs because s/he cannot have it domestically, s/he should not lose out financially by doing so. But if s/he could stay at home and s/he just prefers to have the health care abroad, there is no reason why public funds should have to pay any additional costs as a result. The dual system remains based on this distinction. This line of argument is maintained during the discussions on the text of the draft Directive in the Council.

The Directive is thus relevant to the reimbursement rules on the basis of the freedom of services Treaty Article. Although the Directive will not change the system, its rules are important, since even after the *Kohll* and *Decker* and later judgments, there remained uncertainty on the reimbursement rules. The Directive is made in order to create more clarity; of course, it will have to remain consistent with the case law of the Court of Justice, as it has to abide with Article 56 TFEU. The reimbursement rules are laid down in Article 6 of the draft Directive; in the Presidency proposal in Articles 8–10. According to the text of the draft Directive, the Member State of affiliation shall ensure that insured persons travelling to another Member State with the purpose of receiving health care there will not be prevented from receiving this care where the treatment in question belongs to the benefits of the Member State of affiliation to which the insured person is entitled. The Member State of affiliation has to reimburse the costs to the insured person if it would have been paid for by its statutory social security system had the same or similar health care been provided in its territory. The level of reimbursement is up to the level of costs that would have been assumed had the same or similar health care been provided in the Member State of affiliation, without exceeding the actual costs of health care received. The Member State of affiliation may impose on this patient the same conditions, criteria of eligibility and regulatory and administrative formalities for receiving health care and reimbursement of health care costs as it would impose if the same or similar health care was provided in its territory, in so far as they are neither discriminatory nor an obstacle to freedom of movement of persons. These texts are the same in the draft Directive and in the Presidency proposal. A difference is made, however, in the distinction between hospital care and non-hospital care.

6.5.3.2 Reimbursement without Prior Authorisation

Like the Court of Justice, the draft Directive makes a distinction between non-hospital care and hospital care. The Memorandum to the Directive argues that it is not appropriate to establish or maintain the requirement of any prior authorisation for *non-hospital care* provided in another Member State. In so far as the reimbursement of such care remains within the limits of the cover guaranteed by the sickness insurance scheme of the Member State of affiliation, the absence of prior authorisation requirement will not undermine the financial equilibrium of social security systems. The memorandum further states that Member States may have limitations on the choice of provider or other domestic planning mechanisms which are applied domestically, including conditions, criteria of eligibility and regulatory and administrative formalities. These may also be applied to cross-border non-hospital health care, provided they respect internal market freedoms and any such restrictions on access to non-hospital health care abroad are necessary, proportionate and non-discriminatory.

This is laid down in Article 7 of the draft Directive (Article 8 of Presidency text), which provides that the Member State of affiliation shall not make the reimbursement of the costs of non-hospital care provided in another Member State subject to prior authorisation, where the cost of that care, if it had been provided in its territory, would have been paid for by its social security system. The Presidency text adds that the reimbursement does not exceed the actual costs of health care received.

Member States must make a mechanism for calculation of costs that are to be reimbursed to the insured person by the statutory social security system for health care provided in another Member State. This mechanism has to be based on objective, non-discriminatory criteria known in advance and the costs reimbursed according to this mechanism shall be not less than what would have been assumed had the same or similar health care been provided in the territory of the Member State of affiliation.

A major point of discussion on the draft Directive is whether Member States of application may limit the application on rules on reimbursement that are, by contract, accreditation or otherwise part of the *statutory* social security system of the Member State of treatment. This limitation seems to be contrary to the case law of the Court of Justice, as this case law allows limitations only on grounds of safety and quality of the care. One of the text proposals requires that the provider has a contract with the statutory system; this excludes providers who work independently. An alternative to this text was that the reimbursement may be limited to health care providers that meet at least the same or equivalent standards and guidelines, including provisions on supervision, as defined for providers that are part of the statutory system in the Member State of treatment, and who participate in liability insurance. The latter alternative wishes to guarantee the quality of treatment which it was intended to ensure by the former alternative text. It is not sure yet which text will survive the political discussions.

6.5.3.3 Reimbursement for Which Authorisation can be Required

General

It must be kept in mind that the Directive itself does not introduce a general prior authorisation system, but allows Member States to have such a system on condition that Member States can provide evidence that the conditions of the Directive are met. Article 9 provides that health care which may be subject to prior authorisation is limited to health care which (a) is made subject to planning in so far as it involves overnight hospital accommodation of the patient in question for at least one night or (b) is made subject to planning in so far as it requires use of highly specialised and cost-intensive medical infrastructure or medical equipment, or (c) involves treatments presenting a particular risk for the patient or the population. These situations were also found in the draft Directive, but in that text the care mentioned in (b) and (c) was to be included in a specific list set up by the Commission. Under the Presidency text, this is left to the individual Member States and that may mean a broader list of care subject to authorisation. This may lead to tensions with the case law of the Court, which solely made the distinction between hospital and non-hospital care.

Criteria to Allow Refusal Prior Authorisation in Draft Directive

Very important are the criteria mentioned in the text which allow Member States to refuse authorisation. Article 8(3) of the draft Directive mentioned:

- had the treatment been provided on its territory, it would have been assumed by its social security system; and
- the consequent outflow of patients seriously undermines or is likely to seriously undermine the financial balance of the social security system and the planning and rationalisation of hospital capacity, the maintenance of a balanced medical and hospital service open to all, or the maintenance of treatment capacity or medical competence on the territory of the concerned Member.

Furthermore, Article 8(4) provides that the prior authorisation system shall be limited to what is necessary and proportionate to avoid such impact, and shall not constitute a means of arbitrary discrimination. The Member States have to make publicly available all relevant information on the prior authorisation systems, as is provided by Article 8(5).

In such cases, the Directive provides that the introduction of a prior authorisation scheme is allowed under the following conditions.

A system of prior authorisation may be justified by the following elements: the need to plan the number of hospital infrastructures, their geographical distribution, the mode of their organisation, the equipment with which they are provided and even the nature of the health care which they are able to offer. The aim of such planning is to ensure, the Directive continues, within each Member State, access to a balanced range of quality hospital care, to secure efficient cost management and, so far as is possible, to avoid wastage of financial, technical or human resources.

Criteria to Allow Refusal Prior Authorisation in Presidency Proposal

The Presidency proposal gives more broadly defined escape routes. Article 9(5) reads that the Member State of affiliation may refuse to grant a prior authorisation for reasons including, but not limited to the following:

(a) the patient is not entitled to the treatment in question, in accordance with Article 8 of this Directive;
(b) if this health care can be provided on its territory within a time limit which is medically justifiable, taking into account the current state of health and the probable course of the illness of the person concerned;
(c) if the patient according to a clinical evaluation with reasonable certainty will be exposed to a patient safety risk that cannot be considered to be normal, taking into account the potential benefit for the patient of the sought cross-border health care;
(d) if the general public with reasonable certainty will be exposed to a substantial safety hazard as a result of the cross-border health care in question.

These elements are considerably broader than those of the draft Directive and are not exhaustive. Whereas the draft Directive referred to the planning arguments as established by the Court of Justice, the Presidency proposal refers to new elements and is not limitative. As we have seen in Sect. 6.4, the Court gave a set of limitative criteria which have to be satisfied in the case of refusal of authorisation, so it is unclear whether the new ones will meet a test by the Court on Article 56 TFEU.

Definition of Hospital Care

Following the Court's case law, there have been various discussions on the meaning of the term hospital care, as this may vary throughout the different health systems of the EU. This gives rise to different interpretations. The draft Directive gives 'a minimum EU definition' of hospital care. It defines hospital care as inpatient care: treatment that requires at least one night of stay in a hospital or clinic. This is laid down in Article 8(1) of the draft Directive. Thus, if a person is treated in a clinic and has to be checked the following day again by the clinic, or the second part of the treatment is to be given on this day, whereas he can stay in a hotel or with friends, that is not hospital care. In the Presidency proposal this is worded clearly: health care which is made subject to planning in so far as it involves overnight hospital accommodation of the patient in question of at least one night.

As we have seen, the draft Directive allows also considering certain other kinds of treatment as hospital treatment, if that treatment requires use of highly specialised and cost-intensive medical infrastructure or medical equipment, or involving treatments presenting a particular risk for the patient or the population. Article 8(1) stipulates that a regularly updated technical list of such treatments may be specifically defined by the Commission. The Presidency proposal also mentions this type of care, but does no longer leave the Commission to draw up the list; this is now the task of each Member State.

Reimbursement Rules

Some Member States do not have a set of defined reimbursement levels for particular types of care. This is, for example, the case in health systems with integrated public financing and provision. In this instance, Member States have to put in place a mechanism for cost calculation for cross-border health care, provided that this mechanism is based on objective, non-discriminatory criteria known in advance (Article 8(3) of Presidency text). This provision will remind the readers of the *Watts* case law.

Administrative Procedures

It is important also that Member States of affiliation have to ensure that administrative procedures related to authorisation, reimbursement of costs of health care and other conditions and formalities, are based on objective, non-discriminatory criteria, which are necessary and proportionate to the objective to be achieved. These criteria have to be publicly available in advance (Article 10 Presidency text). Procedural systems have to be easily accessible and capable of ensuring that requests are dealt with objectively and impartially within time limits set out and made public in advance by the Member States. Member States also have to specify in advance and in a transparent way the criteria for refusal of the prior authorisation.

In the draft Directive it was provided that Member States, when setting out the time limits within which requests for the use of health care in another Member State must be dealt with, have to take into account: (a) the specific medical condition, (b) the patient's degree of pain, (c) the nature of the patient's disability, and (d) the patient's ability to carry out a professional activity. These elements, introduced by the Court for assessing the duration of the waiting period, were now mentioned for the handling of the request. In Article 10 of the Presidency text this is limited to a much simpler text: urgency and individual circumstances shall be taken into account when dealing with such requests. In the text there are no longer criteria for assessing the waiting lists; thus this important part of the case law is not codified.

Finally, Member States have to ensure that any administrative decisions regarding the use of health care in another Member State are subject to administrative review and are also capable of being challenged in judicial proceedings, which include provision for interim measures.

6.5.4 Information

The Commission's Working Paper and the Memorandum to the Draft Directive acknowledge that it is often difficult for patients and professionals to identify what rights exist for reimbursement for cross-border health care. This was confirmed by a *Eurobarometer* survey,[22] which showed that 30% of the citizens in the European Union are not aware of the possibility to receive health care outside their country. The Member States' answers to a Commission's questionnaire also mentioned this

[22] Flash Eurobarometer Series #210, Cross-border health services in the EU, Analytical report, conducted by The Gallup Organisation, Hungary, upon the request of the European Commission, the Health and Consumer Protection Directorate-General (DG SANCO), 2007.

uncertainty.[23] This uncertainty and confusion on reimbursement rules is likely to make it more difficult for patients to use their rights in practice.

In addition it was reported that there were problems with the exchange of information between the care providers in the host State and the State of affiliation and with the availability at home of drugs and medical devices prescribed abroad.[24]

The drafters of the draft Directive wished, therefore, to ensure a clear framework for cross-border health care by providing sufficient clarity about rights to be reimbursed for health care provided in other Member States for those rights to be realised in practice and ensuring that the necessary requirements for high-quality, safe and efficient health care are also ensured for cross-border care.

The draft Directive also sets out the requirements for information on all essential aspects of cross-border health care to be provided to patients in order to achieve the objectives of the internal market. For this purpose national contact points for cross-border health care have to be established. The national contact points will have appropriate facilities to provide information on possibilities for cross-border health care and to provide practical assistance to patients if needed. In the Presidency text the task of these information points became limited: the Member State has to give information on its own system, and no longer also on a system of another Member State. The obligation to give information on solving transborder legal procedures and on extralegal solutions was also deleted.

6.6 Conclusions

The draft Directive (the text published by the Commission) followed very closely the case law of the Court of Justice. Thus, it left the dual system and the ensuing problems intact. One of these was that in the *Kohll* and *Decker* case law it was decided that the level of reimbursement would not be higher than what would have been paid under the national system. This approach of the Court was understandable: after all, it ruled that, despite the authorisation system of Regulation 1408/71, reimbursement had to take place, which was quite revolutionary. Therefore, it was logical that the Court was reluctant to rule that Member States had to pay higher bills than under their own rules. Neither had the Court room to decide that the settling of bills could be done in a way other than by advance payments, since the Regulation was not applicable and Article 49 EC (now Article 56 TFEU) did not have such effect.

[23] Commission Staff Working Document, accompanying the proposal for the patient mobility directive, SEC(2008) 2163, p. 12.

[24] Commission Staff Working Document, p. 14.

The drafters of the Directive were, however, able to rethink the system. It is unsatisfactory that not more progress has been made than merely following the case law. Now the proposed Directive lies down that in the case of non-hospital care no authorisation is needed, why not also introduce here a system that the costs are paid by the Member State of affiliation directly to the host State? The problem with the reimbursement under the present rules is that it is primarily to the advantage of wealthier and well-informed European citizens because it requires pre-payment and later reimbursement. This means that a person must have the financial means to be able to advance the payments for medical treatment. Given these rules citizens with expensive systems are more likely to migrate to countries with low cost systems, but the other direction is practically excluded.

Furthermore, the fact that patients are reimbursed only to the level of the rates of the State of affiliation is problematic in light of the principles of equal treatment and the free movement of persons. The patient has to pay the difference between the actual costs and the amount of reimbursement and thus patient mobility is restricted. Patient movement will, therefore, primarily take place to States in which treatment is provided at similar or lower costs structures than in the State of affiliation.

The relationship between the Directive and the Regulation is still awkward to the extent that elements relevant to the Regulation, including criteria for authorisation and for refusal of authorisation, are found in the Directive. It would be preferable to include these in the Regulation, but for political reasons this appears to remain difficult. Still, problems can arise if the Directive is not correctly implemented in a Member State, for instance the provisions on authorisation. How to apply the Regulation in that case? Suppose that the Directive is correctly implemented, but it is not in line with the previous case law. How to interpret the Regulation in that case? Thus the double source of reimbursement rules can lead to important difficulties.

Thus, the Directive leaves the dual system, which resulted from the case law of the Court of Justice, intact. It follows the *Kohll* and *Decker* case law and is thus mainly a conservative operation. Still, the Directive can have positive effects. As can be seen from the cases before the Court, Member States were very reluctant to accept the case law in this area, the *Watts* case, for instance, concerned the question whether the national health service, as public system with benefits in kind (instead of reimbursement) was subject to Article 49 EC (now Article 56 TFEU), whereas this question had already been answered in the *Müller-Fauré* judgment. National courts thus asked questions on issues which had been dealt with before by the Court of Justice. It is, therefore, useful that the Member States will be obliged to lay down important elements of the case law of the Court, including the objective criteria, in their authorisation procedures and the system for calculation of reimbursement in their national laws. After all it makes a serious difference between the situation where a Member State can be criticised and even be brought to Court since it failed to implement the directive fully and the situation in which an individual has to go to Court to claim reimbursement, like Mrs. Watts. Therefore, a Directive can be helpful to reinforce the position of the patient seeking cross-border health care. The obligations to make information points are also important: after all, there is a large difference between law in the books and law in practice, and the information points may help patients to realise their rights.

Other advantages of the draft Directive are still uncertain, since the initial text is under discussion. During the negotiation process some elements of the draft which implemented the case law were amended or left out from the text. This makes the problems with the dual system even bigger, since the text of the directive no longer fully clarifies uncertainties of the case law or terms of the Regulation and since there are now also discrepancies between the case law and the directive, and it is uncertain how the Court will deal with these.

One of the changes is that the text no longer mentions the criteria applicable in respect of the waiting lists.[25] Mentioning them was important for the application of the authorisation criteria mentioned in the Regulation. The lack of these criteria is unfortunate, as now the chance is missed to oblige Member States to make rules on waiting lists in their national law. Furthermore the Directive did not implement the aspect in the *Watts* case that the setting of waiting times should be done flexibly and dynamically, so that the period initially notified to the person concerned may be reconsidered in the light of any deterioration in his state of health occurring after the first request for authorisation. Moreover, the time limit for the waiting list must not exceed a medically acceptable period in the light of the patient's particular condition and clinical needs. Of course the criteria following from the case law are still valid, as they are based on the Treaty, but the criteria for the application of the authorisation procedure have now to be found in several sources.

The automatic priority of beneficial effects of the coordination Regulation in comparison with application of Article 56 TFEU was also abandoned and the possibilities of Member States to subject care to prior authorisation procedures were increased. Moreover the obligations to assist patients in information were reduced. This is unfortunate, as the advantages of the Directive were thus considerably reduced.

From these comments it follows that cross-border health care is a very sensitive issue. Member States are so fearful of the effects of opening the borders that the chance of harmonising the dual system was not taken and the negotiations of the Council widen the gap created by this system even more. Given the lack of support for making a more unified system, the Directive is, however, better than nothing, as it requires Member States to adjust their legislation and thus makes access to EU rights more accessible for the citizens.

[25] Sauter (2009), p. 3 assumes that this means that the case law of the Court is done away with, but of course Article 56 TFEU continues to apply and the Court will interpret the instruments discussed here in the light of this Article.

References

Jorens Y (2003) Cross-border health care in the European Union: up to a free movement of patients? In: Gesellschaft für Versicherungswissenschaft und –gestaltung, Soziale Sicherheit der Grenzgänger in Europa (Social security for frontier workers in Europe). Akademische Verlagsgesellschaft Aka, Berlin

Pennings F (2010) European social security law. Intersentia, Antwerp

Sauter W (2009) Patiëntenrechten bij grensoverschrijdende zorg. NTER, p. 3 ff

Stergiou HM (2006) Op één been kan men niet lopen. Het arrest Watts een stap dichterbij de harmonisatie van patiëntenmobiliteit? (Standing on one leg is not possible. From Watts to harmonising cross border health care?), NTER, p. 219

Van der Mei AP (2003) Free movement of persons within the European Community. Cross-border access to public benefit. OUP, Oxford

Chapter 7
Cooperation Between Health Care Authorities in the Proposed Directive on Patients' Rights in Cross-Border Healthcare

Tamara Hervey

Contents

7.1 Introduction

Lawyers focus on rights. EU lawyers focus on rights in EU law. The focus of most[1] books on EU law is on the development of rights, through 'negative integration' (the interpretation by the Court of Justice of the European Union (Court of Justice) of the directly effective (hence, rights-giving) provisions of the EU Treaties) and 'positive integration' (the adoption, using the 'classic Community method', of binding legislation (often rights-giving) by the EU legislature). This

[1] With some notable exceptions, for example of Craig and de Búrca (2008), Chapter 5.

T. Hervey (✉)
School of Law, University of Sheffield, Sheffield, UK
e-mail: t.hervey@sheffield.ac.uk

J. W. van de Gronden et al. (eds.), *Health Care and EU Law*,
Legal Issues of Services of General Interest, DOI: 10.1007/978-90-6704-728-9_7,

perspective suggests that the most important features of the proposed Directive on patients' rights in cross-border health care are those outlined in Chaps. 4–6 of this book. The proposed Directive seeks to consolidate and clarify case law of the Court of Justice on the application of Article 56 TFEU to cross-border receipt of health care services and its interaction with the social security Regulation 883/2004/EC (former Regulation 1408/71/EEC).[2] The 'meat' of the proposed Directive is found in Chapter II (responsibilities of Member States with regards to cross-border health care) and Chapter III (reimbursement of costs of cross-border health care). These sections of the proposed Directive, plus much of Chapter I (general provisions, including definitions), concern rights in EU law. Why, then, have the editors of this book included an entire chapter on Chapter IV of the proposed Directive, which concerns 'Cooperation on Healthcare'? Why have I agreed to write it?

I believe that, at least since the 1990s, in addition to and alongside the rights-focus of EU law, a range of cooperative activities that are based neither on negative integration nor on positive integration in the sense of the 'classic Community method' have proliferated amongst the European Union and its institutions, and in interactions between those institutions and various state, sub-state (for example, regional) and non-governmental actors. The collective term usually employed to describe these activities is 'new governance'.[3] I think that these 'new governance' activities are or will turn out to be as significant for the EU and its legal order as activities that fit neatly within the model of the 'classic Community method'. Moreover, I think that EU lawyers, especially academic lawyers, should pay attention to 'new governance' activities, even though they challenge the dominant analytical model for EU law, which implicitly sees the EU as hierarchical, supranational, *sui generis* and either constitutionalised or constitutionalising.[4] In some ways, these activities remind us that the EU is a creation of public international law, for these kinds of mechanisms have long been used by international organisations.[5] But in other ways, these activities leave the analysis of the EU implicitly as if it were a state, or a state-in-waiting, untouched, as they echo

---

[2] Regulation 883/2004 of the European Parliament and the Council of 29 April 2004 on the coordination of social security schemes *OJ* 2004 L166/1, which repealed Regulation 1408/71/EEC, and came into force on 1 May 2010, on the adoption of the implementing legislation, Regulation 987/2009 of the European Parliament and of the Council of 16 September 2009 laying down the procedure for implementing Regulation (EC) No 883/2004 on the coordination of social security systems *OJ* 2009 L 284/1, Article 97.

[3] See, for instance, Scott and Trubek (2002), pp. 1–18; de Búrca and Scott (2006); Walker and de Búrca (2007), pp. 519–538; Trubek and Trubek (2007), pp. 539–564; Sabel and Zeitlin (2008), pp. 271–327; NeJaime (2009), pp. 323–399; Gunningham (2009), pp. 145–166.

[4] For a classical exposition, see Weiler (1991), p. 2403. For a critique, see Hunt (2007), pp. 135–155.

[5] For instance, 'OMC-like' processes have long been used by the OECD and the IMF; see, e.g., Schäfer (2006), pp. 70–88.

activities that are being used within states[6] (as an alternative to, or alongside, the market or traditional top-down state regulation) to tackle the 'wicked problems'[7] of the day.

For me, the chapter in the proposed Directive on 'Cooperation in Healthcare' is an important part of the unfolding story of the EU's engagement with health care.[8] Even if the Directive had not been proposed. I think that most of the proposals in Chapter IV would have survived in some form or other. That is why it is worth analysing them: what is their provenance, what are their aims, what actors do they engage and what, in general, do they envisage as the future direction of European Union involvement in health care? The chapter looks at each of the key provisions in Chapter IV in turn: the duty of cooperation (Sect. 7.3.1); recognition of prescriptions (Sect. 7.3.2); 'European reference networks' (Sect. 7.3.3); 'E-health' (Sect. 7.3.4); and health technology assessment (Sect. 7.3.5). Before turning to these questions, a brief outline of the story of the proposal, as at the date of submission of this chapter (30 June 2010), is set out (Sect. 7.2). Finally, some conclusions are drawn about the likely future direction of the matters discussed in the chapter (Sect. 7.4).

7.2 The Proposed Directive on Patients' Rights in Cross-Border Healthcare: Where are We Now?

Nobody disagrees that it was the application by the Court of Justice of what is now Article 56 TFEU on free movement of services to cross-border healthcare litigation that prompted the eventual development of the proposed Directive on

---

[6] For discussion of 'new governance' in the USA and Australia, see, for example, Loebel (2004), pp. 262–390; Trubek (2006); Karkkainen (2006); Alexander (2009), pp. 117–185; Gunningham (2009), pp. 145–166.

[7] A 'wicked problem' is one where the process of understanding or defining the problem cannot be achieved without developing solutions, so 'top down' 'scientific' approaches to solving the problem are not feasible; there is no clear moment when a solution is reached; it is not possible to evaluate solutions objectively as 'right' or 'wrong', only 'better' or 'worse', depending upon one's ideological standpoint; every attempt to solve the problem has significant consequences, many of which are unforeseeable; it is not possible to classify problems into types and thus apply similar solutions to similar types of problems; each problem is a symptom of another, interconnected problem; and alternative descriptions of the problem, explanations of the cause of the problem or the nature of the problem itself point to different solutions. See Rittel and Webber (1973), pp. 155–169 and Conklin (2005), Chapter 1. Authors such as Charles Sabel and Neil Gunningham have used the concept of 'wicked problems' in their work on new governance (see Sabel (2004), pp. 173–195 at p. 181 (available http://www2.law.columbia.edu/sabel/papers.htm)); Gunningham (2007).

[8] See Hervey (2006) for an earlier account of the story and Hervey and Vanhercke (2010) for more recent picture. See also Greer (2009, 2008), pp. 219–231; Steffen (2005); Randall (2000).

patients' rights in cross-border healthcare. The Court was the driver in this story.[9] However, the proposal, as eventually promulgated, picks up a number of pre-existing strands of activity that would probably have continued to gain momentum even without the proposed Directive. Their incorporation into the Directive will strengthen their resource base and their visibility, and, hence, their importance.

The case law of the Court of Justice on free movement of patients[10] has increased levels of uncertainty, both for individual patients, who may not be entirely sure what their entitlements are, but also more importantly for the governments of Member States, and the authorities of their public health care systems. By the early to mid 2000s, the case law had built up a sufficient head of steam that the governments of the Member States were keen to deal with the resultant uncertainties.[11] However, the difficulty in this instance was that the obvious route, through internal market legislation, was not politically acceptable. This is because health care is not seen as an economic 'service' in European societies, and to attach health care to the general Directive on services in the internal market was politically impossible. The so-called 'Bolkestein Directive' on services in the internal market was watered down from the Commission's original proposal, Article 23 of which codified the case law on free movement of health care services. Directive 2006/123/EC[12] does not apply to 'health care services whether or not they are provided via health care facilities, and regardless of the ways in which they are organised and financed at national level or whether they are public or private.'[13]

The European Parliament and Council then called for a specific legal instrument on health care services in the internal market. The European Commission (DG Sanco) ran a public consultation in 2006–2007, consulting a wide range of stakeholders, both in person and via an on-line consultation, on the way forward.[14]

---

[9] See, for example, Sauter (2008).

[10] ECJ, Joined Cases 286/82 and 26/83 *Luisi and Carbone* [1984] *ECR* 377; ECJ, Case C-159/90 *Society for the Protection of Unborn Children Ireland* v. *Grogan* [1991] *ECR* I-468; ECJ, Case C-120/95 *Decker* [1998] *ECR* I-1831; ECJ, Case C-158/96 *Kohll* [1998] *ECR* I-1931; ECJ, Case C-157/99 *Geraets-Smits and Peerbooms* [2001] *ECR* I-5473; ECJ, Case C-368/98 *Vanbraekel* [2001] *ECR* I-5363; ECJ, Case C-385/99 *Müller-Fauré/Van Riet* [2003] *ECR* I- 4509; ECJ, Case C-56/01 *Inizan* [2003] *ECR* I-12403; ECJ, Case C-8/02 *Leichtle* [2004] *ECR* I-2641; ECJ, Case C-145/03 *Keller* [2005] *ECR* I-2529; ECJ, Case C-372/04 *Watts* [2006] *ECR* I-4325; ECJ, Case C-466/04 *Herrera* [2006] *ECR* I-5341; ECJ, Case C-444/05 *Stamatelaki* [2007] *ECR* I-3185; ECJ, Case C-208/07 *von Chamier-Glisczinski*, *ECR* I-6095; ECJ, Case C-336/08 *Reinke* n.y.r. 14 October 2010.

[11] Initiatives included the High Level Process of Reflection; the Commission's 2003 Review; and the Commission's 2006–2007 stakeholder consultation. For discussion see Sauter (2008); Hervey (2006, 2007), pp. 303–333.

[12] Directive 2006/123/EC of the European Parliament and Council of 12 December 2006 on services in the internal market *OJ* 2006 L 376/36.

[13] Directive 2006/123/EC, Article 2(2)(f).

[14] European Commission, *Communication on the consultation regarding Community action on health services* SEC (2006) 1195/4, September 2006.

The Commission was supposed to bring forward a proposal for health care services in the internal market in 2007. Although an unofficial version of a proposal was circulating around Brussels in late 2007, it was never formally promulgated as a proposal, probably because the Council and Commission were concerned not to derail the Treaty of Lisbon. The Commission proposal eventually appeared in July 2008.[15] The proposal was unveiled alongside (yet another) review of the EU's social policy agenda, which was tied to the Lisbon strategy on growth and employment. It was promulgated along with DG-Employment-sponsored proposals on works councils; incorporating international maritime working standards into EU law; and anti-discrimination. Nevertheless, DG Sanco was very much in the driving seat for the proposed Directive on patients' rights in cross-border health care. The then new Health Commissioner Androulla Vassilou, a Cypriot and lawyer by training, had taken up her post in February of 2007.

The legal basis of the proposal was originally simply Article 114 TFEU, so the Directive was subject to what is now known as the 'ordinary legislative procedure', following the amendments to the EU Treaties made by the Treaty of Lisbon. Under the 'ordinary legislative procedure', Articles 289 and 294 TFEU provide that the Commission proposal must be agreed by both the European Parliament and the Council. The Council acts according to qualified majority voting.[16]

The proposal was discussed in the EPSCO Council (Council for Employment, Social Policy, Health and Consumer Affairs) in December 2008, under the French Presidency, and again in June 2009 under the Czech Presidency, where views were divided. The French Presidency reportedly sought to remove any mention of increased transparency around quality and safety standards in health care. The Council also sought to change the Commission's proposals on the prior authorisation system. The Council's compromise texts included strengthened references to subsidiarity, national competence over the organisation of health care systems, and the explicit exclusion of 'long-term care'. Disagreements over the legal basis led to Commissioner Vassilou agreeing to re-examine the possibility of Article 168 TFEU as a joint legal basis, alongside Article 114 TFEU. Several Member States also expressed concerns that the detail of the implementation of the proposal was to be entrusted to comitology processes.

The Swedish Presidency (July–December 2009) considered the proposal one of its priorities. The proposal was discussed at an informal EPSCO Council in July 2009. Over the course of its Presidency, Sweden tabled no less than four compromise texts. In addition, the original proposed text was subject to a technical amendment by Council, to take into account changes to the legislative procedure and competence made by the Treaty of Lisbon 2009.[17] Nevertheless, when the

---

[15] Proposal for a Directive of the European Parliament and of the Council on the application of patients' rights in cross-border health care COM(2008) 414 final.

[16] Article 16(3) TEU and Protocol No. 16 on Transitional Provisions, TFEU, Article 3(3).

[17] Council of the European Union, Note from the Committee of Permanent Representatives to the Council, Interinstitutional File 2008/0142; 16005/09, Brussels 26 November 2009 ('Council text, November 2009').

EPSCO Council discussed the text on 1–2 December 2009, they failed to reach a political agreement on a common position. EU health ministers met again on 16 December 2009, but remained divided. Concerns ranged from national competence over health care to a wide range of views about the scope and implementation of the Directive. As the blocking minority, which included Hungary, Ireland, Portugal and five other Member States, was led by Spain, which was the next holder of the Council Presidency, it was considered unlikely that the proposal would progress further in Council during the first half of 2010.

However, although the Spanish presidency programme did not explicitly mention the proposed Directive,[18] Spain took the lead in forging a compromise text that would be acceptable to sufficient Member States. Following an informal meeting of health ministers in April 2010,[19] the EPSCO Council meeting of June 2010 agreed the proposal.[20] Amongst the significant changes was a new provision clarifying the situation of pensioners living in another Member State, but returning to their country of origin for their health care. With its large population of pensioners from northern Member States, Spain was particularly concerned at the possible ramifications of the proposal, as it originally stood, for its national health care system. A revised legal basis was agreed, of both Article 114 and Article 168 TFEU, which was said to strike a balance between the application of internal market law to health care services and the competences of the Member States for the organisation and provision of health care services, as recognised by Article 168(7) TFEU.

In the meantime, the proposal has completed the first reading by the European Parliament. The complexity of the text led the rapporteur, John Bowis MEP,[21] to postpone the vote in the Committee on Environment, Public Health and Food Safety (ENVI), in agreement with his shadow rapporteurs: Dagmar Roth-Behrendt, Jules Maaten, Kartika Liotard and Kathy Sinnott, MEPs. The ENVI Committee adopted Bowis's report, with over 800 amendments, on 31 March 2009, with a vote taking over 90 min. Although one of Bowis's key groups of amendments was driven by a concern to ensure that the Directive meets the needs of all patients, including under-privileged patients, and not just patients with the financial means to avail themselves of cross-border health care, this failed to convince the Socialist group of MEPs (PES). The Socialist group abstained in committee, on the grounds that they take the view that Article 114 TFEU, is not an appropriate legal basis for the measure. The European Parliament then adopted the proposal in plenary on

---

[18] http://www.eu2010.es/export/sites/presidencia/comun/descargas/Spanish_Presidency_Program.pdf. The programme says that the presidency will 'foster patients' quality and security improvement initiatives' and 'promote e-health', p. 34.

[19] Council of the European Union, General Secretariat of the Council note to Working Group on Public Health, Interinstitutional File 2008/0142; 9001/10, Brussels, 26 April 2010.

[20] Council of the European Union, Council Meeting (Employment, Social Policy, Health and Consumer Affairs), Interinstitutional File 2008/0142; 9948/10, Brussels, 28 May 2010 ('Council text, June 2010').

[21] Member of the Christian Democrat/Conservative European People's Party Group in the European Parliament. Former UK Health Minister.

23 April 2009, by 297 votes for, 120 against and 152 abstentions, mainly from the Socialist group, on the legal basis issue. Following Bowis's retirement from the European Parliament, Françoise Grossetete MEP[22] took over the dossier in September 2009.

Even if the significant opposition to the proposal had prevailed, and the proposal had not been adopted, most of the provisions in Chapter IV on cooperation in health care are likely to continue in some form or other. The following section considers why this is the case, by exploring the provenance and history of each provision, its aims, and the actors it engages. This approach draws on Scott Greer's observation that EU governance mechanisms, including those in the health care field, will continue to flourish only if they promote some kind of tangible benefit for participants, either involving learning or governance or both.[23] Finally, some conclusions will be drawn about the likely future directions of European Union involvement in health care policy in these areas.

7.3 Chapter IV Cooperation on Healthcare

7.3.1 Duty of Cooperation[24]/Mutual Assistance and Cooperation[25]

Article 13 of the Commission's proposal provides:

(a) Member States shall render such mutual assistance as is necessary for the implementation of this Directive.
(b) Member States shall facilitate cooperation in cross-border health care provision at regional and local level as well as through information and communication technologies, cross-border health care provided on a temporary or ad hoc basis and other forms of cross-border cooperation.

The European Parliament proposes to add the following provisions:

(c) Member States, particularly neighbouring countries, may conclude agreements with one another concerning the continuation or potential further development of cooperation arrangements.
(d) Member States shall guarantee that registers in which health professionals are listed can be consulted by relevant authorities of other Member States.

---

[22] Also Member of the Christian Democrat/Conservative European People's Party Group in the European Parliament.

[23] Greer (forthcoming).

[24] COM(2008) 414 final, Commission, July 2008; Resolution A6-0233/2009, European Parliament, April 2009.

[25] Council texts, November 2009 and June 2010; European Parliament text Jan 2011.

(e) Member States shall immediately and proactively exchange information about disciplinary and criminal findings against health professionals where they impact upon their registration or their right to provide services.

The Council's November 2009 and June 2010 texts propose a more detailed and specific first paragraph, and a less detailed second paragraph:

(1) Member States shall render such mutual assistance as is necessary for the implementation of this Directive, including the exchange of information about standards and guidelines on quality and safety, including provisions on supervision, in order to facilitate the implementation of Article 8.7, and including mutual assistance aiming to clarify the content of invoices.
(2) Member States shall facilitate cooperation in cross-border health care provision at regional and local level.

The original Commission proposal does not seem controversial. It simply repeats in this specific context the general duty of sincere cooperation to which Member States have agreed in Article 4(3) TEU. However, discussions at the Council revealed that several Member States were unsure about the legal basis of this whole section of the Commission proposal, and whether it is within the EU's powers to mandate cooperation in the field of health care. The addition of Article 168 TFEU as a joint legal basis may have removed these objections. However, several matters remain unclear in the somewhat 'telegraphic' text. There is particular lack of clarity (and disagreement) about whether this section applies only to support *cross-border* health care, or whether it applies to developing the quality and safety of *all* health care within the EU. The specific reference to Article 8.7 in the Council's November 2009 text suggests the former; cooperation is specifically 'in order to' facilitate the limitation of the obligation to reimburse *cross-border* health care to situations where providers meet 'at least the same or equivalent standards and guidelines on quality and safety', where providers are subject to professional liability insurance or equivalent, and other 'overriding reasons of general interest'. The cooperation duty in this provision is, therefore, simply to promote sufficient transparency and cross-border understanding to assess questions of whether quality and safety arrangements are equivalent, or whether insurance is in place. It does not involve a duty to share information or cooperate over quality or safety arrangements in health care provision more generally. And, of course, the mere duty to cooperate in exchanging information will not in itself resolve disagreements about whether quality and safety standards and procedures are indeed equivalent. Some Member States have gone much further than others in developing such procedures, and those with well-developed arrangements are unlikely to accept those whose arrangements involve a lighter touch.

That said, the Member States have already used EU level institutional structures to cooperate in cross-border health care. For instance, in 2005 the High Level Group on Health Services and Medical Care (composed of senior officials from

Member States and chaired by the Director General of DG Sanco,[26]) developed the *EU Guidelines for Purchase of Treatment Abroad*. The Guidelines form a framework for commissioners of health care established in different Member States to use when purchasing or providing cross-border health care. They cover applicable law, liability arrangements, data protection, pricing, public procurement, and specific contractual matters. In addition, a number of arrangements to share health care provision border areas have already been established, such as in Valka (Latvia)/Valga (Estonia), Gorizia (Italy)/Nova Gorica (Slovenia), and the shared hospital in Cerdania (France)/Cerdanya (Spain), a sparsely populated area of the Pyrenees.[27] Perhaps more fundamentally, the health care strand of the OMC on social inclusion involves the development of indicators on quality and safety that apply to all health care within the EU. The OMC promotes the idea that Member States share problems in health care fields (the ageing population; balancing financial sustainability of health care systems with patient choice in the context of technological development) and can, therefore, profitably share solutions. Quality of care and patient safety are seen as part of the solution in the OMC narrative. Evidence-based, targeted medical interventions, within systems that are focused on primary care and health promotion, are presented as representing greater 'value for public money' in the OMC-social's documentation. The aspiration is that the health care systems of the Member States will converge around models of best practice, which emerge from the comparative iteration that is inherent in the OMC's mandatory processes. The EU is also using its structural funds to support health care reform and capacity-building in under-developed regions of the EU.

The European Parliament's concern for the transparency of registers of health professionals to health authorities in other Member States, and the obligation 'immediately and proactively [to] exchange information about disciplinary and criminal findings against health professionals where they impact upon their registration or their right to provide services', reflects the position of the patients' rights lobby. The possibility of health care professionals providing treatment to patients from other Member States in a situation where they are no longer permitted to provide treatment to home patients is one that in theory would not be feasible, as the home state would be the place where licensing or registration had to be satisfied. However, public fears of 'rogue doctors' run strong, and a cross-border health care situation might make it easier for a health care professional to hide the fact that her licence to practice had been revoked. The proposal here simply requires transparency of matters which, as good practice, ought to be transparent in any event.

---

[26] European Commission, *Communication from the Commission Follow-up to the high level reflection process on patient mobility and health care developments in the European Union* COM(2004) 301 final.

[27] Bertinato et al. (2005) and Rosenmöller et al. (2006).

7.3.2 Recognition of Prescriptions Issued in Another Member State

Article 14 of the Commission proposal concerns recognition of prescriptions issued in another Member State. It applies only to medicinal products that are authorised to be marketed[28] in the territory of the Member State in which the prescription has been presented for dispensing. This makes sense, otherwise the entire system of marketing authorisation which applies to medicinal products in the EU could be bypassed. Restrictions on cross-border recognition of prescriptions are to be prohibited unless they:

(a) 'are limited to what is necessary and proportionate to safeguard human health and are non-discriminatory; or
(b) are based on legitimate and justified doubts about the authenticity of content of an individual prescription.'

Cross-border recognition of prescriptions concerns free movement of both goods and services within the EU. Regulation of pharmacists can also engage freedom of establishment and free movement of capital. The Court of Justice has already considered the application of the Treaty rules (now Articles 34, 49, 56, 63 TFEU) to national laws on pharmacies and the supply of pharmaceuticals, including prescription pharmaceuticals.[29] The proposal consolidates the emerging principles in this case law, in particular the respect for what are regarded as necessary and proportionate restrictions on cross-border movement.

For instance, the *DocMorris* case[30] concerned German law on sale of medicinal products, which provided that medicinal products that can only be bought in pharmacies (which, of course, include prescription-only pharmaceuticals), may not be sold over the internet. DocMorris, a Dutch pharmacy, set up an internet business, aimed at consumers in other Member States, including Germany. A German association of pharmacies challenged the practices of DocMorris. The question before the Court of Justice was: was the German law in breach of Article 30 TFEU? The Court found that national law prohibiting sale of pharmaceuticals by internet and mail order inhibited the free movement of goods. The restriction could in principle have been justified with respect to prescription-only pharmaceuticals, because of the greater risks posed to consumers and the system of fixed prices

[28] Under Directive 2001/83/EC of the European Parliament and of the Council of 6 November 2001 on the Community code relating to medicinal products for human use *OJ* 2001 L 311/67, Article 21. Or under Regulation 726/2004/EC of the European Parliament and of the Council of 31 March 2004 laying down Community procedures for the authorisation and supervision of medicinal products for human and veterinary use and establishing a European Medicines Agency *OJ* 2004 L 136/1.

[29] For instance, ECJ, Case C-322/01 *Deutscher Apothekerverband eV* v. *0800 DocMorris NV and Jacques Waterval* [2003] *ECR* I-4887.

[30] ECJ, Case C-322/01 *DocMorris* [2003] *ECR* I-4887.

applicable to them as part of the German health system.[31] However, the Court found that no evidence of the necessity of the national rule had been submitted to the Court.[32]

Several pharmacists and a pharmacists' professional association established in Germany also challenged a decision by the Saarland authorities to the effect that DocMorris was permitted to open a branch pharmacy in Saarbrucken.[33] German legislation provided that the right to own and run a pharmacy is limited to professionally qualified pharmacists only. The Saarland authorities, and DocMorris, argued that this national law must be 'disapplied', as being inconsistent with EU law on freedom of establishment.[34] The Court found that there was a restriction on freedom of establishment. However, the Court went on to hold that the restriction could be justified by 'the objective of ensuring that the provision of medicinal products to the public is reliable and of good quality'.[35] Adopting a precautionary approach, the Court confirmed that a Member State need not wait until a risk becomes fully apparent, but, where there is uncertainty about risks to human health, Member States may take protective measures.[36] Pharmaceuticals are different from other goods, because their misuse causes serious harm to human health, and is also a burden on public financial resources, because in most Member States the prescription of medicinal products is borne financially by public insurance or taxation-based health care systems.[37] The Court distinguished an earlier case,[38] on the basis that pharmaceuticals are more harmful to health if misused than optical products. Pharmacists, professionally trained and responsible, are different from non-pharmacists who operate in the pharmaceutical retail sector. Therefore, a Member State may justifiably license only pharmacists to sell pharmaceuticals, on the grounds of protection of public health and the financial balance of social security systems.[39]

A similar approach is found in *Commission* v. *Germany* (*Pharmacies*),[40] in which a German rule making it impossible in practice for German hospitals to be supplied on a regular basis by pharmacies established in other Member States was found to be justified on the ground of protection of public health. It is also found in

---

[31] Para 117.

[32] Para 123.

[33] ECJ, Joined Cases C-171 and 172/07 *Apothekerkammer des Saarlandes and Others and Helga Neumann-Seiwert* v. *Saarland and Ministerium für Justiz, Gesundheit und Soziales (joined party DocMorris)* [2009] *ECR* I-0000 (n.y.r.), 19 May 2009.

[34] In line with ECJ, Case 6/64 *Costa* v. *ENEL* [1964] *ECR* 585; ECJ, Case 106/77 *Simmenthal* [1978] *ECR* 629.

[35] Para 28.

[36] Para 29.

[37] Para 33.

[38] ECJ, Case C-140/03 *Commission* v. *Greece* (*Opticians*) [2005] *ECR* I-3177.

[39] Paras 34–39.

[40] ECJ, Case C-141/07 *Commission* v. *Germany* (*Pharmacies*) [2008] *ECR* I-6935.

Commission v. *Italy* (*Pharmacies*),[41] involving Italian laws allowing only pharmacists to own and operate private pharmacies. The Court also held that this national law was a restriction on freedom of establishment.[42] But again, relying on the same reasoning, the Court found the national rules to be justified.

The Court's approach is likely to continue, as it hears further cases on related topics. For instance, the Commission launched enforcement proceedings against Estonia for its national rules prohibiting recognition of medical prescriptions made out by medical practitioners who are qualified to act in their Member State of establishment but are not registered in Estonia.[43] In this case law, the Court, whilst in principle promoting the free movement implicit in an internal market, in practice (at the justification stage of its reasoning) respects the special nature of prescriptions, and the role of pharmacists in dispensing prescriptions, both as elements of public health or consumer safety policy within the Member States, and as elements of the public financing of health care, given the relationships in the relevant Member States between pricing arrangements and prescription-only medicinal products.

The Commission's proposal echoes this approach, providing that restrictions on recognition of individual prescriptions must be 'limited to what is necessary and proportionate to safeguard human health', 'non-discriminatory' and 'based on legitimate and justified doubts about the authenticity or content of an individual prescription.' In order to bring this provision into effect, the Commission is charged with developing 'measures enabling a pharmacist[44] to verify' whether a prescription is authentic. Verification is to be supported through what was originally described an EU 'prescription template' (but is now 'a non-exhaustive list of elements to be included in prescriptions'); and also by the interoperability of e-prescriptions. The practical implications of the original proposed measures would have been quite far reaching for prescribing practice and the operation of pharmacies within Member States across the EU. However, the Council's June 2010 text has dropped the idea of an EU level 'prescription template' and only requires the Commission to develop 'guidelines supporting the Member States in developing the inter-operability of e-prescriptions.' The use of soft law here, but without even a soft EU level measure to be used as a template or implied best practice, is likely to slow the rate of Europeanisation here in practice. Furthermore, whether the Directive will open up the types of markets at issue in the *Commission* v. *Germany* or *Commission* v. *Italy* cases is much less clear. In the first instance, the mutual recognition of prescriptions will probably only be of assistance to individual migrant workers and other frequent travellers. Some individuals may seek lower co-payments by sourcing prescription-only drugs over the internet, in the

---

41 ECJ, Case C-531/06 *Commission* v. *Italy* (*Pharmacies*) [2009] *ECR* I-4103.

42 Para 45.

43 See European Commission, Free movement of services: infringement proceedings against Estonia and Portugal, IP/08/1033, Brussels, 26 June 2008.

44 A 'health professional' in the Council text, June 2010.

same way as medical tourists now buy non-prescription drugs in states where they are cheaper. But over time, the interoperability of prescriptions across borders may assist large health care providers who seek to reap benefits of economies of scale by operating across more than one Member State, and seek to use litigation to remove national regulatory measures that impede this. The proposal as currently framed seeks to operate as a brake on such potential future developments.

One of the elements of the Commission's proposal that has proved problematic in Council is the use of delegated power to determine the detail of provisions. This was the case for verification measures, e-prescriptions, and the correct identification of medicinal products or devices prescribed in one Member State and dispensed in another. A committee of representatives of Member States, chaired by the Commission, in accordance with Decision 99/468/EC,[45] is to assist the Commission in implementing the proposed Directive. The 'regulatory procedure' of Decision 99/468/EC, Article 5, applies in this instance. Under that procedure, the Commission may only adopt a measure if it is in accord with the Opinion of the committee (voting in accordance with the qualified majority voting rules). Otherwise, or if there is no Opinion delivered within the time frame set (3 months), then the matter goes to Council.[46] In practice, therefore, it is likely to take quite some time before these things actually come to fruition, as the very wide disparities between prescriptions and prescribing practice across the Member States, and the significant vested interests[47] in the national status quo, mean that agreement in committee, or in Council, is likely to be difficult to achieve.

The Council's June 2010 text has circumscribed the Commission's delegated powers under the Directive. Use of the comitology procedure is for a 5-year period, in the first instance, towards the end of which the Commission must report. Delegated acts must be notified to both Council and the European Parliament.[48] Furthermore, the use of comitology for cross-border recognition of prescriptions and for the e-health provisions is subject to a revocation procedure. Either the European Parliament or the Council may prospectively (not retrospectively) revoke the Commission's delegated powers here.[49] Moreover, the European Parliament and Council also have the power to object, giving reasons, to a delegated act adopted under the Directive, within a period of 2 months of its adoption.[50] This formulation has been used in recent EU legislation, particularly in areas

[45] *OJ* 1999 L 184/23.

[46] The European Parliament must also be informed.

[47] For instance those of the pharmaceutical industry, medical professional organisations, national funding authorities and patients' groups.

[48] Council text, June 2010, Article 16a.

[49] Ibid., Article 16b.

[50] Extendable by a further 2 months, Council text, June 2010, Article 16c.

concerning energy and the environment,[51] and reflects a compromise in terms of the need for the Member States to retain control over the Commission's delegated authority (even as circumscribed as it already is in the context of the comitology procedure), yet the need to establish EU level regulatory detail.

The European Parliament sought to amend the proposal to allow restrictions on cross-border recognition of prescriptions also on grounds of 'the status of the prescriber'. This would seem to be consistent with the Court's developing case law on the special position of pharmacists in EU law. The European Parliament also seeks to add text to the effect that cross-border recognition of prescriptions 'shall not affect':

(i) National rules on prescribing and dispensing (such as rules on generic substitution—these rules are used as cost-containment measures in the Member States);
(ii) National rules on reimbursement of cross-border prescriptions; and
(iii) 'Any professional or ethical duty that would require the pharmacist to refuse to dispense had the prescription been issued' in the home Member State.

Several of these proposals are now in the Council's June 2010 text, which states that the recognition of prescriptions shall not affect national rules governing dispensing or rules governing generic or other substitution. The text also now makes it explicit that the rules on reimbursement are covered by Chapter III of the proposed Directive on patients' rights in cross-border health care, and are not affected by this section.

Also the European Parliament sought to add a provision to the effect that where a prescription is issued in the Member State of treatment for a medicinal product not normally available on prescription in the Member State of affiliation, it is up to the Member State of affiliation to decide whether to 'authorise exceptionally' or 'to provide an alternative medicinal product deemed to be as effective'. This is about cost-containment, because Member States use lists of products that can be reimbursed, and these differ from Member State to Member State. The European Parliament is seeking to ensure that the Member State that pays, gets to decide, and patients cannot effectively 'forum shop' and force their home state to pay for a prescription that they could not have got at home.

Another cost-containment driven proposal is found in the Council's November 2009 and June 2010 texts. This provides that the Commission (again acting through comitology procedures) shall take measures to ensure the correct identification of pharmaceutical products, especially where the legislation of the dispensing Member State permits substitution of another, equivalent, product for the prescribed product. Given the significant differences in price between proprietary brands and generics, the ability to substitute is an important measure for cost-containment within some national health care systems. The Council's text states that the International Non-

[51] See, for instance, Proposal for a Regulation of the European Parliament and of the Council on European environmental economic accounts COM(2010) 132 final; Directive 2010/31/EU of the European Parliament and of the Council of 19 May 2010 on the energy performance of buildings, *OJ* 2010 L 153/13.

proprietary Name and dosage should be considered as models. Again, when this is implemented, it will suggest a change of practice in at least some Member States.

Overall then, although the proposals on recognition of prescriptions have the potential to lead to more of a single market in pharmaceuticals and medical devices, with the efficiencies that implies, in practice, vested interests of both patients and health care authorities (particularly those bodies that pay for health care under the national health (insurance) system) have been protected in the text. This is consistent with the Court's case law on related questions, which gives a significant discretion to Member States to justify restrictive national policies or practices on the grounds of objective public interests such as public health protection and financial stability of welfare systems. Future developments in this area may, therefore, continue to be Court-driven, although the Court is likely to interpret the Treaty in the context of the agreed legislation, respecting the political settlement here.

7.3.3 European Reference Networks

Article 15 of the Commission's proposal concerns 'European reference networks'. It proposes that Member States should 'facilitate the development of the European reference networks of health care providers.' It lists the objectives of such European reference networks as:

(a) to help to realise the potential of European cooperation regarding highly specialised health care for patients and for health care systems from innovations in medical science and health technologies;
(b) to help to promote access to high quality and cost-effective health care for all patients with a medical condition requiring a particular concentration of resources or expertise;
(c) to maximise cost-effective use of resources by concentrating them where appropriate;
(d) to help to share knowledge and provide training for health professionals;
(e) to provide quality and safety benchmarks and to help develop and spread best practice within and outside the network;
(f) to help Member States with an insufficient number of patients with a particular medical condition or lacking technology or expertise to provide a full range of highly specialised services of the highest quality.

Under the proposal, the Commission is to adopt criteria and conditions for membership of European reference networks, to ensure capacity; quality; and links to and collaborations with, for instance, patients' networks and institutions involved in epidemiological surveillance. Again, a comitology procedure is envisaged for the implementation of this provision.

The concept of a European reference network in the context of health care for rare diseases has been around for some time. It is estimated that between 5,000 and 8,000 different rare diseases affect or will affect around 29 million people in the European

Union.[52] As a proportion of the total EU population of 500 million,[53] this makes it worthwhile taking common action at EU level, even though within a single Member State the proportions of people affected by a rare disease might not be sufficient to warrant disbursement of significant public resources. This version of the idea of European reference networks thus responds to the notion that the EU can 'add value' to health care provision in individual Member States, in particular in areas of medical expertise where the incidence of the medical problem is very low within a single Member State. Economies of scale of tackling rare diseases at EU level should thereby be achieved. The idea of EU 'added value' is also reflected in the European Parliament's proposal that patients suffering from rare diseases should not only have the right to access health care in another Member State, but should also get reimbursement, without the need for prior authorisation, even if the treatment in question is not included in the benefits covered by the national health system of the home Member State.[54] This proposal, if adopted, would have taken rare diseases outside of the general principle to the effect that the Member State which pays gets to determine the basket of benefits that are reimbursed.

Emergent networks of specialised providers of care for rare diseases, and research into 'orphan medicines',[55] have already been supported through EU funding under the public health programmes administered by DG Sanco.[56] European reference networks share expertise, innovation and best practice in the specialised areas in which they work. An example is Orphanet,[57] co-sponsored by the EU, which provides a portal with information for health care professionals, the pharmaceutical industry, researchers and patients, on over 5,000 rare diseases. The countries involved in Orphanet range beyond the Member States of the EU.

---

[52] European Commission, *Communication to the European Parliament, the Council, the European Economic and Social Committee and the Committee of the Regions on Rare Diseases: Europe's challenges*, COM(2008) 679 final.

[53] Eurostat, Data in Focus, 31/2009, 'EU-27 population continues to grow' http://epp.eurostat.ec.europa.eu/cache/ITY_PUBLIC/3-03082009-AP/EN/3-03082009-AP-EN.PDF.

[54] Resolution A6-0233/2009, European Parliament First Reading Text, April 2009, Article 6(1) and 8.

[55] Medicines for the treatment of conditions affecting a very small proportion of the population. The European Union considers diseases to be rare when they affect not more than 5 per 10,000 persons in the European Union, see European Commission, *supra* n. 52.

[56] Decision 1786/2002/EC of the European Parliament and of the Council of 23 September 2002 adopting a programme of Community action in the field of public health (2003–2008) *OJ* 2002 L271/1; Decision 1295/1999/EC of the European Parliament and of the Council of 29 April 1999 adopting a programme of Community action on rare diseases within the framework for action in the field of public health (1999–2003) *OJ* 1999 L 155/1; Council Decision 82/616/EEC of 17 August 1982 adopting a sectoral research and development programme of the European Economic Community in the field of medical and public health research (1982–1986) *OJ* 1982 L 248/12; Council Decision 80/344/EEC of 18 March 1980 adopting a second research programme in the field of medical and public health research, consisting of four multiannual concerted projects *OJ* 1980 L 78/24.

[57] http://www.orpha.net/consor/cgi-bin/index.php. Explicitly mentioned in the European Parliament's Jan 2011 text, Article 13.

Moreover, a special legislative framework already exists for the approval for marketing of orphan medicines within the EU.[58] The European Medicines Agency's Committee for Orphan Medicinal Products considers, first, applications for orphan medicine status. If successful, an orphan medicine enjoys special treatment in the European Medicines Agency's authorisation procedures, including protocol assistance (scientific advice) and reduced fees. The proposed Directive's provisions on European reference networks are consistent with the EU's legislative approach to orphan medicines, in that they give special treatment to rare diseases, on the grounds that it is necessary to overcome the barriers to development of treatments for such diseases in ways that go beyond straightforward (national) market models.

The 'High Level Group on Health Services and Medical Care' worked from 2004 to 2006 on the concept of European reference networks.[59] It had a task force on centres of reference for rare diseases, which reported in September 2005[60] and December 2006.[61] In its final report,[62] the High Level Group recommended the development of criteria for identifying reference networks, and a methodology to assess the benefits of establishing and supporting a European reference network from the perspective of different stakeholders. The High Level Group has now ceased to exist, but this aspect of its work has been taken forward by the Commission in other *fora*, including the proposed Directive and a 2008 Communication on Rare Diseases.

The Commission's 2008 Communication on Rare Diseases[63] seeks to provide a more integrated strategy to what has hitherto been rather piecemeal activity at EU level. The Communication refers explicitly to the shared commitment of European health care systems to equal access and solidarity, as expressed in the Council Conclusions on Common values and principles in European Union Health Systems.[64] It points out that expertise in rare diseases is scarce, and notes that some Member States have 'centres of expertise' or 'centres of reference/centres of

---

[58] Regulation 141/2000/EC of the European Parliament and Council of 16 December 1999 on orphan medicinal products *OJ* 2000 L 19/1, as amended, and Commission Regulation 847/2000/EC of 27 April 2000 laying down the provisions for implementation of the criteria for designation of a medicinal product as an orphan medicinal product and definitions of the concepts 'similar medicinal product' and 'clinical superiority' *OJ* 2000 L 103/5.

[59] See the report of the High Level Group on Health Services and Medical Care on European Reference networks http://ec.europa.eu/health/ph_threats/non_com/rare_8_en.htm.

[60] Report from an expert group of the Rare Diseases Task Force, *Overview of Current Centres of Reference on Rare Diseases*, September 2005, http://ec.europa.eu/health/ph_overview/co_operation/mobility/docs/high_level_wg_001_en.pdf.

[61] Report from an expert group of the Rare Diseases Task Force, *Centres of Reference for Rare Diseases in Europe: State of the art 2006, and Recommendations of the Rare Diseases Task Force,* http://ec.europa.eu/health/ph_threats/non_com/docs/contribution_policy.pdf.

[62] Final Report of the High Level Group on Health Services and Medical Care, HLG/2006/8 final, http://ec.europa.eu/health/ph_overview/co_operation/mobility/docs/highlevel_2006_007_en.pdf.

[63] European Commission, *supra* n. 52.

[64] *OJ* 2006 C 146/1.

excellence' whose knowledge and protocols are widely used by health care professionals in other Member States and internationally. The Council responded to the Commission's Communication by recommending in June 2009 that all Member States develop plans and strategies for rare diseases by the end of 2013, and gather expertise through pooling information at European level.[65] As at June 2010, only five Member States[66] had lodged their plans with the Commission.[67]

The Commission's proposed Directive on Patients' Rights in Cross-border Health care and the Council's November 2009 and June 2010 texts both reflect the idea of 'European reference networks' being focused upon rare diseases, and the added value that collecting expertise at EU level on such diseases can bring. However, the European Parliament's April 2009 text takes the idea of European reference network further. The European Parliament proposes that European reference networks should 'contribute to the pooling of knowledge regarding sickness prevention and the treatment of major commonly occurring disorders.'[68] The European Parliament, therefore, also wants to see European reference networks developed for the big health disorders that are most common in Europe. This would again pick up existing work done via the EU's public health programmes, for example, in cancer, cardiovascular disease, and chronic obstructive respiratory disease. The idea here is that there is added EU value in sharing good practice towards agreed quality standards for management of common (and well understood) diseases, or even in redeploying resources more efficiently across the EU in the treatment of those diseases.

These parts of the European Parliament's proposed amendments pick up an issue of contention in terms of the Proposed Directive as a whole. To what extent is the Directive only about *cross-border* health care and to what extent is it about the governance of health care in the EU *in general*? In terms of the numbers of people involved, and the consequent changes to national practice within health care systems, cross-border health care, be it about the movement of patients, professionals or services themselves, or about the pooling of expertise in areas where there is insufficient expertise within one particular Member State, is a relatively insignificant issue. The governance of health care *in general* is much more significant. Taking into account the proposal as a whole, this is an issue that is fudged in the Commission's proposal, and which MEPs disagree upon. The change of legal basis in the Council's June 2010 text, to include Article 168 TFEU, better supports the idea of a more general brief for the Directive.

The Council also includes members that are unhappy about the facets of the Directive concerning health care governance in general. The Council's text changes the obligation to form European reference networks to being an obligation

---

65 Council Recommendation of 8 June 2009 on action on the field of rare diseases *OJ* 2009 C 151/7.

66 France, Bulgaria, Greece, Portugal, Spain.

67 http://ec.europa.eu/health/rare_diseases/national_plans/detailed/index_en.htm.

68 European Parliament First Reading text, Article 17(2).

of the Commission, to support Member States to form these networks,[69] rather than an obligation of the Member States, which is what the Commission text originally proposed. Council wants to focus only on 'medical conditions requiring a particular concentration of expertise' (rather than a 'particular concentration of resources or expertise'), so not on common diseases.

Under the Commission's proposal, the Commission is to adopt criteria and conditions that the European reference networks must fulfil, in order to ensure that they meet a specific list of capacities and abilities (such as diagnostic capacity; quality of service; research contribution; involvement in epidemiology). The Council's June 2010 text does not list the specifics, but merely obliges the Commission to 'develop and publish criteria that the European reference networks should fulfil in order to receive support from the Commission' and 'criteria for evaluating European reference networks'.[70] An earlier version of the Council text suggested that the Commission should do this through evaluation of currently running pilot projects[71] and then 'in cooperation with the Member States' identify and implement the necessary criteria and conditions. The underlying idea of the Council's text is that existing European regulation on the structure, operation and monitoring of specialised networks shall prevail. Council has added explicit text on non-harmonisation and to the effect that national competences and rules on recognition of expertise must be respected.[72] The Commission's proposal talks of 'measures' to be adopted on the criteria and conditions for European reference networks. 'Measures' is a loose word, and can mean binding legal texts. The Council replaced the word 'measures' with 'guidelines', to be clear that it there is power only to adopt soft law in this context.

In other words, the Council's text suggests that these matters have already been set up in a more 'intergovernmental' mode than the Commission envisages for the future, and that the Council is resistant to move towards greater use of the instruments of the classic Community method, particularly hard law. However, there is no disagreement over the underlying idea of sharing of good practice and pooling of resources, at least with respect to rare diseases. Using the tools and processes of EU 'new governance', this idea has been put into effect in areas other than rare diseases. As Louise Trubek and others[73] have shown in the field of cancer, over time, with only small amounts of money being used to 'steer' policy

---

[69] Council November 2009 text, Article 13(1) 'The Commission shall support Member States in the development of European reference networks between health care providers and centres of excellence in the Member States.'

[70] Council June 2010 text, Article 13(4)(a) and (b).

[71] This is surprising as presumably this is precisely the methodology that the Commission would in any event employ.

[72] Council June 2010 text, Article 13(6) 'Measures adopted under this Article shall not harmonize any laws or regulations of the Member States and shall fully respect the responsibilities of the Member States for the organisation and delivery of health services and medical care.'

[73] Trubek et al. (2008, pp. 804–843; forthcoming).

development, these modes of governance can lead to significant convergence effects between national policies and practices. Networked new governance, particularly when embedded in appropriate institutional frameworks, can lead to learning, enhanced stakeholder engagement and development of best practice benchmarks in the form of clinical guidelines in specific areas. The proposed Directive, if adopted, will form part of the institutional framework supporting continued new governance in the area of rare diseases across the EU. But even without a Directive, the Council's integrated strategy will sustain developments in this direction, and other 'new governance' processes will continue in fields including, but not limited to, rare diseases.

7.3.4 'E-Health'

Article 16 of the proposal gives the Commission, again through comitology, power to introduce specific measures necessary to achieve 'interoperability of information and communication technology systems in the health care field.' This is to take place 'whenever Member States decide to introduce them', which suggests a lack of urgency, or perhaps better, a recognition that there are significant practical, as well as political and legal,[74] barriers to realising such interoperability. The Council's text changes the obligation to one for Member States,[75] and simply envisages the Commission as in a supporting role.

'E-health' in the context of the EU is a topic on its own, and indeed has been the subject of book-length treatment,[76] so there is insufficient space to treat it in detail here. Both the Commission and the Council text of the proposed Directive suggest that the Directive itself is unlikely to make a difference to existing activities at EU level, and within and between Member States, in the development of information and communication technology systems to support health care. There is significant opposition from several powerful Member States, such as the UK and Germany, to EU involvement in patient data systems.

---

[74] For instance with respect to the right to privacy in the storage or sharing of medical data electronically.

[75] Council November 2009 text, Article 14 'Member States shall, supported by the Commission, aim at interoperability of information and communication technology systems, in particular through specifying the necessary standards and terminologies for interoperability.'

[76] Callens (2003, 2010).

7.3.5 Cooperation on Management of New Health Technologies/ Cooperation on Health Technology Assessment; and Data Collection for Statistical and Monitoring Purposes

Article 18 of the Commission's proposal concerns data collection for statistical or monitoring purposes. Under this provision, Member States would be obliged to collect statistical data on the provision of cross-border health care, and to share it with the Commission. The idea behind this is to provide information on cross-border flows of patients for planning purposes. One of the difficulties faced by the Commission in coming up with this proposal (and also faced by the Court in ruling on objective public interest justifications) is that robust data on numbers of patients moving across borders in the EU have not been available.[77]

The Council text omits this provision entirely. The Council view is that it would be a duplication of activities under Regulation 1338/2008/EC[78] on statistics on public health and health and safety at work. If this is accurate, then 'public health' (which usually means population health, epidemiology) is being defined very widely indeed in that Regulation.

Article 17 of the Commission's proposal states that:

> Member States shall facilitate the development and functioning of a network connecting the national authorities ... responsible for health technology assessment.

It sets out the objectives of such a network, and provides that a comitology procedure should be used to adopt measures necessary to set up and manage the network, including specifying the nature and type of information to be exchanged.

This part of the proposal is again an example of added value at EU level, in the sense of promoting efficient use of resources across the EU. At the moment each Member State individually assesses whether a new medical technology, new drug, or new treatment, represents 'value for money' in the public health system. This assessment involves balancing several competing objectives: access of patients to new medicines or health technologies; the need to reward innovation in health care

[77] Bertinato et al. (2005), pp. 5–6. The most widely used data derive from a study on the flows of financial transfers (rather than actual movement of patients) for cross-border care within the EU: see Hermesse et al. (1997), p. 4, updated to 1998 in Palm (2000). These data suggest that expenditure on cross-border health care represents between 0.1 and 0.2% of overall public spending on health care in the EU. However, the data do not take into account waiver agreements between certain Member States (e.g., UK and Germany). There is also under-reporting of actual cross-border health care (one study (Rosenmöller et al. 2006, p. 68) reported boxes of unprocessed E111 (now EHIC) forms sitting in a Spanish hospital). Moreover, national data do not match the available EU data (Bertinato et al. 2005, pp. 14–15). The available data seem to show that patient mobility has not in fact increased in the wake of increased public awareness following the high profile *Kohll* litigation (Bertinato et al. 2005, p 13); see European Commission Staff Working Paper, '*Report of the application of internal market rules to health services. Implementations by the Member States of the Court's jurisprudence*', SEC(2003)900.

[78] *OJ* 2009 L 354/70.

technology; and the need to balance public health care budgets. Health technology assessment is not purely a 'scientific' matter, but is highly politically charged within the Member States, as the outcome of the assessment, if it means that a new treatment or medicine is approved for reimbursement under national public insurance or taxation-based health care systems, will be critical for the success of a new product or procedure. Even the sharing of information or practice that the Commission proposal suggests could result in significant challenges for national health technology assessment procedures, particularly if such procedures currently lack full transparency. The availability of comparable data on health technology assessment across the EU would, for instance, provide political capital for patients' rights groups, and may, therefore, change the balance of power within national health care systems. This is one of the ways that 'new governance' processes, which mandate the reporting of comparable information, can change policies over time.

To date, the EU has had some involvement with projects concerned with the comparability of health technology assessment.[79] The EUnetHTA project 2006–2008 and 2010–2012[80] is financed by the EU's public health programme. It has developed models for health technology assessment of diagnostic technologies and medical and surgical interventions.[81] A great deal of detailed work has to be done before shared practice on health technology assessment could be achieved across the EU. Key barriers are differences in the extent and scope of health technology assessment analysis; and differences in reporting the results. For instance, because terms differ from national system to system, a glossary of common terms[82] is necessary. A 'toolkit' (a 'series of checklists and resources that identify or clarify the relevance, reliability, and transferability of data and information from existing reports'[83]) is needed in order to achieve comparability of health technology assessments. New information infrastructures must also be agreed and designed.[84] But the prize is significant: the EU has many health technology assessment agencies, each producing its own health technology assessment reports, and consequently multiple reports are produced on the same health technology. If these reports could be used in different contexts, across different Member States, there would be a significant saving in time (crucial for patients with diseases for which no, or sub-optimal, treatments are currently authorised) and resources (crucial for

---

79 An international network, the International Network of Health Technology Agencies, was established in 1993. It promotes collaboration between health technology agencies. See http://www.inahta.org/ The EU agenda seeks to go further than the INHTA is able to go, through the development of, in the first instance, comparable, and ultimately, common practices in health technology assessment.

80 http://www.eunethta.net/

81 See the discussions in the special issue, especially Lampe et al. (2009), pp. 9–20 and Kristensen et al. (2009), pp. 1–8.

82 See Rosten et al. (2009), pp. 42–47.

83 Turner et al. (2009a, pp. 28–36; 2009b, pp. 37–41).

84 Neikter et al. (2009), pp. 92–98.

all Member States, given pressures on public funding).[85] Such an approach stops short of a common EU level health technology assessment process, which would of course involve even greater savings, but for which there is neither significant political support, nor legal competence.

A pilot study of its proposed model, undertaken by EUnetHTA, suggested that the work done to date needs to be developed further, but that this is feasible.[86] EUnetHTA started work on a 'Joint Action' in early 2010,[87] involving 33 partners in 23 EU Member States and Norway. It will also bring in work done through the Commission's Pharmaceutical Forum, on 'relative effectiveness' of health technologies.[88] The Commission's proposal would further embed that work in EU activities. But even without the Directive, this work looks set to continue.

The European Parliament seeks consultative status over matters pertaining to the network.[89] The European Parliament proposes that the network to be explicitly based on 'the principles of good governance, including transparency, objectiveness, fairness of procedures, and broad and full stakeholder participation of all relevant groups.' Stakeholder participation, through transparent and collaborative procedures, is part of the 'new governance' approach to wicked problems, such as how to decide what medical treatments, products or technologies will be available to patients under publicly funded health care systems. The relevant stakeholders listed in the European Parliament's text include 'health professionals, patient groups, social partners, scientists and industry.'[90]

The Council has reservations about this part of the proposal. The Council's June 2010 text envisages that participation in the network should be voluntary, and that:

> the members of the network shall participate and contribute to the network's activities according to the legislation of the Member State where they are established.[91]

Its text proposes an obligation on the EU (not on the Member States) to 'facilitate cooperation and the exchange of scientific information amongst the Member States' in a network of health technology assessment authorities. The network's objective is, in the Council's version, to support *Member States* (rather than to support cooperation per se).

The Council has agreed that EU aid can be given to the health technology assessment network. The terms of the aid are set out, but detailed arrangements are

---

85 Turner et al. (2009a), pp. 28–36 at p. 28.

86 Pasternack et al. (2009), pp. 21–27.

87 http://ec.europa.eu/health/technology_assessment/policy/index_en.htm and http://www.eunethta.net/Public/Communication/Press_Releases/Starting-a-new-phase-European-network-for-HTA-Joint-Action/.

88 http://ec.europa.eu/pharmaforum/effectiveness_en.htm.

89 European Parliament First Reading text, Article 20(1).

90 Ibid.

91 Council June 2010 text, Article 15(1).

entrusted to comitology decisions. Council's June 2010 text explicitly adds that measures adopted under this Article 'shall not interfere with Member States' competence in deciding on the implementation of health technology assessment conclusions'[92]—in other words, Member States are to continue to make the cost-benefit analysis implied in health technology assessment. It also explicitly states that harmonisation of national law is prohibited here, and that the responsibilities of the Member State for the organisation and delivery of health care services must be respected.

The very fact that Council has changed the wording of this provision, and therefore, the scope of what was envisaged, suggests that the governments of the Member States take the view that the kinds of 'new governance' activity proposed by Chapter IV of the Directive on patients' rights in cross-border healthcare have the potential to lead to changes in national practices. This is not European integration through the 'classic Community method' of granting legal rights to individuals within the EU. It involves promoting convergence of approaches through mandatory transparent sharing of practices, which allows for the recognition of practices that are successful, and their development into benchmarks of best practice. The consequent pressure to conform to European standards comes from the 'carrot' of the benefits that could be expected from doing so (be they access to EU funds, economies of scale, or simply greater efficiency), rather than the 'stick' of enforceable legal obligation.

7.4 Conclusions

The analysis above suggests that, even if the proposed Directive had not been adopted, most of the proposals in Chapter IV would survive in some form or other. The least likely to survive are those on cross-border prescribing, as there is little existing legislative activity in this area, and strong doubts about the value of such measures, taking into account the consumer protection and cost-containment features of many national rules on prescription-only medicine. Future momentum in the area of cross-border prescribing may well continue to come from the Court of Justice, rather than the legislature. The proposed Directive's provisions on data collection for statistical and monitoring purposes and the provisions on 'e-health' are being taken forward through other legislative provisions. Provisions on European reference networks and cooperation in management of new health technologies pick up activities that the Member States are already permitting the EU to steer. Whilst their embedding into a legislative text will help secure their

92 Ibid., Article 15(6).

future, it is not necessary to achieve this. Taking into account the Commission's original proposal, the European Parliament's First Reading text and the Council's agreed text, a number of overall conclusions can be drawn to summarise where we are with Chapter IV of the Proposed Directive and what trends are likely for the future.

The idea of mandatory cooperation, supported by comitology, which is implicit in the Commission's draft, has been moved away from in Council. Over half of the Member States oppose comitology in this context. The comitology procedures are subject to revocation and an objection procedure. Rather Council prefers a model based on incentives for cooperation (although what exactly those incentives are, other than the opportunity to learn through the process, is not spelled out in the proposal text). Some Member States perhaps want something more like the framework used in the Open Method of Coordination[93] to be explored. This underlines that health care is a national competence. But the debate in Council over these proposals, and their rewording in the Council's text, is also a tacit admission that even these sorts of governance activities can have an effect on the way Member States direct and pursue their policies.

These doubts are related to the ongoing debate about the point of this part of the Directive. Is it about cooperation in *cross-border* health care, or is it about fostering cooperation in matters ultimately relating to quality and safety of health care independently of any cross-border element? This is a fundamental question, which goes both to legal points (for instance, the proper legal basis of the Directive) and to political points (is there a will, or enough of a will, to share and cooperate amongst EU Member States, using the structures of the EU, in the area of health care?) Is this really about governance of the internal market for health care? Is there an 'internal market for health care'? Or is there an opportunity to share expertise and good practice, to tackle common problems, through discussion, benchmarking, collaboration and so on, *without* thinking of health care (except cross-border health care services) as part of 'the internal market'?

If the latter, then comitology (which was set up to support internal market law, and which involves a very narrow range of stakeholders) does not seem to be the

---

[93] The OMC process was first used in the 1990s to coordinate the Member States' economic and fiscal policies. It was subsequently applied to the European Union's employment strategy. OMC uses mutual learning, benchmarking, best practice and peer pressure to steer national policies towards objectives, expressed in 'guidelines' agreed at EU level. The EU guidelines are translated into 'national action plans', with the support of various actors (including non-governmental actors) at national and sub-national level. Each Member State's performance is then evaluated against the EU objectives, using quantitative (or qualitative) indicators, and examples of best practice are identified, to serve as benchmarks as the process of guideline-setting begins anew. For a recent analysis, see Velluti (2010).

appropriate institutional mechanism. Something more akin to the 'new governance' mechanisms of the Open Method of Coordination would seem more appropriate. And of course, in addition, the joint legal basis of the Directive seems necessary to support the latter. The European Parliament is very keen on the idea of involving an expanded range of stakeholders in determining the detailed implementation of the Directive.

Whatever happens to the proposed Directive, and it may yet fail to be adopted, the activities to be supported by its proposed Chapter IV may turn out to be more significant aspects of future EU health care policy than a traditional EU lawyers' focus suggests. After all, cross-border patient movement, or even health professional movement, or health service movement, is likely to affect only a small minority of the citizens of the EU. Collaboration and cooperation in developing quality and safety standards in health care, in assessing new health technologies, in sharing best practice in (rare) disease management and treatment, especially if underpinned by EU structures mandating cooperation, reporting, transparency and comparability of data, are likely to be far more significant into the future, not for the individual 'rights' of patients in the EU, but for the systems that provide their health care and, ultimately, for their health.

Post Script Since the chapter was completed, the European Parliament has adopted a resolution on a revised consolidated text of the proposed Directive (19 January 2011, 11038/2/2010 – C7-0266/2010 – 2008/0142(COD)). The principal changes pertinent to this chapter are as follows:

The provision on mutual assistance and cooperation now includes the phrase 'cooperation on standards and guidelines in quality and safety', not simply information exchange. Given that it is unclear what is happening with the health and long term care strand of the OMC-social under the *Europe 2020* provisions, it may be that sharing of information towards greater quality and value for public money continues under the proposed Directive's arrangements. The European Parliament's text also strengthens the exchange of information about fitness to practice of health care professionals, proposing that the IMI system (See Commission Decision 2008/49/EC of 12 December 2007 concerning the implementation of the Internal Market Information System (IMI) as regards the protection of personal data OJ 2008 L 13/18) be used, which will include safeguards for health care professionals' rights to privacy.

The European Parliament has sought to strengthen the special position of pharmacists in EU law still further, by adding that 'the recognition of prescriptions shall not affect any national rules recognizing for ethical reasons the right of the pharmacist to refuse to dispense, had the prescription been issued in the Member State of affiliation'.

The idea that patients suffering from rare diseases should have the right to access health care in another Member State, and be reimbursed even if the treatment is not included in the basket of benefits reimbursed in the Member State of affiliation has been significantly watered down. When a patient with a suspected rare disease applies for authorization, 'a clinical evaluation *may* be carried out by experts in that field' (my emphasis). If there are no experts in the Member State, or the evaluation is inconclusive, 'the Member State of affiliation *may* request scientific advice'. It is unclear what the point of this proposal is, as there are no consequences in terms of authorization of being diagnosed with a rare disease, except the general rules to the effect that the home Member State must grant prior authorization when the patient is entitled to health care under the national rules that determine entitlements, and when health care cannot be provided in the home

Member State within a medically justifiable time limit. So, *if* these matters are satisfied *and* the patient can persuade the home Member State to carry out a clinical evaluation, or to request advice, if the national entitlement rules are drawn up in such as way that this evaluation constituted *de facto* evidence of an entitlement, then the patient could go elsewhere for the health care, and the home Member State would have to pay. *However*, the home Member State still has the opportunity to control its liabilities by determining entitlements under its health care system, and of course need not seek any evaluation.

On the question of whether the 'European reference networks' are only for rare diseases, the Parliament's texts seeks to depart from this narrow approach. The proposed text '*in particular* in the area of rare diseases' (my emphasis) and on the objectives of European reference networks makes it clear that such networks could also emerge around the common diseases of European societies. European reference networks must meet at least three of a list of possible objectives, only five of which concern rare diseases only. If this version of the text is adopted, Parliament will have won this point

Acknowledgments I would like to thank the participants at the conference *Health Care and EU Law* Radboud University Nijmegen, Netherlands 1–2 October 2009. Work on this chapter has been supported by the ESRC Seminar Series *European Law and New Health Technologies* REF-451-26-0764 (PI Dr Mark Flear).

References

Alexander LT (2009) Stakeholder participation in new governance: lessons from Chicago's public housing reform experiment. Georgetown J Poverty Law Policy 16

Bertinato L et al (2005) Policy brief: cross-border health care in Europe. World Health Organisation, Brussels (On behalf of the European Observatory on Health Systems and Policies)

Callens S (2003) E-health and the law. Kluwer Law International, Deventer

Callens S (2010) The EU legal framework on E-health. In: Mossialos E, Permanand G, Baeten R, Hervey T (eds) Health systems governance in Europe: the role of EU law and policy. Cambridge University Press, Cambridge

Conklin J (2005) Dialogue mapping: building shared understandings of wicked problems. Wiley, London (Chapter 1)

Craig P, de Búrca G (2008) EU law: text, cases and materials. Oxford University Press, Oxford (Chapter 5)

De Búrca G, Scott J (eds) (2006) Law and new governance in the EU and US. Hart, Oxford

Greer S (2008) Choosing paths in European Union health care policy. J Eur Soc Policy 18

Greer S (2009) The politics of European Union health policies. Open University Press, Maidenhead

Greer S (forthcoming) Constitutional asymmetry, supranationalism, and supporting coalitions in European Union health care services policy. Regulation Governance

Gunningham N (2007) The New Collaborative Environmental Governance. Paper presented at Law and Society Association annual conference, Berlin, July

Gunningham N (2009) The new collaborative environmental governance: the localization of regulation. J Law Soc 36

Hermesse H et al (1997) Patient mobility within the European Union. Eur J Public Health 7(3 Suppl)

Hervey T (2006) The European Union and the governance of health care. In: de Búrca G, Scott J (eds) Law and new governance in the EU and US. Hart, Oxford

Hervey T (2007) New governance responses to health care migration in the EU: the EU guidelines on block purchasing. Maastricht J Eur Comparative Law 14(3)
Hervey T, Vanhercke B (2010) Health care and the EU: the law and policy patchwork. In: Mossialos E, Permanand G, Baeten R, Hervey T (eds) Health systems governance in Europe: the role of European Union law and policy. Cambridge University Press, Cambridge
Hunt J (2007) The end of judicial constitutionalisation? Croat Yearbook Eur Law Policy 3(3)
Karkkainen BC (2006) Information-forcing regulation and environmental governance. In: de Búrca G, Scott J (eds) Law and new governance in the EU and the US. Hart, Oxford
Kristensen F et al (2009) Practical tools and methods for health technology assessment in Europe. Int J Technol Assess Health Care 25
Lampe K et al (2009) The HTA core model: a novel method for producing and reporting health technology assessments. Int J Technol Assess Health Care 25
Loebel O (2004) The renew deal: the fall of regulation and the rise of governance in contemporary legal thought. Minnesota Law Rev 89
Neikter S et al (2009) Toward a new information infrastructure in health technology assessment: communication, design, process and results. Int J Technol Assess Health Care 25
NeJaime D (2009) When new governance fails. Ohio State Law J 70
Palm W (2000) Implications of recent jurisprudence on the coordination of health care protection systems. Summary Report produced for DG Employment and Social Affairs. AIM, Brussels
Pasternack I et al (2009) Testing the HTA core model: experiences from two pilot projects. Int J Technol Assess Health Care 25
Randall E (2000) The European Union and health policy. Palgrave Macmillan, Basingstoke
Rittel H, Webber M (1973) Dilemmas in a general theory of planning. Policy Sci 4
Rosenmöller M et al (eds) (2006) Patient mobility in the EU: learning from experience. World Health Organisation, Copenhagen (European Observatory on Health Systems and Policies). Available at: www.iese.edu/en/files/6_22160.pdf
Rosten C et al (2009) Enhancing understanding: the development of a glossary of health technology assessment adaptation terms. Int J Technol Assess Health Care 25
Sabel C (2004) Beyond principal–agent governance: experimentalist organizations, learning and accountability. In: Engelen E, Sie M, Dhian H (eds) De Staat van de Democratie. Democratie voorbij de Staat. Amsterdam University Press, WRR Verkenning 3 Amsterdam, (Available: http://www2.law.columbia.edu/sabel/papers.htm)
Sabel CF, Zeitlin J (2008) Learning from difference: the new architecture of experimentalist governance in the EU. Eur Law J 14
Sauter W (2008) The proposed patient mobility directive and the reform of cross-border health care in the EU. Tilec Discussion Paper DP 2008-34, September, SSRN http://ssrn.com/abstract=1277110
Schäfer A (2006) A new form of governance? Comparing the open method of coordination to multilateral surveillance by the IMF and the OECD. J Eur Public Policy 13(1)
Scott J, Trubek DM (2002) Mind the gap: law and new approaches to governance in the European Union. Eur Law J 8
Steffen M (ed) (2005) Health governance in Europe. Routledge, Abingdon
Trubek L (2006) New governance practices in US health care. In: de Búrca G, Scott J (eds) Law and new governance in the EU and the US. Hart, Oxford
Trubek L et al (2008) The construction of a healthier Europe: lessons from the fight against cancer. Wisconsin Int Law J 26
Trubek L et al (forthcoming) Better: fighting cancer through improved governance in the United States and the European Union. Regulation and Governance
Trubek D, Trubek L (2007) New governance and legal regulation: complementarity, rivalry and transformation. Columbia J Eur Law 13
Turner S et al (2009a) The adaptation of health technology assessment reports: identification of the need for, and development of, a toolkit to aid the process. Int J Technol Assess Health Care 25

Turner S et al (2009b) The health technology assessment adaptation toolkit: description and use. Int J Technol Assess Health Care 25
Velluti S (2010) New governance and the European employment strategy. Routledge, London
Walker N, de Búrca G (2007) Reconceiving law and new governance. Columbia J Eur Law 13
Weiler JHH (1991) The transformation of Europe. Yale Law J 100

Chapter 8
Legislating for Patients' Rights

Gareth Davies

Contents

8.1 Introduction

The proposed Directive on patients' rights is, at the time of writing, trapped in a political and legislative limbo. The embodiment of the existing case law in legislation has inspired protest from various parties and various perspectives, two dominant criticisms being that the Directive undermines national health care systems, and that it provides an over-economic view of the patient and neglects the human, constitutional and social aspects of health care.[1] In some cases, the eruptions of protest are no doubt caused by an unawareness of the existing law and a genuine, but misguided, belief that the proposed Directive is radically new. In other cases, it is precisely an awareness of the legal history which has provoked such passion. The limited participatory possibilities in Court cases has led to

[1] For overviews of some of the arguments, see Newdick (2006), p. 1645; Montgomery (2005), p. 145; Hatzopoulos (2002), p. 683.

G. Davies (✉)
European Law, VU University, Amsterdam, The Netherlands
e-mail: g.t.davies@vu.nl

J. W. van de Gronden et al. (eds.), *Health Care and EU Law*,
Legal Issues of Services of General Interest, DOI: 10.1007/978-90-6704-728-9_8,

frustration on the part of lobby groups who now seize enthusiastically upon the chance to make their mark in the legislative process, and undo, via the political arm of the EU, the alleged harm done by its independent judicial organs.

Yet, whether the proposed Directive is resurrected or abandoned, it deserves a certain consideration for the same reasons that a good academic article on patients' rights would: it highlights pithily the unavoidable issues and problems raised by patient mobility. The EU and its Member States will have to grapple with these, whether they choose to do so via this piece of legislation, another, or solely via the reactive path of litigation before the Court of Justice and national courts applying EU law.

These issues and problems can be considered on two levels. As a practical matter, there is the question of how migration is to be organised, and what the consequences will be for the institutions and individual involved. This is the subject of the largest part of this chapter. For convenience and, it is hoped, explanatory power, it is considered under four headings: rights of exit, rights of entry, the facilitation of movement, and harmonisation. 'Rights of exit' is the phrase used for the right of patients to opt out of their national health care system and go abroad. To what extent does the proposed Directive add to the rights provided by existing case law and legislation? 'Rights of entry' is the phrase used to describe the rights which a patient needs to ensure that she/he can gain access to medical facilities in other Member States. These may not always welcome foreign patients, and local rules may hinder their treatment via price disadvantages, priority for local patients or other mechanisms. To what extent does the directive address these problems? The section on 'facilitation' considers the various ways in which the exercise of substantive rights of exit and entry is made easier. A patient may have a formal right to treatment abroad but find that in practice obstacles arise from bureaucratic procedures, and a lack of information about possibilities and prices. An effective patient migration regime requires that alongside substantive migration rights there be rules concerning enforcement of those rights, access to information, and the speediness, accessibility and transparency of the relevant bureaucratic processes. Such facilitating measures are the subject of Sect. 8.4. Finally, Sect. 8.5, 'harmonisation' considers the extent to which the directive is a step towards harmonising health care systems. The mantra of patient migration has always been that it is about coordination, not harmonisation, yet coordinating systems which lack any common legal elements or framework is a sometimes insurmountable challenge. In particular, as in other areas of the Internal Market, free movement without a shared level of the protection of basic interests is difficult to achieve. Accordingly, Sect. 8.5 suggests that the proposed Directive takes first steps towards harmonising quality standards and patients' rights within the EU.

After considering these questions of mechanism, the conclusions to this chapter draw upon the proceeding parts to ask the broader question of what the proposed Directive is all about: what migration of patients is all about in the eyes of the EU. Is this primarily a phenomenon reflecting and embodying an idea of economic freedom, or an idea of European citizenship, or is it merely the instrumentalisation of individuals in the goal of EU integration, a phenomenon to be primarily understood in institutional and structural terms?

The discussion below refers to the text in the Commission proposal of 2nd July 2008.[2] Amendments were proposed by the Parliament on 30th April 2009.[3] At the time of writing, the matter has not been substantively handled by the council, and the future of both Directive and amendments is uncertain. The proposed amendments are discussed where they raise interesting issues.

8.2 Rights of Exit

The proposed Directive provides in Article 3(2) that its central provisions (Articles 6–9) are not to apply to situations where authorisation for treatment abroad under Regulation 1408/71 would be possible.[4] This is odd.[5] Where treatment is not available in a patient's home state without undue delay that Regulation provides for a right to seek treatment abroad.[6] This right has been extensively discussed in the case law, alongside the right directly deriving from Article 56 TFEU, the difference between the two essentially lying in the mechanisms and degree of reimbursement. The Regulation provides for reimbursement as if the patient were insured in the state of treatment, whereas the Treaty, the Court has found, requires that the patient's costs be covered to the same extent that they would be if similar treatment were provided at home.[7] This latter regime is quite often more advantageous to patients, which is why the free movement of services has featured so prominently in the lawsuits on cross-border medical care. Nevertheless, Regulation 1408/71 is the most obvious first point of call for the individual wishing to avoid unduly long domestic waiting lists by going abroad.

Excluding the Directive from situations where Regulation 1408/71 could be used limits the importance and effects of the Directive considerably. It will not apply to patients who experience domestic undue delay, but only apply to those who could be treated at home within a reasonable time, but nevertheless wish to go

---

[2] Commission Communication of 2 July 2008, *Proposal for a directive on the application of patients' rights in cross border health care*, COM(2008) 414 final. See Sauter (2009), p. 109.

[3] Amendments proposed by the Parliament after its first reading in Inter-institutional File 2008/0142 (COD), 30 April 2009.

[4] Regulation 1408/71 of the Council of 14 June 1971 on the application of social security schemes to employed persons, to self-employed persons, and to members of their families moving within the Community, *OJ* 1971 L 149/2. On the relationship between the Directive and the Regulation see Sauter (2009). See also Regulation 883/2004 of the European Parliament and of the Council of 29 April 2004 on the coordination of social security systems, *OJ* 2004 L 166/1; Sindbjerg Martinsen (2005).

[5] See Sauter (2009).

[6] See Hatzopoulos (2002); Dawes (2006), p. 67; ECJ, Case C-368/98 *Vanbraekel* v. *ANMC* [2001] *ECR* I-5363.

[7] See Sauter (2009); ECJ Case C-385/99 *Müller-Fauré* v. *Onderlinge Waarborgmaatschappij OZ Zorgverzekeringen* [2003] *ECR* I-4509; Case C-372/04 *Watts* v. *Bedford Primary Care Trust* [2006] *ECR* I-4325.

abroad. This may be for personal reasons, because of a desire to be treated without even a reasonable delay, or because of a perception that treatment is of a higher quality in other Member States. In all of these cases it is possible for the Member State to paint a picture of a selfish patient trying to claim unnecessary advantages. The Directive only applies to cases which are normatively more complex than the case of the individual who must go abroad if she/he is to be treated within a medically responsible time.

This legislative limitation is no doubt because of a desire not to disturb the integrity of the Regulation 1408/71 system, yet the effect is to apparently doom the Directive to a marginal role. The greatest reason for health care migration *is* undue domestic waiting times. Indeed, there is something paradoxical in the fact that the central Article of the Directive reaffirms the absence of an automatic right to hospital treatment abroad in situations to which the Directive applies (where there is no domestic undue delay).[8] Article 8(3) provides that States may, under certain conditions, provide for a system in which patients can only go abroad for hospital treatment after authorisation. Such a system may be applied, according to Article 8(3)(b) where its purpose is to prevent the outflow of patients from undermining, or being likely to undermine, the financial balance of the health care system or 'the planning and rationalisation carried out in the hospital sector to avoid hospital overcapacity, imbalance in the supply of hospital care and logistical and financial wastage, the maintenance of a balanced medical and hospital service open to all, or the maintenance of treatment capacity or medical competence on the territory of the concerned Member State'.

At first reading, therefore, the headline message of the Directive is not that patients to which it applies have the right to hospital treatment abroad, but that states have the right to say no. The justifications for restricting exit which Article 8(3)(b) permits follow the case law closely, and are relatively open-ended. Initially it will be easy for states to control outflows in the name of 'balance' and 'stability'.[9]

However, Article 8(4) goes on to emphasise that any such restrictions must be limited to what is 'necessary and proportionate to avoid such impact', and it can only be a question of time before evidential questions come to the fore. As Sauter argues, it is not the intention of the law that Member States simply be able to assert a need for restrictions.[10] On the contrary, the intention is that they apply these when they have good evidence of necessity. He cites recital 31 of the preamble, which provides:

> The evidence available indicates that the application of free movement principles regarding use of health care in another Member State within the limits of the cover guaranteed by the statutory sickness insurance scheme of the Member State of affiliation

---

[8] Article 8 of the proposed Directive.

[9] Ibid.

[10] See Sauter (2009).

will not undermine the health systems of the Member States or financial sustainability of their social security systems.

These evidential issues have been glossed in the cases, as is so often the case in free movement law. Partly because of the nature of the preliminary reference procedure the Court provides somewhat open instructions which national courts are left to apply to the facts as best they can. Whether States can show necessity has until now been a matter for national judges who have probably tended to follow the tradition of respect for governmental assertions. However, the recital suggests that despite the formal coherence of the infrastructural argument for restricting hospital care abroad (most hospital care costs are fixed, so foreign treatment means a state has to pay twice), which the Court has accepted, there is considerable scepticism as to whether in fact the threat is as dramatic as Member States have painted it.[11]

The presence of Article 8(4), in substance a legislative proportionality obligation, may therefore open up this issue to adjudication, and make it clearer that the necessity of restrictions is itself a litigable subject. In any case, the increased flow of cases which the directive would be likely to cause means that eventually the Court will be forced to address this point, and if it is not to turn Article 8 into a trump card for states it will have to require them to show at least reasonably convincing evidence on this point.[12]

That raises the possibility that the position may not be the same in all states, or even within states. For example, it is inevitable that the degree to which patients want to exit will vary from State to State, as will the opportunities. The presence of neighbouring states with shared or similar languages, for example, lowers the threshold to movement. The stability of health care systems will also vary considerably. Thus an unrestricted right of exit might seriously threaten one country, but not another: Swedish patients may have a right to go where they want, while Irish ones may not. Yet some States have locally organised health care, with finance and management decentralised. One region may not be threatened by migration, it may have solid finances, and be far from the border, and have well-regarded facilities, while another region would be, it may have wobbly finances, a bad reputation, and adjoin another state with temptingly modern and efficient hospitals. In another other economic law context the Court has ruled that the legality of tax rebates can only be assessed in their constitutional context, taking into account the structure of government and the extent to which tax power is centralised or decentralised.[13] In other contexts it has ruled that the justifiability of

[11] See ECJ, Case C-385/99 *Müller-Fauré* v. *Onderlinge Waarborgmaatschappij OZ Zorgverzekeringen* [2003] *ECR* I-4509; ECJ, Case C-372/04 *Watts* v. *Bedford Primary Care Trust* [2006] *ECR* I-4325; Davies (2004), p. 94.

[12] Cf., Sauter (2007), on the possible impact of SGEI status on evidential issues, slightly at odds with his argument quoted in the text above.

[13] ECJ, Case C-88/03 *Portugal* v. *Commission* [2006] *ECR* I-7115; see Greaves (2009), p. 779; Winter (2008), p. 183; ECJ, Joined Cases C-428/06 to C-434/06 *Unión General de Trabajadores de La Rioja* [2008] E*CR* I-6747.

restrictions on the free movement of services may depend on local market circumstances.[14] It would not be inconsistent to rule that the necessity of authorisation schemes can only be assessed in the light of the structure and organisation of the health care system, and local health care markets, and may in fact be a regionally variable issue.

Even where authorisation is permitted, the proportionality requirement should inhibit its blanket use. Some treatments are more expensive than others, and some require major investments in infrastructure. There is no basis in Article 8 above for concluding that because unrestricted movement would be a system-threat it follows that authorisation may be required for all hospital treatment. On the contrary, States or health care organisations must make systematic assessments in order to conclude what degree of authorisation and restriction protects system viability with the least impact on mobility.

Thus while the right of patients to exit their national system may be limited, the major added value of the directive will perhaps be its highlighting of the obligation on Member States to justify those limitations. If taken seriously, then this moves patient mobility from the plane of rhetoric to that of enforceable and objectively measurable rights.

Non-hospital treatment, by contrast to hospital treatment, is permitted without authorisation, in Article 7, but this is much less expensive and controversial.[15] Once again, the legislation here follows the Court.

8.3 Rights of Entry

Some health care institutions see foreign patients as clients to be welcomed. They pay for their care, and add to the institutional and national coffers. Other institutions tend to regard incoming patients as parasites, seeking to make use of an infrastructure developed for residents, and funded by their taxes. This difference partly depends on whether the fees charged for care cover the costs or not, and partly on political and institutional perspectives. The financing of health care is too murky and complex for economic rationality to be entirely determinative of the patient-hospital relationship.

The draft Directive does not actually state a right for patients to receive health care in another Member State. This is of course implicit in Article 56 TFEU, but the extent of the right remains open to argument: which restrictions could be justified by the receiving state threatened with an excessive influx, and facing similar system shocks to those states sending many patients abroad? One assumes

[14] ECJ, Joined Cases C-94/04 and C-202/04 *Cipolla and Meloni* [2006] *ECR* I-11421.

[15] See ECJ, Case C-385/99 *Müller-Fauré* v. *Onderlinge Waarborgmaatschappij OZ Zorgverzekeringen* [2003] *ECR* I-4509; ECJ, Case C-372/04 *Watts* v. *Bedford Primary Care Trust* [2006] *ECR* I-4325.

that, on the basis of standard free movement doctrine, the reasons for restrictions, which the Court and Article 8 of the Directive, have acknowledged as legitimate in the context of exit, could be applied *mutatis mutandis* to control entry.

The proposed Directive's contribution to this discussion is found in Article 5(1)(g), which provides that 'patients from other Member States shall enjoy equal treatment with the nationals of the Member State of treatment, including the protection against discrimination provided for according to Community law and national legislation in force in the Member State of treatment'. The Parliament has proposed amending this so that the ban on discrimination against foreign patients covers also discrimination on grounds of racial or ethnic origin, sex, religion or belief, disability, age or sexual orientation.[16]

This discrimination ban should serve as a limited right of access to health care in other Member States. At its narrowest, it is a ban on nationality discrimination, a mere embodiment of Article 18 TFEU. In that case, it will prevent states or health care institutions from distinguishing between residents and non-residents unless they can show an objective justification. Given the context and purpose of the directive, and the equality policy which Article 5 clearly reflects, we may expect the threshold for such justifications to be high. The systemic or financial threat will have to be imminent and significant.

Article 5 can also be read more broadly. 'Patients from other Member States' are not necessarily nationals of their state of residence, merely residents. Article 5 could be understood as a prohibition on discrimination on grounds of non-residence. This accords more precisely with the policy goals of the directive, but sits a little oddly with the reference in the same sentence of the article to 'nationals of the Member State of treatment'. Moreover, a prohibition on residence discrimination would prevent measures being taken even where system stability was threatened, which would be perhaps disproportionate, and would put the state of treatment in a more vulnerable position than the State of residence, which may limit exit. On balance, it is most plausible that Article 5 simply reflects the ban on nationality discrimination, but will be read strictly, so that residence-based preferences are hard to justify.

The Parliament's proposed amendments raise more complex and challenging issues. They refer to the protection against discrimination which is provided by 'EU law and national legislation' as if to suggest that nothing new is being added. However, it is far from self-evident that EU or national law will always prevent discrimination on this range of grounds within the sphere of health care. Since the policy of the addition is so clear, it is most likely that it would in practice be read as a guarantee against discrimination on these grounds, rather than the mere commentary on the status quo that it pretends to be.

Although the proposed amendment only refers to discrimination against migrant patients, it is hard to imagine that a State would extend protection from

[16] Amendments proposed by the Parliament after its first reading, in Inter-institutional File 2008/0142 (COD), 30 April 2009.

discrimination on grounds of race or religion to these, but not to domestically resident ones. Implementation in practice would therefore amount to a harmonisation measure, creating a European-wide non-discrimination framework for health care. The question then arises when exactly such discrimination should be considered to occur. For example, does a local choice to invest in a breast cancer clinic but not a prostate cancer centre amount to potential sex discrimination? Would religious patients have the right to choose the sex of their doctor? Would an absence of available female specialists amount to religious discrimination? And given the varying prevalence of some diseases between different ethnic groups, could funding and treatment decisions by health authorities be challenged on the grounds of possible underlying racial bias, not necessarily conscious, but *de facto*? Would transport to, and from, hospitals become an issue of disability discrimination? Much would turn in all these cases on the issue of justification, but discrimination law in other fields has been a rich source of creative litigation, and the ability to found a *prima facie* case of indirect discrimination on the presence of statistical disparities showing a greater impact on one group than another means that numerous challenges would be possible.[17]

8.4 Facilitation

Articles 6 and 9 are about the facilitation of migration. They address the procedural and information issues which make rights practical and enforceable. They stick very closely to the judgments of the Court. Article 6 provides that patients will be reimbursed for health care received abroad where they would have had a right to similar health care at home, and that the tariff for reimbursement shall reflect the level of costs which would have been assumed by the domestic system. Article 6 also provides that the information on these tariffs will be made clearly available in advance, so that patients can know what their rights are. Finally, Article 6 provides that patients shall have a right to their medical records, since without these it may be difficult for them to continue treatment at a foreign institution.

Article 6 highlights two difficult aspects of patient mobility: which treatment is to be paid for, and how much is to be paid for it. The way in which these questions are to be addressed can be extracted from the case law, and Article 6 introduces no shocking deviations, but there is a new level of urgency created by the explicit legislative imposition of obligations on Member States to define their treatment, and define their tariffs.

At the heart of the question of which treatment is to be paid for is a tension: on the one hand, States are free to define the scope of their health care systems, so the starting point is that a patient should get reimbursement for foreign treatment if

[17] See ECJ, Case C-167/97 *Seymour-Smith and Perez* [1999] *ECR* I-623; Tobler (2005).

that treatment would have been paid for at home.[18] Yet on the other hand, one of the reasons for migration is that different, perhaps better treatments for the same conditions may be available elsewhere. These will not even necessarily be more expensive. If reimbursement for foreign treatment is limited to treatment which would also have been available at home, then this amounts to the establishment of a right to migration that is only enforceable where it is largely superfluous. The usefulness of the right would be limited to cases where treatment at home is not available without undue delay. However, as noted above, in such circumstances the draft Directive does not apply.[19] Therefore, if the Directive were to limit reimbursement for foreign treatment to treatments also available at home, then it would be of very little additional value to a patient.

An alternative approach, more compatible with the underlying policy of migration as a tool for improving patient welfare, would be to say that where a state accepts responsibility for treating a condition, then within the financial limits that the health care system sets, the patient should be able to receive treatment abroad that is different from that which she/he would have received at home, and still be reimbursed, provided that the foreign treatment is medically effective and responsible.[20] Reimbursement should not so much turn on the degree of similarity between the manner of treatment at home and abroad, as on the question of whether the State accepts the obligation to pay a certain amount for the condition in question, in which case the patient who is able to use those funds for preferable or better treatment abroad should be able to.

Yet Member States are suspicious of such an approach because in reality the extent to which a health care system pays for treatment is not determined by the condition, but by the treatment. There is no figure of x euros for a certain disease, but rather price tags on the various forms of treatment. Thus, paying for treatment abroad that is not yet available at home may well add to total health care costs.

The draft Directive does not fully resolve the tensions, and its text retains an unsatisfactory ambiguity. It is captured in Article 6(1) which provides that migrant patients

> ... will not be prevented from receiving health care provided in another Member State where the treatment in question is among the benefits provided for by the legislation of the Member State of affiliation to which the insured person is entitled. The Member State of affiliation shall reimburse the costs to the insured person, which would have been paid for by its statutory social security system had the same or similar health care been provided in its territory. In any event, it is for the Member State of affiliation to determine the health care that is paid for regardless of where it is provided.

In the first sentence, the Article provides that payment is limited to treatment abroad that could also have been obtained at home. In the next and subsequent

[18] See *Watts*, *supra* n. 7.

[19] See Sect. 8.2, 'Rights of Exit' *supra*.

[20] Cf. ECJ, Case C-157/99 *Geraets-Smits* v. *Stichting Ziekenfonds; Peerbooms* v. *Stichting CZ Groep Zorgverzekeringen* [2001] *ECR* I-5473.

sentences, the word 'similar' makes its entry, suggesting that one can indeed go abroad for improved treatment, within the limits of the concept of similarity. This concept is highly contestable. A patient might reasonably argue that there is a huge difference between treatment by pills and treatment by surgery, but different surgical approaches should nevertheless be seen as 'similar' in the context of treatment of a given disease. A surgeon might disagree, taking the view that consequences, techniques, risks and philosophies vary significantly between the two types of operation. A financial officer might be inclined to view 'similarity' in this context in the light of whether one operation is much more expensive than the other. In any case, having raised more doubts than it removes about what precisely is to be paid for, the sub-article concludes with a slightly despairing summing up: in case the preceding text is a bit messy, it seems to say, let us conclude by remembering that the big idea here is that states choose the scope of their health care coverage. That is all very well, except that the relationship between this big idea and the notion of similar treatment is precisely the unanswered question. The use of the words 'In any event' in legislation is unusual, and it seems not unlikely that the article reflects a not-entirely-successful attempt to bash out a compromise between different views.

The Parliament took a somewhat more assertive approach in its amendments. It suggested that Article 6 provides that treatment should be paid for 'which would have been paid for had equally effective health care been provided in its territory'.[21] If one ignores the problematic grammar of the sentence, clearly if equally effective treatment had been provided, then there would be no *need* to pay for the treatment in question, the underlying idea is clear: where a state did not provide adequate treatment not because of principled exclusion, but just because it was not available, it should pay for that treatment abroad. This is confirmed by the following amendment sentence: 'If a Member State of affiliation rejects the reimbursement of this treatment, that Member State shall have to give a medical justification for its decision'. The situation of a patient who can only receive the most effective treatment by going abroad, is not to be compared with the patient wanting to go abroad for other reasons. The latter may be restricted on systemic grounds, but the former may not. The order of hierarchy is (1) medical necessity, (2) the financial health of the system, and (3) other preferences for foreign treatment. This is further reflected in the parliament's proposal that patients with rare diseases have a right to treatment abroad 'even if the treatment in question is not among the benefits provided for by the legislation of the Member State of affiliation'.[22] The treatment of rare diseases is often expensive, and many states, particularly smaller ones, will find that the absence of patients fails to justify the costs. This amendment recognises the logic of European centres of excellence, a pooling of resources to achieve the treatment scale necessary for rare diseases. Not only

[21] Proposed amendment to Article 6(1), in 'Amendments proposed', *supra* n. 3.

[22] Ibid.

may this serve patients, but it also helps medical science and industry in the EU remain at the cutting edge.

Closely linked to the first problem, what should be paid for, is the second one raised by Article 6, that of the scope of reimbursement. Once again, the idea is very simple: the State must reimburse up to the same extent that it would do at home. However, making this work in practice requires established tariffs for treatments, which must be clearly and publicly available in advance if patients are to be able to exercise their rights. If they cannot know whether the treatment they are being offered in another Member State falls within the financial limits of their insurance, then they will be significantly deterred from accepting it. Prior information is central to creating real mobility opportunities. Hence Article 6(4) provides that

> Member States shall have a mechanism for calculation of costs that are to be reimbursed to the insured person by the statutory social security system for health care provided in another Member State. This mechanism shall be based on objective, non-discriminatory criteria known in advance and the costs reimbursed according to this mechanism shall be not less than what would have been assumed had the same or similar health care been provided in the territory of the Member State of affiliation.

The requirement of a 'mechanism for calculation' is a little obscure. It must surely include, among other aspects, a list of the costs of domestic treatment. Without such a list it will be difficult to make the comparison between the costs of domestic and foreign treatment, yet such a comparison is what determines the extent of the right to reimbursement. The other aspect of such a mechanism is likely to be, as discussed below, a system for comparing prices, since they may well not be presented in a way that makes this easy. Once again, the Parliament is much more direct and transparent. In its amendments it proposes that the Directive should explicitly state that Member States must 'have a transparent mechanism for the calculation of costs that are to be charged for the health care provided',[23] and that Member States of affiliation 'may offer patients a voluntary system of prior notification whereby, in return for such notification, the patient shall receive a written confirmation of the maximum amount that will be paid. That written confirmation can then be taken to the hospital of treatment and reimbursement would then be made directly to that hospital by the Member State of affiliation'.[24] These are both deeply practical and patient-friendly amendments that would do a great deal to facilitate movement. This is no doubt one objection that Member States will have to them, but it is to be hoped that the non-threatening inclusion of the word 'may' will assuage these fears, and that then the Member States will in fact, as a result of patient pressure, adopt the suggested approach.

The ease of the demand, 'there shall be a mechanism', belies the intense difficulty of achieving the goal which is aspired to. The tariff issue is one which offers joy only to lawyers. Firstly, for a given Member State to establish a tariff list will

[23] Proposed amendment, introduction of a new Article 5(3)(a).

[24] Proposed amendment, introduction of a new Article 9(a).

be a complex and contested exercise. Secondly, comparing tariffs between Member States requires a certain harmonisation of methodology which is neither present nor imminent. Article 6 cannot work without, at the very least, intensive coordination between states in a spirit of flexibility and goodwill. More realistically, it will probably take harmonising legislation to make its requirements fully workable.

The problem with establishing tariffs is practical, legal, and political.[25] As a matter of substance, it is hard to determine the true cost of a treatment since the way that fixed costs should be allocated can be contested.[26] Moreover decisions have legal consequences. Since hospitals often receive money both from the state and from patients and insurers, they are vulnerable to claims that they are using public money to improve their position on a competitive market: state aid.[27] Also, if they come up with a price that is artificially low, then this will deter exit by patients, since their budget abroad will also be low, but that means the tariffs may be challenged as barriers to free movement. They will also have the unwelcome side effect of attracting incoming patients who will, as a result of the low tariffs, be a net burden on the system. On the other hand, if tariffs are high, then incomers will be deterred, and those who come will be profitable, but domestic patients will be encouraged to go abroad because of the generous budget available to them. High tariffs encourage the export of funds, and also threaten the finances of the system. Conceivably, patients from other countries might claim that high tariffs were a concealed protectionist measure, tending to keep foreign patients out. Alternatively, such high tariffs might amount to covert discrimination since while domestic patients would pay the same tariffs the resulting profitability in the health care sector might well reduce the domestic tax burden. Patients can pay the costs of health care via tax, or via payment per treatment, and an excess of the latter is naturally compensated for by a diminution of the former. It moreover has the advantage of extracting the maximum from the incoming migrant patient.[28]

If a State establishes plausible tariffs, it then has to deal with the political consequences of laying bare the efficiency of its health care system. Whether treatment is cheaper or more expensive than in neighbouring States, this will raise questions that the public will want answered. Notably, some of the states that have traditionally enjoyed waiting lists (the UK and the Netherlands) are also States that have relatively expensive health care and relatively highly paid doctors. The exposure of this combination to public scrutiny could be uncomfortable.

The completion of the domestic price list is just the beginning of the migration problem, rather than its solution. There is no uniquely correct or rational way to decide how care should be priced. One state may have a price for an operation

---

25 See for discussion Davies (2007), p. 158.

26 See Buendia Sierra and Hancher (1998), p. 901.

27 See Sauter and Schepel (2009), Chapter 8.

28 For analogous considerations in the context of education funding (grants or subsidised fees), see Davies (2005), p. 217.

including all recuperation and after-care. Another may have a price for the surgical procedure, a price per night in hospital, and a price per consultation. One may treat material costs as separate from personnel ones.[29] The differences between states will mean that the patient shopping with a price list from one state will find it difficult to work out what this buys him in another state. If she/he goes ahead and gets treatment, then reimbursement will inevitably be full of challenges and conflicts. The principle of mutual recognition and the obligation to respect free movement mean that states cannot simply refuse to pay bills that are not in a form reflecting their domestic price structure. They must try and get behind the tariffs to make objectively justifiable comparisons, and show the reasonable flexibility and openness that free movement demands. However, the transparent cross-border purchasing which the Directive demands and aspires to cannot be achieved by the single-state focus of Article 6.

Other, although similar, procedural issues are raised by Article 9. It sets out the procedures applicable to authorisation schemes, imposing an obligation on Member States to ensure that these operate in an way which is authentically accessible and fair: the criteria on which decisions are to be based must be objective, non-discriminatory, and published in advance (Article 9(1) and 9(3); time limits for dealing with requests must be published in advance and adhered to (Article 9(2)); those time limits must take into account medical circumstances, but also the patient's ability to do their work or profession (Article 9(4)); and finally there must be the possibility of appeal to the courts and the facility for interim measures (Article 9(5)).

These provisions are, like many aspects of the Directive, a codification of the case law.[30] However, that does not make them unimportant. Directives require implementation, whereas in practice a Court judgment is less likely to be fully accommodated within national practices. Codification of the case law may be seen as a very useful completion of the process of embedding principles of free movement concretely and effectively in national law. In the context of an issues such as patient migration, where both conscious state resistance and institutional inertia are high, this may be particularly so.

Article 9 is therefore carefully constructed to ensure that states cannot effectively block free movement by having slow and inaccessible procedures. Nevertheless, the Article shows how difficult it is to close off all the paths of resistance open to states and institutions. Firstly, many of the terms and obligations stated are relatively open: this article provides principles to be translated, rather than precisely measurable and unambiguous rules. What is transparent, what is medically necessary, and how are the factors mentioned in Article 9(4) to be weighed? There will inevitably be disputes and a recalcitrant health care system can adopt a stance

---

[29] A flavour of the complexity is provided by Schreyogg et al. (2006), p. 215.

[30] For example, ECJ, Case C-157/99 *Geraets-Smits* v. *Stichting Ziekenfonds; Peerbooms* v. *Stichting CZ Groep Zorgverzekeringen* [2001] *ECR* I-5473; ECJ, Case C-385/99 *Müller-Fauré* v. *Onderlinge Waarborgmaatschappij OZ Zorgverzekeringen* [2003] *ECR* I-4509; ECJ, Case C-372/04 *Watts* v. *Bedford Primary Care Trust* [2006] *ECR* I-4325.

which is superficially reconcilable with Article 9 but not with its spirit, nor its underlying policy. If the article is to be a success, then the principles of procedural accessibility and timeliness must apply not just to the initial decision but also to appeals to a court. It must be possible to appeal without having to wait so long that the point of the appeal is lost. The obligation to provide interim measures in Article 9(5) is therefore particularly important: without interim measures rights of free movement would be barely enforceable, since patients would often not be able to pay upfront themselves, but would usually not be able, or prepared, to wait for treatment until the judicial path is exhausted. Waiting lists for treatment may be long, but the time taken to reach an appeal court is often longer. On the other hand, recovery of medical costs from a patient that has made use of an interim measure but then finally lost before the courts will often be unrealistic, or cruel: the scale of such costs may be beyond the average individual's means. Courts will therefore be reluctant to be over-generous with their interim decisions, while far-thinking patients may be cautious before exercising a right which could, perhaps, lead to a large bill in the future.

Article 9(4) is interesting when combined with *Geraets-Smits and Peerbooms*.[31] That case established that the concept of medically necessity is to be decided not in accordance with local idiosyncracies but by reference to international medical science. One may therefore expect that the criteria in Article 9(4) are to be read independently of local medical traditions. The fact that in some states it is customary to make patients wait months in pain or discomfort does not in itself show that this is reasonable, when other states, and the international medical consensus, take a different approach.[32] The time which Article 9(4) allows institutions to take depends on the medical and personal context of the patient. States and institutions will want to read this as requiring them not to keep patients waiting for decisions any longer than is normal in their system, as a 'right to the national norm'.[33] However, *Geraets-Smits* suggests that the Court will read it as requiring them to keep patients waiting no longer than international medical science and international good practice allow: a right to international good practice. For states where long waiting is a veritable national tradition (the UK, notably) it may be a shock to see this dismissed as unreasonable in the light of objective internationally accepted good medical practice. Still, it may be commented that the UK patients surely have the right to know that the waiting times they have traditionally been subjected to would be considered violations of basic rights, and of good medical practice, in most of their neighbour states.

It must however be remembered in this context that Article 9(4) only applies to the time taken to make a decision, it is not concerned with the definition of 'undue

---

[31] ECJ, Case C-157/99 *Geraets-Smits* v. *Stichting Ziekenfonds; Peerbooms* v. *Stichting CZ Groep Zorgverzekeringen* [2001] *ECR* I-5473.

[32] Ibid.

[33] See the Member State arguments in ECJ, Case C-385/99 *Müller-Fauré* v. *Onderlinge Waarborgmaatschappij OZ Zorgverzekeringen* [2003] *ECR* I-4509; ECJ, Case C-372/04 *Watts* v. *Bedford Primary Care Trust* [2006] *ECR* I-4325.

delay' in Regulation 1408/71 or the case law on Article 56 TFEU. Yet the criteria for determining a reasonable time to take a decision in Article 9(4) mirror closely the criteria for determining undue delay which the Court has used. They are, in both cases, primarily patient-centred. In reality the question of how long a patient may be kept waiting for treatment and how long a patient may be kept waiting for a decision on authorisation will often be substantively the same, so a broadly parallel approach makes sense. The limitation of Article 9(4) to decision-making time limits, and not treatment time limits, is merely a result of the limited scope of the directive: if the patient's claim is that domestic treatment is not available without undue delay, then it is Regulation 1408/71 or Article 56 TFEU to which she/he should turn.

8.5 Harmonisation

Under the heading 'responsibilities of the Member State of Treatment', Article 5(1) of the proposed Directive contains several provisions which can only be understood as substantive harmonisation of health care. They concern the rights of patients within a medical system, and establish certain shared EU principles governing the status of the individual patient and her or his relationship to her or his doctor and treating institution. These provisions may be grouped into three categories. Articles 5(1)(a), (b), (d) and (e) concern the enforcement of quality standards within the domestic health care system, and require states to police and maintain these, and ensure that patients have effective remedies and redress when things go wrong. This reflects the conventional free movement approach that openness can only be premised upon mutual trust, which is in turn built upon shared basic standards. Secondly, Article 5(1)(c) addresses the rights of patients to information about their treatment and situation. These may be considered as based upon the same free movement logic as the first group. Thirdly, Article 5(1)(g) creates a European patients' non-discrimination right, as discussed above.[34]

Insofar as this non-discrimination right extends beyond migrants, and beyond nationality discrimination—as the parliament wants[35]—it is a quite significant harmonisation measure. While it is often difficult to object in principle to anti-discrimination rules, their open texture can lead to unexpected and controversial interpretations, so that a normatively unobjectionable basic rule can lead to policy results which are far more contestable. Encompassing health policy within a framework of open-ended non-discrimination rights is certainly a defensible approach, but not a self-evident one. If states are required to do this, as Article 5(1)(g) seems to suggest, then this is no mean EU achievement.

---

[34] Section 8.3, 'Rights of entry', *supra*.

[35] Ibid.

Article 5(1)(c) is also somewhat more impactful than may be initially apparent. It provides that Member States will ensure that:

> health care providers provide all relevant information to enable patients to make an informed choice, in particular on availability, prices and outcomes of the health care provided and details of their insurance cover or other means of personal or collective protection with regard to professional liability.

Making an informed choice is something that can only be achieved if the patient understands their prognosis, the possible treatments, and their risks and side-effects. Article 5(1)(c) can therefore only be sensibly read as requiring states to ensure their doctors fully inform patients about all these things.

Once again, it is hard to object to this idea in the abstract, but translated to concrete rules it may well conflict with well-established medical traditions. The idea that doctors should fully inform patients about risks, side-effects, or prognoses may be well-accepted in some states, but will not be the practice in others.[36] Indeed, until relatively recently, it was common practice in most jurisdictions for a doctor to withhold distressing information from a patient and/or their family in circumstances where that doctor felt it would do no good, and might cause more suffering. Such paternalism is generally seen as old-fashioned today, but is far from extinct in all states. It would seem to be the target of attack by Article 5(1)(c), although one might perhaps comment that the patient who is judged not able to deal with the truth about their condition will not generally be the patient most likely to make use of cross-border health care.

Legislating for a patient's right to information is also an intervention in the autonomy and freedom of the doctor. The judgment about how much information to give a patient will typically be a matter for the individual doctor, and the degree to which states feel it is their right or responsibility to intervene in this will depend upon their view of the role of the liberal professions and of the state. In this sensitive context therefore, an EU demand for national implementing legislation addressing such matters may be expected to provoke some resistance, perhaps intermittently outrage.

Both non-discrimination rights, and rights to information, are about the position of the patient within the health care system; they emancipate him or her, and introduce an individualistic element into the system as a whole.[37] This harmonisation of patient rights is not quite the same thing as substantive harmonisation of institutions. Nothing in Article 5 requires particular structures or organisation. However, it may be suggested that aligning the position of patients in different Member States may be a useful precursor to aligning the structure of the relevant national institutions, if only via a contribution to a shared European patient mentality. Thus, even though the non-discrimination obligation does not as such dictate any institutional form, it may help pave the way for EU-wide health care system regulation in the future.

---

[36] Leenan (1993), Chapters. 4, 8 and 9, especially pp. 41–45.

[37] Newdick (2006), p. 1645.

The significance of these provisions may, therefore, lie not just in their substance, but to a large extent simply in the fact that they exist.[38] They are not in themselves necessarily very controversial or far-reaching, but they amount to a concession that coordination without any substantive convergence of health care regimes is unrealistic, and help break the taboo against harmonisation in this field.

8.6 Conclusions

It can be argued that the proposed Directive on patient mobility is, in substance, a 'Citizenship Directive', and one that fits within a social market tradition. It effectively entrenches a right to good quality health care, by making it practically possible for patients to receive that when it is not available at home, or even when it is, but they would rather go abroad. It is, therefore, a Directive that is concerned with one of the most important aspects of membership of a modern welfare State, and tries to balance market and control mechanisms to enrich that membership. Nor should the query as to how many patients will want to, or be able to, exercise the rights it protects, particularly as a result of its odd relationship to Regulation 1408/71, be allowed to entirely obscure its importance as a European statement of principle, about the obligation of States to citizens. The cases show, moreover, that EU action to entrench access to good quality health care is not superfluous. That fact of growing litigation by patients seeking help abroad is evidence that states have not been able to guarantee this on their own.

The proposed Directive is also a 'Citizenship Directive' in a particularly European sense. It instrumentalises the citizen, creating a situation where, by exercising his or her rights, he or she also achieves the integrative goals of the EU. This technique is ubiquitous in EU law, and central to the mechanisms of the Internal Market. By acting, we create society. The EU aims to finesse the opposition between individual rights and collective solidarity, by using the former to create an open Europe which, it may at least be argued, will be more realistically able to guarantee the latter. The rights in the Directive then, like other free movement rights, are a form of substantive constitution building, harnessing the needs and wishes of individuals to re-constitute the European space.

Yet this coherent and harmonious broader picture does not mean that the Directive will not cause considerable pain and upset. Although to a great extent the codification of case law, by forcing States to take implementing action and amend institutions it is likely to be, if adopted, the catalyst that actually makes patient mobility happen on a meaningful scale. That will create pressures and changes which will not be without costs, and an appropriate question to ask, in the light of the various aspects of the directive considered above in this chapter, is who will be

---

[38] Dawes (2006), p. 67; Davies (2007a) p. 215.

the winners and who will be the losers if the directive is adopted in something close to the form discussed here?

Top of the list of winners are clearly mobile patients, provided they get what they expect and treatment abroad does not turn out to be more different and less satisfactory than they had hoped. The information and equality requirements and the procedural protection of the reimbursement rights aim to prevent this. The facilitation measures are thus at the heart of whether this Directive will be a success or not.

The EU is also potentially a winner. Mobility of patients will tend to lead to greater integration of health care systems, not to mention greater social and economic integration. Apart from taking us closer to the open-ended integration ambitions of the TEU, there are also concrete policy advantages to such health care integration. Health care is one of the largest emerging global industries, its economic size being nothing new, but its status as a (quasi) market activity being relatively novel, and as with other industries, the removal of internal obstacles to movement may place EU actors in a better position on the global stage.[39] Patient mobility may be a step towards seeing health care not just as a national social service, but as a transnational service industry in which European organisations undoubtedly have much to offer: apart from their medical expertise, expertise in health care system creation and management, and in the reconciliation of economic goals with social ones, is probably concentrated in Europe as nowhere else, as a result of the prevalence of universal welfare states. European health care systems will increasingly be a part of global health care, not just national.

Yet the established national health care systems will undoubtedly have a hard time dealing with this transition.[40] Free movement almost always causes organisational stress, and in health care, with its rigidities and traditions, and tight budgets this is likely to be more so than usual. It remains, moreover, an open question whether we should regard this national pain as an inevitable part of the move to something better, or as a sign that national solidarity and institutional coherence is being sacrificed to transnational economic ends. One may have successful industries providing top quality care to patients with initiative, but will the average patient be the loser? It may be noted that while the Court has been consistent in permitting states to protect the financial stability of their health care systems, and the Directive does not remove this right, there are more subtle pressures involved than the mere cost of foreign treatment.[41] The exit of the most mobile patients from the national system may reduce domestic lobbying for that system to improve. As Hirschman argued, if the most critical customers exit an organisation, then this gives it a licence to decay.[42] The mobile patient may well be the critical and influential patient, precisely the group that is capable of steering

[39] Davies (2006).

[40] See n. 1 *supra*.

[41] Discussed in Davies (2006).

[42] Hirschman (1970).

national institutions in the right direction. If they have an option, then they may care less about the domestic system, and the less active majority may be abandoned to depressed and indifferent monopoly providers.

Seen in this light, one may wonder if the Directive reflects an over-narrow policy vision. While it contains provisions protecting the financial stability of the health care system, it does not consider the wider costs of individualising health care on a European scale. This is inevitable: such individualisation is a premise of patient mobility without harmonisation. The political choice to liberate patients from collective constraints is what made, or may make, the directive possible. However, just as it is hard to predict patient flows and the financial consequences of migration, it seems plausible to claim that it is hard to predict the social and institutional consequences of the directive too. Given the difficulties of repealing or amending EU legislation once adopted, it may be suggested that adopting the Directive without providing for derogation on broad grounds such as public policy and social cohesion is taking a certain risk. Such derogations require strict policing, but they are a common feature of EU law for a good reason; even well-intentioned law may have unintended consequences. And yet, there is also a certain courage and principle in this risk. It entrenches an integrationist momentum. Where problems arise as a result of patient mobility under the directive the only option of states, given the limited possibilities for individual Member State derogation, is to solve those problems collectively, via further EU measures. Once again, in a most typically European way, the directive is best understood as the beginning of an EU health care integration process which will almost certainly acquire a momentum of its own.

References

Buendia Sierra J-L, Hancher L (1998) Cross-subsidization in EC law. CML Rev 35

Davies G (2004) Health and efficiency: community law and national health systems in the light of Müller-Fauré. Mod Law Rev 67

Davies G (2005) Higher education, equal access, and residence conditions: does EU law allow Member States to charge higher fees to students not previously resident in that state. Maastricht J Eur Comp Law 5 12(3)

Davies G (2006) 'The process and side-effects of harmonisation of European welfare states', Jean Monnet Working Paper 2/06. Available at http://www.ssrn.com

Davies G (2007a) The Community's internal market based competence to regulate health care: scope, strategies and consequences. Maastricht J Eur Comp Law

Davies G (2007b) The effect of Mrs Watts' trip to France on the National Health Service. King's Law J 18

Dawes A (2006) Bonjour Herr Doctor: National Health care Systems, the internal market, and cross-border health care within the European Union. LIEI 33

Greaves R (2009) Autonomous regions, taxation and EC state aids rules. EL Rev 34

Hatzopoulos V (2002) Killing national health and insurance systems but healing patients? The European market for health care services after the judgments of the ECJ in *Vanbraekel* and *Peerbooms*. CML Rev 39

Hirschman AO (1970) Exit voice and loyalty: responses to decline in firms, organizations and states. Harvard University Press, Cambridge

Leenan H (1993). The rights of patients in Europe. Kluwer law and Taxation, The Hague. Chapters 4, 8 and 9

Montgomery J (2005) The impact of European Union law on English health care law. In: Dougan M, Spaventa E (eds) Social welfare and EU law. Hart, Oxford

Newdick C (2006) Citizenship, free movement and health care: cementing individual rights by corroding social solidarity. CML Rev 43

Sauter W (2007) 'Services of general economic interest and universal service obligations as an EU law framework for curative health care', TILEC Discussion paper 2007–29. Available at http://www.ssrn.com

Sauter W (2009) The proposed patients' rights directive and the reform of (cross-border) health care in the EU. LIEI 36

Sauter W, Schepel H (2009) State and market in EU law. CUP, Cambridge (Chapter 8)

Schreyogg J et al (2006) Methods to determine reimbursement rates for diagnosis related groups (DRG): a comparison of nine European countries. Health care Manag Sci 9

Sindbjerg Martinsen D (2005) Social security regulation in the EU: the de-territorialization of welfare. In: de Búrca G (ed) EU law and the welfare state. OUP, Oxford

Tobler C (2005) Indirect discrimination: a case study into the development of the legal concept of indirect discrimination under EC law. Intersentia, Antwerp

Winter JA (2008) Annotation. CML Rev 45

Chapter 9
Disrupting the Community—Saving Public Health Ethics from the EU Internal Market

Christopher Newdick

Contents

9.1 Introduction

EU Institutions have misconceived the relationship between the economics of free market individualism and the politics of social welfare in the EU. The consequence of this misconception is especially serious with respect to cross-border access to health care because of the risk of damaging public health ethics. Public health concerns collective policies to promote community health and often involves the distribution of rights and duties in society.[1] Its *ethical* dimension can be explained

[1] See Dawson and Verweij (2007a, b); Bayer et al. (2007) and Gostin (2004), p. 509.

C. Newdick (✉)
University of Reading, Reading, UK
e-mail: c.newdick@reading.ac.uk

J. W. van de Gronden et al. (eds.), *Health Care and EU Law*,
Legal Issues of Services of General Interest, DOI: 10.1007/978-90-6704-728-9_9,

on a spectrum of values which puts at each extreme the objectives *of freedom of choice, individual rights* and *liberty* on the one hand, and *democracy, equality* and *community* on the other. Each may be characterised as the 'liberal' and 'republican', presumptions of citizenship.[2] Of course, there are dangers inherent at both extremes of the spectrum; as to unrestricted individualism, as much as blind communitarianism. Scharpf suggests that balance is preserved because they serve as 'mutual antidotes' against the other's excesses. 'Republican collectivism is moderated by the protection of individual liberties, whereas libertarian egotism is constrained by the institutions of collective determination.'[3] Recognising the pull in both directions, we can better understand the proper balance between them, especially with respect to cross-border access to health care in the EU.

Social welfare helps to measure the extent to which nation states lean towards one end of this political spectrum or the other. It is part of the fabric of constitutional norms and expectations within which governments balance the tensions between individual *market freedoms* and broader *civic virtues*[4] and which permit a redistribution of resources to reflect social need. Redistribution is said to be warranted by virtue of the moral bond which 'connects the strong to the weak, the lucky and the unlucky, the rich and the poor, creating a union that transcends all differences of interest, drawing its strength from history, culture, religion, language and so on.'[5] As Esping-Andersen has so elegantly shown,[6] the way in which this understanding affects national welfare policy differs because the 'social contract' between government and governed varies from place to place.[7] For example, contributory mechanisms of social insurance used in the 'Bismarkian' systems may be considered more regressive in terms of tax burdens than 'Beveridgean' systems in which benefits are financed from progressive taxation.[8] Whichever model we examine, the *politics* of each describes the community-based sense of civic republicanism embedded within EU Member States and national policy-making is inevitably constrained by the political environment in which those systems have evolved.[9]

In the EU, however, current Institutional presumptions heavily predispose the European Court of Justice towards the *libertarian* end of this spectrum and the protection of individual rights. Its mission is to promote fair market competition

---

[2] Discussing the evolution of these concepts, among the vast literature, see Sandell (2009), Dagger (1998) and Epp (1998).

[3] Scharpf (2009), p. 7. Discussing the dialectics of individualism, civic allegiance and nationalism in post war Germany, see Muller (2007), Chapter 1.

[4] Bellamy (2009), p. 13. On 'constitutional rights norms', see Alexy (2004), Chapter 2.

[5] Walzer (1983), pp. 82–83.

[6] Esping-Andersen (1990).

[7] According to his 'liberal', 'conservative', and 'social democratic' models, with the Scandanavian countries being the most progressive.

[8] See the illuminating study of Baldwin (1993), p. 52.

[9] See Somek (2008a, b), Chapter 3.

among Member States. However, because 'political' and democratic components in EU decision-making are weak, *civic republican* values, and the forces which affect *national* identity may be neglected. As a result, claims of individuals and companies may override democratic national institutions and political legacies. This poses a problem for the doctrine of EU supremacy because it transforms

> ... the hierarchical relation between European and national law into a hierarchical relationship between liberal and republican constitutional principles. Subjective rights [of individuals] may override all countervailing national objectives, regardless of their salience as manifestations of democratic self-determination.[10]

These concerns are especially pertinent to European national welfare systems and ideas of *public* health ethics.

Health care priority setting is one element of public health ethics. In the EU, it raises the question whether Member States should normally retain control over patients' cross-border access to health care, or whether individuals should largely be free to seek care elsewhere in the EU. In EU law, the contrast between these two approaches to public health ethics can be expressed on the *republican* and *liberal* spectrum. Each is illuminated by two opinions of Advocate General Jarabo Colomer in 2001 and 2007. As to the first, he said:

> Sickness funds must be able to expect that, barring *rare exceptions subject to their consent*, any health care which insured persons require will actually be provided by the practitioners and institutions contracted ...[11]

Prior authorisation for treatment abroad is necessary because the allocation of finite resources in any public health care system involves distributive ethics. When individuals claim access to finite public resources, the dispute is not between two parties alone—the individual and the state. It is between three parties, the third being 'the public'; indeed, the tensions are 'polycentric' because they touch all those who may be affected by decisions to divert resources from one purpose to another. Courts are not well-informed in matters of health care resource allocation, nor do they have a democratic mandate to discriminate between competing community interests. Health care priority setting is best left to national policy-making and the experts appointed to the task. Therefore, the principles of freedom of movement which apply to commerce and the *private* exchanges between businesses and individuals cannot work in the same way in public health care systems. The planning essential within national sickness funds means that prior approval of treatment should be necessary when patients seek treatment outside hospitals with which arrangements have been made. These concerns are community-based and republican in nature. They emphasise how public health care

[10] Scharpf (2009), p. 25, discussing the attempt by Austria to increase the numbers of its own nationals qualifying as medical students and the onerous burden of proof demanded to demonstrate that the restriction on German students was necessary.

[11] ECJ, Case C-157/99 *Smits and Peerbooms* [2001] ECR 1-5473, para 72, emphasis added. The ECJ rejected this advice. It did not explain why.

systems serve the community and, therefore, market-based rules cannot automatically apply to them.

Now compare the new *liberal* and *individualist* approach to public health care rights stated by the same Advocate General in 2007. He said:

> Being a fundamental asset, health cannot be considered solely in terms of social expenditure and latent economic difficulties. This right is perceived as a personal entitlement, unconnected to a person's relationship with social security.[12]

This divorces the legal 'right' from its political and financial source and disregards the concerns discussed above. It presents a two-way dispute between the individual and the state which ignores 'other' interests. What prompted this change of judicial opinion? The phrase 'fundamental asset' may have come from the *Opinion of the European Economic and Social Committee on Healthcare.*[13] However, in that document the words appear in a different context. This document states that 'Health is often defined as a fundamental asset *for society*'[14] and that: 'Safeguards must be put in place to ensure the quality of healthcare systems, their universal accessibility as far as possible and their financial sustainability.'[15] Read in context, therefore, the document does not convey an 'individualistic' meaning or promote rights to a 'personal entitlement'. On the contrary, it is community-based and acknowledges our relationship to each other. Yet, the Advocate General uses the phrase to promote a libertarian agenda from the opposite side of the political spectrum. He did not refer to his previous opinion, or explain why the 'public' dimension of the problem was being ignored. His conclusion, with which the ECJ agreed, was stated as matter of legal conclusion; almost, as an article of faith.

I will argue that this second approach is mistaken. Of course, from a *microscopic* perspective, rights to travel abroad for care may appear attractive. A patient who can achieve more rapid access to hospital may be thrilled to have the opportunity. However, if we look only through the microscope, we will be misled. If we instead use a *telescope* we see that the wider concerns of public health ethics present a very different picture. It shows that health care is constrained by finite resources; that a *public* health agenda has to prioritise certain health care objectives over others; that investment in *preventive* care is important, as is the need to promote *equality* of access to care; that if health policy adopts no particular *strategy*, little progress can be made at community level; and that a decision to invest in one group of patients will inevitably involve '*disinvestment*' from others. In this context, 'the others' tend to mean the same groups, for example, those who are inarticulate and invisible to public attention; in practice this means infirm, frail and vulnerable patients,

[12] ECJ, Case C-444/05 *Stamatelaki* [2007] ECR 1-03185, para 40.

[13] OJ 2003 C 234/11.

[14] At para 1.1.1., emphasis added.

[15] At para 2.3.

especially those who are elderly and mentally ill.[16] If the EU encourages public services to sanctify autonomy and market-individualism, we will damage the ethical foundations on which European health care systems are founded by becoming deaf to the interests of people unable to enforce their rights in this way.[17]

So the following considers the impact of the EU internal market on public health care ethics. I disagree that the EU's new 'liberal' approach has been beneficial either for patients, or the systems on which they depend. I argue that it undermines the sense of community between patients and interferes with policies to improve standards of public health. If we look only through the microscope, we ignore the tensions clearly visible through the *telescope* and disrupt efforts to raise standards of public health. This would be unintended, unplanned and unwanted. I make this argument by examining first, *national* agendas for public health, second, the disruptive impact of the ECJ, third the ECJ's motivation, fourth, the draft Patients' Rights in Cross-Border Healthcare *Directive* and the 'individualist' approach, and fifth, communitarian values and procedural rights.

9.2 National Agendas for Public Health

How will the more recent *individualist* agenda apply in Member States? Unsurprisingly, national agendas for health care priorities vary. As statistics from the OECD demonstrate, the incidence of mortality and morbidity differs from place to place.[18] Heart disease and stroke are of more concern in the UK, Germany and Austria than France, Spain and the Netherlands. Obesity is a particular worry for the UK, but the Netherlands is less successful at treating cancers. Given these differences, Member States will obviously wish to address their own health priorities. I will describe the public health agenda in England to illuminate how and why governments have balanced the needs of communities of patients with individual patient rights. The point is not to elaborate on policy choices specific to the NHS, but to demonstrate how national agendas for public health are always likely to effect *individual* rights of access, and may do so for sound reasons which promote community interests. I distinguish two levels of priorities: NHS performance *standards* and the commitment to make *transparent* patients' rights to NHS care.

As to performance standards, the NHS is subject to a number of policies. Perhaps most significant is the commitment to reduce NHS waiting times. In 1997, patients might have waited up to 18 months for admission to hospital for elective

---

[16] For an extensive survey of the literature, current policy and proposals for the future, see *Fair Society, Fair Lives* (*The Marmot Review*) (London, The Marmot Review 2010), which was commissioned by the UK government in 2008. See also Herring (2009) and idem (Herring 2007)

[17] See generally, Gaylin and Jennings (2003): 'Although autonomy is not an ideal of selfishness or disorderly self-indulgence, it is always self-centred, self-expressive, and individualistic ... Autonomy's mood is always possessive. It speaks in the first person singular, rather than the first person plural.' (at p. 72).

[18] See *Health at a Glance* (OECD Statistics, 2007).

care. By 2008, they should have waited no longer than 18 weeks and will often be treated much sooner. This has not come about simply as a result of government rhetoric. Since 1997, there has been considerable investment in training additional doctors and nurses, building new hospitals and purchasing new facilities. In addition, patients have the benefit of *Choose and Book*, in which they must be offered a choice of at least four hospitals in which to receive their elective care at a time to suit them. Notice that the preference of this latter policy is towards an 'individualist' agenda in that patients may choose the time and location of their treatment (but not the treatment itself, which is subject to medical referral).[19] The point is that investment of this nature requires a significant funding commitment which effectively 'disinvests' from other possible areas of the NHS. It is part of a deliberate, coherent, long-term strategy which has identified waiting times and patient choice as a key priority.

The National Institute for Health and Clinical Excellence (NICE) has a similar strategic impact. NICE recommends to the Department of Health the treatments and pharmaceutical 'technologies' that the NHS should provide to everybody. One of the reasons for creating NICE was to reduce the variability that could arise in the NHS (called the 'post-code lottery'). This arises because (152) individual health authorities, exercising their statutory powers, could in law identify different local strategies and priorities. NICE has been introduced to encourage consistency by identifying which treatments *must* be provided by all health authorities. However, the corollary is that some very expensive drugs and treatments which have limited clinical effects on health outcomes will not be recommended by NICE (and so will often not be funded by the NHS). Notice that this does not formally exclude the treatment from the NHS and doctors may still seek to persuade local health authorities to purchase it. Nevertheless, the rationale is the same: that of a national strategy to reduce differentials in access to treatment, the consequences of which may favour some aspects of health care over others.

Another long-term priority is the commitment, again since 1997, to reduce social inequalities in health status and access to health care services.[20] As we noted above, we should not ignore disadvantaged, inarticulate and socially invisible groups, especially frail, older people, and those suffering mental illness. Thus, to promote this policy, some regions of the UK receive higher *per capita* health funding than others. Part of this is pursued through *preventive* medicine, especially in connection with policies to tackle smoking, alcoholism, obesity and drug abuse.

---

[19] However, the potential disadvantage of Choose and Book is that it may favour some (better) hospitals at the expense of others (which are worse). As in any 'market', for those who are able to travel to the better provider, this is good. But this will divert income from the less good hospital and deplete its resources still further. For those who wish to be treated in the local hospital, this is not good. Rather than leaving the pressure for improvement to market forces, an alternative response would be to introduce a 'turn-around team' to improve the standards of the failing hospital.

[20] *Tackling health inequalities: 10 years on* (Department of Health, 2009). Promoting the same agenda, see Closing the gap in a generation (Commission on Social Determinants of Health, WHO, 2008).

Inescapably, this is the product of a choice about *values*. Indeed, the European Commission supports an identical commitment to equality. In *Quality in and Access to Healthcare Services*[21] the Commission acknowledges the variability of access to care throughout the EU and urges Member States to share good practice to respond to health inequality.[22] Notice, however, that our need for treatment when we become frail and elderly is not necessarily by doctors in a hospital. Rather, we need *community* care at home and the attention of nurses and carers. Inescapably, the expansion of community care services to treat *chronic* illness absorbs the funds that might otherwise have been invested in the more expensive technologies in *acute* hospitals. Here too, national policy balances the competing demands for hospitals and doctors on the one hand, with community care and nurses on the other.

These three examples make the same point, that coherent policy-making requires a long-term strategy in which particular objectives take priority. Put the other way round, if health policy is only *reactive,* in the sense of responding to the clinical needs of individuals as and when it arises, then nothing is a priority. To have a significant beneficial impact on public health policy, hard choices are inevitable. Precisely this point has been made by the European Court of Auditors in respect of the EU's involvement in developing public health strategy. Criticising the failure to identify coherent priorities, it said:

> If spending programmes are to have any measurable impact, they need to be concentrated on selected activities that are identified through strategic planning according to a rigorous set of priorities. The number of priorities should be commensurable with the available budget, as having too many priorities will reduce the chances of achieving impact in any individual area.[23]

It seems that the impact of this idea has been lost on the ECJ. Yet to undermine the planning function is to risk depleting finite public funds before the end of the financial year and damaging the egalitarian objectives of public health ethics.[24]

A second level of NHS strategy is to generate a closer, more candid relationship between the NHS and its patients within a 'transparency agenda'. It encourages a transparent dialogue between resource allocators, the public and patients. The commitment is illustrated in the duty to involve the public in decisions about the planning and development of the NHS and a new *NHS Constitution* (which is effectively a Bill of health care rights) which openly acknowledges priority setting in the NHS. Its purpose is to give patients specific rights of access to information

[21] European Commission, 2008.

[22] Mayor (2009), p. 339:b5158.

[23] Court of Auditors, *The EU's Public Health Programme* (2003-07): an effective way to improve health (Special Report no. 2/2009), para 22.

[24] The risk is the more severe in times of economic recession and public spending cuts. Discussing the extent to which public health strategy will have to respond to the changed financial environment, see Appleby et al. (2009).

and an appeal if the patient, or their representative, believe the rationing decision is wrong. Thus, the *NHS Constitution* promises that:

> You have the right to expect local decisions on funding of… drugs and treatments to be made rationally following a proper consideration of the evidence. If the local NHS decides not to fund a drug or treatment you and your doctor feel would be right for you, they will explain that decision to you.[25]

And

> Where a PCT makes a decision to refuse a request for the funding of a healthcare intervention, where the PCT's general policy is not to fund that intervention, the PCT must provide that individual with a written statement of its reasons for that decision.[26]

Clearly, these are not substantive rights of access to treatment. They are *procedural* rights of patients to be engaged with the process. This does not mean they are useless. They are enforceable in an action for judicial review in the sense that the court may refer the decision back to the decision-maker to be taken again in the light of judicial guidance.[27] In taking this approach, the government candidly acknowledges that health resources are finite, demand for care exceeds the supply of resources and that priority setting inevitably has consequences that benefit some, but not others. Rather than hiding behind the mistaken claim that patients have a 'personal entitlement' to care, the *NHS Constitution* makes plain the tensions by introducing duties of candour and explanation on the part of resource allocators.

9.3 The Disruptive Impact of the ECJ

The advantage of a transparent approach to public health strategy is that it illuminates the process of priority setting and the need for cooperation in deciding how these issues should be resolved. Provided it operates fairly and openly, transparency fosters community and a sense of 'belonging' to a system. It may reduce the sense of *competition* for resources and adversity between groups. By its capacity to recognise the need for community-based principles and public engagement, it enhances awareness of the needs of others and contributes to social

---

[25] NHS Constitution, principle 2a (www.dh.gov.uk/en/Healthcare/NHSConstitution/index.htm).

[26] Direction to PCTs and NHS trusts concerning decisions about drugs and other treatments 2009.

[27] For the many cases in which the courts have encouraged fair and reasonable procedures in the UK, see Newdick (2005). For similar resistance to the 'substantive' approach to health care rights, see Daniels (2008), '… what entitlements follow from a right to have a broad set of health needs met? The answer is system relative and depends on resource allocation decisions that are made using a fair, deliberative process' (145) '… the content of a right to health and health care … cannot be specified except through a fair process that takes specific features of a society into account' (147).

cohesion. This is the sense of social solidarity which is at the heart of Member States' social welfare policy and is widely acknowledged by the EU.[28]

By contrast, the contribution of the ECJ to the challenge of community interests has been disruptive. Its policy is demonstrated by the latter Opinion of Advocate General Jarabo Colomer discussed above as indifferent (even hostile) to republican, or community interests in public health. Perhaps it is sufficient to summarise the ECJ's contribution as follows: firstly, patients have cross-border rights to hospital care which cannot be modified solely by reference to economic constraints, secondly, the right may become enforceable once the patient has a health need generally recognised by international medical science which cannot be treated at home without undue delay.[29] If these conditions are satisfied, then the patient may obtain treatment in a 'host' state and return to present the bill to his 'home' health authority. Clearly, this promotes an *individualistic* approach to health care resource allocation. Although the cases acknowledge a need for the rational planning and management of health care services generally, the articulation of the *principle* on which the right is based fails to incorporate this constraint. Of course, the ECJ cannot require further funds to be devoted to social welfare, but it effectively prioritises the investment of finite resources and increases competition between patients for access to care.[30] In this way, the sense of market-individualism it conveys is less familiar to European values and more in tune with the absence of social solidarity in access to health care in the US.[31]

Its disruptive impact can be illustrated both with respect to particular patients and treatments and the way it can undermine health care strategy generally. As to the first, consider NICE guidance. NICE may refuse to recommend some drugs on the grounds of their cost, the extent of the therapeutic benefit available from using them, or the incomplete state of the clinical evidence that they will be effective. Imagine a new drug called *Genomab* developed to treat cancer about which the clinical evidence of effectiveness is still incomplete. Although it cannot cure cancer, it may extend some patients' lives for 3 months, but it also has side-effects which reduce the quality of life. It is expensive and costs £100,000 per quality

[28] See for example, *Together for Health—Strategic Approach for the EU, 2008-2013* (COM(2007) 630 final) and generally, Michalski (2006).

[29] See for example, ECJ, Case C-157/99 *Geraets-Smits* v. *Stichting Ziekenfonds Vgz, Peerbooms* v. *Stichting Cz Groep Zorgverzekeringen* [2001] *ECR* 1-5473. I have considered elsewhere the inadequacy of the threshold assumption that there is some objective notion that medical opinion is often supported 'international medical science', or that 'undue delay' is a useful criterion with which to distinguish different categories of deserving patient. See Newdick (2006a, b, c), p. 1645.

[30] As the English Court of Appeal said in *R* (*Watts*) v. *Bedfordshire PCT* [2004] 77 *BMLR* 26, 'We consider that the court should proceed on the assumption that, if the NHS were required to pay the cost of some of its patients having treatment abroad at a time earlier than they would receive it in the United Kingdom, this would require additional resources. In theory, these could only be avoided if those who did not have treatment abroad received their treatment at a later time than they otherwise would or if the NHS ceased to provide some treatments that it currently does provide.' (at para 105).

[31] See Jost (2003).

adjusted life year (QALY).[32] NICE uses a broad rule of thumb which means that it is unlikely to approve treatments which cost over £30,000 per QALY unless the evidence of clinical effectiveness is robust. Say NICE refuses to approve *Genomab* on this basis. This reflects a judgement about the 'opportunity costs' of spending finite resources in one way rather than another and that to divert such a sum from patients on other effective treatments would be unreasonable. The decision is reached by a public authority, within a transparent process which involves clinicians and health economists. This contributes to the sense of public concern that finite NHS resources should be invested prudently. Note that NICE does not 'ban' treatments from use by the NHS and they are still available to a small number of patients who can demonstrate that they are likely to have *exceptional* benefit from the treatment. However, by comparison to other treatments, *Genomab* is considered to be a low priority.[33]

What view should the EU take of this mechanism? Let us say that *Genomab* is available in some other EU Member States. For example, some Member States may focus much more on acute and hospital care, and much less on chronic and community care. After all, the *politics* of health care is not identical throughout the EU and some Member States may devote less attention to issues of 'inter-generational' equality than others. For these States, the cost of expensive cancer treatment may not present significant difficulty because resources are allocated to different priorities. Surely, these 'strategic' (or macro) factors are relevant to rights of cross-border access. If so, then the availability of the treatment outside a particular Member State is not decisive. One should also consider how much funding should be set aside to accommodate the new demand, the impact on local priorities at home and on those patients who may be *adversely* affected as a result.[34] This may be the more important for new accession Member States with smaller *per capita* investment in health care and for whom equivalent expenditure on such a treatment would be the more serious for others. Differences of this nature are surely relevant to the fair and equal distribution of health care rights, yet, it seems, they are disregarded by the ECJ.

The *Genomab* example concerns a particular treatment, but its implications also apply more generally to long-term planning and strategy. As we have discussed above, national health policy may seek to reduce waiting times for

---

[32] QALYs measure quantity and quality by assessing (1) the duration during which the patient will enjoy benefit from a medicine and (2) the extent to which their condition will be alleviated. See Newdick (2005), pp. 26–37.

[33] Newdick (2006b), p. 205.

[34] At present, the cost of cross-border hospital care is limited. However, in Brazil, where substantive rights to health care have developed, in 2005 the State of Sao Paulo devoted some 30% of its budget to high cost drugs for treatment ordered by the courts through litigation, and the proportion is increasing. See Ferraz (2009). The supposition that substantive rights of access in Brazil would especially assist the poor and other less advantaged members of society to obtain health care is not supported by the evidence, see Afonso da Silva and Vargas Terrrazas (2008). Although the risk is also present with respect to procedural rights, see Epp (1998).

hospital admission, adjust the balance between hospital and community care, or reduce inequalities in access to health care. Each tends to prioritise health care policy so as to promote public interests and inevitably effects the way finite resources can be made available to other patients. In contrast, by conceiving the issues as rights-based, economic freedoms the ECJ disrupts national policy and hollows out the ethical foundation which underpins decision-making in this area.[35]

9.4 What is the Motivation of the ECJ?

What explains the ECJ's one-dimensional view of health care rights? Given the absence of explanation for its policy preferences, the following analysis is inevitably speculative. It is surely wrong to think that this is what EU law *demands.* As the first extract from the Opinion of Advocate General Colomer (discussed above) explains, until 2001, social welfare policy was considered to be within the discretion of the Member States and outside of the ECJ's jurisdiction. Only thereafter was the organisation of social welfare made subject to internal market principles. Although the ECJ has never said why, the change was introduced as a deliberate policy initiated by judges.[36] The Court concedes that:

> ... it is possible for the risk of seriously undermining the financial balance of a social security system to constitute an overriding reason in the general interest capable of justifying an obstacle to the freedom to provide services.[37]

However, as we discuss below, it is mistaken to think that this addresses the problem raised here. Individuals seeking treatment elsewhere in the EU are unlikely to expose *entire* health systems to serious financial imbalance (although hospitals close to major ports will be more seriously affected). Rather, notwithstanding the more limited financial impact involved, the danger is to the principles of *equity* and *community* which underlie the system. The risk is not normally financial imbalance, but dilution of the *political* and *ethical* integrity of the system as a whole. As I discuss below, reforms which tend to favour some groups rather than others will be criticised for eroding the principle of universalism which lies at the heart of any system of public health care. The problem for the EU is not the

---

35 See Montgomery (2006), p. 185 and Coggon (2007), p. 798.

36 As the English Court of Appeal said in *Watts* v. *Bedfordshire PCT* [2004] 77 *BMLR* 26, para 31 the ECJ 'put in place on the foundation of Article 49 [EC] a substantial edifice not immediately clear from its literal terms ... There has been much judicial policy-making, and the policy goes well beyond the words of the Article.' And compare the ECJ's non-interventionist approach with respect to public education in ECJ, Case 263/86 *Belgium* v. *Humbel and Edel* [1988] *ECR* 5365 and ECJ, Case C-109/92 *Wirth* v. *Landeshauptstadt Hannover* [1993] *ECR* I-6447.

37 ECJ, Case C-372/04 *R(Watts)* v. *Bedford Primary Care Trust and Secretary of State* [2006] *ECR* 1-4325, para 103-06.

dictates of legal logic but, as we noted above, the ECJ's insensitivity to 'republican' ideals which promote the idea of *community*.

Another possible explanation is that the court has misunderstood the important distinction between *civil and political rights* and *social and economic* rights. Civil rights are largely individual and 'negative' in character, for example, freedom of speech, religion and assembly. To a much larger extent (but not exclusively) they can be enforced without reference to their impact on other people. Thus, we are entitled to presume that *my* freedom of speech, religion, or assembly should be protected as a fundamental right provided there are no countervailing reasons connected with the rights of others (for example, the law of defamation, the health of others, or the security of the state). Civil and political rights, and the market-based freedoms they promote, tolerate significant inequalities in the way they are used and expressed.

By contrast, *social and economic* rights involve access to public goods and services which inevitably engage issues of distributive justice. The same libertarian presumption of access cannot apply because my rights cannot be properly understood without also considering yours. Republican rights of this nature are not normally absolute, but *relative*. They are based on a presumption of *equality* of access. For this reason, in English law, they are not normally substantive, but *procedural*.[38] Has the ECJ made an error of legal *theory* by being so rights-oriented, so 'drenched' in Dworkin,[39] that it has misunderstood the crucial distinction between civil and political rights on the one hand, and social and economic rights on the other? Contrast the European Court of Human Rights which recognised the distinction in a claim for positive, substantive access to health care in another contracting state. Refusing the right to a patient suffering from HIV/AIDS, it said:

> Although many of the rights it contains have implications of a social or economic nature, the Convention is essentially directed at the protection of civil and political rights...Furthermore, inherent in the whole of the Convention is a search for a fair balance between the demands of the general interest of the community and the requirements of the protection of the individual's fundamental rights... Advances in medical science, together with social and economic differences between countries, entail that the level of treatment available in the Contracting State and the country of origin may vary considerably...[40]

This is not to say that there is an easy, black and white distinction between these two forms of rights, nor that social and economic rights are not *rights*. For

[38] See my discussion in Newdick (2006a, b, c) and idem (Newdick 2008), p. 844.

[39] With acknowledgement to West (2006), p. 221 at p. 253. Speaking of the failure of the US Constitution to promote positive freedoms: 'This Dworkinian drenching of law with moralism can limit our moral sense and dull our capacity for criticism. Part of what the [US] Constitution might be faulted for is its understatement with respect to the affirmative moral duties of legislatures.'

[40] *N* v. *United Kingdom* (2008) (App no. 26565/05), para 3. Although the Preamble of the Charter of Fundamental Rights of the EU states that: 'The Charter reaffirms ... the rights ... from the European Convention ... and the case-law of the Court of Justice ...'.

example, the right to life may impose a *positive* duty to protect individuals from foreseeable harm from others,[41] and access to the courts may require legal assistance to persons during litigation.[42] Competing claims require judgment about which principles should predominate.[43] However, the distinction explains that while some rights may be enforced without significant impact on others, social and economic rights are *always* likely to have this effect if they arise from finite, public funds. Therefore, in fairness to those whose interests are not before the court, they are enforceable as *procedural,* rather than substantive rights. This right entitles the individual to the court's scrutiny of the reasons for the decisions and whether the criteria for assessing access are lawful, fair and reasonable. If they do not withstand proper scrutiny, the procedural right is for the matter back to be referred back the decision-maker to be reconsidered in the light of the court's guidance. This way, public, accountable and fair priority setting systems are encouraged and unelected courts are not required to divert resources from one group of patients to another.[44] The nature of procedural *health care* rights is elaborated below. Although the ECJ has not discussed the point, precisely these considerations apply within the EU also.

Alternatively, is the ECJ's policy based on an intuitive mistrust of national governments and anxiety about their willingness to ignore individual rights? Jennings suggests that:

> there remains a wariness in the autonomy perspective about claims asserting the intrinsic value of belonging, communal membership, or public life because connection with others is seen primarily as a source of threats, limits, or the effacement for the self rather than as an enabling or empowering medium of self-realization.[45]

Some may simply reject communitarian notions as too dangerous, or imprecise to be enforceable as legal rights. Are markets naturally preferable for their capacity to diffuse political and economic power? Should public health care rights simply be an aggregation of individual *contractual* interests? Ronald Dworkin, for example, uses the private US health insurance model of health care as a basis for his 'prudent insurance test' which asks 'what people would decide to spend on their own medical care as individuals, if they were buying insurance under free market conditions.'[46] However, this 'virtual insurance' may not capture the

---

[41] See, for example, *Osman* v. *United Kingdom* (2000) *EHRR* 245 (ECHR) on the duty of the state to protect a person who was known to be at risk of attack from another person.

[42] See for example, *Airey* v. *Ireland* (1981) 2 *EHRR* 592 (ECHR).

[43] Alexy (2004).

[44] See Fredman (2004), Chapter 4 and for the risks and benefits of *substantive* judicial intervention in the Indian courts, Chapter 5. The intensity of scrutiny may vary. See Newdick (2005) and in the South African Constitutional Court, see *Soobramoney* v. *Minister of Health, Kaw-Zulu-Natal* 1998 (1) *SA* 765 (CC) and *Minister of Health* v. *Treatment Action Campaign (No. 2)* (2002) 5 *SA* 721.

[45] Jennings (2001), pp. 88, 94.

[46] Dworkin (2000), p. 317

European view of health care funding. It might invest little reducing levels of health *inequality* or in the impact of disease in the *future*. Nor does it deal with the need for responsible priority setting in the public interest. As Amrtya Sen says, Dworkin's 'insurance' uses 'atomistic operators' as the basis for solutions, whereas policy-making should be 'the subject matter of public reasoning'.[47] So, as a description of the momentum which drives *public* health care systems, it underestimates the public dimension of the task and capacity of public authorities to achieve longer term strategic objectives. More generally, this approach avoids the inevitability of hard choices between competing demands for finite resources, or the political choices required in balancing individual and community rights. As Jennings explains:

> Public health [involves] concepts of the right and the good that pertain not to individuals in isolation but to selves in relationships; not atomistic bearers of interest, preference, and desire but social persons whose personal flourishing is inextricably linked to the flourishing of others. In addition to the liberal language of rights, interests and utilities, public health ethics needs the vocabulary of solidarity, mutuality, interdependency, social justice, community and the common good.'[48]

Thus, *public* health ethics are not comfortably embraced by the economics of fee market individualism. The argument can be expressed in a different way by using Albert Hirschman's discussion of *exit, voice* and *loyalty*. Recall that this model describes a range of individual responses to the goods and services they are offered in the market place. They may abandon a supplier and seek an alternative, voice their complaint, or remain loyal. Certainly, this describes the incentives imposed on private, *commercial* enterprise and which drive competition and promote consumer interests. Should EU law use the same model to encourage patients dissatisfied with standards of public health care to 'exit' the system and find better care elsewhere? As Hirschman says, this model cannot apply in the same way to *public* health care. Even in the US context, one cannot simply 'get away' from public goods and services.[49] He was concerned with issues of public concern such as the environment. But his point is more clearly illuminated in respect of public welfare systems constrained by finite resources. As we have seen, the choices required are essentially political, rather than economic. They involve comparing the needs of differing individuals, populations, generations and future generations. Using Hirschman, if I am one from whom resources may be *disinvested* to support your freedom to obtain care elsewhere in the EU, will I be given 'voice' to inform the decision-maker of the consequences for my treatment? Will I be heard to argue against your 'exit'? As democratic accountability is introduced to our health care systems, the answer is surely 'Yes'. By contrast, the ECJ hears

---

[47] See Sen (2009), p. 266. Put another way, the purpose of health care solidarity is not merely economic and *instrumental*, but is *constitutive* of our commitment to the community as a whole. See Sandell (1982), p. 150, comparing 'strong' and 'weak' conceptions of community.

[48] Jennings (2009), p. 37.

[49] Hirschman (1970), p. 104.

only the voice of those enforcing their EU 'freedoms'. It is deaf to those who are unable, or unwilling to travel, yet whose access to care may be adversely affected as a result.[50] Also a big issue in EU consumer law is the knowledge of being able to travel which is an important aspect of empowerment as a citizen

Or has the ECJ overlooked the implications of policies designed to prioritise *hospital* care, or *community* care? As we have said, health care can be provided in hospital and/or in the community. Doctors dominate the former, with nursing care more common in the latter. The proper balance of investment in them inevitably involves judgment. EU cross-border rights to care emphasise *hospital* care. This has two consequences. First, as Van Doorslaer has shown, hospital care and access to specialist doctors provides disproportionate benefit to rich and well-educated patients:

> Everywhere in Europe, the use of specialist visits is higher (than expected on the basis of need) for the rich and lower for the poor.... The higher educated (which tend to be the richest) ... tend to be much more inclined to contact a specialist than the lower educated.[51]

Assuming this pattern is consistent within the EU market for health care, the right to travel to 'host' states for care will tend to benefit rich, well-educated patients much more than poor ones. Thus, it will tend to widen the inequalities we have discussed above. In addition, investment in hospital care generates costs which may be 'disinvested' from long-term *community care*. This is crucial to those who are too elderly, frail, or chronically ill to travel.[52] So the right to hospital treatment elsewhere in the EU favours those who are well-educated, able-bodied and *acutely* ill, but disfavours poor, disabled and chronically ill patients. This unexplained judicial 'preference' for hospital care over community care offends ideas of equality, as well as the express policy of the European Commission which we discussed above,[53] and corrodes the sense of social solidarity which European social welfare systems have always fostered.

Perhaps it is unreasonable to expect a court to be sensitive to these considerations of social policy. Equally, however, it is odd that the ECJ should feel so strongly motivated to develop policy in this area with, it seems, so little understanding of the consequences of its actions in terms of fairness and equality. Whatever its motivation, Greer has explained the intervention of the EU in health policy as:

> ... being made, or constrained, by people who know little, and perhaps care little, about health... The European Union institutions, especially the ECJ and the European Commission, [have] powerfully and effectively created EU health policy without any demand

[50] It is also deaf to the 'voice' against entry. See Ferrara (2005), pp. 28–36 and Hervey (2000).

[51] van Doorslaer et al. (2004), pp. 629, 645–646.

[52] See generally, Held (2006), 'instead of abandoning culture to the dictates of the market place, we should make it possible for culture to develop in ways best able to enlighten and enrich human life' (at p. 18).

[53] See n. 21 *supra.*

> for it. They have their own interests and agendas, and their support for Europe's health systems can often be more theoretical than real.[54]

Inevitably, the ECJ's engagement in this area has prompted the need for a better, more coherent response to cross-border access to health care and, accordingly, the *Draft Directive on the Application of Patients' Rights in Cross-Border Healthcare* is the response. There are two broad arguments as to how the proposed Directive should best respond to the consequences of the Court's involvement, which I have called *individualist* and *communitarian.*

9.5 The Individualist Approach: The European Parliament and the Proposed Directive

The *individualist* approach has been recommended by the European Parliament in its amendments to the proposed *Directive on Patients Rights in Cross-Border Healthcare.* It gives predominant weight to the wishes of individual patients and relatively little recognition to the constraints operating within Member States, or the impact of individual rights on other patients. Thus, it recommends that:

> … the Member State of affiliation shall ensure that insured persons travelling to another Member State with the purpose of receiving healthcare there or seeking to receive healthcare provided in another Member State, will not be prevented from receiving healthcare provided in another Member State where the treatment in question is among the benefits provided for by the legislation, administrative regulations, guidelines and codes of conduct of the medical professions, of the Member State of affiliation to which the insured person is entitled.[55]

Note that this principle is more extensive than that laid down by the ECJ. It is not limited to *normal treatment* which cannot be obtained without *undue delay.* The right to travel extends to all the care provided by the Member State. Let us consider three aspects of this provision to emphasise the obstacles it will put in the way of strategic planning and the fair allocation of finite resources to all members of the national community.

---

[54] Greer (2009), p. 3.

[55] *Proposal for a Directive of the European Parliament and of the Council on the Application of Patients' Rights in Cross-border Healthcare* (COM (2008) 414), amendment 66; available at: http://ec.europa.eu/prelex/detail_dossier_real.cfm?CL=en&DosId=197193.

9.5.1 'The Benefits Provided for by the Legislation of the Member State'

First, let us take the concession that the right of free movement is subject to health care which is 'among the benefits provided for by the legislation of the Member State of affiliation.' In principle, this would permit Member States to refuse to support treatment abroad if it was not included within a central 'list' of approved treatment (a 'white list'). In practice, however, this limitation is unlikely to be effective because countries do not normally compile specific lists of this nature. Although there is relatively little comparative research in this area, Busse and colleagues have demonstrated that the precise contents of the health care basket are not closely defined and one can understand why not. First, although the UK may be the clearest example, many systems describe patients' entitlements to health care in general terms. The English National Health Service Act 2006 requires the Secretary of State to promote a 'comprehensive' health service and makes no detailed attempt to list exactly what that duty entails. Although the UK has adopted this flexible approach to defining health care entitlement, other EU countries have also adopted 'concept-based', rather than 'treatment-specific' modes of definition.[56] In the former group, although there will be significant range of treatments which will be provided without question, there will be many at the margins about which discussion will be required, opinions may differ and health care *policies* will be required.

Second, given the pace of medical and pharmaceutical development there is a danger that such a list could quickly become out of date. And what about treatments which are used 'off-label' that is, in a way that is well understood by clinicians but not formally approved by the licensing authorities or the European Medicines Evaluation Authority? (This is especially common with respect to neonatal and paediatric care where it is obviously difficult to conduct clinical trials.) Would they still be available? For this reason, at a practical and legal level, the concession about 'the benefits provided by the legislation' will often be unworkable.

9.5.2 Rare Diseases

Rare diseases provoke considerable sympathy. The fact of their rarity means that there may be limited commercial incentive for pharmaceutical companies to develop treatments for them. And when treatments are discovered, they are often extremely expensive to produce because of the adverse economies of scale and, yet, may still be of limited proven therapeutic benefit.[57] Treatment costs of

---

[56] See Busse et al. (2008), pp. S1–S8.

[57] Drummond et al. (2007), p. 36.

$435,000 per patient per year have been discussed which, although the total numbers of patients is small, will impact on treatment available to other patients.[58] For this reason, these are referred to as 'orphan drugs' and those who suffer from rare diseases often find it difficult to access treatment for their condition. Yet the European Commission estimates that, throughout Europe, about 15 million people are affected by rare diseases.[59] What should be the policy response?

The European Parliament's solution is simply to remove those with rare diseases from the concession discussed above that the treatments offered should be among the benefits provided at home. Thus, it recommends that:

> Patients affected by rare diseases should have the right to access healthcare in another Member State and to get reimbursement *even if the treatment in question is not among the benefits provided for by the legislation of the Member State* of affiliation.[60]

Apart from the obvious *disinvestment* impact on other patients, this provokes a difficult ethical question: Should we put a premium on 'rarity'?[61] Should patients with rare diseases be entitled to receive expensive care that could not normally be made available to patients without a rare disease and without regard to its cost?[62] Putting to one side our sympathy for patients with rare diseases, should a patient who needs an expensive, but standard treatment for cancer, be less likely to obtain access to treatment because the disease is not rare? Normally, we assess whether treatment can be provided by reference to its therapeutic impact on quality of life, its cost and the other treatments available. The rarity or otherwise of the disease is surely irrelevant. A better solution, therefore, is for European Reference Networks to develop centres of excellence and become the focus of treatment and advice; one advantage of which would be to attract larger numbers of patients to a single location and take the advantage of economies of scale. We should certainly devote attention to setting up systems which will help reduce the cost of treatment for rare diseases, but it is not fair that all patients with rare diseases should have automatic priority over others.

Another way of making the same point is to ask; who will pay for the costs of purchasing 'orphan drugs' for rare diseases? From which category of existing patients will we *divert* affordable and effective treatment in order to accommodate the needs of patients with rare diseases? And should those groups be consulted first, or simply ignored? Uncomfortable though this question is, the policy of the European Parliament will tend to divert finite health care budgets away from the larger numbers receiving established and effective care, to treat fewer patients with

---

58 Hollis (2006), supporting a formula for extra cost to pay for innovative treatments based on average costs of research and development.

59 *Rare Diseases: Europe's Challenges* (COM(2008) 679 final).

60 See n. 53 *supra*.

61 See McCabe et al. (2005), p. 1016 and Hope (2001), p. 179, rejecting the 'rule of rescue'.

62 Hughes et al. (2005), p. 829, questioning whether the 'rule of rescue' should be especially responsive to those with orphan conditions.

expensive care which may promise only marginal therapeutic benefit. On what ethical basis could such a policy be considered proper?

9.5.3 Prior Authorisation and Financial Balance

Much of the foregoing supports the need for balance between the rights of individuals on the one hand, and the rights of 'others' in the community on the other. Those 'others' may have the support of national policies, for example, through the policy to reduce health inequalities, or local policies intended to promote local health care objectives. The argument for prior authorisation is that it is insufficient to respond to the needs of individuals as and when it arises. Effective long-term planning demands a more strategic approach to health care investment responsive to all groups of society, especially those who are less visible and articulate.

The 'individualist' approach of the draft Directive acknowledges the need for strategy in planning. However, the threshold test which permits prior authorisation is put so high that it is likely to undermine effective policy-making. Thus, it says with respect to hospital care that:

> The Member State … may provide for a system of prior authorization … where … the purpose of the system is to … prevent it from seriously undermining, or being likely to seriously undermine (i) the financial balance of the Member State's socials security system; and/or (ii) the planning and rationalisation carried out in the hospital sector …[63]

We alluded to a similar concession by the ECJ, above. The problem with this is that it is disproportionate to the objective it seeks to achieve. It seems to envisage that, before a single patient may be denied access to care elsewhere in the EU, the entire fabric of the social welfare system should be on the edge of collapse. As Sauter rightly suggests:

> Member States will now have to provide actual evidence that the outflow of patients due to cross-border hospital care seriously undermines their social security system or planning in the hospital sector.[64]

But are the interests of 'others' so marginal to the rights of single individuals? An alternative view would be that to marginalise the rights of others in this way would be ludicrous. Indeed, any health care manager that gave priority to patients who wished to travel abroad for their care until the point at which the financial balance of the system had been seriously undermined would be in dereliction of their duty. As Somek has said, referring to the same views of the ECJ, by focusing

---

[63] See n. 53 *supra*, amendment 76. Like the ECJ, the draft Directive excludes non-hospital care from any cross-border restrictions.

[64] Sauter (2009), pp. 109, 125. The UK government also believes that the European Commission's current proposal is wrong and would mean having to wait until healthcare systems were already in difficulty before prior authorisation for patients was required (UK's Responses to the Consultation, para 18).

so intensely on one side of the health care rights equation, EU law has 'successfully fundamentalized citizenship, in the sense of transforming it into the most fundamental freedoms.'[65]

This also suggests that the major thrust of this provision is misconceived because European health care systems supported by around 9% of gross national product are unlikely to find themselves on the verge of financial and managerial collapse. In reality, therefore, this 'financial balance' threshold could never be satisfied because it is 'next to impossible to establish…'.[66] In any case, it ignores the more important issue of devising fair and reasonable *principles and procedures* by which prior authorisation is administered. Therefore, the principle should not rest solely on the economic issues of financial balance and planning, rather it should focus on distributive ethics, fairness and social solidarity between people. This is the bedrock on which European health care systems have been constructed.

These three features of the European Parliament's view of the *Cross-Border Directive* demonstrate the single-minded commitment to a liberal, individualist agenda. Clearly, more must be done to explain and defend the case for community-based solutions to the challenges of public health ethics and it is to this that we turn next.

9.6 Communitarian Values and Procedural Rights in the EU

To 'cosmopolitanists' committed to a united Europe, it is unattractive to speak of *boundaries* within the EU, or to suggest that regard must be given to local preferences and national priorities. However, this may be a profound mistake. As Ferrara so clearly demonstrates: 'Social sharing builds on closure. It presupposes the existence of a clearly demarcated and cohesive community, whose members feel that they belong to the same whole and that they are linked by reciprocity ties vis-à-vis common risks and similar needs.'[67] In locating the boundaries of this 'closure' he explains that:

> Solidarity became slowly institutionalized during the last two centuries in the wider context of territorial system-building. The establishment of redistributive arrangements played a crucial role in stabilizing the new form of political organization (the nation state) that gradually emerged in modern Europe. This stabilization occurred through the anchoring of people's life chances to state-national organisations uniquely dedicated to social protection.[68]

---

[65] Somek (2007), pp. 787, 797.

[66] Somek (2008a, b), p. 211.

[67] Ferrara (2005), p. 2. Who are the 'others' outside the enclosure and how should we distinguish crude *cultural*, or ethno-centric nationalism? See Muller (2007), Chapter 2.

[68] Ferrara (2005), p. 45.

Social rights, therefore, have become the cement that holds communities together within a 'boundary' and membership of public welfare systems is now a hallmark of citizenship. As Bellamy says:

> [the] expectation that a universal entitlement to social welfare will be reciprocated by everyone's doing their bit to contribute to the welfare of others when they can, obtains support in its turn from citizens feeling they belong to a national political community.[69]

This strongly suggests that solidarity and community evolve from cultural, political and economic bonds that have developed over centuries *within the nation states*. By contrast, given the EU's single-minded and *microscopic* attachment to the utility of markets, at EU level there is little support for any of the factors that promote social cohesion; indeed 'a social Europe cannot be created at the EU level because the collective identification among European peoples and the democratic mechanisms that need to give such an identity voice—namely political parties—do not exist…'.[70]

In this chapter I have argued that social solidarity is so central to the fabric of our social welfare systems that it should be preserved against the forces of the EU internal market. What is required is greater sensitivity to the *public* interests engaged in public health systems and a modification of the notion that private market principles alone provide solutions. How should the matter progress? To suggest a way forward, we need to establish a number of propositions. Firstly, the EU should contribute to good and well managed public health care services in Europe through a cross-border Directive, however, primary responsibility for health care resource allocation and priority setting should remain with Member States. Secondly, principles which apply to private and commercial undertakings cannot apply equally to public health services. Thirdly, to recognise this distinction, the proposed Directive on patients' rights in cross border healthcare should recognise the distinction between *substantive* and *procedural* rights. I hope that the observations in the preceding sections are sufficient to support the first two propositions. As we mentioned above, this third proposition about *procedural* rights is crucial and deserves elaboration.

The approach initiated by the ECJ and adopted by the European Parliament in its response to the Commission's draft Directive is to promote *substantive*, individual rights to health. Thus, as we have seen, the draft Directive requires Member States to 'ensure that insured persons … will not be prevented from receiving healthcare provided in another Member State' provided it is provided for by the 'home' legislation. This is substantive in the sense that the right to reimbursement of the cost of care is enforceable against local health insurers. This gives rise to two difficulties. The first we have already noted; at a pragmatic level, it mistakenly assumes a reasonably treatment-specific list for which the health authority is responsible and this may not be reflected in the practice of many member states.

[69] Bellamy (2009), p. 12.

[70] Bellamy (2009), p. 27.

More importantly this 'substantive' approach to health care rights tends to disregard the *disinvestment* costs of treating Peter instead of Paula. How can both have their respective interests considered? The best answer is not to deny that the patient possess social rights of any sort, but to say that his/her rights are enforceable as *procedural* rights.[71] A similar approach is described by Daniels who suggests four structural *values* to frame the decision-making process in health care resource allocation, i.e., that it should be public, relevant, contain a right of appeal and be subject to external supervision.[72] As we have noted, a similar 'transparency agenda' is being promoted in the *NHS Constitution.* Procedural rights guarantee access to procedures which treat patients openly, equally, fairly and consistently. This gives patients rights to understand the process, be given proper reasons for decisions and (at least in the NHS) to influence NHS policy. It imposes on decision-makers the burden of sharing their reasoning and justifying their conclusions.

The advantage for priority setting is that everyone can be involved in the process and the system does not overreact to articulate litigants. This *inclusive* approach encourages a sense of community and solidarity by openly acknowledging that demands for health care require community-based responses. Thus, to Daniels' structural *values*, a system of procedural rights should add specific 'decision-making *criteria'* so that values can be translated into hard choices. These criteria may include, for example, the relative effectiveness of the treatment, the numbers of those likely to benefit from it, the costs (and cost-effectiveness) of the treatment and the cost of the next best treatment. Public policy considerations may also play a role (for example, reducing health inequalities). In sum, this means distinguishing between a number of levels of decision-making. First, at the *macro* level, the general ethical framework within which priority setting decisions are made. Second, within that general framework, at the *meso* level, the specific policy governing a particular treatment. Third within that specific policy, at the *micro* level, the manner in which the decision has been taken with respect to a particular patient. An example of this process in action is available from the South Central Ethical Framework as a template against which priority setting occurs, and its practical application by the Berkshire Priorities Committee.[73] Some such framework has to assist the consistency of decision-making, otherwise the system would surely be condemned as arbitrary, irrational and unfair. This approach elaborates upon the model suggested by Daniels and Sabin in their model of *Accountability for Reasonableness*[74] in which proper *procedures* are recommended as the fairest approach to individual claims to health care, in preference to substantive rights

---

[71] See, e.g., Tushnet (2008), Chapter 8 comparing differing degrees of 'strong' and 'weak form' judicial review and Sabel and Simon (2004), p. 1015 on 'experiments' with judicial review remedies. See generally, Alexy (2004), Chapter 9.

[72] Daniels (2008), Chapter 4.

[73] Of which I am a member. See: www.berkshire.nhs.uk/priorities/_policies/SC-Ethical-framework.pdf.

[74] Daniels and Sabin (1997).

which tend to focus on you and your treatment, without considering me and mine. At every stage this seeks to make transparent the balance between individual and community rights. Contrast the substantive response of the ECJ, with its emphasis on immediate responses to individual need, and one notices the indifference of the Court to public interests and public engagement.

For these reasons, a *community* approach requires the telescope, not a microscope which focuses on individuals alone. For example, an alternative draft *Directive on the application of patients' rights on cross-border health care* from the Council of Ministers states in the Preamble that matters such as 'the cost-effectiveness of a specific treatment for a specific patient, is a matter for the Member State of affiliation.' The acknowledgment of the principle of cost-effectiveness recognises that the needs of one cannot be understood without regard to the needs of other people. Thus, the text continues:

> The Member State of affiliation may impose on a patient seeking reimbursement of planned cross-border healthcare, the same conditions, criteria of eligibility and regulatory and administrative formalities, whether set at a local, national or regional level as it would impose if *that* healthcare was provided in its territory. This may include an assessment by a health professional or healthcare administrator...[75]

This too recognises that health professionals and health *administrators* may both have a legitimate role in determining health care strategy and national and local priorities because distributive ethics are not uniquely concerned with *clinical* issues. This fully embraces the role of the EU in health care. However, it does so by encouraging co-operation between Member States and, as with rare diseases, through developing networks of excellence to which national health authorities and patients should subscribe. This approach understands that Member States may make different judgements about health care priorities (be they to reduce waiting times, improve community care, reduce rates of cardiovascular disease, improve levels of mental health, and so on). These judgements involve a balance between clinical, ethical, economic and political considerations, but they are not essentially judicial (in the sense that they create *substantive rights*). Inescapably, they affect the speed with which different groups can obtain care. They do not discriminate against other EU nationals or undermine freedom of movement, but (provided they withstand *procedural* judicial review) they do respect difference between the reasonable and defensible policies developed by individual Member States.

[75] Article 8(5).

9.7 Conclusion

Constitutional courts throughout Europe are following the US example of asserting authority against the legislature. This suggests that the traditional paradigm of the separation of powers between the various branches of government is being eroded as the courts play an increasing role shaping legislation and we should not be surprised that the ECJ is having a similar impact on the policies of national Parliaments. This phenomenon has been referred to as *governing with judges*.[76] Of course, it puts an obstacle in the way in which democracy can hold law-makers accountable,[77] but it may explain the ECJ's assertiveness in respect of national welfare systems. Note, however, that *national* courts may be equally concerned to uphold their own constitutional traditions by resisting unwelcome encroachment from 'Europe'. This provokes the dispute yet to be clearly resolved between the ECJ and Member States as to *supremacy*: where is the ultimate authority to determine whether EU acts are constitutional?[78]

This is not just a legal question. It also involves politics and the legitimacy of national governments. We have noted above that the history of reassurance provided by 'republican', or community-based welfare solidarity explains the allegiances people have to their nation states. As Scharpf argues, the legitimacy of national governments also depends partly on their capacity to explain the policies they consider necessary and appropriate within this framework of normative expectations. National governments, however, are exposed to risk if they are unable to do so. As he says, governments will be weakened if their national policies violate deeply held normative convictions. Constitutional legitimacy may be undermined and may ultimately be destroyed:

'This is a critical risk if governments are required to implement European law that has been created by institutionally autonomous judicial legislation without involvement of politically accountable actors.'[79]

---

[76] Stone Sweet (2000).

[77] For a warning against such an approach, see Bellamy (2008), p. 9: 'If there are reasonable disagreements about justice and its implications, then it becomes implausible to regard constitutional courts as basing their decisions on the 'correct' view of what democratic justice demands in particular circumstances … They restrict access and unduly narrow the range of arguments and remedies that may be considered, and are neither accountable nor responsive to citizens …' (at p. 12).

[78] National courts and the ECJ continue to dispute the point, see ECJ, Case 6/64 *Falmino Costa* v. *ENEL* [1964] *ECR* 585.

[79] Scharpf (2009), p. 21, discussing the Austrian universities case, ECJ, Case C-147/03 *Commission* v. *Austria* [2005] *ECR* I-5969 in which Austrian authorities were concerned to increase the numbers of Austrians qualifying as doctors. It was forbidden from differentiating between Austrian and German university applicants, even though many German students returned home after graduating in Austria.

Clearly, then, *national* institutions should be alert to the risks of slavishly adopting policies which contradict, or offend, deeply held local sentiment.

Following this argument, and allowing for the way courts now absorb aspects of political decision-making, interest may develop in national courts holding the incursions of the ECJ into social welfare policy to be *ultra vires* for exceeding the jurisdiction granted by Member States. This could be in relation to the specific exclusion by the EC Treaty of EU competence in 'the organization and delivery of health services and medical care',[80] or more generally, as has recently been suggested by the German Federal Constitutional Court. Thus, with respect to the lawfulness of the Treaty of Lisbon 2009, it has said:

> It is true that the Basic Law grants the legislature powers to engage in a far-reaching transfer of sovereign powers to the European Union. However, the powers are granted under the condition that the sovereign statehood of a constitutional state is maintained on the basis of an integration programme according to the principle of conferral and respecting the Member States' constitutional identity, and that at the same time the Member States do not lose their ability to politically and socially shape the living conditions on their own responsibility.[81]

And in connection with EU laws which contradict the distinctly *national* character of rights and duties in society, it continued:

> European unification on the basis of a union of sovereign states under the Treaties may, however, not be realised in such a way that the Member States do not retain sufficient space for the political formation of the economic, cultural and social circumstances of life. This applies in particular to areas which shape the citizens' circumstances of life, in particular the private space of their own responsibility and of political and social security, which is protected by the fundamental rights, and to political decisions that particularly depend on previous understanding as regards culture, history and language and which unfold in discourses in the space of a political public that is organised by party politics and Parliament.[82]

This articulates the legal, political and cultural misgivings surrounding the expansion of the ECJ's jurisdiction in respect of social welfare policy. It invites a dialogue with the Institutions of the EU[83] as to the proper limits of EU

---

[80] See Article 168(5) TFEU (ex Article 152(5) EC Treaty), 'Community action … shall fully respect the responsibility of the Members States for the organisation and delivery of health services and medical care.' The ECJ has never explained how this provision affects its jurisdiction in health care cases.

[81] BVerfG, 2 BvE 2/08, 30 June 2009, para 226, www.bverfg.de/entscheidungen/es20090630_2bve000208en.html. See generally, Thym (2009), p. 1795 and Doukas (2009), p. 866.

[82] Ibid., para 249. The GFCC identified five areas of competence which do not permit extensive transfer of sovereign power: criminal law, monopoly on the use of force abroad, fundamental fiscal decisions, the guarantee of a just social order and the status of religious communities (see para 252).

[83] On various forms of 'constitutional dialogue' see the helpful discussion by Hickman (2005), p. 306.

jurisdiction.[84] Thus far, the ECJ has not explained the logic of its thinking, or the role it perceives for national health care planning. Will the *Charter of Fundamental Rights of the EU* help resolve these tensions? Article 35 promises that:

> everyone has the right of access to preventive care and the right to benefit from medical treatment under conditions established by national laws and practices.

However, this seems unlikely to introduce significant change to current practice and the matter requires more particular attention in the proposed *Directive*. Certainly, the EU should encourage harmony and equal access throughout the EU, but the process must surely be conducted within the republican, or community-based frameworks already in place nationally. This means that any future EU regime should acknowledge the choices endemic to this area and generate transparent, *procedural* rights. This is the fairest way of balancing the interests of all patients. To adopt the contrary proposals of the European Parliament, by promoting market-individualism and letting the devil take the hindmost, will disrupt and divide the community and present an impoverished view of citizenship and the common good.

Post Script *The Directive on Patients' Rights in Cross Border Healthcare* was published, as these essays went to press, on January 2011. My chapter considered the intense focus on individual rights and how it could damage commitments to solidarity and equality in national systems by favouring the mobile and affluent over chronically ill and dependent patients. I am pleased that my worst fears have not been realised, in particular, for the following reasons:

- Member states retain control over the health care benefits available to patients. Rights to cross border treatment will be subject to the same conditions, eligibility criteria and administrative formalities as apply to others. Prior authorisation procedures are justified if they promote access to a balanced range of treatments.
- The right to cross border treatment is not available where care can be provided at home within a medically justifiable time-limit (which may differ from the ECJ's "without delay" principle).
- Rare diseases do not have special status. Instead, member states must form European reference networks which assist co-operation in responding to patients' needs by pooling knowledge, resources and clinical expertise.
- Restrictions may be placed on cross border treatment where there is a safety risk to the patient or serious concern about the standards of another hospital.

This framework preserves a proper balance between individual and community interests. One hopes that the compromises achieved will save public health ethics from the EU internal market.

[84] For a distinctly EU solution to this problem, see Poiares Maduro (2006) (a former Advocate General of the ECJ): 'The recognition of a set of social rights accorded to all European citizens … can no longer be exclusive of those which can more easily make use of the free movement provisions. Otherwise, many Europeans will feel like strangers with regard to European citizenship. But this would require European social rights … founded on a new form of political discourse on social values at the level of the European Union.' (at p. 135). Again, this ignores both the national, historical and cultural foundations of social rights, and the implications for health care 'inequalities' noted in n. 51 *supra*.

Acknowledgments With the usual disclaimer, I thank Mrs Danielle De Costa Leite Borges, doctoral student at the EU Institute, Florence, for helpful discussions during the preparation of this article.

References

Afonso da Silva V, Vargas Terrazas F (2008) Claiming the right to health in Brazilian courts: the exclusion of the already excluded. http://papers.ssrn.com/sol3/papers.cfm?abstract_id=1133620

Alexy R (2004) A theory of constitutional rights. OUP, Oxford Chapters 2 and 9

Appleby J et al (2009) How cold will it be?—Prospects for funding: 2011–17. The Kings Fund, London

Baldwin P (1993) The politics of social solidarity–class bases of the European welfare state 1875–1975. CUP, Cambridge

Bayer R et al (2007) Public health ethics–policy and practice. OUP, Oxford

Bellamy R (2008) The democratic constitution: why Europeans should avoid American style constitutional judicial review. European Political Science 7

Bellamy R (2009) The liberty of the post-moderns?—Market and civic freedom with the EU. LSE Europe in Question Discussion Paper Series No. 01

Busse R et al (2008) Variability in the healthcare treatment costs among nine EU countries—results from the Healthcare Basket Project. Health Econ 17

Coggon J (2007) Harmful rights-doing?—The perceived problem of liberal paradigms and public health. J Med Ethics 34

Dagger R (1998) Civic virtues–rights, citizenship and Republican liberalism. OUP, Oxford

Daniels N (2008) Just health—meeting health needs fairly. Cambridge UP, Cambridge

Daniels N, Sabin J (1997) Setting limits fairly. OUP, Oxford

Dawson A, Verweij M (2007a) The meaning of 'public' in public health. In: Dawson A, Verweij M (eds) Ethics, prevention and public health. OUP, Oxford

Dawson A, Verweij M (2007b) Public health: ethical issues. Nuffield Council on Bioethics, London

Doukas D (2009) The verdict of the German Federal Constitutional Court on the Lisbon Treaty. ELRev 34:866

Drummond M et al (2007) Assessing the economic challenges posed by orphan drugs. Int J Technol Assess Health Care 23

Dworkin R (2000) Sovereign virtue–the theory and practice of autonomy. Harvard UP, Cambridge

Epp C (1998) The Rights Revolution: lawyers, activists and Supreme Courts in comparative perspective. Chicago University, Chicago

Esping-Andersen G (1990) The three worlds of welfare capitalism. Polity Press, Cambridge

Ferrara M (2005) The boundaries of social welfare. OUP, Oxford

Ferraz O (2009) Between usurpation and abdication? The right to health in the courts of Brazil and South Africa. 20 Aug. Available at SSRN. http://ssrn.com/abstract=1458299), text accompanying notes 46–48

Fredman S (2004) Human rights transformed. OUP, Oxford Chapter 4

Gaylin W, Jennings B (2003) The perversion of autonomy, 2nd edn. Georgetown University Press, Georgetown

Gostin L (2004) Health of the people—the highest law? J Law Med Ethics 32

Greer S (2009) The politics of European Union health policies. McGraw Hill, Open University Press, Maidenhead

Held V (2006) The ethics of care–personal, political, and global. OUP, Oxford

Herring J (2007) Death by indifference. Mencap, London, www.oldt.nhs.uk/documents/Death byindifference.pdf
Herring J (2009) Older people in law and society. OUP, Oxford
Hervey T (2000) Social solidarity: a buttress against internal market law? In: Shaw J (ed) Social law and policy in an evolving European Union. Hart Publishing, Oxford
Hickman T (2005) Constitutional Dialogue, Constitutional Theories and the Human Rights Act 1998. Public Law 306
Hirschman A (1970) Exit, voice and loyalty. Harvard, Cambridge
Hollis A (2006) Drugs for rare diseases: paying for innovation. In: Beach R, Chayjowski R, Short S, St Claire F, Sweetnam A (eds) Health services restructuring in Canada: new evidence and new directions. John Deutsch Institute, Kingston
Hope T (2001) Rationing and life-saving treatments: should identifiable patients have higher priority? J Medical Ethics 27
Hughes D et al (2005) Drugs for exceptionally rare disease: do they deserve special status funding? Q J Med 98. http://qjmed.oxfordjournals.org/cgi/content/full/98/11/829
Jennings B (2001) From the urban to the civic: the moral possibilities of the city. J Urban Health 78
Jennings B (2009) Public health and civic republicanism. In: Dawson A, Verweij M (eds) Ethics prevention and public health. OUP, Oxford
Jost T (2003) Disentitlement–the threats facing our public health care progams and a rights-based response. OUP, Oxford
Mayor S (2009) Cancer mortality is falling across Europe, but some countries have twice the death rate of others. BMJ 339
McCabe C et al (2005) Orphan drugs and the NHS: should we value rarity? BMJ 331
Michalski K (2006) What holds Europe together. CEU Press, Budapest
Montgomery J (2006) Law and the demoralisation of medicine. Legal Studies 26
Muller J-W (2007) Constitutional patriotism. Princeton University Press, Princeton Chapters 1, 2
Newdick C (2005) Who should we treat?—rights rationing and resources in the NHS. OUP, Oxford
Newdick C (2006a) Citizenship, free movement and health care: cementing individual rights by corroding social solidarity. CMLRev 43
Newdick C (2006b) Exceptional circumstances—access to low-priority treatment after the *Herceptin* case. *Clinical Ethics* 1
Newdick C (2006c) The positive side of health care rights. In: McLean SAM (ed) First do no harm–law, ethics and healthcare. Ashgate, Farnham
Newdick C (2008) The European Court of Justice, trans-national health care and social citizenship—accidental death of a concept. Wisconsin Int Law J 26
Poiares Maduro M (2006) European constitutionalism and three models of social Europe. In: Hesselink M (ed) The politics of a European Civil Code. Kluwer, The Hague
Sabel C, Simon W (2004) Destabilisation rights: how public law litigation succeeds. Harv LR 117:1015
Sandell M (1982) Liberalism and the limits of justice. CUP, Cambridge
Sandell M (2009) Justice–what's the right thing to do?. Allen Lane, London
Sauter W (2009) The proposed patients' rights directive. LIEI 36
Scharpf F (2009) Legitimacy in the multilevel European polity. MPIfG Working Paper, no. 1
Sen A (2009) The idea of justice. Allen Lane, London
Somek A (2007) Solidarity decomposed. ELRev 32
Somek A (2008a) Citizenship–as essay on the authority of the European Union. OUP, Oxford
Somek A (2008b) Individualism—an essay on the authority of the European Union. OUP, Oxford
Stone Sweet A (2000) Governing with judges—constitutional politics in Europe. OUP, Oxford
Thym D (2009) In the name of sovereign statehood: a critical introduction to the Lisbon judgement of the German Constitutional Court. CMLR 46
Tushnet M (2008) Weak courts, strong rights. Princeton University Press, Princeton. Chapter 8

Van Doorslaer E et al (2004) Explaining income-related inequalities in doctor utilization in Europe. Health Economics 13
Walzer M (1983) Spheres of justice—a defense of pluralism and equality. Basic Books, New York
West R (2006) Unenumerated duties. U Pennsylvania J Constitutional Law

Chapter 10
Health Care, the United Kingdom and the Draft Patients' Rights Directive: One Small Step for Patient Mobility but a Huge Leap for a Reformed NHS?

Jean McHale

Contents

10.1 Introduction

Across EU Member States patients are increasingly resorting to claims regarding their rights in the health care context.[1] Patients assert that they have a 'right to reproduce',[2] a 'right to die'[3] and increasingly a 'right to health care'. In the UK this engagement with patient rights has largely operated at a rhetorical level. Partly this can be seen as due to a traditionally paternalistic culture surrounding the delivery of patient care in the UK National Health Service (NHS). Partly it can be seen as a product of jurisdiction that operated without a comprehensive legislative statement of patient rights and which rendered challenges to health care resource allocation

[1] See, for example, McHale (2010).

[2] *Evans* v. *UK* [2007] 43 *EHRR* 21 and *Dickson* v. *UK* [2006] 46 *EHRR* 437.

[3] *Pretty v. UK* (2002) 35 *EHRR* 1.

J. McHale (✉)
School of Law, University of Birmingham, Birmingham, UK
e-mail: j.v.mchale@bham.ac.uk

J. W. van de Gronden et al. (eds.), *Health Care and EU Law*,
Legal Issues of Services of General Interest, DOI: 10.1007/978-90-6704-728-9_10,

decisions fundamentally problematic. However, in recent years there has been some concern that through application of EU law patients may be developing rights to health care and that this could have an inequitable and destabilising impact upon the allocation of NHS resources.[4] A right to health care is contained in Article 35 of the Charter of Fundamental Rights and Freedoms of the EU. This provides that:

> Everyone has the right of access to preventive health care and the right to benefit from medical treatment under the conditions established by national laws and practices. A high level of human health protection shall be ensured in the definition and implementation of all Union policies and activities.

However, it is not this 'right' to health care which is seen at present as the potentially destabilising factor for the UK National Health Service. First, the UK along with Poland negotiated a Protocol providing that the Charter will not enable the ECJ to hold UK and Polish law inconsistent with fundamental rights.[5] Secondly, the breadth of such a right would in any event prove very difficult to enforce.[6] Nonetheless as Fredman has commented

> the Charter is likely to function as a source of values and norms ...to influence the interpretation of EU legislative and other measures and to feed into policy-making and into EU activities more generally.[7]

Interestingly the trigger for re-evaluating patients' health care rights in the EU has come not from the Charter but rather from the evolving jurisprudence regarding free movement and medical treatment. The EU has now gone further and proposed a draft Patients' Rights Directive. This chapter explores first, the background to the Directive, the evolution of the free movement cases and how these came to impact upon the delivery of NHS patient care. It questions how radical the impact of cases in this area upon the NHS has been to date. Secondly, the chapter explores the draft Directive proposals concerning patient mobility and what their impact could be upon the NHS. It examines the implications of recent developments in the form of the NHS Act 2006 which introduce new provisions concerning patient reimbursement for treatment. Thirdly, it explores some of the broader ramifications of proposals in the draft Directive for the UK in relation to issues such as standards of patient care. It suggests that while the rise in patient mobility by itself does not seem, in the short-term at least, to have radically undermined resource allocation decision making in the NHS some of the other proposals in the Directive could prove more influential in relation to evolving standards of patient safety and quality of care in the future.

---

[4] See, for example, Montgomery (2005).

[5] Protocol No. 7 Treaty of Lisbon 2009.

[6] See generally Hervey (2003).

[7] Fredman (2006), p. 41 at p. 57.

10.2 Free Movement, Medical Treatment and the UK

During the last decade patients across the EU have been increasingly using their free movement rights in EU law to assert claims to medical treatment. Article 56 TFEU (ex Article 49 EC) Treaty provides that:

> Within the framework of the provisions set out below restrictions on the freedom to provide services within the Union shall be prohibited in respect of nationals of Member States who are established in a Member State of the other than that of the person for whom the services are intended.[8]

Medical treatment is regarded as a 'service'.[9] Claims under the Treaty have also been combined with Article 22 of Regulation No. 1408/71 which concerns cross-border social security provisions and is discussed in greater detail in the chapter by Pennings. (This has recently been replaced by Regulation 883/2004. The new Regulation will not be considered here further but the amendments do not affect the analysis in this chapter as they equally make provision for individuals to claim reimbursement of care where they have been subject to undue delay in their home member state). This enables EU citizens to seek to access medical treatment in another Member State and claim reimbursement for the cost of that treatment. While Member States have some discretion under this Regulation to determine reimbursement Article 22 provides that authorisation:

> may not be refused where the treatment in question is among the benefits provided for by the legislation of the Member State on whose territory the person concerned resides and where he cannot be given such treatment within the time normally necessary for obtaining the treatment in question in the Member State of residence, taking account of his current state of health and the probable course of the disease.

In a number of cases patients have challenged the refusal of national social insurance systems to reimburse costs of treatment in another Member State. So for example, in *Kohll* a refusal by the Luxembourg social insurance scheme to refund the cost of orthodontic treatment in Germany was held to be contrary to free movement principles and not objectively justifiable.[10] This approach was later extended to hospital services.[11] Nonetheless the ECJ in *Müller-Fauré and Van Riet* indicated that Member States could impose some forms of restriction such as

---

[8] Article 57 TFEU (ex Article 50 EC) further provides that:'Services shall be considered to be 'services' within the meaning of the Treaties where they are normally provided for remuneration...'Services' shall in particular include... (d) activities of the professions.'

[9] See further ECJ, Joined Cases 286/82 *Luisi and Carbone* v. *Ministero del Tesoro* [1984] *ECR* 377 and ECJ, Case C-158/96 *Kohll* [1998] *ECR* I-1935.

[10] ECJ, Case C-158/96 *Kohll* [1998] *ECR* I-1935.

[11] ECJ, Case C-157/99 *Geraets-Smits* v. *Stchting Ziekenfonds VGZ and Peerbooms* v. *Stichting CZ Groep Zorgverzekerigen* [2001] *ECR* I-5473, and ECJ, Case C-368/98 *Abdon Vanbraekel and others v. Alliance nationale des mutualities chretiennes* [2001] *ECR* I-5363.

prior authorisation in those situations where otherwise there may be consequent instability to the operation of national health systems.[12] However, the Court drew the distinction in difference in approach between extra-mural and hospital care, in the former prior authorisation was not needed whereas its use in relation to the latter was upheld. In relation to the latter, it was suggested that without such authorisation there was the danger that this would fundamentally undermine the planning of hospital services. Nonetheless the Court indicated that the operation of such prior authorisation procedures could themselves be the subject of scrutiny. Article 22 enables consideration of the time period in which a patient may be expected to wait for treatment in their home Member State. The ECJ stated that it would scrutinise what constitutes 'undue delay' to the patient in receiving treatment. In ascertaining undue delay attention needed to be given to the condition of the individual patient. The fact that there were waiting lists was not to be determinative. This line of cases was subsequently confirmed by the ECJ in *Inizan*.[13]

For a number of years the proliferation of the free movement cases where patients seek treatment in other jurisdictions and claim reimbursement of the cost of the treatment in their home Member State did not appear to create ripples across the English Channel.[14] The practicalities of travelling abroad or simple lack of awareness of the growing jurisprudence may have deterred patients. It was really only after the decisions in *Geraet Smits and Peerbooms* that the implications of these cases for the NHS began to be fully discussed. This led to the then UK Health Minister Alan Milburn introducing a scheme which led to patients being sent from South East England to France and Belgium for 'low risk' procedures.[15] This scheme was headlined by the fact that this was something now required by EU law when in fact the case law did not mandate this.

While there was considerable jurisprudence recognising that treatment may be given in another Member State, uncertainties remained as to the extent to which these principles were applicable in the context of a state national health service such as the UK NHS. At the ECJ in *Müller-Fauré* the UK government argued unsuccessfully that this jurisprudence did not, and ought not, apply to the UK, since the NHS did not provide services for 'remuneration' and to sanction reimbursement in this way would be economically damaging for the UK.[16]

Since the establishment of the NHS in 1948 the majority of health care services have been free at the point of delivery. While the NHS Act 2006 places statutory obligations upon the Secretary of State in relation to the NHS and provision of

---

[12] ECJ, Case C-385/99 *Müller-Fauré and van Riet* [2003] *ECR* I-4509.

[13] ECJ, Case C-56/01 *Inizan* v. *Caisse primarie d' Assurance Maladie des Hauts de Seine* [2003] *ECR* I-12403.

[14] For discussion regarding the development of the case law in this area for example, Hervey and McHale (2004), Chap. 4; Cabral (2004), p. 673; Koutrakos (2005); Palm and Glinos (2010).

[15] See further McHale and Bell (2002), p. 39.

[16] *Supra* n. 4.

various health services such obligations are discretionary in nature.[17] The courts have confirmed that there is no right to demand a particular treatment.[18] Furthermore they have been prepared to allow a wide margin of interpretation to NHS bodies in terms of how they have interpreted their statutory obligations.[19] This position is one which was not radically impacted by the coming into force into UK law of the Human Rights Act 1998 on 1 October 2000. This Act made certain provisions of the ECHR binding for the first time upon public bodies such as the NHS. However, the courts have interpreted the ECHR provisions consistent with earlier jurisprudence and there is no 'human right to treatment'. Clinicians have clinical discretion as 'gatekeepers' in assessing patients and determining clinical need for treatment. Unless it is an emergency situation referrals to secondary care are typically made by general practitioners.

Decisions in relation to which treatment to support are affected by rationing. While the NHS remains a centralised health care service a number of major changes have been introduced over the last two decades. After the National Health and Community Care Act in 1990 an internal market in care was introduced with 'purchasers' and 'providers' of care. Primary care services are provided under the auspices of Primary Care Trusts.[20] These Trusts commission medical, dental and ophthalmic services for their area. These contracts can be either with other NHS providers or with the private sector. Discretion is given to local Primary Care Trusts in relation to certain treatments. Different Primary Care Trusts may take different approaches in relation to priority setting in relation to the funding of particular treatments. So for example, provision of NHS funded fertility treatment varies widely across the country. In exercising treatment decisions clinical decisions are also affected by central rationing processes through the involvement of the National Institute for Health and Clinical Excellence.[21] This has the task of providing appraisals of existing and proposed treatments. It also provides best practice guidance. It can recommend that treatments should be available, not provided or be restricted in use. While the guidance is not binding in practice some NHS bodies do treat it as such.[22] It should be noted, however, that once the decision that treatment is needed has

---

[17] Sections 1 and 3 NHS Act 2006.

[18] *Re J (a minor)* [1992] 4 *All ER*.614, though see *R* v. *Portsmouth Hospitals NHS Trust ex parte Glass* [1999] *Lloyd's Rep Med* 367, per Lord Woolf.

[19] *R* v. *Secretary of State for Social Services, ex p Hincks*. ([1980] 1 *BMLR* 93); *R* v. *Central Birmingham HA, ex p Walker* (1987) 3 *BMLR* 32; *R* v. *Central Birmingham Health Authority, ex p Collier*. (Unreported, Court of Appeal 6 January 1988. LEXIS transcript); *R* v. *Cambridge DHA, ex p B* [1995] 1 *WLR* 898; *R* v. *North Derbyshire HA ex parte Fisher* [1997] 8 *Med LR* 327; *R* v. *Secretary of State for Health ex parte Pfizer Ltd* ([1999] *Lloyds Rep Med* 289); Cf., *R (on the application of Rogers)* v. *Swindon NHS Primary Care Trust and another* [2006] *EWCA* Civ 392. See further Brazier (2003); Newdick (2004); McHale (1999); Newdick (2007), p. 236.

[20] National Health Service Act 2006 s.18.

[21] National Institute for Clinical Excellence (Establishment and Constitution) Order 1999, SI 1999, No 220 and SI 1999, No 2219. For challenges in relation to the operation of NICE see *Eisai Ltd* v. *NICE* [2007] *EWHC* 1941. See further Syrett (2007), p. 127.

[22] See further Rawlins (2005), p. 904.

been made there has been some movement at least towards the rhetoric of 'patient choice'. In 2004 UK Government announced that patients were to have a choice in the context of non-emergency care between four and five health care providers-hospital and, e.g., special clinics such as allergy clinics.[23] A 'choose and book' facility was introduced so patients could book their own treatment appointments.

Up until the mid-2000s it appeared that the EU free movement cases had had a very limited impact upon the NHS and its resource allocation. Despite the case law UK patients did not seem to be seeking treatment in another EU Member State in large numbers. So for example, the figures for 2005 indicated that there were approximately 281 requests for treatment in the EU by UK citizens.[24] However, much greater publicity was given to the possibility of seeking treatment in another jurisdiction by the case of *Watts v. Bedford PCT* decided by the ECJ in 2006.[25] Here Mrs. Watts a 72 year old woman with osteoarthritis in both her hips sought a hip replacement operation. She sought access to treatment in another EU Member State under the E112 scheme which enabled patients to seek prior authorisation to receive treatment in another Member State. However, this was refused. This refusal was made first, on the basis that her consultant orthopaedic surgeon did not specifically support her case. Secondly, it was stated that this was a routine operation and here the standard NHS waiting list time did not constitute 'undue delay' to her in receiving such treatment. Despite this refusal she travelled to Lille in France in January 2003. Here the surgeon and anaesthetist who examined her expressed concern that as she had been rapidly losing weight there was a danger that she was approaching a point where she would not be suitable for surgery. The surgeon recommended the operation be undertaken in March 2003. In the UK she brought initial proceedings for judicial review. At this point a UK consultant reclassified her case to 'soon' which had the effect of reducing the waiting time to between three and four months. However, while the NHS operation was thus now due in April or May because she was concerned as to the deterioration in her condition Mrs. Watts travelled to France where the operation was undertaken in March 2003 and then claimed reimbursement of the cost of the treatment, an amount of some £3900 from Bedford Primary Care Trust. The Trust refused to reimburse the cost. Mrs. Watts challenged this under Article 49 EC.

In the English Court at first instance it was held that while Article 49 EC was applicable in relation to the NHS in this particular case Mrs. Watts had not suffered 'undue delay' as her condition had been reclassified and the operation was as a

---

23 Department of Health, *Chose and Book- Patient's Choice of Hospital and Booked Appointments,* London, Department of Health, 2004.

24 Health and Consumer Protection Directorate General European Commission Summary Report of the responses to the consultation regarding community action on health services, SEC 2006, 1195/4 of 7 September 2006.

25 ECJ, Case C-372/04 *R (on the application of Watts)* v. *Bedford Primary Care Trust, Secretary of State for Health* [2006] *ECR* I-4325 and see further on this case Bois-Pedain, du [2007], p. 66; Davies, (2007a), pp. 160, 162; McHale [2007a], p. 99.

consequence due to take place within 3–4 months.[26] The period of delay between October and February 2003 was not taken into account. In the Court of Appeal the court accepted that in *Müller-Fauré* the argument that Article 49 did not extend to the NHS had been rejected. However, the policy implications of the case led to the Court of Appeal to make an application for a preliminary ruling to clarify the application of Article 49 EC and Article 22 of Regulation No. 1408/71. The ECJ stated that 'it is not in dispute that the corollary of the Secretary of State's duty under Sections 1 and 3 of the NHS Act is the right to obtain treatment available under the NHS.' This remains a controversial statement because, as noted above, the English Courts have long confirmed the statutory duties under the NHS Act 2006 placed upon the NHS are discretionary and clinicians are the 'gatekeepers' to the NHS. In *Watts* the ECJ held that:

> Article 49 EC applies where a person whose state of health necessitates hospital treatment, goes to another Member State and there receives such treatment for consideration, there being no need to determine whether the provision of hospital treatment within the national health service with which that person is registered is in itself a service within the meaning of the Treaty provisions on the freedom to provide services.[27]

The ECJ also confirmed that where patients would be subject to 'undue delay' in receiving treatment in their own Member State they may travel and receive treatment in another Member State and then claim reimbursement of the cost of treatment. The test for undue delay under Article 49 EC, or within Article 22(2) of Regulation 1408/71, was the same.[28] Waiting lists could be scrutinised to ascertain that the target did not exceed a period which was acceptable on the basis of an objective medical assessment of the patient's medical circumstances and clinical needs.[29] The Court emphasised that this should take into account all those factors which characterise the medical condition when the request for authorisation is made or renewed.[30] In addition it was noted that the impact of the illness on the patient's work may be relevant in ascertaining what constitutes 'undue delay'. In ascertaining undue delay this is something to be ascertained on an individual basis. The assessment should be made objectively and with reference to impartial medical evidence. Earlier authority would also suggest that this should be interpreted consistent with international principles of medical science. However, this is a relative issue as has been argued elsewhere. There are huge variations in relation to perceptions as to what is 'illness', 'treatment' and indeed, what is ethically acceptable treatment.[31] The ECJ also held that Member States could operate

---

[26] *R* v. *Bedford PCT* v. *the Secretary of State for Health ex parte Watts, EWHC* 2228. See further the discussion of the judgement of Munby J in McHale (2006), p. 169.

[27] *Supra* n. 26, para 123.

[28] Ibid., para 60.

[29] Ibid., para 75.

[30] Ibid., para 76.

[31] See Davies (2007), p. 162 and Newdick (2006), p. 1661 at p. 1646 and further discussion in McHale (1999), p. 273.

systems such as prior authorisation systems which would facilitate resource allocation. However, such systems would need to satisfy the requirement of proportionality.[32] The existing NHS system was criticised because of the absence of criteria for prior authorisation.

Finally, the ECJ held that in relation to reimbursement of costs where the hospital treatment in the state of residence under the NHS was free of charge and did not provide for the reimbursement in full of the cost of treatment that had or should have been authorised then a patient should be reimbursed with any difference between the cost of equivalent treatment in a hospital covered by the service in question up to the total amount invoiced for the treatment provided in the host state, and the amount which the institution of the latter state was required to reimburse under Article 22 of Regulation No. 1408/71 of the competent institution pursuant to the legislation of that state. This covered the cost of hospital treatment, the cost of medical services strictly defined and the inextricably linked costs relating to his stay in the hospital.

These freedom of movement cases sparked considerable concern across the EU in general and the UK itself in particular.[33] The focus of the current discussion in this chapter is upon the UK situation. Most obvious was the fear that the resource allocation policy of individual Member States could be undermined by individuals seeking to by-pass waiting lists and seek treatment abroad. Newdick has argued that:

> Should EU law seek to undermine national policy by encouraging 'low priority' patients to obtain treatment abroad? Given the need to make difficult choices, surely national governments are best placed to determine national health priorities?[34]

In contrast others were of the view that the decision could be seen as justifiable in policy terms. For example, Davies has argued, when commenting on *Watts*, that:

> Such a use of waiting list times was only legally problematic if the waiting time was so long that it could not be clinically justified and that for individual patients it was medically indefensible. Was the UK government really arguing for its right to act against the medical interests of patients waiting for treatment? It was but it lost the point and can do so no longer.[35]

In the initial aftermath of the judgement the NHS issued new Guidance on treatment abroad for patients and Commissioners.[36] Commissioners were informed that their arrangements must be aligned with the decision in *Watts* and that,

---

[32] *Supra* n. 26, para 116.

[33] See further Newdick (2006).

[34] Newdick (2005), p. 244. See also his chapter in this book.

[35] See further Davies (2007).

[36] Department of Health, 'Going to Another European Country to Get Treatment', http://www.dh.gov.uk/en/PolicyandGuidance/Healthadvicefortravellers/Gettingtreatmentaroundtheworld/EEAandSwitzerland/DH_4114804 (Department of Health, May 2007) and Department of Health *Patient Mobility: Advice to Local Health Care Commissioners on Handling Requests for Hospital Care in other European Countries following the ECJ judgement in the Watts case.* Gateway reference 8010, Department of Health, April 2007.

moreover, it was important that as far as possible arrangements in relation to treatment were agreed before patients went abroad. Nonetheless it appears that the NHS did not at that time envisage a large number of challenges and indeed suggested that bringing down waiting times would consequently reduce the number of challenges.[37]

10.3 Patient Mobility, the UK and the Draft Directive

While case law itself could have led to changes to UK approaches to patient mobility the impact of this case law on structural issues concerning the EU and the delivery of health care may yet prove much more fundamental and long lasting on Member States. The implications of patients using free movement rights to obtain services in other Member States caused concern at EU level. In 2005 the European Parliament asked the Commission to take steps concerning patient mobility and the co-operation of health systems.[38] In June 2006 the Council of Ministers in a *Statement of Common Values and Principles in EU Health Systems* stated that importance of 'protecting the values and principles that underpin health systems in the EU.'[39] This in itself raises, of course, a broader fundamental question as to whether such fundamental principles can effectively be identified: something very challenging given the breadth of EU Member States today. Furthermore if such principles are cast too broadly they could be meaningless. While originally health care and the reimbursement of costs for cross-border patient care was included in the EU Services Directive it was subsequently withdrawn.[40] The European Commission issued a consultation regarding Community action on health care services following the free movement cases.[41] This consultation document was considered by the UK House of Lords European Union Committee in February 2007.[42] In evidence to the Committee the UK Government stated that it was necessary that Member State treatment referral processes were respected. So for example, current UK practice which is to require a General Practitioner referral to secondary care would be needed in order to seek such care in another EU Member States. In addition they stated their view that an individual should only be able to travel to receive treatment which was available in the UK not necessarily in the Member

[37] See further discussion in McHale (2007b), p. 263.

[38] *Report on Patient Mobility and Health care Developments in the EU* (2005).

[39] *Council Conclusions of Common Values and Principles in EU Health Systems* 2733rd Employment, Social Policy, Health and Consumer Affairs Council Meeting, Luxembourg 1–2 June 2006.

[40] Directive 2006/123 [2006] *OJ* L 373/36. See the discussion in the chapter by Szyszczak.

[41] Communication from the Commission, *Consultation Regarding Community action on Health Services*, Commission of the European Communities, Brussels, SEC (2006) 1195 of 26 September 2006.

[42] House of Lords, EU Committee 8th Report of Session 2006–7, *Cross-Border Health Services in the European Union Report with evidence*, HL Paper 48.

State where treatment was sought. The UK Government stated that Member States should be able to limit the cost of treatment abroad to that which would be the case if the treatment was delivered in the UK. They took the view that they would not support legislation which simply restated existing case law. In addition they were clear they would not support any mechanisms which complicated the existing situation. Concerns also related to the prospect of litigation should treatment procedures go wrong and patients suffer harm while in another Member State.

Responses to the Consultation were split as to whether existing private international law rules here are sufficient or whether there was need for greater clarity in dealing with these issues.[43] Suggestions included the prospect of a flexible dispute resolution system along with a European Ombudsman or mediation.

Following the consultation the Commission indicated that it intended to prepare a package of measures which includes legislation with the aim of clarification of the conditions under which cross-border health care may be undertaken and reimbursed.[44] This has now been taken forward in the form of the proposed draft Directive on the application of patient rights in cross-border health care.[45] The draft Directive is part of the renewed Social Agenda. The Commission's expressed intention is to provide legal certainty.[46] The proposals include a legal framework for cross-border care clarifying the case law in this area. The broader implications of the draft Directive for provision of health care in the UK are considered in the next section. Here we focus upon the impact of the draft Directive and the free movement cases upon the NHS.

The draft Directive provides in Article 6(1) that insured persons who travel to other Member States will not be prevented from receiving health care provided in another Member State where it is included in their own state package of health care. It also provides in Article 6(2) for reimbursement

> up to the level of costs which would have been assumed had the same or similar health care had been provided in the Member State of affiliation without exceeding the actual costs of health care received.

As with the pre-Directive case law Article 7 provides that reimbursement in relation to the cost of non-hospital care is not to be subject to prior authorisation. The principle of prior authorisation remains in relation to Article 8(3) of the draft Directive. This can be utilised if the system is to:

> prevent it from seriously undermining or being likely to seriously undermine:

---

[43] Health and Consumer Protection Directorate-General, European Commission *Summary Report of the responses to the consultation regarding Community action on health services* (SEC 2006, 1195/4 of September 2006), 23–24.

[44] Watson (2007), p. 974.

[45] Proposal for a Directive of the European Parliament and of the Council on the application of patients' rights in cross-border health care COM(2008) 414 final. See the discussion in the chapter by Szyszczak.

[46] Commission Press Release IP/08/1080 and MEMO/08/473, 2 July 2008.

(i) The financial balance of the Member State's social security system; and/or
(ii) The planning and rationalization carried out in the hospital sector to avoid hospital overcapacity, imbalance in the supply of hospital care and logistical and financial wastage, the maintenance of a balanced medical and hospital service open to all or the maintenance of treatment capacity or medical competence on the territory of the concerned Member State.

However, Article 8(4) provides that the criteria shall be 'what is necessary and proportionate to avoid such impact.' In addition Article 8(5) of the draft Directive requires that Member States are to publicise the information concerning prior authorisation systems.

It appears that the UK decided to pre-empt the Directive coming into force by making statutory provision for those patients seeking treatment overseas. This also provides a statutory basis for the procedures for authorisation of treatment in another EU Member State following the *Watts* case. The existence of the draft Directive triggered the Department of Health to provide further Guidance in relation to those seeking treatment overseas in the form of the National Health Service (Reimbursement of the Cost of EEA Treatment) Regulations 2010 and related directions and Guidance.[47] NHS providers are reminded in the Guidance document that reform is needed not least because of the prospect that the UK will be subject to infraction proceedings as well as to judicial review.[48]As the current Guidance makes clear, there are two routes for NHS patients claiming reimbursement for the cost of treatment. These are the E112 route and the Article 56 TFEU route. The E112 route applies only to state provided treatment. In contrast the Article 56 TFEU relates to all treatment including private care. As the Guidance notes numbers accessing care in other Member States are low. Around 1,000 seek treatment via the E112 route each year. There are not specific figures available in relation to the Article 56 TFEU route but as the Guidance states:

> the Department of Health does not have exact data on the numbers but is not aware that a significant number of NHS patients have used this route or intend to do so.

Nonetheless it goes onto state that:

> However, whilst there is limited data available as to the number of NHS patients who are currently seeking treatment under Article 56 it is essential that patient mobility is managed in a sustainable manner.[49]

The regulations insert new Sections 6A and 6B into the primary legislation with the aim of providing clarification on the position of cross-border care. The regulations set out the conditions which must be complied with before there is a

47 SI 2010, National Health Service (Reimbursement of the Cost of EEA Treatment) (England) Directions 2010.

48 Department of Health, *Cross-border healthcare and patient mobility; revised advice on handling requests from patients for treatment in countries of the European Economic Area-Guidance to the NHS* London, Department of Health (2010), para 3.9.

49 *Supra* n. 48, para 3.5.

statutory obligation to provide reimbursement. In relation to treatment where there is the requirement of prior authorisation the Guidance is careful to make clear that authorisation as such does not constitute authorisation of a particular practitioner. As it states

> Patients need to be aware that prior authorisation does not imply clinical approval of a patients planned health care in another Member State, nor implies acceptance of any responsibility for that treatment. No duty of care attaches to that authorisation.[50]

Interestingly the Guidance also comments in relation to travel insurance that there appears to be some diversity in the travel insurance market with the development of 'niche' practitioners who are providing new insurance packages.[51] The Guidance goes onto state that: 'It is in the patient's interests to ensure that they have the appropriate cover and commissioners should play their part in reminding people of this.'[52]

Primary Care Trusts are required to both establish and publish procedures on the issue of claiming reimbursement of health care where treatment is undertaken in another jurisdiction.[53] The Directions provide that advice and assistance is to be given to those persons who are intending to travel to receive treatment in another Member State. A form for making such claims is to be specified. PCTs are required under the directions to make this form available. Details of the information needed in respect of such a claim must also be published.

The Guidance and Directions differentiate between those procedures where prior authorisation should be sought. The Guidance suggests that before seeking treatment in another Member State patients should contact local NHS Commissioners to determine whether prior authorisation is needed and the level of cost reimbursement involved.[54] Interestingly the Guidance states that: 'This should happen before the patient accesses treatment in another Member State though retrospective applications may also be considered.'[55] The Guidance also emphasises that as part of this procedure it will give Commissioners the opportunity to provide patients information regarding treatment options within the NHS although they cannot insist upon these options being preferred by the patient.[56]

One interesting aspect of the Guidance relates to what actually are 'primary care services' and which services should be subject to prior authorisation. This was left as an issue after the *Watts* case. Recently in the UK there has been a movement towards providing services which in the past would have been solely available in a hospital setting in a primary care context. These are referred to as being 'special

---

[50] Ibid., para 5.4.
[51] Ibid., para 5.7.
[52] Ibid., para 5.7.
[53] Ibid., para 6.3.
[54] Ibid., para 7.3.
[55] Ibid., para 7.4.
[56] Ibid., para 7.4.

services' under the Guidance. The DOH notes that such services provide easier access to care but at the same time they are costly in relation to both their initial provision and their subsequent operation.[57] As a consequence the DOH has taken the approach that 'certain specialised services' (for example, PET scans and specialist radiography services) which may be provided in a non-hospital setting should be subject to prior authorisation on the same basis as if they were provided in hospitals. The Guidance set out what will constitute special services and as a result prior authorisation will be required before these are authorised. They are defined as follows:

(a) A service that involves a stay in hospital accommodation for at least one night;
(b) Medical treatment that involves general anaesthesia, epidural anaesthesia or intravenously administered sedation;
(c) Dental treatment that involves general anaesthesia or intravenously administered sedation; or
(d) A service whose provision involves the use of specialised or cost intensive medical infrastructure or medical equipment.[58]

This is a clear attempt to delimit the impact of the free movement cases. The final category will prove particularly controversial. There is considerable scope for argument in relation to the definitions set out here. In many respects a lot of NHS care will involve specialised/cost intensive infrastructure/equipment. Where will the dividing line be drawn? Could this, for example, exclude a lot of dental care which inevitably involves expensive equipment? Does it mean that prior authorisation would really only not be required where a person was seeking basic GP care, precisely the type of care which they would be unlikely to travel overseas to receive? Interestingly the DOH has not provided a conclusive definition of such services instead and again potentially controversially this is an issue which is being left to individual PCT's. They are required to publish information identifying those services which are special services and thus require prior authorisation. This raises the prospect of differing definitions of such services from PCT to PCT with in effect a 'postcode lottery' should some PCTs decide to interpret this generously. Where treatments are sought which are not under the classification of 'special treatments' nonetheless the Guidance still emphasises the need for patients to discuss in advance their plans regarding this treatment.[59]

A further part of the process will be that health professionals may apply what is known as 'gatekeeping' to those patients who wish to access treatments.[60] The Guidance states that the aims are both to ensure that patients have a clinical need for treatment but that in addition patients can only access treatment which they would be entitled to access in the NHS.[61] Under Article 56 TFEU prior

[57] Ibid., para 7.5.

[58] Ibid., para 7.8.

[59] Ibid., para 7.9.

[60] Ibid., para 8.5.

[61] Ibid., para 8.5.

authorisation the commissioner should require the issue to be determined in 20 days unless additional information is needed.[62]

The determination of each case is left to PCT's. Interestingly the Guidance specifically states that it is for PCT's to determine their own procedures.[63] However, some parameters are established under the Guidance. These are stated as being

> The PCT has determined that the service the patient has requested is not one that would be provided by the NHS, in the circumstances of the patient's case the treatment is experimental.
>
> The PCT considers that there is a proven or well evidenced clinical risk to the patient or to the wider public health if the patient travels abroad.
>
> The PCT considers that there are inadequate after care or follow up arrangements in place for the treatment in question.
>
> The PCT has evidence that the provider is unsuitable because it has evidence of its previous neglect or fraudulent actions (this criterion is expected to be used only in very rare cases where accurate and substantiated information/evidence is available.[64]

Section 6A of the NHS Act 2006 provides that the maximum level of reimbursement which is allowed is limited to either:

> the cost of the equivalent NHS service or the actual cost of treatment where this is lower than the NHS cost. PCT's are expected to reimburse patients at tariff price where this exists plus the appropriate local Market forces factor.[65]

In relation to those treatments which require prior authorisation PCTs are required to also both specify and make this form available. The Direction also makes provision for claims to be dealt with within specific time limits. Once a decision is reached applicants are to be notified both of the decision and of reasons for the decision. Interestingly the Primary Care Trusts are advised in the Guidance that a decision may be subject to challenge either through judicial review or through the submission of a complaint to the European Union.[66]

As was noted above, following the ECJ cases patients may not be refused treatment where there has been 'undue delay'. Specific provision is now made for the situation in which there has been such delay. The DOH Guidance specifically makes reference to the ECJ jurisprudence and states that where has been undue delay then this may mean that a patient may be successful following the ECJ judgements in claiming retrospectively for the cost of treatment abroad.[67] The Guidance states that:

[62] Ibid., para 8.11.

[63] Ibid., para 9.3.

[64] Ibid., para 9.3.

[65] Ibid., para 9.3.

[66] Ibid., para 4.7.

[67] Ibid., para 11.4.

(a) The requested service is necessary to treat or diagnose the medical condition of the patient;
(b) The requested service is the same as or equivalent to a service that the Secretary of State or the patient's PCT or Strategic Health Authority would make available to the patient in the circumstances of the patients case; and
(c) The Secretary of State or the patients PCT or SHA cannot provide to the patient a service that is the same as or equivalent to the requested service within a period of time that is acceptable on the basis of medical evidence as to the patients clinical needs taking into account the patient's state of health at the time the decision under this section is made and the probable course of the medical condition to which the service relates.[68]

The new Section 6B of the NHS Act 2006 provides that PCTs must have regard to:

the patient's medical history

(a) The extent of any pain, disability, discomfort, or other suffering that is attributable to the medical condition to which the service is to relate;
(b) Whether any such pain, disability, discomfort or suffering makes it impossible or extremely difficult for the patient to carry out ordinary daily tasks; and
(c) The extent to which the provision of the service would be likely to alleviate or enable the alleviation of the pain, disability discomfort or suffering.

The full implications of *Watts*, the free movement cases and what will happen post the draft Directive remain of course the source of speculation. What is clear is that the UK was concerned to ensure that Guidance and procedures are in place. While new structures are operational as has been seen above this may still ultimately prove problematic. Discretion has been left to PCTs. While some Guidance has been issued they have been granted considerable discretion and this may lead to inconsistency in approach across the NHS as a whole. The extent to which this may also have a radical impact upon resource allocation remains still uncertain due to the limited data which is available. This author has in the past suggested that perhaps the *Watts* judgement may, in the longer term, prove less radical than first feared. In 2008 a widespread consultation process was undertaken by the NHS European Office to ascertain the impact of the draft Directive proposals upon the NHS.[69] This interestingly found that most respondents were not anticipating that there would be a large expansion in cross-border care. The NHS took the view that the impact of these cases would not be major when placed in context of broader considerations which included demographic change and migration patterns. Moreover, the success in reducing waiting list targets may mean that there are fewer prospects of claims in relation to undue delay. However, events since the May 2010 election may mean that some caveats may now be added to this original statement. The UK Government have, at the time of writing, announced their intention to abandon certain NHS targets. This may have a knock on impact in relation to the delivery of care to specific patients. If it is the case that treatment

68 Ibid., para 11.2.

69 See further Bowden (2009), p. 18.

targets are increased then more patients may seek more rapid treatment in other EU countries. This could then have consequent cost implications for the NHS. Furthermore it could also have implications for priority settings. Bowden comments that in relation to entitlements, as she noted, unless there is prior needs assessment it would be in practice very difficult to ascertain whether a particular treatment would be available due to the fact that instead of defined designated treatments the decision to go ahead with treatment is a matter of clinical judgement.[70] Furthermore as the survey noted different treatments could be regarded differently in different jurisdictions. Concerns were expressed in relation to the provision in the draft Directive which allowed costs to be recovered if 'same or similar' costs were available in the patient's home system. While Bowden suggests that one way round this is to provide clarification on limits for entitlements and how eligibility should be determined. Nonetheless it remains highly questionable that this could be done in practice.

Interestingly responses to the NHS European Office survey saw the cross-border health care cases as an extension of the idea of Patient Choice which was already part of NHS policy.[71] In contrast, as Bowden notes, in relation to Patient Choice this simply relates to those providers who are operating under contracts to the NHS as opposed to the broad range of providers which operates in the context of the EU.

10.4 Broader Issues Concerning Standards of Patient Care

What is particularly interesting are the broader implications of those recommendations in the draft Directive.[72] If enhanced patient mobility becomes a major issue then this forces Member States, not simply to address the resource implications which may flow from this, but also to look at broader issues relating to delivery of health care and its impact upon the home Member State. Article 5 places several responsibilities on the Member State of treatment. These include under Article 5(1)(a) the requirement for mechanisms in order to meet standards of quality and safety for health care 'taking into account medical science and generally recognised good medical practices.' Article 5(1)(b) provides for the monitoring of such standards. The Directive will establish a cooperation framework which will include such things as health technology assessment, data collection and quality and safety. While much will be left to Member States Article 5(3) makes provision for the Commission to develop standards and guidelines which will facilitate the implementation of such standards. As the chapter by Hervey demonstrates, the draft Directive also proposes in Article 15 the development of new 'European reference networks'. These would aim to join on a voluntary basis

[70] Ibid.

[71] Bowden (2009), p. 19.

[72] See Palm and Glinos (2010), p. 551.

specialised health care centres across Member States. The aim would be that such networks could provide 'focal points' for purposes such as research, evaluation and the dissemination of information.[73] Pilot projects are being funded to test the concept of such networks. Article 17 provides for 'co-operation on the management of new health technologies'. The EU is currently providing support for a pilot network considering health technology assessment, EUnetHTA.[74] The Commission has also noted the potential for information and communication technologies to improve quality, safety and efficiency of health care.[75] Article 16 of the draft Directive also contains recommendations on e-health. Concerns regarding the use of such technologies include the different types of technology and formats and it is recommended that harmonisation is needed across the EU to facilitate use of such technologies.[76]

A further potential impact of the draft Directive is in relation to patient standards of care and patient safety in general. The NHS European office undertook a consultation following the draft Directive. Respondents to this consultation expressed concern in relation to standards of health care where health care was delivered by potentially a wide range of providers in other EU countries.[77] Several potential issues can be identified here. First, there is the question of who has responsibility for the care provided? A UK House of Lords Select Committee Report which considered the draft Directive in 2009 highlighted the importance of the 'pathway of care' in relation to patient safety.[78] Respondents to the Report commented that where care is provided through a multi-disciplinary team someone needs to have ultimate responsibility for that care. Ascertaining where such responsibility may lie is something which can be complex in relation to a standard NHS package of care but this complexity is magnified where treatment is provided in another jurisdiction. Furthermore care can be seen very often as a continuum rather than being regarded a 'one off' package of care. So for example, in evidence to the House of Lords Select Committee in 2009 the British Dental Association commented that in relation to dentistry that this is also not often a 'snap shot' event and that consequently seeking one-off episodes of care elsewhere can be very dangerous.[79]

Secondly, concerns have been expressed by the UK General Medical Council that even if the Directive was not seen as necessarily problematic to a pathway of care in a particular situation the diversity of culture and language was an issue

[73] *Supra* n. 45, para 2.3.1.

[74] Ibid., para 2.32.

[75] Ibid., para 2.3.2.

[76] Ibid., para 8.4.

[77] Bowden (2009), p. 19.

[78] House of Lords European Union Committee, *Healthcare across EU borders; a safe framework*, CM 7580 April 2009, para 124.

[79] Ibid., para 124.

which needed to be engaged with.[80] The House of Lords Select Committee Report concluded that: 'clarity is required about the responsibilities of all those involved in the pathway of care'[81] They emphasised that this was important to ensure that patients would then be in the best position to make an informed decision in relation to their treatment. The process of providing prior authorisation of treatment may enable the issue of the package of care to be identified and possible concerns addressed at that time. But the issue of diversity of culture and of language raise further fundamental issues. This relates to the broader policy question as to how care is actually delivered in practice.

Currently there are no central standards of patient care across the EU. There are no clear centralised 'benchmarks' here. In the UK as noted earlier Guidance as to particular treatments is provided by the National Institute for Health and Clinical Excellence. In addition within the UK standards of health care delivery are monitored by a statutory body the Care Quality Commission operational since 2009.[82] This body has powers of inspection and investigation. What is interesting is the extent to which developments consequent upon the Directive may impact upon standard setting in health care at single jurisdictional level.

If differential standards of care are provided across different Member States then there is the consequent possibility that litigation might result.[83] Furthermore there was a real possibility that home Member States would be left to deal with the consequences if something went wrong in another Member State as continuing care would fall inevitably within the province of the home Member State. The draft Directive states that there should be mechanisms in place to provide compensation for harm although the precise forms of such mechanisms are left to the individual Member States to determine.[84] This is inevitable given the wide ranging difference between complaints and civil litigation procedures across Member States. In the UK responses to this recommendation contained in the draft Directive have been critical. The General Medical Council stated that: 'there have to be effective systems that lead to regulatory action or redress for patients if they have been harmed.'[85] The UK Government Minister Dawn Primarole also criticised this provision and stated that 'Our view is that Article 5 is not clear enough with regards to how complaints, liability and negligence fit together'.[86] One possible consequence of this provision may be that individual EU Member States begin to reappraise their civil redress and complaints systems in the light of those in other jurisdictions. It is possible that transfer of information on such issues

---

[80] Ibid., para 125.

[81] Ibid., para 134.

[82] S.1 Health and Social Care Act 2008. See further discussion in McHale (2010).

[83] McHale and Bell (2002), p. 39.

[84] Article 5(d) and *supra* n. 45, para 8.6(16).

[85] House of Lords European Union Committee, *supra* n. 78.

[86] Ibid., para 144.

could in the longer term lead to greater alignment across the EU both in relation to complaints processes but also more generally in relation to civil compensation.

A related issue is that where mistakes arise abroad this can lead to costs for the NHS. A patient with botched surgery abroad may seek NHS treatment. The cost of this treatment will divert other resources from an already overstretched NHS. In evidence to the House of Lords Select Committee in its examination of the draft Directive the then Minister of State Dawn Primarole stated that this issue needed to be clarified.[87] The doctors' professional organisation the British Medical Association has proposed the introduction of a procedure enabling the home Member State to claim costs of remedy of a difficult procedure from the other Member State.[88]

However, litigation can be seen very much as a final step. It is a better approach to attempt to consolidate standards of quality in health care delivery across the EU as a whole to provide reassurance to patients and Member States alike. Prophetically, as it now appears, as early as 2001 Nys commented that the free movement cases might result in development of a 'harmonised package' of comparable health care services across the EU.[89] The draft Directive now introduces a 'duty of cooperation' under Article 13. The proposal for the Directive states that:

> Realising the potential of the internal market for cross-border health care requires co-operation between providers, purchasers and regulators of different Member states at national, regional or local level in order to ensure safe, high quality and efficient care across borders.[90]

This is with the aim of making clear as to which Member State is responsible for compliance with common principles for health care. The draft Directive provides that there should be appropriate provision of patient information on access to cross-border health care and national contact points for such information.[91] It states that:

> Whenever health care is provided it is vital for patients to ensure:
>
> – clear information that enables people to make informed choices about their health care;
> – mechanisms for ensuring the quality and safety of health care that is provided;
> – continuity of care between different treating professionals and organizations;
> – and mechanisms to ensure appropriate remedies and compensation for harm arising from health care.[92]

The aim is to ensure clarity in responsibilities of Member States in relation to quality and safety of care.

87 Ibid., para 145.

88 Ibid., para 145.

89 Nys (2001), p. 317.

90 *Supra* n. 45, para 8.1.

91 Ibid., para 7.5.

92 Ibid., para 4(a).

A further broader impact of enhanced patient mobility may be the need to facilitate the exchange of information concerning patient records. The proposed Directive also while indicating how transfer of medical records may be necessary to facilitate patient care also illustrates the problems with such an approach in that there remain tensions between access to data and protection of personal data which is also required under EU law through Directive 95/46/EC of the European Parliament and of the Council of 24 October 1995 on the protection of individuals with regard to the processing of personal data and on the free movement of such data. Following the draft Directive a Recommendation has been published on the cross-border interoperability of electronic health systems.[93] This is aimed at facilitating access to patient data when the patient is being treated in another Member State but the issue of data security will inevitably still remain a fundamental concern for individuals and Member States. The House of Lords Select Committee recommended a 'clearer system is established for the transfer of patients' medical records.'[94] This is, however, certainly not an uncontroversial recommendation. The UK NHS has been establishing an electronic database for medical records. This has been criticised due to the risk that this poses to data security.[95] There would potentially be an even broader risk here to data security should this be taken further. It remains to be seen whether the recommendations in relation to e-health contained in the Directive impact upon the UK. The draft Directive does not require that such systems are introduced but to facilitate their use where they operate. Concerns as to the impact upon the UK included safeguards for patient health and the need for explicit regulation of telemedicine.[96]

Some further practical issues raised as concerns also include the issue of the cross-border recognition of prescriptions under Article 14 of the draft Directive. Although generally welcomed in the UK some concerns were raised.[97] One issue was due to the diversity of languages across the UK, questions of translation of different medication, etc., arose as problematic. The House of Lords Select Committee recommended that the Commission developed detailed rules regarding prescriptions. These would include procedures enabling a prescription to be verified to ensure that it came from a recognised prescribe.[98]

---

93 Commission Recommendation C (2008) 3282 of 2 July 2008 on cross-border interoperability of electronic health record systems.

94 *Supra* n. 78, para135.

95 BBC News, 'Calls to halt England NHS patient database development', http://news.bbc.co.uk/1/hi/health/8559045.stm.

96 *Supra* n. 78, para 177.

97 Ibid., para 167.

98 Ibid., para 178.

10.5 Conclusions

The UK has become increasingly engaged with the prospect of enhanced patient mobility across the EU. Concerns expressed by commentators in this area relate to the prospect of the impact upon NHS resource allocation. This could lead to inequitable distribution of health care resources if resources are diverted to patients who are simply able to be more mobile than others whether due to their physical condition or due to their economic circumstances if they are in the fortunate position of being able to pay money 'up front'. To date, however, despite these concerns there still does not seem to have been a large number of patients seeking treatment in other EU jurisdictions. This may be due to a range of factors, lack of awareness that this is an option, the fact that patients may not wish to 'risk' treatment by health care providers outside the EU, the fact that delays within the NHS are not such that patients feel that they need to seek treatment abroad and simply that illness itself is an inhibitor to travel. The EU draft patient's rights directive may impact upon the delivery of UK health care in two respects. First, its very existence and the publicity generated by it coming into force may mean that more people are encouraged to seek treatment in other EU Member States. It remains to be seen, however, whether this is a realistic prospect given that since *Watts* there still does not seem to have been a large increase in patients travelling to other EU states. Secondly, it is suggested that perhaps the draft Directive if it is implemented may have longer term a greater impact in the alignment of health law and policy both at EU level and at Member State level. It may result in a trend towards greater uniformity in health care standards; it may long-term impact upon medical training and education. There are of course some caveats here. At EU level the diversity of health care systems across Member States will present considerable challenges to moving towards EU standards in this way. It does not, however, appear that these cases have not to date provided a catalyst to nudge the UK towards the general re-evaluation of the feasibility of a National Health Service and to move it towards a social insurance system.

Post Script This chapter was written in the light of the Draft Patients Rights Directive as published in 2008. The Directive has been subsequently amended and a revised version of the Directive was adopted in January 2011.

References

Bowden H (2009) EU cross-border health care proposals: implications for the NHS. Eurohealth 15(1), 18

Brazier M (2003) Rights and health care. In: Blackburn R (ed) Rights of citizenship. Mansell, London

Cabral P (2004) The internal market and the right to cross-border medical care. EL Rev 29(5)

Davies G (2007) The effect of Mrs. Watts trip to France on the national health service. KLJ 18, 160

Du Bois-Pedain A (2007) Seeking health care elsewhere, Camb Law J, 66

Freedman S (2006) Transformation or dilution: fundamental rights in the EU social space. ELJ 12, 41
Hervey TK (2003) The right to health in European Union law. In: Hervey TK, Kenner J (eds) Economic and social rights under the EU charter of fundamental rights: a legal perspective. Hart Publishing, Oxford
Hervey TK, McHale JV (2004) Health law and the European Union (chapter 4). Cambridge, CUP
Koutrakos P (2005) health care as an economic service under EC law. In: Dougan M, Spaventa E (eds) Social welfare and EU law. Hart Publishing, Oxford
McHale JV (1999) Enforcing health care rights in English Courts. In: Burchill R, Harris D, Owers A (eds) Economic, social and cultural rights: their implementation in English law. University of Nottingham, Nottingham
McHale JV (2006) Law, patient's rights and NHS resource allocation: is Eurostar the answer? Health Anal 14(2), 169
McHale JV (2007a) The right to medical treatment in EU law. Med Law Review 15, 99
McHale J (2007b) Framing a right to treatment in English law. Watts in Retrospective. Maastricht J Eur Comp Law 14(3), 263
McHale J (2010) Fundamental rights and health care. In: Mossialos E, Permanand G, Baeten R, Hervey TK (eds) Health systems governance in Europe. CUP, Cambridge
McHale J, Bell M (2002) Traveller's checks. Health Ser J 60, 39
Montgomery J (2005) The impact of European Union law on English health care law. In: Dougan M, Spaventa E (eds) Social welfare law and EU law. Hart, Oxford
Newdick C (2004) The organisation of health care. In: Grubb A (ed) Principles of medical law. OUP, Oxford
Newdick C (2005) Who shall we treat? 2nd edn. Oxford University Press, Oxford
Newdick C (2006) Citizenship, free movement and health care: cementing individual rights by corroding social solidarity CML Rev 43, 1661
Newdick C (2007) Judicial review: low priority treatment and exceptional case review. Med Law Rev 15(2)
Nys H (2001) Comparative health law and the harmonization of patients rights in Europe. Eur J Health Law 8, 317
Palm W, Glinos I (2010) Enabling patient mobility in the EU: between free movement and coordination. In: Mossialos E, Permanand G, Baeten R, Hervey TK (eds) Health systems governance in Europe. CUP, Cambridge
Rawlins M (2005) Five NICE years Lancet 365
Syrett K (2007) NICE and judicial review: enforcing accountability for reasonableness through the courts. Med Law Rev 16, 127
Watson R (2007) Europe is to legislate on cross-border health care. BMJ 334, 974

Part III
Competition Law and Health Care Issues

Chapter 11
The Treaty Provisions on Competition and Health Care

Johan W. van de Gronden

Contents

11.1 Introduction

A couple of years ago the Dutch Ministry of Health Care organised an international workshop on competition law in health care. At the end of this workshop, one of the speakers, a specialist in health care issues, compared competition law with a 'fat cat'. The health care sector has had a difficult time in welcoming competition law because the 'fat cat' seemed to be mainly interested in competition issues and not in the special features of health care. But after a certain elapse of time the sector has developed some skills to cope with the presence of this cat

J. W. van de Gronden (✉)
Faculty of Law, Radbouw University, Nijmegen, The Netherlands
e-mail: j.vandegronden@jur.ru.nl

J. W. van de Gronden et al. (eds.), *Health Care and EU Law*,
Legal Issues of Services of General Interest, DOI: 10.1007/978-90-6704-728-9_11,

and has even managed to like it from time to time, as this 'fat cat' is capable of enhancing efficiency.

This example shows that coping with competition law could be problematic in health care since it is believed that it could interfere with essential health care arrangements. However, the views on the role of competition have changed over the last decade and as a result it is acceptable that even in health care European competition law is applied. So, health care is starting to take into account the silly and peculiar moods of the 'fat cat' called competition law.

But what about the 'fat cat' itself? How does it behave? Does it like health care and is it prepared to take into account what is special about health care? Does it only emphasise issues of efficiency or does it acknowledge that in special circumstances cooperation is necessary in order to offer health care services of high quality to patients? It cannot be ruled out that tensions between competition law and health care could occur. After all, the point of departure of the European competition rules is to stimulate rivalry between undertakings, whereas in relatively many cases the provision of health care to patients may require cooperation between health care operators or at least avoidance of rivalry between these operators. Consequently, if applying competition law to health care entails rivalry at all cost, it may be argued that the 'fat cat' does not respect the special features of health care. In contrast, if European competition law acknowledges that some forms of cooperation are allowed in health care, it is clear that the 'fat cat' is starting to like health care, and that the ties between European competition law and health care are based 'on mutual respect'.

Hence, this contribution will examine whether health care objectives are accommodated in the application of the Treaty provisions on competition.[1] The focus will be on the cartel prohibition and the prohibition of the abuse of a dominant position. So far the most important cases dealing with competition law and health care have not dealt with merger control.[2]

---

[1] On 1 December 2009 the Treaty of Lisbon entered into force. As a result, the EC Treaty is renamed the Treaty on the Functioning of the European Union (hereafter: TFEU) and the provisions on competition are renumbered. The cartel prohibition is contained in Article 101 TFEU (former Article 81 EC) and the prohibition on the abuse of dominance is laid down in Article 102 TFEU (former Article 82 EC). As virtually all important case law (so far) is based on the old Treaty provisions, this chapter will refer to both the new and old numbers of these provisions.

[2] So far, no significant case law on mergers between hospitals or other health care operators is available. The cases handled by the Commission mainly concern mergers between pharmaceutical companies. In these cases the Commission's investigations concentrate on the consequences of the mergers for competition between original and generic medicines and for the Research and Development. See, e.g., Decision of the Commission of 27 May 2005 in Case No. COMP/ M.3751—Novartis/Hexal, available at: http://ec.europa.eu/competition/mergers/cases/decisions/ m3751_20050527_20212_en.pdf and the Decision of the Commission of 28 February 1995 in Case No. IV/M.555—Glaxo/Wellcome, available at: http://ec.europa.eu/competition/

The present chapter will start with exploring the general approach adopted in EU law towards health care objectives (Sect. 11.2). Which objectives are acknowledged as significant values that EU law should respect? Subsequently, it will be scrutinised whether these objectives are accommodated in judgements in which the EU competition rules are applied in health care cases. To start with, it will be examined what role health care objectives play in the case law on the concept of undertaking (Sect. 11.3). This case law tackles one of the most principal problems of competition law: is an activity of an economic nature and therefore subject to the rules of the market (the competition rules)? Then, case law dealing with the cartel prohibition (Sect. 11.4), the prohibition of the abuse of a dominant position (Sect. 11.5) and health care will be analysed. This chapter ends by drawing conclusions (Sect. 11.6).

11.2 The Role of Health Care Objectives in EU Law

Health care concerns a wide variety of issues such as the relationship between doctor and patient.[3] As a result, a great many objectives could potentially play a role in applying competition law to health care. However, famous cases like *Kohll*,[4] *Decker*,[5] *Smits–Peerbooms*,[6] *Müller-Fauré*[7] and *Watts*[8] show that cases involving economic integration[9] and health care have raised mainly organisational issues (for example, the reimbursement of costs of health care services received in another Member State). Hence, it may be argued that competition law could influence mainly the organisation of health care, as it targets arrangements set up by entities such as private enterprises and public authorities. Consequently, for the

(Footnote 2 continued)
mergers/cases/decisions/m555_en.pdf. Further, a couple of hospital mergers and mergers of companies that offer hospital related products or services were notified to the Commission. Given the low markets shares and the limited overlap of the activities of the parties concerned, the Commission cleared these mergers. See, e.g., Case COMP/M.4788—Rozier/BHS, available at: http://ec.europa.eu/competition/mergers/cases/decisions/m4788_20070821_20310_en.pdf; Case COMP/M.4418—Nycomed Group/Altana Pharma, available at: http://ec.europa.eu/competition/mergers/cases/decisions/m4418_20061213_20310_en.pdf, http://ec.europa.eu/competition/mergers/cases/decisions/m4418_20061213_20310_en.pdf; and the Press Release of the Commission of 9 December 2005 on the merger between Helios and Fresenius, IP/05/1553.

3 Hervey and McHale (2004), p. 14.

4 ECJ, Case C-158/96 *Kohll* [1998] *ECR* I-1931.

5 ECJ, Case C-120/95 *Decker* [1998] *ECR* I-1831.

6 ECJ, Case C-157/99 *Smits en Peerbooms* [2001] *ECR* I-5473.

7 ECJ, Case C-385/99 *Müller-Fauré* [2003] *ECR* I-4509.

8 ECJ, Case C-372/04 *Watts* [2006] *ECR* I-4325.

9 At issue in these cases was the application of the free movement rules to health care. See the chapter by Baquero Cruz in this book.

purposes of this contribution it is only necessary to focus on organisational aspects of health care and not on issues such as the relationship between doctor and patient, the right to privacy and human rights and health care.

At the heart of the question that is addressed in the present contribution is the national health care organisation of the Member States. However, the organisation and the delivery of health care services belong to the competences of the Member States pursuant to Article 168(7) TFEU (ex Article 152(5) EC). As a result, it is difficult to outline in detail which health care objectives are acknowledged by European law, since it is for the Member States to set these objectives. Nevertheless, it is possible to sketch the main lines of these objectives from the perspective of European law. It goes without saying that given the constitutional dimension of this issue, primary EU law should be explored. Hence, Treaty provisions and other sources of primary law will be analysed. However, in this writer's view, the case law of the ECJ on free movement and health care is of special interest as it deals with clashes between health care and EU Internal Market law. So, the way the ECJ has applied the Treaty provisions on free movement (the primary law dealing with the internal market) to health care indicates as well which objectives are of interest. As no massive body of secondary law having considerable impact on the national organisation of health care is in force (yet), the current Directives and Regulations dealing with health care matters are not capable of providing convincing evidence with regard to the issue of the health care objectives.

Article 34 of the Charter of the Fundamental Rights of the European Union,[10] which has become legally binding with the entry into force of the Treaty of Lisbon,[11] stresses the importance of solidarity. One could 'translate' this concept of solidarity to health care by analysing the ECJ's case law on free movement and health care. From this case law it could be derived that the financial equilibrium of social security systems is regarded as a mandatory requirement (Rule of Reason) that may justify restrictions of free movement. Social security schemes, such as health care schemes, are set up in order to ensure access for all to particular benefits and, are therefore, a manifestation of solidarity. In this approach solidarity could relate to the situation, in which healthy persons support unhealthy persons and to the situation, in which the costs of treatment which cannot be afforded by needy people are financed by the contributions of wealthy people. As in the ECJ's free movement case law on health care no clear distinction is made between these two aspects of solidarity, it may be assumed that—at least in this writer's view—both forms of solidarity are acknowledged. All in all, solidarity is a health care objective that is considered of great importance in European law.

Furthermore, of great interest is that Article 35 of the Charter of the Fundamental Rights of the European Union provides that:

---

[10] *OJ* 2003 C 303/1.

[11] See Article 6(1) of the TEU, as amended by the Treaty of Lisbon 2009, *OJ* 2007 C 306/1.

> … everyone has the right of access to preventive health care and the right to benefit from medical treatment under the conditions established by national laws and practices.

This provision clearly reflects the health care objective of universal coverage. In its case law on free movement and health care the ECJ also refers to this objective. In *Smits–Peerbooms*, for example, it has been accepted that a Member State must be entitled to plan a network of hospitals covering its whole territory since '… the survival of the population…' is dependent on such a network.[12] A balanced medical and hospital service open to all must be guaranteed.[13] Case law on state aid and health care endorses the finding that universal coverage is acknowledged in European law, as well. In the state aid case of *BUPA*[14] arguments related to community rating and open enrolment made the Court of First Instance (CFI), renamed the General Court by the Treaty of Lisbon, decide that the funding of health insurance companies was justified.[15] It is clear that in the CFI's view the universal provision of health care is of importance: all the inhabitants of a Member State should have access to medical treatment and that, therefore, universal access should be financed. All in all, it could be concluded that universal coverage is seen as a health care objective that should be respected in EU law.

Furthermore, it should be pointed out that Article 168(1) TFEU (ex Article 152(1) EC) contains a policy-linking clause stipulating that a high level of human health protection shall be ensured in the definition and implementation of all policies and activities of the EU. Moreover, according to the same Treaty provision, if action taken by the EU complements national policies, it must be directed towards improving public health. Moreover, pursuant to Article 6 sub a EU (former Article 3(1) sub p EC) the activities of the EU should contribute to the attainment of a high level of health protection. In its case law, the ECJ has drawn conclusions from these provisions (in so far as they were laid down in the EC Treaty)[16] by, for instance, deciding that national requirements concerning eyesight examinations, which restrict free movement, are justified in the light of the Rule of Reason.[17] In addition, the ECJ has linked the issue of universal coverage to the need to offer high-quality hospital treatment in *Müller-Fauré*[18]: the access for all to hospital services should concern services of outstanding quality. Therefore, quality is also a health care objective that is considered of great importance in European law.

---

[12] See para 74 of *Smits–Peerbooms*.

[13] See para 73 of *Smits–Peerbooms*. See also para 67 of *Müller-Fauré* and para 104 of *Watts*.

[14] CFI, Case T-289/03 *British United Provident Association* [2008] *ECR* II-81.

[15] The *BUPA* case is discussed in the chapters by Neergaard and De Vries in this book.

[16] At the time of writing of this chapter no case law on the new Treaty provisions on health care was available.

[17] See ECJ, Case C-108/96 *Mac Quen* [2001] *ECR* I-837, especially para 30.

[18] See para 79 of *Müller-Fauré*.

Hence, it is apparent from the foregoing analysis that solidarity, universal coverage and high quality are objectives that European law adhere to. In this respect, it must be pointed out that the health care objectives that are acknowledged in the case law of the European Courts and in the Treaty provisions are reflected in the much-debated draft Directive on the application of patients' rights in cross-border health care.[19] This draft[20] stipulates that national health care systems should be in line with the principles of universality, access to good quality care, equity and solidarity.[21] However, it should be noted that at the end of 2009 the Swedish presidency did not manage to clinch a deal on this draft in the Council.[22] Therefore, it is up to the Spanish Presidency to try to reach agreement on this matter. At the time of the writing of this chapter the outcome of this negotiating process was unknown.

In any event, solidarity, universal coverage and high quality are important health care objectives in European law. It may, therefore, be expected that the application of the European competition rules pay due consideration to these objectives. After all, as already mentioned, the EU institutions, in applying European law, must take into account requirements of human health protection according to Article 168(1) TFEU. In this regard, it must be pointed out that apart from Article 168(1) TFEU policy-linking clauses connected with health care are also laid down in other Treaty provisions. Article 9 of the Treaty establishing the EU, as it stands since the entry into force of the Treaty of Lisbon, provides that in defining and implementing its policies the EU is obliged to take into account requirements linked to, *inter alia,* the protection of human health. By stressing the importance of this objective at the beginning of the Treaty establishing the EU, which sets out the general principles of EU law since 'Lisbon', the Treaty framers have made it clear that human health protection is one of the top priorities of the EU. Hence, the policy-linking principles oblige the EU institutions, such as the Commission and the European Courts, to integrate health care objectives into, *inter alia*, the way EU competition law is applied. On top of that, it should be noted that the principle of loyal cooperation laid down in Article 4(3) TEU (ex Article 10 EC) also imposes on the EU Institutions the duty to carry out the tasks entrusted with them by European law.

Below it will be examined to what extent health care objectives are accommodated in European competition law. What role do solidarity, universal coverage and high quality play in competition law cases on health care? The question of whether the European Courts and the Commission have taken these objectives into account, when deciding on the concept of undertaking, and applying the cartel

---

[19] COM(2008) 414 final.

[20] This draft is discussed in the contributions of Szyszczak and Hervey to the present volume.

[21] See Article 5 of this draft.

[22] See for example the next Internet site: http://www.se2009.eu/en/meetings_news/2009/12/22/we_have_succeeded_in_putting_focus_on_patients.

prohibition and the prohibition of the abuse of dominant position, will be addressed.

11.3 The Concept of Undertaking and Health Care

EU competition law only applies to undertakings. It is well-known case law that every entity engaged in economic activities is an undertaking within the meaning of Article 101 TFEU (and Article 102 TFEU).[23] An economic activity is defined as the offering of goods or services on the market.[24]

In order to apply the concept of undertaking properly attention should be paid to the organisation of health care in the EU Member States. The systems in the EU can be divided into two main categories: National Health Services and Social Insurance Systems.[25] National Health Care services are financed by public taxation and operate according to a benefits-in kind system. This system is found in, for instance, the UK and Spain. Social Insurance Systems are based on compulsory insurance. All citizens or particular categories of person are obliged to be affiliated with a health insurer, such as a sickness fund. This system operates for instance in Belgium, France and Germany. In the Netherlands a market-oriented system of health insurance operates. All citizens are obliged to conclude agreements with private insurance companies. This system is based on open enrolment and private insurers are the managing bodies (with regard to the basic health care scheme).[26] To what extent do the bodies managing these various national health schemes and the health care providers operating in these systems fall within the ambit of the European rules on competition?

From the case law of the ECJ it could be derived that in health care cases a distinction should be made between bodies managing social security schemes and health care providers.[27] Remarkably, the objective of solidarity plays a major role in decisions dealing with managing bodies, whereas references to this objective seem to be completely absent in rulings regarding health care providers. From cases such as *Poucet et Pistre*[28] and *Cisal*[29] it is apparent that managing bodies are not regarded as undertakings in so far as the principle of solidarity is predominant in the schemes they administrate. In the recent case, *Kattner Stahlbau,*[30] the ECJ

---

[23] See for example, ECJ, Case C-41/90 *Höfner* [1991] *ECR* I-1979.

[24] See for instance ECJ, Case 118/85 *Commission* v. *Italy* [1987] *ECR* 2599.

[25] See for instance Hervey and McHale (2004), p. 21.

[26] See for a discussion of this system: Hamilton (2005), p. 8 et seq.

[27] See van de Gronden (2008), p. 743 et seq.

[28] ECJ, Joined Cases C-159/91 and C-160/91 *Poucet et Pistre* [1993] *ECR* I-637.

[29] ECJ, Case C-218/00 Cisal [2002] *ECR* I-691.

[30] ECJ, Case C-350/07 *Kattner Stahlbau* v. *Maschinenbau-und Metall-Berufsgenossenschaft*, 5 March 2009, *ECR* I-0000 (n.y.r.).

has confirmed this approach by examining whether the statutory disability insurance scheme at issue was predominantly based on the principle of solidarity and to what extent this scheme was subject to supervision by the State.[31] Conversely, if these schemes are based on a mix of solidarity and competition, it seems to follow from rulings in *FFSA*[32] and the *Albany* cases[33] that the managing bodies are supposed to be engaged in economic activities.

Of special interest is the *AOK* case.[34] Here the ECJ decided that German sickness funds are not engaged in economic activities for the following three reasons: the benefits, which the affiliated persons are entitled to, are determined by national legislation,[35] the funds concerned are not allowed to be for profit[36] and these funds were compulsorily engaged in a system of risk equalisation.[37] So, in the view of the ECJ, it was of great importance that German sickness funds were not able to influence the level of the benefits or the amount of contributions paid by the affiliated persons. In this writer's view this element was decisive in the *AOK* case and made the ECJ rule that competition law was not applicable. Also in cases like *Poucet et Pistre*,[38]*FFSA*[39] and *Albany* the ECJ scrutinised how the benefits and the contributions of the schemes concerned were framed in national law.

So, bodies managing health care schemes based on benefits and contributions that are solely determined by national laws are not undertakings, and as a consequence they escape from the reach of competition law. It could be argued that it is inherent in a National Health Care System that the level of benefits is completely determined by national legislation. The same holds true for the amount of contribution, since such a system is tax-based. So, it may be assumed that European competition law is not applicable to at least the core activities of these bodies. Unsurprisingly, in the *FENIN*[40] cases it did not take much effort for the European Courts to decide that the Spanish NHS bodies were not engaged in economic activities, as they were funded from social security contributions and other State funding and provided services free of charge to affiliated persons on the basis of

---

31 See para 43 of *Kattner Stahlbau*. State supervision must ensure that bodies managing the schemes concerned observe the principle of solidarity.

32 ECJ, Case C-244/94 *FFSA* [1995] *ECR* I-4015.

33 See ECJ, Case C-67/96 *Albany* [1999] *ECR* I-5751; ECJ, Joined Cases C-115/97, C-116/97 and C-117/97 *Brentjens* [1999] *ECR* I-6025 and ECJ, Case C-219/97 *Drijvende bokken* [1999] *ECR* I-6121.

34 ECJ, Joined Cases C-264/01, C-306/01, C-351/01 and C-355/01 *AOK* [2004] *ECR* I-2493. See the chapter by Welti in this book.

35 See para 52 of the *AOK* judgement.

36 Ibid., para 51.

37 Ibid., para 53.

38 ECJ, Joined Cases C-159/91 and C-160/91 *Poucet and Pistre* [1993] *ECR* I-637.

39 ECJ, Case C-244/94 *FFSA* [1995] *ECR* I-4015.

40 See CFI, Case T-319/99 *FENIN* [2003] *ECR* I-357 and ECJ, Case C-205/03P *FENIN* [2006] *ECR* I-6295.

universal cover.[41] However, it cannot be excluded that NHS bodies carry out supplementary activities in a commercial setting. In that case they are undertakings in so far as they carry out these activities.

The implementation of social insurance systems, however, may amount to economic activities. After all, it is possible that the national legislature of a Member State has given some freedom to managing bodies in granting benefits to patients. If for instance elements of competition have been introduced into a national health care system, the bodies administrating this system may be undertakings within the meaning of Article 101 TFEU. However, it is of great importance which kinds of competition elements have been introduced. If these elements concern the freedom to set prices, it is likely that the managing bodies involved are not undertakings. After all, in *AOK* the ECJ decided that the introduction of price competition does not call into question the social task of the managing bodies concerned, as it only stimulates these bodies to operate in an efficient way.[42] This remarkable and peculiar decision[43] shows that what matters in the ECJ's view is the possibility to influence the level of benefits.

To conclude: objectives of universal coverage and solidarity play an important role in the ECJ's case law on the concept of undertaking. In this case law due account is taken of these objectives. However, so far arguments about high quality have not played any role at all in the concept of undertaking.

The predominant role of solidarity in a health care scheme may lead to the non-applicability of competition law. Furthermore, in *AOK* the aim of providing universal cover to the affiliated persons was a reason to decide that German sickness funds were not engaged in economic activities. As already pointed out, given the main characteristics of National Health Care Systems it may be assumed that the managing bodies of these systems fall outside the ambit of the European competition rules, at least in so far as they carry out their core tasks. The main reason for this is the determination of the level of the benefits in the relevant national laws. As a result, social insurance systems delegating discretionary powers related to benefits are likely to be governed by competition law. In the next section it will be examined whether objectives of universal coverage, solidarity and quality are accommodated in the application of the competition rules to health care cases.

Remarkably, the ECJ has adopted a different approach towards health care providers. It is settled case law that these providers are engaged in economic activities because they offer services (or goods) for economic consideration.[44] Consequently, the ECJ has held that health care providers are undertakings

[41] See para 39 of the CFI judgement in *FENIN*.

[42] See para 56 of *AOK*.

[43] It has been put forward that the ECJ's view on price competition in *AOK* does not match legal doctrine as enhancing efficiency is at the heart of the objectives of competition law, which implies that the possibility of price competition would amount to an economic activity. See Belhay and van de Gronden (2004), pp. 684 and 685.

[44] See for example, ECJ, Joined Cases C-180 & C-184/98 *Pavlov* [2000] *ECR* I-6451 and ECJ, Case C-475/99 *Glöckner* [2002] *ECR* I-8089.

irrespective of the fact of how their health care system is designed. So, it does not matter whether hospitals, doctors, etc., operate in a NHS setting or are paid by (social) insurance companies. They do in any case fall within the ambit of competition law. In the case of a NHS or a social insurance system that predominantly is based on solidarity, this finding could lead to odd results, as has become clear in the *FENIN* cases. In these cases the European Courts have decided that the subsequent use of the purchased goods or services determines the qualification of the buying activities of the entity concerned. Since the performance of the social tasks entrusted to NHS bodies does not constitute economic activities, these bodies are also not undertaking when purchasing goods and services on the market. As a result health care providers when negotiating with for example NHS bodies must comply with the European competition rules, whereas 'the burden of competition law' is taken off the hands of their counterparts.

11.4 The Cartel Prohibition and Health Care

Health care providers and various health insurers are undertakings within the meaning of Article 101 TFEU (ex Article 81 EC). Consequently, they have to comply with the cartel prohibition contained in this Treaty provision. They are not allowed to conclude agreements that restrict competition. Does this mean that many forms of cooperation that exist in health care are forbidden under European competition law? For example, in order to share know-how and capacity various hospitals work together. Strict application of Article 101 TFEU could have severe consequences in health care, as such an application may put under pressure these forms of cooperation. This is even true in cases that lack an effect on intra-Community trade. After all, many national competition law systems are aligned with Articles 101 and 102 TFEU and are, as a result, interpreted in the light of these Treaty provisions.[45] So, the fair chance exists that agreements (concluded between hospitals, health care insurers, etc.) that are prohibited under European competition are also unlawful in many national competition law systems.

In some cases health care operators working together may benefit from the policy measures that have been adopted with regard to horizontal and vertical agreements in EU competition law. For example, they can cooperate under the Research and Development Block Exemption[46] and the Specialisation Block

[45] See, e.g., Vedder (2004), p. 5 et seq.

[46] Regulation 1217/2010 of 14 December on the application of Article 101(3) of the Treaty on the Functioning of the European Union to certain categories of research and development agreements, *OJ* 2010 L 335/36.

Exemption.[47] Furthermore, the Guidelines on horizontal agreements[48] set out under which circumstances horizontal agreements are not contrary to the cartel prohibition. Health insurance companies may benefit from the Block Exemption Regulation for the insurance sector,[49] which exempts insurance agreements that meet criteria of a highly technical nature. Moreover, health care undertakings may jointly set-up facilities and networks without violating Article 101(1) TFEU if these facilities and networks can only be realised through cooperation between the parties concerned. If this is the case, health care operators have demonstrated that the conditions of the concept of ancillary restraints are fulfilled, which implies that the cartel prohibition is not violated.[50] Similar forms of cooperation that do not meet this strict test of the ancillary restraints may be justifiable under the 'legal exception'[51] of Article 101(3) TFEU. When health care providers and/or insurers operating at different levels of the markets work together, the block exemption on vertical restraints[52] and the guidelines on these restraints[53] may offer solutions as how to deal with competition law.

However, it should be noted that these Commission measures set out general principles of competition law and are not tailor-made for health care. As a result, many health care operators may be uncertain as to whether their agreements are compatible with EU competition law.

11.4.1 The Approach Developed in **Wouters** *and* **Meca-Medina**

How could this problem be solved? In this writer's view, the solution can be found in a famous case dealing with standards set up by professionals.

---

[47] Regulation 1218/2010 of 14 December 2010 on the application of Article 101(3) of the Treaty on the Functioning of the European Union to certain categories of specialisation agreements, *OJ* 2010 L 335/43.

[48] See the Commission Guidelines on the applicability of Article 101 TFEU to horizontal cooperation agreements, *OJ* 2001 C 11/1.

[49] Commission Regulation No 267/2010 of 24 March 2010 on the application of Article 101(3) of the Treaty on the Functioning of the European Union to certain categories of agreements, decisions and concerted practices in the insurance sector, *OJ* 2010 L 83/1.

[50] See paras 28–31 of the Commission's Guidelines on the application of Article 81(3) of the Treaty, *OJ* 2004 C 101/97 and CFI, Case T-112/99 *Métropole Télévision* [2001] *ECR* II-2459, especially para 124.

[51] See para 31 of the Guidelines Article 81(3) EC (now Article 101(3) TFEU).

[52] See Regulation 330/2010 on the application of Article 101(3) of the Treaty on the Functioning of the European Union to categories of vertical agreements and concerted practices, *OJ* 2010 L 102/1 (The former block exemption was laid down in Regulation 2790/1999 on vertical agreements, *OJ* 1999 L 336/21).

[53] See the Commission Guidelines on Vertical Restraints, *OJ* 2010 C 130/1.

11.4.1.1 The *Wouters* Case

In *Wouters*[54] the ECJ developed a special approach that is capable of taking into consideration the special context of an agreement. At stake was a regulation of the Dutch Bar Association that prohibited attorneys from setting up professional partnerships with accountants. The reason for this regulation was that such partnerships could lead to conflict of interests.

The ECJ had to decide whether this regulation was in violation of Article 101(1) TFEU. It found that the Dutch Bar Association was an association of undertakings, that its measures were, therefore, subject to European competition law and that the regulation at stake restricted competition as it prevented attorneys and accountants from offering multi-disciplinary services, which would be capable of satisfying the needs created by the increasing interpenetration of various (national and international) markets.

The ECJ stressed that the market context needed to be taken into account in an assessment based on the cartel prohibition. This point of view was not revolutionary, as in many cases the ECJ had already found agreements not to be in violation of the cartel prohibition because of the market context.[55] However, the ECJ went on by moderating the 'market context test' and pointed out that for the purposes of the application of Article 101 (1) TFEU:

> … account must first of all be taken of the overall context in which the decision of the association of undertakings was taken or produces its effects. More particularly, account must be taken of its objectives, which are here connected with the need to make rules relating to organisation, qualifications, professional ethics, supervision and liability, in order to ensure that the ultimate consumers of legal services and the sound administration of justice are provided with the necessary guarantees in relation to integrity and experience.[56]

These considerations transform the market context test in such a way that non-competition objectives are accommodated in the review based on the cartel prohibition. The ECJ went on by putting forward that it must be examined whether '… the consequential effects restrictive of competition are inherent in the pursuit of those objectives.'[57] Subsequently, the ECJ reviewed the regulation adopted by the Dutch Bar Association in the light of these considerations and decided that due to problems of conflicts of interests this regulation was not in violation of Article 101 TFEU.[58] Of special importance was that the measures taken by the Dutch Bar Association did not go beyond what was necessary.[59]

---

54 ECJ, Case C-309/99 *Wouters* [2002] *ECR* I-1577.

55 See Faull and Nikpay (2007), p. 234.

56 See para 97 of *Wouters*.

57 Ibid.

58 See paras 98–110 of the *Wouters* case.

59 See para 109 of the *Wouters* case.

It is apparent from the *Wouters* case that agreements dealing with professional ethics that are inherent in the pursuit of particular professional objectives are allowed, even in cases where competition is restricted. The way the ECJ dealt with professional ethics has similarities with the Rule of Reason developed under the Treaty provisions on free movement.[60] After all, a general interest objective is balanced against the aim to ensure a system of undistorted competition.[61] Because the ECJ's reasoning departed from the close relationship between the agreements at hand and the objective to be achieved, this contribution refers to this approach as the inherent restrictions approach.

It should be noted that the approach developed in *Wouters* should not be confused with the US anti-trust law Rule of Reason. According to the 'US' Rule of Reason anti-competitive effect are balanced against pro-competitive effects.[62] In contrast, the line of reasoning deployed by the ECJ in *Wouters* aims at striking a good balance between competition and a non-competition goal (related to professional ethics). In *Métropole Télévision*[63] the CFI rejected the existence of an US like Rule of Reason in European competition law, as pro-competitive effects must be taken into account under Article 101(3) TFEU, which provides that restrictive agreements that amount to efficiencies are allowed provided that certain conditions are fulfilled. It should be kept in mind that so far, the ECJ has not confirmed this CFI ruling. What is more important, the matter at issue in *Métropole Télévision* does not have any consequences for the *Wouters* approach, as the latter does not concern the balancing of anti-competitive and pro-competitive effects.

Further, from the *Wouters* case it could be derived that three criteria must be met in order to apply the inherent restrictions approach.[64] Firstly, the overall context of the agreement concerned must justify restriction of competition. It must be examined what the factual circumstances of the agreement at stake are and which (national) laws and principles constitute the legal framework. Secondly, it must be examined whether the pursuit of the objectives to be achieved is inherent in the restrictions concerned. So, a close connection must exist between these objectives and the restrictions resulting from the agreement that is under review. Thirdly, the agreement may not go beyond what is necessary (proportionality).

11.4.1.2 The *Meca-Medina* Case

The approach developed in *Wouters* is confirmed by the *Meca-Medina* judgement of the ECJ.[65] In this case the Commission had approved anti-doping rules

---

60 Appeldoorn and Vedder (2010), p. 59.

61 See Townley (2009), p. 130.

62 See, e.g., Hovenkamp (2005), p. 116 et seq.

63 CFI, Case T-112/99 *Métropole Télévision* [2001] *ECR* II-2459.

64 Cf., also Faull and Nikpay (2007), p. 186.

65 ECJ, Case C-519/04P *Meca-Medina* [2006] *ECR* I-6991.

adopted by sports associations; this decision was appealed against. In its judgement the ECJ held that these anti-doping rules were in line with Article 101 TFEU since they are justified by a legitimate objective.[66] In such circumstances limitation of competition is inherent in the organisation and proper conduct of competitive sport.[67] Since it was not proven that the Commission had made a manifest error in assessing the anti-doping rules, the ECJ decided that these rules were not disproportionate.[68] Compared to *Wouters* it is notable that the ECJ uses the term 'legitimate objectives' and not the term objectives, which are '... connected with the need to make rules relating to organisation, qualifications, professional ethics, supervision and liability ....' Apparently, the pursuit of objectives other than those that are at issue in regulations of professional activities could justify restrictions of competition.[69] It seems that in *Meca-Medina* the CFI has extended the scope of the inherent restrictions approach and has accepted that this approach could be applied to various issues of general interest. This finding is supported by Commission practice, as this EU Institution has already applied a '*Wouters*-like approach' in some cases.[70] Another novelty in *Meca-Medina* is related to the principle of proportionality. In this case the ECJ carried out a marginal review with regard to this principle.[71] It stated that the Commission had not made a manifest error in finding that the anti-doping rules concerned were justified.

In sum, since *Meca-Medina* it could be argued that the ECJ has adopted an inherent restrictions approach, which may be applied when objectives of general interest are at stake. Three conditions must be checked in order to apply this approach: (1) the overall context of the agreement concerned justifies restriction of competition, (2) the achievement of the objectives concerned is inherent in the restrictions caused by the agreement at stake and (3) the proportionality principle is fulfilled.

11.4.2 The Inherent Restrictions Approach and Health Care Cases

In this writer's view, the inherent restrictions approach developed in *Wouters* and *Meca-Medina* could be of great interest for health care cases.[72] In the first place

---

[66] See para 45 of the *Meca-Medina* case.

[67] Ibid.

[68] See paras 47–55 of the *Meca-Medina* case.

[69] On this issue, see also Faull and Nikpay (2007), p. 238 and 239.

[70] See the Decision of the Commission on the EPI Code [1999] *OJ* L 106/14 and the Commission Press Release on the case of the UEFA multi-ownership rule, IP/02/942 (27/06/2002). See also Faull and Nikpay (2007), p. 237 and 238.

[71] See paras 50–55 of *Meca-Medina*.

[72] See also Houdijk (2009), p. 543 et seq.

the context for agreements in health care has special characteristics. It is clear from the outset that the setting of the agreements concluded for instance by hospitals and insurance companies is special: health care providers and insurers must comply with standards laid down in health care laws and pay due consideration to professional standards. Furthermore, in health care the factual circumstances, such as the need to plan infrastructure, set largely the content of an agreement. In the second place significant objectives must be achieved in health care. It has already been mentioned that universal coverage, solidarity and high quality of treatment are goals that are in the forefront in health care. In applying the competition rules, the European Courts and the Commission must take these objectives into account, since, as already pointed out above, policy-linking clauses oblige these institutions to accommodate objectives of general interest such as health care in the implementation of European law.[73] Hence, the EU Institutions have the duty to incorporate health care objectives into the way they deal with EU competition law.[74]

Therefore, the writer of this contribution would like to argue that the inherent restrictions approach is of great relevance for health care cases. This approach is capable of striking a balance between the aim of ensuring undistorted competition and the need to achieve health care objectives. This raises the question to what extent traces of this approach in health care cases could be found in EU competition law. In order to address this question, a few important cases are examined below. These cases concern tensions between health care objectives and competition law. Their discussion gives a representative overview of the way health care objectives are dealt with in the assessments of agreements in the light of the cartel prohibition. Part of this overview is case law on practices that are common in the pharmaceutical sector. However, since the present chapter focuses on the issue of accommodating health care objectives in the application of the European competition rules, no complete picture of the cases dealing with pharmaceuticals and competition law will be given.[75]

---

[73] Odudu argues that policy-linking clauses may not play a role in a competition law analysis, as these clauses are incapable of direct effect. See Odudu (2006), p. 166 and 167. However, he ignores the fact that in European law general principles that do not have direct effect give guidance as to how to interpret provisions of EU law that do have such effect. Townley rightly points to the role that the precautionary principle plays in interpreting EU law. See Townley (2009), pp. 96–98. Furthermore, the ECJ based the 'useful effect rule' (which precludes Member States from deriving the useful effect of the Treaty provisions on competition) on a general principle: Community loyalty contained in Article 10 EC, now Article 4(3) TEU. It is settled case law that this rule has direct effect, as it must even be applied by the national competition authorities. See ECJ, Case C-198/01 *Consorzio Industrie Fiammiferi* (CIF) [2003] *ECR* I-8055.

[74] See also Townley (2009), p. 54, 94 and 95.

[75] On pharmaceuticals and competition law see, e.g., Dawes (2006), p. 269 et seq.; Pautke (2005), p. 24 et seq. and Rey and Venit (2004), p. 153 et seq.

11.4.2.1 The CFI Judgement in *GlaxoSmithKline*

The first case relates to the Commission Decision with regard to the *Glaxo-SmithKline* policy on parallel trade in medicines.[76] In 2006 the CFI handed down its judgement in this case. In October 2009 it was the turn of the ECJ to take a decision. First the CFI judgement will be discussed, and subsequently the ECJ ruling will be explored. These two judgements are of special interest, as the principal issue of the aims of competition law was raised. It was examined which goals the Treaty provisions on competition are supposed to pursue. Given this principal background one would have expected that attention was paid to the role that health care objectives play in applying competition law in this case involving the distribution of medicines.

What was the approach adopted by the CFI? In *GlaxoSmithKline*[77] it examined whether restrictions of parallel trade in medicines contained in distribution agreements that this pharmaceutical company had concluded with wholesalers was in violation of Article 101 TFEU. It put forward that this agreement must be examined in its specific context.[78] It decided that in this specific case the agreement at hand did not have the object of restricting competition (although according to the 'classic approach' in EU competition law agreements preventing companies from being engaged in parallel trade are supposed to have this effect).[79] The reason for this remarkable finding was related to the specific health care context.[80] It was argued, *inter alia*, that in many Member States not the final consumers/patients but the national sickness insurance scheme bears the essential parts of the costs of the medicines.[81] As in the CFI's view consumer welfare is at the heart of competition law,[82] the agreements concerned did not have the object of restricting competition. However, at the end of the day the CFI deduced from the facts of the case that the agreement concerned did have the effect of restricting competition, and therefore, did fall within the scope of Article 101(1) TFEU.[83] Finally, the CFI annulled the decision of the Commission, as it had not adequately addressed the parties' arguments that their agreement was justifiable under Article 101(3) TFEU. In essence, the parties claimed that their dual pricing system that causes restrictions

---

[76] See the Decision of the Commission of 8 May 2001 in Cases: IV/36.957/F3 Glaxo Wellcome (notification); IV/36.997/F3 Aseprofar and Fedifar (complaint); IV/37.121/F3 Spain Pharma (complaint); IV/37.138/F3 BAI (complaint); IV/37.380/F3 EAEPC (complaint), *OJ* 2001 L 302/1.

[77] CFI, Case T-168/01*GlaxoSmithKline* [2006] *ECR* II-2969.

[78] See para 171 of the CFI judgement in *GlaxoSmithKline*.

[79] This is the outcome of the famous ECJ judgement in ECJ, Joined Cases 56 and 58–64 *Grundig/Consten* [1966] *ECR* 299. The point of departure of this judgement is that agreements aiming at restricting parallel trade are hard core restrictions in European competition law.

[80] See paras 124–147 of the CFI judgement in *GlaxoSmithKline*.

[81] Ibid., para 131.

[82] Ibid., paras 118, 135 and 147.

[83] Ibid., paras 148–192.

of parallel trade in pharmaceuticals would result in high revenues that are necessary in order to fund research and development.[84]

In *GlaxoSmithKline*, the CFI adopted a principled approach by stressing that the cartel prohibition must be assessed in the light of the only aim that—in its view—seems to matter in European competition law: consumer welfare. This way of dealing with competition law entailed that the CFI scrutinised the context of the agreement at issue. Or to put it in the terms of the inherent restrictions approach: the CFI started reviewing this agreement in the light of the first condition of the *Wouters/Meca-Medina* judgements (the overall context of the agreement concerned justifies restriction of competition). But it then stopped and failed to verify whether the other two conditions of these judgements were fulfilled (the pursuit of the objectives at issue is inherent in the restrictions concerned and the proportionality test). Hence, the CFI confined itself to developing a contextual analysis and did extend its review to other aspects of the inherent restrictions approach.

11.4.2.2 The ECJ Judgement in the *GlaxoSmithKline* Case

What was the response of the ECJ to the remarkable approach of the CFI in *GlaxoSmithKline*? Given the disapproving reception of the CFI judgement in both legal literature[85] and by the Advocate General,[86] it was not a surprise that the ECJ adopted a very critical stance towards this approach. The ECJ started by stressing that there is a sharp distinction between the object and the effect of restricting competition.[87] In order to assess the anti-competitive nature of the agreement the content of the provisions, the objective of the agreement and its legal and economic context need to be examined. Then the ECJ recalls that according to settled case law restrictions on parallel trade are regarded as hard core restrictions and are deemed to have the object of restricting competition. These considerations made the ECJ reject the CFI's view that an agreement restricting parallel trade has the object of restricting competition in so far as it may be presumed to deprive final consumers of the advantages of effective competition.[88] In the view of the ECJ the nature of such agreements is anti-competitive irrespective of the fact of whether

[84] See the Case Comment of Eccles (2007), p. 137.

[85] In academic legal writing the CFI judgement in *GlaxoSmithKline* was not well received. See for example, Whish (2009), p. 121 and 122 and Jones and Sufrin (2008), p. 232 and 233.

[86] In his Opinion the Advocate General firmly argued that the CFI erred in law by deciding that the agreements concluded by GlaxoSmithKline did not have the object of restricting competition. In his view the notion of restriction of competition by object focuses on the impact of competition and not on overall assessment of the harmfulness to consumers. See paras 102–118 of the Opinion of Advocate General in Joined Cases C-501/06 P, C-513/06 P, C-515/06 P and C-519/06 P *GlaxoSmithKline,* 30 June 2009, *ECR* I-0000 (n.y.r.).

[87] See para 55 of the ECJ ruling in *GlaxoSmithKline*.

[88] Ibid., para 62.

consumer welfare is at stake or not. So, all agreements restricting parallel trade are deemed to have the object of restricting competition.

How did the ECJ support this finding? The ECJ referred to the objectives of competition law and based its decision on the line of reasoning that was put forward in the *T-Mobile* judgement of June 2009.[89] In *GlaxoSmithKline* the ECJ contended that the EU competition rules do not only aim to protect the interests of consumers or competitors but also the structure of the market and the competition as such.[90] In *T-Mobile* the ECJ had already given this view on the objectives of EU competition law.[91]

Hence, in *GlaxoSmithKline* the ECJ took the principal point of view that European competition law aims at various goals and rejected the CFI's decision regarding the predominant role of consumer welfare. However, it is remarkable that in this case involving the distribution of medicines it did not pay any attention to health care objectives. It did not give any clue on the role that the inherent restrictions approach, which was developed by the ECJ itself in *Wouters* and *Meca-Medina*, may play in this regard. It is a missed opportunity that in *GlaxoSmithKline*, which was a case of principle, the ECJ did not shed any light on this matter. However, it should be pointed out that the judgement of the ECJ did not call into question the need to analyse the context of the agreements concerned. On the contrary, in *GlaxoSmithKline* at stake was how to apply the competition rules in a particular context. The objective of consumer welfare turns out not to be dominant in the ECJ's view and in applying the European competition rules the Commission should take due account of the structure of the market and competition as such. By its nature, this approach does leave room for taking into account the special context of health care agreements: after all the structure of the market is one of the elements of this context. So, from this perspective there is a striking similarity between the judgements of these two European courts: both confined themselves to analysing the context and did not apply the other conditions of the *Wouters* and *Meca-Medina*.

On top of that, at the end of the day the consequences of the rejection of the CFI's approach by the ECJ were not serious, as both European courts were of the opinion that the agreement at stake did fall within the scope of the cartel prohibition contained in the Treaty. Furthermore, the ECJ supported the line of reasoning of the CFI with regard to Article 81(3) EC, now Article 101(3) TFEU. The ECJ stressed that reviewing the agreement concerned in the light of this Treaty provision requires that the nature and the specific features of the pharmaceutical sector must be taken into account. So, the Commission was obliged to examine the request for the exemption by scrutinising the factual arguments and evidence

---

[89] ECJ, Case C-8/08 *T-Mobile Netherlands BV, KPN Mobile NV, Orange Nederland NV, Vodafone Libertel NV* v. *Raad van bestuur van de Nederlandse Mededingingsautoriteit*, 4 June 2009, *ECR* I-0000 (n.y.r.).

[90] See para 63 of the ECJ Ruling in *GlaxoSmithKline*.

[91] See para 38 of the judgement in *T-Mobile*.

provided by the parties. By not doing so, the Commission had infringed its obligations under European law.

Apparently, in the view of the ECJ the special context of health care agreements may play also a role in the review under Article 81(3) EC, now Article 101(3) TFEU. However, it should be noted that the main problem with the Commission decision was that it did not adequately address the parties' arguments related to this Treaty provision. Basically, this is a procedural problem and, as a result, the issue of how health care agreements should be reviewed under Article 101(3) TFEU was not addressed by the ECJ. So, it is not clear what the opinion of the ECJ is on this issue.

11.4.2.3 The *Pavlov* Case

Another case that raises important issues of health care and the cartel prohibition is *Pavlov*. Here a national organisation of medical specialists had set up a collective supplementary pension scheme for their members. The question arose whether this arrangement could lead to restriction of competition, since this professional body was regarded as an association of undertakings (within the meaning of the Treaty provisions on competition).

The ECJ put forward the argument that due account must be taken of the economic context in which the undertakings concerned operate, of the products or services covered by the decisions of those undertakings, of the structure of the market concerned and of the actual conditions in which this market functions.[92] It was stated that the arrangement standardised in part the costs of the services of the medical specialists and therefore restricted competition. However, this cost factor is insignificant in comparison with other factors, such as medical fees or the cost of medical equipment. Hence, the arrangement at issue did not appreciably restrict competition.[93] Of interest was even that the implementation of collective supplementary pension schemes could lead to economies of scales[94]; apparently these positive effects mitigated the negative effects. However, the (possible) role of health care objectives was not explored in *Pavlov*.

So, as in *GlaxoSmithKline* the ECJ carried out only a contextual analysis and did not pay any attention to health care objectives. In *Pavlov* the context of the medical services concerned was decisive in ruling that the cartel prohibition was not violated, although a restriction of competition was discernible to a certain extent. However, the ECJ did not base its assessment in this case on a comprehensive view on the relationship between competition and health care objectives. Admittedly, given the minor effects of the pension arrangements at issue the ECJ did not need to develop such a view. Nonetheless, the *Pavlov* judgement is not

---

92 See para 91 of *Pavlov*.

93 Ibid., paras 94, 95 and 97.

94 Ibid., para 96.

capable of giving guidance on the possible role of health care objectives in cartel prohibition cases.

11.4.2.4 Evaluation

The conclusion is that the European Courts have started to develop an approach towards the application of Article 101 TFEU to health care cases. The cases analysed above only focus on the first condition of the inherent restriction approach, that is, the context. My point is that so far the European Courts have confined themselves to examining the specific context of health care cases. While assessing agreements in this sector they have scrutinised the factual and legal circumstances. In this regard it must be pointed out that the recent Commission Inquiry into the pharmaceutical sector shows that mapping out the market circumstances of a particular sector is also high on the agenda of the Commission.[95]

So far, no case law discusses agreements in health care cases in the light of the objectives that these agreements pursue. So, it is not clear from the outset how the European Courts deal with the question of whether health care agreements that restrict competition may be justified by legitimate health care objectives. That is remarkable because objectives related to universal coverage, solidarity and good quality are considered to be of great value in EU law, as set out above, and, therefore, they could serve perfectly well as objectives in the sense of the inherent restrictions approach. Such an approach is capable of providing a framework for assessing health care agreements that are, in spite of their restrictive nature, necessary in order to achieve legitimate objectives. In my view it should be avoided that legitimate interests that are acknowledged in EU law, such as universal coverage, solidarity and good quality, are put under pressure by competition law.

Another important issue that is not addressed in the case law on competition and health care is how the principle of proportionality has to be applied. Must the proportionality test be based on a full or marginal review? As already pointed out, in the case *Meca-Medina*, which concerned regulations of a sport association, the point of departure was marginal review. Due to the significance of health care (compared to sports) it could be argued that a similar test should apply in health care cases. Furthermore, Article 168(7) TFEU (ex Article 152(5) EC) explicitly stipulates that the organisation and the delivery of health care belong to the competences of the Member States. Hence, when it comes to health care agreements the position could be defended that the necessity of restrictions that are inherent in the pursuit of objectives related to universality, solidarity and high quality must be subject to a marginal proportionality review.

---

[95] See the Communication of 8 July 2009 from the Commission. Final Report of the Pharmaceutical Sector Inquiry Report at: http://ec.europa.eu/competition/sectors/pharmaceuticals/inquiry/index.html.

But how would this work in practice? Many agreements that are concluded by insurers and health care providers will enjoy the (rebuttable) presumption of compatibility with Article 101 TFEU. As long as they seem reasonable in the light of the objectives to be achieved, it would not make any sense to make them subject to a harsh and strict competition law review. However, things are different with hard core restrictions such as price fixing and market sharing. Such restrictions normally have adverse effects on competition, not only in terms of consumer welfare but also in terms of the structure of the market and competition as such. Consequently, even if they are marginally reviewed, it is likely that an infringement of Article 101 TFEU will be found. It goes without saying that measures taken by health care operators in order to deliberately eliminate competition cannot be justified by the inherent restrictions approach. For example, patents settlements leading to generic competitors being paid off by an originator company for delayed market entry, which are the subject of recent investigations carried out by the Commission,[96] or other actions aiming at obstructing the entry of generic drugs on the market,[97] do not fall within the scope of this approach.

Another issue that needs to be addressed is the role that Article 101(3) TFEU could play. Pursuant to this Treaty provision agreements are exempted from the cartel prohibition if they contribute to the production, distribution and innovation, give a fair share of this improvement to consumers, are indispensible, and do not totally eliminate competition. However, so far the Commission has not developed a policy that accommodates health care objectives in the application of this Treaty provision. As pointed out above, the Commission was even criticised by both the CFI and the ECJ in *GlaxoSmithKline* for not taking seriously the arguments that the parties concerned had put forward in relation to Article 101(3) TFEU. The CFI and the ECJ were not able to shed any light on the role that this provision could play in health care, as they annulled the Commission Decision for procedural reasons.

Moreover, it should be noted that in its Communication on Article 101(3) TFEU (ex Article 81(3) EC) the Commission has indicated that agreements realising non-competition goals could only benefit from this exemption in so far as they also contribute to the attainment of the economic objectives mentioned in Article 101(3) TFEU.[98] In other words, this Treaty provision is not an independent head of justification for general interest objectives and can, therefore, not serve as a 'tool' for integrating health care objectives in competition law. This point of view seems to be (partly) at odds with the position that the Commission took in the

---

[96] See Press Release of 12 January 2010 (Commission launches monitoring of patent settlements concluded between pharmaceutical companies), IP/10/12.

[97] See the Press Release of 7 January 2010 (Commission opens formal proceedings against pharmaceutical company Lundbeck), IP/10/8.

[98] See para 42 of the Commission's Guidelines on the application of Article 81(3) of the Treaty, *OJ* 2004 C 101/97. This passage reads as follows: 'Goals pursued by other Treaty provisions can be taken into account to the extent that they can be subsumed under the four conditions of Article 81(3)'.

Guidelines on horizontal agreements[99] and in the *CECED* case.[100] Here the Commission accepted that agreements pursuing goals of environmental protection (such as energy saving) could be justified under Article 101(3) TFEU.

Hence, Commission policy on the relationship between this Treaty provision and general interest issues such as health care objectives is in a state of flux,[101] to put it mildly. Given the significance of health care objectives and the interests involved, basing health care agreements on this 'Article 101(3) TFEU policy of the Commission' would entail great risks. As the ECJ has developed the inherent restrictions approach and seems to have accepted that legitimate objectives may be balanced against a system of undistorted competition under Article 101(1) TFEU, agreements concluded by health care providers and insurers will likely benefit more from this approach than from relying upon Article 101(3) TFEU.[102]

11.5 Dominant Positions and Health Care

What role do health care objectives play in Article 102 TFEU cases concerning health care? Unlike Article 101 TFEU the ECJ has not developed an inherent restrictions approach towards the prohibition of the abuse of a dominant position. Admittedly, it goes without saying that in defining the relevant market the Commission and the European Courts must pay due consideration to the special features of health care markets. It is inherent in the concept of the relevant market that these characteristics are taken into account. But measures taken by dominant firms are only forbidden if they constitute abusive behaviour. Consequently, addressing the question of whether health care objectives are accommodated in the application of Article 102 TFEU boils down to examining which role these objectives play in establishing an abuse of a dominant position.

Like the discussion of the cases on the cartel prohibition this part of the chapter focuses on tensions resulting from the application of Article 102 TFEU in health

---

[99] See paras 179–198 of the Commission Guidelines on the applicability of Article 81 of the EC Treaty to horizontal cooperation agreements, *OJ* 2001 C 3/2.

[100] See the Commission Decision 2000/475 in Case IV.F.1/36.718, CECED *OJ* 2000 L 187/47.

[101] See also Monti (2002), p. 1090 et seq.

[102] Townley argues that non-competition goals should be balanced under Article 101(3) TFEU, as the application of the cartel prohibition contained in Article 101(1) TFEU should solely be based on a consumer welfare test. See Townley (2009), p. 251 et seq. To my mind, however, it makes more sense to incorporate health care objectives in the analysis carried out under the cartel prohibition, as long as the ECJ has not changed its *Wouters* and *Meca-Medina* case law and the Commission has not sorted out the problems caused by its confusing points of view on the place of non-competition goals in Article 101(3) TFEU. After all, what matters is that a reliable solution that will not expose the realisation of health care objectives to great risks of uncertainty is developed. Furthermore, in the already mentioned case *GlaxoSmithKline* and *Pavlov* the ECJ explicitly rejected the view that the application of the cartel prohibition should only be based on a consumer welfare test.

care. As a result, a complete overview of cases concerning dominance and health care will not be given but rather a couple of representative cases will be discussed.

Two cases are worth mentioning, when it comes to a clash between the Treaty provision on dominance and health care: *Sot.Lelos kai Sia EE*[103] and *Ambulanz Glöckner.*[104] First *Sot.Lelos kai Sia EE* will be discussed, since this is a classic and, to a certain extent, a straightforward Article 102 TFEU case. But in this case the ECJ explicitly addressed the question whether undertaking could justify their behaviour by referring to objectives of general interest. Subsequently, *Ambulanz Glöckner*, in which the implementation of an important health care task, the transport of ill people, was at stake, will be explored. This case is to a certain extent atypical as the ECJ was called upon to apply Article 106 TFEU, which contains rules governing undertakings having exclusive or special rights.

11.5.1 The Sot.Lelos *Case*

The *Sot.Lelos* case concerned a measure taken by the pharmaceutical company GlaxoSmithKline. It had stopped supplying medicines to particular wholesalers in Greece because these wholesalers were engaged in parallel trade. At first the Greek competition authorities put preliminary questions to the ECJ on this matter but in its *Syfait* judgement[105] the ECJ ruled that these questions were inadmissible as the authority concerned was not an independent judicial body. Interestingly, however, the Advocate General did address the substantive issues of *Syfait* and contended that given the special characteristics of the pharmaceutical sector GlaxoSmithKline was allowed to stop supplying the Greek wholesalers that export medicines to other Member States, as parallel trade could put under pressure research and development.[106]

From the perspective of health care objectives this is an interesting conclusion, as it seems that in this Advocate General's view these objectives are of particular interest when assessing a health care case in the light of Article 102 TFEU. However, the story continued and in the *Sot.Lelos* case the Athens Court of Appeal put preliminary questions on the same matter. Given the independent status of this domestic court the ECJ was now obliged to look into the substantive aspects of the case.

Unlike the Advocate General in *Syfait,* the Advocate General in the *Sot.Lelos* case rejected the claim that the refusal to supply wholesalers exporting medicines to other Member States was necessary in order to prevent research and

---

[103] ECJ, Joined Cases C-468/06 to C-478/06 *Sot.Lelos kai Sia EE,* 16 September 2008, *ECR* I-0000 (n.y.r).

[104] ECJ, Case C-475/99 *Ambulanz Glöckner* [2002] *ECR* I-8089.

[105] ECJ, Case C-53/03 *Syfait* [2005] *ECR* I-4609.

[106] See the Conclusion of Advocate General Jacobs in *Syfait,* ibid., most notably paras 89–104.

development from being put under pressure. In his view GlaxoSmithKline had not proved the existence of a causal link between parallel trade and the aggravating position of research and development in the pharmaceutical sector.[107] Furthermore, the Advocate General examined GlaxoSmithKline's argument that parallel trade had led to perverse consequences on the planning and distribution of medicines in Greece. He also rejected this argument, by putting forward that this enterprise had not succeeded '... to point to anything capable of tipping the balance in its favour, despite the fact that matters relating to the welfare of patients and the reduction of public health costs are deserving of special attention in the main proceedings....'[108] Remarkably, this quotation shows that the Advocate General of the *Sot.Lelos* case did not explicitly exclude the possibility that such matters may justify the conduct of dominant companies such as at issue in the present proceedings.

Then it was the turn of the ECJ to shed light on the substantive aspects of this case. It stated that an undertaking with a dominant position like GlaxoSmithKline cannot stop supplying a long standing customer, if the orders placed are not out of the ordinary.[109] However, it had to be examined whether the special context of the pharmaceutical sector would justify the policy of GlaxoSmithKline.[110] This enterprise had pointed out that the market for medicines was subject to strict price regulation. The ECJ, however, replied that this regulation did not preclude the EU competition rules from applying. It decided that, although the degree of price regulation may differ from Member State to Member State, a dominant pharmaceutical company is not allowed to prevent wholesalers from exporting medicines to Member States where the prices are set at a low level.[111]

In contrast, a dominant pharmaceuticals company may protect its own commercial interests if certain wholesalers place orders that are out of all proportion to the amount previously sold by the same wholesalers.[112] In other words, pharmaceutical companies may only take into account their legitimate interests.[113] The argument put forward by GlaxoSmithKline that it also had responsibilities with regard to the planning and distribution of medicines was rejected, as it is for the national authorities to take action in cases of shortage.[114] The approach taken by the ECJ in *Sot.Lelos* is fairly comparable with the way it dealt with health care cases under the cartel prohibition. The ECJ confined itself to a contextual analysis

---

107 See paras 106–115 of the Conclusion of Advocate General Ruiz-Jarabo Colomer in *Sot.Lelos kai Sia EE.*

108 Ibid., para 119.

109 Ibid., para 49.

110 Ibid., para 51.

111 Ibid., paras 66 and 67.

112 Ibid., paras 71, 72 and 76.

113 However, Turner-Kerr has rightly pointed out that this is not the end of the debate, since it is not clear from the outset how to determine that orders are out of the ordinary. See Turner-Kerr (2009). p. 59.

114 See para 75 of *Sot.Lelos kai Sia EE.*

without accommodating health care objectives and a proportionality test in its assessment.

Unlike its Advocate General, the ECJ seems to rule out that health care objectives may lead to the finding that a particular conduct of a dominant firm is not of an abusive nature. Furthermore, it is striking that the ECJ sidestepped the research and developments arguments of GlaxoSmithKline,[115] whereas these arguments had played an important role in the line of reasoning of the Advocates General in *Syfait* and *Sot.Lelos,* and which arguments were appreciated in a considerably different way by these Advocates General. The ECJ seems to reject the idea that the pursuit of health care objectives may justify refusal to supply. On the one hand, it could be pointed out that GlaxoSmithKline had not substantiated adequately its claim that stopping supplying wholesalers engaged in parallel trade was necessary in order to ensure access to medicines for all in Greece. On the other hand, unlike its Advocate General, the ECJ did not confine itself to merely concluding that this claim was not supported by overriding evidence but it put forward the principal view that it was not up to a private party to take measures in order to achieve the general interest objective at issue (the planning and distribution of medicines). One cannot help thinking that in the ECJ's view dominant undertakings should not take due account of issues of general interest while operating on the market. However, ensuring access to medicines for all contributes to universal coverage in health care, which is, as outlined in Sect. 11.2 of this chapter, acknowledged as a valuable objective, which should be respected in EU law. On top of that, it is a pity that the ECJ did not address the research and development arguments of GlaxoSmithKline. It is clear from the outset that the issue of research and development is a specific characteristic of the pharmaceutical sector and results in health care services of high quality. By not discussing these arguments the ECJ has missed an opportunity to contribute to the development of a health care objectives based approach in dominance cases. Consequently, the development of the inherent restriction approach in the context of Article 102 TFEU is still at an initial stage and in comparison with Article 101 TFEU even in a state of underdevelopment.

In this regard, however, it should be pointed out that in its Guidance on Article 102 TFEU[116] which aims at modernising EU competition policy on dominance, the Commission seems to accept that reasons external to a dominant firm may be capable of justifying abusive behaviour. In this policy document the Commission outlines that it intends to apply an objective necessity test to cases of dominance. It explicitly states that '(e)xclusionary conduct may, for example, be considered objectively necessary for health or safety reasons related to the nature of the

[115] See the case comment of Turner-Kerr (2009).

[116] Guidance on the Commission's enforcement priorities in applying Article 82 of the EC Treaty to abusive exclusionary conduct by dominant undertakings (Communication from the Commission), *OJ* 2008 C 45/7.

product in question.'[117] Consequently, the objective of health care may serve as a reason for not applying Article 102 TFEU to abusive behaviour. However, it should be noted that, to this point of view, the Commission has added that it is normally up to the public authorities to set and enforce health (and safety) standards. This should be taken into account when an undertaking relies on the objective necessity test. All in all, the main difference between the ECJ's decision in *Sot.Lelos* and the Commission's Guidance is that, unlike the ECJ, the Commission does not rule out from the outset that health care objectives may be invoked as an exception under Article 102 TFEU, although relying on this exception is subject to strict requirements. It should be awaited whether the ECJ will accept the objective necessity test as developed by the Commission in its Guidance and will be, in other words, prepared to deviate from its point of view as pointed out in *Sot.Lelos*.[118]

11.5.2 The **Ambulanz Glöckner** *Case*

In *Sot.Lelos* the arguments of the dominant firm involved that health care objectives were at stake was not accepted. However, things are different with the case *Ambulanz Glöckner*. In Germany the provision of ambulance services is regulated at regional/non-federal level: the *Länder* are responsible for the delivery of these services. In the *Land* Rheinland-Pfalz the market for the emergency transport of ill people was reserved to two medical aid organisations. Conversely, state authorities could grant an authorisation for non-emergency transport to other companies. However, this authorisation was not given, if the two companies entrusted with the task of emergency transport regarded such an authorisation as a danger to their special tasks. Hence, these companies were able to leverage their market power from the reserved market to the market that was open to competition, which amounted to an abuse of a dominant position. As a state body caused this restriction of competition, the infringement concerned Article 102 TFEU in conjunction with Article 106 TFEU (ex Article 86 EC), which precludes Member States from forcing or making undertakings having exclusive or special rights to violate the European competition rules. Then again, this infringement was justified in the light of the health care objectives concerned.

Here universal coverage played a crucial role. It was put forward that commercially oriented enterprises would only offer ambulance services in urban areas at daytime, leaving the provision of services in remote areas (at night) to the undertakings entrusted with special tasks. As a result, these undertakings would

[117] See para 29 of the Guidance.

[118] However, in legal doctrine it is pointed out that in *Sot.Lelos* the ECJ has made clear that as long as the purpose of a dominant firm is to abuse its position by restricting parallel trade, it must be assumed that Article 102 TFEU is infringed. See Lovdahl Gormsen (2010), p. 48.

not be able to carry out their tasks under economically acceptable circumstances,[119] which would put under pressure the universal coverage of the emergency transport of ill people. After all, the revenue resulting from the non-emergency transport helps the undertakings entrusted with a special task to finance the provision of the emergency transport, which is costly in remote areas.[120] Given the special characteristics of the services concerned, the transport in emergency cases and the non-emergency transport were so closely linked that it was not possible to dissociate them from each other.[121] The German competition authorities had not made a manifest error in deciding that the rights conferred upon the companies entrusted with a special task concerned not only the reserved market of emergency transport of patients but also the market of non-emergency transport that, in principle, was open to competition. Hence, in cases concerning Services of General Economic Interest, the ECJ does not carry out a full proportionality review.[122] Finally, in *Ambulanz Glöckner* the conclusion was that restricting competition was justifiable. However, it was put forward that relying upon Article 106(2) TFEU requires that the companies entrusted with the task of transporting patients are able to meet the demand for emergency and non-emergency ambulance services. Consequently, in *Ambulanz Glöckner* the ECJ seems to suggest that undertakings entrusted with Services of General Economic Interest must operate with a minimum level of efficiency.[123]

In sum, in *Ambulanz Glöckner* the context of the services that were under consideration made the ECJ decide that the restriction of competition at issue was justified. Moreover, a significant argument in reaching this decision was the health care objective of universal coverage. Unlike the other cases discussed in this contribution due account was taken of the health care objectives that were at stake. Furthermore, attention was paid to the proportionality test. What is the difference between *Ambulanz Glöckner* and other cases? In *Ambulanz Glöckner*, the competent national authorities had decided to entrust two companies with a special task, which implied that these companies performed Services of General Economic Interest. The advantage of this is that Article 106(2) TFEU could be invoked in order to justify restrictions of competition. The case law of the

[119] The ECJ has developed a flexible approach and in the words of Neergaard has accepted that privileged undertakings may offset profitable sectors against less profitable sectors. See Neergaard (2009), pp. 212–217. As a result, it may be argued that the application of Article 106(2) TFEU is mainly deployed to solve problems of cherry picking. See van de Gronden (2006), p. 125.

[120] See para 58 of *Ambulanz Glöckner*.

[121] Ibid., para 60.

[122] See Sauter (2008), p. 187. In this regard it must be noted that in Neergaard's view the proportionality test and the assessment based on the criterion of the economically acceptable circumstances are different tests. However, she points out that in the present stage of the developments related to Article 106(2) TFEU the 'separate proportionality test' is not clearly defined. See Neergaard (2009), pp. 217–219.

[123] See Buendia Sierra (2007), p. 638.

European Courts enables Member States and undertakings having special tasks to derogate from the prohibitions laid down in the Treaty provisions on competition. Consequently, the concept of Services of General Economic Interest could serve as a tool for accommodating health care objectives in the application of these Treaty provisions. However, it should be noted that not in all circumstances this concept is capable of striking a balance between the objective of undistorted competition and the need to achieve health care objectives. After all, not every health care operator is entrusted with a special task within the meaning of Article 106(2) TFEU.

11.6 Conclusions

From the analysis carried out in the present contribution it could be derived that universal coverage, solidarity and high quality have a special status in EU law. Do the European Courts and the Commission accommodate these health care objectives in the application of the EU competition rules? At the jurisdictional stage of the assessment, which concerns the question of the applicability of competition law (the concept of undertaking), the objectives of solidarity and (to a lesser extent) universal coverage are of importance. If social security schemes are largely based on these objectives, competition law is not applicable to bodies managing these schemes. However, it may be assumed that, as a rule, health care providers do fall within the scope of competition law. Furthermore, so far objectives of high quality did not lead to the non-applicability of competition law in the ECJ's case law.

It appears that in *Wouters* and *Meca-Medina* (both cases already mentioned) the ECJ has developed the inherent restrictions approach, which provides an adequate basis for integrating these objectives into competition law. This approach is capable of justifying restrictions of competition, if in the first place these restrictions are closely related to the context of the agreement at stake, in the second place the restrictions are inherent in the pursuit of legitimate objectives and in the third place these restrictions do not go beyond what is necessary. The analysis of the case law on competition law and health care shows that traces of the inherent restrictions approach are discernible in this case law. However, the application of this approach in health care needs to be further developed. It is not clear from the outset to what extent universal coverage, solidarity and high quality may be regarded as objectives in the sense of the inherent restrictions approach. Furthermore, the question remains open as to what the level of proportionality review is (marginal or full review).

On the one hand it could be tempting for the Commission to argue that the organisation and the delivery of health care belong to the competences of the Member States and that, therefore, action at EU level is not appropriate. On the other hand, a process of spontaneous harmonisation has been taking place in the majority of the Member States, when it comes to competition law. As a result, national competition authorities and national courts are or will be confronted with health care cases to which they will have to apply national competition rules that are shaped in accordance with the Articles 101 and 102 TFEU. The chapters of Welti and Sauter to the present volume show how competition law is applied to health care in Germany and the Netherlands. If the Commission does not give more guidance on the relationship between health care and competition law, these 'Euro-national competition rules' will be applied in a divergent way. This could have negative effects on the provision of health care services to patients.

It is not this writer's view that the EU legislature should come up with hard law measures harmonising the application of competition rules to health care. The point that should be stressed is that the EU needs a clear and transparent soft law approach towards this subject. The Commission should take action and start developing Communications and Guidelines as to how EU competition law has to be applied in health care. Such action could be taken in close cooperation with the competent competition authorities of the Member States, for example in the framework of the European Competition Network. Further, the Commission could even consider taking decisions on the basis of Regulation 1/2003,[124] in order to clarify important issues. The following questions should be addressed in such a soft law approach. What role does the inherent restriction approach as developed in *Wouters* and *Meca-Medina* play? What is the status of health care objectives such as universal coverage, solidarity and high quality? Is the concept of Services of General Economic interest of any help in this respect?

As the chapter of Cortez reinforces, health care is at the top of the agenda in the Western world. Enhancing efficiency will be one of the challenges to meet in the future. But it is also clear that due account must be paid to universal coverage, solidarity and high quality. Therefore, it must be clarified how competition law must be applied in health care. Hence, it is necessary that a coherent concept on the application of the competition rules to health care is not only developed at national level but also in European law.

References

Appeldoorn JF, Vedder HHB (2010) Mededingingsrecht. Beginselen van Europees en Nederlands Mededingingsrecht [Competition Law. Principles of European and Dutch Competition Law]. Europa Law Publishing, Groningen

Belhay S, van de Gronden JW (2004) Some room for competition does not make a sickness fund an undertaking. Is EC competition law applicable to the health care sector? (ECJ Joined Cases C-264/01, C-306/01, C-453/01 and C-355/01 *AOK*)', Europ Compet Law Rev

Buendia Sierra JL (2007) Article 86 (2): Services of general interest and other public interest objectives. In: Faull J, Nikpay A (eds) The EC Law of Competition, 2nd edn. Oxford University Press, Oxford

Dawes A (2006) Neither head nor tail: the confused application of ec competition law to the pharmaceutical sector. Europ Compet Law Rev

[124] Regulation 1/2003 of the Council 16 December 2002 regarding the execution of the competition rules of Articles 81 and 82 of the Treaty, *OJ* 2003 L 1/1.

Eccles R (2007) The CFI judgement in *GlaxoSmithKline*. Eur Compet Law Rev 28(2)
Faull J, Nikpay A (2007) The EC Law of Competition, 2nd edn. Oxford University Press, Oxford
Hamilton GJ (2005) A new private universal health insurance in the Netherlands. In: den Exter A (ed) Competitive I 2004, Erasmus University Press, Rotterdam
Hervey TK, McHale JV (2004) Health law and the European union. Cambridge University Press, Cambridge
Houdijk JCA (2009) Publieke belangen in het mededingingsrecht: een onderzoek in vijf domeinen (public interests in competition law. A study in five areas) Kluwer, Deventer
Hovenkamp H (2005) The antitrust enterprise. Principle and execution Harvard University Press, Harvard
Jones A, Sufrin B (2008) EC competition law 3rd edn. OUP, Oxford
Lovdahl Gormsen L (2010) why the European commission's enforcement priorities on article 82 EC should be withdrawn. Eur Compet Law Rev
Monti G (2002) Article 81 EC and public policy. CMLRev
Neergaard U (2009) Services of general (economic) interest: what aims and values count? In: Neergaard U, Nielsen R, Roseberry LM (eds) I DJØF Publishing, Copenhagen
Odudu O (2006) The boundaries of EC competition law. The Scope of Article 81 Oxford University Press, Oxford
Pautke S (2005) Competition law limitations for the distribution of pharmaceuticals—rough guide to the brave new world. Eur Compet Law Rev
Rey P, Venit JS (2004) Parallel trade and pharmaceuticals: a policy in search of itself. Eur Compet Law Rev
Sauter W (2008) Services of general economic interest and universal services in EU law. Europ Law Rev
Townley C (2009) Article 81 EC and Public Policy. Hart Publishing, Oxford
Turner-Kerr P (2009) Finally a bit of clarity for pharmaceutical companies: but uncertainties remain: judgement of the ECJ in Sot.Lelos Kai Sia EE v GlaxoSmithKline AEVE. Europ Compet Law Rev
Van de Gronden JW (2006) The internal market, the state and private initiative. A legal assessment of national mixed public–private arrangements in the light of european law. Legal Issues Econ Integration
Van de Gronden JW (2008) Cross-border health care in the EU and the organization of the national health care systems of the member states: The dynamics resulting from the European court of justice's decisions on free movement and competition law. Wisconsin Int Law J
Vedder HHB (2004) Spontaneous harmonisation of national (competition) laws in the wake of the modernisation of EC competition law. Compet Law Rev
Whish R (2009) Competition Law. 6th edn. Oxford University Press, Oxford

Chapter 12
BUPA; A Healthy Case, in the Light of a Changing Constitutional Setting in Europe?

Sybe A. de Vries

Contents

Contribution received in 2010.

S. A. de Vries (✉)
European Law at the Europa Institute of Utrecht University, Utrecht, The Netherlands
e-mail: S.A.deVries@uu.nl

J. W. van de Gronden et al. (eds.), *Health Care and EU Law*, 295
Legal Issues of Services of General Interest, DOI: 10.1007/978-90-6704-728-9_12,

12.1 Introduction

The much-debated and intensely explored *BUPA* case does not only shed light on the application of the *Altmark* conditions in the field of state aid law, but may also have reinforced the merely ancillary and supportive role of the EU in the field of health care.[1] It fits well in the 'sovereignty debate' in Europe[2] and appears to meet Member States' or even citizens' demands to increasingly decide for themselves how social issues, like health care, must be handled by their government.

The judgment led to divergent reactions: from positive, to mildly critical or even exceptionally negative responses.[3] Controversial as the case may be, the *BUPA* judgment is important as it further defines the margins within which the Member State may regulate and finance services of general economic interest, in this particular case health insurance.

In this chapter the primary focus is on the implications of the *BUPA* judgment for EU law in general and, the secondary focus, is how this judgment fits with other judgments concerning financing of services of general economic interest. The judgment of *BUPA* will be viewed through the prism of a changing constitutional setting in Europe, which is partially the result of the entry into force of the Treaty of Lisbon in 2009.

First, the background and facts of the *BUPA* case will be established (Sect. 12.2). Then the question as to whether the *BUPA* judgment increases the wide margin of discretion for Member States to regulate and finance services of general economic interests in general and healthcare services in particular will be addressed. How does *BUPA* relate to other judgments and Commission Decisions concerning the financing of public service interests, and will *BUPA* be able to provide some coherence in the approach to financing services of general economic interest (Sect. 12.3)?

Then the possible impact of the Treaty of Lisbon on (the financing of) services of general economic interest will be discussed (Sect. 12.4). The *BUPA* case will be placed in the light of the new Treaty of Lisbon 2009. In addition there will be consideration of the possible impact of the Charter of Fundamental Rights (especially Article 36) and other important principles of EU law on the financing of services of general economic interest. Will *BUPA* induce the *EU* to take legislative action in this field, a possibility now offered by the Treaty of Lisbon 2009? Lastly, the conclusions and final assessment will be given (Sect. 12.5).

---

[1] GC, Case T-289/03, *BUPA* v. *Commission* [2008] *ECR* II-81.

[2] Vedder (2008), p. 1.

[3] Sauter, for instance, takes a critical stance: Sauter (2009), pp. 269–286. For a more positive response: Ross (2009), pp. 125–140.

12.2 Background: State Aid, Healthcare, and *BUPA*

12.2.1 The Importance of State Aid for the Health Care Sector

A key value of each health care system in the Member States of the European Union, which applies to welfare services generally,[4] is universal access or coverage (see Sect. 12.4.1).[5] To guarantee universal coverage the national government also plays a vital role in market-oriented systems. After all, the healthcare market is characterised by several instances of market failure, for instance information asymmetry and risk selection.[6] In market-oriented systems where healthcare is no longer determined by government regulation of the supply side, like in the Netherlands, public interests, such as affordability, accessibility and good quality of care, must be protected, for instance, by a system of regulated competition. In both State- and/or market-oriented health care systems, the Member State provides for subsidies or other forms of financial measures to support the healthcare sector, ultimately with a view to guarantee universal coverage. The question is accordingly whether these supportive measures fall within the scope of the EU state aid rules and, if so, whether they are ultimately compatible with the Treaty rules on state aid. In *BUPA* the General Court (GC) was confronted precisely with this question.

With respect to state aid in the field of healthcare a distinction can be made between *providers of healthcare*, which receive financial assistance from the national government and *managing bodies* responsible for healthcare schemes. Although *BUPA* concerns the latter situation, a few observations are made with respect to the financing of healthcare providers. In order to assess whether state aid for the healthcare sector will be exposed to the Treaty rules in the first place, the concept of an 'undertaking' plays a crucial role. It is settled case law that every entity engaged in an economic activity is an undertaking within the meaning of EU competition law.[7] In cases where healthcare providers, like doctors and hospitals, are involved, the European Court of Justice (ECJ) assumes that healthcare is usually provided for economic consideration and that, as a result, healthcare providers are considered as undertakings.[8] State aid granted to health care providers may therefore easily fall within the scope of the Treaty provisions on state aid.

In cases where managing bodies of health care systems, like health insurers, are involved, the Court adopts a different approach. Managing bodies are undertakings depending on the degree of solidarity or competition built in the system. If the

---

[4] Neergaard (2009a, b).

[5] The Council Conclusions on Common values and principles in European Health Systems, *OJ* 2006, C 156/1; van de Gronden (2009), p. 7.

[6] Lavrijssen and de Vries (2009), p. 388.

[7] ECJ, Case C-41/90 *Höfner* and *Elser* [1991] *ECR* I-1979.

[8] van de Gronden (2009), at p. 9; ECJ, Joined Cases C-180/98 to 184/98 *Pavlov* [2000] *ECR* I-6451; ECJ, Case C-475/99 *Ambulanz Glöckner* [2001] *ECR* I-8089.

principle of solidarity is predominant, the managing bodies are, according to the case law of the Court, not performing economic activities.[9] The more competition brought into the health care system, the greater the economic connotation will be and hence the higher the chance that the competition rules will apply. It is not surprising that in a more market-oriented system, or mixed State- and market-oriented system, like in Ireland, the state aid rules may also come into play where some form of financial assistance to health insurers is involved. It will then depend on the conditions mentioned in Article 107 TFEU whether aid granted by the Member State is compatible with the internal market. One of these conditions elaborated in the Court's case law is that the company involved should have obtained a financial advantage that it would not have received in the normal course of business. As health insurance undertakings involved in the management of healthcare schemes will most probably be subject to solidarity obligations, the question arises whether these undertakings can be characterised as public service undertakings and, if so, whether financial benefits to these undertakings truly constitute state aid. Assuming that the undertakings in question are public service undertakings, the *Altmark* case becomes significant, where the Court held:

> where a state measure must be regarded as compensation for the services provided by the recipient undertakings in order to discharge public service obligations, so that the undertakings do not enjoy a real financial advantage and the measure does not have the effect of putting them in a more favourable competitive position than the undertakings competing with them, such a measure is not caught by Article 87(1) of the Treaty.[10]

In addition four conditions, mentioned in paragraph 95 of the judgment, have to be fulfilled for such compensation to fall outside the scope of Article 107(1) TFEU. This means that notification will not be necessary and that Article 106(2) TFEU containing the exception for services of general economic interest will not need to be invoked, if all *Altmark* conditions are indeed fulfilled. How eventually the state aid rules and *Altmark* are applied in the health care sector, will be illustrated by an analysis of the *BUPA* case.

12.2.2 The BUPA *Case*

The *BUPA* case concerned the Irish risk equalisation scheme (RES), which, according to the Commission and the General Court of the EU, did not constitute state aid within the meaning of Article 107 TFEU. Whereas the Commission had to base its decision on pre-*Altmark* case law, the General Court, blessed with the Court of Justice's judgment in *Altmark*, could apply the four *Altmark* conditions to this case and easily came to the conclusion that they were all fulfilled.

---

[9] van de Gronden (2009), at p. 8. For example, ECJ, Joined Cases C-264/01 C-306/01, C-351/01 and C-355/01 *AOK* et al. [2004] *ECR* I-2493.

[10] ECJ, Case C-280/00 *Altmark Trans* [2003] *ECR* I-7747, para 87.

Particularly interesting features of this case are that, firstly, the Irish aid scheme provides for *ex post* compensation of costs incurred by insurance companies and, secondly, that in Ireland a private insurance system operates alongside a tax based system.[11]

According to the facts of the case, approximately 50% of the Irish population had taken out private insurance with one of the three private insurers. BUPA was one of the three insurance companies, but withdrew from the market in 2007 after its appeal against the introduction of a RES was rejected.[12] The idea of setting up a RES was that it should contribute to the attainment of the public interest objectives served by private insurance, which are: open enrolment (anyone under the age of 65 must be accepted), lifetime cover, community rating and minimum benefits policy.

According to the GC the RES:

> is essentially a mechanism which provides for payment of a charge to the Health Insurance Authority (HIA) by Private Medical Insurance (PMI) insurers, whose risk profile is healthier than the average market risk profile, and for a corresponding payment by the HIA to PMI insurers whose risk profile is less healthy than the average market risk profile. Those payments are made through a fund specially established for that purpose and administered by the HIA.[13]

Determination of RES payments is directly linked to the differential between the risk profiles of the PMI insurers, taking into account a number of risk factors. Those factors include, first, the age and sex of the persons covered and, if appropriate, a weighing known as the 'health status weight', which is based on hospital bed utilisation.[14]

As the costs PMI insurers incur may differ considerably, there is a cost differential, which is determined on the basis of the comparison between the actual costs (on the basis of the insurer's real risk profile) and the hypothetical costs (on the basis of the insurer's average market risk profile). This ultimately provides the basis for calculating the equalisation payments.[15] On the basis of this scheme insurance companies are compensated for the costs after they have been incurred, so-called *ex post* compensation, and this is criticised for wiping out incentives to contract and purchase care in a more efficient manner.[16] In this sense, the Irish scheme differs considerably from the Dutch scheme, which is mainly based on an *ex ante* scheme.[17]

A comparison with the Dutch RES offers a good insight in the (flexible) reasoning of the Court in *BUPA* as the Dutch scheme was also subject to a Commission Decision (discussed in Sect. 12.3.3). This scheme differs from the Irish

---

[11] van de Gronden (2009), at p. 17.

[12] For example, Sauter (2009), at p. 274.

[13] Para 27 of *BUPA*.

[14] Ibid., para 32.

[15] Ibid., para 33.

[16] For example, Sauter (2009), at p. 283.

[17] See with regard to the Dutch scheme the chapter of Sauter in this book. Cf., van de Gronden (2009), at pp. 16–17.

scheme in two respects. Firstly, in the Netherlands the healthcare system is wholly based on private insurance, constituting an obligatory scheme encompassing income solidarity and affordability of health care for everyone, whereas in Ireland the private insurance system operates alongside the tax-financed healthcare system. And secondly, as stated above, the Dutch scheme provides for *ex ante* compensation, that is, when risks are known but no costs have been incurred yet.[18]

The GC applies the *Altmark* conditions to assess whether the RES scheme constitutes state aid. Regarding the first condition, the GC concluded that, irrespective of the alleged optional, complementary and luxury nature of the PMI services, the PMI obligations aim to ensure a certain level of PMI services to all persons living in Ireland, at an affordable price and on similar quality conditions. The Commission was therefore right in considering these obligations to fall under the *service of general economic interest mission* (paras 204–207).

Before it came to this conclusion the GC also referred to *minimum* criteria that must be taken into account:

> In that regard, the Court notes at the outset that even though the Member State has a wide discretion when determining what it regards as an SGEI, that does not mean that it is not required, when it relies on the existence of and the need to protect an SGEI mission, to ensure that that mission satisfies certain minimum criteria common to every SGEI mission within the meaning of the EC Treaty, as explained in the case-law, and to demonstrate that those criteria are indeed satisfied in the particular case. These are, notably, the presence of an act of the public authority entrusting the operators in question with an SGEI mission and the universal and compulsory nature of that mission (para 172).

Regarding the second *Altmark* condition, the GC held that it is established case law that:

> the Member State has a wide discretion not only when defining an SGEI mission but also when determining the compensation for the costs, which calls for an assessment of complex economic facts [...]. It is precisely because the determination of the compensation is subject to only restricted control by the Community institutions, moreover, that the second *Altmark* condition requires that those institutions must be in a position to verify the existence of objective and transparent parameters, which must be defined in such a way as to preclude any abusive recourse to the concept of an SGEI on the part of the Member State (para 214).

Hence, this condition was also fulfilled in the present case.

Regarding the third condition, whether the compensation is necessary and proportionate for discharging the SGEI mission, the Court states that its review of the proportionality of the RES scheme is necessarily limited and only amounts to a marginal review of the Commission Decision:

> Given the discretion enjoyed by a Member State in defining an SGEI mission and the conditions of its implementation, including the assessment of the additional costs incurred in discharging the mission, which depends on complex economic facts, the scope of the

[18] van de Gronden (2009), at p. 17.

> control which the Commission is entitled to exercise in that regard is limited to one of manifest error (para 220).

Furthermore, the GC acknowledged that the RES cannot strictly fulfil the third condition of *Altmark*, as the RES is not intended to compensate for an identified cost occasioned by the supply of the service in question.

Regarding the fourth and last condition, the Court held that:

> … accordingly, the Commission was entitled in this case to consider that in the context of the analysis of the existence of State aid within the meaning of Article 87(1) EC, there was no need to draw a comparison between the potential recipients of the RES payments and an efficient operator (para 248).

The reason is that the RES does not intend to offset the costs which might result from inefficiencies on part of the insurers.

12.3 A Wide Margin to Regulate and Finance SGEI

12.3.1 Different Approaches in the Case Law to Financing Services of General Economic Interest

At the time the ECJ was to deliver its judgment in *Altmark*, two approaches could be found to the question how financial benefits to public services undertakings should be assessed: the state aid approach and the compensation approach.[19] The state aid approach implies that State funding of a public service undertaking ought to be regarded as State aid within the meaning of Article 107 TFEU. However, such funding can be approved under Article 106(2) TFEU. Much of the Commission's practice in the field of state aid still departs from this approach. Even the recently revised Communication on the application of the State aid rules to public service broadcasting, for example, is based on the state aid approach as it further clarifies the conditions under which financing of public service broadcasting can be justified on the basis of Article 106(2) TFEU.[20]

With *Altmark* the Court, by considering that financial aid to public service undertakings falls outside the scope of the state aid provisions altogether, provided that four conditions are fulfilled, at last opted for another approach, the compensation approach. The compensation approach implies that state funding of services of general economic interest amounts to state aid within the meaning of Article 107(1) TFEU only if, and to the extent that, the economic advantage it provides

---

[19] With respect to the 'state aid approach', see, for example, GC Case T-46/97 *SIC SA* v. *Commission* (here the General Court annulled the Commission Decision, which was based on the 'compensation approach'); with regard to the 'compensation approach' (before *Altmark*), see, for example, ECJ, Case C-53/00 *Ferring SA* [2001] *ECR* I-9067 and ECJ, Case 240/83 *ADBHU* [1985] *ECR* 531; see also de Vries (2006), pp. 125–130.

[20] *OJ* 2009 C 257/1.

exceeds an appropriate remuneration of such additional costs. Since much remained unclear, especially where *Altmark* 'fails to address the situation where a Member State does not satisfy the four conditions',[21] in 2005 the Commission adopted a Decision and Framework with a view to clarifying the Court's case law (the '*Altmark* package').[22] On the basis of the Decision aid granted to certain undertakings is exempted from the notification requirement as laid down in Article 108(3) TFEU. But the Decision is limited in scope as it only applies to companies whose turnover is limited and, particularly relevant for the subject matter, to hospitals and social housing undertakings carrying out services of general economic interest irrespective of their turnover. The purpose of the Framework is to specify under what conditions public service compensation not meeting all four *Altmark* requirements can still be justified on the basis of Article 106(2) EC.

The Decision and Framework of 2005 were not able to answer all remaining questions that were raised by *Altmark,* meanwhile, the Commission continued to carefully examine state aid measures under Article 107 TFEU. The consequences were that, if the state undervalued its aid scheme and did not therefore notify the scheme to the European Commission, the aid would have to be recovered from the recipient.[23] The Commission was probably so sensitive about illegal subsidies that it wanted to keep control of the process. Some help came a few years later when, in the wake of its single market strategy 2007, the Commission addressed questions on state aid ('The frequently asked questions on state aid and public service obligations'),[24] aiming to elucidate the Decision and Framework of 2005. Here the Commission takes a flexible stance by tolerating a broad definition of services of general economic interest and by moderating the fourth condition of *Altmark.* A public procurement procedure, or defining the amount of compensation by a comparison with the costs of a well run company, are, according to the Commission, not necessary.[25]

12.3.2 BUPA: *The Introduction of a New Approach for All Services of General Economic Interest?*

With *BUPA* the GC has gone a step beyond *Altmark* by introducing a new, third, approach: how to assess aid measures in respect of public service undertakings.

---

[21] See Szyszczak (2004), pp. 982–1011 at p. 991.

[22] *OJ* 2005 L 312/67; *OJ* 2005 C 297/4.

[23] For example, Szyszczak (2004), at p. 992; but the consequences may have been mitigated as a result of the Court's judgment in *CELF* (ECJ, Case C-199/06 *Centre d'esportation du livre français (CELF)* [2008] *ECR* I-469), see below Sect. 12.4.3.

[24] SEC(2007) 1516 final.

[25] See also, for example, van de Gronden (2009), at p. 21.

Considering the flexible way in which the GC interprets the *Altmark* conditions, one can but conclude that the Court has indeed been willing to give Member States considerable discretion in regulating public interests in the healthcare sector.[26] It is argued that the GC in *BUPA* adopted a 'jurisdictional approach', which entails that the application of Article 107 TFEU finally depends on the *characterisation* of the undertaking involved and the services of general economic interest it performs rather than on a substantive and in depth (economic) assessment of whether the public service mission is discharged in a proportionate manner.

Such a jurisdictional approach is more in accordance with Article 168(7) TFEU, leaving Member States' competences to organise and finance healthcare unfettered. Of course, this does not mean that Member States are given a *carte blanche* to exercise their competence in the field of healthcare, without giving due respect to the requirements of the Internal Market. In the same vein, the fact that the EC Treaty, now the Treaty on the Functioning of the European Union, excludes a certain area from the Union's competence is no reason in itself to exclude the application of the Internal Market rules, which also include the state aid provisions.[27] Besides, the GC clearly held that in defining and entrusting services of general economic interest certain minimum criteria must be taken into account by the Member State. SGEI are, according to the Court in paragraph 172 of its judgment, normally concerned with activities which, due to their special characteristics, can be distinguished from other economic activities.[28] According to the Commission in its Staff Working Document on state aid in the form of public service compensation:

> the more precisely an entrustment specifies the mission assigned, the greater level of protection from challenge under the state aid law (for example, by competitors) for the compensation granted.[29]

The fact that public health in the first place falls under the responsibility of the Member State may certainly have induced the GC to take a more self-restraint rather than activist approach (see below, Sect. 12.4).

This wide discretion for Member States to finance services of general economic interests without being concerned by the application of Article 107 TFEU also appears from the judgment of the GC in *TV2/Danmark*.[30] In this case the GC

[26] See, for example, van de Gronden (2009), at p. 12; also Lavrijssen and de Vries (2009), p. 397.

[27] See Prechal et al. (2010).

[28] See in this regard: Ross (2009), pp. 125–140, at p. 134. Ross argues that 'this observation makes the CFI's previous endorsement of a wide discretion for Member States sound somewhat hollow and opens up the possibility that, after all, the concept of SGEI indeed has a EU-community core.'

[29] SEC(2007) 1516 final, p. 22.

[30] GC, Joined Cases T-309/04, T-317/04, T-329/04 and T-336/04 *TV2 Danmark* [2008] *ECR* II-2935.

endorsed the Member States' broad powers to define *public service broadcasting*, whilst referring to the Amsterdam Protocol on public broadcasting, a resolution of the Council[31] and relevant case law. In *TV2/Danmark* the GC confirms its lenient approach towards services of general economic interests and the manner in which they are entrusted to a group of (or in this particular case only one) undertaking(s).

Interestingly, in paragraph 123 the Court rejects the argument brought forward by the commercial broadcasters that the definition of services of general economic interest must be dependent on a comparative analysis of programming. Such an approach comes close to a *market impact assessment*, or *ex ante* evaluation of new media activities, which is now included in the revised Broadcasting Communication of the Commission on the application of Article 86(2) EC (now, Article 106(2) TFEU) to financing public service broadcasting. The introduction of such an *ex ante* evaluation for new media activities in the broadcasting communication seems to fit in with the Commission's plans, which have been introduced by the State Aid Action Plan, to review state aid instruments and to introduce a more economic approach.[32]

But the original proposal of the Commission for such a broadly applied market-based test met with strong criticism from the Member States. At the instigation of the Dutch Minister for Cultural Affairs, a common position paper was adopted, inspired by responses of a number of Member States (17), taking a firm stand against, *inter alia,* the introduction of an *ex ante* market impact assessment. This 'political crusade' was intended to safeguard the application of the principle of subsidiarity in this respect as the Member States must remain firmly in charge of the remit, organisation and funding of their public service broadcaster.[33] The Commission seems to have taken into account some of the concerns of the Member States, for instance by referring to *significant* new audiovisual services for which a market assessment is needed and by leaving it up to the Member States how such a market impact assessment should be conducted. However, the Communication states in paragraph 89:

> Such an assessment would only be objective if carried out by a body which is effectively independent from the management of the public service broadcaster, also with regard to the appointment and removal of its members, and has sufficient capacity and resources to exercise its duties.

Similarly to the field of public health, the regulation of the media as part of cultural policy traditionally belongs to the competence of the Member States. This is recognised by Article 167 TFEU. Or, in the words of the Treaty of Lisbon 2009,

---

[31] *OJ* 1999 C 30/1.

[32] COM(2005) 107 final.

[33] See Common Position Paper (Draft 5 August 2008) *Main principles for a revision of the broadcasting communication of the European Commission*. Available at: http://www.minocw.nl/documenten/44541b.pdf; see also the letter of the Minister of Education, Culture and Science on the Broadcasting Communication, to be found on the website of the Ministry of Education, Culture and Science, http://www.minocw.nl/eumedia/index.html.

the EU shall have competence to carry out actions to (just) *support*, *coordinate* or *supplement* the actions of the Member States in the areas of culture and public health. Nevertheless, the EU legislator has displayed some legislative activity in the field of media policy, most notably through the adoption of the Television without Frontiers Directive (now revised by the Audiovisual Media Services Directive), which clearly sets limits on the exercise of national competence in this area.[34] Such legislation in the field of healthcare is still in its infancy, although steps have been made into this direction through the proposal for a Directive on patient mobility,[35] which, if adopted in its original form, will considerably limit Member States' competences in the field of healthcare as well.[36]

12.3.3 No Coherent Approach How to Assess State Aid for the Discharge of SGEI Missions

One of the main criticisms at the time the ECJ delivered its judgment in *Altmark* was that, although by definitely choosing the compensation approach and thereby offering more discretion for the Member States to regulate and finance a service of general economic interest, the Court at the same time caused considerable (legal) uncertainty. It is questionable whether *BUPA* and the flexible stance of the GC will eventually contribute to the desired legal clarity. In fact two conflicting developments can be discerned in current state aid policy and practice. On the one hand, the Commission's more economic approach to the application of the state aid rules as laid out in its State Aid Action Plan entails for the assessment of SGEI that:

> compensations granted should make the performing of public service missions feasible without leading to overcompensation and undue distortions of competition. Point (i).[37]

On the other hand, there is the more reticent, 'jurisdictional', approach of the GC in cases such as *BUPA*. This appears in sharp contrast with a more economic application of the state aid rules, as it does not take efficiency arguments into account. Point (ii).

Regarding Point (i), it is striking to see that the Commission's state aid policy in the field of media policy appears to be more in accordance with the basic assumptions of the State Aid Action Plan than its policy in respect of healthcare. The Broadcasting Communication insists on an *ex ante* evaluation of significant new media activities offered by public service broadcasting corporations. Several Commission Decisions in the field of public service broadcasting show that the Commission does not accept merely formal, jurisdictional (or should they be said

---

[34] *OJ* 1989 L 298/23.

[35] On this Directive, see the chapters of Szyszczak, Hervey and Pennings in this book.

[36] COM(2008) 414 final. See, for example, van de Gronden (2009), at pp. 21–22.

[37] COM(2005) 107 final, p. 10.

to be more political and even opportunistic) arguments of the Member States, but requires a well-substantiated standpoint. This is particularly evident in the German *ZDF* case, where the Commission was of the opinion that the definition of the public service remit for additional digital channels and new media services in German legislation was not sufficiently precise. With respect to the definition for new media services the Commission stated that:

> a general authorisation of public service broadcasters to offer such loosely defined media services and the resulting lack of predictability for third parties bears the risk that other market operators are discouraged to develop and offer such new media services.[38]

The Commission observed that the definition of new media services could not be regarded as a service of general economic interest. In response to these remarks Germany and the Commission entered into negotiations, which resulted in commitments submitted by Germany, one of which was the establishment of an evaluation procedure for new or modified digital offers of public service broadcasters.[39]

In another case, *BBC News 24*, the Commission, in assessing whether the aid to the BBC to launch a special interest channel was proportionate under Article 106(2) TFEU, considered that other companies or potential competitors must not be precluded from entering the market.

Most recently in approving the annual financing system for Dutch public service broadcasters, the Dutch government committed itself by stating:

> that new audiovisual services, including pay services, will be subject to a prior evaluation before being entrusted to public service broadcasters. The Dutch authorities will ensure that the prior evaluation process will take place in a transparent way. As part of this prior evaluation process interested parties will be consulted and the market effects of new audiovisual services will be assessed and balanced against the benefits of the new service for the Dutch society.[40]

In the field of health care, an elaborate Commission Decision practice is lacking. So far the focus has been on the case law of the EU Courts, having to decide whether, depending on the degree of solidarity and universal coverage, managing bodies in the field of healthcare should or should not be considered undertakings within the meaning of the competition rules.[41] In addition, there are well-known cases on the application of the free movement rules in the healthcare sector.[42]

---

38 State aid E 3/2005—Financing of public service broadcasters in Germany, C(2007) 1761 final, para 230.

39 See also, for example, Lavrijssen and de Vries (2009), at p. 416.

40 See Press Release, IP/10/52, 26 January 2010.

41 For example, ECJ, Case C-475/99 *Ambulanz Glöckner* [2001] *ECR* I-8089; ECJ, Joined Cases C-264/01, C-306/01, C-453/01 and C-355/01 *AOK* [2004] *ECR* I-2493; ECJ, Case T-319/99 *FENIN* [2003] *ECR* II-357. Belhaj and van de Gronden (2004), pp. 682–687.

42 See, for example, ECJ, Case C-158/96 *Kohll* [1998] *ECR* I-1931; ECJ, Case C-120/65 *Decker* [1998] *ECR* 1831; ECJ, Case C-157/99 *Smits en Peerbooms* [2001] *ECR* I-5473 and ECJ, Case C-372/04 *Watts* [2006] *ECR* I-4325.

The *Zorgverzekeringswet* case is interesting as it concerned the Dutch health-care system, which for that matter is a striking example of a 'mixed solidarity and competition based system.'[43] The Commission came to the conclusion that the state aid provisions were applicable, as the Dutch health insurance companies can be considered as 'undertakings' and that the involved RES, which is managed by a State body and which provides for the compensation of the differences in risks health insurance companies incur, falls within the scope of Article 107 TFEU. On the one hand, the Commission in its Decision showed a flexible approach, as it acknowledged that health insurers can be qualified as undertakings entrusted with services of general economic interest, without being explicitly charged with such a mission by a legislative act or a public concession.[44] On the other hand, the Commission was of the opinion that not all four *Altmark* conditions were fulfilled. In particular the last condition, the efficiency requirement, was not fulfilled, as all insurers, irrespective of how efficient they were, receive compensation. But the Commission eventually decided in favour of the RES by applying the exception contained in Article 106(2) TFEU. According to the Commission, the RES is necessary to deal with the danger of risk selection by the health insurers and to ensure the stability of the health insurance system.[45]

Regarding Point (ii), the judgments in *BUPA* and *TV 2/Danmark* are clear evidence of another development, as they obviously represent greater reluctance on the part of the GC in applying the *Altmark* criteria.[46] It has even been argued that the GC may have introduced an alternative *Altmark* test, where 'compensation is not directly based on the costs, receipts, and profits of the services of general economic interest that are being compensated.'[47] The GC is particularly flexible in applying the third and fourth conditions of *Altmark,* which require that compensation is necessary for the expenses made in discharging public service obligations and that the costs of an efficient undertaking are taken into account (in the absence of a public procurement procedure).[48] Irrespective of the particularities of the health insurance sector (the fact that health *risks* are being compensated) the *BUPA* case has, not wholly unsurprisingly, been criticised for insufficiently taking efficiency arguments into account. The RES in Ireland was therefore said to be more involved in compensating inefficiency and overcompensation, rather than risk compensation.[49] Particularly the fact that the Irish scheme was based on *ex post* risk equalisation of the actual costs incurred means that inefficiency is by definition also compensated.[50]

---

[43] See, for example, van de Gronden (2009), at p. 14.

[44] See also, for example, Lavrijssen and de Vries (2009), at p. 395.

[45] Europese Commissie, Steunmaatregelen nr. N 541/2004 en N 542/2004 Nederland.

[46] For example, Vedder (2008), at p. 25.

[47] For example, Sauter (2009), at p. 282.

[48] Ibid.

[49] For example, Vedder (2008), at p. 26.

[50] For example, Sauter (2009), at p. 283.

Hence, *BUPA* (and *TV2/Danmark*) do not appear to offer the preferred economic approach to the application of the state aid rules. Rather, the Commission's possibilities to intervene on the basis of the state aid rules are narrowed down.[51] It has even been argued that the 'jurisdictional approach' of the GC may open the door to all kinds of competition distorting measures and for compensation of inefficiency and overconsumption.[52]

An argument has also been made that in the EU competition rules *BUPA* recognises:

> social concerns mediated through national measures. The heart of the purpose of the RES was intergenerational solidarity—itself one of the avowed goals of the Union according to the Lisbon Treaty.[53]

BUPA is perhaps exemplary for the evolvement of social concerns in competition law (or EU law in general). It also touches upon the question of what model of competition the EU is actually looking for, a question, which is not just hypothetical considering, on the one hand, the deletion of the reference to a 'system of undistorted competition' in the objectives of the Treaty of Lisbon 2009 and, on the other, the adoption of a Protocol on the Internal Market and Competition to the Treaty. In addition, the Treaty of Lisbon 2009 includes the concept of a 'social market economy'; it recognises social rights and contains important references of services of general economic interest.[54] It will thus be interesting to see how *BUPA* fits in with the Lisbon Treaty 2009 and whether the changed constitutional setting, considering the rather blurred picture of diverging trends in state aid policy, offers some 'grips' to help explain the Court's approach.

12.4 BUPA and the Treaty Context: The Constitutional Dimension

12.4.1 The Treaty of Lisbon 2009 and Services of General Economic Interest

Both the former EC Treaty as well as the Treaty of Lisbon 2009 contain a variety of provisions, which are, to a more or lesser extent, relevant for the discharge of services of general economic interest in general and for healthcare in particular. In the following a closer look will be given to these provisions and to the Charter of Fundamental Rights, which, according to Article 6 TEU, has the same legal value as the Treaties, and also contains references to SGEI.

---

[51] See, for example, van de Gronden (2009), at p. 18.

[52] Cf., Vedder (2008), at p. 26.

[53] Cf., Ross (2009), at p. 140.

[54] See also Joerges (2009), pp. 41–42.

12.4.1.1 Charter of Fundamental Rights

Under Chapter IV 'Solidarity' of the Charter of Fundamental Rights two provisions come into the picture. First, Article 35 on Healthcare states:

> Everyone has the right of access to preventive healthcare and the right to benefit from medical treatment under the conditions established by national laws and practices. A high level of human health protection shall be ensured in the definition and implementation of all Union policies and activities.

As already stated in Sect. 12.2 of this chapter, inherent in the right of access to preventive healthcare is the concept of universal coverage, which, of course, is an important feature of the concept of a service of general economic interest.[55] Based on this provision two preliminary observations can be made. First of all, universal coverage, access to healthcare for each EU citizen, is a shared value in the healthcare systems of the Member States. The importance of universal access for EU citizens was also stressed by the Council in its Communication on common values and principles in European Union Health Systems.[56] Second, it is left to the individual Member States, due to the lack of a coherent set of principles of EU Health law and of EU competence in this field, *how* to realise universal access.[57]

Article 36 of the Charter of Fundamental Rights is not only relevant for the public health sector but for *all* sectors where services of general economic interest are at issue. It states that:

> the Union recognizes and respects access to services of general economic interest as provided for in national laws and practices, in accordance with the Treaty [...], in order to promote the social and territorial cohesion of the Union.

Although not couched in terms of individual enforceable rights for individuals, it does emphasise the importance of services of general economic interests in the EU and should therefore have an impact on how Community Institutions, including the Community Courts, should act or abstain from taking action.[58]

The fact that the Charter, since the Treaty of Lisbon 2009 came into force, is now legally recognised and binding is significant:

> as it can now more easily and more vigorously be deployed as a standard for judicial review of Union measures and national measures implementing Union law and as an aid to interpreting national and Union measures.[59]

But even before the Treaty of Lisbon 2009 the Charter, since its proclamation at the Treaty of Nice in 2000, had been increasingly relied upon by the EU Courts as

---

[55] See also para 163 of *BUPA*.

[56] *OJ* 2006, C 156/1.

[57] Cf., van de Gronden (2009), at pp. 6–7.

[58] Cf., Prechal (2009), p. 68. See also Prosser (2005), p. 173.

[59] Chalmers and Monti (2008), p. 69.

an authoritative source of fundamental rights.[60] The question remains, however, whether the Charter is still merely a codifying document adding little to the existing case law or an autonomous, self-standing source of law generating its own meaning.[61]

In any event, the inclusion of services of general economic interest in the Charter, as well as a reference to access to healthcare, emphasise the fundamentality and universality of access to health services, which should steer the orientation and interpretation of State aid rules in this field. Of course, the question remains: *how*?

12.4.1.2 Treaty Provisions Relevant to SGEI

As a preliminary remark it must be stressed that the core provision on services of general economic interest, that is, Article 106(2) TFEU, has been left untouched. But the Treaty of Amsterdam introduced another provision, Article 16 EC (now Article 14 TFEU), which could at the time be seen as a 'first step in the constitutionalisation of the services of general economic interest.'[62] According to Article 16 EC services of general economic interest are given a place in the shared values of the Union and have a role in promoting social and territorial cohesion. Furthermore, 'the Community and the Member States, each within their respective powers and within the scope of application of this Treaty, shall take care that such services operate on the basis of principles and conditions which enable them to fulfil their missions.'

It was held at the time that Article 16 EC in combination with Article 86(2) EC (now Article 106(2) TFEU) merely articulated the value of services of general economic interest to Member States and the Community. Apart from this, Article 16 EC had an independent and additional role and function in Community law.[63] The additional value of Article 16 EC was considered twofold. First, it made clear that the function of services of general interest stretched beyond the field of competition. And second, it entailed that the traditional approach to interpret derogations from the free movement and competition rules restrictively should be abandoned.[64]

The Treaty of Lisbon 2009 introduced three new features to Article 14 TFEU. First, the provision has been inserted in the Chapter on Principles and under Title II (provisions having general application). These provisions have a transversal character and require, more than the EC Treaty did, the EU to take account of these principles in all of its activities.[65]

---

60 Cf., Chalmers and Monti (2008), at p. 65.

61 Cf., Chalmers and Monti (2008), at p. 69.

62 Cf., Prechal (2009), at p. 67.

63 Ross (2000), pp. 22–38.

64 Cf., Ross (2000), at p. 38.

65 Cf., Prechal (2009), at p. 68.

Second, Article 14 TFEU is rendered more specific by including a reference to *particularly economic and financial conditions* as part of the principles and conditions on which basis services of general economic interest must operate to fulfil their public service mission, although it is as yet unclear what the precise impact of the insertion of this reference will be.[66] It is assumed that it emphasises the Member States' broad discretionary powers in this respect.

Third and last, Article 14 TFEU offers a legal basis for the adoption of Regulations at EU level, which shall establish the principles and conditions, without prejudice to the competence of Member States, in compliance with the Treaties, to provide, to commission and to fund such services. This provision is more weakly formulated than the previously proposed provision of the Constitution, Article III-122, stipulating that:

> European laws shall define these principles and conditions.

However, it still provides for an important (additional) legal basis granting the Council and European Parliament the power to develop comprehensive rules at EU level.[67] Two points of criticism, however, have been raised regarding this provision. Firstly, the fact that Article 14 TFEU only refers to *principles and conditions* would possibly exclude the adoption of detailed provisions at EU level, for example, with a view to modify the outcome of *Altmark* (or *BUPA*). And secondly, the fact that the provision only enables the adoption of *Regulations* and not of *Directives* seems to be at odds with the idea that Member States must remain primarily responsible for the definition and entrustment of services of general economic interest.[68] And for that matter it was a Framework *Directive* that was proposed by the Socialist Group in the European Parliament a couple of years ago.[69] But apart from Article 14 TFEU, there are other legal bases for Framework Directives, the use of which Article 14 TFEU does not preclude.[70] Article 106(3) TFEU offers the possibility for the Commission to adopt Directives or Decisions, and Article 114 TFEU constitutes a general legal basis for the adoption of a Directive within the framework of the Internal Market. Article 114 TFEU should not be interpreted as only offering a limited market-based view on SGEI, but in fact:

> … as offering a real challenge to make the different and competing values of economic integration and protection of public services compatible in the wake of an emerging European social society.[71]

[66] See also Amtenbrink and van de Gronden (2008), p. 325.

[67] See also Neergaard (2009b), p. 204.

[68] Krajewski (2008), pp. 392–393.

[69] To be found at: http://www.socialistgroup.org/gpes/media3/documents/1917_EN_public_services_en_november_2006.pdf

[70] Rodrigues (2009), pp. 261–262.

[71] See de Vries (2009), p. 151. See with regard to the possibilities to legislate on the basis of Article 106(3) TFEU, Krajewski (2008), at p. 393 and Sauter (2008), pp. 167–193 at p. 172.

12.4.1.3 The Protocol Attached to the Treaty

The importance of services of general economic interest also appears from the Protocol on Services of General Interest, which is attached to the Treaty of Lisbon (Protocol No. 26). Article 1 of the Protocol states the following:

> The shared values of the Union in respect of services of general economic interest within the meaning of Article 16 of the Treaty on the Functioning of the European Union (now Article 14 TFEU) include in particular:
>
> - the essential role and the wide discretion of national, regional and local authorities in providing, commissioning and organising services of general economic interest as closely as possible to the needs of the users;
> - the diversity between various services of general economic interest and the differences in the needs and preferences of users that may result from different geographical, social or cultural situations;
> - a high level of quality, safety and affordability, equal treatment and the promotion of universal access and of user rights.

Article 2 of the Protocol states:

> The provisions of the Treaties do not affect in any way the competence of Member States to provide, commission and organise non-economic services of general interest.

On the one hand the Protocol can be seen as a particular expression of the Member States' wish to keep control over services of general economic interest.[72] On the other hand it can be viewed as an incitement for the EU to develop a European approach to services of general economic interest.[73] The question is whether this Protocol in fact adds something substantial to the concept of services of general economic interest. Although the Protocol may indeed not as such alter the law as it stands, it does contain interpretative provisions, which confirm the central role of national (and sub-national) entities to provide services of general economic interest.[74] The value of the Protocol may therefore well be that the effect is that services of general economic interest will as a result be differently adjudicated under the state aid provisions.

12.4.2 The Treaty of Lisbon 2009, the Concept of a Social Market Economy and Health Care

Apart from the above-mentioned important provisions on services of general economic interest it can be observed that the Treaty of Lisbon 2009 includes other provisions, which may entail that the state aid provisions should in some cases be

---

72 Cf., Sauter (2008), at p. 173.

73 Amtenbrink and van de Gronden (2008), at p 326.

74 Cf., Prechal (2009), at p. 68.

applied in a more flexible way. There is the concept of a 'social market economy' to start with, which has been included in the objectives of the EU and which can be viewed as an expression that market integration must also include social and solidarity concerns.[75] This may also be relevant for the assessment of cases such as *BUPA*, for a EU model of competition should more than before include elements of solidarity.[76] But the launch of this concept cannot in itself solve the tension between public service interests and free competition and it is unclear what a social market economy precisely involves and which steps are needed to further its advance.[77] In my opinion it does allude to the fact that the European economic integration process should at least *not* be perceived as a 'neo-liberal project'.

Furthermore, the fact that the TFEU Treaty no longer refers to a system of undistorted competition in Article 3 TFEU, which the EC Treaty included as one of the central tasks of the Community in Article 3(1)(g) EC, could imply that the EU Courts are less inclined to develop groundbreaking case law in the field of competition law.[78] But whether the significance of competition policy as a cornerstone of the Internal Market will diminish is questionable. After all, the notion of a system of undistorted competition has now been laid down in Protocol No. 27, attached to the Lisbon Treaty 2009 and hence with binding force.[79]

From the Treaty of Maastricht 1993 onwards the EC Treaty has included a specific provision on health. Article 169(7) TFEU stipulates that Union action shall respect the responsibilities of the Member States for the definition, organisation and delivery of health services and medical care. Member States retain their responsibility for the allocation of resources. Although the scope of EU law, for instance the scope of the state aid rules with respect to financial measures in the field of healthcare, should not be conflated with the competence the EU, or its Member States, has in regulating the health care sector. But the fact that healthcare is first of all the full responsibility of the Member States must play some role also in the case law of the Courts and the decision practice of the Commission on state aid. This is furthermore emphasised by the duty to integrate an adequate social protection and a high level of human health in other EU policies as laid down in Article 9 TFEU. Although this provision is less forcefully formulated than Article 11 on environmental protection requirements, it does mean that a kind of 'health impact assessment' of all EU policies and activities, including state aid policy, should be carried out.[80] It is also important to note that the health integration clause of Article 9 TFEU is now placed at the same footing as the other integration clauses under the Title on provisions having general application. This 'upgrading'

[75] See also, for example, Neergaard (2009b), at p. 203.

[76] Cf., Ross (2009), at p. 140.

[77] For example, Neergaard (2009a, b) at p. 48 and pp. 203–204, respectively.

[78] Cf., Amtenbrink and van de Gronden (2008), at p. 327.

[79] Cf., Joerges (2009), at p. 30.

[80] Cf., de Vries (2006), at p. 22.

since the Treaty of Lisbon 2009 further underlines the importance of taking account of health protection requirements in other EU policies.

12.4.3 BUPA *and the TFEU*

Some would argue that, irrespective of the insertion of Article 16 EC, the Protocol on Services of General Interest, accompanying documents and the amendment of Article 16 by the Treaty of Lisbon 2009 by Article 14 TFEU, from a strictly legal perspective nothing has changed. After all Article 14 TFEU clearly states that it applies without prejudice to Articles 93, 106 and 107 TFEU. The concept of services of general economic interests seems highly politicised.[81] The rhetoric surrounding services of general economic interest could simply be understood as merely political fireworks. In this 'scenario' it is not difficult to imagine that judicial bodies may easily become *captured* by politics, of which *BUPA* would be an illustration.

But the legal developments described in this chapter cannot be left wholly unnoticed or merely classified as 'political'. It has also been argued that the insertion of Article 16 in the EC Treaty at the time constituted a first important step in the constitutionalisation of services of general economic interest. Furthermore, attention has been given to the fundamental notion according to which each person should have a certain minimum of guaranteed access to certain services.[82] This in combination with the other novelties of Lisbon showing more consideration for social concerns and solidarity, could certainly constitute a self-standing explanation of the restrained approach of the GC in *BUPA*. After all the Treaty should guide the Courts in how to interpret the norms of Treaty Articles, like Articles 106 and 107 TFEU, without them being necessarily captured by politics.[83] *BUPA* may thus be seen as recognition of a competition model which includes social concerns, including healthcare concerns, albeit that these services are delivered nationally and locally.[84]

However, this is not the end of the story. The fact that the Treaty of Lisbon 2009 and the changed constitutional setting may explain the reserved attitude of the Court in a case like *BUPA* does not elucidate *how* reserved or 'silent' the Court should be in assessing state aid cases. If we look at *BUPA* we see that the Court's reasoning is flawed on some points. The GC does not shed light on the question of how *general* the obligations may be, which are laid down in national legislation for

---

[81] Cf., Vedder (2008), at p. 25.

[82] Cf., Prechal (2009), at p. 66; see also, for example, Ross (2000).

[83] For example, de Vries (2006), at p. 373; a comparison could be made with the application of the free movement rules and public interest exception, whereby the Court is advised to take account of the (inherently substantive) differences between horizontal and flanking policies.

[84] For example, Ross (2009), at p.140.

health services to qualify as services of general economic interest.[85] But at the same time the Court held that certain *minimum criteria* common to every SGEI mission must be taken into account. In this sense *BUPA* is not exactly instrumental in taking away the existing confusion, that is, whether financial aid for the delivery of services of general economic interest should or should not be notified to the Commission. A blessing in disguise may have been the Court's judgment in *CELF*, which entails that, in cases where the Member States failed to notify the aid scheme to the European Commission and the Commission finally adopts a positive decision declaring the aid compatible with Article 107 TFEU, the national courts are not required to recover unlawfully implemented aid, but merely the interest on the state aid.[86]

In addition, there is case law indicating that there are limits to the Court's flexible approach as well. Not only can the Court seriously check whether the Commission's appraisal of the compensation in question is correct. This was the case in *SIC II*, which involved financing of the Portuguese public service broadcaster. Although the GC took a flexible approach as regards the application of the *Altmark* conditions, in particular the fourth condition, it did place the Commission *under a strict duty* to investigate all relevant documents provided by the Member State to assess whether the use of public funds amounted only to a compensation of costs.[87] In another case, *Italy* v. *Commission*, the GC held that a SGEI cannot be derived from the mere fact that the undertakings concerned pursue activities in the public economic interest.[88]

Nevertheless, we are still faced with a rather incoherent approach to the application of the state aid rules in areas where public service interests are at issue. Although the Commission is certainly induced to take a more flexible stance to state aid cases in the field of healthcare, it is not sure, considering its Decisions in, for example, the field of media policy, whether it will do so in practice. *BUPA* makes apparent the need to further clarify the scope of the state aid rules in respect of SGEI. It may reopen the debate on the adoption of a Framework Directive (or Regulation), which must stipulate certain basic obligations and principles, which all SGEI must comply with in Europe. Lisbon now offers an explicit legal basis for such a framework instrument, but even other (internal market) legal bases could be used, if we accept that the internal market is, certainly after Lisbon, more than a narrowly construed concept with trade liberalisation as its priority.[89]

---

85 For example, van de Gronden (2009), at p. 19; see also, for example, Sauter (2009), at p. 286, who argues that the main problem of BUPA is that competition is ignored: '[...] especially when the distinction between the public and private spheres blurs (...) the process of competition should be protected.'

86 ECJ, Case C-199/06 *Centre d'exportation du livre français (CELF)* [2008] *ECR* I-469.

87 ECJ, Case T-442/03 *SIC II* [2008] *ECR* II-1161; see, for example, Vedder (2008), at p. 24.

88 Case T-222/04 *Italy* v. *Commission,* Judgment of 11 June 2009, ECR I-0000 (n.y.r.); see, for example, van de Gronden (2009), at p. 19.

89 For example, de Vries (2009), at pp. 139–158.

12.5 Conclusion

BUPA has certainly raised dust in many respects. The reticent attitude of the GC in the field of healthcare can be explained when taking into account the various provisions included in the Treaty of Lisbon 2009 and other legal developments in the field of SGEI. Most European lawyers tend to argue from the logic of the case law in the field of state aid and competition policy. But the Treaty now offers a base for more critical reflections on this logic. From the perspective of health care and the Member States' competences in this area, a flexible stance to the application of the state aid provisions is desirable. In that sense the GC in *BUPA* appears to have taken an advance on the Treaty of Lisbon 2009 and its constitutional dimension.

This does, however, not take away the fact that undistorted competition, although absent in the catalogue of Treaty objectives, must still be considered an important task of the EU, as otherwise the process of market integration would be seriously undermined. This means that the Commission in assessing state aid cases should continue to be under a strict duty to present evidence that public service undertakings are not being overcompensated. In that sense *BUPA*, although considerably relaxing the *Altmark* conditions, still imposes upon the Member State the duty to formulate in their national legislation minimum criteria in respect of health services; something they were probably never, or hardly ever, required to do before. This may unquestionably lead to changes in the health care systems of the Member States, offering a more transparent policy on the control and definition of SGEI and thereby ensuring both legal certainty for the market parties and protection of public interests. These effects on the organisation and financing of healthcare, which competence, according to Article 168 TFEU belongs to the Member States, are noticeable and cannot be prevented. But it is intolerable, in the light of the constitutional dimension of the Treaty, that, due to an increasing degree of incoherence in the application of the state aid rules, *inter alia*, as a result of *BUPA*, national healthcare systems are slowly being deconstructed.[90] The judgment in *BUPA*, therefore, unmasks the need to further clarify the scope of the concept of SGEI, which should incite the Union legislator to take action.

Acknowledgments The author would like to thank Wies Smit and Marloes Ramp for their assistance.

References

Amtenbrink F, van de Gronden JW (2008) Economisch recht en het Verdrag van Lissabon I: mededinging en interne markt (Economic law and the Treaty of Lisbon I: competition and the internal market), 9 SEW

[90] Hatzopoulos (2009).

Belhaj S, van de Gronden JW (2004). Some room for competition does not make a sickness fund an undertaking. Is EC competition law applicable to the health care sector? (Joined cases C-264/01, C-306/01, C-453/01 and C-355/01, AOK), ECLR

Chalmers D, Monti G (2008) European union law—updating supplement. CUP, Cambridge

De Vries S (2006) Tensions within the internal market—the functioning of the internal market and the development of horizontal and flanking policies. Europa Law Publishing, Groningen

De Vries S (2009) Harmonization of services of general economic interest: Where There's a Will There's a Way!. In: Van de Gronden JW (ed) EU and WTO law on services, limits to the realization of general interest policies within the services markets? Kluwer Law International, Alphen a/d Rijn

Hatzopoulos V (2009) Services of general interest in healthcare: an exercise in deconstruction? In: Neergaard U, Nielsen R, Roseberry LM (eds) Integrating welfare functions into EU law—from Rome to Lisbon. DJØF Publishing, Copenhagen

Joerges C (2009) A renaissance of the European economic constitution. In: Neergaard U, Nielsen R, Roseberry L (eds) Integrating welfare functions into eu law—from Rome to Lisbon. DJØF Publishing, Copenhagen

Krajewski M (2008) Providing legal clarity and securing policy space for public services through a legal framework for services of general economic interest: squaring the circle. 14 European Public Law

Lavrijssen S, de Vries S (2009) Chapter 19, Netherlands. In: Krajewski M, Neergaard U, van de Gronden JW (eds) The changing legal framework for services of general economic interest—between competition and solidarity. Asser Press, The Hague

Neergaard U (2009a) Services of general economic interest: the nature of the beast. In: Krajewski M, Neergaard U, van de Gronden JW (eds) The changing legal framework for services of general interest in Europe. Asser Press, The Hague

Neergaard U (2009b) Services of general (economic) interest: what aims and values count? In: Neergaard U, Nielsen R, Roseberry LM (eds) Integrating welfare functions into EU law—from Rome to Lisbon. DJØF Publishing, Copenhagen

Prechal S (2009) Fundamental rights and the liberalization of services markets. In: van de Gronden JW (ed) EU and WTO law on services—limits to the realization of general interest policies within the services markets. Kluwer Law International, Alphen a/d Rijn

Prechal S et al (2010) The principle of attributed powers and the ‚scope of EU law'. In: Prechal S, Widderhovenen R, Besselink L (eds) European monographs. Kluwer Law International, Alphen a/d Rijn

Prosser T (2005) The limits of competition law—markets and public services. OUP, Oxford

Rodrigues S (2009) Towards a general EC framework instrument related to SGEI? Political considerations and legal constraints. In: Krajewski M, Neergaard U, van de Gronden JW (eds) The changing legal framework for services of general interest in Europe—between competition and solidarity. Asser Press, The Hague

Ross M (2000) Article 16 E.C. and services of general interest: from derogation to obligation? 25 ELRev

Ross M (2009) A healthy approach to services of general economic interest? The BUPA judgment of the Court of First Instance. 34 ELRev

Sauter W (2008) Services of general economic interest and universal service in EU law. 33 ELRev

Sauter W (2009) Case note on case T-289/03, British United Provident Association Ltd (BUPA), BUPA Insurance Ltd, BUPA Ireland Ltd v. Commission of the European Communities, Judgment of the Court of First Instance of 12 February 2008, nyr'. 46 CMLRev

Szyszczak E (2004) Financing services of general economic interest. 67 MLR

Van de Gronden JW (2009). Financing healthcare in EU law: do the European state aid rules write out an effective prescription for integrating competition law with healthcare? 6 CompLRev

Vedder H (2008) The constitutionality of competition—EC internal market law and the fine line between markets, public interests and (self-)regulation in a changing constitutional setting. http://papers.ssrn.com/sol3/papers.cfm?abstract_id=1282035

Chapter 13
EU Law and the Organisation of Health Care: Experiences from Germany

Felix Welti

Contents

F. Welti (✉)
Professor of Social law at the Universität Kassel, Room 3109, Arnold-Bode-straße 10, 34109, Kassel, Germany
e-mail: schulz.welti@t-online.d
e-mail: mail@felix-welti.de

J. W. van de Gronden et al. (eds.), *Health Care and EU Law*,
Legal Issues of Services of General Interest, DOI: 10.1007/978-90-6704-728-9_13,

13.1 Introduction

Since the ECJ rulings in *Kohll* and *Decker* in 1998[1] it has been clear for German legislation, jurisprudence and academic discussion that EU law, especially the freedom of services, has had an impact on the system of the German public health insurance. It is even more controversial, how far other parts of EU economic law, especially competition law and public procurement law, have an influence on the German health care system, especially in regard to the ECJ decisions in the cases *AOK*[2] and *Oymanns.*[3]

In Germany public procurement law is seen as a part of competition law, because public procurement can influence the competition of providers. Public procurement, as far as implementing the EC Directive 2004/18, is regulated in the German law against restrictions of competition (Gesetz gegen Wettbewerbsbeschränkungen—GWB, Sect. 98). The applicability of the GWB on the public health insurance funds has been a controversial subject in German legislation and jurisprudence in the past few years.

In this chapter first, the role of competition in the German health care system is discussed in general Then the (non-)application of the concept of an undertaking in the German health insurance funds following the *AOK* case will be analysed; after this the impact of EU state aid rules and of public procurement rules is discussed. Finally the latest developments and further prospects after the ruling of the German Federal Constitutional Court on the Treaty of Lisbon 2009 and after the federal elections in September 2009 are examined.

13.2 The German Health Care System and the Role of Competition

The German health care system is divided into a public sector, which is composed of 72 million members of the public health insurance funds, and a private sector, which consists of about 8.5 million customers of private health insurance. The public sector is part of the social insurance system founded through the ‘Bismarck reforms’ in 1881. In principle, today, the private sector is only open for self-employed persons, for persons with an income of more than 49.500 € *per annum* and for civil servants who have a special status in health care. The public health insurance funds are regulated by the Social Code Book V (*Sozialgesetzbuch V*) and strictly supervised by the administration.

---

[1] ECJ, Case C-120/95 *Decker* [1998] *ECR* I-1871; ECJ, Case C-158/96 *Kohll* [1998] *ECR* I-1935.

[2] ECJ, Case C-264/01 *Ichthyol* v. *the groups of sickness funds—AOK Bundesverband* [2004] *ECR* I-2493.

[3] ECJ, Case C-300/07 *Oymanns* [2009] *ECR* I-0000 (n.y.r.).

Ownership and organisation of hospitals can be private or public: Some hospitals are owned by private corporations, some are run by free welfare organisations. Public hospitals are run by the municipalities or the federal states. Practitioners and specialists work in private practice. The public health insurance funds do not provide benefits in cash, but benefits in kind through contracts with hospitals and the doctors' associations. There is free choice of physicians and in most cases also of hospitals and there are almost no waiting lists.

13.2.1 Competition Between Public Health Insurance Funds

Since 1994, the law establishes competition between the public health insurance funds. Most people can now choose freely between about 160 different public health insurance funds. Contributions and benefits are fixed by law and there are few differences between the funds. The number of funds has been decreasing continuously since the start of competition. Public health insurance funds are bodies governed by public law. The public health insurance funds and their members are not bound by contracts. The membership status is established by law and, in most cases, is compulsory. Public health insurance funds are forced to cooperate and have to establish a common central organisation on federal and on state level, especially with regard to cooperation and contracting with the hospitals, doctors and health services. In cooperation with the representative associations of doctors and hospitals, this central organisation fixes in a legal framework, under supervision of the federal government, the scope of the public health insurance system.

Between the public health insurance funds there is a state regulated system of risk structure compensation (Risikostrukturausgleich). All contributions are collected in a central pool (Gesundheitsfonds) by a state authority and the public health insurance funds get certain risk-adjusted amounts per capita of insured persons. The criteria are age, gender, and since the recent reform, morbidity, measured according to the incidence of 80 of the most common diseases.

The last reform (in 2007) strengthened the public health insurance funds' duty to cooperate. A fixed common contribution rate for all funds was set by the 'Act to Strengthen Competition in the Statutory Health Insurance System (GKV-WSG)'. The rate is now 15.5% of the work income up to 44.550 € *per annum*. The funds are allowed to charge an extra contribution (Zusatzbeitrag) as a *per capita* payment. The first health insurance fund to charge an extra contribution was a very small fund that was forced to charge the extra contribution from all members, because of two cases of haemophilia. This shows that the problem of risk selection still has not been completely solved. There are some incentives for public health insurance funds not to provide good care of chronically ill, disabled and other 'expensive' patients. In early 2010, several big health insurance funds also started charging the extra contribution, in most cases 8 € per month.

Competition in the public system has some similarities with competition in the private sector. For example, regarding risk selection, competition in the public sector has similar negative effects as competition in the private system. However, whether there is an increased efficiency of the system has not yet been measured. Yet, costs rose and contribution rates have been increased since the introduction of the public competitive system. Of course there are several reasons for this development. The system of competition in the public sector resembles New Public Management strategies, but, until now, the system has not been privatised and the market has not been opened up for entry by private insurance companies. Nevertheless, it is debated whether German national competition law, influenced by EU competition law, becomes applicable to public health insurance funds as a result of competition between the funds in Germany.[4]

13.2.2 Competition Between Public and the Private Health Insurance

In Germany there is little competition between public funds and private insurance companies. Self-employed persons and persons with an income of more than 49.500 € *per annum* are not mandatory members of the public health insurance funds. They are allowed to join them voluntarily, if they were insured initially on a mandatory basis and so continue their membership in the public system. Persons with a higher income normally stay in the public health insurance funds only in case they have several children, because these are insured in public funds without contribution, or in case they are chronically ill and would have to pay high contributions to private health insurance. Private companies call the 49.500 € threshold the 'borderline of peace', because they are 'left in peace' with the business of wealthy and healthy persons.

The 'Act to Strengthen Competition in the Statutory Health Insurance System (GKV-WSG)' of 2007 provided that persons may only leave the public system if their monthly income was higher than the threshold in three successive years. The newly elected coalition of Christian Democrats and Liberals has abandoned this requirement to make it easier to swap into the private system. The GKV-WSG also included the opportunity for the public health insurance funds to offer special contribution schemes which would pay refunds to those who did not need health care services. These reforms strengthened the public funds in the small area of competition with the private insurance companies. The Federal Constitutional Court[5] declared the Act to be in accordance with the constitutional freedom of conducting business and one social court also found it in accordance with EU competition law.[6] However, the implementation of elements not following the principle of solidarity,[7] as well as applying the law of bankruptcy on the public

---

[4] Mühlhausen (2002), p. 80.

[5] BVerfG 10 June 2009, Case 1 BvR 706/08; *Neue Juristische Wochenschrift* (2009), p. 2033.

[6] SG Dortmund 21 January 2008, Case S 40 KR 236/07.

[7] Krogull (2008), p. 240; Lamping and Sohns (2007), pp. 368–371.

funds,[8] is seen as a problem in political and academic debates, because the funds no longer keep their status as public funds and gradually change their character.

During the debates on the 2007 health care reform the integration of private health care insurance into the system of risk structure compensation (Risikostrukturausgleich) was a controversial issue between the then governing parties, the Christian Democrats (CDU/CSU) and the Social Democrats (SPD). The Christian Democrats were strongly opposed to this plan and it was not realised in the 2007 reform. Following the line of the European Commission Decisions in relation to the reform in the Netherlands and the *BUPA* decision of the European Court of First Instance[9] on the Irish health care system, this type of reform would not have been a *prima facie* violation of EU competition Law, because health insurance offered by private providers can be a service of general economic interest.

13.2.3 Competition Between Health Care Services

In Germany, hospitals, practitioners, specialists and other health care services are mostly private business or belong to free welfare organisations. They are subject to regulated competition, and there has been an intensive discussion on how the public health insurance system influences this competition and if this influence is in accordance with EU law.

Originally, the public health insurance funds contracted separately with practitioners and specialists. After the physicians' collective organisation and strike of 1913 a public physicians' organisation was established by law which contracts collectively with the funds and can be seen as a cartel. Patients are allowed to choose their own physician. This is still the regular way of organising outpatient treatment. Hospitals, including the private ones, receive State funds for their investments whilst their running costs are financed by the public funds. Hospitals which are incorporated into the public hospital plan are entitled to treat patients on the account of the public funds. All physicians and hospitals are integrated in this system subject to the requirement of an economic needs test. Under a constellation like this which is governed by public law, there was no impact of competition law, even if some practitioners and specialists would have liked to earn more and attempted to take legal action against the alleged cartel of the public funds.[10]

Assumptions of ineffectiveness of the German system led to more criticism in the 1990s. Claims were made that there was not enough cooperation between practitioners, specialists, hospitals and rehabilitation units, a lack of gate-keeping to benefits and not enough innovation because of a lack of competition.[11] In

---

8 Heberlein (2009), p. 141 at p. 146.

9 General Court, Case T 289/03 [2008] *ECR* II-81. See the chapters by Neergaard and de Vries in this book.

10 LSG Bayern 12 February 2003, *Gesundheitsrecht* (2003), p. 316.

11 Cassel et al. (2008).

addition, the former East German system of outpatient clinics (Polikliniken) could not be integrated adequately in the West German system. In 2000 the then governing majority of Social Democrats and Green Party started with health care reforms in an attempt to establish so-called 'Integrated Medical Care': a system, in which practitioners, specialists, hospitals and rehabilitation units would contract with each other and with individual public health insurance funds to form alternatives to the traditional system. It was connected with 'Disease Management' in the case of chronic illnesses and extra funds were provided in the reforms of 2004 and 2007. Over the past few years the system of 'Integrated Medical Care' has gained some importance, but it still only represents a small part of the whole system. Whilst Integrated Medical Care is discussed mostly from the point of effectiveness and quality, cost cutting is also a relevant subject in German health care reforms. Therefore, public health insurance funds were also allowed to contract separately with pharmaceutical companies and with suppliers of therapeutic aids like prostheses or orthopaedic footwear to negotiate lower prices.

13.3 The (Non-)application of the Concept of Undertaking to German Health Insurance Funds

In the decision '*AOK Bundesverband e.a.*'[12] the ECJ decided that the former groups of health insurance funds, now united into one, could not be characterised as undertakings or associations of undertakings in the sense of Article 81 EC (now Article 101 TFEU) in relation to the pharmaceutical undertakings on the German market. Their right to fix a common price for drugs was therefore maintained. The decision was based on the fact that the public health insurance funds serve an exclusive social objective and are non-profit organisations which are not engaged in an economic activity. The ECJ also considered the fact, that every fund offers essentially identical obligatory benefits to their members and the existence of a solidarity mechanism, which enables an equalisation of costs and risks between different funds. The health insurance funds are under State supervision when fixing common prices.

This ECJ ruling coincides with the decisions of the court in the *INAIL*,[13] *FENIN*[14] and *Kattner Stahlbau*[15] cases. Competition in the system does not change the public character of the funds, which is based on the principle of solidarity and on the non-profit character of the funds.

---

[12] ECJ, Case C-264/01 *Ichthyol* v. *the groups of sickness funds* [2004] *ECR* I-2493.

[13] ECJ, Case C-218/00 *INAIL* [2002] *ECR* I-691.

[14] ECJ, Case C-250/03 *FENIN* [2006] *ECR* I-6295.

[15] ECJ, Case C-350/07 *Kattner Stahlbau* [2009] *ECR* I-1513.

The German proponents of including the public health insurance funds in European competition law have criticised this jurisprudence of the ECJ.[16] Sodan[17] referred to the differences of contribution and benefits and to the segment of competition between public health insurance funds and private health insurance companies. He stressed that the ECJ had not decided on the application of EU competition law on the relation between public health insurance funds and private health insurance companies. Koenig and Engelmann[18] pointed out that an increasing freedom of free and selective contracting with providers and of variable benefits for members could lead the health insurance funds into being undertakings. Other German authors supported the ECJ's ruling. Bieback[19] stressed, that the competition between the public health insurance funds is governed by public law and cannot justify the application of competition law. Fuchs[20] pointed out, that fixed prices are valuable instruments of cost control in health care and that the pharmaceutical undertakings have enough legal protection according to German social law. Pruns[21] explains that the 'economic' activities of the public health insurance funds in relation to their partners in Integrated Health Care do not constitute activities of an undertaking in the meaning of European competition law.[22] Krogull[23] sees changes after the last reforms and now supports categorising public health insurance funds as undertakings in the competition with private health insurance companies in the range of voluntary insurance. In my opinion this idea is to be rejected. Voluntary insurance in the public system in Germany is still an annex to the mandatory insurance and it still follows the principles of solidarity for those who chose the public option.

13.3.1 The Impact of the European State Aid Rules on German Health Care

Another relevant question concerns the qualification of public payments to German hospitals as state aid prohibited by Article 107 TFEU. After the Commission Decision of 28 November 2005 (2005/842/EC) it seems to be clear that compensatory payments by the Member State for hospitals, which carry out activities qualified as services of general economic interest, are not state aid. However, some

[16] Kluckert (2009), p. 352.

[17] Sodan (2005), p. 145–151.

[18] Koenig and Engelmann (2004), pp. 682, 686.

[19] Bieback (2004), pp. 57–60.

[20] Fuchs (2005), pp. 87–90.

[21] Pruns (2008), p. 196.

[22] Becker and Kingreen have a different opinion (2008).

[23] Krogull (2008), p. 177.

doubts remain. The Commission adopted the criteria of the *Altmark Trans* ruling[24] and demands from the Member States to specify the nature and duration of the public service obligations and parameters for calculating, controlling and reviewing the compensation. At least according to the Directive on the application of Patient Rights in Cross-border Health Care (2008/0142/EG)[25] it is possible that neighbouring states or hospitals in neighbouring states may ask how far the public subsidies help German hospitals in the acquisition of patients from elsewhere in Europe. In fact, hospitals in Northern Germany have patients from Sweden and Norway, which helps the public systems of these countries to minimise waiting lists. But private hospitals in Sweden could ask if German state aid to German private hospitals is justified.

A second problem could be the fact that about one-third of German hospitals are run by the State as university hospitals or by the municipal or county administration. Where there are economic losses, these public owners compensate them. It may be a potential conflict if this compensation would be classified as prohibited state aid or if there is a necessity for more transparent payments.[26] The CFI (now the general Court) did not see any reason to condemn the inactivity of the Commission in this case.[27]

It should be added, that municipal and county hospitals provide only a deficiency guarantee for the system. The communities are obliged to provide a hospital if no other provider is willing to. University hospitals serve a special function with regard to the connection of medical research, medical training and medical supply in difficult cases.

13.3.2 The Impact of Articles 101 TFEU, 102 TFEU and the European Merger Control Rules on German Health Care

During the past decade a few hospitals in Germany have been privatised and have mostly been taken over by large companies, becoming even larger. Thus in some areas a public monopoly may be succeeded by a private monopoly.

In 2004 the European Commission found that the notified take over of the HELIOS hospital federation by the Fresenius cooperation (COMP/M.4010) falls within the scope of the Merger Regulation 139/2004/EC. However, the Commission decided that the concentration in the German hospital sector was compatible with the Internal Market.

---

[24] ECJ, Case C-280/00 *Altmark Trans* [2003] *ECR* I-7747.

[25] Kingreen (2009), p. 109 at p. 119; Röbke (2009), p. 79 at p. 82.

[26] Bauckhage-Hoffer (2009), p. 393 at p. 400.

[27] General Court, Case T-167/04 [2007] *ECR* II-2379.

A takeover of a county hospital in a sparsely populated north Bavarian area by a private group was halted in 2008 by German Federal Cartel Office,[28] and the Federal Court of Justice (Bundesgerichtshof),[29] deciding that this group would have controlled all hospitals in the area. Experts criticised the decision, claiming that the hospital market could not be compared to other markets. Hence, it should be noted that competition law can have an impact on the organisation of the health care sector, even if, in this particular case, the takeover hardly had an effect on the Internal Market.[30] Thus EU law did not apply in this case.

After the last health care reforms the market for outpatient treatment has been opened for hospitals and also for a new kind of outpatient hospitals, the medical supply centres. Hospitals began to establish such medical supply centres. They hope to optimise 'patient management' at the transition from outpatient to hospital care, which means directing patients to their hospitals. In the past few months the German public for the first time discussed the subject of unlawful payments from hospitals to practitioners who send them patients. With the new structures such payments could subside because patients stay inside the same undertaking. Maybe this kind of integration could be seen as building new vertical monopolies.

13.3.3 The Impact of European Public Procurement Law on German Health Care

Another debate in this context concerns the application of public procurement law, which is associated with competition law in the German domestic context due to its function of ensuring fair competition according to public contracts. Traditionally public procurement law did not apply to the relations between public funds and suppliers of health care services. The dominance of some public funds on the health care market representing up to 40% of patients was an important argument for the providers to call for the application of procurement rules. On their way from payer to player the funds were seen as following their own organisational interests and not only carrying out a health care policy prescribed by public law.

But following the judgment in *AOK Bundesverband e.a. (Ichthyol)* the discussion concentrated on procedures and the applicability of procurement law, in particular EC Directive 2004/18. If the funds insisted on being non-profit public entities to be excluded from competition law, why should they not be subject to the

---

28 Bundeskartellamt, 10 March 2005, Case B 10—123/04.

29 BGH, 16 January 2008, Case KVR 26/07.

30 Bruckenberger et al. (2006), p. 172 at p. 182.

public procurement law?[31] Opponents pointed out that the funds were not the consumers of health care but it was the individual patients who were the consumers. Ultimately, market decisions were not taken by the funds but by the patients themselves as long as participation in Integrated Health Care remained voluntarily.[32] This argument was combined with scepticism against the 'brave new world' of competition in health care and the fear that patients' interests could be disregarded leaving them fewer choices than in the public system which allows a free choice of physicians and hospitals.[33] On the contrary, contract specialists of the public funds fear that the flexibility and the innovative potential of Integrated Health Care could be lost due to the application of public procurement rules. They point out that the public funds often do not exactly know which services they want to include in a new contract but wait for innovative offers and develop the new schemes in a cooperative process.[34]

Most specialists of social security law, including myself, are still sceptical about the benefits of applying procurement law in the healthcare system.[35] Unsurprisingly it was not a social court, but a court competent for competition law cases (the OLG Düsseldorf) which asked the ECJ for preliminary ruling regarding the application of procurement law.[36] In the case of *Oymanns Orthopädie Schuhtechnik* a supplier of orthopaedic footwear wanted to participate in a programme of Integrated Health Care of the AOK Rheinland, an important public fund, for the supply of products to diabetics suffering health problems with their feet as a result of diabetes. In June 2009 the ECJ gave its judgment and stated, that the German health insurance funds are bodies governed by public law and therefore have to apply to the rules of the Directive 2004/18.[37] The Court assumed that the public health insurance funds were indirectly financed by the state, because they are mainly financed by contributions from their members which are imposed, calculated and collected according to rules of public law. This judgment referred to a time, where the funds still could calculate their contributions themselves with the consent of their state board of control. Nowadays, the contribution is fixed by law. So this aspect seems to be even clearer. In his Opinion Advocate General Mazák pointed out that the German health insurance funds are also subject to management supervision by the State. However, the Court did not address this issue because the other condition, financing by the state, was fulfilled. But most experts agree that this is an important point which future cases should address.

31 Mühlhausen and Kimmel (2008), p. 30 at p. 35; Hartmann and Suoglu (2007), p. 404 at p. 414; Kingreen (2004), p. 659 at p. 669.

32 Engelmann (2009), p. 137 at p. 168.

33 Wallrabenstein (2009), p. 36 at p. 61.

34 Bollmann and Zimmermann (2009), p. 201 at p. 204.

35 Bernhardt (2008), p. 128 at p. 139: 'over-regulation'; Bittner (2008), p. 352 at p. 353; Baltzer (2007), p. 573 at p. 579, p. 638 at p. 644.

36 OLG Düsseldorf, 23 May 2007, Case VII-Verg 50/06, *Gesellschaftsrecht* (2007), p. 429.

37 ECJ, Case C-300/07 *Oymanns* [2009] ECR I-0000 (n.y.r.).

Referring to additional questions of the OLG Düsseldorf the ECJ stated, that a contract is to be seen as a framework agreement within the meaning of Directive 2004/18, if the payment is fixed and carried out only by the fund, if the duration of the agreement is determined and if the supplier undertakes an obligation to implement the agreement upon demand by the insured persons. Many commentators in the German discussion were of the opinion that this type of contract should be regarded as concession which would not be subject to EC Directive 2004/18. The Court did not follow this opinion, stating that this kind of agreement did not confer an economic risk to the supplier whilst a concessionaire would have to bear an economic risk. Hence, contracts are regarded as framework agreements as long as Integrated Health Care is a voluntary and additional part of the supply of German health care. If a public health insurance fund would allow all medical supply in one area or for a group of patients to be in the hands of one supplier in a population-related health care provision scheme, then this situation may be seen as different.

Meanwhile, the social courts[38] and the legislator have also applied procurement rules to special contracts with pharmaceutical undertakings and with suppliers of medical aid. Therefore, the integration of social security law and public procurement law seems to be on its way in these special cases. The German Federal Court of Justice (Bundesgerichtshof) decided in 2008 that emergency transport service has to be tendered if it is organised by using third-party organisations.[39]

The problems of gradual changes of a running system remain. For example, the regulations for public contracts and the possibility of legal protection can be used to challenge new contracts, thereby preserving the old system of collective contracts. New contracts can be stopped effectively through tactical use of legal protection. Paradoxically, this allows those who are not interested in more competition and cost reduction for the public funds to use procurement law to slow down the implementation of a new system which could be more competitive.

13.4 Reactions to the Impact of EU Law on German Health Care

13.4.1 Reactions of the Legislator

Just before the *Oymanns* judgment, the German legislator reacted to the discussion on competition law and health care and opened the Social Code Book V for the applicability of national and EU competition law. With the 'Act to Strengthen Competition in the Statutory Health Insurance System (GKV-WSG)' of 2007 a

[38] LSG Baden-Württemberg, 23 January 2009, Case L 11 WB 5971/08.

[39] BGH, 1 December 2008, Case X ZB 31/08, BGHZ 179, 84; Ruthig (2010), p. 12 at p. 21.

few minor parts of competition law were applied by analogy in the health care system. At the start of 2009 the next reform changed the SGB V again and now declares that the law of procedures for public contracts has to be applied if its requirements are met. However, this only applies to the small field of selective contracting where public health insurance funds can choose their contractors and are not obliged to contracting with every suitable supplier. The law also determines the competent courts for these cases. After a long struggle between the different courts, the social courts had exclusive jurisdiction on these issues. This showed the political aim to ensure that the decisions are made in accordance with the goals and rules of the social health care system. However, the new coalition of Christian Democrats and Liberals has changed this determination of jurisdiction and given the jurisdiction to the courts responsible for competition law cases.

For contracts concerning therapeutic aids the law now explicitly requires the use of the provisions for public contracts if they are suitable. The application of procurement law is seen as unsuitable in cases of special manufacture and for mixed contracts with a major share of services (Sect. 127 SGB V). This shows that German legislation still regards selective contracting as unsuitable in many cases. This was specified after protests of patients' organisations and organisations of disabled persons which had experienced a worsening of supply after the first tendering procedures.

13.4.2 Reactions of the Courts

For some time, the German jurisprudence seemed to be occupied with the question of competence regarding the applicability of competition law in health care cases. A number of diverging views of the social courts and the courts responsible for competition claims emerged before the legislator referred these cases to the social courts.[40] However, before coming to the social court, a preliminary decision about the claim has to be made by an administrative chamber located at the department of commerce, not at the department of health.

Before the legislative decision on applicability of procurement law at the end of 2008 the social security tribunals began to accept principles of procurement law in cases of selective contracting by the health insurance funds. The State Social Security Tribunal of Baden-Württemberg decided in a case concerning pharmaceutical supply contracts,[41] that even without taking EU Law into account, the funds had to apply fair and transparent tendering procedure under constitutional law.[42] This decision demonstrates one current element of the debate putting the EU

[40] Ebsen (2008), p. 9 at p. 24; BGH 15 July 2008, Case: X ZB 17/08; BSG 22 April 2008, Case: B 1 SF 1/08 R.

[41] LSG Baden-Württemberg 27 February 2008, Case L 5 KR 507/08 ER-B.

[42] Kingreen (2008), p. 51 at p. 72; Sormani-Bastian (2008), p. 73 at p. 82.

Law into perspective and showing alternative reasons for German law, especially constitutional reasons.[43] In line with this the Federal Social Security Court decided that a private ambulance service may claim equal treatment with public services on the basis of constitutional freedoms and not of on the basis of EU law.[44]

13.4.3 Reactions in Political Discussions

The impact of EU competition law on the political discussion has been visible but hardly measurable, because interests and ideas about competition and markets in health care systems exist regardless of the EU law. It should also be kept in mind that there were very few cross-border aspects. Health care systems still remain national in character and display a number of national specificities. Also multinational pharmaceutical companies or hospital groups are used to finding a specific strategy for every national market. EU law, in particular competition law, can be used as an additional argument in legal and political discussions. However, most of the relevant arguments can also be phrased in constitutional terms in the German discourse. Neither the German legislator nor the German courts have (up to now) openly accepted genuine EU reasons for the application of competition law in social security cases. The *Oymanns* decision may increase the impact of EU law in the future debate.

EU Law does not hold the necessary answers to the questions of German health care reforms. German health care politics has to find its way between competition and solidarity by itself. Yet, EU law shows the protagonists that competition and solidarity cannot be combined freely and without consequences. It is not possible to give public health insurance funds monopoly advantages without binding them to the requirements of public law, including fair and transparent proceedings in relation to private undertakings. For the future, this may help to catalyse finding reform paths. It may impede reform strategies which imply a transition from public to private monopolies.

13.4.4 The Decision of the Federal Constitutional Court on the Treaty of Lisbon

On 30 June 2009 the German Federal Constitutional Court decided on the constitutionality of the Treaty of Lisbon 2009. The judgment[45] had been expected with high tension and may not only be relevant for the further German position in the development of the EU but also for the jurisprudence and the discourse in other

[43] Bloch and Pruns (2007), p. 645 at p. 652.

[44] BSG 20 November 2008, Case B 3 KR 25/07 R.

[45] BVerfG 30 June 2009, Case 2 BvE 2/08; *Neue Juristische Wochenschrift* (2009), p. 2267.

Member States. The claimants were the MPs of the German Left Party (Die Linke), an MP of the Bavarian Christian Democrats (CSU) and some conservative academics and individuals. The Court rejected their claim that the Treaty of Lisbon 2009 was not in accordance with the German Constitution. However, the Court used the opportunity to define constitutional law boundaries for the European integration. It pointed out that:

> The European unification on the basis of a union of sovereign states under the Treaties may, however, not be realised in such a way that the Member States do not retain space for the political formation of the economic, cultural and social circumstances of life.

It also established the principle of democracy as a baseline for integration. Central political aspects regarding the freedom of personal development and the shaping of the circumstances of life by social policy have to remain in the competence of the Member States unless a new German constitution would allow the substantial transfer of power to a democratic European Union. For the first time in its decisions concerning the European integration, the court referred to the principle of the social state, which is irrevocable according to the German constitution. The securing of the individuals livelihood was considered as an essential decision which must be made by the German legislative bodies based on their own competence. In this context, the court also refers to the legally and factually limited possibilities of the European Union to shape the structures of a social state.

This judgment can be seen as a strong warning to the German government and Parliament to maintain Germany's sovereignty on essential areas of social policy. It may also contain a warning to the European Commission and the European Court of Justice to respect national competences and not to overstretch the competences of the EU. The German Federal Constitutional Court explicitly refers to the jurisprudence of the ECJ and points out, that in its case law the ECJ has developed principles which strengthen the social dimension of the European Union, naming the cases *Müller-Fauré*[46] and *Sodemare,*[47] the first restricting the freedom of services, the second restricting the freedom of establishment and also the scope of EU competition law and both stressing the Member States' competence for social security policy. The judgment on the Treaty of Lisbon may be a new argument to take Articles 151, 168 and 345 TFEU seriously and to respect the political will of the Member States to maintain the sovereignty in matters regarding social security and health care policy and the system of property ownership, including public property.[48] The basic decisions of Member States on health care systems, including the decision for public health insurance, regulated supply and public hospital financing and ownership shall be made by the legislation of Member States and shall not be the result of the interpretation of EU law by European Institutions. The EU shall not decide whether Member States open

---

[46] ECJ, Case C-385/99 *Müller-Fauré/van Riet* [2003] *ECR* I-4509.

[47] ECJ, Case C-70/95 *Sodemare* [1997] *ECR* I-3395.

[48] Compare Deutscher Bundestag, BT-Drs. 16/10911.

their health care system for market and competition. But if there is an opening for market and competition, this has to be done in accordance with the rules governing the Internal Market, including competition law.[49]

13.4.5 The Next Health Care Reforms After the Elections

The federal elections on 27 September 2009 brought the coalition of Christian Democrats and Liberals (FDP) into power. The Christian Democrats remembered that the reform plans they offered to the electorate in 2005 proved to be unpopular and so they abstained from suggesting health care reform plans this time. The Liberals were the only German party calling for more competition and the opening of the market for private insurance companies in the health care sector, which could also mean privatisation of the public health insurance funds. The Liberals have been strengthened in the recent elections. However, it is not clear which position, the Liberal or the social wings of Christian Democrats, will take in the field of health care and how strong these wings will be.

The Liberals now lead the Ministry of Health with Minister Philipp Rösler. The coalition government announced a reform to establish a new system with *per capita* contributions and additional state aid for compensatory payments. At the beginning of 2010 some large public health insurance funds announced that they will charge an extra fee because of the underfunding of German health system.

The result in the long run could be a reform, following the Dutch pattern, including the privatisation of the public health insurance funds. This would raise new questions of EU competition law. It is possible that the opening of a large national insurance market in Germany may have important cross-border aspects.

The liberal swing in German politics could also bring a new wave of privatisation and concentration in the sector of hospitals and outpatient hospitals. But maybe finally the Liberals will not be that 'liberal' in this field because traditionally many physicians in Germany vote for the Liberal Party as their political representatives. It may be more difficult for them to now to hold the tension between corporate interests and market results, between the ideology and the reality of competition in health care.

13.5 Conclusion

EU competition law is not applicable to the German health insurance funds and their central organisation. Their character has not changed fundamentally since the ECJ ruling on the fixed prices in the 'AOK' case. On the other side of the coin

[49] Fisahn and Viotto (2007), p. 98 at p. 201; Höpner (2009), p. 407 at p. 415; Wunder (2008), p. 196; Schlegel (2007), p. 700 at p. 712.

since the ECJ's ruling in *Oymanns* public procurement law is applicable to the public health insurance funds as far as they can contract selectively and do not have to contract with all suitable providers. State aid to German hospitals is not in conflict with EU competition law as far as it follows the *Altmark Trans* criteria. EU competition law may become more important in German health care politics and legislation during the current period of legislation, if the legislators will follow some of their announcements of liberalisation and privatisation. Then competition law may help to avoid new monopoly structures of private insurance and private providers.

Acknowledgements Thanks to Henning Groskreutz and Tim Golke for support in research.

References

Baltzer J (2007) Das Sozialrecht als Wettbewerbsordnung (Social security law as competition regulation). Die Sozialgerichtsbarkeit 10

Bauckhage-Hoffer F (2009) Grenzüberschreitende Gesundheitsversorgung in der EG und Europäisches Beihilferecht (Cross-border health care provision in the EC and European state aid law). Gesundheitsrecht

Becker U, Kingreen T (2008) Sozialgesetzbuch V, § 69, Rz 44, C.H. Beck, München

Bernhardt D (2008) Doppelte Regulierung im Leistungsbeschaffungsrecht der GKV (Double regulation in benefit procurement of the public health insurance funds). ZESAR 3

Bieback KJ (2004) Remark to ECJ C-264/01 e.a. 56 Recht der sozialen Dienste und Einrichtungen 4

Bittner R (2008) Ware Gesundheit – Auswirkungen von Wettbewerb im Gesundheitswesen auf die medizinische Versorgungsqualität (Health as a commodity—Results of competition in health care on the quality of medical supply). Das Gesundheitswesen 6

Bloch E, Pruns K (2007) Ausschreibungspflichten bei der Leistungserbringung in der GKV (Procurement obligations for public health insurance funds). Die Sozialgerichtsbarkeit 11

Bollmann C, Zimmermann I (2009) Die Zukunft der Integrierten Versorgung (The future of integrated health care). Die Krankenversicherung 8

Bruckenberger E et al (2006) Krankenhausmärkte zwischen Regulierung und Wettbewerb (Hospital markets between regulation and competition). Springer, Berlin

Cassel D et al (2008) Vertragswettbewerb in der GKV (Contract competition in the public health insurance funds). Wissenschaftliches Institut der AOK, Bonn

Ebsen I (2008) Das GKV-Vergaberecht nach dem Gesetz zur Weiterentwicklung der Organisationsstrukturen in der gesetzlichen Krankenversicherung (The public health insurance funds procurement law after the law of development of organisational structures of public health insurance funds) (GKV-OrgWG). In: Cassel D et al (eds) Vertragswettbewerb in der GKV (Contract competition in the public health insurance funds) Wissenschaftliches Institut der AOK, Bonn

Engelmann K (2009) § 69 SGB V und das Kartellvergaberecht. In: Ebsen I (ed) Vergaberecht und Vertragswettbewerb in der Gesetzlichen Krankenversicherung (Procurement law and contract competition in public health insurance funds). Lang, Frankfurt am Main

Fisahn A, Viotto R (2007) Anforderungen an eine demokratische Europäische Union (Standards for a democratic European Union). Zeitschrift für Rechtspolitik 6

Fuchs M (2005) Remark to ECJ C-264/01 e.a. Juristenzeitung 2

Hartmann P, Suoglu B (2007) Unterliegen die gesetzlichen Krankenkassen dem Kartellvergaberecht nach §§ 97 ff. GWB, wenn sie Hilfsmittel ausschreiben? (Are the public health insurance funds underlying the procurement law when putting therapeutic aids out to tender?). Die Sozialgerichtsbarkeit 7

Heberlein I (2009) Die Insolvenz von Krankenkassen aus der Sicht von Versicherten – ein verfehltes Paradigma (Insolvency of public health insurance funds from the view of the members—a failing paradigm). Gesundheitsrecht 3

Höpner M (2009) Integration durch Usurpation - Thesen zur Radikalisierung der Binnenmarktintegration (Integration by usurpation—theses on the radicalisation of common market integration). WSI-Mitteilungen 8

Kingreen T (2004) Vergaberechtliche Anforderungen an die sozialrechtliche Leistungserbringung (Procurement law demands to social security benefits). Die Sozialgerichtsbarkeit 11

Kingreen T (2008) Fairness und Transparenz als vergaberechtsunabhängige Pflichten bei der Auswahl von Vertragspartnern (Fairness and transparency in the choice of contractors as obligations independent from procurement law). In: Cassel D et al (eds) Vertragswettbewerb in der GKV (Contract competition in the public health insurance funds). Wissenschaftliches Institut der AOK, Bonn

Kingreen T (2009) Der Vorschlag der Europäischen Kommission für eine Patienten-Richtlinie (The proposal of the European Commission for a Patient Rights Directive). ZESAR 3

Kluckert S (2009) Gesetzliche Krankenkassen als Normadressaten des Europäischen Wettbewerbsrechts (Public health insurance funds addressed by European competition law). Duncker & Humblot, Berlin

Koenig C, Engelmann C (2004) Das Festbetrags-Urteil des EuGH: Endlich Klarheit über den gemeinschaftsrechtlichen Unternehmensbegriff im Bereich der Sozialversicherung? (The fixed-price-ruling of the ECJ: finally clarification of the community law's concept of undertaking in the sector of social insurance?). Europäische Zeritschrift für Wirtschaftsrecht 22

Krogull J (2008) Wettbewerbsstrukturen im Selbstverwaltungssystem der gesetzlichen Krankenversicherung (Competition structures within the autonomous administration system of the public health insurance funds). Nomos, Baden-Baden

Lamping W, Sohns A (2007) Die GKV in Europa – Von der Ökonomisierung in die Wettbewerbsfalle? (The public health insurance funds in Europa—from economization to the competition trap?). Die Krankenversicherung 12

Mühlhausen K-H (2002) Mitgliederwettbewerb innerhalb der gesetzlichen Krankenversicherung (Competition on members within the German public health insurance funds). Baden-Baden, Nomos

Mühlhausen K-H, Kimmel F-P (2008) Die gesetzliche Krankenversicherung zwischen Sozialrecht, Vergaberecht und Kartellrecht – der notwendige Weg zu einem Sozialvergaberecht (Public health insurance funds between social security law, procurement law and antitrust law—the necessity of a social security procurement law). Gesundheits- und Sozialpolitik 4

Pruns K (2008) Kartell- und vergaberechtliche Probleme des selektiven Kontrahierens auf europäischer und nationaler Ebene (Antitrust law and procurement law problems of selective contracting on European and national level). LIT, Münster 10

Röbke M (2009) Grenzüberschreitende Gesundheitsdienstleistungen innerhalb der Europäischen Union (Cross-border health care services in the European Union). Medizinrecht 27

Ruthig J (2010) Notfallrettung zwischen öffentlicher Aufgabe und öffentlichem Auftrag (Emergency services between public function and public procurement). Deutsches Verwaltungsblatt 12

Schlegel R (2007) Gesetzliche Krankenversicherung im Europäischen Kontext – ein Überblick (Survey of public health insurance in European context). Die Sozialgerichtsbarkeit 12

Sodan H (2005) Europäisches Gemeinschaftsrecht und deutsches Krankenversicherungsrecht (European community law and German health insurance law). Gesundheitsrecht 4

Sormani-Bastian L (2008) Fairness und Transparenz als vergaberechtsunabhängige Pflichten bei der Auswahl von Vertragspartnern – Kommentar zu Kingreen (Fairness and transparency in the choice of contractors as obligations independent from procurement law—comment on

Kingreen). In: Cassel D et al (eds) Vertragswettbewerb in der GKV (Contract competition in the public health insurance funds). Wissenschaftliches Institut der AOK, Bonn
Wallrabenstein A (2009) Wettbewerb in der Sozialwirtschaft: rechtliche Steuerung der politischen Steuerung (Competition in social economics: juridical steering of political steering). Archiv für Wissenschaft und Praxis der sozialen Arbeit 3
Wunder A (2008) Grenzüberschreitende Krankenbehandlung im Spannungsfeld von Grundfreiheiten und vertraglicher Kompetenzverteilung (Cross border health care in the tension of Basic freedoms and the competence order of the treaty). Peter Lang, Frankfurt am Main

Chapter 14
Experiences from The Netherlands; The Application of Competition Rules in Health Care

Wolf Sauter

Contents

W. Sauter (✉)
Dutch Healthcare Authority (NZa), Utrecht, The Netherlands
e-mail: wsauter@nza.nl

W. Sauter
University of Tilburg, Tilburg, The Netherlands

J. W. van de Gronden et al. (eds.), *Health Care and EU Law*,
Legal Issues of Services of General Interest, DOI: 10.1007/978-90-6704-728-9_14,

14.1 Introduction

This chapter is concerned with the role played by various types of competition rules in the context of the recent and ongoing drive toward healthcare liberalisation in the Netherlands. It focuses more specifically upon the relationship between the general competition rules applied by the Netherlands' Competition Authority (NMa) and the sector specific competition policy that is applied by the Dutch Healthcare Authority (NZa). This is also a comparison between an EU inspired regime that will be familiar to most readers, based on the distinction between anticompetitive agreements, dominance abuse, and mergers on the one hand and the more novel sectoral regime that has few parallels elsewhere (with the notable exception of the dominance-based concept of significant market power that is derived from the harmonisation context of electronic communications) on the other hand.

EU competition policy involvement in the health care sector in the Netherlands is so far limited to a crucial state aid decision in 2005 that is touched upon lightly because it will be discussed at length by De Vries chapter in this book. Meanwhile a noteworthy policy *vis-à vis* state aid is emerging at national level which will be discussed briefly.

The structure of this chapter is as set out above: first the main elements of health care liberalisation in the Netherlands are discussed (Sect. 14.2), followed by a comparison between the two competition regimes at systemic level and then by discussing some individual cases by way of example (Sects. 14.3–14.5). Next state aid is touched upon (Sect. 14.6), followed by conclusions on the role of the twin tracks of competition policy in health care, and on their interaction (Sect. 14.7).

14.2 Health Care Liberalisation

14.2.1 The Drivers Behind Liberalisation

The Dutch health care system is essentially market driven.[1] Thus it relies both on exclusively private health insurers and exclusively private health care providers, albeit within a regulatory framework. At the same time the system is consumer orientated: for example, the Healthcare Authority has to adopt the general consumer interest as its first priority guiding all its actions, as set out in the Healthcare Market Regulation Act of 2006.[2] Consumer choice is seen as providing the

[1] Cf., Dutch Ministry of Health, The new care system in The Netherlands: durability, solidarity, choice, quality, efficiency, May 2006 http://www.minvws.nl/en/folders/z/2006/the-new-health-insurance-system-in-three-languages.asp; Dutch Health Authority, Contribution to EU consultation on cross-border health services, October 2006 http://ec.europa.eu/health/ph_overview/co_operation/healthcare/docs/health_services_co201_nl.pdf.

[2] Sauter (2009b), p. 419.

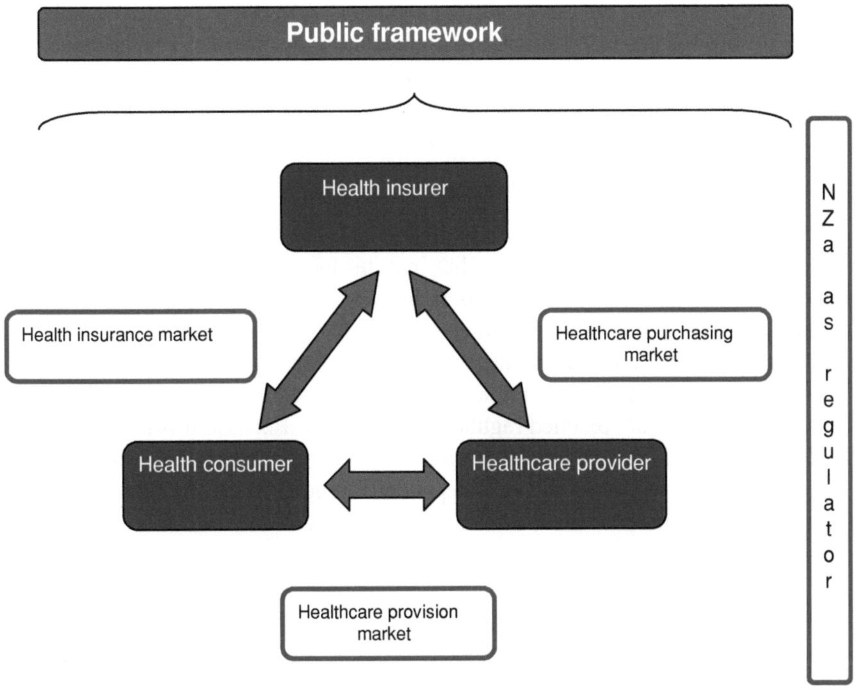

Fig. 14.1 The 'healthcare triangle'. *Source* NZa, various publications

impetus behind a system that relies on competition feeding through different markets and/or market segments. The most important (groups of) markets are pictured in Fig. 14.1 in their regulatory context.

Free consumer choice between insurers that is guaranteed by the regulatory framework is intended to work as an incentive for competitive insurance markets. If such competitive insurance markets emerge successfully, competition is next expected to filter through into markets for health care provision because insurers will try to gain competitive advantage by obtaining the best deal possible from health care providers. This eventually leads to provider combinations such as hospitals putting pressure on their consultants (doctors) to provide competitive high quality services as well.

Crucial to the success of this model is that insurers both have incentives and are able to direct their consumers to particular providers, and to selectively contract providers.[3] In this manner insurers can reward good, or preferred, providers of health care and punish poor ones, by directing more consumers to the former and/or cutting down the numbers destined for the latter (or sending them none).

---

[3] Ideally all parties would have incentives to contract mutually based on the pressures of (potential) competition. However it appears that to reach this stage selective contracting must first be possible. Cf., Capps et al. (2003), p. 737.

A further precondition are good quality indicators. So far these incentives and their results do not appear to be functioning adequately in practice. For instance, the current system of ex post risk equalisation may fatally reduce the incentives involved, and market power of providers in combination with consumers' expectations to be able to see any doctor of their choice may frustrate selective purchasing. For the purposes of this chapter however we will stick to the system as it was designed, not its critique.

In a pattern familiar from the liberalisation of other industries (for example, the utilities), health care liberalisation has not meant fewer rules, but instead an increase in the number of rules. This is because decisions that used to be taken centrally within firms or by government must now be negotiated between different market parties with conflicting interests. At the same time public interest objectives must be secured. Both to reduce transaction costs and to ensure that socially desirable outcomes are reached regulation is required. Because it is not possible to devise all detailed rules needed in advance, and because their application must be supervised, there is a need for an independent 'regulator' on top of the need for 'regulation'.[4] In this manner a measure of flexibility is introduced.

14.2.2 Health Insurance Reform and Price Liberalisation

The first step of the 2005/2006 health care reform was the introduction of a legal framework that provides for mandatory health insurance for all Dutch citizens and a tax subsidy for those on the lowest incomes. All health insurers are under an obligation to provide services to all consumers without risk selection or premium differentiation. This is to avoid insurers competing not on the merits (that is, on quality and price of services) but on obtaining a healthy (or low risk) insured population that does not require treatment. The funding regime is in two parts:

- 50% of the premium is a nominal premium (that is differentiated per insurer not per consumer) and collected directly by the insurers (there is a low variation between insurers in the pricing of this basic insurance package);
- and 50% of the premium is income dependent and collected by the state; this part of the premium is redistributed to insurers based on a risk adjustment system.

This risk adjustment system is intended to avoid adverse selection and moral hazard and to promote competition on the merits. It comprises both *ex ante* (the true 'risk' adjustment) and ex post (reimbursement of costs with no risk component) elements, whereas the ambition is, over time, to eliminate *ex post* adjustment as much as possible. Risk equalisation is discussed further below in the section on 'State aid'.

[4] For additional arguments for regulation see Maskin and Tirole (2004), p. 1034.

The next important development is the progressive ('step by step') liberalisation of prices of curative health care. Fully liberalised prices now account for now 35% of the number of treatments, and this is likely to be 50% by 2011 (subject to a temporary price cap). Long-term care on the other hand remains dominated by regional monopsony purchasers facing private providers with little competition so far. However it is believed there may be scope here to introduce at least competition 'for' (if not 'in') the market by means of auctions and improved public procurement procedures. Also personal care budgets managed by the individual consumer play an important role in increasing consumer choice and thereby provider responsiveness.

14.2.2.1 The Need for Regulation

Just a few more specific remarks about the general need for health care regulation in the Netherlands are made here. In the recent past prior to reform rising costs led to widespread rationing and therefore waiting lists that became politically unsustainable. Apart from rising costs (due to ageing populations, increasing possibilities for treatment due to technological innovation, and rising expectations), health care markets are also burdened by a range of market failures. Of these just three important aspects are mentioned here.

- First the effects of the *third party pays principle* which means that patients are not sensitive to costs, whereas providers have obvious incentives to sell more care (supply induced demand) or to sell at higher prices. There is therefore a problem of moral hazard at the expense of insurers and/or the government as payer of last resort.
- Second is the problem of *adverse selection* which means that insurers would all like to insure exclusively healthy patients who never need care, whereas healthy patients have no incentive to take out insurance. This can lead to a race to the bottom with insurers both weeding out costly consumers and barring them at the gate.
- Third is the strong position of health care providers both in terms of *information asymmetry* and in the form of *market power*: there is reason to believe that market power of health care providers is pervasive in many markets.

All three of these problems are serious ones that, if market-based solutions (as a first choice)[5] are unavailable, regulation must address. Most importantly, in health care, as a market in transition, problems of market power call for a vigorous application of competition policy.

[5] The locus classicus is Arrow (1963), p. 941.

14.2.2.2 The Various Regulators

Finally in October 2006 the Healthcare Authority has been introduced as an independent regulator as well as sector-specific competition authority, an innovation that (with the recent exception of the UK) appears largely unique in the EU today.[6] Apart from the NZa there are a number of other authorities that are involved in health care regulation in the Netherlands. For instance, there is an agency, CVZ, that is responsible for advising on whether specific forms of care should be covered by basic insurance or not and that is also responsible for the administration of the risk adjustment system. The health care inspectorate IGZ is in charge of the quality of health care provision and of developing and/or approving health quality standards. Apart from these health care specific agencies there are a number of regulators that are responsible for the entire economy and therefore also cover health care. These include the (general) Netherlands' Competition Authority NMa as well as the general regulators for behavioural and solvency aspects of financial supervision, the Central Bank DNB and the Securities Authority AFM. Of this panoply of regulators, only the Netherlands' Competition Authority and the Healthcare Authority will be discussed.

The next section examines the two parallel regimes of sector-specific and general competition policy in health care.

14.3 Applying Competition Policy to Health Care

14.3.1 The Relevance of Competition Policy in Health Care

Because it is almost entirely composed of vulnerable transition markets, the health care sector requires special scrutiny under competition policy. Examples are market structure (concerning especially mergers but with implications for aid) and entrenched positions of market power; leveraging and other cross-over effects, especially between liberalised and non-liberalised sectors. As was mentioned above providers' selling power is thought to be pervasive. Moreover a successful competition policy in this field is likely to be of central importance to the success of and/or support for liberalisation. This is because if due to a lack of competition the reforms fail to produce results, that is, improved health care performance in terms of quality, access, and affordability, the overall support for reform is likely to erode.

In the Netherlands there are two applicable competition policy regimes that are implemented by two separate authorities with concurrent powers.

[6] Since 1 January 2009 the Cooperation and Competition Panel (CCP) in the UK performs similar functions especially as a sector-specific competition authority for the NHS. Cf., http://www.ccpanel.org.uk/.

- In the first place general competition policy, implemented by the Netherlands' Competition Authority. This is a system that was created in 1998 in spontaneous harmonisation with the EU system of competition law and that accordingly is based on prohibitions and *ex post* controls (except mergers which are screened *ex ante*).
- Second, in 2006 a system of sector-specific competition policy was introduced by the Healthcare Market Regulation Act. This policy is carried out by the Healthcare Authority and forms a prevention-based system using *ex ante* controls.

Both systems will be discussed in detail below. In addition the EU regime for state aid control is relevant to the liberalisation context and will be touched upon briefly.

14.3.2 General Versus Specific Competition Policy

The two competition policy regimes for health care in the Netherlands that were mentioned above show a number of important similarities, differences, and common problems.

The most important similarities are their common focus on market power, on horizontal instead of on vertical issues, and on hardcore restrictions like price fixing and foreclosure. Also, effects are considered more important than formal (or: '*per se*') restrictions.[7] Finally, the authorities involved are in both cases independent from political control, at least where decisions in individual cases are involved.

The number of differences is larger. The general competition policy covers the entire economy, is prohibition based, and is about policing functioning markets. It derives part of its powers and most of its principles from the EU level (in addition the Netherlands' Competition Authority is empowered to apply Articles 101 and 102 TFEU where there is an effect on trade between the Member States).[8] The system of control is *ex post*, and infringements of the prohibitions of anticompetitive agreements ('cartels') and dominance abuse are sanctioned by fines as well as, in some cases, not only behavioural, but structural remedies: breaking up undertakings.

The sector-specific regime is purely based on national law and regulation and as such more subject to political pressures. Instead of policing existing markets it is more concerned with creating markets where there were none before. For this reason, control is exercised *ex ante*: it is sufficient to prove the existence of

[7] The effects-based approach is especially important regarding Article 102 TFEU. Cf., Guidance on the Commission's enforcement priorities in applying Article 82 of the EC Treaty to abusive exclusionary conduct by dominant undertakings, COM (2009) 864 final. However some per se restrictions remain important, especially in the context of Article 101 TFEU. Cf., Case C-8/08 *T-Mobile* et al., judgment of the Court of 4 June 2009, *ECR* I-0000 (n.y.r.).

[8] Council Regulation (EC) No 1/2003 of 16 December 2002 on the implementation of the rules on competition laid down in Articles 81 and 82 of the Treaty, *OJ* 2003 L 1/1, Article 5 ('The competition authorities of the Member States shall have the power to apply Articles 81 and 82 of the Treaty in individual cases.').

opportunities and incentives to restrain competition in order to impose remedies (that is, effects do not have to be demonstrated). So far remedies are behavioural, for example, price constraints.

The common problems include market definition (especially geographic markets, about which more will be said below), and the especially exacting standards of judicial review that Dutch authorities appear to face compared to their EU counterparts.

14.3.3 Managing Concurrent Powers

As was already mentioned the Netherlands' Competition Authority is an independent authority with the entire economy within its scope. It refers to the Ministry of Economic Affairs. The powers of the Netherlands' Competition Authority are enforcing the cartel prohibition, the abuse of dominance prohibition, and the monopoly on merger control (for mergers below the EU thresholds). To manage concurrence, it has precedence over the Healthcare Authority concerning the interpretation of competition concepts (such as 'dominance' or 'foreclosure') based on the Healthcare Markets Regulation Act. In addition there is cooperation between the two authorities on the contentious issues of geographical market definition, and collaboration governed by a mutual protocol (or inter-institutional agreement) which provides for regular mutual consultation at all levels.

The Healthcare Authority is an independent authority under the Ministry of Health the scope of which is limited to the health care sector. Its competition powers are the ability to determine contract terms and the contracting process, to control significant market power (SMP), and to provide advice on merger control. Apart from the cooperation and collaboration already mentioned, concurrence is managed by the fact that the Healthcare Market Regulation Act provides for the priority of the sector-specific over the general competition rules. So far this is especially important in the case of market dominance, where SMP is considered more effective and less burdensome to prove than is dominance abuse under the general competition rules. In future the ability to determine contracting terms may also become more important, for instance, as will be seen below it was recently used to impose access to electronic networks related to health care, such as related to the exchange of patient records and referrals by general practitioners.

The next sections will provide more detail on each of the two authorities.

14.4 The National Netherlands' Competition Authority (NMA)

We will briefly discuss the experience of the Netherlands' Competition Authority regarding the three branches of its competence in the health care sector: mergers, dominance abuse and cartels.

14.4.1 Merger Review

Until 2004 the Netherlands' Competition Authority elected not to exercise merger review in the health care sector due to what it perceived as the limited scope for competition at that time. In other words it did not take into account potential competition or the relevance of the market structure to future competition, that is, adopting a static rather than a dynamic approach. This is illustrative of divergence with the Healthcare Authority's view that is generally more prospective. The result of the Netherlands' Competition Authority's approach was a merger wave in anticipation of regime change that may have significantly biased the market structure by creating numerous local and regional incumbencies that are resistant to entry and change.

Although since 2004 over 100 health care mergers have been reviewed by the Netherlands' Competition Authority, none were blocked, and only a handful was cleared with conditions. Again the Netherlands' Competition Authority has often used the argument that since little competition remained (following past mergers not vetted) there was not much competition left that could be restricted, thereby favouring further clearances.[9] Recently there has been a public controversy concerning an ex post analysis by the Netherlands' Competition Authority itself that showed in at least one case significant price increases implemented by recently merged hospitals.[10] The Netherlands' Competition Authority has denied this provides evidence that health care mergers generally lead to price increases.

A further complication in merger cases has been market definition. Product market definition has been relatively unproblematic although it may differ based on the level of analysis adopted: for consumers there is little to no substitution between diagnoses (for example, hip treatment is not a useful substitute for heart surgery), although there are 900 different diagnoses for hospital treatment alone; at the provider level however a limited degree of supply substitution is possible (i.e., an orthopaedic surgeon can operate on knees and shoulders alike), so the market can be defined by specialisation or major diagnostic category (there are about 25 of these); and finally it is possible to define the market more abstractly as access to market groups, such as clinical (inpatient) versus non-clinical (outpatient) hospital care. Geographic market definition on the other hand is problematic, not just in the Netherlands but, for example, in the US experience as well.[11]

---

[9] For a critical view see Canoy and Sauter (2010).

[10] Based on the work of Kemp and Severijnen (2009). The authors focused on hip replacement surgery and demonstrated that one set of merged hospitals (in 'het Gooi') significantly increased their prices, whereas another set of merged hospitals (in Rotterdam) did not. Criticism of merger practice based on these data was reported in the daily newspaper *Volkskrant* of 31 December 2009 ('healthcare mergers lead to price increases'), and rebutted by the Netherlands' Competition Authority in a Press Release of 11 January 2010.

[11] I am grateful to Rein Halbersma for his comments on the issue of market definition (see also further below). The usual disclaimer applies. Cf., Varkevisser et al. (2008), p. 7. On the US experience see *Improving Healthcare: A Dose of Competition. Report by the Federal Trade Commission and the Department of Justice*, July 2004. http://www.usdoj.gov/atr/public/health_care/204694.htm.

This problem occurs because the standard hypothetical monopolist or SSNIP test (based on the effects of a small but significant non-transitory increase in price of 5 or 10%) fails due to the prevalence of the 'third party pays' system: because consumers rarely have to meet their hospital bills directly (the insurers do) they are not sensitive to price changes. Initially the Elzinga Hogarty test was used as an alternative, based on the LIFO/LOFI (little in from outside/little out from inside) test looking at travel patterns of patients to and from a particular area. The Elzinga Hogarty test was initially developed for measuring commodity movements (such as coal and corn) and used in health care due to its relative straightforward application. This test (as Elzinga himself testified in US proceedings) however is unreliable in health care because it measures actual travel patterns and not willingness to travel in response to a merger. For similar reasons the Critical Loss method (based on contestable ZIP (postal) codes) fails.

Meanwhile, the Netherlands' Competition Authority and Healthcare Authority have developed two alternatives based on actual consumer preferences. These are the LOCI (logit competition index) based on willingness to travel and the Option Demand method, based on willingness to pay.[12] So far the Netherlands' Competition Authority has not applied these methods to decide actual mergers, although the Healthcare Authority has begun using them in the opinions that it provides to the Netherlands' Competition Authority in such cases.[13]

The most high profile merger case in health care to date was that of *Zeeuwse Ziekenhuizen*[14] in March 2009. This decision was the outcome of a true merger saga that lasted almost four years, starting in September 2005 across two notifications and intensive lobbying at all levels. At issue was a monopoly merger between the only two direct competitors in an isolated estuary region in the South West of the Netherlands which resulted in a market share of well over 80% for clinical and non-clinical hospital care. The parties mounted an efficiency defence that was initially rejected because neither the efficiencies claimed nor the passing on to consumers of the resultant benefits were held to be guaranteed. The Healthcare Authority in its advice to the Netherlands' Competition Authority was highly critical of this monopoly merger which it predicted would have negative effects on all three of the consumer interest variables, quality, affordability, and access. It argued that the merger should only be cleared, if at all, subject to significant structural and behavioural remedies.

A key role in the case was then played by the Healthcare Inspectorate (IGZ) which argued that the merger was necessary to guarantee minimum quality levels and indeed eventually hospital survival in this region. As a result the case was

---

12 An additional method under consideration is the time elasticity approach based on the willingness to travel. Cf., more generally Varkevisser (2009).

13 For example, http://www.nza.nl/104107/138494/Cooperatie_Vlietland_-_Vlietland_Ziekenhuis.pdf on a vertical merger involving a hospital in the Rotterdam area and http://www.nza.nl/binaries/21047/42909/87232/Openbare_NZa-zienswijze_voo1.pdf with regard to the *Zeeuwse Ziekenhuizen* case discussed below.

14 Decision of 25 March 2009, Case 6424 *Ziekenhuis Walcheren—Oosterscheldeziekenhuizen*.

cleared based on behavioural remedies, notably the imposition of a price cap at the level of the national average for hospital prices, and with guarantees for securing the claimed quality improvements. The Netherlands' Competition Authority found that these remedies ensured the requirements for the efficiency defence would be met and cleared the merger conditionally on that basis. Remarkably given the structural problems caused by this merger between closest rivals, the structural remedies recommended by the Healthcare Authority (such as hiving off services that were not key to quality improvements and hospital survival) were not considered.

Fuelled by events such as these there is an ongoing debate in the Netherlands on whether or not merger review in health care must be restructured, for instance by introducing a merger prohibition based on a mandatory 35% market share threshold. This particular proposal appears to have been shelved following a negative opinion in April 2009 by the Dutch Council of State on the grounds that there was not necessarily a correlation between size and performance and that the 35% test fits ill with existing national and EU merger review standards.[15] However this is unlikely to end the debate, with the government currently preparing a proposal to give an increased vetting role to the Healthcare Inspectorate including the power to block mergers on grounds of quality and accessibility (evaluating the latter in cooperation with the Healthcare Authority). This screening, which would not cover affordability, or price, would take place before the Netherlands' Competition Authority is involved. The increasingly complex nature of the test proposed bears testimony to the political sensitivity of this subject.

14.4.2 Dominance

So far no noteworthy dominance cases involving health care have been brought under the general competition rules, at least following the creation of the Healthcare Authority.[16] Based on the above-mentioned statutory priority rule dominance issues are left for the Healthcare Authority to deal with under SMP.

14.4.2.1 Anticompetitive Agreements

The Netherlands' Competition Authority has been more active with regard to anticompetitive agreements.

---

[15] Dutch Council of State, 17 April 2009, Annex to Parliamentary Documentation II 2008/9, 27 247, No 90.

[16] For an exception preceding the creation of the NZa cf., the Decision of 3 September 2002, Case 2554 *Molenpad Health Services* v. *ZAO Zorgverzekeringen*. Here the Netherlands' Competition Authority rejected a complaint of dominance abuse by a physical therapist against the standardised contracting practices of a health insurer.

- In the *Thuiszorg't Gooi* case it fined parties active in various forms of long-term care for carving up markets between closest competitors.[17] The Specialisation Block Exemption was found not to be applicable as the purpose of the contested market sharing agreement was the allocation of customers and territories.[18] An efficiency defence based on the notion that 'integrated care' was at issue was rejected because the primary relations concerned were horizontal, not vertical, in nature.
- In *Dienstapotheek Assen* local pharmacists were found guilty, *inter alia*, of excluding entrants from local/regional information systems with patient and medication records and denying them access to backup schedules.[19] It is worth noting that because in subsequent years it turned out that this precedent had hardly any effect on similar exclusionary practices elsewhere, the Healthcare Authority has recently adopted a general regulation on access to electronic networks in health care (see further below).
- In *Brancheverenigingen van psychologen en psychotherapeuten*, the branch organisations of psychologists and psychotherapists were found guilty of price coordination by means of price recommendations.[20] Remarkably this decision was overturned on appeal by the Rotterdam District Court which held that the Netherlands' Competition Authority could not treat this as a per se (hardcore) infringement, but should instead have investigated more fully whether in this sector price was a relevant competition parameter.[21]

In addition the Netherlands' Competition Authority has issued extensive guidelines for the health care sector (focusing on horizontal agreements) in 2002 and 2007 and it will provide revised guidance in 2010. A live issue at present is the relationship between insurers and liberalised professions (for example, physical therapists, psychotherapists), with the latter accusing the former of exercising abusive buying power because insurers typically refuse to negotiate with individual practitioners, working instead with standard contracts on a 'take it or leave it' basis. Another topical issue is integrated care, that is, vertical chains of treatment for chronic diseases, which tend to involve large horizontal groups of general practitioners as well. In this case the insurers are faced with selling power and few or no regional and local alternatives. Hence, the 2010 Guidelines are likely to focus on the issues of buying power and of selling power in the context of vertical

---

[17] Decision of 19 September 2008, Case 5851 *Thuiszorg't Gooi*.

[18] Commission Regulation (EC) No 2658/2000 of 29 November 2000 on the application of Article 81(3) of the Treaty to categories of specialisation agreements, *OJ* 2000, L 304/3.

[19] Decision of 16 November 2004, Case 2501 *Dienstapotheek Assen*.

[20] Decision of 20 April 2005, Case 3309 *Brancheverenigingen van psychologen en psychotherapeuten*.

[21] Decision of 17 July 2006, LJN: AY4928. The subsequent appeal by the Netherlands' Competition Authority to the Administrative High Court for Trade and Industry was turned down as unfounded. Decision of 8 October 2008, LJN: BF8820.

agreements. In any event health care will continue to be one of the main areas of focus of the Netherlands' Competition Authority.

We now move on to a discussion of the Healthcare Authority.

14.5 The Netherlands' Healthcare Authority (NZA)

In this section we will look at the tasks of the Healthcare Authority, at its approach to SMP, and its power to intervene in contract terms and contracting processes.

14.5.1 The Healthcare Authority's Regulatory Tasks

The health care authority is responsible for market supervision as well as market development relating to the three types of markets set out in the diagram earlier in this chapter (the 'healthcare triangle'): that is, health insurance markets; health care provision markets; and health care contracting markets. It is also charged with the more traditional tasks of a rate regulator such as tariff and performance regulation; setting prices (including maximum and minimum rates as well as bandwidth rates, various forms of price caps and/or unregulated prices) and budgets; and defining standard product categories (Fig. 14.1 at p. 339).

Furthermore the Healthcare Authority supervises the application of the 2006 Health Insurance Act, notably the key elements of the system, that is, the duty of care; open enrolment; and community rating.[22] Similarly relating to long-term care (e.g., nursing homes and care for the handicapped) the Healthcare Authority is charged with supervising the lawful and effective execution of the Act on Long-Term Care. Finally the Healthcare Authority is responsible for advising the Health Minister both on request and *ex officio*. This latter role tends to take the form of competition advocacy.

14.5.2 Sector-Specific Competition Policy for Health Care

Of primary interest for the purposes of this section are two types of relevant powers enjoyed by the Healthcare Authority:

- The power to impose specific obligations on individual parties with SMP. This power is based on EU principles developed in the context of electronic

[22] This branch of its activities and indeed the legal basis for the obligations involved is thought to be covered by the exception in Article 54 of the Third Non-life Insurance Directive 92/49/EEC, *OJ* 1992, L 228/1. This reading was confirmed by a letter to the Dutch Health Minister from the then Commissioner for the Internal Market, Frits Bolkestein, dated 8 October 2003.

communications and may for that reason perhaps be more relevant outside the Netherlands.
- The power to impose general obligations on all market parties by intervening in contract terms and the contracting process, which is discussed last. This power so far appears to be unique to the Netherlands as an instrument of sector-specific competition policy.

These two powers will now be discussed in more detail.

14.5.3 Significant Market Power (SMP)

A finding of SMP empowers the Healthcare Authority to impose specific obligations on the party or parties with SMP in order to promote effective competition. As mentioned above, the concept of SMP was borrowed from electronic communications. It is applicable across the entire health care sector (hence both to the regulated and the liberalised segments) and is applied to individual undertakings based on an in-depth (and time-consuming) analysis. The key criterion for a finding of existence of significant market power is dominance.

There are three steps to determining SMP:

- First, the definition of the relevant (product and geographical) market, on a case-by-case basis, as in the case of merger analysis. The product market is less contested, as mentioned above from the perspective of the patient different treatments are unlikely to be in the same market, whereas from the perspective of the provider they may be grouped together by specialisation or even more abstractly as clinical versus non-clinical care: the results do not so far lead to significant problems or discussion, whereas the geographical market is highly problematic due to the third party pays principle. The same new methods devised for mergers that were mentioned above will be used here as well.
- The second element is dominance analysis. The question here is whether the party (or parties, in the case of collective dominance) concerned has the ability to determine its behaviour independent from other market participants, that is, customers, suppliers, and competitors. The necessary analysis is based on a combination of market share (with a presumption of dominance at shares that are over 55%),[23] market structure, and effects. Unlike dominance abuse in general competition law, proof of abuse is not necessary for an SMP finding. Nevertheless, based on national electronic communications case law with regard to SMP where

[23] This is an unexplained (if minor) deviation from the 50% market share familiar from general competition law. Cf., ECJ, Case C-62/86 *AKZO Chemie BV* v. *Commission* [1991] *ECR* I-3359.

showing 100% market share was not considered sufficient, the existence of 'opportunities' and 'incentives' to restrict competition must be shown.[24]

- Third a proportionate remedy (obligations) must be imposed. These remedies will be dealt with in more detail in the next paragraph.

14.5.4 SMP Remedies

A finding of SMP triggers proportional *ex ante* obligations. These are intended to be preventive, and not punitive. Unlike dominance abuse, which involves a legal transgression that is met with sanctions, a finding of SMP does not mean any legal rule has been breached. On the other hand if SMP obligations are nor met or respected a breach will occur, and sanctions can be meted out accordingly.

The possible remedies are the following: transparency; non-discrimination; the obligation to deal; providing a reference offer; the obligation to provide unbundled services; apply cost accounting principles; accounting separation; and individual price regulation (in case of a risk of excessive or predatory pricing). In each case the maximum term of an obligation (prior to renewed examination of its continued justification) is three years. The Health Minister can add new categories of obligations, one of which, structural separation, is regularly debated as a possible supplement to the current toolbox. From a perspective of effectiveness and least intrusive intervention it might make more sense to provide the Healthcare Authority with more powers regarding mergers, that is, *ex ante* to avoid competition issues arising, rather than with draconic divestiture powers *ex post.*

SMP remedies must always be tailored to the specificities of the case at hand. The proportionality of the remedy to the competition problem involved is one key to judicial review, the 'opportunities and incentives' for anticompetitive behaviour that were mentioned above are the other. Finally, it is possible for the Healthcare Authority to impose interim measures in those cases where there is an irredeemable risk of harm as a result of a presumptive SMP position. In this case it is the former rather than the latter dimension that is likely to be strictly scrutinised.

14.5.5 Significant Market Power (SMP): Policy Context

The policy priorities of the Healthcare Authority towards SMP are exclusion and selling power. Where possible it would combat exclusion of competitors as a first order effect rather than the exploitation of consumers which is a second order effect. That is to say it considers promoting competition a more effective way of fighting

[24] CBB, AWB 05/903 and 05/921 to 05/931, Judgment of 29 August 2006 ('Mobile terminating rates').

exploitation than regulation which is likely to create dependency, is likely to throw up entry barriers, and perpetuates itself. Likewise the Healthcare Authority intends to concentrate on selling power and not buying power especially where the benefits of buying power are eventually passed on to consumers. This would appear to be the case as long as health insurance markets are competitive.

The Healthcare Authority would tend to concentrate on horizontal instead of on vertical restraints of competition, and on leveraging of market power (for instance, leveraging of SMP from the regulated into the liberalised sector). In the event of horizontal and vertical integration it would focus on foreclosure. The Healthcare Authority would address issues such as low prices and discrimination only in the presence of clear-cut foreclosure effects. This approach is broadly in line with the general competition policy priorities as expounded by the European Commission, albeit applied to the health care context. It is worth noting however that these are so far largely points of principle rather than examples of actual practice, which is slow in emerging. This also means that many pending issues have not yet been subjected to judicial scrutiny—an important caveat given the harsh reputation of Dutch administrative law courts when dealing with market authorities.

14.5.6 Practical Experience of SMP so far

The practical application of its SMP powers by the Healthcare Authority has seen a slow start. Since Spring 2007 about 30 cases have been registered and screened, resulting in five formal decisions (of which three in the curative sector and two in long-term care). The Healthcare Authority has taken two further decisions on administrative (internal) review. In none of these cases were SMP positions found to exist. Most recently however it has taken a preliminary measure based on a presumption of SMP in the pharmacy section—about which more details are given below.

Some examples of cases that were examined are the following:

- *Espria*: in this case, concerning a prospective merger between a grouping specialised in long-term care and a large housing cooperative, the Healthcare Authority investigated the risk of exclusion of competitors from the market for housing long-term care facilities. However because the probable SMP position was located outside health care sector (i.e., in the housing market) the Healthcare Authority was not competent to act.[25]
- *VieCurie*: this case concerned vertical cooperation between a general practitioners' collective and a general hospital in the market for primary care diagnostics. Both parties enjoyed high local market shares of above 50%, hence

[25] Although this merger was indeed cleared by the Netherlands' Competition Authority, it was nevertheless subsequently blocked by the Housing Minister who has special powers regarding mergers involving housing cooperatives.

meeting the threshold for a presumption of SMP.[26] Because it appeared that there was nevertheless no possibility for independent behaviour by the hospital, this case was not pursued further.

- *Ozis*: this concerns several cases of collaborating pharmacists excluding entrants from their systems with electronic medication and patient records (the 'Ozis' system). This system was also at issue in the Netherlands' Competition Authority Case *Dienstapotheek Assen* described above. Because this problem was found to be widespread and as the earlier intervention by the Netherlands' Competition Authority had not prevented it from spreading, the Healthcare Authority decided not to address this problem by using SMP in yet another individual case but based on a horizontal measure that will be discussed in the next section.
- *Apotheek Breskens*: this recent case concerns a pharmacy in an isolated border region of the Netherlands that boycotts insurers' preference schemes for cheaper generic drugs by refusing to contract with them, forcing consumers to pay for their drugs directly and claim (whole or partial) restitution from their insurers.[27] Here the Healthcare Authority has used its interim measures powers with respect to SMP for the first time by imposing an obligation to deal with pending further investigations.

Finally vertical chains of integrated treatment for chronic diseases (including horizontal groupings) are being scrutinised at present. The measures under consideration do not just involve SMP but also (potentially) intervening in contract terms and the contracting process. The latter instrument will be discussed further below after a short diversion into the Community law implications of SMP in health care.

14.5.7 Compatibility with EU Competition Law?

As has been seen above the priorities of and general approach to SMP as identified by the Healthcare Authority are in line with general competition law. Nevertheless there is a question whether the SMP instrument as such breaches EU competition rules which provide that national rules are not allowed to be more strict than the EU regime. This discussion boils down to the question of whether these powers are in line with Article 3 of Regulation 1/2003. (The issue did not arise in relation to SMP in electronic communications because this is based on a harmonised EU regime, unlike the purely national SMP regime for health care in the Netherlands.) However there is an exception to this rule in relation to unilateral conduct which is thought to apply here.[28] This makes sense

[26] Decision of 18 June 2007, *AMM VieCurie Ziekenhuis*.

[27] Decision of 18 November 2009, *Menzis-Apotheek J.D. van Dalen*.

[28] Regulation 1/2003, *supra* n. 8, Article 3 sub 3.

because the ability to act independently is at the heart of any finding of SMP, and it is the ability to abuse this independence which the proportional obligations imposed are intended to forestall.

14.5.8 Intervening in Contract Terms and/or the Contracting Process

This power of the Healthcare Authority does not appear to have any precedents elsewhere. It can only be used in order to promote competition and/or in order to promote transparency of health care markets. In the pursuit of these objectives the NZa may either intervene directly in contracts, that is to say by setting and/or adjusting or striking out contract terms and conditions, or it may intervene in the contracting process, for example, by imposing an obligation to negotiate, to follow certain procurement rules, or to auction care. In addition to the objectives of promoting competition and/or transparency the main condition for the use of these powers is that structural problems are involved, although it is not yet clear if this means nationwide problems or only in particular markets.

The applications so far have been a regulation to increase contracting transparency in long-term care and a regulation introducing access obligations for electronic networks concerning the provision of health care (although literally 'facilitating' rather than 'imposing' access). The latter enables access to electronic networks under reasonable, objective, and non-discriminatory conditions for the purposes of exchanging patient records and medication records, facilitating electronic prescriptions as well as for the use of referral networks including access to information on waiting lists. This is intended to solve a nationwide problem of which two examples are pharmacists excluding entrants from the exchange of patient and medication records (which raised issues of patient safety as well as market entry), and hospitals excluding new entrants (specialised clinics) from referral networks used by general practitioners.

Although applying the power to intervene in contract terms and the contracting process in this way is clearly highly useful to facilitate entry in transition markets, the interpretation used by the Healthcare Authority to underpin the electronic networks′ regulation has not yet been tested in court. If it stands up in court (and there are good arguments to think that it should), other access issues may also come to the fore.

14.6 State Aid

In the interest of providing a full picture of the relationship between competition policy of health care liberalisation in the Netherlands, the state aid dimension will be covered briefly.

14.6.1 EU Involvement

As is described in greater detail in the chapter by De Vries in this book, a crucial state aid decision taken by the European Commission in 2005 in the context of risk equalisation is one of the pillars of the Dutch system.[29] As was mentioned above the Netherlands has introduced mandatory universal health insurance that is provided by exclusively private health insurers. These insurers operate subject to a set of obligations, notably to provide a legally defined minimum set of services, the duty to contract sufficient care and most importantly they are prohibited from applying risk selection to their consumers and, in line with this prohibition on risk selection, premium differentiation for the basic set of services is likewise prohibited.

To underpin this system the Netherlands has introduced a system of risk equalisation in order to avoid overt and/or covert risk selection and to promote competition on the merits (for example, efficiency and quality) instead. By compensating for an above average risk profile and doing so *ex ante* insurers are encouraged to improve their performance instead of refusing all other than healthy consumers (who, being healthy, would in a process of adverse selection not be interested in taking out insurance). In practice however there is an important element of ex post compensation as well, which is less ideal from a theoretical point of view as it constitutes a refund of costs actually incurred instead of risks engaged in, and hence compromises the incentive structure of the scheme, and, thereby, its purpose.[30]

As mentioned above, the funding for health insurance in the Netherlands is based on individual insurance premiums (50%) on the one hand, and based on income-related premiums withheld at base on the other, which covers the funding based on risk equalisation through a public fund (the remaining 50%).

This system was duly notified as a potential state aid and subjected to Commission scrutiny based on the four *Altmark* criteria.[31] It failed on the fourth condition, which requires the beneficiary undertaking to have an efficiency that is at least equivalent to that of a well run operator. Consequently the Commission next considered the scheme based on the Article 86(2) EC (now Article 106(2) TFEU) exception for services of general economic interest. In the absence of an express designation of a service of general economic interest, it was prepared to

[29] Decision of 3 May 2005 relating to State aid N 541/2004 and N 542/2004—The Netherlands—Risk equalisation scheme and retention of reserves.

[30] Cf., Ministry of Health, Welfare and Sport, Risk Insurance under the Health Insurance Act in The Netherlands, Summary of 7 July 2008 (original report August 2007).

[31] ECJ, Case C-280/00 *Altmark Trans GmbH and Regierungspräsidium Magdeburg* v. *Nahverkehrsgesellschaft Altmark GmbH, and Oberbundesanwalt beim Bundesverwaltungericht (Altmark)* [2003] *ECR* I-7747.

accept that the investiture could be derived from the general legal context in the Netherlands,[32] emphasising the minimum set of services and the fact that premium differentiation was prohibited. Following the necessity and proportionality test (and in spite of the ex post equalisation also involved) the system was accepted as falling within the scope of the exemption.

By way of evaluation it would seem that the Netherlands took a huge gamble by proceeding in this way as 50% of Dutch hospital financing was at risk in the Commission's decision. Possibly this is one explanation for the Commission's circumspect approach. A much sounder approach in Community law would have been designating a proportional service of general economic interest explicitly, and a much sounder approach on the merits would have been to eliminate the ex post compensation as much as possible. The latter is currently under consideration by the Dutch Ministry of Health and would appear to be a good idea from both perspectives.

14.6.2 Aid: Recent Developments at National Level

Perhaps surprisingly, the Healthcare Authority, although a sector-specific Netherlands' Competition Authority, is itself in the business of doling out state aid. This has not been widely recognised and in fact so far state aid in health care in the Netherlands is usually not notified. The reason why the Healthcare Authority is involved is because it is still responsible for fixing the budgets of hospitals for the 65% of health care services that are not yet liberalised. To provide aid to struggling hospitals it fixes the budget at a higher level, accordingly imposing higher financial outlays on the insurers involved who are then compensated ex post from the risk equalisation fund. Because (as was just discussed) the latter is financed by income-based (collective) premiums state aid would in most cases appear to be involved.

Increasing awareness of this problem has led to several developments. In the first place there is discussion about formally defining services of general economic interest (i.e., by law), which would notably include defining the dimension of 'continuity' of care. Safeguarding continuity is generally the argument invoked to justify providing aid but objective criteria do not exist yet—which leads to ad hoc solutions under political pressure. Most likely elements of ambulance services and emergency services will be defined as key from a continuity perspective, but not all hospitals services, as is *de facto* the case at present.

Further ambitions include the introduction of an early warning system, that is, monitoring which health care providers are in dire straits financially so

---

[32] ECJ, Case C-393/92 *Municipality of Almelo* et al. v. *NV Energiebedrijf IJsselmij* [1994] *ECR* I-1477. Cf., CFI, Case T-289/03 *British United Provident Association Ltd (BUPA), BUPA Insurance Ltd, BUPA Ireland Ltd* v. *Commission of the European Communities* [2008] *ECR* II-81. Annotated by Sauter (2009a), p. 269.

intervention may be possible before they collapse under the weight of their debts, and introducing modalities of intervention that combine the provision of continuity with competitive incentives, for example, auctioning of care or of capacity. Reasons to be concerned about state aid in a liberalisation context are obviously the resulting barriers to entry, and the distortions of competition involved: poor performance is rewarded, and thereby well-performing competitors are penalised, all at the ultimate expense of the consumer/taxpayer. It is therefore crucial that policy in this field is improved.

14.7 Conclusions

The arguments in favour of a regulatory framework to facilitate competition in health care markets are strong, given the existence of pervasive market failures, the fact that liberalisation is taking place step by step, so we are dealing not just with a transition market but with a drawn out transition process, and given the serious risk of anticompetitive effects between the liberalised and non-liberalised sections. These are among the reasons why the Netherlands has adopted a dual system of competition policy in the health care sector, that is, both general and sector-specific competition policy. Given the need for a coherent application of sector-specific competition policy with other regulatory duties in the sector this task has been attributed to the Healthcare Authority, which enjoys an independent status as regards its decisions in individual cases, a degree of independence comparable to the general Netherlands' Competition Authority.

Concurrence between the two regimes is managed by intensive inter-institutional cooperation, by a priority rule favouring the Netherlands' Competition Authority on the interpretation of competition concepts, thereby safeguarding the coherence with EU competition thinking, and a second priority rule favouring the Healthcare Authority where enforcement is concerned—thereby safeguarding the coherence of sectoral policy for health care as a whole.

Because sector-specific competition policy is largely about promoting entry and competition, there is a focus on exclusion not exploitation, selling power not buying power and horizontal not vertical restraints. This is in line with general competition policy trends. A difference is that the Healthcare Authority attributes more importance to even a minor degree of competition remaining in a market (as a possible stepping-stone for entry), to potential competition and to a dynamic view of the market more generally. The Healthcare Authority also appears more sensitive than the Netherlands' Competition Authority is to the effects on market structure as a result of merger activity. This is a logical consequence of the former's broad powers and responsibilities for the health care sector that require a holistic perspective.

The interaction between competition and regulation is complex but so far appears to favour application of general regulation instead of pursuing individual competition cases. This is also because at least initially the focus is most likely to be on competition problems that are widespread, and hence require general solutions such as regulation of contract conditions and contracting processes, rather than those that are more individualised and incidental (unless they are of particular and exemplary gravity). There should be more scope for individual cases now that new methods for market definition have been developed. In any event, for the time being it will remain an open question whether the 'Dutch model' of twin tracks of general and sector-specific competition policy in the health care sector will be successful. Much would appear to depend on the scope that the administrative courts in the Netherlands will be prepared to accord to the Healthcare Authority in the first cases on SMP and intervention in contract terms and the contracting process.

Acknowledgments I am grateful to Misja Mikkers and Ilaria Mosca for helpful comments. All views presented here are personal.

References

Arrow KJ (1963) Uncertainty and the welfare economics of medical care. Am Econ Rev 80
Canoy M, Sauter W (2010) Hospital mergers in the Netherlands and the public interest: What standard for merger control? Eur Compet Law Rev 377
Capps C et al (2003) Competition and market power in option demand markets. Rand J Econ 34
Kemp R, Severijnen A (2009) Ex post analysis of the actual effects of a Dutch hospital merger on prices: a case study. In: Proceedings of the Conference Ex-post evaluation of competition policy, Mannheim, Germany, 3–4 June 2009 (Mannheim)
Maskin E, Tirole J (2004) The politician and the judge: accountability in government. Am Econ Rev 94
Sauter W (2009a) Annotation. CML Rev 46
Sauter W (2009b) Is the general consumer interest a source of legitimacy for healthcare regulation? An analysis of the Dutch experience. European Journal of Consumer Law/Revue Européenne de Droit de la Consommation 8(2–3)
Varkevisser M (2009) Patient choice, competition and antitrust enforcement in Dutch hospital markets. Optima, Rotterdam
Varkevisser M et al (2008) Defining hospital markets for antitrust enforcement: new approaches and their applicability to The Netherlands. Health Econ Policy Law 3(1)

Chapter 15
The Elusive Ideal of Market Competition in United States' Health Care

Nathan Cortez

Contents

15.1 Introduction

What role does market competition play in the United States' health care system, and what might the United States (US) and the European Union (EU) learn from each other's experiences? Market competition remains a persistent but elusive ideal in American health care. More than its peers, the US health care system looks to market-inspired theories and policy instruments to solve its problems. But decades of policies promoting this ideal have not given Americans the health system they

N. Cortez (✉)
Dedman School of Law, Southern Methodist University, Dallas, Texas, USA
e-mail: ncortez@smu.edu

J. W. van de Gronden et al. (eds.), *Health Care and EU Law*, Legal Issues of Services of General Interest, DOI: 10.1007/978-90-6704-728-9_15,

desire.[1] Most recognize that equity is not what markets provide,[2] yet markets have also failed to produce a more efficient US health care system. Ironically, the ideal of market competition has both driven and undermined contemporary health reform efforts in the United States. Even reforms designed to stimulate more competitive markets have faced considerable resistance because the political branches could not agree how to balance the public and private sectors.[3]

Markets versus government remains the 'basic dividing line and dominant theme in American health policy'.[4] Academics and policymakers have long struggled to identify the appropriate role for markets in health care.[5] And there remains 'deep social ambivalence about whether health care should be considered a public good or a commodity'.[6]

Of course, the United States is not alone in this struggle. Because there has never been a purely public or private health care system,[7] every country must determine the appropriate relationship between markets and government in health care. Even countries with robust public health care systems are trying to use markets to squeeze more efficiency out of their systems without jeopardizing other priorities, such as universal coverage or solidarity. For example, Canada recently considered whether to open its public system to more private sector participation.[8] Most countries labor to find the appropriate role for market competition in health care.

This chapter explores how the ideal of market competition both drives US health policy and sets it apart. I begin by reviewing how the US health system remains an international outlier, examining so-called 'American exceptionalism' in health care. Second, I discuss how several EU Member States have embraced market instruments, and explain how these efforts qualitatively differ from US efforts. Third, I evaluate notable market-based trends in the United States, such as managed competition, privatization, and consumer-driven health care, and describe how these models have failed to live up to their promises. Fourth, this chapter discusses how contemporary health reform in the United States has been both driven and undermined by market ideals. I conclude by considering the appropriate role for competition in health care, given its many limitations.

---

[1] White (2007), pp. 395, 434.

[2] Pauly (1998). On the whole, US economists seem less comfortable than economists in Europe talking about justice and equity in health care. Callahan and Wasunna (2006), p. 10.

[3] Cutler and Keenan (2008), p. 472.

[4] White (2007), at pp. 395, 396; Hyman (2006), p. 265. Of course, the 'market' and 'market mechanisms' can mean many things, including different instruments that bear on the behavior of different health care actors and institutions. See Callahan and Wasunna (2006), at p. 4.

[5] For a particularly insightful analysis nearly thirty years ago, see Rosenblatt (1981), p. 1067.

[6] Hunter (2008), p. 20.

[7] Chernichovsky (1995), p. 340; Callahan and Wasunna (2006), at pp. 41, 92.

[8] *Chaoulli* v. *Quebec* (Attorney General), [2005] 1 S.C.R. 791 (Can.); Bobinski (2008), pp. 355–369; Flood, et al. (2005), pp. 257–277.

15.2 American Exceptionalism in Health Care

The US health care system is exceptional. So-called 'American exceptionalism', the idea that the United States is unique in the world, has been controversial since Alexis de Tocqueville published his observations in the 1830s.[9] But the health policy world generally agrees that the US health care system is singular.[10] Among developed countries, the United States is the only one without a single health care system organized around 'a common philosophy about coverage, access, and cost'.[11] Ours is a fragmented pastiche of health insurers, providers, and facilities, each of which is regulated primarily by states rather than the federal government.[12] Indeed, calling ours a 'system' is charitable; its defining feature may be its extreme decentralization.[13]

So precisely how is the US health care system exceptional? Health care systems are generally evaluated along three dimensions: cost, quality, and access.[14] As one scholar notes, 'enhancing quality, lowering cost, and broadening access' is the 'holy grail' or 'holy trinity' of health care policy.[15] Compared to its peers, the US health care system does not fare particularly well along any of these three dimensions.

The first and increasingly central criterion is cost. How expensive is the health care system? What does it spend *per capita*, and what percentage of the economy does health spending occupy? The US health care system is by far the most expensive in the world, both in aggregate and *per capita* terms. In aggregate terms, the United States spends as much on health care as every other nation in the world *combined*. In 2007, worldwide health care spending reached around $4.1 trillion, and the United States alone accounted for over *half* of that amount ($2.3 trillion).[16] Moreover, most predict that US spending will continue to rise, potentially to as much $4.3 trillion by 2018—equal to *total* worldwide health spending today.[17] Unsurprisingly, the United States spends a much larger portion of its gross domestic

---

9 See, e.g., Schuck and Wilson (2008), p. x.

10 'Volumes have been written on the topic of American exceptionalism in health policy'. Jost (2004), p. 437.

11 Cutler and Keenan (2008), at p. 449.

12 Bloche (2009), pp. 452–454. Of course, the same might be said about the EU, as health care remains a competency of the Member States.

13 Brown (2008), p. 325; Cutler and Keenan (2008), at p. 451.

14 Cortez (2008), p. 95.

15 Hyman and Silver (2001), p. 1452.

16 World Health Organization (2007); Centers for Medicare and Medicaid Services, Office of the Actuary, National Health Statistics Group, *National Health Expenditures Aggregate, Per Capita Amounts, Percent Distribution, and Average Annual Percent Growth, by Source of Funds: Selected Calendar Years 1960–2008* (2008), at Table 1.

17 Centers for Medicare and Medicaid Services, Office of the Actuary, National Health Statistics Group, *National Health Expenditures and Selected Economic Indicators, Levels and Annual Percentage Change: Calendar Years 2003–2018* (2008), at Table 1.

product (GDP) on health care than other countries. In 2008, health care spending accounted for 16.2% of the US economy, and experts predict it could reach 20.4% by 2018.[18] By contrast, health spending occupies significant but much more modest portions of the economies in Germany (10.6% of its GDP), Canada (10.1%), the Netherlands (9.8%), Denmark (9.8%), Spain (8.5%), and the United Kingdom (8.4%).[19] Moreover, US health care is exceptionally expensive in *per capita* terms. In 2007, US residents spent an average of $7,290 on health care, roughly twice what their counterparts spent in Canada ($3,895), Germany ($3,588), the Netherlands ($3,837), Denmark ($3,512), the United Kingdom ($2,992), and Spain ($2,671).[20] Again, experts largely project US spending to rise,[21] though other countries certainly also struggle with rising costs.

The second criterion for evaluating health systems is quality. Does the health care system provide necessary, appropriate, and high quality care? Does it ensure that health care professionals, facilities, and products meet minimum quality standards? What results does the system generate, and how healthy are residents? The US system does not provide high quality care commensurate with its spending. Although the 'quality' of health care is notoriously difficult to measure, most metrics show that the United States lags behind its peers. For example, in 2000 the World Health Organization (WHO) famously and somewhat controversially ranked 193 countries by the quality and performance of their health systems.[22] The United States ranked 37th in overall performance[23] and 24th in the overall health of its population.[24] More specific comparisons show that the United States does not score well compared to other developed countries on several health-related metrics, such as life expectancy and infant mortality rates, which are admittedly imperfect barometers of quality.[25] Yet, virtually every comparison of

---

[18] Centers for Medicare and Medicaid Services, *supra* n. 16, at Table 1; Centers for Medicare and Medicaid Services, *supra* n. 17, at Table 1.

[19] Organization for Economic Cooperation and Development, *OECD Health Data 2009: Statistics and Indicators for 30 Countries* (2009) (citing 2007 data).

[20] Ibid.

[21] The potential causes for high health care spending in the United States are many, and are beyond the scope of this chapter. For excellent discussions, see Jost (2007), pp. 174–177, and Cutler and Keenan (2008), at pp. 450–454.

[22] WHO (2000).

[23] Ibid., at p. 155. The WHO measured 'performance' through eight criteria, including how responsive and fair the health system is, how healthy residents are, and health spending per capita. Commentators from the United States often criticize these criteria as being unfairly weighted against the US health care system.

[24] Ibid. at p. 176. The WHO measured 'health attainment' by comparing disability-adjusted life expectancy (DALE) years between countries.

[25] Cutler and Keenan (2008), at p. 452, 453 (noting that the United States ranked 23rd out of 30 countries measured in life expectancy at birth).

'quality' shines an unfavorable light on the US health care system.[26] The US system does certain things very well. It is good at providing innovative, extraordinary, life-saving treatments. But it struggles to provide basic care and prevent common illnesses.[27] As two notable scholars conclude, 'there is precious little evidence that the United States does better than other countries in any material outcome'.[28]

The third criterion is access to care. How difficult is it for people of ordinary means to access health care goods and services? What percentage of the public has health insurance, and what percentage can obtain basic care? How long must patients wait for care? Does the system make care reasonably available to those who need it? Again, despite ample spending, access to health care in the United States is exceptionally erratic. In 2008, 46.3 million people lacked health insurance in the United States,[29] and undoubtedly more have lost insurance during the recent recession. Another 25 million Americans are 'underinsured', defined as those with insurance that requires relatively high cost-sharing obligations (such as premiums, deductibles, and other out-of-pocket spending) relative to income.[30] Although some argue that the uninsured can always get care somewhere, the uninsured do face consequences—in 2002 the Institute of Medicine estimated that 18,000 adults aged 25–64 die each year from treatable conditions because they lack insurance.[31] The United States is the only modern industrialized democracy that relies primarily on private, voluntary health insurance[32]; every other such country approximates universal coverage.[33] United States' residents who are not offered or cannot afford health insurance typically go uninsured. Although it is true that the uninsured do not lack access to all necessary care,[34] they must rely on an unorganized patchwork of 'safety net' providers with precarious funding.[35] Moreover, there are significant disparities in access to care and the quality of care received depending on one's race, ethnicity, and socioeconomic status.[36] Even among the insured, there is

---

26 See, e.g., Hussey et al. (2003), pp. 89–99 (comparing the US health care system to four others using 19 quality criteria, such as survival rates from common procedures); American College of Physicians (2008), pp. 1–21; Docteur and Berenson (2009); Commonwealth Fund Commission on a High Performance Health System (2008).

27 Nolte and McKee (2008), p. 58.

28 Cutler and Keenan (2008), at p. 453.

29 DeNavas-Walt et al. (2009), pp. 20, 21 (Table 7).

30 Schoen et al. (2008), p. w298 (web exclusive). Moreover, Families USA (2007) estimated that during 2006–2007, up to 89.5 million people under age 65 lacked health insurance for at least one month. Families USA (2007).

31 Institute of Medicine of the National Academies (2002), p. 165.

32 Jost (2004), at p. 433.

33 Jost (2007), at p. 178.

34 Ibid., at p. 2.

35 See Institute of Medicine of the National Academies (2000).

36 American College of Physicians (2008), at p. 2.

significant variation in health care costs, quality, and access.[37] Although no country's health care system is completely equitable—wealthier residents tend to access higher quality care more quickly than non-wealthy residents virtually everywhere, the United States is alone among developed countries in allocating health care *primarily* based on one's ability to pay.[38] For decades, US policymakers have tried unsuccessfully to approximate universal insurance coverage.

The US health care system is exceptional in countless other ways. It spends markedly more on administrative costs than any other system.[39] Its medical malpractice compensation system is notorious for being excessive and punitive.[40] And it uses 'one of the most regressive approaches to financing of any country in the world'.[41]

In sum, the US health care system is exceptional: exceptionally expensive, exceptionally inefficient, and exceptionally uneven in distributing care to its population. As Jost concludes, other countries demonstrate that they can 'provide universal access at much lower cost without sacrificing quality'.[42] Indeed, the experience of other countries 'tends to show that in this one particular corner of the economy, government often outperforms the private sector'.[43] Yet the US health care system still clings to the ideal that market competition can solve its problems.

15.3 Market Competition in Europe: Proceeding from a Different Baseline

Despite its exceptional nature, the US health care system is far from the only one to embrace market competition. Virtually every health care system in the EU relies on at least *some* market-based tools and incentives, typically to reduce costs, enhance efficiency, and give patients greater choice.[44] Indeed, health reforms in

---

37 Ibid., at p. 1.

38 Jost (2007), at p. 178, 182 (noting that in most other countries 'health care resources are distributed primarily on the basis of other criteria, though rarely is wealth irrelevant'.).

39 American College of Physicians (2008), at p. 9; Cutler and Keenan (2008), at p. 452; Jost (2007), at pp. 175–176.

40 Studdert et al. (2004), p. 283; Leflar (2009), p. 3. Note that despite repeated declarations that the US medical malpractice system significantly contributes to high health care spending, most studies suggest that it contributes no more than 5% to overall spending, even when factoring in the costs of defensive medicine (e.g., ordering tests and procedures motivated by the fear of malpractice liability rather than a judgment that the procedure is medically appropriate or necessary). Cutler and Keenan (2008), at p. 453; Jost (2007), at p. 175.

41 Jost (2007), at p. 191.

42 Ibid., at p. 188.

43 Ibid., at p. 201.

44 Callahan and Wasunna (2006), at p. 90, 92.

Member States have generally converged around the common trend of introducing market-based incentives.[45]

Of course, some Member States embrace market incentives in health care more than others. For example, Callahan and Wasunna have identified certain States as 'market rejectors' (Denmark, France, Ireland, Italy, Sweden, and the United Kingdom), and others as 'market accommodators' (Belgium, Germany, Israel, the Netherlands, and Switzerland), with others falling in between.[46] Market 'accommodators' generally try to utilize market instruments without sacrificing principles of solidarity or universal coverage.[47] But even the market 'rejectors' (States that historically reject broader, more invasive market mechanisms in health care) generally 'accept some limited role for the market'.[48]

The 'accommodators' have embraced market instruments in several ways. Most notably, the Dutch health care system relies on individual insurance mandates and competition between private insurers (often referred to as 'regulated competition'), building on theories of managed competition developed originally by American economist Enthoven.[49] The Dutch Health Insurance Act, which entered into force on 1 January 2006, requires private managed care organizations to compete annually for individual patients, implementing concepts like selective contracting, using general practitioners as gatekeepers, and vertically integrating with providers.[50] The Dutch system is also notable for the government's efforts to provide objective price and quality information to consumers.[51] Likewise, reforms in Germany, with one of the most expensive health care systems in the world, have tried to encourage competition among both providers and the sickness funds that pay for them.[52] Switzerland, another expensive system, has also encouraged competition among its insurance funds.[53] In fact, the Dutch and Swiss health care systems both have inspired US reform discussions.[54] Thus, although only the

45 Ibid., at p. 91.

46 Ibid., at pp. 91–108.

47 Ibid., at p. 92.

48 Ibid., at p. 91.

49 Ven, van de and Schut (2008), pp. 771, 773–774 (noting that the Netherlands 'is the first country that is consistently implementing Alain Enthoven's model of national health insurance based on managed competition in the private sector'); Callahan and Wasunna (2006), at pp. 43, 101–103. Enthoven originally presented his views in a 1977 memo to the US Secretary of Health, Education, and Welfare, subsequently published in two parts in *The New England Journal of Medicine*. See Rosenblatt (1981), at p. 1076 n. 34. See also the chapter by Sauter in this book.

50 Ven, van de and Schut (2008). Importantly, the Dutch government finances many of the most expensive and least affordable health care goods and services, such as long-term nursing care, hospitalizations over a certain duration, and inpatient mental health care. Jost (2007), at p. 193.

51 Ven, van de and Schut (2008), at p. 780 (noting that the Dutch government established a website to provide consumers information about insurers, at http://www.kiesbeter.nl).

52 Freeman (1998b), pp. 179–191; Callahan and Wasunna (2006), at pp. 100, 101. See the chapter by Welti in this book.

53 Callahan and Wasunna (2006), at 103, 104.

54 Harris (2007).

Dutch system relies primarily on private insurers, other systems in the EU implement market-inspired policies.

Even the market 'rejectors' have experimented with market instruments in health care. Sweden—with its robust welfare state and general wariness of market influences in health care—has tried easing cost pressures by (i) encouraging hospitals to compete with one another, (ii) utilizing private providers, and (iii) shifting costs to patients via co-payments.[55] Italy has tried to encourage equal competition among public and private providers and, like other countries, has tried to use co-payments to contain costs.[56] Denmark, which has one of the most comprehensive health systems in Europe, increasingly relies on private supplemental insurance.[57] Likewise, 80% of the population in France relies on supplemental private health insurance.[58] Even the United Kingdom's National Health Service (NHS), a well-known paradigm for public, centralized health care, has implemented market-based reforms. Prime Ministers Thatcher and Major both encouraged 'internal competition' among NHS hospitals.[59] The NHS has also tried to encourage managed competition by introducing primary care trusts to pay for care.[60]

Despite these examples, and there are many more, the United States and EU Member States have implemented market-based tools from very different baselines. While the United States is alone among developed countries in relying primarily on private, voluntary health insurance, Member States generally cover everyone, usually through national or social health insurance.[61] Historically, the arguments for more competition in European health care systems 'overwhelmingly took for granted that universal entitlement to health insurance was a given'.[62] Even the Netherlands, with its entrepreneurial traditions and reliance on private insurers, operates from the baseline of solidarity.[63] In contrast, there has been significant disagreement in the United States whether universal coverage is 'desirable and implementable'.[64]

These baselines derive from different priorities. Although every country generally aims to provide quality care to everyone for a reasonable price, the US

---

[55] Diderichsen (2000), pp. 931–935; Saltman (1998), pp. 164–178; Callahan and Wasunna (2006), at pp. 95–96.

[56] Callahan and Wasunna (2006), at p. 98 (noting that Italy has some of the highest co-payments in the EU (30%), although nearly half the population does not have to pay them).

[57] Callahan and Wasunna (2006), at pp. 98–99.

[58] Ibid., at p. 99.

[59] White (2007), at p. 401. The NHS 'survived the Thatcher years', when railroads, airlines, and other public services were privatized. Callahan and Wasunna (2006), at p. 93.

[60] Callahan and Wasunna (2006), at p. 94 (noting that market-based reforms in the United Kingdom have ebbed and flowed with Labour party); Ranade (1998b), pp. 101–118.

[61] Jost (2006), at pp. 433–434. Note, however, that like the United States, the Dutch system relies primarily on private insurers.

[62] Marmor (1998), p. 68.

[63] Callahan and Wasunna (2006), at p. 103; Robinson (1998), pp. 147–162.

[64] Marmor (1998), at p. 68.

health care system places a higher priority on independence and entrepreneurship than its peers.[65] Patients are responsible for themselves. Americans generally trust private industry and distrust the government to solve problems.[66] Unsurprisingly, our health care system reflects these values.

In contrast, health systems in the EU are generally based on social solidarity, the belief that citizens are responsible to each other, not just themselves, and that all citizens should have equal access to care, regardless of their ability to pay.[67] There is less distrust of government and less faith that the market can solve all problems. Indeed, '[s]olidarity is fundamentally a rejection of markets as the best means to distributing health care goods and services'.[68] Logically, EU health systems reflect these values.[69]

Among Member States, market-based reforms are intended to reduce costs, increase efficiency, and give patients greater choice—all pragmatic goals. In the United States, proponents tout the same pragmatic goals, but also cling to market-based solutions on ideological grounds, seeking to increase the private sector's role at the expense of the public sector. Thus, market-based solutions are propelled in the United States much more by ideological forces.[70]

Yet, as in the United States, health care systems in the EU (varied as they are) must determine the extent to which health care is an economic, commercial endeavor versus a non-economic, public good. Article 168 of the Treaty on the Functioning of the European Union (TFEU) states that health care is the responsibility of Member States. However, EU law, enunciated through Treaties, Directives, Regulations, and landmark decisions by the European Court of Justice (ECJ), prohibits Member States from restricting the free movement of goods, services, persons, and capital within the internal common market, and bans anti-competitive or protectionist arrangements.[71] Thus, EU law sometimes requires

---

[65] Gawande (2009); Jost (2007), at p. 15 (noting that the US health care system typically scores high when evaluating creativity and innovation).

[66] Jost (2007), at p. 117.

[67] Newdick (2008), pp. 844–845 ('Solidarity animates the European idea of health care to this day'.)(internal quotations omitted); Callahan and Wasunna describe 'solidarity' as 'a communal or communitarian moral promise' rather than a publicly recognized right expressed in more individualistic terms. Callahan and Wasunna (2006), at pp. 90, 105. Newdick also contrasts solidarity from 'a modern rights based approach'. Newdick (2008), at p. 845.

[68] Jost (2007), at p. 172.

[69] Callahan and Wasunna (2006), at p. 87.

[70] Ibid., at p. 109.

[71] Several articles of the Treaty on the Functioning of the European Union prevent Member States from restricting the free movement of goods (Articles 34–36 TFEU), persons (Articles 45–48 TFEU), services (Articles 56–62 TFEU), and capital (Articles 63–66 TFEU). Two Articles prohibit anti-competitive arrangements (Articles 101 and 102 TFEU). See Treaty of Lisbon amending the Treaty on the European Union and the Treaty Establishing the European Community, 13 December 2007, *OJ* (C 306) 1, 10, 42; see also Gronden, van de (2008), pp. 705–760.

Member States to consider whether internal health policy decisions restrict free movement or are otherwise anti-competitive.

However, as van de Gronden notes:

> it is difficult and sometimes nearly impossible to draw a distinction between elements of the internal market and features connected with the organization and delivery of health care.[72]

Although EU law dictates that States shall retain responsibility for managing services of general interest like health care and social security, judicial opinions have circumscribed this authority in several high-profile cases by applying free movement and competition requirements.[73] For example, a series of landmark court rulings by the ECJ has held that Member States have limited authority to prevent their residents from traveling to other Member States for non-hospital care, or even to require prior authorization before reimbursing residents for that care back home.[74] These rulings are affecting the basic tradeoffs Member States make in their health care systems, including decisions regarding hospital capacity, waiting lists, and even whether to cover new treatments.[75]

The ECJ is drawing some fine lines here by developing a complicated and technical set of tests for determining the circumstances under which national health care systems violate free movement and competition law. Indeed, in the competition cases, it seems that the more Member States embrace principles of market competition, rather than solidarity, in their health systems, the less claim they have that health care is a non-economic activity not subject to the EU's competition laws.[76] This distinction is the biggest grey area for EU health care systems,[77] reflecting perhaps the broader tensions between economic and social integration in Europe.

---

[72] Gronden, van de (2008), at p. 707.

[73] Ibid.; Hatzopoulos (2008), pp. 761–803; Newdick (2008), at pp. 844–867.

[74] ECJ, Case C-158/96 *Kohll* v. *Union des Caisses de Maladie* [1998] *ECR* I-1931; ECJ, Case C-120/95 *Decker* v. *Caisse de Maladie des Employés Privés* [1998] *ECR* I-1831; Case C-157-99 *B.S.M. Geraets-Smits* v. *Stichting Ziekenfonds VGZ and Peerbooms* v. *Stichting CZ Groep Zorgverzekeringen* [2001] *ECR* I-5473; ECJ, Case C-385/99 *Müller-Fauré* v. *Onderlinge Waarborgmaatschappij OZ Zorgverzekeringen UA, and E.E.M. van Riet* v. *Onderlinge Waarborgmaatschappij ZAO Zorgverzekeringen* [2003] *ECR* I-4509; ECJ, Case C-372/04 *Watts* v. *Bedford Primary Care Trust* [2006] *ECR* I-4325; ECJ, Case C-368/98 *Vanbraekel* v. *Alliance Nationale des Mutualités Chrétiennes* [2001] *ECR* I-5363.

[75] Gronden, van de (2008), at pp. 717, 724–725; Newdick (2008).

[76] Gronden, van de (2008), at pp. 740–742, 751 ('[The ECJ has] scrutinized how much room a national social security scheme leaves for competition in the implementation of a social security scheme, and what role the principle of solidarity plays. When a social security scheme is almost completely based on solidarity, the institution managing the scheme cannot be regarded as an undertaking [subject to competition law]. In contrast, if the implementation of a social security scheme is based on a mix of competition and solidarity elements, the institutions concerned do perform an economic activity and can, as a result, be seen as an undertaking [subject to competition law]'.); Hatzopoulos (2002), pp. 710–713.

[77] Hatzopolous (2008).

Thus, although health care systems in the United States and EU both rely on market instruments, these jurisdictions generally proceed from very different baselines. In Europe, market competition enhances more cohesive, comprehensive systems; in the United States, it forms the philosophical foundation. Nevertheless, the United States need not look to Europe or even Canada for examples of efficient, 'government-run' health care (the US Veterans Health Administration) has been hailed as our most successful health care system after major reforms over the past 10–15 years,[78] providing perhaps the most recent domestic example of how non-market alternatives can outperform market instruments in health care.

15.4 Market-based Instruments and Their Limitations

Over the past few decades, the United States' health care system has embraced several market-based techniques to address its problems.[79] However, these tools generally have failed to reduce spending or the number of uninsured.

First, the United States' health care system was transformed in the 1980 and 1990s by 'managed competition', which shifted away from incentives provided by traditional indemnity insurance and fee-for-service medicine, relying instead on competition among insurers to incentivize physicians and other providers to make wiser, more prudent spending decisions.[80] Managed care organizations such as health maintenance organizations (HMOs) began using several tools to lower spending, including: selective contracting with providers; using primary care physicians as gatekeepers to limit access to more expensive specialty care; shifting more financial risks to patients and providers; and using utilization reviews to verify that treatments were 'medically necessary'.[81]

In the 1990s, HMOs, PPOs, and other incarnations gradually supplanted conventional indemnity insurance.[82] Evidence suggests that managed competition actually helped control spending in the United States between 1993 and 1997, although some argue that this was due more to panic by providers anticipating managed care reforms than to organizations actually managing care.[83] But despite

[78] Longman (2007); Jost (2007), at p. 192.

[79] Callahan and Wasunna (2006), at p. 35 ('Market thought made a great political leap in the 1980s and 1990s. Health care had become an obvious arena to test its applications and implications').

[80] Jost (2007), at p. 18; White (2007), at p. 398; Ranade (1998a), pp. 6, 7.

[81] White (2007), at p. 402, 403; Ranade (1998a), at pp. 6, 7; Cutler and Keenan (2008), at p. 469–470.

[82] White (2007), at p. 410 (Table 2).

[83] Ibid., at pp. 430, 431; Callahan and Wasunna (2006), at pp. 75–77, 206, 207 (managed care was 'an economic success and a political failure', meaning that it successfully suppressed costs, but was unpopular politically, largely because it constrained patient choice) (quoting Robinson (2001), p. 2622).

the decade-long shift toward managed care, spending has continued to rise dramatically since 1997.[84] Moreover, the managed care 'revolution' also failed to reduce the number of uninsured in the United States, which jumped from 34.7 million in 1990 to 46.3 million in 2008.[85] Thus, although managed care introduced several market-based innovations to the US health care system, these innovations generally failed to lower spending or reduce the number of uninsured.[86] Finally, as policymakers and academics on both sides of the political spectrum acknowledge, managed 'competition' requires extensive government regulation and aggressive enforcement of antitrust laws to work.[87]

The second major market-based trend in US health care system has been privatization: increasing the private sector's role in health care and reducing the government's.[88] In most developed countries, health care is traditionally viewed as a public good rather than a commodity subject to the vagaries of the market. The US view differs. Indeed, the long history of American medicine has pointed toward the 'coming of the corporation'.[89] Proponents of privatization believe that private businesses can insure patients, run hospitals, and provide health care more efficiently than the public sector.

Many hospitals have transitioned from not-for-profit to for-profit enterprises.[90] Physicians have become more entrepreneurial, establishing physician-owned hospitals, surgery centers, and laboratories, all of which have proliferated in recent years.[91] But rather than reduce spending, privatization and entrepreneurialism have encouraged a complex web of financial relationships between physicians, hospitals, pharmaceutical companies, and other income-generating ventures. In fact, federal and state governments have sewn together a complicated patchwork of laws that govern financial conflicts of interest by providers, most notably the federal self-referral and anti-kickback statutes.[92]

Even Medicare, the federal health insurance program for the elderly and chronically disabled,[93] has become more privatized in recent years, despite evidence that Medicare generally outperforms private insurers.[94] Indeed, Medicare frequently finds itself as 'the battleground of the market versus government

---

[84] White (2007), at p. 407 (noting that except between 1993 and 1997, managed care reforms failed to control costs as well as Medicare); Cutler and Keenan (2008), at p. 470.

[85] DeNavas-Walt et al. (2009), at p. 59 (Table C-1). The percentage of uninsured went from 13.9% in 1990 to 15.4% in 2008.

[86] White (2007), at p. 407, 416.

[87] Marmor (1998), at pp. 56, 57.

[88] However, as Richard Freeman notes, 'privatization' and 'marketization' can be distinct phenomena. Freeman (1998), at p. 190.

[89] Starr (1982), pp. 420–449.

[90] Callahan and Wasunna (2006), at pp. 78, 79.

[91] White (2007), at p. 425; Gawande (2009).

[92] 42 U.S.C. §§ 1320a-7b(b), 1395nn.

[93] Cutler and Keenan (2008), at p. 455.

[94] White (2007), at p. 432.

struggle'.[95] Since its inception in 1965, Medicare has delegated responsibilities to private insurers, and Congress has explicitly incorporated private insurers into Medicare.[96] For example, Congress has tried to encourage beneficiaries to receive their Medicare benefits through a private HMO, first through Medicare Part C, then through Medicare+Choice, and later Medicare Advantage.[97] Although private HMOs were supposed to control costs better than traditional Medicare's fee-for-service model, these efforts have proven to be incredibly expensive and almost complete failures.[98]

More recently, when Congress created a new Medicare prescription drug benefit in 2003, it entrusted private companies to run these new plans, believing that elderly Medicare beneficiaries would shop online and compare plans that competed for customers.[99] The thinly-veiled goal was 'to privatize as much of the drug benefit as possible'.[100] Today, Medicare beneficiaries have to choose between more than 2,400 plans offering a staggering variety of co-payments, drug prices, and formularies.[101] Relying on the private sector has not saved Medicare money: the prescription drug legislation gave private insurers $46 billion in incentives to participate, and cost $134 billion over initial estimates.[102] Thus, privatization has also failed to reduce spending.[103]

Third, free-market advocates have touted consumer-driven health plans (CDHPs) as a panacea for the US spending crisis. Consumer-driven theorists claim they can cut spending by requiring patients to spend their own money more wisely (rather than insurers'), thereby reducing demand for care and eliminating waste.[104] CDHPs generally use high deductibles that require patients to pay for most routine care until the high deductible has been met. For example, a family may have to spend $5,000 out-of-pocket before the insurance policy begins to cover expenses. These CDHPs are usually combined with tax-exempt health or medical savings

---

[95] Oberlander (2003); Callahan and Wasunna (2006), at pp. 83–85.

[96] Hess (1968), pp. 119–122; Field and Stefanacci (2007), pp. 208–210.

[97] Field and Stefanacci (2007), at pp. 208, 209. Note that enrollment among Medicare beneficiaries was never particularly high, beginning with 8% of beneficiaries in 1995 and peaking at 16% in 1999-2000 before declining back to 11% in 2003. Callahan and Wasunna (2006), at p. 84.

[98] Callahan and Wasunna (2006), at pp. 207, 208; Jost (2007), at p. 201 (noting that the government has dumped billions subsidizing uncompetitive private Medicare Advantage plans).

[99] Medicare Prescription Drug, Improvement, and Modernization Act of 2003, Pub. L. No. 108–173, 117 Stat. 2066.

[100] Callahan and Wasunna (2006), at p. 84.

[101] Centers for Medicare and Medicaid Services (2009); Schneider and Hall (2009), pp. 25, 26 (citing a Medicare expert struggling to help an elderly parent select a prescription plan).

[102] Jost (2006), at p. 439; Callahan and Wasunna (2006), at p. 167.

[103] There is also evidence that increased commercialization within Medicaid, the federal-state insurance system for the poor, is problematic and has failed to reduce spending. See Watson (2001), p. 53.

[104] Jost (2007), at pp. 17, 32; Cutler and Keenan (2008), at pp. 470, 471; Marmor (1998), at p. 56.

accounts (HSAs or MSAs).[105] The rationale behind consumer-driven health care is that patients can be turned into consumers if they are forced to pay a larger share of their own health expenses.[106] Today, many insurers offer some form of high-deductible plan in conjunction with health savings accounts. But again, consumer-driven health care has failed to reduce spending, and has not proven to be a viable option for the uninsured.[107]

Thus, none of these market-based innovations (managed competition, privatization, or consumer-driven health care) has reined in spending or solved the problem of the uninsured in the United States. But why? Though the answers are many and complex, the bottom line is that health care is not like other goods and services.

First, market-based innovations in health care depend heavily on principles of neoclassical microeconomics that do not work particularly well in health care.[108] Taking one example, advocates of consumer-driven health care assume that patients can and will make rational, utility-maximizing decisions when spending their own money.[109] But research shows that most patients often do not—and indeed cannot—make perfectly rational decisions about their own health care. Patients' rationality is 'bounded' rather than perfect.[110] Patients' decisions derive as much from behavioral, historical, sociological, and psychological factors as from economic ones.[111] Decisions about diagnoses and courses of treatment are mired in uncertainties.[112] Most patients are not capable of evaluating complex medical information, so they often rely on physicians and other professional intermediaries to make decisions for them.[113]

Health care markets are also saddled with information asymmetries between payers and providers.[114] Information about the price and quality of health care goods and services is scarce.[115] Providers have little incentive to produce unbiased

---

[105] Federal laws in 1996 and 1997 encouraged these plans, but it was not until Congress passed the Medicare Modernization Act in 2003 that they proliferated. See Health Insurance Portability and Accountability Act (HIPAA), Pub. L. 104–191, 110 Stat. 1936; Balanced Budget Act of 1997, Pub. L. No. 105–33, 111 Stat. 251; Medicare Prescription Drug, Improvement, and Modernization Act of 2003, Pub. L. No. 108–173, 117 Stat. 2066.

[106] Jost (2007), at pp. 31, 32.

[107] For a devastating critique of the consumer-driven movement, see Jost (2007).

[108] Jost (2007), at pp. 86–118; Cutler and Keenan (2008), at p. 459.

[109] Jost (2007), at pp. 87, 93.

[110] Madison (2007), p. 1584; Simon (1979), p. 502.

[111] Jost (2007), at p. 31.

[112] Ibid., at p. 93; Appleby (1998), p. 39.

[113] Schneider (1998), pp. 35–46; Jost (2007), at pp. 98–100; Gawande (2009) ('Any plan that relies on the sheep to negotiate with the wolves is doomed to failure', quoting a doctor).

[114] White (2007), at p. 419; Jost (2007), at pp. 97, 98.

[115] Jost (2007), at p. 90.

information and may often have an incentive to conceal it.[116] And many segments of the health care industry still frown upon price advertising.[117]

Predictably, transaction costs are significant in health care.[118] Health insurance serves a valuable function, but it complicates transactions, particularly because most Americans purchase it through yet another intermediary: employers.[119]

Finally, health insurers and providers often enjoy local or regional monopolies, which leads to anticompetitive behavior.[120] For example, there are considerable concentrations of market power in the pharmaceutical, medical device, hospital, physician, and insurance markets.[121]

In summary, neoclassical microeconomics depends on so-called 'perfect' markets, but markets are far from perfect in health care.[122] Health care simply is not like other industries.[123]

Second, several market-based innovations in health care are geared toward discouraging 'moral hazard'—the concern that patients with insurance will over-consume health care precisely because they are insured.[124] Indeed, many market advocates believe moral hazard is the primary problem in health care, and that insurance 'is the problem, not the solution'.[125] But again, health care is not like other goods and services. Seeking health care is often 'time-consuming, inconvenient, unpleasant, uncomfortable, and sometimes just plain painful'.[126] Most insured patients have better things to do than consume health care.[127] Thus, market-based innovations like consumer-driven health care that seek to limit patient demand are not likely to rein in spending.

---

116 Ibid., at p. 90.

117 Ibid., at p. 98.

118 Ibid., at p. 91.

119 As Cutler and Keenan aptly note 'Employers writing checks to health insurance companies fear that they will be made to bear the cost; workers are afraid to leave their jobs because health insurance is tied to work; and everyone is a pink slip away from losing coverage'. Cutler and Keenan (2008), at p. 459.

120 Jost (2007), at p. 91.

121 Ibid., at pp. 100, 101; White (2007), at p. 415 ('Overall, a period of market-led transformation of American medical care resulted in the consolidation of both insurers and hospital systems …').

122 Of course, noted health economist Mark Pauly has argued that the correct comparison is not perfect markets versus perfect government, but imperfect ones. See Pauly (1997), p. 470. See Rice (2002), for a criticism of how market competition works in health care *vis-à-vis* government.

123 Jost (2007), at p. 32.

124 Appleby(1998), at p. 39; Gladwell (2005); Jost (2007), at p. xv.

125 Jost (2007), at pp. 34, 35, 70.

126 Ibid., at p. 35; Gladwell (2005).

127 Jost (2007), at p. 35.

In summary, market-based innovations in health care often underestimate how different health care is from other industries.[128] Market incentives are limited, particularly demand-side incarnations like consumer-driven health care. Patients are not 'consumers' in any true sense and providers are not true 'sellers'. The economics of health care is unconventional, and market-based incentives are often a crude and imperfect tool for allocating scarce health care resources. As Joseph White notes, '[t]he market did not control costs, increase access, or help rationalize the American health care system'.[129] Indeed, 'market theory' has been called an 'intellectually spent explanatory paradigm' for health care policy.[130]

But this has not deterred free-market advocates. When the approaches above fail, they argue that it is because we have not created perfect enough markets,[131] or that government regulation still impedes the market. Recognizing the limitations of market-based tools in health care is paramount. But there continues to be a strong pro-market slant among health economists and policymakers in the United States.

15.5 The Ideal of Market Competition in United States Health Reform

Contemporary reform efforts in the United States reveal the extent to which market ideals retain their vigor. Ironically, market ideals have both driven and obstructed recent health reform proposals. Both the 1993 Clinton plan and the 2009 Obama plan took pains to promote competition between insurers and increase patient choice, but each was heavily criticized by market advocates and others concerned that the plans would irreversibly amplify the government's role in health care, perhaps even leading to 'socialized medicine' (a frequently voiced but frequently misunderstood criticism).[132] It is notable that the defeat of the Clinton plan and the significant resistance encountered by the Obama plan both occurred in otherwise favorable political settings: both were championed by Democratic lawmakers that enjoyed a Democratic House, Senate, and Presidency. Yet both plans were bogged down and heavily influenced by criticisms animated by free-market rhetoric. And though reasons for the intense resistance to these plans are numerous and complex,

---

[128] Cutler and Keenan note that '[e]conomic transactions can happen smoothly or with rough edges. [Health care] is as rough as it gets'. Cutler and Keenan (2008), at p. 459; Jost (2007), at p. 189.

[129] White (2007), at p. 426.

[130] Hunter (2008), at p. 18 (citing Symposium, 'Rethinking Health Law', 41 *Wake Forest Law Review* (2006), p. 341) (internal quotations omitted).

[131] White 2007), at p. 399.

[132] Jost (2006), at p. 99 (citing fears over the Clinton plan); Bobinski (2008), at pp. 372, 373.

many derive from the basic disagreement over the appropriate balance between markets and the government in health care.

In 1993, the Clinton plan relied heavily on theories of managed competition to control costs and improve access to insurance[133] (though as noted above, fostering such competition generally requires extensive government regulation).[134] The legislation was long and complex, in part because of the nature of health reform, but also in part because of 'the lengths to which it went to appease all possible political constituencies', including market advocates.[135] Despite these overtures, opponents won the political debate by seizing on two firmly held beliefs in the United States: first, that achieving universal coverage will require significant government expenditures; and second, that the private sector can more efficiently provide health insurance than the government.[136] However, as several American commentators have noted, 'international evidence in fact provides striking proof that the opposite can be true'.[137] Thus, despite relying on a framework of managed competition, the Clinton plan failed spectacularly. In fact, some speculated that its demise might preclude future reform efforts in the United States.[138]

Sixteen years later, health reform continued to be both driven and shackled by the ideal of market competition. In September 2009, President Obama convened a special joint session of Congress to push for health reform and answer criticisms that the proposed bills would sacrifice competition for government control. His speech mentioned 'competition' four times, reaching the following crescendo:

> My health care proposal has also been attacked by some who oppose health reform as a 'government takeover' of the entire health care system. ... So let me set the record straight. My guiding principle is, and always has been, that consumers do better when there is choice and competition. ... Without competition, the price of insurance goes up and the quality goes down.[139]

In March 2010, after nearly a year of rancorous debate, President Obama finally signed into law landmark health reform legislation, the Patient Protection and Affordable Care Act.[140] The Act is more accurately cast as health *insurance* reform rather than health *system* reform, as it generally targets access to health

---

[133] Health Security Act, H.R. 3600, 103d Cong. (1st Sess. 1993).

[134] Skocpol (1995), pp. 66, 69; Jost (2006), p. 580; Marmor (1998), at pp. 60–61.

[135] Jost (2006), at p. 609 note 411.

[136] Marmor (1998), at p. 67.

[137] See, e.g., ibid., at p. 67; Jost (2006).

[138] See, e.g., Marmor (1998), at p. 62.

[139] President Barack Obama's Remarks to a Joint Session of Congress (9 September 2009), at http://www.whitehouse.gov/the_press_office/Remarks-by-the-President-to-a-Joint-Session-of-Congress-on-Health-Care/.

[140] H.R. 3590, 111th Cong. (2nd Sess. 2010), codified as Public Law 111–148. On 30 March 2010, President Obama also signed the Health Care and Education Reconciliation Act of 2010, H.R. 4872, 111th Cong. (2nd Sess. 2010), which makes several amendments to the Patient Protection and Affordable Care Act.

insurance, rather than reforming how the system organizes or delivers care.[141] The Act includes several major reforms that should significantly expand access to health insurance in the United States.

First, beginning in 2014, the Act requires uninsured individuals to purchase health insurance, and those who remain uninsured must pay an additional tax based on their income. In return, the Act outlaws some of the more controversial insurance company practices, such as rescinding policies when patients become sick, imposing lifetime dollar limits on coverage, and denying policies based on preexisting medical conditions.[142]

Second, also beginning in 2014, the bill expands eligibility for Medicaid (the joint federal-state health insurance program for the poor) particularly to uninsured individuals without dependent children who previously were ineligible despite meeting income limits.[143] The bill thus turns Medicaid into a genuine insurance program for the poor, as only half of all poor residents are currently eligible under diverging state eligibility requirements.

Finally, the bill creates state-based health insurance 'exchanges' that allow uninsured individuals to purchase policies that meet minimum coverage requirements.[144] States will receive money from the federal government to establish these exchanges, or states can rely on the federal government to establish a multi-state exchange. Individuals will receive tax credits to pay for insurance premiums, as well as federal subsidies to pay for cost-sharing obligations such as deductibles and co-payments. The bill creates separate insurance exchanges for smaller, self-insured businesses to purchase plans for employees, and these plans are also subsidized federally.

Together, these reforms are expected to reduce the number of uninsured by 32 million over ten years, leaving roughly 23 million uninsured, 'about one-third of whom would be unauthorized immigrants'.[145] Thus, the Act would raise the percentage of 'legal non-elderly residents' with insurance coverage from roughly 83 to 94% nationally.

The Act specifically targets competition in the insurance market. One of the Act's major features is creating health insurance exchanges in which individuals and smaller employers can shop among competing plans.[146] Realizing that health

---

141 Although the Act includes provisions that do target the delivery system (e.g., Title III, Subtitle A, 'Transforming the Health Care Delivery System'), few believe that the Act will in fact fundamentally change how health care is delivered in the United States.

142 H.R. 3590, *supra* note 140, at Title I, Subtitle A, Part A ('Individual and Group Market Reforms').

143 Ibid., at Title II, Subtitle A ('Improved Access to Medicaid').

144 Ibid., at Title I, Subtitle D ('Available Coverage Choices for All Americans').

145 Letter from Douglas M. Elmendorf, Director, U.S. Congressional Budget Office, to Hon. Nancy Pelosi, Speaker of the U.S. House of Representatives, 20 March 2010, at http://www.cbo.gov/.

146 H.R. 3590, *supra* n. 140, at Title I, Subtitle D.

insurers dominate local markets,[147] the Act tries to subject these markets to regional or even national competition to encourage insurers to offer more generous benefits for lower prices. The Congressional Budget Office estimates that roughly 24 million residents would purchase individual insurance through the exchanges by 2019.[148]

Throughout the legislative process, Republicans and Democrats generally agreed that more competition in the insurance market would improve the price and perhaps the quality of insurance. But unsurprisingly, the parties disagreed pointedly over the precise role the government should play to promote such competition. Most Democrats argued that a public insurance plan (the so-called 'public option') would force private insurers to offer better plans at better rates; most Republicans countered that a public plan would ultimately drive private insurers from the market, inevitably leading to a single payer system. Thus, although both parties generally agreed in principle that reforms should try to make the insurance market more competitive, they disagreed significantly about how to do so. Moreover, many Americans broadly support universal insurance coverage in theory, but there has never emerged anything close to a public consensus on how to achieve it.[149] A single payer system has never seriously been considered.

As a compromise, the Act replaced the so-called 'public option', which generated fierce debate and threatened to undermine passage of the legislation, with a series of alternatives. First, the Act creates local, non-profit health care 'cooperatives' called 'Consumer-Oriented and Operated Plans' (CO-OPs) that will offer insurance.[150] The Act would have created a state-based 'community health insurance option', but this provision was later stricken from the bill.[151] Finally, the Act allows the US Office of Personnel Management to contract with health insurers to offer 'multi-state' health plans in each state exchange.[152] These three programs seem designed to offer consumers alternatives to plans offered by private health insurance companies—without creating anything that could be cast as 'public option'. Nevertheless, not a single Republican Representative or Senator voted for the Patient Protection and Affordable Care Act or the Reconciliation Act that finalized the legislation.

Thus, despite major insurance reforms, the US health care system continues to tether itself to private health insurance, even though this has not and will not produce universal coverage. Indeed, some argue that the ideal of market competition in American health care has 'siphoned energy away from more appropriate

[147] Robinson (2004), pp. 11–24.

[148] Letter from Douglas M. Elmendorf, *supra* note 145, at p. 9.

[149] Cutler and Keenan (2008), at p. 472; Blendon et al. (2003), pp. W3-405-09 (noting that roughly half of Americans surveyed would support single-payer insurance and half would oppose it).

[150] See H.R. 3590, *supra* n. 140, at § 1322.

[151] Ibid., at § 1040 (amending Title I, Subtitle D, § 1323).

[152] Ibid., at § 10104 (amending Title I, Subtitle D, § 1334).

strategies of reform'.[153] Ironically, the ideal has both animated and burdened contemporary health reform efforts.

15.6 Markets in Health Care: Toward a More Perfect Union?

What is the appropriate role for market competition in health care? For the United States, this is the $2.3 trillion question. Unfortunately, given the nature of health care, there are no reliable formulae that might guide us. And the experiences of peer countries, most of which seem to have found a better balance, are so varied and complex that it is difficult to extract many useful lessons.[154] In each system, the goal is to use the market 'without doing harm to the moral values of medicine, most notably the primacy of patient welfare and professional integrity'.[155] But in the United States, another, more basic goal continues to elude us: using the market not only to control spending, but to increase access to care.

Fortunately, there seems to be relatively broad support to pursue the following principles, even though there remains significant and possibly even intractable disagreement over precisely how to implement them.

15.6.1 Insurers Should Compete

Data reveal that there is not much local competition between health insurers in the United States, and many locales show significant concentrations of market power.[156] Thus, contemporary reform efforts have often placed a high priority on stimulating competition between insurers, or least removing existing barriers to it. To some, this means shifting away from employer-based insurance toward a more flexible individual market, as in the Netherlands.[157]

Regardless of the tactic, both domestic and international experiences suggest that creating a competitive insurance market requires significant government involvement. For example, the Patient Protection and Affordable Care Act would create state insurance exchanges for those without access to affordable group insurance.[158] The Act relies on significant government oversight to achieve the dual purposes of controlling costs and expanding access to coverage, recognizing that a less encumbered insurance market does neither. Regulators can facilitate the

---

153 Marmor (1998), at p. 69.

154 Callahan and Wasunna (2006), at pp. 4, 203.

155 Ibid., at p. 36.

156 American Medical Association (2006); Jost (2007), at pp. 100, 101; White (2007), at p. 415.

157 Ven, van de and Schut (2008).

158 See *supra* n. 140.

market by addressing various market failures, for example by requiring risk pooling, community rating, guaranteed issue, portability, renewability, and limiting rescissions.[159] Some of these interventions are more controversial than others, but none generate as much intense debate as the proposal to provide a public, government sponsored insurance plan to compete with private insurers.

15.6.2 Providers Should Compete

Data also reveal significant concentrations of market power among health care providers.[160] As with the insurance market, there is no easy solution. But the following two philosophies might create a more transparent, competitive market. First, because price advertising is still taboo in much of the health care industry, many recommend that we require providers to list their prices publicly in order to facilitate comparison shopping.[161] Indeed, encouraging price transparency has been perhaps the most important and realistic contribution of the consumer-driven movement.[162] Second, a growing contingent calls for financing reforms like 'pay-for-performance' that could better align the incentives of providers with those of patients and payers by explicitly linking payments to outcomes and quality benchmarks.[163] Providers that improve the health of their patients would receive higher payments than those who did not, particularly providers with higher complication or hospital readmissions rates.[164] The goal is to use financial incentives to improve care, encouraging quality over quantity (the bane of fee-for-service models).[165]

15.6.3 Competitive Markets Require Accurate, Objective Information

Competitive health care markets require not only better price information, but also better information about quality than these markets currently provide. For example, in an ideal world, patients and insurers could access a database or website that

159 See, e.g., Arrow, et al. (2009), p. 493; Marmor (1998), at p. 67.

160 Jost (2007), at p. 100.

161 See, e.g., American College of Physicians (2008), at p. 13; Jost (2007), at p. 194.

162 Jost (2007), at p. 85.

163 Cutler and Keenan (2008), at p. 464.

164 Ibid.

165 Ibid.; Arrow et al. (2009), at p. 493; Gawande (2009) ('As economists have often pointed out, we pay doctors for quantity, not quality').

would allow them to compare the quality of service providers.[166] There is little disagreement in principle that we need better quality information.[167] On the other hand, recent efforts to generate better information about the quality of health care goods and procedures have generated controversy. Comparative effectiveness studies and technology assessments cure at least some information asymmetries by allowing patients, professionals, and payers to compare goods and services.[168] The market alone does not reliably produce this information,[169] which may be why many countries seem to be embracing these studies.[170] In the United States, comparative effectiveness research has generated controversy, in part because some believe that it leads to government 'rationing',[171] despite evidence that governments rarely use such research to deny coverage for effective technologies.[172] Thus, although the Patient Protection and Affordable Care Act would support comparative effectiveness research, it would not allow the government to make coverage or reimbursement decisions based on these findings.[173]

15.6.4 Modest Cost-sharing

Many countries have found that modest cost-sharing can be an effective method of controlling costs and encouraging more responsible, cost-sensitive consumption of health care—but only if it does not deny access to care for poorer populations or deter patients from obtaining necessary care.[174] For example, tiered pharmaceutical plans with varying co-payments can encourage patients to use less expensive generics in appropriate circumstances, and co-payments also encourage more judicious visits to physician offices and emergency rooms.[175] But cost-sharing is not very effective for services like hospitalization, over which patients exercise very little control.[176] Thus, modest cost-sharing with payments based on income

166 Jost (2007), at p. 200.

167 For a discussion on the limits of this approach, see Schneider and Hall (2009), at pp. 7–65.

168 Arrow et al. (2009), at p. 493. For a critique of technology assessments, see Elhauge (1996), p. 1525.

169 Callahan and Wasunna (2006), at p. 173 (citing studies); Jost (2007), at p. 198 (noting that political pressure hampers Medicare payment and coverage determinations).

170 Callahan and Wasunna (2006), at pp. 172, 173; Dickson et al. (2003), p. 3; European Network for Health Technology Assessment, at http://www.eunethta.net/.

171 See, e.g., Gottlieb (2009), p. A15.

172 Jost (2007), at p. 185.

173 H.R. 3590, *supra* n. 140, at § 6301(j).

174 Hall and Schneider (2009), p. 743; American College of Physicians (2008), at pp. 13-14; Jost (2007), at pp. 130, 131, 191.

175 Jost (2007), at pp. 196, 197.

176 Ibid., at p. 197.

can encourage patients to consume certain health care goods and services responsibly.

It is important to keep in mind that not all health care goods and services are created equal. For example, expensive acute and longer term care can be financially catastrophic for patients, and it is this type of capricious risk that health insurance is well designed to handle.[177] We should subsidize this type of care for those who cannot afford it and be wary of market mechanisms, particularly demand-side incarnations like consumer-driven health care, that promise to reduce costs here. On the other end of the spectrum, more predictable, low-cost health care goods and services seem to be more responsive to demand-side incentives, at least for those with sufficient income.[178] Other services that are more susceptible to moral hazard, such as cosmetic surgery, also seem to respond to cost-sharing incentives and provider competition.[179]

There is evidence that supply-side competition works best 'with the help of demand-side control imposed by government monopsonistic purchasing clout',[180] reflected in efforts to introduce a public health insurance option to compete with private insurers.[181] The United States uses both supply-side and demand-side incentives, 'perhaps the worst of both worlds' because cost-sharing is not complete enough to restrain demand, and care is not managed systematically enough to restrain supply.[182] Supply-side limits are much more common in other countries, but demand-side limits like consumer-driven health care seem to be the device *du jour* of the pro-market crowd.[183] Nevertheless, there seems to be a growing consensus that market-based incentives work better on the supply side (where, for example, they can encourage providers to offer better prices and higher quality care) than on the demand side (which relies, for example, on patients to make wise spending decisions).[184]

15.6.5 Retail Care

There has been a proliferation of private retail clinics in the United States that provide basic care in retail chain pharmacies, supermarkets, and discount stores.[185]

177 Ibid., at pp. xii, 192, 193.

178 Ibid., at pp. 193–194.

179 Ibid., at pp. xvii, 193.

180 Callahan and Wasunna (2006), at p. 209.

181 The legislation passed by the US House of Representatives included such an option. See Affordable Health Care for America Act, H.R. 3962, 111th Cong. (1st Sess. 2009); Jost (2007), at p. 195.

182 Cutler and Keenan (2008), at p. 470, 471.

183 Ibid., at p. 471.

184 Saltman and Figueras (1996), p. 20; Schneider and Hall (2009), at pp. 10, 11.

185 Sage (2007), pp. 1233–1334.

These clinics employ a number of market-based innovations that make them attractive to the uninsured and under-insured, thus potentially expanding access to care. For example, retail clinics typically accept cash payments rather than insurance; openly post prices; have low overhead and maintain expansive hours; provide basic care for common ailments; employ mid-level practitioners such as physicians assistants and nurse-practitioners; make use of electronic medical records and computerized practice guides; and focus on customer service.[186] Retail clinics generally expand access to care and introduce a modicum of competition in the *delivery* of care.[187] The retail movement has delivered several innovations, though the government should still cover routine health care for the poorest among us.[188]

Together, these market-facilitating philosophies underscore the reality that competition in health care works best when coupled with relatively strong government regulation to guide it.[189] Competitive insurance markets require extensive government regulation to combat market failures like adverse selection and moral hazard. Competitive provider markets require robust enforcement of antitrust and fraud and abuse laws.[190] Markets alone do not provide reliable comparative information about the price or quality of health care goods and services. Indeed, some argue that for any market-based reforms to successfully improve cost, quality, and access in the United States, they 'would have to include such substantial restrictions on the normal ways of doing business in US markets that it would be barely recognizable as market-oriented in the American context'.[191] White echoes this sentiment, arguing that '[e]ffective reform will require restraining the market, not relying on it'.[192] Finally, facilitating competition is not costless: the 'transaction costs' of regulating and promoting competition can often 'mean that the efficiency gains of competition are used to sustain the system of competition itself'.[193]

In short, the logic and goals of markets do not produce the type of health care system that most Americans want.[194] The basic market for health care in the United States gives providers wide latitude to pursue profits, requires patients and payers to shop intelligently for health care goods and services, and grants entrepreneurs broad access to capital.[195] But these features 'do not appear to be helping

[186] Ibid., at pp. 1238–1242.

[187] Ibid., at p. 1235.

[188] Jost (2007), at p. 194.

[189] Callahan and Wasunna (2006), at p. 209.

[190] Haas-Wilson (2003).

[191] White (2007), at p. 399 (internal quotations omitted).

[192] Ibid., at p. 436.

[193] Freeman (1998a), p. 400.

[194] White (2007), at pp. 395, 434.

[195] Ibid., at p. 434.

the health care system attain its goals'.[196] The United States' health care market does provide a wide array of choices and does offer sophisticated, high-end care.[197] But it does so at a significant cost. Our system encourages innovation, but the immense innovation over the last twenty years has not markedly improved our system.[198]

Markets alone will not adequately insure the elderly or sick among us. Universal coverage requires some people to subsidize others, and no country provides universal coverage without the government compelling such subsidies.[199] Equity is not what markets provide, and markets have failed to provide a more equitable and efficient system.[200]

15.7 Conclusion

The United States remains an international outlier in health care, both functionally and philosophically. Though EU Member States also rely on market instruments in health care, and similarly struggle to locate the appropriate boundaries, these nations generally implement market-based policies from a baseline of universal coverage that the United States does not enjoy, even after major health insurance reform. The ideal of market competition in the US health care system persists, but continues to elude us, as demonstrated by contemporary reform efforts. The evidence suggests that market theories and policy instruments have yet to produce the health care system most Americans want. Recognizing the limits to market competition in health care—including learning to distinguish where it is helpful from where it is not—will be necessary to further improve our system.

References

American College of Physicians (2008) Achieving a high-performance health care system with universal access: what the United States can learn from other countries. 148 Ann Intern Med

American Medical Association (2006) Competition in health insurance: a comprehensive study of US markets. 2005 Update (Chicago, AMA)

Appleby J (1998) Economic perspectives on markets and health care. In: Ranade W (ed) Markets and health care: a comparative perspective, Longman, New York

Arrow K et al (2009) Toward a 21st-century health care system: recommendations for health care reform. Ann Intern Med 150

[196] Ibid.

[197] Ibid.; Jost (2007), at pp. 15–16.

[198] White (2007), at p. 438.

[199] Ibid., at p. 432; Cutler and Keenan (2008), at p. 455.

[200] Pauly (1998); White (2007), at p. 397.

Blendon RJ et al (2003) 'Americans' views of the uninsured: an era for hybrid proposals. Health Affairs (web exclusive) (27 August)
Bloche MG (2009) The emergent logic of health law. South Calif L Rev 82
Bobinski MA (2008) The health insurance debate in Canada: lessons for the United States? Conn Ins L J 14
Brown LD (2008) The amazing noncollapsing US health care system—is reform finally at hand? New Engl J Med 358
Callahan D, Wasunna AA (2006) Medicine and the market: equity v. choice. Johns Hopkins University Press, Baltimore
Centers for Medicare and Medicaid Services (2009) 2010 medicare part d stand-alone prescription drug plans (data as of 20 November) at http://www.cms.gov/PrescriptionDrug CovGenIn/.
Chernichovsky D (1995) health system reforms in industrialized democracies: an emerging paradigm. The Milbank Quarterly 73
Commonwealth Fund Commission on a High Performance Health System (2008) Why not the best? Results from the national scorecard on U.S. health system performance, 2008 (Commonwealth Fund).
Cortez N (2008) Patients without borders: the emerging global market for patients and the evolution of modern health care. Indiana L J. 83
Cutler D, Keenan P (2008) Health Care. In: Schuck PH, Wilson JQ (eds) Understanding America: The anatomy of an exceptional nation. Public Affairs, New York
DeNavas-Walt C et al (2009) Income, poverty, and health insurance coverage in the United States: 2008 (U.S. Census Bureau 2009), (Table 7)
Dickson M et al (2003) Survey of pharmacoeconomic assessment activity in eleven countries. OECD Working papers (Paris, Organization for Economic Cooperation and Development)
Diderichsen F (2000) 'Sweden', 25 J Health Polit Policy L
Docteur E, Berenson RA (2009) How does the quality of U.S. health care compare internationally? (Robert Wood Johnson Foundation and Urban Institute)
Elhauge E (1996) The limited regulatory potential of medical technology assessment. Virginia L Rev 82
Families USA (2007) Wrong direction: one out of every three americans are uninsured. Publication no. 07–108
Field RI, Stefanacci RG (2007) Beyond drug coverage: the cumulative effect of privatization reforms in the medicare modernization act. 1 St. Louis University J Health L Policy
Flood CM et al (eds) (2005) Access to care, Access to justice: The legal debate over private health insurance in Canada. University of Toronto Press, Toronto
Freeman R (1998a) competition in context: the politics of health care reform in Europe. Int J Qual Health Care 10
Freeman R (1998b) The German model: the state and the market in health reform. In: Ranade W (ed) Markets and health care: a comparative analysis. Longman, London
Gawande A (2009) The cost conundrum: what a texas town can teach us about health care. The New Yorker (1 June)
Gladwell M (2005) The moral hazard myth: the bad idea behind our failed health care system. The New Yorker (29 August)
Gottlieb S (2009) Governments always ration care. Wall Street J (25 June)
Gronden van de JW (2008) Cross-border health care in the EU and the organization of the national health care systems of the member states: the dynamics resulting from the European court of justice's decisions on free movement and competition law. Wisconsin Int L J 26(3)
Haas-Wilson D (2003) Managed care and monopoly power: the antitrust challenge. Harvard University Press, Cambridge
Hall MA, Schneider CE (2009) When patients say no (to save money): an essay on the tectonics of health law. Conn L Rev 41(3)
Harris G (2007) Looking at the Dutch and Swiss health systems. New York Times (30 October)

Hatzopoulos V (2002) Killing national health and insurance systems but healing patients? The European market for health care services after the judgments of the ECJ in Vanbraekel and Peerbooms. CML Rev 39
Hatzopoulos V (2008) Financing national health care in a transnational environment: the impact of the European community internal market. Wisconsin. Int L J 26
Hess AE (1968) Medicare after one year. J Risk Ins 35
Hunter N (2008) Risk governance and deliberative democracy in health care. Georgetown Law J 97
Hussey PS et al (2003) How does the quality of care compare in five countries. Health Affairs 23
Hyman D (2006) Getting the haves to come out behind: fixing the distributive injustices of American health care. L Contem Probl 69
Hyman DA, Silver C (2001) You get what you pay for: result-based compensation for health care. Washington Lee Law Rev 58
Institute of Medicine of the National Academies (2000) America's health care safety net: intact but endangered.
Institute of Medicine of the National Academies (2002) Care without coverage: too little, too late.
Jost TS (2004) Why can't we do what they do? National Health Reform Abroad. J L Med Ethics 32
Jost TS (2006) Our broken health care system and how to fix it: an essay on health law and policy. Wake Forest L Rev 41
Jost TS (2007) Health care at risk: a critique of the consumer-driven movement. Duke University Press, Durham
Leflar RB (2009) Unnatural deaths, criminal sanctions, and medical quality improvement in Japan. Yale J Health Policy Law Ethics 9
Longman P (2007) Best care anywhere: why VA health care is better than yours. PoliPoint Press, Sausalito
Madison K (2007) Regulating health care quality in an information age. U.C. Davis Law Rev 40
Marmor TR (1998) The procompetitive movement in American medical politics. In: Ranade W (ed) Markets and health care: a comparative analysis. Longman, London
Newdick C (2008) The European court of justice, trans-national health care, and social citizenship—accidental death of a concept? Wisconsin Int Law J 26
Nolte E, McKee CM (2008) Measuring the health of nations: updating an earlier analysis. Health Affairs 27
Oberlander J (2003) The political life of medicare. University of Chicago Press, Chicago
Pauly M (1997) Who was that straw man anyway? A comment on evans and rice. J Health Polit Policy Law 22
Pauly M (1998) Trading cost, quality, and coverage of the uninsured: what will we demand and what will we supply? The future U.S. healthcare system: who will care for the poor and uninsured?. Health Administration Press, Chicago
Ranade W (1998a) Introduction. In: Ranade W (ed) Markets and health care: a comparative analysis. Longman, London
Ranade W (1998b) Reforming the British national health service: all change, no change? In: Ranade W (ed) Markets and health care: a comparative analysis. Longman, London
Rice T (2002) The Economics of health care reconsidered, 3rd edn. Health Administration Press, Chicago
Robinson R (1998) Managed competition: health reform in the Netherlands markets and health care: a comparative analysis. In: Ranade W (ed) Longman, London
Robinson JC (2001) The end of managed care. J Am Med Assoc 285
Robinson JC (2004) Consolidation and the transformation of competition in health insurance. Health Affairs 23
Rosenblatt R (1981) Health care, markets, and democratic values. Vanderbilt Law Rev 34
Sage WM (2007) Might the fact that 90% of Americans live within 15 miles of a wal-mart help achieve universal care? Kansas Law Rev 55

Saltman R (1998) Health reform in Sweden: the road beyond cost containment. In: Ranade W (ed) Markets and health care: a comparative analysis. Longman, London
Saltman RB, Figueras J (1996) On solidarity and competition: an evidence-based perspective. Eurohealth 2
Schneider CE (1998) The practice of autonomy: patients, doctors, and medical decisions. Oxford University Press, Oxford
Schneider CE, Hall MA (2009) The patient life: can consumers direct health care? Am J L Med 35
Schoen et al C (2008) How many are underinsured? Trends among U.S. adults, 2003 and 2007. Health Affairs 27 (web exclusive)
Schuck PH, Wilson JQ (eds) (2008). Understanding America: The anatomy of an exceptional nation Public Affairs, New York
Simon H (1979) Rational decision making in business organizations. Am Econ Rev 69
Skocpol T (1995) The rise and resounding demise of the clinton health plan. Health Affairs 14
Starr P (1982) The social transformation of American medicine. Basic Books, New York
Studdert DM et al (2004) Medical malpractice. New Engl J Med 350
Ven WPMM van de, Schut FT (2008) universal mandatory health insurance in the Netherlands: a model for the United States? Health Affairs 27
Watson SD (2001) Commercialization of medicaid. St. Louis Univ L J 45
White J (2007) Markets and medical care: The United States, 1993–2005. 85 The Milbank Quarterly
WHO (2000) World Health Report 2000, Health systems: improving performance, at http://www.who.int/whr/2000/en/.
World Health Organization (2007) Spending on health: a global overview at http://www.who.int/mediacentre/factsheets/fs319/en/index.html.

Part IV
Further Issues of EU Health Care Law

Chapter 16
The Compatibility of Health Care Capacity Planning Policies with EU Internal Market Rules

Rita Baeten and Willy Palm

Contents

16.1 Introduction

The interplay between EU internal market rules and health system regulation has generated heated debates for over more than a decade. Initiated by the seminal case law of the European Court of Justice on the use of prior authorisation systems to control the access to, and statutory reimbursement of, health care services

R. Baeten (✉)
European Social Observatory (OSE), Brussels, Belgium
e-mail: baeten@ose.be

W. Palm
European Observatory on Health Systems and Policies, Brussels, Belgium
e-mail: wpa@obs.euro.who.int

J. W. van de Gronden et al. (eds.), *Health Care and EU Law*,
Legal Issues of Services of General Interest, DOI: 10.1007/978-90-6704-728-9_16,

purchased outside the Member State of affiliation, the discussion went beyond the scope of patient mobility to also question the compatibility of other regulatory measures with EU principles of free movement and freedom of establishment.

Indeed, the controversy provoked by the inclusion of health care services in the horizontal Directive on Services in the internal market, proposed by the European Commission in 2004,[1] did not only, or maybe even not in the first place, concern the stipulations with regard to the reimbursement of health care treatment received in another Member State.[2] The proposed application of the principle of freedom of establishment to health care services provoked heavy reactions and concerns.[3] These provisions obliged the Member States to organise a major screening exercise, identifying and assessing procedures and conditions that service providers should comply with for entering the market, including regulations with regard to quantitative or territorial restrictions limiting the number of care providers, price fixing, the legal form of the health care provider, staff norms and referral systems. If these were found to be discriminatory, or if their necessity and proportionality could not be justified, Member States were required to simplify and remove authorisations and licensing procedures.

As the provisions contained in the Services Directive were deemed too drastic and unfit to reflect the complexity and specific nature of health care systems, the European Parliament and the Council decided to exclude health services from the scope of the Directive. The European Commission announced that it would develop a proposal better suited to health care services,[4] and in July 2008 presented a proposal for a Directive on the Application of Patients Rights in Cross-Border Health Care.[5] Contrary to what it claims, the latter proposal only focuses on the needs of patients searching for medical care in another Member State and leaves aside important other aspects related to the application of the free movement rules to health care services. In particular the situation of health care providers wishing to provide their services occasionally in another Member State or willing to permanently establish in another Member State are not clarified. Thus the primary TFEU rules continue to apply on a residual basis alongside relevant secondary law on mutual recognition of qualifications.

Strikingly, the policy debate on these controversial issues has become silent since the removal of health care services from the scope of the Services Directive, as if it was assumed that 'the danger' for national health systems was cleared. Nevertheless, authorisation schemes required for the establishment of health care providers in general and quantitative and territorial planning norms in particular

---

1 Proposal for a Directive of the European Parliament and of the Council on services in the internal market, COM(2004) 2 final of 13 January 2004.

2 Article 23 Proposal *supra* n. 1.

3 See the chapter by Szyszczak in this book.

4 Amended proposal for a Directive of the European Parliament and of the Council on services in the internal market, COM(2006) 160 final of 4 April 2006.

5 Proposal for a Directive of the European Parliament and of the Council on the application of patients' rights in cross-border health care, COM(2008) 414 of 2 July 2008.

are increasingly subject to scrutiny of the Court and are assessed on their conformity with the TFEU, mainly, but not exclusively, with the provisions on the freedom of establishment.

In this chapter we analyse this case law and sketch the lines the Court has drawn so far. Focusing on the jurisprudence related to capacity planning through quantitative or territorial restrictions limiting the number of health care providers, the chapter starts in Sect. 16.2 by exploring *why* capacity planning is generally considered necessary to preserve the basic objectives of health care systems. In Sect. 16.3 we show that licensing and authorisation schemes limiting the number of care providers through quantitative or territorial restrictions can easily be considered to hinder the freedom of establishment in the EU. In Sect. 16.4, we explain which grounds the Court accepts to justify these restrictions for hospital care; outpatient care and human resources. Finally, in Sect. 16.5 we analyse how the Court assesses the proportionality of the measures. In this section we will demonstrate that the Court leaves a wide margin of discretion to the Member States in the definition of their policies and especially assesses whether the legislation is suitable to effectively protect public health and the financial sustainability of the social security system in a coherent and consistent way and whether it circumscribes the discretion of the national authorities.

We consider as health care providers both health professionals and health care institutions and providers providing both outpatient care and inpatient care.

16.2 Capacity Planning in Health Care

Almost all developed health systems have set up mechanisms for planning health care resources, aiming to ensure access to health care for the whole population, preserve its quality, avoid wastage of resources and guarantee its long-term financial sustainability.[6] The basic objective of health care capacity planning is to tune health care supply to the national populations' needs, by defining the availability and distribution of health care services and the health care workforce. Planning policies do not necessarily mean to restrict or limit supply.

Health care capacity planning can take many forms and realise several functions. Planning measures can be taken at the level of training, the entrance into the profession, the authorisation to set up practice or to build or open facilities. But also by reserving certain interventions to providers of a certain type or with a certain activity level or through selectively contracting with providers, authorities can effectively plan the capacity of health systems to provide health care. By setting a quantitative and territorial quota of care providers, policy makers generally aim to ensure accessibility to care for the whole population, including remote areas; to ensure quality of care provision, for example, through the

[6] See also Gekiere et al. (2010), pp. 461–508.

preservation of a sufficient concentration of experience and to cater for the rational use of the limited public budgets. Information asymmetry between the producers and recipients of health care is generally considered as one of the root causes for market failures in the health sector by which competition does not necessarily lead to optimal allocation of resources nor to balanced price setting. In addition payment systems often provide financial incentives to increase the volume of services and to provide the whole spectrum of services, leading to overcapacity, supply-side imbalances, wastage through provider-induced demand and loss of investments in underused capacity. Without regulatory intervention, provider-induced demand can lead to a high density of sophisticated diagnostic equipment while basic needs remain unmet.[7] Quantitative and geographical planning norms defining the number of health care providers can avoid a situation where care providers only select the 'easiest to treat' patients or exclusively provide treatments that are well-remunerated and for which income is predictable.[8] It can also avoid the situation where health care provision is concentrated only in the most profitable areas, ensuring that health care services are available for all groups and geographical areas.

The extent and nature of capacity planning varies greatly between countries, reflecting the health systems institutional and regulatory framework. Quantitative and territorial planning norms in principle include health care providers that provide publicly funded care and have an agreement or contract with the health authorities with regard to the price, quality, effectiveness and quantity of the health provision. However, it can also relate to non-contracted private care providers who operate outside the statutory health care system, as will be illustrated by the *Hartlauer* case, discussed below.

Capacity planning is often focused on hospitals and usually includes capital investments, investment in expensive equipment, service delivery and the allocation of human and financial resources. Traditionally, bed capacity has been the preferred unit of capacity planning. Some countries, including France and England, substituted bed capacity planning with service volumes and activity planning, given the decreasing relevance of hospital beds as a measure of health care capacity. It is expected that, with the changing role of the hospital, plans confined to hospitals will be increasingly limited in scope with many traditionally hospital-based services now being provided in ambulatory care facilities.[9] Some countries also plan ambulatory and primary care. Many EU Member States also regulate the number of pharmacies expressed as a ratio of the population in a certain geographical area.[10] Access to the pursuit of health care professions is in most countries indirectly limited, through controlling access to training places, in

[7] Ettelt et al. (2008), pp. 47–67.

[8] Ibid.

[9] Ibid.

[10] Taylor (2004), pp. 196–212.

particular for medical doctors.[11] Conditions for access to health care training and/or the pursuit of the profession aim to protect both patients and licensed health care professionals.[12]

Where all these conditions and mechanisms for controlling access to health care practice and provision are meant to serve higher goals of public health, safety and quality, efficiency and financial sustainability, planning can also be subject to regulatory capture. Regulatory capture refers to the phenomenon whereby regulation or regulatory bodies set up to safeguard the public interest may be captured instead by the regulated to favour specific corporate or private interests that dominate in the sector it is charged with regulating. Focused resources devoted to a particular policy outcome can be successful at 'capturing' influence with the staff or commission members of the regulatory agency, so that the preferred policy outcomes of the special interest are implemented. Since captured regulation serves the interests of those with the bargaining power to create new rules, it is argued that a captured regulatory agency, with the power of the government behind, is often worse than no regulation whatsoever.[13] Health care providers may thus use regulation to avoid competition and sustain their incomes, which may result in the scarcity of certain necessary services and inefficiencies. This is especially the case where the regulation of entry criteria is the responsibility of health professional groups.[14] In countries with a strong corporatist tradition, health care provider associations can be involved in the capacity planning process.[15] Such consultation mechanisms can facilitate the cooperation of private actors to mainly publicly funded systems. However, they do render the system more vulnerable for regulatory capture.

As a derivative of regulatory capture, Member States may also use regulation and specifically planning policies to privilege their own providers and protect their health care markets from any influx of foreign competitors.

It is within the context of this delicate balance between the defence of the general interest in health systems on the one hand and the removal of corporatist private interest as well as protectionist national interest on the other hand that the European Court of Justice had to judge on certain national entry requirements and authorisation schemes for health care providers. We focus specifically on the jurisprudence related to capacity planning in health care through quantitative and territorial restrictions limiting the number of health care providers. There are other important recent rulings concerning, inter alia, ownership of pharmacies, confining the exploitation of pharmacies to pharmacists; limiting the numbers of pharmacies to be owned by one pharmacist or requiring pharmacists to hold a minimum share

11 Bloor and Maynard (2003).

12 de Bijl and Nederveen-Van de Kragt (1997), pp. 5–18.

13 See for example, Levine and Forrence (1990), pp. 167–198.

14 Dubois (2006) , pp. 175–176.

15 Ettelt et al. (2008).

of pharmacies.[16] We will refer to this case law where it is relevant for our topic of health care capacity planning.

16.3 Is Capacity Planning a Hindrance to Free Movement?

In this section we explain how entry requirements limiting the number of health care providers through quantitative and territorial restrictions are caught by the EU free movement principles, in particular by the freedom to provide services and the freedom of establishment.

In its assessment on whether a measure is compatible with the free movement principles, the Court has to first decide whether the regulated activity falls within the ambit of the TFEU. The determining criterion for this is the economic character of the activity. Services within the meaning of the TFEU are defined by Article 57 TFEU as any activities 'where they are normally provided for remuneration, insofar as they are not governed by the provisions relating to freedom of movement for goods, capital and persons'. The Court has made clear that health care provided for remuneration, irrespective of the way in which it is funded, is an economic activity and thus has to comply with the EU Treaty rules on the freedom of establishment (Article 49 TFEU) or free provision of services (Article 56 TFEU). The freedom of establishment guarantees the ability of health care providers to establish themselves in a stable and continuous way in one or more Member States.

In its assessment of whether a specific measure would form a barrier to free movement, the Court has gradually broadened the scope. Where the concept of a hindrance was initially limited to direct discriminatory measures on the basis of nationality, the concept was gradually extended to indirect discrimination: measures that are applicable, without distinction, to domestic and foreign operators alike but would ultimately have the same discriminatory effect. For the freedom of establishment provisions the Court even went to consider all national measures liable to 'hinder or render less attractive' the exercise of the fundamental freedom of establishment guaranteed by the Treaty,[17] even if the measures were not discriminatory on grounds of nationality. In this way nearly any kind of regulation can be regarded as a potential hindrance to freedom of establishment; this risks affecting the regulatory autonomy of Member States to organise health care and related national social security systems.[18]

That the application of the EU internal market rules to regulation on entry requirements and in particular to measures restricting the number of health care

---

[16] ECJ, Joined Cases C-171/07 and C-172/07 *Apothekerkammer des Saarlandes and Others* [2009] *ECR* I-0000 (n.y.r.).

[17] ECJ, Case C-299/02 *Commission* v. *Netherlands* [2004] *ECR* I-9761, para 15, and ECJ, Case C-140/03 *Commission* v. *Greece* [2005] *ECR* I-3177, para 27.

[18] See also Gekiere et al. (2010).

providers is very sensitive was already illustrated in the debate on the Commissions proposal for a Directive on Services in the Internal Market in 2004. Article 15 of this proposal introduced a systematic and pre-emptive screening of authorisation schemes. Member States were required to evaluate whether the access to the exercise of a (health care) service was subject to a series of requirements including.

> quantitative or territorial restrictions, in particular in the form of limits fixed on the basis of population or on the basis of a minimum geographical distance between service-provider.

As a next step Member States had to assess whether these requirements were justified and proportionate. If this was not the case they had to be altered or the Member States had to withdraw the measure. This Article became one of the most controversial aspects of the proposal and ultimately led to the total exclusion of health care provision from the scope of the Directive. Not surprisingly, the number of infringement actions brought by the Commission then increased.

In one of these cases, the *Hartlauer* case, a scheme of capacity planning limiting the supply of health care providers was challenged. It concerned an authorisation requirement for setting up an independent outpatient dental clinic, the attribution of which was based on the assessment of the health needs of the population. *Hartlauer*, a German-based company was denied this authorisation. In its judgement of 10 March 2009, the Court did not leave any doubt that:

> … a national rule under which the establishment of an undertaking from another Member State is subject to the issue of a prior authorisation constitutes a restriction within the meaning of Article 43 EC, since it is capable of hindering the exercise by that undertaking of freedom of establishment by preventing it from freely carrying on its activities through a fixed place of business.[19]

According to the Court, any grant of such an authorisation involves additional administrative and financial costs and the pursuit of a self-employed activity is reserved to certain economic operators who satisfy predetermined requirements.[20] Such legislation deters, or even prevents, economic operators from other Member States from pursuing their activities in the host Member State through a fixed place of business.[21] In line with earlier case law the Court underscores that national legislation under which the pursuit of an activity is subject to a condition linked to the economic or social need for that activity constitutes a restriction in that it tends to limit the number of providers of services.[22]

The Joined Cases *Blanco Pérez and Chao Gómez* concern the legislation on the establishment of pharmacies in the Spanish region of Asturias, limiting the number

[19] ECJ, Case C-169/07 *Hartlauer* [2009] *ECR* I-0000 (n.y.r.), para 34.

[20] Ibid., para 35.

[21] Ibid., para 38, see also ECJ, Case C-531/06 *Commission* v. *Italy* [2009] *ECR* I-0000 (n.y.r.), para 44.

[22] *Hartlauer*, ibid., para 36.

of pharmacies in an area by reference to the population of that area, that is to say, a minimum number of 2,800 or 2,000 inhabitants per pharmacy, and a on a geographical restriction preventing the opening of a pharmacy within 250 metres of another pharmacy.[23] The legislation sets out criteria for distinguishing between competing candidate pharmacists, awarding points based on the professional and teaching experience of the candidates. More points are awarded for professional experience gained in towns with a population under 2,800.

In these cases, the Court based itself on the same arguments as in the *Hartlauer* case, to conclude that the conditions under scrutiny constitute a restriction on the freedom of establishment.[24] This confirms the observed trend in the jurisprudence to apply a low threshold for the application of EU internal market rules.

The application of free movement rules is not unconditional. Regulatory measures hindering free movement can be justified. In this respect it needs to be proven that the measure is necessary to protect the public interest objective (necessity test); is appropriate for securing the attainment of the objective pursued and does not go beyond what is necessary in order to attain it (proportionality test).[25] The delicate balance between the Member States regulatory autonomy and the application of free movement rules will be found in the context of justifying impediments to free movement. In its recent health care case law, the Court has been asked to draw some lines with regard to these conditions.

16.4 Is Capacity Planning Justified in the Light of General Interest?

In this section we clarify the extent to which the Court accepts health care planning measures as justified on legitimate grounds or by an overriding reason in the public interest.

A restriction may comply with EU law if it meets the following conditions. First, it must be justified on either legitimate grounds derived directly from the EU Treaty or by an overriding reason in the public interest drawn from ECJ case law.

Based on the legal exception contained in Article 46 TFEU for regulation aimed at protecting public health, the Court accepted that Member States could justify measures maintaining a balanced medical and hospital service open to all and a treatment facility or medical competence within a national territory that is essential

[23] ECJ, Joined Cases C-570/07 and C-571/07 *José Manuel Blanco Pérez and María del Pilar Chao Gómez* v. *Consejería de Salud y Servicios Sanitarios, Principado de Asturias* [2010] *ECR* I-0000 (n.y.r.).

[24] Ibid., para 53–60.

[25] ECJ, Case C-55/94 *Gebhard* [1995] *ECR* I-4165, para 37. See also ECJ, Case C-170/04 *Rosengren and Others* [2005] *ECR* I-4071, para 43, and ECJ, Case C-500/06 *Corporación Dermoestética* [2008] *ECR* I-0000 (n.y.r.), para 35.

for the public health and even the survival of the population.[26] Interestingly, in the most recent analysed cases, issued after the entering into force of the TFEU, the Court additionally refers to Article 168(1) TFEU and Article 35 of the Charter of Fundamental Rights of the European Union, under which, inter alia, a high level of protection for human health is to be ensured in the definition and implementation of all policies and activities of the European Union.[27] Furthermore, in these joined cases the Court explicitly weighs the internal market objectives against the imperative requirements of the protection of public health. The Court argues that:

> the seriousness of the objectives pursued in that domain may justify restrictions which have adverse consequences, and even substantial adverse consequences, for certain operators.[28]

Additionally, based on the so-called 'Rule of Reason'[29] restrictions to the freedom of establishment which are applicable without discrimination on grounds of nationality can be justified as well by overriding reasons of general interest, such as the risk of seriously undermining the financial balance of the social security system.[30]

16.4.1 Hospital Care

In the patient mobility case law, based on the free movement of services principles, the Court acknowledged the planning argument of the national health authorities and accepted it as a justification for submitting the reimbursement of cross-border hospital care to the condition of prior authorisation, which is restricting the freedom to provide services.

The Court argued that the number of hospitals, their geographical distribution, the way in which they are organised and the facilities with which they are provided, and even the nature of the medical services which they are able to offer, are all matters for which planning must be possible.[31] It acknowledged that this kind of planning generally meets a variety of concerns: it seeks to achieve the aim of ensuring that there is sufficient and permanent access to a balanced range of high-quality hospital treatment in the state concerned and assists in meeting a desire to control costs and to prevent, as far as possible, any wastage of financial, technical and human resources.[32] The Court accepted that, if patients were at liberty,

---

[26] ECJ, Case C-158/96 *Kohll* [1998] *ECR* I-1931, para 46.

[27] *José Manuel Blanco Pérez and María del Pilar Chao Gómez, supra* n. 23, para 65.

[28] Ibid., para 90.

[29] Rosas (2010), pp. 433–446.

[30] *Kohll*, supra n. 26, para 41.

[31] Ibid., para 76.

[32] ECJ, Case C-385/99 *Müller-Fauré and van Riet* [2003] *ECR* I-4509, paras 77, 78 and ECJ, Case C-157/99 *Smits and Peerbooms* [2001] *ECR* I-5473, paras 76, 78, 79.

regardless of the circumstances, to use the services of hospitals with which their health insurance fund had no agreement, whether those hospitals were situated in the Member State or in another Member State:

> all the planning which goes into the system of agreements in an effort to guarantee a rationalised, stable, balanced and accessible supply of hospital services would be jeopardised at a stroke.[33]

In particular the Court acknowledged that large outflows of patients would be liable to put at risk the very principle of having agreements with hospitals and, consequently, undermine all the planning and rationalisation carried out in this vital sector in an effort to avoid the phenomena of hospital overcapacity, imbalance in the supply of hospital medical care and logistical and financial wastage.[34]

According to the Court primary EU law allows Member States to restrict the freedom to provide medical and hospital services if the maintenance of treatment capacity or medical competence on the national territory, essential for the public health, or even the survival of the population, is at stake and if it would seriously undermine the necessary planning for medical services that is intended to control costs and prevent, as far as possible, any wastage of financial, technical and human resources.[35] The Court accepted that waiting times can arise from objectives relating to the planning and management of the supply of hospital care and that national authorities are entitled to institute a system of waiting lists, to set priorities on the basis of the available resources and capacities.[36]

In a recent case concerning German rules establishing a degree of geographical proximity between the pharmacy supplying medicinal products and the hospital for which those products are intended, the Court confirmed that this planning argument can also justify restrictions on the free movement of products.[37]

16.4.2 Outpatient Care Practices

For the assumption of the costs of non-hospital care provided in another Member State, the Court ruled in its patient mobility case law that a prior authorisation system could not be justified since it had not found specific evidence that, where insured persons were at liberty to go without prior authorisation to another Member State for outpatient treatment, this would give rise to such large outflows of patients, that this could seriously undermine the financial balance of the social

[33] *Smits and Peerbooms*, *supra* n. 32, para 81 and *Müller-Fauré and van Riet*, *supra* n. 32, para 82 and ECJ, Case C-372/04 *Watts* [2006] *ECR* I-4325, para 111.

[34] *Smits and Peerbooms*, *supra* n. 32, paras 105, 106.

[35] *Hartlauer*, *supra* n. 19, para 49.

[36] *Watts, supra* n. 33, paras 67 and 68.

[37] ECJ, Case C-141/07 *Commission* v. *Germany* [2008] *ECR* I-6935.

security system.[38] According to the Court, unlike the services provided by practitioners in their surgeries or at the patients home, those provided in a hospital take place within an infrastructure with, undoubtedly, certain very distinct characteristics, since the number of hospitals, their geographical distribution, the mode of their organisation and the equipment with which they are provided, and the nature of the medical services which they are able to offer, must all be planned for.[39] Although suggesting that planning is specific for the hospital sector, the Court did not a priori exclude that there are outpatient services for which planning is necessary.

Hartlauer was the first case in which the Court had to rule on the compatibility of capacity planning measures for non-hospital services, that is, national legislation making the establishment of outpatient health care providers subject to planning. According to Austrian law authorisation for the establishment of private outpatient dental clinics could be granted only if 'there was a need' to set up a new institution, having regard to the care already available, inter alia, from medical practitioners contracted to sickness funds. As it was for the decentralised authorities of the provinces to ensure that the legislation was enforced, the governments of Upper Austria and Vienna rejected the application by *Hartlauer* arguing that dental care was already adequately ensured by existing public and private non-profit-making health institutions and other contractual practitioners offering comparable services. On that basis, they concluded that there was no need to set up an additional private outpatient dental clinic.

Referring to the patient mobility case law, the Court recalls that the planning of medical services is intended to control costs and to prevent, as far as possible, any wastage of financial, technical and human resources, since the medical care sector generates considerable expenses and must satisfy increasing needs, while the financial resources available for health care are not unlimited, whatever the mode of funding applied.[40] In its opinion, planning of outpatient care services may prove to be indispensable for filling up possible gaps in the access to outpatient care as well as for avoiding duplication of structures in order to ensure medical care which is adapted to the needs of the population, covering the entire territory, including geographically isolated or otherwise disadvantaged regions.[41]

In this context the Court accepts that a Member State can organise medical care in such a way that it gives priority to a system of benefits in kind, so that all patients have easy access, throughout national territory, to the services of contracted practitioners.[42] The Advocate General pointed out that the assessment protects the existence of persons and institutions which carry out their activities as part of the public service task of the sickness insurance system.[43] According to the

[38] *Müller-Fauré and van Riet, supra* n. 32, paras 93, 95.

[39] *Smits and Peerbooms, supra* n. 32, para 76.

[40] *Hartlauer, supra* n. 19, para 49.

[41] Ibid., para 52.

[42] Ibid., para 53.

[43] *Hartlauer, supra* n. 19, Opinion of the Advocate General, para 105.

Austrian government an uncontrolled expansion of services on offer by the establishment of new independent outpatient dental clinics would have harmful consequences for the economic situation of the practitioners having concluded a contract with the sickness funds, since these private health institutions would only concentrate on the more profitable services, leaving the former with the task of offering the full range of services.[44] The Court appears to follow this reasoning.

The Court seems to withdraw from its earlier position in which it only acknowledged the need for planning for hospital services, with their very distinct characteristics. It acknowledges that providing outpatient care such as doctors surgeries and outpatient clinics can also be the subject of planning which requires prior authorisation for setting up new providers of services. In *Blanco Pérez and Chao Gómez* these findings are considered fully transposable to the provision of public health services in the field of pharmacy.[45]

It should be noted that the Advocate General in the *Hartlaue*r case took a slightly different approach, arguing that the Court's reasoning on the need to restrict cross-border provision of hospital care could also be extended to dental care, which also takes the form of actual surgery, such as extractions, the elimination of aesthetic deformations or certain orthodontic care, requiring qualified staff.[46] For this he explicitly referred to the concept of 'hospital care' as defined in the draft Directive on the application of patients rights in cross-border health care,[47] which extends the possibility for using prior authorisation to health care that requires the use of highly specialised and cost-intensive medical infrastructure or medical equipment or treatments that present a particular health risk for the patient or the population.[48] In the amended version that the Council adopted on 8 June 2010, reference to the hospital setting has been replaced by a broader reference to health care which is subject to planning. This approach has also been followed by several Member States—for example Belgium and France—when implementing the patient mobility case law. Further clarification as to whether an extended definition of 'hospital care' would be upheld by the ECJ could be expected from an action brought by the Commission, challenging French legislation that makes the reimbursement of medical services provided in a general practitioners surgery in another Member State, requiring the use of the extensive material supplies, conditional upon the grant of prior authorisation.[49]

---

[44] Ibid., para 42 and Opinion of the Advocate General, para 74.

[45] José Manuel Blanco Pérez and María del Pilar Chao Gómez, *supra* n. 23, para 70–71.

[46] Hartlauer, *supra* n. 19, para 42 and Opinion of the Advocate General, para 92.

[47] *Supra* n. 5.

[48] Hartlauer, *supra* n. 19 and Opinion of the Advocate General, fn 44.

[49] ECJ, Case C-512/08 Commission of the European Communities v. French Republic. In this recent case, the Court accepted that the considerations expressed in respect of medical services provided in a hospital setting, can be reproduced with regard to medical services involving the use of major medical equipment, even if those services are supplied outside such a setting. [2010], para 34, (n.y.r.), 5 October 2010.

16.4.3 The Health Care Sector Workforce

The Court has also had the opportunity to rule on cases relating to workforce planning in health care. One case concerned a German Law creating a quota system for psychotherapists wishing to practice under the statutory sickness insurance scheme, defining the number of psychotherapists corresponding to the needs of the region.[50] The Commission challenged the transitional provisions or 'established rights' of this quota system, which permitted psychotherapists to obtain an authorisation to practice independently of the quota system, solely to psychotherapists who had practised in a region under the statutory sickness insurance schemes during a reference period. Comparable or similar professional activity performed by psychotherapists under the sickness insurance schemes of another Member State, was not taken into account.

In this case it is not the quantitative restrictions on access to the profession of psychotherapist themselves, in the form of quotas based on the actual need for care, that are questioned, but the arrangement with regard to the acquired rights. The Court acknowledged the protection of an established right, namely the retention of patients following several years of professional activity, as an overriding ground of public interest. A Member State may consider it necessary to protect a practice and, by the same token, the professional activity of the persons concerned by means of the adoption of appropriate measures.[51] This case provides a good example to illustrate that conditions for access to the pursuit of health professions aim to protect both patients and licensed health care professionals. In this case the protection of public health is not at stake and not invoked as a justification.

A more recent case relates to a law of the Belgian French Community limiting in principle the total number of non-resident students, for each university institution for nine paramedical training courses to 30% of all enrolments in the preceding academic year.[52] Once that percentage has been reached, the non-resident students are selected with a view to their registration by drawing lots. This law was issued after the French Community of Belgium had noted for some years a significant increase in the number of students from other Member States, in particular France, enrolling in its institutions of higher education, in these paramedical courses. The Court states in this case that the link between the training of future health professionals and the objective of maintaining a balanced high-quality medical service open to all is only indirect and the causal relationship is less well established than in the case of health professionals who are already present on the market. The assessment of such a link will depend, inter alia, on a prospective analysis which will have to extrapolate, on the basis of a number of contingent and

[50] ECJ, Case C-456/05 *Commission* v. *Germany* [2007] *ECR* I-10517.

[51] Ibid., para 63.

[52] ECJ, Case C-73/08 *Bressol* and *Chaverot* [2010] *ECR* I-0000 (n.y.r.).

uncertain factors and take into account the future development of the health sector concerned, but also depend on an analysis of the situation at the outset.[53]

It should be noted that the cases with regard to human resources planning discussed here do not concern the national quota systems commonly referred to as *numerus clausus*, including measures such as restricting the number of candidates having access to training for a specific health profession; measures limiting the number of training places or quantitative restrictions on access to the pursuit of the profession. Most Member States establishing *numerus clausus* measures do not take into account candidates coming from other Member States when establishing these quotas, in order to comply with EU law. This thus constitutes an example of reverse discrimination: whereas domestic candidates are subject to the quota system, candidates coming from another Member State are not subject to it. This leads to situations in which candidates exceeding the quotas in their home Member State try their luck in neighbouring Member States that are not allowed to limit the inflows from abroad. Furthermore, candidates studying abroad can, when returning home to exercise their profession, thwart the planning policies domestically. For instance, it is argued that the extremely high proportion of students in physiotherapy and paramedical fields in the Belgian French community coming from France is due to the limits in the access to similar educational programmes in France.[54]

16.5 Are the Measures Proportionate?

As was previous shown in the previous section of this chapter, the Court recognises that capacity planning in health care through territorial and quantitative restrictions limiting the number of care providers can indeed be justified on the grounds of protecting public health or preserving an overriding reason of general interest. This is the case where it proves indispensable for:

- filling in possible gaps in access to public health services. This includes giving priority to a system of benefits in kind and preserving the contractual system, so that all patients (thus also the less well-off) have easy (and free) access to health care and to ensure sufficient and permanent access to high-quality services, throughout national territory (thus also in remote areas) by forcing providers to spread throughout the country;
- avoiding the duplication of structures and preventing any wastage of financial, technical and human resources;
- protecting a practice and the professional activity of the persons concerned.

---

[53] Ibid., para 69.

[54] Simonet (2006a, b).

So far the Court has not explicitly linked quantitative or territorial restrictions with the need to ensure that providers are able to gain sufficient experience or to avoid a situation that competition would reduce the quality of the services, nor on limiting the number of providers to avoid provider-induced demand.

Obstacles to the freedom of establishment must not only be justified by an imperative requirement in the general interest and be applied in a non-discriminatory manner, they must also be suitable for securing the attainment of the objective which they pursue and not go beyond what is necessary in order to attain it.[55] The core of the justification lies in this next step, the 'proportionality' test.[56] The case law discussed in this chapter with regard to health care provides clear examples of the application of this principle. Even if the Court gives the Member State a rather wide margin of discretion in assessing that the measure under scrutiny does not exceed what is necessary to attain the objective and that it cannot be achieved by a less restrictive measure, meeting the 'appropriateness test' is more difficult.

16.5.1 The Margin of Discretion for the Member States

When assessing whether restrictions on the free movement are appropriate, account must be taken, according to the Court, of the fact that the health and life of human beings rank foremost among the assets and interests protected by the Treaty,[57] and Member States have, in the absence of common or harmonised rules, the power to determine the level of protection they wish to afford to public health and the way in which that level is to be achieved. Since the level of protection may vary from one Member State to another, Member States must be allowed discretion[58] and, consequently, the fact that one Member State imposes less strict rules than another Member State does not mean that the latter's rules are disproportionate.[59]

In the case on quantitative and territorial restrictions of pharmacies in the Spanish region of Asturia, the Court acknowledges that neither Directive 2005/36 on professional qualifications[60] nor any other measure implementing the fundamental freedoms lay down rules concerning access to activities in the pharmacy field, which seek to set the conditions for opening new pharmacies in Member

---

[55] *Gebhard, supra* n. 25, para 37.

[56] Gekiere et al. (2010).

[57] *Commission* v. *Italy, supra* n. 21, para 36.

[58] *Hartlauer, supra* n. 19, para 30; *Commission* v. *Germany, supra* n. 38, para 51; *Apothekerkammer des Saarlandes and Others, supra* n. 16, para 19; *Commission* v. *Italy, supra* n. 21, para 36.

[59] *Commission* v. *Germany, supra* n. 37, para 51, *José Manuel Blanco Pérez and María del Pilar Chao Gómez, supra* n. 23, para 44.

[60] *OJ* 2005 L 255, p. 22.

States.[61] The Court refers to the Preamble of Directive 2005/36 stating that territorial distribution of pharmacies, in particular, remains a matter for the Member States.[62]

Furthermore, the Court notes that where there is uncertainty as to the existence or extent of risks to human health, a Member State should be able to take protective measures without having to wait until the reality of those risks becomes fully apparent,[63] for instance without having to wait for the shortage of health professionals to materialise. The same applies with regard to the risks to the quality of education in that field.[64] The Court takes the view that, when there is uncertainty about the efficacy of alternative or less restrictive measures to protect public health, the inherent risks can be invoked to justify the maintenance of their measure.[65] In the same line of reasoning the Advocate General argued that the Court is required to give considerable deference to the Member State particularly when there is conflicting evidence, including the experience in different Member States[66] and when the absence of a policy consensus is supported by the existence of important policy differences among Member States.[67]

The Court thus applies the precautionary principle. According to the European Commission, this principle may be invoked when the potentially dangerous effects of a phenomenon have been identified by a scientific and objective evaluation, and this evaluation does not allow the risk to be determined with sufficient certainty. The measures resulting from the use of the precautionary principle may take the form of a decision to act or not to act. The response depends on a political decision and is a function of the level of risk considered 'acceptable' by the society on which the risk is imposed.[68]

The Court seems to assign the responsibility to assess the existence or extent of the risks to the Member States, and does not require the provision of substantial evidence, when there is a clear link between the measure and the objective protecting public health. Most of these cases passed this test quite easily. In the *Bressol and Chaverot* case, however, which dealt with limiting access of students residing abroad to medical training, the Court appears to have been stricter. The causal relationship between the training of future health professionals on the one hand, and the objective of maintaining a balanced high-quality medical service open to all that contributes to achieving a high level of protection of health on the

---

61 *José Manuel Blanco Pérez and María del Pilar Chao Gómez, supra* n. 23, para 45.

62 Ibid., para 50.

63 *Commission* v. *Italy, supra* n. 21, para 54, *José Manuel Blanco Pérez and María del Pilar Chao Gómez, supra* n. 23, para 74; *Bressol and Chaverot, supra* n. 52, para 70.

64 *Bressol and Chaverot, supra* n. 52, para 70.

65 *Commission* v. *Italy, supra* n. 21, para 84.

66 *José Manuel Blanco Pérez and María del Pilar Chao Gómez, supra* n. 23, Opinion of the Advocate General, para 17.

67 Ibid., Opinion of the Advocate General, para 18.

68 Communication from the Commission on the precautionary principle, COM(2000) 1 final of 2 February 2000.

other hand, is not clear-cut. Therefore, the Court requested that competent national authorities would prove that there exists a real risk of shortage of health professionals and of impairment of the quality of education of health professionals. The appropriateness and proportionality of the measure would need to be substantiated by an objective, detailed analysis, supported by solid and consistent data, clearly demonstrating a genuine risk to public health.[69]

Most cases were also found, after an in-depth assessment, not to go beyond what is necessary to attain the objective pursued.[70] Only in the case of the German legislation on acquired rights for psychotherapists the Court found that the measure under scrutiny went beyond what was necessary to attain its stated objective. Clearly, the precautionary principle did not apply since the objective of this transitional measure was not the protection of public health. The transitional provisions only applied to psychotherapists who had practised under the German statutory sickness insurance scheme during the reference period and did not take account of comparable activity performed by psychotherapists under the statutory sickness insurance schemes of other Member States. The Court argued that the number of the latter psychotherapists was limited and that Germany had provided no evidence to suggest that taking account of this group would have jeopardised the objective that the transitional provisions were designed to achieve. It concluded, therefore, that it was disproportionate not to take them into account.[71]

The Court thus seems not to interfere heavily in the substance of the policies pursued, by assessing whether the measure is appropriate, or whether the objective could be pursued by less restrictive measures, when the aim of the measure is to protect the public health.

As we show in the next section, the Court is more severe when it comes to assessing the coherence and consistency of the investigated measures and their procedural aspects.

16.5.2 Coherence and Consistency

The Court assesses whether the legislation is suitable to protect public health and the financial balance of the social security system effectively against the risks connected with an uncontrolled expansion of providers. To conclude on the appropriateness, the Court assesses whether the legislation genuinely reflects a concern to attain this objective in a consistent and systematic manner.[72] Referring to the risk of regulatory capture, the Advocate General in the *Blanco Pérez and*

---

[69] *Bressol and Chaverot*, *supra* n. 52, para 71.

[70] See for example, *José Manuel Blanco Pérez and María del Pilar Chao Gómez*, *supra* n. 23, para 112.

[71] *Commission* v. *Germany*, *supra* n. 50, para 72.

[72] *Hartlauer*, *supra* n. 19, para 55.

Chao Gómez case clarifies that this requirement allows the Court to distinguish legislation that might even have been originally aimed at the pursuit of such a goal but has become captured by certain specific interests, such as those of the already established pharmacists.[73] It is a requirement that can be said to protect the integrity of the regulatory and legislative process and proper political accountability.[74] The Court seems especially to rely on the assessment of whether the legislation was applied in a coherent and consistent way when assessing legislation that places limits on the number of licences or authorisations attributed in a certain sector.[75]

In the *Blanco Pérez and Chao Gómez* case the Court regarded the quantitative and territorial restrictions on the establishment of pharmacies in the Spanish region of Asturia coherent and consistent for as long as the rules would not prevent, in any geographical area which has special demographic features, the establishment of a sufficient number of pharmacies to ensure adequate pharmaceutical services.[76]

In the *Hartlauer* case the Austrian authorisation scheme failed the test of coherence and consistency. The Court criticised the fact that prior authorisation based on an assessment of the needs of the market which was required for setting up and operating new independent outpatient dental clinics did not apply to the setting up of new doctors' group practices. The Court argued that those two categories of providers of services may have comparable features and are thus liable to affect in an equivalent manner the economic situation of contractual practitioners in certain geographical areas and, in consequence, the attainment of the planning objectives pursued by the competent authorities.[77] This inconsistency also affects the attainment of the objective of preventing a risk of serious harm to the financial balance of the national social security system.[78]

It could be argued that the Court concluded differently on the difference in behaviour between self-employed health professionals and health professionals employed by a company in the Austrian *Hartlauer* case on dental clinics and in the Italian and German cases on pharmacies.[79] In Austria, the practitioners who provide medical services within group practices have the status of personally liable partner and are authorised to practice independently as dental practitioners, whereas the practitioners in an outpatient clinic have the status of employee. According to the Court the documentary evidence does not show that that circumstance has any definite effect on the nature or volume of the services

---

[73] *José Manuel Blanco Pérez and María del Pilar Chao Gómez, supra* n. 23, Opinion of the Advocate General, para 32.

[74] Ibid., Opinion of the Advocate General, para 21.

[75] See for example, ECJ, Case C-360/04 *Placanica and Others* [2007] *ECR* I-1891, para 55.

[76] *José Manuel Blanco Pérez an d María del Pilar Chao Gómez, supra* n. 23, para 94–103.

[77] *Hartlauer, supra* n. 19, para 60.

[78] Ibid., para 61.

[79] *Apothekerkammer des Saarlandes and Others, supra* n. 16 and *Commission* v. *Italy, supra* n. 21.

provided.[80] On the other hand, with regard to pharmacies the Court held that a self-employed pharmacist operates a pharmacy not with a purely economic objective, but that his private interest connected with the making of a profit is tempered by his training, by his professional experience and by the responsibility that he owes, given that any breach of the rules of law or professional conduct undermines not only the value of his investment but also his own professional existence.[81] The Court concluded that a Member State may take the view that the operation of a pharmacy by a non-pharmacist may represent a risk to public health, in particular to the reliability and quality of the supply of medicinal products at retail level, because the pursuit of profit in the course of such operation does not involve moderating factors such as those, noted for independent pharmacists.[82]

16.5.3 Circumscribing the Exercise of the Discretion of National Authorities

In the assessment of the proportionality of the capacity planning measures procedural elements play an important role. The Court assigns the Member States a relatively wide margin of discretion in choosing their policy options, but these should be applied in a consistent and coherent way and have to adequately circumscribe the exercise of discretion by the national authorities. It is indeed settled case law that prior administrative authorisation schemes must be based on objective, non-discriminatory criteria known in advance.[83]

In the *Hartlauer* case, the Court found that in practice different criteria were used, depending on the province, to ascertain whether the condition of the existence of a need for the services offered by the new institution is satisfied.[84] In the province of Vienna, the existence of a need was assessed on the basis of the number of patients per dental practitioner in the area covered, without the number of patients in question being fixed or brought in advance to the notice of the persons concerned in any way. In the province of Upper Austria, the relevant assessment was made on the basis of the answers given by practitioners practicing in the catchment area of the independent outpatient dental clinic intended to be set up, even though they were potential direct competitors of that clinic. The Court pointed out that such a method was liable to affect the objectivity and impartiality of the treatment of the application for authorisation.[85] The Court therefore concluded that the assessment of the needs of the market was not based on a condition

80 *Hartlauer, supra* n. 19, para 59.

81 *Apothekerkammer des Saarlandes and Others,supra* n. 16, para 37.

82 Ibid., para 39.

83 *Hartlauer, supra* n. 19, para 64.

84 Ibid., para 66.

85 Ibid., para 69.

capable of adequately circumscribing the exercise by the national authorities of their discretion.[86]

Interestingly, the Advocate General reached the opposite conclusion stating that with regard to the assessment of the health needs of the population, a national law sets out the criteria which are to be taken into account, that is to say, the purpose of the institution, the services which it proposes to offer, the health institutions' plan of the province concerned and, finally, the existing provision of care.[87] The assessment is a tool used at provincial level in the implementation of the 'plan for health institutions', an instrument of health care planning in the light of guidelines laid down by the Republic of Austria.[88]

It can be questioned what the impact of this approach would be on decentralisation in health systems. Whereas the powers for health care policies are often shared between different governance levels, for instance with framework legislation at national level and interpretation and implementation at regional level, the Court's requirement to adequately circumscribe the exercise by the national authorities of their discretion could indeed force national authorities to more carefully define the criteria that the regions would apply when implementing national legislation. This could lead to decreased policy margin for the regions, and thus to more centralisation in health care policy.

16.6 Conclusions

Our analysis shows that quantitative and territorial restrictions limiting the number of health care providers are invariably caught by the free movement provisions, in particular by the freedom of establishment.[89] The Court recognises the need, and thus the right for Member States, to regulate and plan the national health service capacity and professional workforce in order to preserve the public interest.

Territorial and quantitative restrictions limiting the number of care providers can be justified by the need to protect public health; the financial viability of the social protection system and the professional activity of the persons concerned. This is particularly the case when the measures aim to prevent wastage of financial, technical and human resources; to ensure affordable care to all patients; to ensure universal access to care, including for patients in remote areas and to protect a practice and the professional activity of the persons concerned. For all these reasons it can be necessary to limit establishment of providers in order to give priority to other providers who are able to meet these objectives.[90] It is, however,

86 Ibid., para 70.

87 Ibid., Opinion of the Advocate General, para 99.

88 Ibid., para 93.

89 See Sect. 16.3.

90 See Sect. 16.4.

not clear whether the number of health care providers can be limited in order to ensure that providers are able to gain sufficient experience or to avoid that competition would reduce quality of the services, nor on limiting the number of providers to avoid provider-induced demand.

The Court assigns the Member States with a relatively wide margin of discretion in choosing their policy options. It allows Member States to take protective measures where there is uncertainty as to the existence or extent of risks to human health, without having to wait until the reality of the risks becomes fully apparent and thus applies the precautionary principle.

The Court seems not to interfere heavily in the substance of the policies pursued, by assessing whether the measure is appropriate, or whether the objective could be pursued by less restrictive measures, when the aim of the measure is clearly to protect the public health.[91]

The Court is more severe when it comes to assessing whether the measures are applied in a consistent and coherent way and adequately circumscribe the exercise by the national authorities of their discretion. The assessment of the consistency and coherence of the policy aims to reveal whether the policy has been well thought through and to make sure it has not been the subject of regulatory capture. Regulatory capture occurs when a state regulatory agency created to act in the public interest instead acts in favour of the commercial or special interests that dominate in the sector it is charged with regulating. In particular the Court seems to rely on the assessment of whether the legislation was applied in a coherent and consistent way when assessing legislation that limits the number of licenses or authorisations attributed in a certain sector. In the assessment as to whether the exercise by the national authorities of their discretion is adequately circumscribed, procedural elements play an important role.[92]

This jurisprudence shows that the authorisation requirements that should have been systematically screened, if health care services had remained within the scope of activity of the Services Directive, are now scrutinised on a case-by-case basis by the Court, based on complaints of interested competitors. The Court suggests that if health care services had remained under the scope of the Services Directive, Member States would, pursuant to Article 14(5) of this Directive, not be allowed to take measures which make the granting of an authorisation subject to the case-by-case application of the existence of an economic need or market demand.[93]

The Court seems to take into account the political message of the exclusion of health care services from the scope of the Services Directive, underscoring that health care should not be treated as any other commodity, due to its specific characteristics. The Court acknowledges the risks of unbridled de-regulation in this sector and attributes the Member States with a wide margin in choosing their

---

[91] See Sect. 16.4.

[92] See Sect. 16.5.

[93] Hartlauer, *supra* n. 19, Opinion of the Advocate General, Fn 37.

policy instruments, as long as they are applied in a coherent and consistent way and based on objective criteria, known in advance.

Finally, we could question whether the Court itself does not introduce some degree of inconsistency when ruling that patients are at liberty to go to the care provider of their choice in another Member State, whereas, domestically they only can receive reimbursement of treatment from contracted providers.[94] Even if this could seem to create an inconsistency in the policy, the Court does, however, not forbid this so-called reverse discrimination since EU law does not deal with purely internal situations. Reverse discrimination arises when nationals of a Member State are disadvantaged because they are subject to a national measure, while foreign (EU) nationals are protected from that national measure by virtue of EC law.[95]

Acknowledgment Thanks to Herwig Verschueren, Miek Peeters, Marleen Steenbrugghe, and Irene Glinos for comments on an earlier draft of this chapter.

References

Bloor K, Maynard A (2003) Planning human resources in health care: towards an economic approach. An international comparative review. Canadian Health Services Research Foundation, Ottawa

De Bijl N, de Nederveen-Van Kragt I (1997) 'Legal safeguards against medical practice by not suitably qualified persons: a comparative study in seven EU countries. Eur J Health Law 4

Dubois CA (2006) Reshaping the regulation of the workforce in European health care systems. In: Dubois CA, McKee M, Nolte E (eds) Human resources for health in Europe. Open University Press, Berkshire

Ettelt S et al (2008) Planning health care capacity: whose responsibility? In: Rechel B et al (eds) Investing in hospitals of the future. WHO on behalf of European Observatory on Health Systems and Policies, Copenhagen

Gekiere W et al (2010) EU law and the freedom to provide services and health care. In: Mossialos E, Permanand G, Baeten R, Hervey T (eds) Health systems governance in Europe: the role of EU law and policy. Cambridge University Press, Cambridge

Levine M, Forrence J (1990) Regulatory capture, public interest, and the public agenda: toward a synthesis. J Law Econ Organ. 6(2)

Ritter C (2006) Purely Internal situations, reverse discrimination, Guimont, Dzodzi and article 234. Available at SSRN: http://ssrn.com/abstract=954242

Rosas A (2010) Life after Dassonville and Cassis: evolution but no revolution. In: Poiares Maduro M, Azoulai L (eds) The past and future of EU law. The classics of EU law revisited on the 50th anniversary of the Rome treaty. Hart Publishing, Oxford

Simonet MD (2006a) Avant-projet de décret régulant le nombre d'étudiants dans certaines filières: le Gouvernement poursuit la concertation. Press release of the Minister for Higher Education of the Communauté française (9 March)

---

[94] *Müller-Fauré* and *van Riet*, *supra* n. 33.

[95] Ritter (2006), accessed on 17 June 2010.

Simonet MD (2006b) Préserver un enseignement supérieur de qualité et de proximité pour les étudiants de la Communauté française: limitation à 30% du nombre d'étudiants non-résidents, Press release of the Minister for Higher Education of the Communauté française (3 February)
Taylor D (2004) Regulating pharmaceutical distribution and retail pharmacy in Europe. In: Mossialos E et al (eds) Regulating pharmaceuticals in Europe: striving for efficiency equity and quality. Open University Press, Buckingham

Chapter 17
Public Procurement Law and Health Care: From Theory to Practice

Vassilis Hatzopoulos and Hélène Stergiou

Contents

V. Hatzopoulos (✉)
Democritus University of Thrace, Thrace, Greece
e-mail: vasshatz@socadm.duth.gr

V. Hatzopoulos
College of Europe, Bruges, Belgium

V. Hatzopoulos
University of Nottingham, Nottingham, UK

H. Stergiou
Department of International and European Law, Radboud University, Nijmegen, The Netherlands
e-mail: H.Stergiou@jur.ru.nl

J. W. van de Gronden et al. (eds.), *Health Care and EU Law*, Legal Issues of Services of General Interest, DOI: 10.1007/978-90-6704-728-9_17,

17.1 Introduction

Recent literature explores the impact of EU Law on national health care systems through an analysis of the application of EU competition law, EU internal market law and EU state aid rules.[1] In this chapter the impact of the fast-growing field of EU public procurement rules on health care will be explored. Public procurement rules are a concrete expression of the fundamental freedoms, in particular the free provision of services (Article 56 TFEU). According to settled case law:

> the purpose of coordinating at Community level the procedures for the award of public contracts is to eliminate barriers to the freedom provide services and goods and therefore to protect the interests of traders established in a Member State who wish to offer goods or services to contracting authorities established in another Member State.[2]

EU public procurement policy mainly consists of EU secondary law. Since the 1970s the EU has been regulating public procurement through Directives in all of its Member States in order to accomplish a single market and remove restrictions on goods, services, establishment and capital. However, it is not until recently that both the application and enforcement of EU public procurement law have been rapidly expanding. In 2007 public procurement accounted for an important proportion of economic activity: over € 2,000 billion or around 17% of EU GDP.[3] Local and cross-border competition in this area is delivering savings, with contracting authorities spending on average between 5 and 8% less than they had

[1] See, among many, (a) for the impact of the internal market rules, Hatzopoulos (2002), pp. 683–729, and more recently, Hatzopoulos (2005), pp. 123–160; Davies (2002), pp. 27–40; Cabral (2004), pp. 673–685, and van der Mei (2002), pp. 289–215 and van der Mei (2004), pp. 57–67; Dawes (2006), pp. 167–182; (b) for state aid see Hatzopoulos (2009), pp. 761–804 and Hatzopoulos (2010, forthcoming); (c) for a full account of the relationships between EU and Health Law see Hervey and McHale (2004).

[2] For example, ECJ, Case C-380/98 *University of Cambridge* [2000] *ECR* I-8035, para 16; ECJ, Case C-19/00 *SIAC Construction* [2001] *ECR* I-7725, para 32; Case C-92/00 HI [2002] *ECR* I-5553, para 43; and ECJ, Case C-507/03 *Commission* v. *Ireland* (*An Post*) [2007] *ECR* I-9777, para 27.

[3] European Commission working document: measurement of Indicators for the economic impact of public procurement policy of 27 April 2010. Available on: http://www.ec.europa.eu/internal_market/publicprocurement/index_en.htm.

originally earmarked.[4] Both on a national and EU level the number of court cases is increasing.[5] The Commission has stepped up the efforts of monitoring compliance with public procurement law.[6]

The current developments with regard to the (potential) influence of EU public procurement concern the definitions of a contracting authority and a public sector contract in relation to health care. For EU public procurement law to be applicable, both definitions are decisive.

First, public entities that qualify as contracting authorities in terms of the procurement Directives need to tender in accordance with the rules of these Directives. The entities covered by the Directive fall within two broad categories: (i) the State, regional or local authorities (public authorities), associations formed by one or several of such authorities; and (ii) bodies governed by public law and associations formed by one or several of such bodies governed by public law.[7] Health care entities, such as hospitals and sickness funds, which qualify as contracting authorities under the procurement directives, may face the compulsory application of procurement rules while purchasing medical supplies, goods and services.

Second, in order to determine whether the procurement Directives are applicable, a public sector contract should be at stake. Following recent case law of the European Court of Justice a growing number of services escaping the full applicability of the Directives, among which health care services, are subject to the transparency principle, under the condition that these services are of 'certain cross-border interest'.[8] This may result into tendering obligations, even for excluded public contracts, such as health care services.

In this chapter we explore the possible effects of EU public procurement on national health care systems by analysing both procurement definitions in relation to health care. We start our analysis by summarising the applicable EU public procurement legislation, principles and soft law and its exact scope in relation to health care (Sect. 17.2). Subsequently, we turn to the parties in a contract, subject to procurement rules in the field of health care, addressing both the definition of contracting authorities and relevant case law (Sect. 17.3). This will then lead to an analysis of possible justifications for not holding a tender procedure in the field of

---

4 Ibid.

5 See also Drijber and Stergiou (2009), pp. 805–846, in which the 'specialist' case law on public procurement is placed in the wider context of the 'general' case law on the free provision of services.

6 Ibid.

7 Article 1(9) Public Sector Directive.

8 ECJ, Case C-324/98 *Telaustria* [2000] *ECR* I-10745; ECJ, Case C-59/00 *Vestergaard* [2001] *ECR* I-9505; ECJ, Case C-231/03 *Coname* [2005] *ECR* I-7287; ECJ, Case C-264/03 *Commission* v. *France (social housing)* [2005] *ECR* I-8831; ECJ, Case C-458/03 *Parking Brixen* [2005] *ECR* I-8585; *Commission* v. *Ireland (An Post)*, cited *supra* n. 2; ECJ, Case C-6/05 *Medipac-Kazantzides* [2007] *ECR* I-4557; ECJ, Case C-220/06 *Asociación Profesional de Empresas de Reparto y Manipulado de Correspondencia* v. *Administración General del Estado (Correos)* [2007] *ECR* I-12175; ECJ, Joined Cases C-147/06 & C-148/06 *SECAP SpA and Santorso Soc. Coop. Arl* v. *Commune di Torino*[2008] *ECR* I-3565.

health care (Sect. 17.4). Finally, we illustrate the impact of EU public procurement rules on health care by analysing a Dutch case study, in which the question whether general hospitals in the Netherlands, which operate in a market-orientated health care system since the 1 January 2006, qualify as contracting authorities in terms of 2004/18/EC Directive (Sect. 17.5). Our conclusions will follow in Sect. 17.6.

17.2 Health Care and EU Public Procurement: Rules and Principles

The rules on contract award procedures are currently contained in two Directives of 2004. Directive 2004/17/EC provides rules on the procurement procedures of entities operating in the water, energy, transport and postal services sectors (Utilities Directive).[9] The Utilities Directive does not apply to public contracts in the field of health care. For all other public contracts the rules are found in Directive 2004/18/EC (Public Sector Directive).[10] First, the scope of this Directive will be explored (Sect. 17.2.1). Subsequently, the scope of the Directive in relation to health care will be explored (Sect. 17.2.2). Finally, relevant case law of the ECJ with regard to the applicability of the transparency principle to public health care services is discussed (Sect. 17.2.3).

17.2.1 The Scope of Directive 2004/18/EC

The scope of the Public Sector Directive is determined by (i) the nature of a public contract and (ii) the value of a public contract. Depending on the nature and value of a contract, it should be tendered in accordance with the rules of the Directive. In other words, a public contract that *ratione materiae* falls under the scope of this Directive and the value of which exceeds the applicable financial thresholds must be tendered by a contracting authority in accordance with the Directive.

Public contracts are divided into three main categories: public service contracts, public works contracts and public supply contracts. In this contribution we focus on the procurement of public services. The Directive does not define public

---

[9] Directive 2004/17/EC on the coordination of the procurement procedures of entities operating in the water, energy, transport and postal services sectors (*OJ* 2004, L 134/1).

[10] Directive 2004/18/EC on the coordination of procedures for the award of public works contracts, public supply contracts and public service contracts (*OJ* 2004, L 134/114).

services.[11] For the purposes of the Directive, the meaning of services is very wide. All services are covered. It includes all 'public contracts other than public works or supply contracts having as their object the provisions of services referred to in Annex II of the Directive'.[12] This Annex makes a distinction between Part A- and Part B-services. The threshold values have been set at levels, which are intended to reflect those contracts which are likely to attract bidders from other Member States.[13] Currently, the threshold for the award of service contracts by government departments and entities closely associated with these departments lies at € 125.000. For contracting authorities, such as regional and local authorities, the Directive applies to all Part A services contracts with a value equal to or greater than € 193.000.[14]

A number of public contracts is excluded from the scope of the Public Sector Directive. This Directive does not apply, for example, to below-threshold contracts, to secret contracts and contracts requiring special security measures (Article 14), employment contracts, research and development services, financial services (Article 16), service concessions (Article 17) or service contracts awarded on the basis of an exclusive right (Article 18). A general provision in the Directive exempting health care from the application of the Directive does not exist. However, recital 6 of the Directive gives contracting authorities the possibility to implement 'measures necessary to protect public (...) health, human and animal life (...)' provided that these measures are in conformity with the Treaty.

17.2.2 A Light Procurement Regime for Health Care Services Under Directive 2004/18/EC

The Directive does not explicitly regulate the procurement of health care services. However, health care services are listed in Annex II B of the Directive and therefore a special 'light' procurement regime applies.

[11] In its Guide to the Community rules on public procurement of services, the Commission states: 'Within the meaning of the EC Treaty services are considered to be services where they are normally provided for remuneration, insofar as they are not governed by the provisions relating to the freedom of movement for goods, capital and persons.' See *Guide to the Community rules on public procurement of services other than in the water, energy, transport and telecommunications sectors.* Directive 92/50/EEC, p. 5. This approach is in line with settled case law of the ECJ, in which the Court has held that Article 56 TFEU (ex Article 49 EC) is applicable to services normally provided for remuneration. ECJ, Case 263/86 *Humbel* [1988] *ECR* 5365, para 17 and ECJ, Case C-157/99 *Smits and Peerbooms* [2001] *ECR* I-5473, para 58.

[12] Article 1(2)(d) Public Sector Directive.

[13] New thresholds entered into force on 1 January 2010. See Regulation (EC) No 1177/2009, amending Directives 2004/17/EC and 2004/18/EC in respect of their application thresholds for the procedures for the award of contracts (*OJ* 2009, L 314/64).

[14] Article 7(b) first indent Public Sector Directive.

Since the adoption of the Directive 92/50/EEC on the coordination of procedures for the award of public service contracts[15] (now consolidated and amended by the Public Sector Directive), a so-called 'two-tier' approach exists towards the procurement of public service contracts. This approach was maintained in the Directives of 2004.[16] This means that the Public Sector Directive applies in its entirety only to contracts designated as 'Part A-service contracts' also referred to as contracts for 'priority services'.[17] In effect, these services were identified as being of priority interest from the point of view of development of cross-border operations.[18] In other words, Part A-services are those on which the open internal market regime is likely to have the most impact (and conversely), taking into account factors such as the potential for cross-border trade and economic importance.[19] The services, including health care services, listed in Annex II B ('non-priority services' or 'Part B-services'), do fall within the scope of the Directive but they are subject to a 'light' procurement regime. This only requires (a) non-discriminatory technical specifications to be used in the tendering documents (Article 23) and (b) the ex post publication of the results of the award (Article 35(4)).[20] There exists no tendering obligation for Part B-services. It is therefore in principle lawful to grant Part B-service contracts without organising any form of procurement procedure.[21] This light Part B-regime has been based on the assumption that from an internal market perspective the services in question

---

[15] Council Directive 92/50/EEC of 18 June 1992 relating to the coordination of procedures for the award of public service contracts as amended by Directive 97/52/EC.

[16] In its review of the procurement Directive on public service contracts 92/50/EEC under Article 43 of that Directive, the Commission was obliged within three years of adoption to consider applying all the provisions of the Directive to Part B-services and make proposals for adapting the Directive. But no changes had been made since the adoption of Directive 92/50. During the legislative process of the new Directives no revision took place and no proposals were made. According to an EU Commission official, Member States were at that time reluctant to discuss a more 'liberalised' regime of Part B-services.

[17] Annex II A of the Directive covers, *inter alia*, maintenance and repair of equipment and vehicles, some transport services, financial services, computer services, research and development for the authority's own purpose, accounting services, management consultancy, computer services, architectural and planning services, advertising, building cleaning and property management, publishing and printing and sewerage and sanitation services.

[18] Guide to the Community rules on public procurement of services, *supra* n. 11, p. 7.

[19] Recital 21 of Services Directive 92/50/EEC. See also Arrowsmith (2005), p. 314, para 6.44.

[20] Article 21 Public Sector Directive.

[21] Annex II B to the Directive lists 11 categories of public services, which are subject to a 'light' procurement regime. The following services are currently included in Annex II B: hotel and restaurant services, rail and transport services, water transport services, supporting and auxiliary transport services, legal services, personal replacement and supply services, except employment contracts, investigation and security services, except armoured car services, education and vocational education services, health and social services, recreational, cultural and sporting services and other services, except contracts for the acquisition, development, production or co-production of programmes by broadcasting organisations and contracts for broadcasting time. A service falls in the last category 'other services' only in the exceptional case where it is not possible to place it in any of the categories of Annex IIA or Annex IIB.

have no priority in terms of establishing the internal market. These types of services are considered to be less capable of attracting international competition either because of the nature of the services (for example: legal and administrative services which are based on knowledge with national laws and jurisdictions) or because of the location in which they are provided (hotel and restaurant services). With regard to these categories of services it was considered necessary merely to give service providers the minimum information needed to explore the market, and to create an information base which would permit informed judgments to be made about possible application of the procedural and other rules of the former procurement directive on public service contracts to some or all of these categories.[22]

In order to further assess which health services are included in Annex II B, one has to look at the applicable categorisation and sub-categorisation. Annex II B refers to a specific form-based category. Health care services are grouped in category 25 of Annex II B, together with social work services. The following main categories of health services are, based on the Common Procurement Vocabulary (CPV) 2008, included in category 25 of Part B:

85100000-0 Health services
85110000-3 Hospital and related services
85120000-6 Medical practice and related services
85130000-9 Dental practice and related services
85140000-2 Miscellaneous health services
85150000-5 Medical imaging services
85160000-8 Optician services
85170000-1 Acupuncture and chiropractor services

The CPV, adopted by Regulation (EC) No. 213/2008, is in use since 17 September 2008 and consists of a main vocabulary for defining the subject matter of a contract, and a supplementary vocabulary for adding further qualitative information. The main vocabulary is based on a tree structure comprising codes of up to 9 digits (an 8 digit code plus a check digit) associated with a wording that describes the type of services forming the subject of the contract. As indicated on the website of the EU, the use of the CPV is mandatory in the EU as from 1 February 2006: 'Contracting authorities should try to find the code that suits their envisaged purchase as accurately as possible. Although in some occasions contracting authorities may find themselves having to select several codes, it is important that they select a single code for the title of the contract notice'.[23]

In case a service falls both within Annex II A and II B or a public contract has as its object both products and services within the meaning of Annex II, it must be considered a Part B-public service contract if the value of the services in question exceeds that of the products or the Part A-services covered by the contract.[24] In

[22] See Guide to the Community rules on public procurement of services, *supra* n. 11, p. 9.

[23] http://simap.europa.eu/codes-and-nomenclatures/codes-cpv/codes-cpv_en.htm.

[24] Article 7(a)(b) Public Sector Directive.

such cases the general rule applies, that it is not possible to avoid the application of the Directives by including the service in a contract, which for some reason would not be subject to the Directive.[25] It is, therefore, necessary to examine whether the contracting authority could have split the transactions into separate contracts, one or more of which would have been subject to the Directives.[26] So, in assessing whether Part A- and Part B-services are artificially packed together or split up, the intention of the contracting authority in a specific case should be scrutinised. 'If the services naturally combine to achieve a single purpose, then splitting them up would be artificial (...). On the other hand, if the services do not naturally combine to achieve a single purpose, then packaging them together (where the value of the non-priority services is greater) would be artificial'.[27]

This has also been the approach by the Court in the *Tögel* case, which dealt with health care services.[28] In this case an integrated service contract was at stake (services consisting in the transport of injured and sick persons with a nurse in attendance), which involved some components covered by Part A (land transport services) and some by Part B (ambulance services). The Court ruled with reference to Article 9(3) of the Directive that it is prohibited to artificially group in one contract both Part A- and Part B-services 'without there being any link arising from the a joint purpose or operation', with the sole purpose of increasing the proportion of Part B-services and thus avoiding the full application of the Directive. According to the Court not only the artificial splitting, but also the artificial grouping of contracts is prohibited.

Arrowsmith has criticised the 'greater value rule' for facilitating circumvention of the full procurement regime of Part A-services in the case that Part A-services are of a value above the threshold, but the Part B-services are of greater value. In that way the Part A-services are exempted from the full regime, although the rules would apply if the Part A services were purchased separately.[29] However, in the *Felix Swoboda* case[30] the Court decided that there does not exist an obligation for the contracting authority to separate in that case the Part B-services from the Part A-services and to award separate contracts in respect of them.

As health care services qualify as Part-B services, paragraph 2.3 deals with the obligations resulting from recent case law by the ECJ on the application of the transparency principle.

---

[25] Article 9(3) of the Public Sector Directive prohibits the artificial splitting of contracts for the purpose of avoiding the application of the Directive.

[26] See Guide to the Community rules on public procurement of services, *supra* n. 11, p. 12.

[27] Trepte (2007), pp. 230–231, para 4.98.

[28] ECJ, Case C-76/97 *Walter Tögel* v. *Niederösterreichische Gebietskrankenkasse* [1998] *ECR* I-5357.

[29] Arrowsmith (2005), p. 315, para 6.47.

[30] ECJ, Case C-411/00 *Felix Swoboda GmbH* v. *Österreichische Nationalbank* [2002] *ECR* I-10567.

17.2.3 General Principles Applicable to the Award of Health Care Services: Change of Procurement Regime Following the Transparency Case Law?

When assessing the impact of EU Public Procurement Law on national health care systems, general principles of law applicable to the award of health care services should be taken into account. The Treaty contains general rules that prohibit Member States from discriminating against the undertakings of other Member States and from having in place other barriers to market access (Article 34 TFEU (ex Article 28 EC), Article 45 TFEU (ex Article 39 EC) and Article 56 TFEU (ex Article 49 EC).[31] As we concluded it is lawful under the Directive to grant health care services and other Part B-service contracts without organising any form of procurement procedure.

However, in a series of recent judgments the Court has intervened and has developed a special *Transparency* case law, in which it has decided that the award of excluded public service contracts, such as Part B-services, must respect the principle of transparency, as a means of ensuring equal treatment of potentially interested parties.[32] The Part B-procurement regime of health care services has been mostly affected by this case law, since this case law may lead to an obligation to tender.

In the cases *Telaustria, Coname* and *Parking Brixen* the award of service *concessions* was a central issue.[33] Service concessions, that is, the situations where the service providers do not get fully paid by the contracting authority for their services, but are remunerated by the users, thus participating in the operational risk of the services offered, are not covered by the Directive.[34]

---

[31] By the same token, recital 2 of the Directive states that 'the award of contracts concluded in the Member States on behalf of the State, regional or local authorities and other bodies governed by public law entities, is subject to the principles of the Treaty and in particular to the principle of freedom of movement of goods, the principle of freedom of establishment and the principle of freedom to provide services and to the principles deriving there from, such as the principle of equal treatment, the principle of non-discrimination, the principle of mutual recognition, the principle of proportionality and the principle of transparency.' Furthermore, Article 2 of the Public Sector Directive stipulates that operators can benefit from opportunities in other Member States by stating that Member States have to comply with the principles of non-discrimination and transparency when awarding public contracts.

[32] The equal treatment principle in relation to public procurement was first mentioned in ECJ, Case C-243/89 *Commission* v. *Denmark* (*Storebaelt*) [1993] *ECR* I-3353, para 33. It was further developed in ECJ, Case C-21/03 *Fabricom* v. *Belgian State* [2005] *ECR* I-1559, para 14. The principle of equal treatment entails an obligation of transparency. See, for the first time, ECJ, Case C-275/98 *Unitron Scandinavia and 3-S* [1999] *ECR* I-8921, para 31. See for general literature on the transparency case law: Arrowsmith (2005), p. 354; Arrowsmith (2006), p. 344; McGowan (2007), pp. 274–283 and Brown (2007), p. 1.

[33] *Telaustria*, para 62, *Coname* and *Parking Brixen*, *supra* n. 8.

[34] See for literature on the transparency principle and service concessions: Neergaard (2007), pp. 387–409 and Stergiou (2009), pp. 159–184.

According to the Court, in *Telaustria,* the first of this series of judgments, transparency 'consists in ensuring for the benefit of any potential tenderer, a degree of advertising sufficient to enable the services market to be opened up to competition and the impartiality of the procurement process to be reviewed'.[35] Unfortunately, the Court did not specify what kind or degree of publicity is necessary; for example, whether it is sufficient to publish an announcement for a list of approved suppliers or if publicity must be Europe-wide.[36] Nor was it clear whether 'a sufficient degree of advertising' implies an obligation to tender. It was not until 2005 that the Court had an opportunity to clarify what 'a sufficient degree of advertising' actually means. In *Coname,* it held that transparency does not necessarily involve 'an obligation to hold an invitation to tender'.[37] Rather it implies that the contracting authority is obliged to ensure that an undertaking located in the territory of another Member State has access to appropriate information regarding the concession before it is awarded. In other words, the contracting authority must ensure that any interested party has the opportunity to manifest its interest, but a procedure in accordance with the Directives is not required.

In the next relevant ruling, *Parking Brixen*, the Court stressed that some kind of call for competition is necessary:

> (...) a complete lack of any call for competition in the case of the award of a public service concession such as that at issue in the main proceedings does not comply with the requirements of Articles 43 EC and 49 EC any more than with the principles of equal treatment, non-discrimination and transparency.[38]

Again, it was clear that doing nothing was not enough, but unclear what a contracting authority should positively be doing to satisfy the transparency principle.[39] Following the *Transparency* case law (up until *Parking Brixen*) the Commission, in 2006, issued an Interpretative Communication.[40] According to the Commission, in order to comply with the obligation to ensure adequate advertising, the advertising should mention the 'essential details of the contract to be awarded and of the award method' and 'should provide as much information as an undertaking from another Member State will reasonably need to make a decision on whether to express its interest in obtaining the contract.' In view of the vagueness of the Commission's formulation it comes as no surprise that Member

---

[35] *Telaustria, supra* n. 8, para 62.

[36] Arrowsmith (2005), p. 366.

[37] *Coname, supra* n. 8.

[38] *Parking Brixen, supra* n. 8, para 50.

[39] Public authorities had expressed a need for clarification of the obligations deriving from the principle of openness, since the application of this principle is subject to interpretation. The vagueness of the obligations on how to act had been experienced problematic. See *Social Services of General Interest: Feedback Report to the 2006 questionnaire of the Social Protection Committee*, pp. 10–12, available at: http://ec.europa.eu/employment_social/spsi/docs/social_protection/2008/feedback_report_final_en.pdf.

[40] *Interpretative Communication on the Community law applicable to contract awards not or not fully subject to the provisions of the directives* (*OJ* 2006, C 179/2).

States were left with numerous questions unresolved.[41] An obvious antinomy lies on the fact that the Directive, an instrument of hard law, specifically submits Part B-services to the 'light' procurement regime, while the Communication, through the back door (that is, Articles 49 and 56 TFEU and the principle of transparency), imposes on them a much heavier procedural burden.[42]

The Commission's position, nonetheless, has been partly confirmed by the Court in its landmark case, *Commission* v. *Ireland* (*An Post*). In this case the Court further spelled out the requirements of transparency limiting, by the same token, the scope of their application. The Court dealt with the question whether the award of a Part B-service contract to An Post concerning payments under social benefit schemes, without any prior advertising, was contrary to the Treaty.[43] The Court considered that service contracts come within the scope of Treaty provisions on free movement only when these contracts present a 'certain cross-border interest' to an undertaking located in another Member State. It held that these provisions are breached if such an undertaking 'was unable to express its interest in that contract because it did not have access to adequate information before the contract was awarded.' The Court seems to focus on the likelihood that a company established in another Member State would have been interested in making an offer, had it been properly informed about the public contract through any form of advertisement. In the framework of an action against a Member State it is for the Commission to show that the criterion of 'certain cross-border interest' is fulfilled.[44] In the case of *An Post*, the ECJ found that the Commission had not provided the

---

[41] See also McGowan (2007). The Commission has been criticised by several Member States and the European Parliament for creating new rules on tendering, which go beyond the current obligations under Community law. Germany challenged the legality of the Communication (Case T-258/06, *OJ* 2006, Ruling of 20 May 2010, C 294/52).

[42] See also Interpretative communication on the application of Community law on Public Procurement and Concessions to institutionalised PPP (IPPP) (*OJ* 2008 C 91/02), in which the Commission emphasises the application of 'the principle of equal treatment and the specific expressions of that principle, namely the prohibition of discrimination on grounds of nationality and Articles 43 TEC on freedom of establishment and 49 TEC on freedom to provide services' when choosing a third party for the supply of economic activities. See also *Communication on Mobilising private and public investment for recovery and long-term structural change: developing Public Private Partnerships*, COM (2009) 615 final, p. 5, para 3.1.

[43] *An Post*, *supra* n. 2. In a similar infringement procedure between the Commission and Ireland, the Court was asked to assess whether Ireland had failed to fulfil its obligations on the principle of transparency. The Dublin City Council (DCC) had awarded a Part B-service contract to provide emergency ambulance services to the Eastern Regional Health Authority without undertaking any prior advertising, ECJ, Case C-532/03 *Commission* v. *Ireland* (*ambulance services*) [2007] *ECR* I-11353. See for a case note, Browne (2008), pp. 92–95.

[44] *An Post*, *supra* n. 2 at para 33: 'According to settled case law, it is the Commission's responsibility to provide the Court with the evidence necessary to enable it to establish that an obligation has not been fulfilled and, in so doing, the Commission may not rely on any presumption.'

required evidence and the Commission's application was dismissed.[45] It is unclear how this finding will affect the onus of proof in disputes between individuals. The ruling in *SECAP* explains further the exact meaning of 'certain cross-border interest'[46]: 'in view of its particular characteristics, a given contract is likely to be of certain cross-border interest and therefore attract operators from other Member States'.[47] This depends, *inter alia*, on 'the estimated value [of the contract] in conjunction with its technical complexity or the fact that the works are to be located in a place which is likely to attract the interest of foreign operators'.[48]

This recent development on the application of the transparency obligation has raised certain practical questions: What is the meaning of the adverb 'certain?' How should a certain cross-border interest be established? Does a public authority have a *duty* to assess whether the contract in question presents 'certain cross-border interest?' Obviously, there is not one single circumstance that determines whether a given contract is of certain cross-border interest. The test is inevitably a very factual one.[49] One conclusion can be drawn: depending on the individual characteristics of a public service contract, this case law on transparency could lead to an obligation to advertise health care services. However, it remains uncertain whether this case law introduces the full application of the Directive in terms of a tender obligation.

Whether a health care service is of 'certain cross-border interest' will highly depend on the size and estimated value of the contract. Further, the complexity of the contractual obligation, requiring a high degree of expertise unlikely to be found at the local level, would justify interest from other Member States. Moreover, it is considered that a contract, which is performed in a border region, attracts foreign service providers.[50] For example, a contract to provide ambulance services in the southern region of the Netherlands, with an estimated value of € 300 million a year, will probably attract the attention of German and Belgian ambulance service providers. In that case it is advised to organise a procurement procedure in accordance with the Directive. However, a supply contract with an estimated value of € 42.000, to deliver medical supplies to a middle-sized hospital in a centrally located and small town in the Netherlands, will probably, based on its value and geographical characteristics, not qualify as a contract of 'certain cross-border

[45] The ECJ applied the same reasoning to contracts whose value falls below the thresholds of the Directive. Case C-412/04 *Commission* v. *Italy* [2008] *ECR* I-619.

[46] *SECAP SpA and Santorso Soc. Coop. Arl* v. *Commune di Torino*, cited *supra* n. 8.

[47] Ibid., para 24.

[48] Ibid., para 24.

[49] See also Drijber and Stergiou (2009), pp. 809–815.

[50] Due to the mobility of service providers and service recipients active in these markets, the dynamics of this service market has changed and they are considered to be, from a service recipient perspective, increasingly of cross-border interest. The case law on patient's rights to cross-border health care shows that patients are willing to travel in order to undergo treatment in another Member State. See for example ECJ, Case C-444/05 *Stamatelaki* [2007] *ECR* I-3185 and ECJ, Case C-372/04 *Watts* [2006] *ECR* I-4325.

interest'. Future case law is expected to flesh up the criteria in order to determine which health care services are of 'certain cross-border interest'. In the meanwhile, it is difficult to draw a general conclusion with regard to the question to what extent the EU procurement rules and principles currently affect the national health care systems. As indicated above, this currently depends on the individual characteristics of every single public contract concerning health. Notwithstanding this conclusion, it is clear that the *Transparency* case law is of influence on the scope of the Directive of health care services. For sure, this case law can lead to a more significant role of EU Public Procurement Law in the field of health care.

17.3 Entities in Health Care Subject to EU Public Procurement Rules and Principles

For determining the applicability of the procurement rules in health care, the concept of a contracting authority, together with the value and nature of the public contract, is regarded the most important element of the public procurement legal framework.[51] For the EU Public Procurement rules and principles to be applicable, it is necessary that the health purchaser in question qualifies as a contracting authority in terms of the Directive. Public Procurement rules and principles only bind contracting authorities, other entities are subject to the principle of contractual freedom. The qualification of any entity as being a contracting authority is a highly controversial issue, the more so in the field of health care. This part first introduces the concept of a contracting authority. Relevant case law of the ECJ with regard to this concept is discussed (Sect. 17.3.1). Second, the enumeration, by Member States, in Annex III of the Directive, of entities they deem to be contracting authorities in health care is analysed (Sect. 17.3.2). Finally, case law of the ECJ concerning the procurement practice in different Member States in health care is analysed. From this case law follows that other public entities in the field of health care, however not listed in Annex III, are considered contracting authorities in terms of Article 1(9) of the Directive.

17.3.1 The Concept of a Contracting Authority

The Public Sector Directive is directed at entities that emanate from the State. The entities covered by the Directive fall within two broad categories:

(1) the State, regional or local authorities (public authorities), associations formed by one or several of such authorities;

[51] Bovis (2007), p. 192.

(2) bodies governed by public law and associations formed by one or several of such bodies governed by public law.[52]

All health care entities, which are part of the State, regional or local authorities, are subject to the Directive. Annex IV to the Directive consists per Member State of a non-exhaustive list of central government authorities. Moreover, Annex III contains a non-exhaustive list of 'bodies governed by public law.' The content of both Annexes will be further discussed in part Sect. 17.3.2.

For all other entities active in the area of health care, but not included in Annex III, their qualification as contracting authorities is not automatic. The specific legal and factual situation pertaining to each such entity should be scrutinised in order to determine whether it qualifies as 'a body governed by public law'. This category of contracting authorities is subject to three cumulative criteria, which have generated an extensive body of case law.

17.3.1.1 Specific Purpose of Meeting Needs in the General Interest, Which do not have an Industrial or Commercial Character

First the organisation must be established for the *specific purpose of meeting needs in the general interest, which do not have an industrial or commercial character.* With regard to the first part of this criterion, it has been considered in the case law that this definition excludes entities, which are subject to commercial pressure to purchase efficiently.[53] This applies to public entities providing goods and services in a competitive market.[54] Entities providing services directly to the public often meet needs in the general interest.[55] According to the Court, needs in the general interest are those which for reasons associated with the general interest, the state choose to provide itself or over which it wishes to retain a decisive influence.[56] The definition of the term 'needs in the general interest' has been interpreted very widely. Activities in the field of waste collection and the cleaning of a municipal road network,[57] as well as the activity of a funeral undertaker[58] have all been considered by the Court to meet needs in the general interest. These types of activities can be linked to a public policy or public interest such as hygiene and

[52] Article 1(9) Public Sector Directive.

[53] ECJ, Case C-44/96 *Mannesmann Anlagenbau Austria AG and Others* v. *Strohal Rotationsdruck GmbH* [1998] *ECR* I-73.

[54] Arrowsmith (2005), pp. 264–265, para 5.10.

[55] Ibid., p. 266, para 5.11.

[56] ECJ, Case C-323/96 *Vlaamse Raad* [1998] *ECR* I-5063, paras 50–51 and ECJ, Joined Cases C-223/99 and C-260/99 *Agorà Srl and Excelsior Snc di Pedrotti Bruna & C.* v. *Ente Autonomo Fiera Internazionale di Milano and Ciftat Soc. Coop. arl* [2001] *ECR* 3606, para 37.

[57] ECJ, Case C-360/96 *Gemeente Arnhem and Gemeente Rheden* v. *BFI Holding BV* [1998] *ECR* I-6821.

[58] ECJ, Case C-373/00 *Adolf Truley GmbH* v. *Bestattung Wien GmbH* [2003] *ECR* I-1931.

public health. If an activity does meet needs in the general interest, it falls then to be considered whether these needs have an industrial or commercial nature. In applying this test the ECJ has mainly focused on the question whether the entity carries out the activity on a commercial basis,[59] In that respect, the Court examines both the characteristics of the marketplace in which the entity operates (in competition with other undertakings, which can influence its commercial behaviour, commercial side-activities), and the nature of the entity itself.

The second criterion that an entity needs to satisfy in order to qualify as a body governed by public law under the Directive is the existence of *legal personality*. This requirement has not provoked any great amount of legal debate. The Court has constantly held that it is irrelevant whether the entity in question has been established under private or public law.[60]

17.3.1.2 Financed or Supervised or Appointed by Another Contracting Authority

Third, the Directive applies to entities which are either *financed* or *supervised* or *appointed* by another contracting authority. This condition is used primarily to determine the degree of dependency of the entity in question from the State and the degree of State control. The condition is satisfied where *any* of the three criteria is met. The term 'financed for the most part' means, according to the judgment in *Cambridge*, more than the half and is to be re-appraised constantly.[61] There is no requirement that the activity of the bodies in question should be directly financed by the State or by another public body; the Court has held indirect financing to be sufficient.[62] The managerial dependency condition concerns the direct participation of public authorities and officials in the management of the entity. According to the Court in *Commission* v. *France* (*social housing*) it is necessary to considers whether the controls over the entity make them 'dependent on the public authorities in such a way that the latter are able to influence their decisions in relation to public contracts'.[63] In this specific case in which an entity was responsible for providing social housing in France, the Court decided that this condition was met in view of the fact that: (a) the activities were highly regulated; (b) the Ministers for finance and construction exercised broad supervisory powers

---

[59] Arrowsmith (2005), p. 269, para 5.14.

[60] ECJ, Case C-214/00 *Commission* v. *Spain* [2003] *ECR* I-4667; ECJ, Case C-283/00 *Commission* v. *Spain* [2003] *ECR* I-11697; Case C-84/03 *Commission* v. *Spain* [2005] *ECR* I-139. See for an analysis of these cases: Trepte (2007), pp. 119–121, paras 2.56–2.59.

[61] *University of Cambridge, supra* n. 2, para 30. See also Article 2 of Directive 2006/111/EC on the transparency of financial relations between Member States and public undertakings (Transparency Directive), *OJ* L 318.

[62] ECJ, Case C-337/06 *Bayerischer Rundfunk and Others* [2007] *ECR* I-11173, paras 34 and 49. See also Arrowsmith (2005), p. 257, para 5.6.

[63] ECJ, Case C-237/99 *Commission* v. *France* (*social housing*) [2001] *ECR* I-939.

and (c) the responsible Minister had the competence to suspend the management and appoint a liquidator or administrator. The Court has ruled in *Adolf Truly* that the condition of 'supervisory dependency' is satisfied where the public authorities supervise not only the annual accounts of the body concerned but also its conduct from the point of view of proper accounting, regularity, economy, efficiency, etc.[64] In *Commission* v. *France* (*social housing*) the Court held that a degree of management supervision is necessary, which permits the public authorities to influence or interfere with the procurement procedures.[65] The Court has described these three alternative criteria of finance, management supervision and appointment as embodying a relationship of close dependency on a contracting authority.[66]

17.3.1.3 Oymanns

Only recently has the Court been asked to apply the above-mentioned criteria of 'a body governed by public law' to entities active in the field of health care. In *Oymanns*, the Oberlandesgericht Düsseldorf asked the Court, *inter alia*, whether the German statutory sickness insurance funds constitute contracting authorities for the purposes of the application of the rules in the Directive.[67] While the first two conditions were fulfilled in this case, the extent to which the funds were financed/supervised/appointed by the State had to be ascertained. Unfortunately, the Court only interpreted 'financed for the most part', since it consider this condition to be fulfilled in this specific case: '[...] when the activities of statutory sickness insurance funds are chiefly financed by contributions payable by members, which are imposed, calculated and collected according to rules of public law'.[68] The Court takes into consideration the fact that the sickness funds in question are financed, for the most part, by compulsory contributions from members[69] for which (contributions) no specific consideration is provided in return[70]: 'no contractual consideration is linked to those payments, since neither the liability to pay contributions nor their amount is the result of any agreement between the statutory sickness insurance funds and their members, since membership of the funds, and payment of contributions, are both required by law'.[71] In that respect the Court considers that the amount of contributions is based solely on

[64] *Adolf Truley supra* n. 58, paras 71–74.

[65] *Commission* v. *France* (*social housing*), *supra* n. 63, para 59.

[66] *Mannesmann supra* n. 53, para 20 and *University of Cambridge, supra* n. 2, para 74.

[67] ECJ, Case C-300/07 *Hans and Christophorus Oymanns*, judgment of 11 June 2009, *ECR* I-0000 (n.y.r.).

[68] Ibid., para 59.

[69] Ibid., para 52.

[70] *University of Cambridge, supra* n. 2, para 74.

[71] *Oymanns supra* n. 67, para 53.

the capacity to contribute of each member, whereas other factors, such as the age of the insured persons, their state of health or the number of co-insured persons, are irrelevant in that regard. Moreover, the setting of the contribution rate by the statutory sickness insurance funds requires, in any event, the approval of the public body which supervises each fund. The Court concludes that the funds' other sources of revenue, the direct payments by the federal authorities, although of a smaller amount, are unquestionably direct financing by the State and that contributions are compulsorily recovered on the basis of the provisions of public law. Thisf amounts, according to the ECJ, to a situation, in which there is financing, for the most part, by the State of the German statutory sickness insurance funds.[72]

17.3.2 Are Member States' Lists on Contracting Authorities Helpful?

Annex III of the Directive lists each Member State's bodies and categories governed by public law. Annex IV to the Directive consists per Member State of a non-exhaustive list of central government authorities. Both lists contain contracting authorities and entities that have to apply EU public procurement rules. From national ministries to local councils, from schools to universities, but also hospitals, airports, railway operators, museums, postal entities, urban transport, water utilities and national lotteries. These lists are non-exhaustive and only have indicative value,[73] while the exact scope of the Directive remains defined by the Court's case law. Therefore it cannot be ruled out that entities listed in one of these Annexes are 'disqualified' in the course of court proceedings. Especially, since it has been left to the Member States themselves to enumerate, in a non-exhaustive manner, the entities they consider to be subject to the Directive and no mechanism for regular revision by the Commission is in place. A fine example is *Oymanns*, in which the question was raised whether German sickness funds are contracting authorities, despite the fact that these funds are expressly listed in Annex III. The German court raised, although not explicitly, a question concerning the validity of the inclusion in the list in Annex III of these funds.[74] Nonetheless, according to the Commission, the lists intend to 'give citizens and businesses the opportunity to identify which public authorities in the EU have to submit their public contracts to EU-wide tender procedures. As well as improving accountability and transparency in this area, the updated lists are intended to offer more

[72] Ibid., paras 54–58.

[73] http://ec.europa.eu/internal_market/publicprocurement/authorities_en.htm.

[74] *Oymanns supra* n. 67, para 46.

opportunities for business to participate in public contracts'.[75] By Decision of 9 December 2008 the Commission has updated both Annexes (including the 'new' Member States).[76]

A comparison of the national lists shows a very wide variety of perceptions concerning the qualification of contracting authorities in the field of health care.[77] Some Member States have submitted their list exclusively in their official language (Bulgaria, Czech Republic, Estonia, Cyprus, Hungary, Malta), thus cancelling the 'transparency' function of the lists. Others have not listed any body or entity in the field of health care (Luxemburg, Denmark), while others merely refer to (parts of) the definition of Article 1(9) of the Directive (Portugal, Slovakia). In practice, therefore, the usefulness of the lists is quite limited, as any helpful comparison is difficult to be carried out. A list of bodies/categories of 13 Member States, illustrates this problem[78]:

- Austria considers all bodies under the budgetary control of the 'Rechnungshof' (Court of Auditors) except those of an industrial or commercial nature to be a contracting entity.
- In Belgium six public hospitals and three sickness funds are indicated as contracting authorities. Private hospitals are not mentioned.
- In France there is one specific health insurance (Caisse nationale militaire de sécurité sociale (CNMSS)) and all public hospitals listed as contracting authorities.
- In Germany social security institutions, such as health, accident and pension insurance funds and hospitals, health resort establishments, medical research institutes, testing and carcass disposal establishments, are indicated as contracting authorities.
- Greece gives only a broad definition of all entities controlled by over 51% of the State.
- Ireland has used the following qualification: 'Hospitals and similar institutions of a public character and agencies established to carry out particular functions or meet needs in various public sectors [for example, Health care Materials Management Board (...), etc.] and Health Service Executive (organisation responsible for providing health and personal services for Irish citizens).'
- In Italy agencies administering compulsory social security and welfare schemes, public welfare and benevolent institutions (and, more general, organisations providing services in the public interest are qualified as contracting authorities). Hospitals are not mentioned.

[75] http://europa.eu/rapid/pressReleasesAction.do? reference=IP/08/1971&format=HTML&aged=0&language=EN&guiLanguage=en.

[76] Commission Decision of 9 December 2008 amending the Annexes to Directives 2004/17/EC and 2004/18/EC of the European Parliament and of the Council on public procurement procedures, as regards their lists of contracting entities and contracting authorities. 2008/963/EC.

[77] See also Hatzopoulos (2008), pp. 177–178 [on file with the author].

[78] Available on http://ec.europa.eu/internal_market/publicprocurement/authorities_en.htm.

- The Netherlands has indicated the former sickness funds as contracting authorities, whereas it has privatised its health system from 1 January 2006. Furthermore, the Netherlands enumerates several bodies involved in the management of hospital facilities and accreditation of health providers. Academic hospitals, which are generally considered to be contracting authorities, are not mentioned.[79]
- In Poland 'Public Autonomous Health Care Management Units whose founding body is a regional or local self-government or association thereof' are mentioned. There is no reference made to hospitals or sickness funds.
- In Romania hospitals, sanatoria, clinics, medical units, legal-medical institutes and ambulance stations are listed as contracting authorities.
- Slovenia has taken a broad approach by indicating that all public institutes in the area of health care are contracting authorities.
- In Spain all bodies and entities governed by Spanish legislation on public procurement and administrative entities and common services of the health and social services are contracting authorities.
- The United Kingdom has enumerated the following entities: National Health Service Strategic Health Authorities, NHS Trusts, Regional Medical Service, Royal Hospital, Chelsea, Community Health Partnerships, Special Health Boards, Health Boards, the Welsh National Health Service Trusts, Local Health Boards. Bodies and National Health Service Strategic Health Authorities.

It is evident that Member States have different perceptions about the entities that in their respective health care systems qualify as contracting authorities. Obviously, this can lead to a different application in each Member State of the Directive in the field of health care.

17.3.3 ECJ Case Law on Procurement Practice in Health Care

In the last decade the ECJ has been increasingly faced with procurement disputes in the field of health care. A growing number of infringement proceedings in this area have been initiated by the Commission. Furthermore, since the financial interests involved are often substantial and the market for health care grows, there is an increasing number of disputes found to be worth fighting in courts.

In a series of judgments the ECJ has ruled on compliance with EU public procurement rules in health care. This 'health care case law' does not necessarily evolve around the question whether certain entities, active in the field of health care, qualify as contracting authorities in terms of the Directive. As discussed, the only case present in that respect is *Oymanns*. Nonetheless, the available case law provides, in addition to the above-discussed Annexes, guidance as to which

[79] http://www.nvz-ziekenhuizen.nl/Actueel/NVZ_Nieuws/Archief/2005/Maart/Nummer_12_d_d_17_maart_2005.

entities are considered to be contracting authorities in the field of health care in national procurement practice.

From *Tögel* it follows that the sickness fund for lower Austria is considered to be a contracting authority.[80] Under national legislation the Austrian social security institutions are required to reimburse to insured persons the costs of transport incurred by them or by members of their families when they have had to call on medical assistance. The relationship between the social security institutions and the transporting undertakings is governed by private-law contracts which must afford insured persons and members of their families adequate access to the benefits provided for by the law and under agreements. Thus, the Niederösterreichische Gebietskrankenkasse entered into framework agreements with the Austrian Red Cross, regional section for Lower Austria, and the Austrian Federation of Samaritan Workers, for the provision of patient transport of all three types. The reasoning of the Court on whether this concerned a Part A- or a Part B-services contract has already been discussed in Sect. 17.2.2.

In *Ambulanz Glöckner*, a case, which also concerned the provision of patient transport services, the question had been raised in German proceedings between Ambulanz Glöckner, a private undertaking established in Pirmasens and the administrative district Landkreis Südwestpfalz, a contracting authority, concerning its refusal to renew authorisation for the provision of ambulance services.[81] This case has become renowned for the Court's reasoning on the justified use of Article 106(2) TFEU (ex Article 86(2) EC) (see Sect. 17.4.3). Based on this exception, the Court ruled that ambulance contracts could be awarded on the basis of prior authorisation, without a tender procedure.

In *Contse* the Instituto Nacional de la Salud (the National Health Institute, 'Insalud') had issued two calls under the then applicable public procurement Directive (92/50/EEC) for tenders for services of home respiratory treatments and other assisted breathing techniques in two Spanish provinces.[82] Contse SA, an oxygen-producing factory, submitted that Insalud had breached former Articles 12 EC, 43 EC, 49 EC (now Articles 18, 49 and 56 TFEU) and Article 3(2) of [Directive 92/50] by including certain criteria and elements in the tendering specifications, special administrative clauses and technical specifications. For example, Insalud had applied an admission condition which required the tenderer at the time the tender was submitted to have an office open to the public in the capital of the province where the service was to be provided. The Court ruled that Article 56 TFEU (ex Article 49 EC) precludes a contracting authority, such as Insalud, from applying this type of admission criterion. All the above findings are based on the assumption that Insalud is indeed a contracting authority.

---

[80] *Tögel, supra* n. 28.

[81] ECJ, Case C-475/99 *Ambulanz Glöckner* [2001] *ECR* I-8089. See the chapter by Welti in this book.

[82] ECJ, Case C-234/03 *Contse* [2005] *ECR* I-9315.

It can be safely adduced from case *Medipac-Katzantzidis* that public hospitals in Greece are contracting authorities.[83] Venizelio-Pananio, which is the general hospital of Heraklion (Crete), had issued a tender for the supply of various surgical sutures. Medipac was one of the nine companies, which submitted a tender. The committee conducting the tendering procedure issued a recommendation to Venizelio-Pananio's Administrative Board, reiterating a suggestion from the surgeons of that hospital that the PGA type sutures proposed by Medipac be excluded. According to that recommendation, it had been found that knots done with PGA type materials slipped easily and closed prematurely, that needles frequently twisted or broke and that sutures did not hold sufficiently. The ECJ decided that, where proposed products, although bearing the CE marking, give rise to concern on the part of the contracting authority, such as Venizelio-Pananio, as to patients' health or safety, the principle of equal treatment of tenderers and the obligation of transparency preclude the contracting authority from being able itself to reject the tender in question. Since harmonisation was in place (Directive 93/42 concerning medical devices, as amended by Regulation No 1882/2003), the contracting authority should, if it considered that those materials could jeopardise public health, inform the competent national authority and set the safeguard procedure of that Directive in motion.

In Italy regions and regional health associations are contracting authorities. In *Commission* v. *Italy* (*health care transport services*), the Commission initiated proceedings against Italy because the region of Tuscany and the Tuscan Aziende Sanitarie (public health authorities) had extended the duration of the regional framework agreement for the supply of health care transport services with several service providers, such as the Confederazione delle Misericordie d'Italia, ANPAS—the Tuscan regional committee and the Croce Rossa Italiana—Tuscan division, without a tender procedure.[84] The Court dismissed the Commission's action for lack of proof. However, the reasoning of the Court with regard to the presence of a public service contract is interesting and will be discussed in Sect. 17.4.4 of this chapter.

Finally, in both *Commission* v. *Ireland* cases from 2007, contracting authorities were involved that are part of the State: in *An Post* the Irish Minister for Social Welfare and in *ambulance services* the Dublin City Council.[85]

All these cases offer some certainty about the authorities they deal with. The authorities concerned, however, did not present any particular difficulty as to their qualification as contracting authorities: they all concerned cases of straightforward state controlled entities. This case law, nonetheless, offers little guidance (if at all) for more complex institutional settings. What about private hospitals funded by public funds (Belgium)? Do private hospitals in the UK and Ireland contracted by

---

[83] *Medipac-Kazantzidis*, *supra* n. 8, confirmed in ECJ, Case C-489/06 *Commission* v. *Greece* [2009] *ECR* I-1797.

[84] ECJ, Case C-119/06 *Commission* v. *Italy* (*health care transport services*) [2007] *ECR* I-4557.

[85] *An Post, supra* n. 2, *Ambulance services*, *supra* n. 43.

NHS Strategic Health Authorities qualify as contracting authorities? In the Netherlands do private health insurers (where affiliation is compulsory according to terms fixed by law) and private hospitals receiving funds from central government need to comply with the Directive? Currently, there are no general answers to these questions. As follows from a Dutch case study, which is carried out in Sect. 17.5 of this chapter, the answers may differ with each individual entity active in the field of health care.

17.4 Possible Exceptions from Tendering Obligations in the Field of Health Care

If the health care service concerned is of cross-border interest and the entity, which purchases the public service, qualifies as a contracting authority, the actual process of public procurement should be initiated and the rules on public procurement apply. The complete failure to advertise or invite competing bids for the purposes of granting a health care service could be considered in violation of the general Treaty provisions on free movement of services, or, more specifically, the principle of transparency. In this part we will explore possible justifications of a violation of the Directive or of tendering obligations arising out of the *Transparency* case law.

Within EU Law, several means of justifying non-competitive tenders exist: Treaty exceptions and the overriding reasons of public interest (Rule of Reason) (Sect. 17.4.1), the accomplishment of some mission of general interest according to Article 106 (2) TFEU (ex Article 86(2) EC) (Sect. 17.4.2) and reasons inherent in the public procurement rules (Sect. 17.4.3). Finally, the theoretical arguments according to which health care should out of principle not be subject to EU public procurement rules at all are discussed (Sect. 17.4.4).

17.4.1 Treaty Exceptions and Overriding Reasons

As we have seen in Sect. 17.1 the ECJ has applied in its *Transparency* case law Treaty principles, such as the principles of non-discrimination equality and transparency, to Part-B services, such as health care services. The foregoing may result into positive obligations for contracting authorities, that is, the obligation to advertise or even tender health care services. In that respect is it interesting to analyse whether Treaty exceptions and the 'Rule of Reason' may justify a case in which the principle of transparency has been violated or a tender procedure has not been initiated.

Article 51 TFEU (ex Article 45 EC), which is extended by Article 62 TFEU (old Article 55 TEC) to cover the Chapter on Services, states that the Treaty provisions shall not apply 'so far as any given Member State is concerned, to activities which in that State are connected, even occasionally, with the exercise of *official authority*'.[86] The Court has interpreted the official-authority exception narrowly. Furthermore, Article 52 TFEU (ex Article 46 EC) in the Chapter on Services provides that provisions of those Chapters 'shall not prejudice the applicability of provisions laid down by law, regulation or administrative action providing for special treatment for foreign nationals on ground of *public policy, public security or public health.*' Recital 6 of the Public Sector Directive provides for a similar exception: 'nothing in this Directive should prevent the imposition or enforcement of measures necessary to protect public (…) health, human and animal life (…).' However, (a) the very recital states that these measures should be in conformity with the Treaty and (b) no corresponding provision is to be found in the operative part of the Directive. Therefore, this recital should be seen as a cross-reference to the Treaty express exceptions. In relation to health care services, *public health* is the most relevant Treaty exception.

Besides the express exceptions contained in the Treaty, the Court has developed a large body of 'overriding reasons of general interest' which may justify national restrictions on the freedom of establishment and services.[87]

Until recently, the relevance of these exceptions for justifying the infringement of the provisions of the Directive or the transparency obligation in EU procurement law practice had not been acknowledged. Nonetheless, there is a trend that these exceptions are being considered as a possible justification for these types of infringements. In public procurement cases the Court is prepared to recognise Treaty exceptions and overriding reasons. This is especially visible in recent case law of the Court. In *Commission* v. *Ireland* (*ambulance services*)[88] Advocate General Stix-Hackl examined whether Ireland, which did not advertise the award to supply emergency services, could in that respect rely on 'one of the Treaty rules providing for a general exemption of measures of the Member States from the application of primary law, whether one of the grounds of justification expressly provided for in the Treaty or a ground of justification recognized by case law'.[89] As a matter of principle, the Advocate General considered that the overriding reasons should also be applied in relation to procurement law. Ireland was unable to demonstrate that grounds of justification or requirements in the general interest, recognised by the Court, such as consumer protection, were at stake. In *Commission* v. *Italy* (*service concessions for horse-betting*), the Italian Government

[86] ECJ, Case 2/74 *Reyners* v. *Belgium* [1974] *ECR* 63. Official authority is that which arises from the sovereignty and majesty of the State; for him who exercises it, it implies the power of enjoying the prerogatives outside the general law, privileges of official power and powers of coercion over citizens.

[87] For example, ECJ, Case C-19/92 *Kraus* [1993] *ECR* I-1663, para 32; ECJ, Case C-55/94 *Gebhard* [1995] *ECR* I-4165, para 37; and ECJ, Case C-243/01 *Gambelli* [2003] *ECR* I-13031, paras 64–65.

[88] *Ambulance services*, *supra* n. 43.

[89] Ibid., Opinion of the Advocate General, paras 86 et seq. The Court concluded that there was no public contract. It therefore did not need to address the issues discussed here.

argued that the automatic renewal of 329 licences for horse-betting operations without inviting any competing bids was:

> justified by the need to ensure continuity, financial stability and a proper return on past investment for licence holders as well as the need to discourage recourse to clandestine activities, until the existing licences could be reallocated on the basis of tendering procedures.[90]

The Court considered that the renewal of the licences may (i) be recognised as an exceptional measure, as provided for in old Articles 45 and 46 EC, or (ii) justified in accordance with case law of the Court for overriding reasons of general interest. Regarding overriding reasons of general interest, the Court referred to consumer protection and 'the prevention of both fraud and incitement to squander on gaming', as well as to the need to preserve public order.[91] However, the renewal of the licences without putting them out to tender was 'not an appropriate means of attaining the objective pursued by the Italian Republic, going beyond what was necessary in order to preclude operators in the horse-race betting sector from engaging in criminal or fraudulent activities'.[92]

An example of the way public health has proved antagonistic to the full application of the procurement rules is offered by the case *Medipac-Katzantzidis*.[93] In this case the Court acknowledged with reference to settled case law 'that the objective of the protection of public health constitutes an overriding public-interest requirement entitling Member States to derogate from the principle of the free movement of goods provided that the measures taken comply with the principle of proportionality'.[94] According to the Court the suspension of a tendering procedure for the supply of medical devices may lead to delays liable to give rise to problems in running a hospital such as Venizelio-Pananio. Consequently, the Court considered that in a situation of urgency, that is, if the implementation of such a safeguard procedure gives rise to delays liable to jeopardise the operation of a public hospital and thereby public health, a hospital such as Venizelio-Pananio is entitled to take all interim measures required to enable it to procure the medical devices necessary for its operation. However, it must be able to show that there is a situation of urgency justifying such derogation from the principle of free movement of goods and demonstrate that the measures taken are proportionate.[95]

---

90 ECJ, Case C-260/04 *Commission* v. *Italy* (*service concessions for horse-betting*) [2007] *ECR* I-4165, para 15.

91 See, in particular, ECJ, Joined Cases C-338/04, C-359/04 & C-360/04 *Placanica* [2007] *ECR* I-1891.

92 *Commission* v. *Italy*, *supra* n. 90, paras 34–35.

93 *Medipac-Kazantzidis*, *supra* n. 8.

94 See ECJ, Case 120/78 *Rewe-Zentral* [1979] *ECR* 649 (*Cassis de Dijon*), para 8; ECJ, Case C-270/02 *Commission* v. *Italy* [2004] *ECR* I-1559, paras 21 and 22; and ECJ, Joined Cases C-158/04 and Case C-159/04 *Alfa Vita Vassilopoulos and Carrefour-Marinopoulos* [2006] *ECR* I-8135, paras 20–23.

95 *Medipac-Kazantzidis*, *supra* n. 8, paras 60–62.

17.4.2 Services of General Economic Interest

Considering the character of Part-B services, it is not ruled out that some of these services, including health care, services, qualify as services of general economic interest ('SGEI'). SGEI are referred to in Articles 14 and 106(2) TFEU. Article 14 TFEU confers responsibility upon the Union and the Member States to ensure, each within their respective sphere of competences, that their policies enable SGEI to fulfil their missions. Article 106(2) TFEU implicitly recognises the right of Member States to assign specific public service obligations to economic operators. Providers of SGEI are exempted from application of the Treaty rules to the extent that this is necessary to allow them to fulfil their mission to pursue activities of general interest. In the Protocol on SGEI annexed to the Treaty of Lisbon 2009, SGEIs are defined as 'services, both economic and non-economic, which the public authorities classify as being of general interest and subject to specific public service obligations'.[96] It is the responsibility of public authorities, at the relevant level, to decide on the nature and scope of SGEI.[97] It is therefore difficult to define one single concept of SGEI, which encompasses the different situations existing in the various Member States. The Court has considered, *inter alia*, the following activities as being SGEIs: the operation of a river port which handles the majority of river traffic in goods in a Member State,[98] the establishment and operation of a public telecommunications network,[99] the operation of television services[100] and of certain transport lines,[101] employment recruitment[102] and basic postal services[103] and ambulance services.[104] In a number of cases the Court has positively applied Article 106(2) TFEU, holding that an exclusive or special right was required for the undertaking in question to perform the universal services under economically acceptable conditions.[105]

---

[96] On the concept of SGEIs and its implications on EU law, especially after the entry into force of the Lisbon Treaty, see, among many, the contributions contained in Neergaard et al. (2009); Krajewski et al. (2009); van de Gronden (2009).

[97] In CFI, Case T-289/03 *BUPA* [2005] *ECR* II-741, the CFI recognised explicitly that Member States have a wide discretion in defining what services on their territory are to be considered as SGEI. The Commission nonetheless scrupulously examines whether a Member State has committed 'a manifest error' when defining a certain service as SGEI. It does so in particular in State aid cases.

[98] ECJ, Case 10/71 *Port of Mertert* [1971] *ECR* 730, para 11.

[99] ECJ, Case 41/83 *Italy* v. *Commission* [1985] *ECR* 888, paras 29–33.

[100] ECJ, Case 155/73 *Sacchi* [1974] *ECR* 409.

[101] ECJ, Case 66/86 *Ahmed Saeed* [1989] *ECR* 853, para 55.

[102] ECJ, Case C-41/90 *Höfner* [1991] *ECR* I-2017, para 24.

[103] ECJ, Case C-320/91*Corbeau* [1993] *ECR* I-2568, para 15.

[104] *Ambulanz Glöckner, supra* n. 81.

[105] In all these cases the Court accepted the argument that the exclusive right protected the undertaking in question against the risk of cream skimming, leaving them with the least profitable services. See *Corbeau, supra* n. 103; ECJ, Case C-67/96 *Albany* [1999] *ECR* I-5751; ECJ, Case C-209/98 *Deutsche Post* [2000] *ECR* I-3743.

The Court has not yet had the opportunity to declare that Article 106(2) TFEU may derogate from public procurement rules and the transparency obligation. However, in *Ambulanz Glöckner* the Court was asked to rule on the application of Article 106(2) TFEU in relation to the authorisation to provide ambulance services.[106] The Landkreis involved relied on former Article 86(2) EC for justifying that ambulance contracts were awarded to public ambulance service providers on the basis of authorisations, not tenders. It argued that some measure of protection of the public ambulance service against competition from independent operators was necessary. According to the Landkreis emergency transport services, which must be provided 24 h a day throughout the territory, require costly investments in equipment and qualified personnel. Such investment may be paid out by the award to the same operations, without any competitive tender, of the authorisation to operate also on the non-emergency transport. According to the Court:

> the possibility which would be open to private operators to concentrate, in the non-emergency sector, on more profitable journeys could affect the degree of economic viability of the service provided by the medical aid organizations and, consequently, jeopardize the quality and reliability of that service.[107]

However, like every exception, Article 106(2) TFEU has to be interpreted strictly. The restriction of the free provision of health services must be proportionate to the general economic interest pursued. Therefore it must be concluded that only in very exceptional cases the test of proportionality is passed and a contracting authority may successfully rely on Article 106(2) TFEU to justify a breach of transparency or tender obligations with regard to health care services. It should also be noted that *Glöckner* is the only case in which Article 106(2) has been successfully pleaded in order to avoid the application of the procurement rules, and that it was decided before the '*Transparency* case law' had been fleshed out.

17.4.3 No Public Service Contract Involved

It goes without saying that only in the case of a public contract the procurement rules apply. According to, and for the purposes of, the Public Sector Directive, public contracts are 'contracts for pecuniary interest concluded in writing between one or more economic operators and one or more contracting authorities (…)'.[108] In summary, the definition of a public contract includes three elements: *a contract, in writing, for consideration* (or in other words: 'for pecuniary interest'). If one of these constitutive elements is absent, there is no public service contract involved and the Directive does not apply. Especially, the notion of 'for consideration' has

---

[106] *Ambulanz Glöckner*, *supra* n. 81.

[107] Ibid., para 61.

[108] Article 1(2)(a) Public Sector Directive.

given rise to a considerable amount of case law. The Directive does not define 'consideration'. In that respect there are two cases in the field of health care procurement, which are relevant.

In case *Commission* v. *Italy* (*health care transport services*) the Court had to decide whether Italian public health authorities had lawfully extended the duration of the regional framework agreement for the supply of health care transport services.[109] These were carried out by voluntary/not for profit associations such as the Red Cross, the Samaritans, etc. Italy argued before the Court that the services provided did not qualify as a public service contract in terms of the Directive, since the involved service providers did not receive any remuneration in return for their services: they only received a reimbursement for their fixed costs. With reference to settled case law,[110] in which the Court interprets the definition of contracting parties' obligations very widely, the Court rejects this argument.[111] The Court rules that the element of consideration is fulfilled when services are rendered on behalf of, and paid by, a contracting authority by virtue of a contract.[112] The Court takes into consideration the fact that the service providers do not only receive payment for specific services they offer, but also for keeping their helicopters on stand-by.[113] To the extent that the amounts received do not strictly correspond to the costs incurred for the provision of services, the element of 'consideration' has been fulfilled.[114] The foregoing means that any approximate calculation of remuneration which is not tailored to reflect the exact cost of a given service, that is, the usual kind of arrangements in the field of health care, gives rise to a public contract even if it is awarded to a non-profit organisation.

Despite the large definition given by the Court to the concept of consideration and, as consequence, to the existence of a contract, there are nonetheless service relations which do not qualify as being contractual. In *Commission v Ireland* (*ambulance services*) the Commission argued that Dublin City Council ('DCC')

---

[109] *Commission* v. *Italy* (*health care transport services*), *supra* n. 84.

[110] ECJ, Case C-399/98, *Ordine degli Architetti delle province de Milano e Lodi* v. *Comune di Milano* [2001] *ECR* I-5409. In this ruling, the city of Milan had given developers permission for a development scheme to build the exterior of the world-known theatre. The Court ruled that there was a contract, although the agreement was governed by public law and involved the exercise of public law powers. Advocate General Léger had reasoned that if something is provided without benefit to the provider there is no potential for the favouritism that the Directives seek to prevent.

[111] The Commission interprets the definition of the contracting parties obligations also very widely. 'All forms of consideration moving from the contracting authority and capable of valuation in money terms satisfy the requirement of pecuniary consideration', according to the Commission in its Guide to the Community rules on public procurement of services, *supra* n. 11, pp. 11–12.

[112] *Commission v Italy*, *supra* n. 84, para 47.

[113] Ibid., para 48.

[114] Ibid., para 50: 'Dans les circonstances précises de l'espèce, la méthode de paiement prévue par l'accord-cadre de 2004 dépasse donc le simple remboursement des frais encourus. Dans cette mesure, il convient de considérer que cet accord-cadre prévoit une contrepartie des services de transport sanitaire qu'il vise'.

had awarded a Part B-service contract to provide emergency ambulance services to the Eastern Regional Health Authority without undertaking any prior advertising.[115] According to the Commission, DCC and the Authority agreed to enter into a service-level agreement and that a contract was drafted to that end. Therefore, DCC provided emergency ambulance services at the behest of the Authority and for remuneration.[116] The Court decided differently. According to the Court 'it is conceivable that DCC provides such services to the public in the exercise of its own powers derived directly from statute, and applying its own funds, although it is paid a contribution by the Authority for that purpose, covering part of the costs of those services'.[117] According to the Court, the mere fact that funding arrangements exist between two public bodies in respect of such services does not imply that the provision of the services concerned constitutes an award of a public contract.[118] Two elements seem to have determined the Court's judgment in this case, although none is clearly expressed in the judgment (by the Grand Chamber). First, that by making arrangements for the provision of ambulance services the DCC was honouring its statutory obligations – not arranging some 'fantasy' service provision. Second, that none of the entities involved seemed to be of a commercial nature.

17.4.4 Arguments Against the Application of Procurement Rules and Principles in the Field of Health Care

More controversial than the technical procurement issues discussed above is the more general question whether health care provision should be, considering the specific character of health care services, subject to EU public procurement rules at all. From the Feedback Report to the 2006 questionnaire of the Social Protection Committee follows that substantive arguments have been put forward against the general application of these rules to health care provision.[119]

First of all, public authorities doing public tenders in the field of health and social services are facing many difficulties according to the responses to the consultation. Drafting tenders is reported as being a difficult and demanding task. Especially, public authorities (and very often municipalities) have difficulties to define the content of the services and to develop requirements in a detailed way, all

115 *Ambulance Services*, *supra* n. 43.

116 Ibid., para 32.

117 Ibid., para 35.

118 Ibid., para 37.

119 *Social Services of General Interest: Feedback Report to the 2006 questionnaire of the Social Protection Committee*, pp. 10–12, available at: http://ec.europa.eu/employment_social/spsi/docs/social_protection/2008/feedback_report_final_en.pdf. Despite the fact that the title of this report only refers to social services, this Report includes health care services.

the more since the services will have to be personalised to the specific needs of each user. These difficulties are reinforced by the fact that public authorities do not necessarily know in detail the needs and specificities of health and social services. Therefore, the risk of public tenders focusing on prices has been often mentioned.[120]

Furthermore, the public procurement rules are seen as not flexible enough regarding inter-municipal cooperation, which in principle falls under the scope of the Directive, resulting from the restrictive concept of 'in-house' contracts.[121] Moreover, the application of public procurement is reported as changing the traditional type of partnership relationship between public authorities and providers into a competitive one. As a result, it has been put forward that private initiatives in social services that require public financing may be difficult to carry out within the framework of public procurement legislations.

Also, the negative effect on establishing long-term trust relationships with suppliers and other partners has been raised, which may ultimately lead to a disruption of the continuity of a public service. Other issues concern the increased transaction costs and delays. The administrative burdens placed on small organisations for organising a tender procedure. Contributors indicate that providers have experienced increased paperwork in the last few years, manifold bureaucratic requirements for applications and reporting. These increased requirements bind a lot of valuable resources of organisations, which is especially difficult for small associations, NGOs, etc., often active in the field of health care.[122]

In light of all these issues, the positive effects of public procurement applied to health and social services (more quality, more choice and reduced prices) are put in question by some contributors. In a perfect market competition may indeed contribute to making the activities more effective and to cost savings, but there are several problems in the field of social welfare and health care that are caused by market failures, particularly by asymmetric information.

It is not easy to rebuff the above arguments. The Commission, however, despite declaring itself concerned about them, favours a different approach. Following a Communication from the Commission on *A Single Market for 21st Century Europe.*[123] a Staff Working Document *Towards the application of public procurement rules to social services of general interest* the Commission confirms its attachment to the application of the public procurement rules and principles in the area of health care. If a public authority decides to 'externalise' a social service of

[120] Ibid., p. 10.

[121] Ibid., p. 11.

[122] Ibid., p. 13.

[123] *Communication from the Commission to the European Parliament, the Council, the European Economic and Social Committee and the Committee of the Regions. Services of general interest, including social services of general interest: a new European commitment.* 20.11.2007 COM (2007) 725 final, p. 11.

general interest against remuneration, it has to follow the Community law rules on the award of public service contracts.[124] In the framework of the consultation process launched following its Communication on Social Services of General Interest of April 2006, the Commission received a number of questions concerning the application of the public procurement rules to social services of general interest. The Staff Working Document provides answers to these queries. In case of Part B-services (for example: health and social services, educational services, etc.), the 'light' procurement regime is applicable. As we have seen in Sect. 17.2.3, contracting authorities should also live up to the transparency principle when a Part B-contract is of 'certain cross-border interest'.

17.5 A Case Study on the Concept of Contracting Authorities: do Public Hospitals in the Netherlands Qualify as Contracting Authorities?

It has been explained above that the applicability of the procurement rules in the field of health care depends on the assessment whether the health purchaser qualifies as a contracting authority in terms of the Public Sector Directive. However, in Sect. 17.3 we have reached the conclusion that such assessment is casuistic and, often, unpredictable. The legal uncertainty ensuing may be illustrated by reference to the *Amphia* series of cases, in the Netherlands. Until 2004, the Dutch general hospitals, united in the Cooperation Dutch Hospitals, were not considered to be contracting authorities (with the exception of academic-teaching hospitals). The *Amphia* case led to proceedings at the Dutch Supreme Court and four years of intensive debate among lawyers and policy makers in the Netherlands. First, a short introduction into the Dutch health care system and into the current procurement practice in the field of health care in the Netherlands is given (Sect. 17.5.1). Then we present (Sect. 17.5.2) and analyse (Sect. 17.5.3) the *Amphia* cases.

17.5.1 A Short Introduction into the Dutch Health Care System and into Procurement Practice in Health Care in the Netherlands

In January 2006 the Netherlands established a new health care system, aiming at introducing a competitive market and increasing patient choice. Currently, private

124 *Commission staff working document. 'Frequently asked questions concerning the application of public procurement rules to social services of general interest.'* SEC (2007)1514 of 20.11.2007.

health insurers operate the system.[125] The insurers are required to provide a standard benefits package covering medical care.[126] The Dutch health insurance system is financed by: (i) income-related contributions and (ii) premiums paid by the insured.[127] Contributions are collected centrally and distributed by the so-called Health Insurance Fund among insurers on a risk-adjusted capitation formula.[128] A system of risk equalisation enables the acceptance obligation and prevents direct or indirect risk selection. General Practioners receive a payment from each patient on their practice list and a fee per consultation. The majority of specialists in the Netherlands work in hospitals. Two-thirds of hospital-based specialists are self-employed, organised in partnerships and paid on a fixed fee for services. Hospital budgets are developed using a formula that pays a fixed amount per bed, patient volume and number of licensed specialists. Additional funds by the government are provided for capital investment, although hospitals are increasingly encouraged to obtain investments via the private market. Recently, a new system of payments was introduced: the Diagnosis and Treatment Combinations ('DTC').[129] A DTC consists of a description of a medical service and the price of this treatment, which a hospital delivers. In 2008, 10% of all hospital services were reimbursed on the basis of DTCs. In the future, it is expected that most care will be reimbursed using DTCs. However, there is still considerable debate about the desired speed of further liberalisation of the hospital market. In the future hospitals may have greater freedom in negotiating the price and quality of DTCs. The quality of care is guaranteed through legislation regarding professional performance. The Netherlands Health Care Inspectorate protects and promotes health and health care by ensuring that care providers, care institutions and companies comply with these laws and regulations.

---

[125] Prior to 2006, a dual system of private a public insurance existed. People with earnings above approximately €30,000 per year and their dependants (around 35% of the population) were excluded from statutory coverage provided by public sickness funds and could purchase cover from private health insurers. See also the chapter by Sauter in this book.

[126] Statutory coverage includes: care by general practitioners (GPs), hospitals and midwives; hospitalisation; dental care (up to the age of 18; coverage from age 18 is confined to specialist dental care and dentures); medical aids; medicines (not all medicines; sleeping pills nor, for example, are not covered); maternity care; ambulance and patient transport services; paramedical care (limited physiotherapy/remedial therapy, speech therapy, occupational therapy and dietary advice).

[127] The income-related contribution is set at 6,5% of the first € 30.000 of annual taxable income. Employers reimburse their employees for this contribution and employees pay tax on this reimbursement. The Dutch insured pay a flat-rate premium (set by insurers) to their private health insurer. The Dutch government has created a safety net for low-income citizens if the average flat-rate premium exceeds 5% of their household income. Furthermore, the Dutch government pays for the premiums of children up to 18 years of age.

[128] http://english.minvws.nl/en/themes/health-insurance-system/default.asp.

[129] Diagnosis and Treatment Combinations (Diagnosebehandelingcombinaties, DBC's, in Dutch) are Dutch health care codes that define and describe all characteristics of particular treatments. See http://nl.wikipedia.org/wiki/Diagnosebehandelingcombinatie.

In the Netherlands there are no figures concerning the extent to which EU public procurement rules are applied in the field of health care. Therefore, it is difficult to conclude what the compliance rate is with regard to the procurement rules in the field of health care. In 2008 a statistical study was published concerning the compliance of eight academic hospitals in the Netherlands with the public procurement rules.[130] Since Dutch academic hospitals qualify as contracting authorities under the Public Sector Directive, they have to comply with the procurement rules, when they purchase works, supplies and services.[131] The outcome was, especially compared to 2004, disappointing. Only 57% of contracts (in 2004: 59%) were tendered in compliance with the Directive. In total 47% of the public services contracts (for example on consultancy) and 67% of the public supplies contracts were tendered.[132] With regard to the construction and exploitation of works the compliance was the highest, at 72%.[133]

17.5.2 The Amphia *Cases: Does a General Hospital in the Netherlands Qualify as a Contracting Authority?*

Amphia, a general hospital, founded after a merger of three hospitals. According to its statutes it has, as its objective, to 'research, treat, nurse and take care of the ill.' In April 2002 Amphia decided to install a new kitchen and food distribution system in its hospitals. It decided to purchase new food distribution trolleys. The total value of the contract was above the then applicable threshold for supply contracts. However, Amphia did not organise a procurement procedure in compliance with the former Supplies Directive 93/36/EEC, but invited several suppliers, who are active in that business, to take part in a business presentation.

[130] Nalevingsmeting Europees Aanbesteden 2006. Onderzoek naar naleving van Europese aanbestedingsregels in Nederland [Compliance Monitor European Tendering 2006. Research on compliance with EU public procurement rules]. By Significant B.V., November 2008. http://www.ez.nl/Actueel/Kamerbrieven/Kamerbrieven_2008/November_2008/Nalevingsonderzoek_aanbesteden.

[131] For the difference between academic and general hospitals in the Netherlands: In Dutch: Essers et al. (2008).

[132] Compared to 2002 and 2004 the compliance rate was lower, especially in the field of public services contracts. Nonetheless, figures show that the amount of public procurement procedures has increased, possibly due to the increased splitting of contracts into different parcels.

[133] This has to do with the important role the Netherlands' Board for Health care has performed in the accommodation of intramural health care. Until 2008 hospitals had to require both a license and a building permit from the Board for new construction projects and major renovations under the Health care Institutions Act. The Board considered applications for building permits by checking compliance with the procurement rules. Currently, government involvement in health care construction diminishes and hospitals and other health care institutions will have to handle their property investments by earning back those investments by means of their activities. See http://www.bouwcollege.nl.

Following these presentations, only two undertakings were invited to take part in the actual price negotiations. Sortrans B.V., who had until then acted as the main supplier of these trolleys, submitted an offer, which was rejected by Amphia.

In the proceedings, initiated by Sortans, before the District Court of Breda, Sortans submitted that Amphia qualifies as a contracting authority and therefore should have organised a tender in accordance with the Supplies Directive. This plea was successful. Both the District Court[134] and the Court of Appeal in Den Bosch[135] ruled that Amphia indeed qualifies as a contracting authority. First, the courts positively answered the question whether Amphia fulfils *specific purpose of meeting needs in the general interest,* which *do not have an industrial or commercial character.* In that respect both courts reasoned that the objective of Amphia consists of meeting needs in the general interest, since it deals with public health. Although Amphia stands in competition with other hospitals, this does not prevent an institution from meeting needs in the general interest. Moreover, the competition was restricted in a sense that, at that time, 90% of the hospitals tariffs were determined by a State body in the Netherlands. Furthermore, sickness funds were obliged to accept Amphia as partner. Second, the Court of Breda decided that Amphia is *an entity, financed, for the most part,* by the state, regional or local authorities or other bodies governed by public law.[136] At that time the old sickness funds system was still in place. Amphia had submitted that, although, it was financed for the most part (60%) out of sickness funds premiums and 40% out of private health insurance premiums, these premiums could not be regarded as financed by the State, since these premiums were based on the principle of solidarity, which means that the premium was related to the income of the insured and not related to the insured activities or risks. Both courts ruled that sickness funds were obliged to contract hospitals and there was no contractual relationship between the former sickness funds and hospitals. Finally, Amphia had put forward that the condition of *'subject to management supervision by the state, regional or local authorities or other bodies governed by public law'* was not fulfilled, since the state did not intervene with the decision which supplier would obtain the contract to supply the trolleys. The Court of Breda, however, decided that, by regulating and supervising quality, tariffs, exploitation, and renovation works, the State supervised a hospital in such a way that a hospital could not be considered independent in that respect.

In its ruling of 1 June 2007 the Supreme Court set aside the decision of the Court of Appeal.[137] In a relatively short judgment it considered that the Court of Appeal should have taken into consideration the factual circumstances, in which

---

134 Voorzieningenrechter Rechtbank Breda, KG ZA 04-486, LJN: AR7227.

135 Gerechtshof's-Hertogenbosch, C0500057, LJN: AU4635.

136 The Court of Appeal found that it was not necessary to scrutinise possible fulfilment of this condition and the third condition 'financed by the state'.

137 Hoge Raad, C06/022HR, LJN: AZ9872. As the highest court in fields of civil, criminal and tax law in the Netherlands, the Supreme Court examines only whether a lower court observed proper application of the law in reaching its decision. At this stage, the facts of the case as

Table 17.1 Comparison of the different Amphia judgments

Criterion for contracting authority	District court of Breda/Court of appeal Den Bosch	Supreme court	Court of appeal Arnhem
Specific purpose of meeting needs in the general interest?	YES because: Public health main objective tariff regulation Compulsory contracting	NO because: Climate of competition Hospitals managed on 'output, effectiveness and profitability'	Not addressed
Financed for the most part by state?	YES because: Financed for 60% out of sickness funds No contractual relationship between funds and hospitals	NO because: Contractual relationship exists Hospitals render health care in return for premiums	Not addressed
Supervised by the state?	Not addressed	Not addressed	NO because: Not a significant influence on its management and influence or interference with the outcome of tender procedures

Amphia operates. The statutes should not be decisive but instead the climate in which Amphia operates should be given consideration in order to answer the question whether Amphia fulfils *specific purpose of meeting needs in the general interest*, which *do not have an industrial or commercial character*. In that respect the Supreme Court considered that from 1 January 2003 onwards, general hospitals in the Netherlands operate in a climate of competition and that they are increasingly in the possibility to compete with other hospitals on prices. Moreover, although Amphia's main aim is to generate as much profits as possible, it is managed (and by health insurers led) on the basis of 'output, effectiveness and profitability'. Therefore, together with the fact that general hospitals are increasingly responsible for exploitations risks, a general hospital is not an entity, which fulfils *specific purpose of meeting needs in the general interest,* which *do not have an industrial or commercial character.* With regard to the question whether Amphia is *an entity, financed, for the most part,* by the State, regional or local authorities or other bodies governed by public law, the Supreme Court decided that there exists a contractual relationship between the former sickness funds and general hospitals, since in return for the premiums, hospitals render care based on Article 44 of the former Sickness Fund Act. According to the court, financing by the State can only be the case when hospitals receive payments for their activities, without rendering anything in return, which was not the case here.[138] The Supreme Court referred the case to the Court of Appeal in Arnhem to decide on the merits of the case. Meanwhile, the Minister of Health advised general hospitals for the sake of legal certainty to apply the procurement rules in the meantime.[139]

The Court of Appeal only scrutinised the third condition under Article 1(9), which is that of the Directive applies to an entity, which must be either *financed* or *supervised* or *appointed* by another contracting authority. With reference to the cases already discussed, *Commission* v. *France* (*social housing*) and *Truly*, for this criterion to be fulfilled, there should be, according to the court, dependency, which amounts to a significant influence on its management and which permits the public authorities to influence or interfere with the procurement procedures.[140] The Court of Appeal decided that this was not the case. The applicable laws only related to the supervision on the construction of hospitals buildings, the purchase of medical equipment and the budget of hospitals, but did not concern the actual choice of a trolley supplier. Nor did the regulation of quality by the Netherlands' Health Care Inspectorate and other laws concerning the quality and safety of food do so. The laws and regulations are of a general character, in other words, they concern the Dutch health care system in general and not specifically Amphia only. These laws and regulations rather create a framework, in which hospitals (which enjoy policy competences) such as Amphia need to organise health care (Table 17.1).

17.5.3 Analysis

It can be concluded following the *Amphia* cases that not all general hospitals in the Netherlands qualify as contracting authorities. However, a general conclusion that all general hospitals do not qualify as contracting authorities has not been drawn. On the contrary, the Minister of Health has responded to parliamentary questions that this case law has left some questions unanswered.[141] General hospitals may, depending on the circumstances, very well qualify as contracting authorities. In other cases than the *Amphia* case the condition of 'subject to management supervision' could be fulfilled. For instance, when the State or a public body significantly influence investment decisions. But based on the current applicable Dutch legislation this will not often be the case. According to the Minister current laws and regulations concern the admission of health care institutions and laws

[138] Hebly (2008).

[139] http://www.minvws.nl/kamerstukken/staf/2007/aanbestedingsplicht-ziekenhuizen.asp.

[140] *Commission* v. *France* (*social housing*), *supra* n. 63, para 59.

[141] http://www.minvws.nl/kamerstukken/staf/2007/aanbestedingsplicht-ziekenhuizen.asp. Letter of 26 January 2009.

concerning the quality of care. This does not result into supervision in terms of the Directive, since they do not create influence or interfere with procurement procedures.[142]

Interestingly, neither the Supreme Court nor the Court of Appeal Arnhem decided to make a preliminary reference to the ECJ. In his conclusions Advocate General Keus considered the relevance of a possible reference.[143] On the one hand, he acknowledged the uncertainty, which exists with regard to the fulfilment of the 'financed by' criterion in relation to other health care entities financed by sickness funds premiums.[144] On the other hand, these cases have been decided under the former Dutch health care system, which was set up around sickness funds and private health insurers. Since the Dutch health care system has been reformed, a preliminary reference in the *Amphia* case would have concerned the former health care system and would have only limited relevance for the future. Furthermore, it is important to note that the Court of Breda, the Court of Appeal Arnhem and the Supreme Court have all made extensive references, in their rulings, to settled case law of the ECJ. However, this case law was interpreted and applied in a different manner. Whereas, the Court of Breda (and the Court of Appeal Den Bosch implicitly) decided, with reference to *University of Cambridge*,[145] that Amphia qualifies as a contracting authority, the Supreme Court and Court of Appeal Arnhem came to a different conclusion by applying *University of Cambridge, Agora, Truley and Commission* v. *France* (*social housing*).[146] The question remains whether *Oymanns* could have changed the outcome in the *Amphia* cases. In other words, is the Dutch case law in line with the recent *Oymanns* ruling? As articulated on many occasions (and again in *Oymanns*) by the Court the concept of a public authority should be interpreted in a functional and broad manner. Both the Supreme Court and the Court of Appeal Arnhem have stressed the fact that the Dutch health care system is undergoing transition, gradually reducing State intervention to a minimum. Both courts had to apply Article 1(9) and its case law to a privatised health care system. Generally, it can be concluded that privatisation of health care decreases the application of public procurement law. The conclusion that under these circumstances the EU public procurement rules are not applicable is reasonable. However, by doing so the Dutch courts have interpreted 'financed for the most part' differently than the ECJ has done in *Oymanns*. By scrutinising the specific funding of the German health care system and the German laws, the

[142] http://www.minvws.nl/kamerstukken/staf/2007/aanbestedingsplicht-ziekenhuizen.asp. Letter of 23 April 2009.

[143] Conclusie A-G Keus, C06/022HR, LJN AZ9872.

[144] Currently, uncertainty evolves around the question whether the so-called 'care offices' (Zorgkantoren) are considered to be contracting authorities. Care offices are responsible for the implementation of the General Exceptional Medical Expenses Act (AWBZ). They have been set up by the jointly operating care insurers, but operate independently.

[145] *University of Cambridge, supra* n. 2.

[146] *Agorà, supra* n. 56, *Adolf Truley supra* n. 58 and *Commission* v. *France* (*social housing*), *supra* n. 63.

Court concluded that a contractual relationship between the sickness funds and the insured was not present. The Dutch Supreme Court ruled in the opposite direction, by stating that, based on Dutch law, the sickness funds render health care in return for the received premiums. Therefore contractual consideration between the funds and the insured exists. Notwithstanding the differences between the two health care systems, the *Amphia* outcome can be seen as being contrary to the *Oymanns* decision with regard to the interpretation of the 'financed for the most part' condition. Therefore, despite the changes which the Dutch health care system currently undergoes, a preliminary reference would have been appropriate. It could have especially created more legal certainty with regard to the applicability of procurement rules to national health care systems, which are (semi-)privatised.

17.6 Conclusions

In 2009 the German Federal Court (FDC) had to decide whether emergency rescue services are subject to public procurement law.[147] In the region of Saxony, several Saxon municipalities provide for rescue services. These services are often delegated to private entities. The question was raised whether this alliance was obliged to apply public procurement rules to their tenders. The FDC ruled that since emergency services qualify as public service contracts, they should be tendered in accordance with the rules of the Directive.[148] In that respect the FDC took a functional approach and set aside national technicalities in administrative law. This goes in the opposite direction from *Amphia*.

Amphia would have been decided differently had it not been brought to the Dutch Supreme Court. Thus, there is no general answer possible to the core question of this contribution: If, how and to what extent EU public procurement rules affect the national health care systems? Certainly, it can be concluded that, EU public procurement rules increasingly affect national health care systems. However, the answers to the question *how* and *to what extent* are unclear. Different outcomes are to be expected not only between different Member States but also within a single Member State. Depending on the judicial and constitutional system of each Member State internal differences will eventually be phased out, but it will take much longer to streamline the application of the relevant criteria at the EU level, especially since the health care systems of Member States are, and will be, in constant transition. The resulting variable geometry and legal uncertainty is clearly against the idea of a single market in the area of health care procurement, especially against the overriding principle governing procurement in the EU, that of

[147] Bundesgerichtshof, Ruling from 29 June 2009, BvR 2959/07.

[148] The Higher Regional Court in Düsseldorf had decided differently. According to this Court, the type of contract did not contain an obligation to provide a service but included a delegation of the exercise of official authority. Higher Regional Court Düsseldorf, Decision from 5 April 2006, VII-Verg 7/06.

transparency (that is, there is an important lack of transparency at the level of the applicable rules). This is an unsatisfactory situation.

What are possible means for the EU to circumscribe the uncertainty? How to clarify the scope of public procurement rules in relation to health care? A first step forward would consist of an updated and complete version of Annexes III and IV to the Public Sector Directive, preferably in English. This list should be closely monitored by the Commission and should be kept up-to-date by including the results of both EU and national case law. Second, the Commission may decide to clarify at the level of the services by, through a text of soft law, defining the content of services of general interest in the field of health care. Furthermore, issuing a soft law document concerning specifically the criteria for the application of procurement in health care could be helpful. In this document the Commission may chose to clarify the *Transparency* case law in relation to health care. On a more general level, the EU could strive for common solutions through coordination or Open Method of Coordination (OMC). This could also provide a platform, whereby best practices in the field of health care procurement could be exchanged. Coordination in the field of health care already in place,[149] is expected to intensify once the draft Patients Rights' Directive is adopted.[150] Such coordination could also extend to procurement practices. By all means, uniform application of EU public procurement in the field of health care remains problematic, since both the organisation and financing of national health care systems and public procurement in health care are not harmonised. However, for the sake of transparency and legal certainty a minimum level of coordination is necessary, in order to keep the competition on these public markets healthy!

References

Arrowsmith S (2005) The law of public and utilities procurement. Sweet & Maxwell, London

Arrowsmith S (2006) The past and the future evolution of EC procurement law: from framework to common code? Public Contract Law J 35

Bovis C (2007) EU public procurement law. Edward Elgar Publishing, Cheltenham

Brown A (2007) Seeing through transparency: the Requirement to Advertise Public Contracts and Concessions under the EC Treaty. PPLR 1

Brown A (2008) Case note. PPLR 17

Cabral P (2004) The internal market and the right to cross-border medical care. EL Rev

Davies G (2002) Welfare as a service. Leg Issues Eur Integr 29(1)

Dawes A (2006) Bonjour Herr doctor: national health care systems, the internal market and cross-border medical care within the EU. Leg Issues Eur Integr 33(2)

Drijber BJ, Stergiou HM (2009) Public procurement law and internal market law. CML Rev 46

Essers MJJM et al (2008) Aanbesteden & Mededinging in de Gezondheidszorg [Public Procurement and Competition in Health Care] (Bohn Stafleu van Loghum)

[149] See for example, Hervey and Trubek (2007), pp. 623–647.

[150] COM (2008) 414.

Hatzopoulos V (2002) Killing national health and insurance systems but healing patients? The European market for health care services after the judgments of the ECJ in *Vanbraekel* and *Peerbooms*. CML Rev

Hatzopoulos V (2005) Health law and policy, the impact of the EU. In: Búrca De (ed) EU law and the welfare state: in search of solidarity. OUP/EUI, Oxford

Hatzopoulos V (2008) Conference paper: health systems governance in Europe: the role of EU law and policy: public procurement and state aid in national health care systems

Hatzopoulos V (2009) Financing national health care in a trans-national environment: the impact of the EC internal market. Wis Int Law J 26(3)

Hatzopoulos V (2010, forthcoming) Public procurement and state aid in national health care systems. In: Mossialos E, Permanand G, Baeten R, Hervey T (eds) Health systems governance in Europe: the role of EU law and policy. CUP, Cambridge

Hebly JM (2008) De Ziekenhuisparabool [The Hospital Parabola]. Tijdschrift Aanbestedingsrecht

Hervey T, McHale J (2004) Health law and the European union. CUP, Cambridge

Hervey T, Trubek L (2007) Freedom to provide health care services in the EU: an opportunity for "hybrid governance". Columbia J Eur Law 13(3)

Krajewski M et al (eds) (2009) The changing legal framework for services of general interest in Europe—between competition and solidarity. TMC Asser, The Hague

McGowan D (2007) Clarity at last? Low value contracts and transparency obligations. PPLR 16

Neergaard U (2007) Public service concessions and related concepts—the increased pressure from community law on member states use of concessions. PPLR 6

Neergaard U et al (eds) (2009) Integrating welfare functions into EU law—from Rome to Lisbon. DJØF Publishing, Copenhagen

Stergiou H (2009) The increasing influence of primary EU law on EU public procurement law: must a concession to provide SGEI be tendered? In: van de Gronden J (ed) EU and WTO law on services. Kluwer, The Hague

Trepte P (2007) Public procurement in the EU. A Practioner's Guide. OUP, Oxford

Van de Gronden J (ed) (2009) EU and WTO law and services–limits to the realization of general interest, policies within the services markets?. Kluwer, Alphen aan de Rijn

Van der Mei AP (2002) Cross-border access to health care within the EU: Some reflections on Geraets-Smits and *Peerbooms* and *Vanbraekel*. Med Law

Van der Mei AP (2004) Cross-border access to medical care: non-hospital care and waiting lists. Leg Issues Eur Integr

Chapter 18
Patient Mobility Beyond Calais: Health Services Under WTO Law

Markus Krajewski

Contents

18.1 Introduction

In 2003, British citizen Yvonne Watts of Bedford travelled to Calais in France for hip surgery. She did so because she did not want to wait until this treatment was offered to her in Britain according to waiting list policy of the National Health Service (NHS). Upon her return, Mrs Watts claimed reimbursement of the costs of her treatment in Calais from the NHS, which was refused. The European Court of

M. Krajewski (✉)
Faculty of Law, University of Erlangen-Nuremberg, Erlangen, Germany
e-mail: Markus.Krajewski@jura.uni-erlangen.de

J. W. van de Gronden et al. (eds.), *Health Care and EU Law*,
Legal Issues of Services of General Interest, DOI: 10.1007/978-90-6704-728-9_18,

Justice (ECJ)[1] decided that this refusal violated the freedom to receive services in the meaning of Article 49 EC Treaty (now Article 56 TFEU).[2] The *Watts* judgment has since become one of the leading cases of the ECJ's jurisprudence on cross-border patient mobility.[3]

Had Mrs. Watts gone to the United States, Singapore or Malaysia matters would have been different because the freedom to receive services does not extend to third countries. Mrs Watts would have been obliged to bear her own costs unless the refusal by the NHS to reimburse the costs of treatment in those countries would have violated other legal rules. Trade in services between EU members and third countries which are members of the WTO is governed by the rules of the General Agreement on Trade in Services (GATS). One may ask how the refusal to reimburse the costs of medical treatment would have been decided under GATS law? The question is not a hypothetical one. Even though the numbers of EU patients travelling to third countries for medical treatment are still marginal, an increasing number of private hospitals in countries like Singapore, Thailand or Malaysia offer specialised medical treatments at an international standard for a fraction of the price required in OECD countries.[4] Could patients travelling to places outside of Europe to receive medical treatment and health services claim reimbursement of the relevant costs from the organisations of their national health systems under GATS law?

This question raises not only difficult doctrinal, but also policy questions, in particular, since the GATS has been subject of an ongoing public debate about the benefits and potential dangers of trade liberalisation in services on a global level. Many contributions to that debate relate to health services: Some commentators claim that the GATS jeopardises the political autonomy of WTO Members to organise and finance their national health systems and puts health systems which are not based on market models under pressure.[5] Others have argued that the GATS does not limit the regulatory choices of the WTO Members and allows them to adapt their GATS commitments to their health policy.[6] While this is not the place to fully engage in this debate and assess the merits of the arguments, it should be noted that the general tone of the debate about the impact of the GATS bears striking similarities to the debate about the impact of EU law on the national health systems. Not least because of the similarities of the arguments, it seems useful for the purpose of this book to extend the analysis of the impact of EU law on healthcare beyond the horizon of internal market and to include the analysis of

---

[1] Throughout this chapter, the term European Court of Justice or ECJ refers to the 'Court of Justice' in the meaning of Article 19(1) EU Treaty (Treaty of Lisbon 2009).

[2] ECJ, Case C-372/04 *Watts* [2006] *ECR* I-4325.

[3] For a comprehensive analysis of that case law see van de Gronden (2009), p. 705, at pp. 708–731 and Sauter (2008).

[4] Arunanondchai and Fink (2007), p. 12.

[5] Price et al. (1999), pp. 1889–1892.

[6] Zeiler-Kligman (2006), pp. 233–276. For a more nuanced view see Chanda (2003), p. 1997 at p. 2006–2007.

WTO/GATS law on the cross-border provision of health services, in particular on patient mobility. The chapter will develop this analysis on the basis of transplanting the *Watts* case into WTO law and assume that Mrs Watts had not travelled to Calais but to Thailand or Malaysia. How would this case have been solved? It is submitted that this method highlights similarities and differences between EU and WTO law clearly and allows for more concrete comparisons.[7]

Accordingly, this chapter is structured as follows: After this Introduction the first section concerns the question whether medical or hospital treatment abroad concerns 'trade in (health) services' in the meaning of the GATS (Sect. 18.2). This part identifies the legal construction of this notion through the four modes of supply and also gives a short factual account of the scope and structure of trade in health services on a global level. The next part will ask more directly which measures fall into the scope of the GATS (Sect. 18.3). In particular, it has to be determined whether the exclusion of services supplied in the exercise of governmental authority from the GATS influences the application of the agreement to health and medical services. Having determined under which circumstances the GATS applies to measures affecting the cross-border supply of health services, the subsequent part of the chapter discusses the substantive obligations of the GATS (Sect. 18.4). After a short overview of the main principles of the GATS, the chapter will provide an in-depth enquiry into the specific commitments in health services of the EU and other WTO Members, because only the exact analysis of the limitations and qualifications of these schedules allows us to clearly determine the impact of the GATS on the cross-border to provision of health services. In addition, the potential of the general exception clause of the GATS to justify regulations of health systems which violate GATS obligations needs to be ascertained. Lastly, the legal status of GATS in the EU legal order, in particular the contentious issue of direct effect, needs to be assessed, because only if the GATS is directly applicable would a patient who received medical treatment abroad be able to rely on the agreement to claim reimbursement of the costs of said treatment (Sect. 18.5).

18.2 The Concept of Trade in (Health) Services

The GATS applies to measures affecting trade in services (Article I:1 GATS). The impact of the GATS on the regulation of health services therefore depends on whether the regulatory measures, for example, the refusal of a national health system or a public sickness fund to reimburse the costs of treatment abroad, affect trade in services. The notion of 'trade in services' is defined in the GATS on the basis of one of four Modes of supply as stipulated in Article I:2 GATS:

[7] For a similar, albeit briefer exercise regarding the *Laval*, *Viking* and *Rüffert* cases of the ECJ see Krajewski (2008), p. 55 at pp. 57–59.

For the purposes of this Agreement, trade in services is defined as the supply of a service:

(a) from the territory of one Member into the territory of any other Member;
(b) in the territory of one Member to the service consumer of any other Member;
(c) by a service supplier of one Member, through commercial presence in the territory of any other Member;
(d) by a service supplier of one Member, through presence of natural persons of a Member in the territory of any other Member.

Health services can be traded through all four Modes of supply.[8] Cross-border supply (Mode 1) concerns the supply of a service from the territory of one Member into the territory of another Member. Normally, this does not involve the movement of the service supplier or consumer across borders. Instead, only the service crosses the border. In health services, Mode 1 is usually associated with telemedicine or diagnosis and medical advice through telecommunications (e-health). The supply of a service in the territory of one Member to the service consumer of another Member (Mode 2) occurs if the consumer of one WTO Member consumes a service in the territory of another member. This Mode therefore covers cross-border patient mobility. The supply of a service by a service supplier of one Member through commercial presence in the territory of another Member (Mode 3) requires the commercial presence of a foreign service supplier in the territory of a WTO Member. Health services trade through Mode 3 involves, *inter alia*, the establishment of hospitals or clinics in another country. Lastly, the supply of a service by a service supplier of one Member through presence of natural persons of a Member in the territory of another Member (Mode 4) is usually associated with the supply of medical services or the services of nurses and midwives through the temporary movement of professionals providing these services in another country. Mode 4 includes the provision of services by self-employed professionals and by posted workers.[9]

A growing number of bilateral and regional trade agreements add an additional layer of rules to the international trading system. Increasingly, these agreements supplement WTO provisions and also apply in the external trade relations of the EU. It is hence interesting to see that the modal approach to the notion of trade in services is also followed in these agreements. The definition of trade in services based on the four Modes of supply has rightfully been called 'canonical' by one commentator.[10] Yet, it has to be remembered that the notion of trade in services encompassing commercial presence (investment or establishment), presence of natural persons and consumption abroad had to be intellectually construed, and actively lobbied for, prior and during the negotiations on trade in services in the Uruguay Round. It has been showed that a growing 'epistemic community' of

[8] Chanda (2002), pp. 158–159.
[9] Herwig (2008), p. 7 at p. 17.
[10] Lang (2009), p. 157 at p. 161.

trade officials, business representatives, professionals, think tanks and individual academics developed, consolidated and finally implemented the idea that 'trade in services' was to be understood as a new field of trade policy, thus defining and socially constructing 'a new reality'.[11]

It is difficult to determine the factual importance of trade in health services on a global level, because reliable empirical data on international trade in services are rare. One of the main difficulties is that the national foreign trade statistics do not contain specific and differentiated data on the various modes of supply of health services.[12] It is assumed that the trade in health services constitutes a small proportion of global trade in services in general. However, there may be significant differences between modes, countries and sectors. Some countries, like the Philippines, are known for the large numbers of nurses working abroad (Mode 4) while others, like the United States, tend to attract patients who are looking for highly specialised and complicated surgeries in order to benefit from the latest technology in the area (Mode 2). On a global level, the proportion of trade in health services through Mode 2, which involves cross-border patient mobility, still seems relatively small.[13] The largest proportion of the notion of trade in health services seems to be supplied through Mode 4.[14]

The modal conceptualisation of the notion of trade in services has no direct equivalent in EU primary law. Instead, the conceptualisation of the cross-border supply of services in EU law covers elements of three fundamental freedoms. Modes 1 and 2 under the GATS are equivalent to the freedom to provide and to receive services. The corresponding freedom to Mode 3 under EU law is the freedom of establishment. Finally, Mode 4 covers parts of the free movement of services if the service supplier is self-employed and of the free movement of workers if the service supplier is an employee. It should be noted that the Commission's Proposal for a Directive of the European Parliament and of the Council on the Application of Patients' Rights in Cross-Border Healthcare of July 2008[15] deviates from the conception of the three freedoms and introduces a notion of 'cross-border healthcare' which is strikingly similar to the four modes of the GATS. It even refers to 'modes of supply', a term which has hitherto not been used in internal EU law.[16] Paragraph 10 of the Preamble reads as follows:

'[T]he concept of "cross-border healthcare" covers the following modes of supply of healthcare:

---

[11] Drake and Nicolaidis (1992), p. 37 at p. 45.

[12] Lindl (2005), p. 156; Zimmermann (2008), p. 201.

[13] Waeger (2008), pp. 10–11.

[14] Waeger (2008), at pp. 14–15.

[15] Proposal for a Directive of the European Parliament and of the Council on the application of patients' rights in cross-border healthcare, COM (2008) 414 final. For an assessment of this proposal see the chapters by Hervey, Szyszczak and Pennings and Hervey in this book.

[16] A search of the term 'modes of supply' in the EUR-Lex databases reveals only references to international trade agreements of the EU with the exception of the Commission Decision in which the term has only be used descriptively (search date: 30 April 2010).

- Use of healthcare abroad (i.e.: a patient moving to a healthcare provider in another Member State for treatment); this is what is referred to as 'patient mobility';
- Cross-border provision of healthcare (i.e.: delivery of service from the territory of one Member State into the territory of another); such as telemedicine services, remote diagnosis and prescription, laboratory services;
- Permanent presence of a healthcare provider (i.e.: establishment of a healthcare provider in another Member State); and,
- Temporary presence of persons (i.e.: mobility of health professionals, for example moving temporarily to the Member State of the patient to provide services).'

The Draft Directive does not only apply to cross-border patient mobility, but also the establishment of health-service suppliers, e-health and the movement of service providers are covered. The scope of the GATS regarding trade in services is therefore almost identical to the scope of the notion of 'cross-border supply of health' as defined in Paragraph 10 of the Draft Patient Directive. It should be noted that the European Parliament rejected this broad conceptualisation of the notion of cross-border healthcare. In its Resolution of 23 April 2009, adopted after the first reading of the Proposal, the Parliament restricts the scope of the Directive to the use of healthcare abroad.[17] It remains to be seen as to whether the Commission's or the Parliament's approach will prevail.

18.3 Scope of the GATS

As shown in the previous section, cross-border patient mobility can be conceptualised as trade in services through Mode 2 (consumption abroad) according to the GATS. The next question to analyse in order to determine whether a patient could claim reimbursement of the costs of medical treatment in another WTO country, concerns the conditions under which the GATS applies to health services, in particular on services supplied in a highly regulated public health system. Furthermore, it needs to be assessed whether measures taken by a national health service or a public sickness funds are measures which are covered by the GATS at all.

18.3.1 Exclusion of Governmental Services

Like most other international trade agreements, the GATS does not define the term 'services'. Article I:3(b) GATS states that the agreement applies to services in all

[17] European Parliament, Patients' rights in cross-border healthcare, Resolution P6_TA(2009) 0286, 23 April 2009.

sectors except services supplied in the exercise of governmental authority. The notion of service supplied in the exercise of governmental authority is further defined in Article I:3(c) GATS as 'any service which is supplied neither on a commercial basis, nor in competition with one or more service suppliers.' Unlike Article 51 TFEU (ex Article 45 EC) which excludes activities that are connected 'with the exercise of official authority' from the scope of the freedom of establishment and the free movement of services,[18] the GATS notion of services supplied in the exercise of governmental authority does not focus on the concept of 'governmental (or official) authority' but on the circumstances of the supply of the service.[19] If a service is supplied on a commercial basis or in competition with other service suppliers it is covered by GATS. In general, an activity can be considered commercial if it involves an economic viable transaction, an act of buying and selling. The second part of the definition of Article I:3 (c) GATS requires that two or more service suppliers compete with each other for the same services market. Apart from these general considerations, there is disagreement and debate about the exact interpretation of the terms 'commercial basis' and 'in competition'.[20] For the purposes of this contribution, it is sufficient to address only those aspects of that debate which have related directly to the question whether this exception clause could apply to the supply of health services.

At the outset, two uncontested cases can be mentioned. It is generally assumed that a service provided free at the point of delivery, that is, without any direct financial contribution from the service recipient, would not be considered a service supplied on a commercial basis. Without paying a price which can be associated with an individual service in return for that service there is no economically valuable transaction and hence no exchange which can be characterised as an act of selling and buying. Hence, a service which is financed exclusively on the basis of tax money through the general public purse would have to be considered as non-commercial. Furthermore, the health services supplied in the framework of a classical national health system are typically provided on the basis of a public (regional or state-wide) monopoly. Hence, they are not provided in competition with one or more service suppliers. Consequently, health services supplied by a national health service would be excluded from the GATS.[21] This does not exclude the application of the GATS to the reimbursement of costs of treatment abroad, because the treatment of a patient from a country with a national health system in another country consists of a supply of a service in the territory of that other country. It is hence only relevant if the activity performed in the other country

[18] On the meaning of this provision see ECJ, Case 2/74 *Reyners* [1974] *ECR* 631; ECJ, Case 147/86 *Commission* v. *Greece* [1988] *ECR* 1637, para 7 and ECJ, Case C-114/97 *Commission* v. *Spain* [1998] *ECR* I-6717, para 34.

[19] Krajewski (2003), p. 341.

[20] Adlung (2006), p. 455; Leroux (2006), p. 345; Van Duzer (2004), p. 287 et seq. See also Krajewski (2009), p.187 at pp. 198–203.

[21] Zeiler-Kligman (2006), at p. 265.

constitutes a service, not if the similar activity at home would be considered a service.[22]

Contrary to a national health system, health services which are provided in a fully commercialised context and against the payment of a price which reflects the costs of the production of the service including a profit for the service supplier (market price) are supplied on a commercial basis. Hence, the supply of such a service would not fall under the exception clause and be covered by the GATS. Examples of these services are obviously manifold and include all services provided in purely commercial contexts. Matters are more complicated if other health systems, such as public insurance systems or hybrid forms, are considered. In this case, it is necessary to carefully analyse and interpret the notions of 'commercial' and 'in competition'. Two aspects of such an exercise will be briefly discussed here, because they are of particular relevance to the health sector.

The first concerns the question whether the financing of the service through a third entity, which is distinct from the public purse and the service consumer, should have an impact on the determination of the commercial character of the service. As is well known, the ECJ held in *Geraets-Smits/Peerbooms* and *Müller-Fauré* that health services provided in social insurance systems either as benefits-in-kind or for reimbursement would be considered services in the meaning of Article 50 EC (now Article 57 TFEU), because the services were paid for by somebody (albeit not the recipient).[23] This view has been criticised for its narrow and formalistic focus on the individual service transaction.[24] It does not take the context of the service, in particular the logic of a solidarity-based health system, into account. The supply of a health service should not be singled out as a stand-alone transaction, because it is embedded in the organisational and financial structure of the health system in general.

The ECJ's perspective should therefore not be applied in the context of Article I:3(c) GATS without adaptation. One possibility would be to distinguish between health systems in which the remuneration of the service supplier (doctor, hospital and other health profession) is determined on the basis of the number and types of services which are actually supplied and systems in which the remuneration is determined by other factors. In the former system, the service could be considered to be supplied on a commercial basis, because the exchange of the service itself would be a valuable economic transaction. Even if the service consumer does not pay for the service directly, the service supplier is paid for the individual transaction. Hence, it is important how many, and what kind, of services the supplier actually supplies. If the number and type of services are irrelevant, for example, because every service supplier receives a certain budget which is determined by

---

[22] In this respect, the GATS approach can be compared with the ECJ's approach to the notion of services in the *Watts* case.

[23] ECJ, Case C-157/99 *Smits and Peerbooms* [2001] *ECR* I-5473; ECJ, Case C-385/99 *Müller-Fauré and van Riet* [2003] *ECR* I-4509.

[24] See for example, Wunder (2009), p. 324 at p. 331.

other factors than the actual services supplier, it seems convincing to assume that the service is not supplied on a commercial basis, because there are no economic incentives to supply more services or supply services of a specific kind.

This interpretation of the GATS would be more nuanced than the approach of the ECJ to health services, which does not differentiate between the different modalities of financing the service. However, like other differentiations discussed so far, the one suggested here may cause problems when applied in practice. In particular, health systems may employ a mix of elements for determining the actual remuneration a health service supplier receives. They may generally use the number and types of services as a basis for the calculation of the remuneration, but apply a maximum sum. In such a case, or in the case of other forms of calculating the remuneration for the service provider, a case-by-case approach would have to determine whether the service is provided on a commercial basis or not.

A second aspect relates to the notion of 'in competition'. Many governmental services which have previously been provided on the basis of monopolies have been subject to transformations in recent years. In particular, governments and administrations have begun to introduce limited aspects of competition. This is especially visible in the health sector. In this context, it may be useful to recall the ECJ's *AOK Bundesverband* judgment[25] a case which dealt explicitly with the notion of 'competition' in order to determine the economic nature of an activity. The Court was faced with the question of whether the fact that the German sickness funds (*Krankenkassen*) were engaged in some competition would make these entities undertakings in the meaning of EU competition law. The ECJ concluded that this was not the case. For the purpose of this chapter it is of particular importance that the ECJ stated that freedom of the sickness funds to 'engage in some competition with one another in order to attract members' does not call the analysis that they are not engaged in an economic activity into question. The Court accepted that the legislature introduced an element of competition:

> in order to encourage the sickness funds to operate in accordance with principles of sound management, that is to say in the most effective and least costly manner possible, in the interests of the proper functioning of the German social security system.[26]

This is an approach which could also be usefully applied in the context of interpreting Article I:3(c) GATS. If there is only 'some competition' and if this element of competition was introduced to improve the efficiency of the service suppliers, but not to introduce market relationships, the service should not be considered to be supplied in competition with one or more service suppliers. The decisive factor in this context is the outcome of the limited competition. If, as in the *AOK Bundesverband* case, the competition between the different service suppliers does not lead to any direct gains or losses because all service suppliers

[25] ECJ, Joined Cases C-264/01 a.o., *AOK Bundesverband* [2004] *ECR* I-2493.

[26] *AOK Bundesverband, supra* n. 25, para 56.

are connected through a scheme which equalises gains and losses, it could be argued that this service is not 'supplied in competition with one or more service suppliers.'

The discussions in this part have shown that the carve-out for services supplied in the exercise of governmental authority does not include any particular sector a priori from the scope of the GATS. It is not surprising that WTO Members consider health services to be covered by the GATS. In fact, the WTO's services classification explicitly includes services provided by medical doctors, dentists, psychiatrists, nurses, midwives and paramedics as well as health services including hospital services.[27] Yet, the organisation and financing of a particular service may lead to the exclusion of that service from the scope of the agreement. The exception clause is based on the economic conditions of the supply of the service. Its scope may therefore vary between countries and at different points in time. Depending on the actual circumstances, a service may be supplied on a commercial basis and in competition with one or more service suppliers in one country, and may therefore fall within the scope of the GATS, whereas the same service could be provided on a non-commercial basis and not in competition in another country and would therefore not be covered by the GATS. As these conditions depend on the regulatory framework of the particular framework, governments may influence the scope of the GATS by modifying the economic conditions of the supply of the service. In particular, deregulation and liberalisation may reduce the number of services that are covered by the GATS exemption clause.[28]

18.3.2 Institutional and Regulatory Scope

As already mentioned GATS applies to 'measures by Members' affecting trade in services. Measures of Members are defined as measures of:

(i) central, regional or local governments and authorities; and
(ii) non-governmental bodies in the exercise of powers delegated by central, regional or local governments or authorities' (Article I:3(a) GATS).

In the present context, this raises the question whether decisions of the organisations of the national health systems fall under this definition.

It can be assumed that the entities of a traditional national health service, which is institutionally not separated from the central government, would normally be considered as authorities at the central or regional level of government in the meaning of Article I:3(a) GATS. Matters are slightly more complicated for

---

[27] See the WTO's Services Sectoral Classification List, MTN.GNS/W/120, 10 July 1991 as attached to the Guidelines for the Scheduling of Specific Commitments under the General Agreement on Trade in Services, S/L/92, 28 March 2001.

[28] Zdouc (1999), p. 295 at p. 321, note 85.

the decisions of public sickness funds, which are not directly part of the government, but are nevertheless public entities with regulatory authority. It seems possible to interpret the notion of 'authorities' in a broader sense and include all public entities which exercise governmental authority in that definition. It could be argued that if even measures of non-governmental can be subject to the GATS if these bodies exercise delegated public authority, measures of public bodies with the same effects must also fall into the scope of the agreement. It is also rather obvious that the decision of a private insurance company not to reimburse the costs of treatment abroad is not a measure falling into the scope of the GATS, because this decision is not based on delegated governmental authority. Instead, it is a normal commercial decision framed in a contractual context. Unlike parts of EU law, GATS does not apply between the contractual relations between private parties ('horizontal effect'). In line with general public international law the activities of a private entity will only be subject to the GATS if the private entity can be attributed to official (that is, regulatory and not commercial) behaviour of the State.

As health systems across the globe currently experiment with mixed public–private forms and move back and forth between a greater reliance on commercialisation and competition and the reintroduction of public elements,[29] the question whether the decisions of the entities of a national health system are covered by the GATS can only be answered depending on the circumstances of the case at hand.

18.4 Substantive Obligations of the GATS

Based on the discussions in the previous section it can be assumed that the decision of the NHS or a public sickness fund not to reimburse the costs of medical treatment in another WTO Member is a measure which falls into the scope of the GATS. The measure affects trade in health services, because it has an effect on the decision of a patient to consume health services through Mode 2. This raises the question whether such a decision also violates a substantive obligation of the GATS.

18.4.1 Main Principles

The main substantive principles of the GATS are the non-discrimination standards which comprise most-favoured nation treatment (Article II GATS) and national treatment (Article XVII GATS) and the obligation to grant market access (Article

[29] Cacace et al. (2008), pp. 5–16.

XVI GATS) which involves the prohibition of quantitative and qualitative restrictions.[30] Market access and national treatment can be considered as functionally equivalent to the prohibition of discrimination and of restrictions contained in the fundamental freedoms of the EU. However, one important feature of the GATS is its distinction between general obligations and specific commitments. The general obligations of Part II of the GATS apply, subject to certain exceptions, to measures affecting all services sectors, whereas the specific commitments of Part III of the GATS only apply if a WTO Member specifically committed a service to these disciplines in its Schedule of Specific Commitments. While the most-favoured national principle is a general obligation, market access and national treatment are specific commitments.

The most-favoured nation principle of the GATS obliges a WTO Member to treat services and service suppliers of one Member no less favourably than it treats like services and service suppliers of another Member. In essence, Article II GATS prohibits the discrimination of services and service suppliers from different foreign countries. The obligation of most-favoured nation treatment does not apply unconditionally. Members can exempt measures from most-favoured nation treatment by listing them in the their lists of Article II exemptions. The EU maintains a number of such exemptions, but none in health or health-related services.[31]

Article XVI:1 GATS requires a WTO Member to grant market access according to the terms, limitations and conditions specified in its Schedule of Specific Commitments. Article XVI:2 GATS specifies that a Member may not maintain or adopt any of the measures specifically mentioned in the six sub-paragraphs of Article XVI:2 GATS. These measures include, *inter alia,* limitations on the number of service suppliers, service transactions or total number of service operations expressed in the form of numerical quotas, monopolies, exclusive service suppliers or the requirements of an economic needs test. Furthermore, Article XVI:2 GATS covers limitations on the total number of natural persons employed in a particular service sector, measures which restrict or require specific types of legal entity or joint venture through which a service supplier may supply a service and limitations on the participation of foreign capital in terms of maximum percentage limit on foreign shareholding or the total value of foreign investment. If a WTO Member made a full market access commitment in a particular sector or sub-sector, all measures mentioned in Article XVI:2 GATS are prohibited. WTO Members may, however, limit their market access commitment by listing those measures which would otherwise violate the market access obligation in their schedules.

---

[30] For an overview see Weiss (1995), pp. 1177–1225 and Footer and George (2005), pp. 799–953.

[31] General Agreement on Trade in Services, European Communities and their Member States, Final List of Article II (MFN) Exemptions, 15 April 1994, GATS/EL/31.

The national treatment provision (Article XVII GATS) requires a Member to treat services and service suppliers of another Member no less favourably than its own like services and service suppliers. Article XVII:2 GATS specifies that the requirement of national treatment can be met through formally identical treatment or formally different treatment. National treatment under GATS therefore includes *de jure* and *de facto* non-discrimination. Article XVII:3 GATS states that:

> Formally identical or formally different treatment shall be considered to be less favourable if it modifies the conditions of competition in favour of services or service suppliers of the Member compared to like services or service suppliers of any other Member.

A footnote to Article XVII GATS states that the national treatment obligation does not require the compensation for 'inherent competitive disadvantages which result from the foreign character of the relevant services or service suppliers.' In other words, national treatment requires the protection of the competitive relationship between a domestic and a foreign service or service supplier in the domestic market, but does not require a Member to provide the preconditions for an economically viable supply of a service from another country.

The GATS also contains other obligations such as transparency requirements (Article III GATS) which oblige WTO Members, *inter alia,* to publish all measures of general application affecting trade in services, the obligation to apply measures affecting trade in services in a reasonable, objective and impartial manner (Article VI:1 GATS) and to provide for judicial or administrative review mechanisms for administrative decisions (Article VI:2 GATS). Furthermore, there are provisions on monopolies and restrictive business practices (Article VIII, IX GATS), government procurement (Article XIII GATS) and subsidies (Article XV GATS). However, these provisions do not contain obligations which go beyond the general principles of non-discrimination and market access. These areas of the GATS are therefore not significant for the impact of the GATS on health services. This shows a major difference between WTO and EU law, because EU public procurement, state aid and competition law influence the financing and organisation of national health systems to a great extent.[32]

18.4.2 Specific Commitments in Health Services

In order to determine whether, and to which, extent trade in health services is subject to the market access and national treatment principles the list of Specific Commitments of each WTO Member must be consulted, because market access and national treatment only apply for sectors with specific commitments and only subject to limitations and qualifications of commitments. The EU maintains a common schedule of commitments, but in those sectors where the internal

[32] Szyszczak (2009), p. 191, at pp. 201–212.

competence rests predominantly with the Member States, the EU list is simply a compilation of the specific commitments of the individual EU Members and lists commitments and limitations on that basis.

The lists of specific commitments are structured according to different sectors and sub-sectors of the services economy. For health services, the following sub-sectors are relevant: Medical and dental services (sub-sector 1.A.h.),[33] services provided by midwives, nurses, physiotherapists and para medical personnel (sub-sector 1.A.j.), hospital services (sub-sector 8.A) and other human health services (sub-sector 8.B.). In addition, the sub-sector life, accident and health insurance services (sub-sector 7.A.a) could be of importance for health services in general. For each of these sub-sectors, WTO Members list their commitments on the basis of the four modes of supply and regarding market access and national treatment, respectively.

The existing level of health-related commitments of WTO Members is generally considered to be relatively low.[34] Most commitments have been made by developed countries. The scope of these commitments varies between the different modes of supply. Similar to other sectors, the lowest level of commitments in health services can be found in Mode 4 (presence of natural persons).[35] Mode 3 also shows a relatively high level of restrictions and limitations of the commitments, while Modes 1 and 2 appear to be the more liberalised modes of supply with regard to health services.[36]

Limitations concerning Mode 3 include general restrictions on foreign direct investment such as foreign equity limitations or joint venture requirements.[37] There are also a number of restrictions in Mode 3 which are direct reactions to the specificities of national health systems. For example, Germany scheduled the following limitation regarding market access in medical services through commercial presence: 'Economic needs test for medical doctors and dentists who are authorized to treat members of public insurance schemes. The criterion is shortage of doctors and dentists in the given region.'[38] This implies that medical doctors and dentists may not rely on Article XVI GATS to challenge the quantitative restrictions which apply for the participation in the German public insurance scheme. Considering that 90% of all German patients are covered by this scheme most doctors will have to be admitted to that system if they want to survive economically. Another example of a restriction regarding the establishment of doctors is the limitation of the United Kingdom which also applies to market

[33] This numerical classification relates to the classification of services sectors according to the WTO's Services Sectoral Classification List, *supra* n. 27. This list also contains the corresponding classification of the UN Central Product Classification (CPC).

[34] Adlung and Carzaniga (2001), p. 352 at p. 356.

[35] Adlung and Carzaniga (2006), p. 83 at p. 88.

[36] Adlung and Carzaniga (2006), at p. 91 and p. 93.

[37] Butkeviciene and Diaz (1998), p. 135 at p. 153.

[38] General Agreement on Trade in Services, European Communities and their Member States, Schedule of Specific Commitments, 15 April 1995, GATS/SC/31.

access for medical services in Mode 3: 'Establishment for doctors under the NHS is subject to medical manpower planning.'[39] This restriction serves the same function as the German restriction. It clarifies that doctors who want to treat NHS patients, which again is the economic basis for most doctors, cannot establish themselves freely but have to accept the conditions and limitations of the manpower planning of the NHS.

Interestingly, the commitments in Mode 2, which covers patient mobility, contain the least number of restrictions.[40] Apparently, many WTO Members did not see particular regulatory needs to restrict the ability of their citizens to receive medical services in another WTO Member.[41] However, one restriction which is of extreme importance for the purposes of this chapter can be found in the schedule of the United States. It concerns a limitation of the US commitment to national treatment in hospital services through Mode 2. According to this limitation, 'federal or state government reimbursement of medical expenses is limited to licensed, certified facilities in the United States.' This means that US citizens receiving hospital services in another WTO Member may not claim reimbursement of those costs from federal or state sources. This applies in particular to the federal health-care programmes of Medicaid and Medicare which do not reimburse costs for treatment abroad.[42]

It should be noted that the EC Schedule of Specific Commitments of 1994 does not contain a restriction on Mode 2 regarding the reimbursement. Interestingly, however, the schedule of Poland, which is still a separate schedule, contains such a restriction. Regarding private medical services and private hospital services, Poland maintained the following limitation for national treatment in Mode 2: 'Public medical insurance programmes do not cover cost of medicare supplied abroad.'[43] This restriction will be abandoned in the new consolidated schedule of the EU which includes the 25 Members of 2004.[44]

---

39 EC Schedule of Specific Commitments, *supra* n. 38.

40 Butkeviciene and Diaz (1998), at p. 145.

41 Adlung and Carzaniga (2001), at p. 357.

42 Cortez (2008), p. 71 at p. 96.

43 General Agreement on Trade in Services, Poland, Schedule of Specific Commitments, 15 April 1994, GATS/SC/71. Poland made no commitments regarding health services offered by the public sector.

44 Council for Trade in Services, Communication from the European Communities and its Member States, Certification, Draft Consolidated GATS Schedule, 9 October 2006, S/C/W/273. This schedule is not yet in force as all 25 EU Members whose commitments are consolidated in this schedule (Bulgaria and Romania are not yet included) will have to ratify the schedule. See ECJ, Opinion 1/08, Opinion of 30 November 2009, *ECR* I-0000 (n.y.r.). It is doubtful, if this continues to be necessary after the entry into force of the Treaty of Lisbon 2009 which confers the exclusive competence in trade in services to the Union (Article 207(1) TFEU).

18.4.3 Non-Reimbursement of Costs for Medical Treatment Abroad as Violation of GATS?

Having established that the decision of a public entity such as the NHS or a public sickness fund not to reimburse the costs of treatment in a non-EU country would fall into the scope of the GATS, it is now possible to assess this decision in light of the aforementioned GATS principles.

To begin with, such a decision could violate the most-favoured nation principle (Article II GATS) if the costs for the treatment in one country would be reimbursed while the costs for treatment in another country would not. Using the concrete example of Mrs Watts: the costs of her treatment in France were reimbursed by the NHS, but the costs of the similar treatment in Thailand or Singapore would not. Arguably, this could be seen as discrimination between services from France and services from Thailand or Singapore. However, such a violation of the most-favoured nation obligation would be justified on the basis of Article V GATS, which allows deviations from GATS obligations in order to establish or maintain an (regional) economic integration agreement. Hence, if members of an economic integration agreement grant each other more favourable treatment compared to the treatment of non-members of this integration agreement and if the requirements of Article V GATS are met, the violation of the most-favoured nation principle could be justified. As the EU is an economic integration agreement within the meaning of Article V, any privileges which EU members grant each other do not have to be extended to all other WTO members.

Next, we move to the specific commitments. Could the refusal to reimburse patients be a restriction of market access in the meaning of Article XVI? As mentioned above Article XVI:2 GATS prohibits a number of specific quantitative and qualitative restrictions such as economic needs tests, quotas and monopolies. At first sight, the refusal to reimburse the costs of medical treatment abroad would not fall under any of those measures. However, the WTO's decision in *US—Gambling and Betting Services* may shed some doubt on this conclusion.[45] The case concerned a US ban on online gambling. The Panel and the Appellate Body of the WTO held that such a ban constituted a numerical quota in the form of a 'zero quota'.[46] The Appellate Body based this interpretation, *inter alia*, on the 'effects' of the total ban on market access. This raises the question whether it might be possible to argue that the refusal to reimburse the costs of treatment abroad has the effect of a total ban, that is, a 'zero quota' regarding Mode 2? Making such an argument would be difficult, because the refusal to reimburse the costs only reduces the number of patients which actually seek medical treatment abroad, but does not amount to an effective ban on treatment abroad. The mere reduction or

---

45 *United States—Measures Affecting the Cross-Border Supply of Gambling and Betting Services*, Report of the Appellate Body adopted on 20 April 2005, WT/DS285/AB/R.

46 *US—Gambling and Betting, supra* n. 45, paras. 227 et seq. For a critical view on this see Regan (2007a), pp. 1297–1317.

impediment of receiving services through a refusal to reimburse the costs would not amount to a market access violation. Article XVI GATS only aims at the quantitative and quantifiable limitations mentioned in its paragraph 2, but not at limitations on trade in services in general.

This distinguishes Article XVI GATS from Article 56 TFEU (Article 49 EC), which not only prohibits formal restrictions but also measures which make the supply of consumption of a service more difficult. The ECJ has stated repeatedly that the free movement of services requires not only the elimination of all discrimination on grounds of nationality, but also the abolition of non-discriminatory restrictions, 'which prohibit, impede or render less advantageous the activities of a provider of services.'[47]

The next question is whether the decision not to reimburse the costs of treatment abroad could be a violation of the national treatment principle (Article XVII GATS) under the assumption of full commitments regarding medical and hospital services in Mode 2. National treatment requires that foreign services and service suppliers are treated no less favourable than like domestic services and suppliers. Considering our concrete example, it needs to be asked whether the decision not to reimburse the costs of hospital treatment in Malaysia or Singapore treats those hospital services less favourable than like domestic services. Two points need to be considered: first, are the services 'like' in the meaning of Article XVII GATS and second, does this rejection treat domestic services less favourable of the Thai and Singaporean services?

The likeness of services and service providers is one of the most contentious issues in GATS.[48] A starting point for the interpretation could be the GATT and WTO practice regarding likeness of goods which is determined, *inter alia*, on the basis of product's end-uses in a given market and the consumer tastes and habits.[49] However, in the case of medical and hospital services end-uses may not provide a sufficient distinction, because the ultimate use of these services is to regain one's health. Consumer tastes and habits may also be of limited value because patients typically do not have the right, let alone the capacity and necessary information to select between different types of services and service suppliers. The traditional GATT approach which has been suggested as a guidance to determine likeness under the GATS[50] is therefore difficult to apply to health and hospital services.

An alternative approach would be to assess the characteristics of the service in question. The starting point would be that the same type of medical or hospital services is in question. Assuming that the service in question is a hip-replacement

---

47 ECJ, Case C-76/90 *Säger* [1991] *ECR* I-4221, para 12; ECJ, Joined Cases C-369/96 and C-376/96 *Arblade* [1999] *ECR* I-8453, para 33.

48 For a comprehensive treatment of the issue see Diebold (2009).

49 See for example, Appellate Body Report, *EC—Measures Affecting the Prohibition of Asbestos and Asbestos Products*, WT/DS135/AB/R, para 101. Other aspects of determining the likeness of goods concern physical characteristics and tariff classifications, which however do not apply to services.

50 Cossy (2006), p. 16 et seq.

surgery involving a given number of days in hospital and carried out by a doctor and staff trained according to international standards, the next questions would relate to the quality of the service including hygiene, patient safety and comfort or other related factors. Again assuming that the treatment in question takes place in a modern hospital which meets international standards, it would be difficult to argue that the services are not like. However, it may be problematic to determine the factual equivalence of the standards of treatment. In this case, international standardisation might help: If a hospital has been approved by an international standardisation organisation, this obstacle may also be overcome.[51]

Furthermore, it has to be asked whether the circumstances of the supply of the service, in particular the context of the national health system, have an influence on the determination of likeness. In particular, the differences between systems providing benefits in kind and systems providing cash benefits or reimbursements need to be considered. Considering systems which are based on reimbursement, it seems that there is no structural difference between receiving treatment in a hospital abroad and at home if in both cases reimbursements are claimed. Matters could be different regarding systems providing benefits in kind. In this context, it could be argued that structural differences between the domestic provision and financing of the service and the provision and financing of the service in another country are so significant that they cannot be considered like. However, it is uncertain whether the dispute settlement institutions of the WTO would follow this line of argument or if they would ignore the context of the national health system in the same way as the ECJ disregarded the differences between the national systems in determining whether medical treatment would be considered a 'service' for the purposes of the free movement of services.

Assuming that the treatment in a hospital abroad and the treatment in a domestic hospital are 'like services' within the meaning of Article XVII GATS, the meaning of the notion of treatment less favourable needs to be determined. The starting point is the distinction between *de jure* and *de facto* discrimination. *De jure* discrimination concerns a distinction which is formally based on the origin of a service or service supplier, while *de facto* discrimination does not require such a distinction.[52] It should be noted that the refusal to reimburse treatment costs concerns a so-called *de jure* discrimination, because it is based purely on the origin of the service and there is a formal difference between the treatment of the service supplied at home and the service received abroad.

However, not every formally different treatment amounts to a less favourable treatment. According to Article XVII:3 GATS which builds on GATT and WTO case law, a treatment is considered less favourable if it 'modifies the conditions of competition' in favour of the service or service supplier from one country over the services or suppliers from another country. In the case at hand, it would be difficult to argue that the refusal to reimburse the costs of the treatment in Thailand or

---

[51] For examples of such an approval see Mattoo and Rathindran (2005), at p. 15.

[52] Krajewski and Engelke (2008), p. 396 at p. 410.

Singapore while reimbursing the costs of a domestic treatment would not modify the conditions of competition to the detriment of the Thai or Singaporean services and service suppliers.

Having determined that the decision not to reimburse the costs for medical treatment outside of the EU could constitute a violation of the national treatment principle, the limitations of the specific commitments come into play. Accordingly, the answer to the question at stake must be nuanced. A country which did not make any commitments in medical or hospital services is free to maintain regulations which violate the national treatment or market access principle. If a country made a full commitment in these services, that is, scheduling no limitations,[53] the refusal to reimburse the costs of treatment abroad would violate the GATS. If a country limited the commitments, the answer depends on the scope of the limitations. If the commitments exclude the reimbursement of the costs, the refusal to reimburse would not violate the GATS. If they do not contain such a limitation, the refusal would remain a violation of GATS. These are by no means theoretical considerations as the variety of schedules in health and hospital services indicate. Hence, while the refusal to reimburse the costs would not violate GATS commitments in the US or Poland, the refusal of the NHS or German sickness funds could violate the GATS because these countries committed Mode 2 fully to the national treatment principle. In this context, the modification of the EU schedule which would hitherto exclude the limitation scheduled by Poland is particularly noteworthy.

18.4.4 Exceptions

If the refusal to reimburse the costs of treatment abroad violates the national treatment principle, the last step of the analysis concerns the possibility to justify such a violation on the basis of the general exception clause of Article XIV GATS. It is structured and worded in a similar way as Article XX GATT and can therefore also be interpreted on the basis of the case law regarding Article XX GATT.[54] Functionally, Article XIV GATS is equivalent to Article 52(1) TFEU (ex Article 46 EC), which is the general exception clause for the free movement of services. It should be noted that the WTO legal order does not contain any justifications which are equivalent to the mandatory requirements which have been used by the ECJ to justify deviations from the fundamental freedoms.[55] Furthermore, it must also be remembered that there is no provision in the GATS which is equivalent to Article

[53] According to the WTO nomenclature this is indicated by inscribing 'none' in the respective part of the schedule, see Scheduling Guidelines, *supra* n. 27, para 42.

[54] *US—Gambling and Betting*, *supra* n. 45, para 295.

[55] ECJ, Case C-19/92 *Kraus* [1993] *ECR* I-1663, para 32 and ECJ, Case C-55/94 *Gebhard* [1995] *ECR* I-4165, para 37.

106(2) TFEU (ex Article 86(2) EC) which contains an exception for services of general economic interest. The options of justifying a violation are therefore arguably more limited under GATS law than under EU law.

For the purposes of the present analysis the justifications of in Article XIV lit. (a) and (b) GATS are most relevant. Article XIV lit. (a) GATS allows for a justification of measures which are necessary to protect public morals or to maintain public order, while lit. (b) applies to measures necessary to protect human, animal or plant life or health.

The refusal to reimburse the costs of treatment abroad could be justified on the basis of Article XIV(a) GATS if it the goals pursued with this refusal concern the protection of public morals or the maintenance of public order. Generally, such a justification requires that there is an obvious and serious threat to the social fabric of a society as alluded to in footnote 5 to the GATS which states: 'The public order exception may be invoked only where a genuine and sufficiently serious threat is posed to one of the fundamental interests of society.' In *US—Gambling and Betting* the Panel as upheld by the Appellate Body found that the term 'public morals' denotes standards of right and wrong conduct maintained by or on behalf of a community or nation.[56] The Panel also found that the definition of the term public order 'refers to the preservation of the fundamental interests of a society, as reflected in public policy and law.'[57] The provision of health services may be part of the fundamental interests of a society, but it seems doubtful that the reimbursement of the costs of medical or hospital treatment abroad would seriously threaten these interests in a fundamental way.

Regarding Article XIV(b) GATS which covers measures necessary to protect human health it could be argued that this includes the financial stability of a healthcare system. Concerning the patient mobility cases the ECJ has explicitly argued that the very similar term of Article 46 EC Treaty should be interpreted to include this possibility.[58] Article XIV lit. (b) GATS could be interpreted in a similar way as the ECJ interpreted the free movement of services. Hence, Article XIV GATS could be invoked by a WTO Member if it could show that the exodus of patients puts the national health systems under severe financial stress.

Assuming that such an argument could be made, the WTO Member invoking Article XIV GATS would also have to show that the measure at hand was 'necessary'. It is generally assumed that this is only the case if there is 'no alternative measure less restrictive of trade which may be *reasonably* available to a member to achieve the same policy goals.'[59] The Appellate Body also stated that necessary involves:

[56] *United States—Measures Affecting the Cross-Border Supply of Gambling and Betting Services,* WT/DS285/R, Panel Report, para 6.465.

[57] *US—Gambling and Betting*, Panel Report, *supra* n. 56, para 6.467.

[58] ECJ, Case C-157/99 *Smits and Peerbooms* [2001] *ECR* I-5473, paras. 72 et seq.; ECJ, Case C-385/99 *Müller-Fauré and van Riet* [2003] *ECR* I-4509, paras. 67 et seq.

[59] *Thailand—Restrictions on Importation of and Internal Taxes on Cigarettes*, Report of the Panel, adopted on 7 November 1990, BISD 37S/200, para 74.

> in every case a process of weighing and balancing a series of factors which prominently include the contribution made by the compliance measure to the enforcement of the law or regulation at issue, the importance of the common interests or values protected by that law or regulation, and the accompanying impact of the law or regulation on imports or exports.[60]

Yet, despite this wording, the Appellate Body has never engaged in a full weighing and balancing exercise.[61] Instead, it has usually accepted the policy choices and level of protection of the respective Member. Hence, a Member relying on Article XIV GATS to justify a measure violating a GATS provision would have to demonstrate that the measure has a positive effect on the ends pursued and that this effect outweighs the trade impact of the measure. In this context, it should also be noted that the notion of 'necessary' cannot be equated with the proportionality principle under EU law.[62] As a consequence, it is unlikely that the WTO Appellate Body would assess a Members' choice to operate waiting lists, because these lists contribute to the ends pursued by the Member, i.e., allocating resources and prioritising treatment in a system with limited capacities.

Lastly, any measure justifiable under Article XIV GATS must meet the requirements of the introductory clause of Article XIV, the so-called 'chapeau'. In general, this means that a measure should not be applied in a discriminatory and arbitrary manner. Based on this understanding of Article XIV GATS it is possible to justify the refusal to reimburse the costs of medical treatment abroad, but it requires the demonstration that the measure contributes to the aim of maintaining financial stability of the national health system and also that the measure is necessary.

18.5 The Application of the GATS in the EU Legal Order

If the refusal to reimburse the costs of medical treatment in another WTO Member would violate the GATS, could a patient directly rely on the GATS in legal proceedings? In order to answer this question, the legal status of WTO agreements in the EU legal order must be determined. The WTO agreements were concluded by the (then) European Community and its Member States as a so-called mixed agreement, because WTO matters fell partly into the scope of the exclusive EC competence of the common commercial policy and partly into the scope of the competence of the Member States.[63] As international agreements concluded by the EC/EU the WTO agreements form an integral part of the EU legal order according

[60] *Korea—Measures Affecting Imports of Fresh, Chilled and Frozen Beef, WT/DS161/AB/R, WT/DS169/AB/R, Report of the Appellate Body* paras. 164–166.

[61] Regan (2007b), pp. 347–369.

[62] On this issue see also Neumann and Türk (2003), p. 199 at p. 224.

[63] ECJ, Opinion 1/94 *WTO* [1994] *ECR* I-5267, paras. 98 and 105.

to Article 216(2) TFEU (ex Article 300(7) EC).[64] As agreements concluded by the Member States, they also form an autonomous part of the legal order of the Member States.

This inclusion of international agreements in the EU legal order does not mean that individuals can directly rely on them. Instead, as the ECJ has held consistently, that the provision of the agreement in question must contain 'a clear, precise and unconditional obligation which is not subject, in its implementation or effects, to the adoption of any subsequent measure' in order to have direct effect.[65] To determine whether this is the case the wording, purpose and nature of the agreement must be taken into account. This coincides with the practice in many other national legal systems. Typically, only those (parts of) international agreements are considered directly applicable which contain clear, precise and unconditional norms which can be applied to a specific case without any intermediate act of the legislature or the administration.

The ECJ has considered a number of international agreements, in particular, accession agreements to be capable of having direct effect in the EU legal order. However, the ECJ has consistently held that GATT and WTO law is not directly applicable.[66] In other words, individuals may not directly rely on WTO provisions in legal proceedings to challenge EU measures. It is only where the Community has intended to implement a particular obligation assumed in the context of the WTO, or where the EU measure refers expressly to the precise provisions of the WTO agreements, that the legality of an EU measure may be reviewed in light of the WTO rules.[67] With regards to the GATS this exception does not apply. Hence, the GATS is not directly applicable from the perspective of EU law.

However, the analysis should not end here. In fact, the ECJ has repeatedly stated that the rejection of the direct effect of WTO law only affects those parts of the WTO which are subject to the exclusive competence of the EU. In fields which fall within the competence of the Member States EU law neither requires nor forbids that the legal order of a Member State should accord to individuals the right to rely directly on the respective rule.[68] Regarding the GATS, it is important to recall that at the time of the conclusion of the Uruguay Round, trade in services

---

[64] ECJ, Case 181/73 *Haegeman* [1974] *ECR* 449, para 5; ECJ, Case 12/86 *Demirel* [1987] *ECR* 3719, para 7.

[65] ECJ, Case 12/86 *Demirel* v. *Stadt Schwäbisch Gmünd* [1987] *ECR* 3719, para 14 and Case C-162/96 *Racke* v. *Hauptzollamt Mainz* [1998] *ECR* I-3655, para 31.

[66] ECJ, Case C-149/96 *Portugal* v. *Council* [1999] *ECR* I-8395, para 47, ECJ, Case C-93/02 *Biret International* [2003] *ECR* I-10497, para 52; ECJ, Case C-377/02 *Van Parys* [2005] *ECR* I-1465, para 39. Most recently ECJ, Case C-120/06 *FIAMM* [2008] *ECR* I-6513, paras. 90 et seq. concerning the decisions of the WTO Dispute Settlement Body.

[67] ECJ, Case 70/87 *Fediol* [1989] *ECR* 1781, paras. 19–22, ECJ, Case C-69/89 *Nakajima* [1991] *ECR* I-2069, para 31, and, as regards the WTO agreements, ECJ, Cases C-149/96 *Portugal* v. *Council* [1999] *ECR* I-8395, para 49 and ECJ, Case C-93/02 *Biret International* [2003] *ECR* I-10497, para 53.

[68] ECJ, Joined Cases C-300/98 *Dior and others* [2000] *ECR* I-11307, para 48; ECJ, Case C-431/05 *Merck Genéricos* [2007] *ECR* I-7001, para 34.

fell into the competence of the Member States with the exception of Mode 1.[69] It was hence for the Member States to determine whether the GATS had direct effect in the three other modes. Some Member States' courts have excluded the direct effect of the GATS.[70] The Treaty of Nice 2000, however, conferred trade in services to the exclusive competence of the (then) EC with the exception of cultural and audiovisual, educational services, social and, importantly, human health services (ex Article 133(5) EC). The Treaty stated that these areas fell into the shared competence of the EC and its Members.[71] It is not clear how this shared competence would influence the issue of direct effect. However, the question is no longer relevant. The Treaty of Lisbon 2009 transferred the entire realm of trade policy, including trade in services into the scope of the exclusive competence of the Union. Consequently, the Member States are no longer free to decide whether the GATS may have direct effect or not. It is therefore safe to conclude that individuals may not rely on the GATS to challenge the refusal of a national health authority to reimburse the costs of treatment abroad.

Two important caveats are called for: First, the exclusion of direct effect does not mean that the GATS cannot be applied at all by the courts. Instead the ECJ held that in areas where WTO law is not directly applicable, the courts must apply national law as far as possible in the light of the wording and purpose of WTO law.[72] This also applies to the interpretation of EU secondary law, because of the primacy of international agreements over secondary EU legislation.[73]

Second, a violation of the GATS by the EU and/or EU Member State may be subject to the dispute settlement proceedings of the WTO. These may, however, only be initiated by other WTO Members. An individual patient could not directly challenge the refusal of the national health authorities to reimburse the costs of treatment abroad in front of the WTO. However, the WTO Member where the treatment took place (in the GATS logic: the exporting country) in question could challenge this refusal as a measure which impedes its exports by violating the GATS commitments of the Union. If this refusal would indeed violate GATS, the WTO Dispute Settlement Body could request the EU and the Member State to change the law which leads to such a refusal. If this request would be ignored, the WTO could allow the other Member to apply trade sanctions against the EU.

---

[69] Opinion 1/94, *supra* n. 63, para 44.

[70] Finanzgericht Hessen, Judgment of 10.12.2002, 4 K 3994/00 and Oberlandesgericht München, Judgment of 17.12.2008, 20 U 3508/08.

[71] Opinion 1/08, *supra* n. 44, para 133.

[72] *Dior and others, supra* n. 68, para 47.

[73] ECJ, Case C-335/05 *Rizeni* [2007] *ECR* I-4307, para 16 (relating to the GATS).

18.6 Conclusion

This chapter intended to demonstrate the impact of the GATS on the regulation of health services in the Member States of the EU. Using the pertinent case of cross-border patient mobility it was shown that the GATS conceptualises the movement of patients in another WTO Member to receive medical or hospital services as trade in services through Mode 2 according to Article I GATS. Furthermore, it was argued that health services fall within the sectoral scope of the GATS unless they are provided by the government on a non-commercial basis and in a non-competitive environment. Hence, a measure of a WTO Member affecting cross-border patient mobility, such as the refusal to reimburse the costs of the treatment by the national health authorities, would be subject to the GATS, which gave raise to the question whether this measure would violate core GATS principles.

It was shown that a violation of the most-favoured nation principle (Article II GATS) by reimbursing costs of treatment in other EU Members, but not in third countries, could be justified on the basis of Article V GATS, which allows the deviation from GATS obligations for the purposes of regional economic integration agreements. Furthermore, such a measure would also not violate the principle of market access (Article XVI GATS). However, it was demonstrated that a refusal to reimburse the costs of the treatment abroad could violate the principle of national treatment (Article XVII GATS) if the medical or hospital treatment abroad and the respective treatment at home could be considered 'like' services. This depends on a number of factors including the characteristics of the service in question, but possibly also on the structural similarities of the respective health systems in which the service is provided.

A violation of the GATS could be justified on the basis of Article XIV(b) GATS if it could be shown that the refusal of reimbursement would be necessary to maintain the financial stability of the respective national health system. If, however, a Member did not undertake specific commitments in health services in the first place or scheduled a special limitation which excluded the reimbursement of costs for treatment abroad such as the United States or Poland, the measure would not violate Article XVII GATS.

Based on these findings we are now in a position to highlight some similarities and differences between EU and GATS law regarding the mobility of patients: The consumption of medical and hospital services abroad falls into the scope of EU and GATS law. Under EU law it is considered part of the free movement of services, under WTO law it is considered trade in services through Mode 2. The refusal to reimburse the costs of a treatment abroad by the competent entities of the national health system could violate both the TFEU and the GATS, in particular Article XVII GATS (national treatment). However, the violation of Article XVII GATS requires that the treatment abroad and the equivalent treatment at home are 'like services'. Furthermore, the home state of the patient would have to include medical or hospital services in its Schedule of Specific Commitments without a relevant limitation concerning the reimbursement of the costs. Contrary to this, the free movement of services applies unconditionally. Lastly, violations of GATS and EU law can be justified on the grounds of the financial stability of the health system. The major difference from a practical perspective is that EU law has direct effect and can be relied upon by individuals while GATS is not directly applicable.

In light of the preceding analysis of the application of the legal framework of the GATS on patient mobility one may ask whether WTO law will have a considerable impact on the the organisation of healthcare on a domestic level. The answer is likely to be negative for two reasons: First, as pointed out above, the scope of GATS commitments in health services remains limited on global level. Second, as long as the GATS does not give raise to individual claims for reimbursement in domestic courts as the EU free movement rules did, countries may not be pressured into changing their systems. It can therefore be assumed that the overall impact of the GATS on healthcare will be limited. But who would have assumed ten years ago that EU law would gain a significant impact on healthcare in Europe? As Niels Bohr and Mark Twain (and others) knew: it is difficult to make predictions; especially about the future.

References

Adlung R (2006) Public services and the GATS. J Int Econ Law 9

Adlung R, Carzaniga A (2001) Health services under the general agreement on trade in services. Bull World Health Organ 79

Adlung R, Carzaniga A (2006) Update on GATS commitments and negotiations. In: Blouin C, Drager N, Smith R (eds) International trade in health services and the GATS. World Bank, Washington

Arunanondchai J, Fink C (2007) Trade in health services in the ASEAN region. World bank policy research paper 4147. World Bank, Washington DC

Butkeviciene J, Diaz D (1998) GATS commitments in the health services sector and the scope for future negotiations. In: Zarrilli S, Kinnon C (eds) International trade in health services. UNCTAD, Geneva

Cacace M et al (2008) Explaining convergence and common trends in the role of the state in OECD healthcare systems. Harv Health Policy Rev 9

Chanda R (2002) Trade in health services. Bull World Health Organ 80

Chanda R (2003) Social services and the GATS: key issues and concerns. World Dev 31

Cortez N (2008) Patients without borders: the emerging global market for patients and the evolution of modern health care. Indiana Law J 83

Cossy M (2006) Determining "likeness" under the GATS: squaring the circle? World Trade Organization staff working paper ERSD-2006-08. WTO, Geneva

Diebold N (2009) Non-discrimination in international trade in services—a contextual and comparative analysis of 'likeness' in WTO/GATS, Ph.D. thesis (University of Bern)

Drake W, Nicolaidis K (1992) Ideas, interests, and institutionalization: "trade in services" and the Uruguay round. Int Organ 46

Footer M, George C (2005) The general agreement on trade in services. In: Macrory P, Appleton A, Plummer M (eds) The World Trade Organization: legal, economic and political analysis, vol 1. Springer, New York

Herwig A (2008) The multiple understandings of conflict between trade in services and labour protection. In: Joerges C, Kjaer P (eds) Transnational standards of social protection, RECON Report No. 4

Krajewski M (2003) Public services and trade liberalization: mapping the legal framework. J Int Econ Law 6
Krajewski M (2008) Competitiveness and labour protection: a comment. In: Joerges C, Kjaer P (eds) Transnational standards of social protection, RECON Report No. 4
Krajewski M (2009) Protecting a shared value of the union in a globalized world: services of general economic interest and external trade. In: van de Gronden J (ed) EU and WTO law on services. Kluwer Law International, Alphen an de Rijn
Krajewski M, Engelke M (2008) Article XVII. In: Wolfrum R, Stoll P-T, Feinäugle C (eds) WTO—trade in services, Max Planck commentaries on world trade law, vol 6. Martinus Nijhoff, Leiden
Lang A (2009) GATS. In: Bethlehem D, McRae D, Neufeld R, Van Damme I (eds) The Oxford handbook on international trade law. OUP, Oxford
Leroux E (2006) What is a "service supplied in the exercise of governmental authority" Under Article I:3(b) and (c) of the general agreement on trade in services? J World Trade 40
Lindl C (2005) Potenziale und Ausschöpfungsmöglichkeiten für den internationalen Austausch von Dienstleistungen–Das Beispiel Gesundheitsdienstleistungen [Potentials and possibilities to utilise the international exchange of services–the example of health services]. Verlag Dr. Kovač, Hamburg
Mattoo A, Rathindran R (2005) Does health insurance impede trade in health care services? World bank policy research working paper 3667. World Bank, Washington
Neumann J, Türk E (2003) Necessity revisited—proportionality in WTO law after Korea—beef, EC–Asbestos and EC—sardines. J World Trade 37
Price D et al (1999) How the World Trade Organisation is shaping domestic policies in health care. Lancet 354
Regan D (2007a) A gambling paradox why an origin-neutral "zero-quota" is not a quota under GATS Article XVI. J World Trade 41
Regan D (2007b) The meaning of 'necessary' in GATT Article XX and GATS Article XIV: the myth of cost–benefit balancing. World Trade Rev 6
Sauter W (2008) The proposed patient mobility directive and the reform of cross-border healthcare in the EU. TILEC Discussion Paper, Tilburg
Szyszczak E (2009) Modernising healthcare: pilgrimage for the holy grail? In: Krajewski M, Neergaard U, van de Gronden J (eds) The changing legal framework for services of general interest in Europe. TMC Asser Press, The Hague
Van de Gronden J (2009) Cross-border health care in the EU and the organization of the national health care systems of the member states. Wis Int Law J 26
Van Duzer JA (2004) Health, education and social services in Canada: the impact of the GATS. In: Curtis JM, Ciuriak D (eds) Trade policy research 2004. International Trade Canada, Ottawa
Waeger P (2008) Trade in health services—an analytical framework, advanced studies Working Paper No. 141. Kiel Institute for World Economics, Kiel
Weiss F (1995) The general agreement on trade in services 1994. CML Rev 32
Wunder A (2009) Zum Vorschlag des Erlasses einer Richtlinie über die Ausübung der Patientenrechte in der grenzüberschreitenden Gesundheitsversorgung—Was ist neu? [The proposal for the adoption of a directive on the exercise of patients' rights in cross-border medical care—What is new?] Medizinrecht
Zdouc W (1999) WTO dispute settlement practice in relation to GATS. J Int Econ Law 2
Zeiler-Kligman B (2006) How i learned to stop worrying and love the GATS: an examination of the impact of the general agreement on trade in services on the Canadian health-care system. Dalhous Law J 29
Zimmermann T (2008) Grenzüberschreitende Gesundheitsversorgung aus der Perspektive des deutschen Gesundheitssystems [Cross-border healthcare from the perspective of the German health system]. Nomos, Baden-Baden

Part V
Conclusion

Chapter 19
Conclusions: Constructing a 'Solid' Multi-Layered Health Care Edifice

Johan van de Gronden and Erika Szyszczak

Contents

Legal issues relating to health care have appeared with increasing regularity before the European Courts. Even as this book was going to press we encountered a number of new cases which we have taken into account in the Conclusions. As the chapters of this book show the range of health care issues touched by EU law is broad. Free movement, competition and public procurement law are the main areas which invite clashes between national health care policies and EU law, but the potential range is even wider, touching upon citizenship and discrimination issues, human rights and data protection. We were even more surprised to find the Commission's proposal for a draft Directive on Patients' Rights[1] unexpectedly followed by a Common Position

[1] Commission Communication of 2 July 2008, *Proposal for a directive on the application of patients' rights in cross-border health care*, COM(2008) 414 final.

J. van de Gronden
Radbouw University Nijmegen, Nijmegen, The Netherlands
e-mail: j.vandegronden@jur.ru.nl

E. Szyszczak (✉)
University of Leicester, Leicester, UK
e-mail: ems11@leicester.ac.uk

J. W. van de Gronden et al. (eds.), *Health Care and EU Law*,
Legal Issues of Services of General Interest, DOI: 10.1007/978-90-6704-728-9_19,

in the Council[2] after months when it seemed the Member States might never reach agreement. In January 2011 the European Parliament adopted this draft in second reading and the council will decide on this draft in March 2011. To the conservative EU lawyer and policy analysts even the hint of health care being a subject area of EU law might seem surprising. The EU has very limited competence in the area and the legal framework for the regulation of health care issues in the EU is fragmented, relying upon soft or new governance techniques to iron out difficulties not only between the Member States but also between the wide range of interested parties affected by cross-border health care issues.

19.1 Developments in Health Care and EU Law

As the chapter by *Szyszczak* shows the legislative competence of the Community/EU was specifically limited in the original EEC Treaty. Indeed references to public health issues were found as *derogations* for the Member States in relation to the free movement principle in the old Article 36 and Article 46 EC. The Treaty of Maastricht 1992 introduced a new Article 129 EC (renumbered Article 152 EC after the Treaty of Amsterdam 1997) setting out the limited competence of the then Community to regulate the area of public health. Essentially the involvement of the EU was to complement the activities of the Member States, encouraging and promoting the coordination and cooperation between the Member States on issues which may have a cross-border effect. The old Article 152(5) EC stated that any action by the Community in the field of public health should fully respect the responsibilities of the Member States for the organisation and delivery of health services and medical care.[3] Article 168(7) TFEU, which is now in place since the Treaty of Lisbon 2009, also acknowledges these responsibilities, although in different wording.[4]

In this regard it should be noted that health care is closely linked to social services and social protection in the EU Member States and viewed as part of the services provided in the (national) general interest.[5] The Protocol [9] on Services of General Interest annexed to the TEU and TFEU by the Treaty of Lisbon 2009[6] emphasises, in Article 2, that the Treaties do not in any way affect the competence

[2] Proposal of 28 May 2010 for a Directive of the European Parliament and the Council on the application of patients' rights in cross-border health care, 9948/10.

[3] The Treaty of Amsterdam 1997 raised the profile of public health issues by adding it to the list of activities of the Community in Article 3(1) (p) EC. The new Article 152 EC also mainstreamed a 'high level of human health protection' through Community policies.

[4] In the next section this different wording will be analysed.

[5] See the *Communication from the Commission: implementing the Community Lisbon programme: social Services of General Interest in the European Union*, COM (2006) 177, 26 April 2006.

[6] The text of this Protocol can be found in *OJ* 2007 C 306/158.

of the Member States to provide, commission and organise non-economic services of general interest.

However, the role of health care as a national responsibility in what Ferrara has termed a 'bounded space' with defined membership and territorial scope has been challenged.[7] Health care borders have become increasingly porous, for example, in continental Europe where travel across a local border brings a range of different medical opportunities and as Europe expanded cheaper medical treatment became available in the central and eastern European states, facilitated by the internet for advertising, cheaper travel, and the acceptance of medical tourism. The limited EU competence to legislate in the field of health care was lost in the use of the fundamental free movement provisions to create a new citizenship right to travel abroad for health care and have the costs reimbursed by the State of affiliation. This went much further than the limited and pragmatic right to seek health care in another Member State coordinated by the Social Security Regulation discussed by Pennings. The development of these rights is discussed by *Davies* and by *Baquero Cruz* and seen in the context of market integration opportunities alongside the deepening of a citizenship concept. In contrast, others, for example, *Newdick*, see this development as a serious challenge to the sacred concepts of solidarity and cohesion at the level of the nation State. However, as *Krajewski* shows the EU may not be the limit of regulation of transborder health care as new medical tourist markets emerge in Central and South America and Asia, and WTO law may provide patients with the 'tools' to break open these markets.

At the same time in Europe, as with almost every other developed country, and especially the US, health care costs have been rapidly raising as a proportion of GDP.[8] Since a large share of these costs are subsidised by the taxpayer, in one way or another, and this share could increase in the US under planned health care reforms discussed by *Cortez*, governments and policy makers are highly focused upon shifting the burden of health care away from the State by experimentation with a different mix of public and private provision.

One of the reasons for the higher costs of health care is social and demographic changes in Europe: citizens are healthier and living longer and the birth rate has declined. Thus an older generation is dependent upon different forms of payment for the costs of health care. Europe has moved away from traditional State involvement and provision of a wide range of welfare or social benefits and social services and in the 1990s began discussing how traditional welfare benefits could be modernised. Included within this debate were issues of social and financial provision of ageing and long-term health care costs. The current economic crisis caused by the credit crunch has even made the need to reform health care more urgent given the cuts on government expenditure that the EU Member States are forced to make.

---

[7] Ferrera (2005).

[8] Hall and Jones (2007), pp. 39–72.

As the traditional welfare states of Europe have experimented with reforms in the shape of 'modernisation' the EU has taken an interest in the use of market-based principles in the provision and delivery of the new social services. As *Hervey* and *Szyszczak* show the EU was able to do this by using new (or soft) governance techniques to allow the Member States, and other interested actors, to discuss co-operation in different *fora*. EU involvement in policy making in health care raises issues of competence and the constitutional principle of the limits of EU law. These issues are discussed by specifically *Neergaard* and *De Vries* but are also a theme running through many other chapters in this book.

19.2 EU Law and National Health Care Systems: Constitutional Issues

All in all, it is apparent from the developments sketched above that a process of 'EU competence creep' into the national health care systems is taking place. As the authors of country analyses show sometimes it is the EU competition law provisions which make a greater impact upon the national health care system, seen, for example, in the analysis of *Sauter* of the Netherlands,[9] whereas in other countries the focus is on the EU public procurement rules, as is pointed out in the analysis by *Welti* of Germany (who also explains that public procurement law is seen as part of competition law in Germany). In other countries it is the application of the EU free movement provisions, which has made the bigger impact, seen in the analyses of *McHale* and *Newdick* of the English NHS.

The 'EU competence creep' raises the question of a constitutional nature: how is at the present stage of the European integration process a balance struck between the EU and national health care powers? Resolving this question starts with pointing out that incrementally, the European Court of Justice of the European Union (ECJ) is seen as the central Institutional actor exercising considerable influence on the health care systems of the Member States. The ECJ has repeatedly stated as 'a mantra' that the responsibility over the organisation and delivery of health care services is the responsibility of the Member States.[10] But the focus of its rulings is to review national health care measures in the light of 'EU market law'. As *Drijber* and *Cadenau* show it does not shy away from deciding that longstanding health care practices of various Member States are incompatible with EU law.

[9] For example, the Netherlands Competition Authority has issued comprehensive Guidelines on the application of competition law to health care cases (in Dutch: richtsnoeren voor de zorgsector, available at: http://www.nmanet.nl/Images/Richtsnoeren%20voor%20de%20zorgsector_tcm16-135479.pdf). These guidelines, which, inter alia, concern the relationship between Articles 101 and 102 TFEU on the one hand and health care practices on the other hand, have a considerable impact on the delivery of health care services.

[10] Seen in ECJ, Case 238/82 *Duphar* [1984] *ECR* 523.

After years of carefully orchestrating new governance techniques the Commission took the bold step of including health care issues in its original proposal for a Directive on Services.[11] At the time this was miscalculated but in fact the second proposal for a Directive on Patients' Rights in Cross-Border Health Care[12] moved beyond an attempt to codify and to modify the free movement patient mobility case law of the ECJ bringing a raft of rights for patients seeking medical care anywhere in the EU, including their own State and 'institutionalising' the soft new governance processes and agendas. This was an ambitious move, modernising the approach adopted by the coordination approach of the social security regime.[13]

The politically sensitive character of health care and the new challenges it was facing due to rising costs stemming from the increased patient-consumer demands, the ageing population and progress made in medical science, led virtually all Member States, but for different reasons opposed to an EU approach. The stumbling adoption process of the Directive and the concessions made by the Commission, especially in the change to a dual legal base, reveal that the Member States are determined to retain competence over the core issue of the organisation and delivery of health care.

As already mentioned, at the writing of these conclusions the Council reached a common position on the (heavily amended) draft Directive,[14] which was forwarded to the European Parliament for its second reading, scheduled for January 2011. This proposal provides, inter alia, that health care that involves overnight hospital accommodation, or is planned due to its highly specialised nature or involves particular risks, may be made subject to prior authorisation. So, this draft reinforces the original point of departure: it is for the Member States to determine when patients are entitled to reimbursement of the costs of cross-border hospital care (as long as patients can be treated without undue delay). Nevertheless, it should be noted that the proposal retains the position that the system of prior authorisation should be limited to what is necessary and proportionate and prior authorisation may not constitute a means of arbitrary discrimination.

Predictably, the Treaty of Lisbon 2009 has also stressed the point that health care belongs to the Member States' competences and even attempts to build in 'safeguards' against EU law influences on national health care.[15] Article 168 TFEU (the Treaty provision on health care) does not only acknowledge that it is

---

[11] See *Proposal of the Commission of 25 February 2004 for a Directive on services in the Internal Market*, COM(2004) 2 final. The first provisions of this draft did not exclude health care services from the Directive's scope. However, the final version of this piece of EU legislation explicitly stipulates that health care services are not covered by it. See Article 2(2 sub f) of *Directive 2006/123/EC of the European Parliament and of the Council of 12 December 2006 on services in the internal market*, *OJ* 2006 L 376/36.

[12] This proposal is discussed in the contributions of Szyszczak and Hervey.

[13] On the relationship between this regulation and the draft directive, see Pennings' contribution.

[14] Proposal of 28 May 2010 for a Directive of the European Parliament and the Council on the application of patients' rights in cross-border health care, 9948/10.

[15] Cf., Szyszczak's contribution.

for the Member States to organise and deliver health care (as did the former Article 152 EC) but is also puts forward that the competences of the Member States include.

> … the management of health services and medical care and the allocation of the resources assigned to them…

A phrase which was absent in Article 152 EC. It remains to be seen to what extent the new wording of the health care provision of the Treaty will be capable of curtailing the effects that result from the ECJ's case law on free movement and competition (and possibly from future groundbreaking European citizenship rulings), as it may, strikingly, also be argued that Article 168 TFEU expands the limits of the EU's role in public health. It should be noted that this provision explicitly states that the EU must 'respect' the Member States' competences, rather than 'fully respect' as Article 152 did. To put it differently, the wording of the present Treaty provision on public health seems to leave open more room for EU involvement than the comparable Treaty provision that was in force until 1 December 2009. So, the Treaty of Lisbon 2009 has introduced a delicate and sophisticated balance between the EU and national competences in health care.

Against this background, it is not a great surprise that in the discussion by *Baeten* and *Palm* of cases such as *Hartlauer*[16] and *José* Manuel Blanco *Pérez*,[17] we see that the ECJ has also adopted a similar sophisticated approach. In these cases the ECJ deployed a marginal review as to whether national health care measures restricting free movement were proportionate. The ECJ mainly examines whether the national measures that intervene on health care markets and impose obligations upon providers are drafted in a consistent and systematic manner. On the other hand, although the ECJ concentrated on these 'institutional' aspects of the national measures concerned and not on substantive issues, it did examine, as is explained by *Drijber* and *Cadenau*, in great detail the consistency and internal logic of these measures. To put it differently, a central issue appears to be how the relevant health care framework has taken shape. It is clear from the outset that the ECJ's review was based on the need to strike a fair balance between the internal market and the national health care competences.

A similar approach may be found in a recent judgement of the ECJ, which concerned an infringement action.[18] At stake were the Spanish health care rules that were related to the costs of persons affiliated to the Spanish NHS who stayed as, for example, a tourist or student in another Member State and were treated in that Member States due to unexpected medical problems. In some cases the reimbursement of the costs by the host state authority may be limited to a maximum level, which leaves the Spanish tourist or student with a deficit. The Spanish

---

[16] ECJ, Case C-169/07 *Hartlauer* [2009] *ECR* I-1721.

[17] ECJ, Joined Cases C-570/07 and C-571/07 *José Manuel Blanco Pérez a.o.* v. *Consejerá de Salud y Servicios Sanitarios and Principado de Asturias*, judgement of 1 June 2010, *ECR* I-0000 (n.y.r.).

[18] ECJ, Case C-211/08 *Commission* v. *Spain*, 15 June 2010, *ECR* I-0000 (n.y.r.).

rules under review did not provide for compensation of these non-reimbursed costs, although similar treatment in a Spanish hospital was eligible for full reimbursement of the costs. On first sight, this practice seemed to be at odds with the ECJ's *Van Braekel* judgement,[19] which, on the basis of the Treaty provisions on the free movement of services, obliges Member States to meet the costs of patients who have received prior approval for treatment abroad but are not fully compensated for the costs connected with this treatment by the host state authorities (where the patients concerned would not have been in the position to pay contributions where they had received similar treatment in a home-State hospital).[20] The ECJ was of the opinion that the adverse effects that such deficits could have on free movement was hypothetical and, as result, the free movement rules were not violated. The Spanish rules at stake were not found to be incompatible with EU law. The major reason for this remarkable finding was that the main aim of persons travelling to another Member State as, for example, students or tourists, is not to undergo medical treatment, and these persons are, as a result, not discouraged from making use of their free movement rights due to possibly limited compensation in the (non-anticipated) case that they fall ill.[21] All in all, the ruling on these Spanish rules could appear as the ECJ stepping back, being more careful than has been seen so far in this area.

Similarly in landmark decisions on state aid and health care the ECJ has shown a great respect for the retained competences of the Member States by developing a flexible approach towards national compensatory measures and Services of General Economic Interest, as was shown by *Neergaard* and *De Vries*. This deference to Member State competence may be explained by the fact that, at the current stage of the European integration process, *organising* health care is still a competence retained by the Member States. Indeed, at a pragmatic level the EU does not have the capacity to legislate in the area.

A tendency which is developed in several chapters, most notably Davies' is, that in recent cases the European Courts linked the *access* to health care benefits to the concept of European citizenship. The ECJ has scrutinised whether national laws that impose restrictions on undergoing treatment abroad may prevent individuals from exercising their rights derived from the Treaty provisions on European Citizenship. Thus, the freedom of choice (of medical treatment) of individuals is a value that is protected in the case law of the EU Courts. However, it is apparent from the ECJ's judgement in *Chamier–Glisczinski*,[22] discussed by *Baquero Cruz* in this book, that not every disparity resulting from differences between national health care systems constitutes an infringement of these Treaty provisions. The ECJ appears aware of the limitations of European citizenship (as it

[19] ECJ, Case C-368/98 *Vanbraekel and others* (2001) *ECR* I-5363.

[20] See Pennings' contribution.

[21] See para 72 of *Commission* v. *Spain*.

[22] Judgement of 16 July 2009, Case C-208/07 *von Chamier–Glisczinski, ECR* I-0000 (n.y.r.).

currently stands) and denies itself the opportunity to interpret this concept expansively.

All the same, one might think that the European Courts, by stressing the freedom of choice in their jurisprudence, have considerable effects on the status of the recipients of health care: they are transformed from patients into (circumspect) consumers or even European citizens when exercising their free movement rights.[23] However, as long as respect for the Member States' competences is one of the underpinning principles of how EU law deals with health care, it is not likely that such a transformation will be the result of the application of the Treaty provisions to health care. In this regard it should be noted that the provisions of the proposed Directive on Patients' Rights that aimed at giving patients generous entitlements to cross-border hospital care were heavily amended.[24] Conversely, it cannot be ruled out that liberalisation measures taken by national governments may be capable of turning patients into (circumspect) consumers, which, of course, means that these governments bear the full responsibility for this process and the EU cannot be held accountable for this.

19.3 Internal Market: Drastic EU Requirements for National Health Care Systems?

Although it is clear that the national health care systems are not immune for EU law, the Europeanisation process, which these systems are subject to, is of a sophisticated nature: as the famous *Echternach* procession two steps forwards are followed by one step backwards. Hence, mapping the consequences of EU law for health care entails a nuanced approach. Therefore, as the chapters in this book reveal, a distinction should be made when analysing the impact of the internal market and competition rules on national health care systems. It is apparent from the case law that internal market law interferes more deeply with national competences in these matters and that competition law takes a more nuanced approach. Therefore, the impact of these two different areas of EU law will be analysed separately, starting with the internal market provisions.

It is settled case law that the Treaty provisions on free movement (especially services) prohibits Member States from having in place prior authorisation schemes for patients seeking cross-border non-hospital care, whereas such schemes are justifiable in case of hospital care, as long as the patients concerned can be treated without undue delay. From an internal market perspective the ECJ has perhaps

---

[23] Cf., Davies' contribution.

[24] The European Parliament has, for example, proposed not to make patients with rare diseases subject to prior authorization. See Article 8(9) of the first reading of this Directive [P6_TA(2009)0286]. The Council draft of 28 May 2010, however, does not confer such generous rights upon patients with rare diseases.

struck a fair balance between free movement and national health care planning. However, *Newdick* argues that from the perspective of national authorities engaged in a complicated and difficult process of setting priorities for cost-intensive treatments, reimbursing costs of cross-border hospital treatments of patients who cannot be cured on time on the national territory may have disruptive effects, as the outcome of this process of setting priorities, which is supposed to be subject to national rules of good governance, seems to be ignored. A particular patient (who may turn out to be a circumspect consumer in the eyes of national planning authorities) may decide to break away from the national system of planning, which is based on sophisticated and detailed national criteria, and seek treatment abroad. *Newdick* fears that the ECJ's case law obliges the national authorities of the Member State of affiliation to reimburse the costs of the treatment given by the hospital in another Member State irrespective of the fact of whether the patient involved was high on priority lists for domestic hospital treatment. The result of this might be that these national authorities are left with considerable deficits on their budgets, which could have adverse effects on financing hospital treatment of patients who do rank high on priority lists (but who are not circumspect consumers but may not have the capacity to take advantage of the free movement opportunities).[25] As long as the figures of the outflow of patients seeking hospital treatment in other Member States are low, as is outlined by *Szyszczak*, we would like to argue that it is not likely that such disruptive effects will occur. Nevertheless, at the moment a flourishing internal market for cross-border hospital care emerges, the problems resulting from the ECJ's case law interfering with national priority setting need to be tackled. In Watts a step towards a solution is made, as the ECJ acknowledges that waiting lists may be used as appropriate means for planning health care (provided that certain conditions are met).[26]

Remarkably, in its case law on free movement and health care providers, such as *Hartlauer* and *José Manuel Blanco Pérez*, the ECJ did not depart from the 'classical divide' between hospital and non-hospital care. In disputes regarding national measures imposing obligations upon health care providers (for example, prior authorisation schemes) the ECJ has decided that such measures may be justified, as they are inherent in national health care planning systems. It does not matter whether these measures aim at regulating hospital care or non-hospital. In other words: whereas in cases concerning the demand side (patient mobility) the ECJ has considerably limited the powers of the Member States to prevent patients from receiving outpatient services, in cases concerning the supply side (national measures directed at health care providers) the Member States' competences remain untouched to a considerable extent. This is even truer, since the ECJ did not make these measures subject to a full proportionality review.[27] Rather, as is already pointed out above, it examined whether the national measures taken in

[25] See the contribution of Szyszczak, Davies and Newdick.

[26] See ECJ, Case C-372/04 *Watts* [2006] *ECR* I-4325, at point 67.

[27] See the contribution of Baeten and Palm.

relation to health care providers were drafted in a consistent and systematic manner.

What is striking is that this approach boils down to monitoring whether national health care measures are in accordance with good governance-based principles. After all, in the view of the ECJ it is of great interest that the national measures under review are shaped in line with principles of an institutional—and perhaps of a constitutional—nature (consistency, systematic approach, transparency, etc.). So, this case law gives an impulse for developing principles of good governance in health care at EU level. *Hervey* points out that the much-debated draft Directive on Patients' Rights also sets principles and rules that are at the heart of good governance.[28] Strikingly, this draft provides that the Member States must have in place a mechanism for calculating costs of cross-border care that is based on objective, non-discriminatory criteria known in advance.[29] It cannot be excluded, as is argued by *Davies*, that introducing such a transparent calculation mechanism will create headaches for many officials of national authorities given the complex administrative structures to which the reimbursement of treatment costs is made subject to national health care systems. Member States will, inter alia, be obliged to outline with great care *which* benefits patients are entitled to and the *maximum* level of reimbursement that is applicable to these benefits. Remarkably, in the *Elchinov* case (pending at the writing of these Conclusions), the ECJ has to address, inter alia, the question *how* a Member State must draft a list that identifies which benefits are granted to affiliated persons and what the level of reimbursement is in relation to cross-border health care.[30]

In any event, the fierce opposition from the Member States towards substantive requirements of EU law for national health care seems to have inspired the EU Institutions to take a different road. Focusing on the development of good governance principles, the shaping of which may be further supported by soft law, could turn out be a way for building a EU approach towards health care, rather than setting strict substantive requirements that force Member States to increasingly open up national health care markets.

In this respect, attention must be paid to the role of EU public procurement law, which constitutes, in essence, an important component of the *acquis communautaire* of EU internal market law ('free movement of public contracts'). In our view,

[28] See Chapter IV of this proposal.

[29] See Article 8(4) of the draft of 28 May 2010.

[30] See Case C-173/09 *Georgi Ivanov Elchinov* v. *Atsionalna Zdravnoosiguritelna Kasa*. In his Opinion of 10 June 2010 the Advocate General has contended that such a list *is* compatible with EU law, as long as it is based on objective, non-discriminatory criteria known in advance. It is not a coincidence that this wording mirrors the provision on calculation mechanisms of the draft patient Directive. However, it must be noted that the ECJ will only have the opportunity to address the health care issues at stake in this case if it decides that the national referring court was competent to ask the questions concerned. The competence matter, which concerns the hierarchical relationship between the national Supreme Court and lower domestic courts, may prevent the ECJ from giving guidance on these significant health care issues.

the application of the public procurement rules to health care may contribute to good governance in this sector, as these rules oblige the Member States to grant health care contracts to market operators in a transparent and non-discriminatory way.[31] Although many questions still need to be resolved, as is explained by *Hatzopoulos* and *Stergiou*, a non-discriminatory and transparent selection of operators for public contracts in health care is without any doubt in perfect tune with the principles of good governance of the internal market.

19.4 Competition Law: Rules of the 'Market Game'

Compared to the Internal Market rules, the ECJ has embarked from a different position as to which role EU competition law should play in health care. *Van de Gronden* argues that in its case law on the application of the competition provisions to health care, the ECJ draws on the will of national legislatures as it examines with great care the role competition and solidarity play in health care systems. If solidarity prevails in a health care scheme, the bodies managing this scheme are not engaged in economic activities and are, as a result, not undertakings, whereas the managing bodies of health care systems based on a mix of solidarity and competition are considered to be undertakings within the meaning of EU competition law.[32] It should be noted that it is settled case law that as a 'hard and fast rule' providers of health care services (and suppliers of health care goods) are undertakings as they are remunerated for the services they provide (or the goods they supply).[33] The point of departure seems to be that EU competition law is only of relevance for national health care schemes that are (considerably) opened up for competition. To put it differently, competition law constitutes the rules of the 'market game' and comes into play at the stage a Member State has made its national health care system subject to market forces.

Given the limited role that competition play in the German health care systems, *Welti* argues that the EU competition law rules are not applicable to German sickness funds and their central organisation. However, in some other Member States these rules do apply to health insurers, as these states (such as the Netherlands) have opened up these insurers to competition. Experiences from these countries have taught us that introducing competition in health care is a complicated process, which will only be successful if it is done with great care. For example, *Sauter* argues that incumbents may jeopardise the proper functioning of health care markets given their great advantages over competitors entering these (new and emerging) markets. So, he is of the opinion that given the persuasive

[31] See the contribution of Hatzopoulos and Stergiou.

[32] See Van de Gronden's contribution.

[33] Ibid.

market failures in health care the arguments for introducing health care specific competition rules (a special regulatory framework) are very strong.

However, making health care markets highly competitive does not automatically lead to universal coverage: introduction of market forces is not a universal remedy for ensuring access to the necessary health care benefits for all. As *Cortez* shows, the attempts made in the US in order to increase coverage by setting up market-driven health care schemes have shown that unregulated markets fail to deliver what is expected from them: access for all. Hence, the most significant lesson to be learnt from US experiences is that competition in health care needs strong government regulation. In health care addressing market failures is not only about improving competitive structures of markets, which are weakened, for example, by strong positions held by incumbents, but also about the achievement of essential objectives of general interest, such as universal coverage. This concern (universal coverage) seems to have been the rationale behind the flexible and stunning state aid judgement handed down by the CFI (now General Court) in the *BUPA* case.[34] After all, as *De Vries* shows, relaxing the strict *Altmark*[35] conditions for compensatory measures on Services of General Economic Interest contributes to improving access to health care benefits for all. In sum, even in health care systems that are (gradually) made subject to market forces state interventions remain necessary in order to let markets work and to deliver the benefits every (European) citizen is entitled to.

However, in the EU the question is *which* State entities have the authority to make the interventions needed in health care, since in Europe an intertwined and complicated structure of European, national and sub-national governance is in place. Is this structure of multi-level governance capable of providing the (legal) framework that health care needs?

19.5 Multi-Level Governance in Health Care

It is clear from the new wording of Article 168 TFEU, the fierce debate caused by the proposed Directive on Patients' Rights and many other instances exposed in chapters in this book showing that Member States will not give up easily their competences to organise and deliver health care. Hence, the national dimension of the health care systems is a fact of life in the EU, which will even not be altered in the long run. National regulations will continue to determine the level of the health care benefits and the conditions that apply to these benefits. Consequently, the one billion million euro question is how to shape national health care systems in such a way that they ensure the proper reception of the EU rules on free movement, procurement, harmonisation, competition and European citizenship. In other

[34] CFI, Case T-289/03 *BUPA* [2008] *ECR* II-81.

[35] ECJ, Case C-280/00 *Altmark Trans* [2003] *ECR* I-7747.

words, how should the second layer of governance (EU law) be placed on the first layer of governance (national health care system)? How should this edifice be constructed so that it will endure without the risk that it will tumble down as soon as it is touched by the challenges that health care systems will face in the years to come?

In our view, an overarching principle is solidarity. As *Newdick* argues, so passionately in modelling their health care systems the Member States should give due interest to the role solidarity plays. The analysis carried out in the present volume has convincingly demonstrated that the ECJ bases both its internal market and competition law approach towards health care on solidarity. The predominant role of solidarity is even capable of depriving health care services of their economic nature (which entails the non-applicability of competition law, as was shown by *Van de Gronden*), whereas in internal market law solidarity provides the national authorities with the arguments to derogate from the fundamental freedoms. Hence, Member States should clearly outline in their national health laws what role solidarity plays. It is of utmost importance that these laws meet good governance principles such as non-discrimination and transparency and that officials who administer them may give due regard to principles of accountability. In its case law the ECJ is increasingly emphasising the importance of these principles. The Union legislature further elaborates on this approach, as is apparent from the draft Directive on Patients' Rights.

However, the good governance approach does not give Member States *carte blanche*. Especially the case law on free movement and public procurement has shown that the stance of EU law towards the national health care organisation is not neutral. To our mind, it is a logic consequence attached to the ECJ's finding that health care amounts to, for example, services within the meaning of the EU free movement rules that market forces should somehow play a role in health care. EU law couples health care with competition. It is a harsh conclusion for many Member States but it results from the principled view taken by the ECJ on the 'market dimension' of health care. The findings of the present volume do not only point to the significance of solidarity but also to the added value of competition in health care.

In sum, solidarity and competition constitute two leading principles for placing the EU layer on the national health care layer. These principles provide the cement for connecting these two layers. Ideas of solidarity developed from national understandings of the concept can be moulded to create a social dimension to the EU market model. This means that the dichotomy of health care services without competition and health care services provided through competition will not be of any help for construing a national-European health care edifice.[36] A sophisticated combination of solidarity and competition will guide Member States to make their national health care systems compatible with EU law. But at the same time, it will enhance the quality of the EU model. It goes without saying that there will be

[36] See Krajewski (2009), at p. 505 and p. 506.

differences from national system to national system as to what the exact components of such a combination are. However, it is clear from the outset that Member States should not shy away from making their health care schemes subject to a critical review and from reconsidering the role of competition in these schemes. What follows from the case law of the ECJ is that in health care schemes considerable room for competition must be built in for the provision of services that do not need to be planned. So, Member States' health care designs must outline as clearly as possible which reasons justify protective measures and why competition could put under pressure the achievement of particular legitimate objectives. What is more, Member States should open up the markets of health care services that do not need to be planned or to be made subject to state control otherwise. So, a balanced approach towards solidarity, competition and health care is needed at national level. Not only does such a national approach enable a successful reception of EU law, it also makes health care systems ready for accommodating the third layer, which is of interest, WTO law. *Krajewski* shows that the dynamics of the (substantive) WTO rules largely compare to those of EU law, also when it comes to health care. Hence, it cannot be ruled out that in the (near) future the health care edifice will compromise of three layers: apart from the national and EU standards, WTO norms could determine health care benefits or otherwise have an impact on health care.

In the light of the foregoing we would like to argue that a model characterised by 'strong government policy' may be the cornerstone helping Member States to build a 'solid' health care edifice. What is meant by 'strong government policy' in this context? We would offer some (non-exhaustive) definitions. First, the competent national authorities must base their interventions on strong and logic ('consistent') causal links between the measures to be taken (such as planning) and the objectives to be attained (such as universal coverage). The arguments for intervening must be convincing and solid. Second, the procedures that must be completed in order to take the measures concerned should be fully in tune with the principles of good governance: the Member States have 'strong procedures' in place. Non-discrimination and transparency are the keywords here. Third, if there is no case for government intervention, the competent national authorities should not hesitate to open-up the market concerned. This does not mean that government has not an important role to play. After all, the special features of a particular health care market may make it necessary to stimulate competition (sector specific regulatory measures) or to impose obligations that, for example, ensure access for all. In other words, even in market-driven settings strong regulatory policy is needed.

Multi-layer governance gives rise to complicated and challenging questions. However, reflecting on these questions, and what is more, resolving them contribute to our understanding of the European social model. The Treaty of Lisbon 2009 explicitly proclaims that the EU is based on 'a highly competitive social market economy' (Article 3(3) TEU). Given the general wording of this provision it is hard to grasp what the European social model and a highly competitive social market economy are about. Therefore, it is of great interest that actors at both national and EU levels (and possibly even at WTO level) continuing with constructing the multi-layered health care building. The recent *Monti* report[37] constitutes an excellent stepping stone for this, as it explicitly recommends to adopt the proposed Directive on Patients' Rights and to take supporting action, which may lead to the launching of a benchmark for health care systems in the EU. By further building upon the present *acquis communautaire* for health care, the EU Institutions and the Member States are able to shed more light on what is meant by 'a highly competitive social market economy' and on the exact contours of the European social model will begin to take clearer shape.

References

Ferrera M (2005) 'Towards an Open Social Citizenship? The New Boundaries of Welfare in the European Union'. In: de Búrca G (ed) EU Law and the Welfare State—In Search of Solidarity. OUP 2005, Oxford

Hall R and Jones C (2007). The value of life and the rise in health spending. Quart J Econ 122(1)

Krajewski M (2009) Conclusion. In: Krajewski M, Neergaard U, van de Gronden J (eds) The changing legal framework for services of general interest in europe—Between Competition and Solidarity, TMC Asser Press, The Hague (referred to in the Introduction of the present volume)

Monti M (2010) A New Strategy for the Single Market. At the Services of Europe's Economy and Society, Report to the President of the European Commission, 9 May 2010 (This report is available at http://ec.europa.eu/bepa/pdf/monti_report_final_10_05_2010_en.pdf)

[37] See Monti (2010), p. 54 and 55. (This report is available at http://ec.europa.eu/bepa/pdf/monti_report_final_10_05_2010_en.pdf).

Table of Cases

Court of Justice of the European Union Index

Court of First Instance/General Court

Index

MIX
Papier aus verantwortungsvollen Quellen
Paper from responsible sources
FSC® C105338

If you have any concerns about our products,
you can contact us on
ProductSafety@springernature.com

In case Publisher is established outside the EU,
the EU authorized representative is:
Springer Nature Customer Service Center GmbH
Europaplatz 3, 69115 Heidelberg, Germany

Printed by Libri Plureos GmbH
in Hamburg, Germany